The Journals of Hipólito Ruiz

Don Hipólito Ruiz, 1754–1816
Courtesy of the Real Jardín Botánico, Madrid

The JOURNALS *of* HIPÓLITO RUIZ

Spanish Botanist in Peru and Chile 1777–1788

Translated by

Richard Evans Schultes

and

María José Nemry von Thenen de Jaramillo-Arango

Transcribed from the original manuscripts by

Jaime Jaramillo-Arango

Timber Press
Portland, Oregon

ISBN 0-88192-407-5

Timber Press, Inc.
The Haseltine Building
133 S.W. Second Avenue, Suite 450
Portland, Oregon 97204, U.S.A.

Printed in Hong Kong

Library of Congress Cataloging-in-Publication Data

Ruiz, Hipólito, 1754–1816.

[Relación del viaje hecho a los reynos del Perú y Chile. English]

The journals of Hipólito Ruiz, Spanish botanist in Peru and Chile, 1777–1788 / transcribed from the original manuscripts by Jaime Jaramillo-Arango ; translated by Richard Evans Schultes and María José Nemry von Thenen de Jaramillo-Arango.

p. cm.

Includes index.

ISBN 0-88192-407-5

1. Peru—Description and travel. 2. Chile—Description and travel. 3. Botany—Peru—Early works to 1800. 4. Botany—Chile—Early works to 1800. 5. Ruiz, Hipólito, 1754–1816—Journeys—Peru. 6. Ruiz, Hipólito, 1754–1816—Journeys—Chile. I. Jaramillo-Arango, Jaime, 1897–1962. II. Schultes, Richard Evans. III. Jaramillo-Arango, María José Nemry von Thenen de. IV. Title.

F3411.R9213 1998

918.504'3-dc21 97-11251

CIP

Dedicated to the Memory of Jaime Jaramillo-Arango, M.D. 1897–1962

The following words on the life of the late Dr. Jaime Jaramillo-Arango are offered as a tribute to this Colombian scholar, who located and published the original, complete Spanish manuscript of the Relación *of Don Hipólito Ruiz. This account is adapted, with permission of the editor, from the tribute by R. E. Schultes that first appeared in the botanical journal* Taxon *in 1963.*

On July 30, 1962, coincidental with the strong earthquake of that day in the northern Andes, Dr. Jaime Jaramillo-Arango died of a heart attack in his home in Bogotá, Colombia. He is survived by his wife and helpmeet, Doña María José Nemry de Jaramillo-Arango, whom he married in 1948 and who devoted most of her time to collaborating with her husband in his researches and cultural activities.

Eminent Colombian surgeon, diplomat, historian, and friend of culture, Jaramillo-Arango was born in Manizales, Colombia, on January 17, 1897. He was educated first in the school of Santo Tomás de Aquino in Manizales and later in San Bartolomé, Bogota, preparing himself in medicine in the Escuela de Medicina of the Universidad Nacional of the same city. He later took specialized medical courses in Paris, Rochester, and London.

Returning to Colombia, he took charge of the department of clinical surgery of the San Juan de Dios hospital (1920–1923 and 1927–1931) and became famous as one of the most skillful surgeons of Colombia. In 1933 and 1934 he served as rector of the Faculty of Medicine of Bogotá. In 1934, he became Minister of Education.

The Colombian government, recognizing his outstanding international reputation in cultural circles, called him to fill several diplomatic posts. He served as minister to Germany in 1938, was Colombian delegate to the League of Nations in 1940, and represented Colombia as minister to Denmark from 1938 to 1945. During the last war, from 1940 to 1945, he was accredited to the London governments-in-exile of Belgium, Holland, Norway, and Poland. From 1940 to 1943 he represented Colombia as minister to Great Britain. During the hard times of the war (1943–1945) he was raised to the rank of ambassador, remaining in London throughout the grim years of the bombardment of the British capital.

In 1944 Dr. Jaramillo-Arango was Colombian delegate to the Preparatory

Commission and First Assembly of UNESCO, which was gathered in London. As vice-president, he proposed the founding of a University of the United Nations, the essential functions of which would be to encourage scientific research, higher technical education, and the study of other branches of human knowledge, and to create a center where students would enjoy the benefits of a cosmopolitan, intimate, and cordial atmosphere with teaching on a universal basis. The proposition was received with great enthusiasm by all the delegates, and a commission was instructed to make preliminary studies and gather information on the subject, but unfortunately nothing came of it, and the proposition was finally pigeonholed.

After his return to Colombia, he served as rector to the Universidad Nacional in 1950, and he later became a senator in the Colombian parliament, during some of the most trying years of the Republic.

Dr. Jaramillo-Arango was representative of that kind of scholar so typical of Colombia—outstanding in many different subjects completely apart from his main field of activity. Botanically, he has made several important contributions. In 1950 he published *The Conquest of Malaria*, a meticulous historico-medico-botanical study based upon an assiduous and careful reevaluation of all the published literature on the subject, past and present, and upon a painstaking, thorough search in European libraries for unpublished manuscripts. This book received unqualified praise from authorities and reviewers in the various fields that it covers, and is prefaced by Sir Philip Manson-Bahr, the great authority on tropical diseases.

Jaramillo-Arango's search for manuscripts on malaria and quinine took him and his wife to the partly bombed library of the British Museum (Natural History), where he discovered the original and complete manuscript of Hipólito Ruiz's *Relación histórica del Viage, que hizo á los Reynos del Perú y Chile el Botánico dn. Hipólito Ruiz en al año de 1777 hasta el de 1788, en cuya epoca regresó á Madrid*. This he and Mrs. Jaramillo-Arango copied and edited with the greatest of care, and in 1952 the Real Academia de Ciéncias Exactas, Físicas y Naturales of Madrid published it in a sumptuously illustrated edition of two volumes.

The ensuing years saw the publication of a number of short papers and monographs on botanical history, devoted in particular to quinine and to the Spanish botanical expeditions of the late eighteenth century sent by King Carlos III to study the flora of the Spanish domains in the New World.

At the time of his death, Dr. Jaramillo-Arango had just finished correcting the proofs of a new book about trees, written for school children between the ages of 13 and 15. His deep feeling and love for plants is apparent throughout the pages of this book. The original idea of the book was to stimulate the study of tropical natural history in the secondary schools of Colombia, and to bring about better understanding, love, and care of trees as man's best friends and allies in his perennial struggle against the elements in the tropics.

Dr. Jaramillo-Arango had become interested in the study of the real causes of the last illness and death of the liberator Simón Bolívar, and he was already laying his usual plans for a thorough investigation into this controversial topic once his book on trees was published.

As a close personal friend of Jaime Jaramillo-Arango, I wish to point out the great debt which botany owes to this man of so many facets. His influence was, naturally, very strongly felt in Colombian botany, but the international character of his interests has assured him a significant place in the worldwide history of botany.

Dr. Jaramillo-Arango at work on the journals of Ruiz in the Colombian Embassy in London, ca. 1950.

Contents

Foreword

by
Santiago Castroviejo
Director, Real Jardín Botánico, Madrid

Upon receiving a letter from the well-known Harvard professor, Dr. Richard Evans Schultes, I found myself very surprised by its contents. My good friend Schultes suggested that I write the foreword to his English translation—finished after many years of labor—of the work of the distinguished Colombian, Dr. Jaime Jaramillo-Arango, of the journals of Don Hipólito Ruiz. At first I declined the offer, as I believed that I was not the person best qualified to write the foreword to such a book.

We again spoke of the matter during a visit that Dr. Schultes made to Madrid in September of 1992. Two months later, when I visited Bogotá, I was contacted by María José, widow of Jaime Jaramillo-Arango. Though we had never met before, we soon established an easy rapport. She told me about all the ups and downs of the celebrated manuscript that had appeared by chance in London, and how she had copied it word for word when she had not yet learned Spanish and when, of course, there were no photocopiers. She also told me about the voyage to Madrid she and her husband had made to edit the manuscript, about their visit to the Real Jardín Botánico del Prado, and so on. When we had finished our conversation, I realized I could no longer refuse; I therefore wrote to Professor Schultes and offered to write the foreword to his book.

In 1952 a numbered edition of 1050 copies was made of the two-volume work of Dr. Jaramillo; the two volumes of number 31 belong to the library of the Real Jardín Botánico. This work, according to the bill provided by my colleague Juan Armada, cost 64,703.15 pesetas, with the first volume costing 38,887.90 pesetas and the second 25,815.25 pesetas. It is also specified that 980 copies would be bound in paper, 65 in cloth, and 5 in leather. The aforementioned bill includes 230 pesetas (165 for each volume) to defray the cost of sending a copy to Señor Jaramillo.

I remember that I found the work of Jaime Jaramillo-Arango especially interesting because it not only consisted of the printed Ruiz journal, as had the work previously published by Agustín J. Barreiro, but also offered ample additional documentation—maps, itineraries, and so on. Above all, it included a meticulous study comparing this version of the journal to that first published. The merit of Dr. Jaramillo-Arango's work was not merely in identifying the manuscripts, but rather in having recognized their value and having brought to them the additional documentation necessary for understanding the whole of the expedition at that time.

I had the opportunity to follow the trail of the latest research on this topic, thanks to the work done in the Real Jardín to prepare for the exposition and book titled *La Expeditión Botánica al Virreinato del Perú (1777–1788)*, and thanks to the work of the Ecuadorian professor Eduardo Estrella, who wrote a very important introductory study to the *Flora Huayaquilensis* of Juan Tafalla, Ruiz's disciple, to whom we will dedicate a few words later.

It might be worthwhile to remember two events of 1774 that, although happening at opposite ends of the world, helped to provide the primary steps in the organization of the first of the great Spanish overseas scientific expeditions. The first of those events was the discovery, by S. J. López Ruiz, of cinchona trees not far from Colombia, and the second was the naming of R. J. Turgot as the prime minister of King Louis XVI. Turgot, possibly under the influence of the Jussieus, proposed the organization of a grand expedition to America, for various reasons. Among these were finding the location of the manuscripts, lost in Peru, of the French botanist Joseph de Jussieu, a participant in the French-Spanish expedition directed by La Condamine (1735–1745); collection of data about the utility of several plants that had not yet been extensively studied; and compilation of reliable information about the state of the Spanish colonies after the administrative reorganization of the Hispanic territories (the division of the Viceroyalty of Peru, the creation of the Viceroyalty of La Plata and of the Intendency of Caracas, etc.) in the period when movements for independence began to appear in the British colonies.

However, it was J. E. B. Clugny, not Turgot, who took it upon himself to solicit the necessary permission for Joseph Dombey to travel through the Viceroyalty of Peru; this he did by pleading an exclusive interest for the scientific journals of Jussieu. The Spanish government responded by organizing the expedition and inviting Dombey, at the same time making it very clear that the expedition would be led by the young Spanish botanist Hipólito Ruiz and that he would be accompanied by, among others, the botanist José Pavón and the artists José Brunete and Isidro Gálvez.

It could be said that the history of the field journals begins with a document to be found in Appendix I of the Spanish edition of Dr. Jaramillo's work: "Instrucción a que deberán arreglarse los sugetos destinados por S. M. para pasar a la América meridional, . . ." (Instructions to be followed by the subject destined by His Majesty to South America, . . .), which was approved on the 9th of April 1777. The fourth article of that document states,

> so that the useful rivalry that feeds them in their discoveries, of which there will often be opportunity, not degenerate against all hope into discord, it would be well that, as they encounter genera or species that are new or as yet badly defined by botanists, they record in their respective journals the name of the discoverer following the name that has then been attributed to the plant, and that when they are first able to communicate their findings to each other, each adds his signature in each journal to establish who has the first rights of publication.

It is not certain that such a standard had been applied, but it might have avoided the troublesome diplomatic incident created around the publication of the *Stirpes novae . . .* of Charles L'Héritier in Paris, 1784–1805. It seems more than probable that there existed some "diarios de campos" (field journals) to which Hipólito Ruiz refers in his writings. Dombey, contrary to the desire expressed by the Spanish Crown, was able to send his journals out of Cádiz before they could be submitted to the registration carried out by J. Cuéllar in April of 1785, and they arrived in France on the French frigate *La Bellone*, which had been docked in the port of Cádiz. On the other hand, nothing is known of any "diarios" of Pavón, but we know of at least three versions of those of Ruiz, successively corrected, which contain the narration of what happened on the expedition.

The 123-page folio manuscript entitled *Relación del Viaje hecho á los Reynos de Perú y Chile por los Botánicos y Dibuxantes enviados por el Rey para aquella Expedición, extractada de los diarios por el orden que llevo a cabo su autor dn. Hipólito Ruiz* contains the oldest known version. It was donated to the Museo Nacional de Ciencias Naturales in Madrid by Father Augustín Jesús Barreiro, O.S.A., who had obtained it from Isabel Pascual of Aravaca, Madrid, who in turn had inherited it from her father, Tomás Pascual de Miguel. He had already used it in 1867 in the writing of his doctoral thesis, which was read that same year in the college of pharmacy of the Universidad Central; the same manuscript was referred to by Marcos Jiménez de la Espada in a message in the Real Sociedad Española de Historia Natural in 1872. This text, which is written in a hand corresponding to that of Hipólito Ruiz, was transcribed by Barreiro and published in 1931 by the Comisión de Estudios Retrospectivos de Historia Natural of the Real Academia de Ciencias Exactas, Físicas y Naturales de Madrid. It was translated into English by B. E. Dahlgren and published in 1940 by the Field Museum of Natural History, Chicago.

From then on, all that we know about the "diarios" we owe to Jaime Jaramillo-Arango, who published a combined edition of two more versions he had discovered by chance while looking for information on quinine in the natural history section of the British Museum in London. The second version is a manuscript of 88 folio sheets with corrections and crossings out, with its handwriting also attributed to Hipólito Ruiz. It is entitled *Compendio del Viage que hizo á los Reynos del Perú y Chile el Botánico Español dn. Hipólito Ruiz en el año de 1777 hasta el de 1788* (Prologue, Figure 1). Included in the text are commentaries about the exact work of the members of the expedition, which allow us to date this copy between 1793 and 1801.

A third version of the same text was also kept in the aforementioned natural history section of the British Museum and is entitled *Relación histórica del Viage, que hizo á los Reynos del Perú y Chile el Botánico dn. Hipólito Ruiz en al año de 1777 hasta el de 1788, en cuya época regresó a Madrid* (Prologue, Figure 2). This 75-sheet folio manuscript has handwriting similar to that of the *Compendio* and seems to be a copy, incomplete but revised, with some of the stylistic and spelling corrections from the previous manuscript. It can be reasonably supposed to have been done after the year 1801.

To prepare his version, Jaime Jaramillo-Arango used the third manuscript as far as he could with the existing sheets (the 75 sheets of the third manuscript correspond to the first 57 of the second); he then continued his editing with the second manuscript.

The manuscripts kept in the British Museum appear to have come from the collection of Aylmer Bourke Lambert, bought by the museum at an auction after the death of their owner. It is still unknown how the "diarios" fell into the hands of the English naturalist. The absence of notes in the handwriting of Pavón, who always had a propensity to add his name to the manuscripts of the expedition that were edited by Ruiz, makes one think they were not sold by him. Indeed, there is absolutely no reference to these texts in the correspondence between Lambert and Pavón (1814–1825). One thinks of the possibility of a sale by the family of Ruiz to the English naturalist, although it appears, according to Dr. Antonio González Bueno, that no documented proof of this exists. It is known, however, that successive donations of archeological objects from the expedition were made on later dates to the Museo Arqueológico Nacional in Madrid.

We also do not have clear documentation that would allow us to calculate the quantity and quality of materials sold by the successors of the members of the expedition, although it is certain that Pavón was not the only one who sold off the collections of the expedition.

Returning to the study of the three written documents, we see that, despite the organizational unity of all three, a comparative analysis of the texts shows that additions were made in the last two texts that are more significant than one would think from a first reading. Indeed, although the three manuscripts present long lists of plants collected in the described places, they are not the same in the two previously published editions. The document transcribed by Jaramillo-Arango presents lists shorter than those in the one published by Barreiro. The elimination of plants does not seem to have been made by chance: some plants that in the first version had not been assigned a special utility were left out of the second version, and the allusions to the modes of use and the virtues of herbal plants were amplified, in some cases in an obvious manner. I will cite as an example the entry on *Cinchona hirsuta*, collected in Chacahuassi, which is dispatched in the first version with a simple allusion to its common name (Barreiro, page 230 in the translation published by Dahlgren), while the second gives a short description of the plant, its uses, its habitat, and references to the studies that were made of it by members of the expedition (Jaramillo-Arango, here, Chapter 55, "Trip to Chacahuassi, or House at the Bridge," under the heading, "Cascarillo Fino Delgado, Cascarilla Azahar, and Cascarilla Boba de Hoja Morada").

This adaptation of the texts is not superficial; it seems rather to respond to the concept of botany developed by Casimiro Gómez Ortega and defended by Hipólito Ruiz and also, in some ways, by the "Madrid botanical-sanitary school" of the end of the eighteenth century, in which the plant's utility begins really to take an important place in the objectives of this discipline. This is quite different from the position maintained by Antonio José Cavanilles, who became director of the Real Jardín Botánico de Madrid in 1801.

Studying the journals, the reader can give himself an idea of the work accomplished by the members of the expedition, the difficulties, problems, and dangers that they encountered, the material collected, the field information compiled, and so on. With all that, one would expect a work of still greater importance than that made public, despite the fact that before the death of Ruiz the Sancha printing house published the *Quinología*, the *Prodromus Flora Peruvianae et Chilensis*, one volume of the *Systema Vegetabilium Florae Peruvianae et Chilensis*, and the first three volumes of the transcendent *Flora Peruviana et Chilensis sive Descriptiones et Icones Plantarum Peruvianarum et Chilensium*. Of the last-mentioned work, nine remaining volumes and three supplements, in which it had been planned to publish descriptions of about 5000 species and more than 2220 color plates of plants, lamentably remained in the archives, unpublished. In this collection of papers, sample sheets, and letters one also finds the *Flora Huayaquilensis*, which was unknown until the 1980s, when Dr. E. Estrella was able to reconstruct it after following the trail of Juan Tafalla, the disciple of Ruiz and continuator of his work in the Real Audiencia de Quito. It was published only in 1991.

A consequence of the problem of a lack of continuity in the work of the participants in the various botanical expeditions organized by the Spanish Crown at the end of the eighteenth century was that the fruits of these noble labors were to go no further, in the best of cases, than the archives. This can be deduced from information taken from the unpublished manuscripts kept in the archives of the Real Jardín Botánico and summarized in the accompanying table, which indicates the name of the botanist responsible for each expedition, the area and period in which they worked, the number of plates of botanical drawings, and the complete or incomplete written floras.

The immense majority of these original manuscripts are still waiting for their opportunity to see the light of day. Of them all, only the *Flora Huayaquilensis*, the *Flora de Cuba*, and nearly a third of the so-called *Flora de Mutis*, or *Flora de la Expedición Botánica al Reyno de Nueva Granada*, have been published.

One has to look at the social and political reality of Spain to understand such an abandonment of scientific activity. In effect, Spain was suffering from problems of internal political instability as a consequence of the French Revolution, the fall of Godoy, the Napoleonic invasion, the War of Independence, the persecution of liberals and intellectuals by Fernando VII, and so on. Thus Malaspina was jailed, Mociño had to flee from Spain, and the Count of Mopox lost his position. In addition, there was much fault to be found with the governments of that period, as shown by Mariano Lagasca when he wrote,

> knowledge that was as precious as it was unduly forgotten, scorned, or at best valued very little, and always by the government, for rarely was this knowledge sufficiently nourished to give the abundant fruit that had been promised. Indeed, the government repeatedly suffocated it in the cradle that the same government had prepared. These are the results of carelessness and little enlightenment in a government: they spoil the fruit of an infinite number of expeditions, after having spent more riches on them than possibly all the other nations together!

Manuscript Floras in the Archives of the Real Jardín Botánico, Madrid

AUTHORS	AREAS AND DATES	NUMBERS OF PLATES	FLORAS
P. Loefling	Orinoco (Venezuela), 1754–1756	115 botanical, 81 zoological, 2 ethnological, 2 maps	*Flora Cumanensis*, 2 volumes with 211 descriptions; first draft, 260 descriptions
H. Ruiz, J. Pavón	Peru and Chile, 1777–1788	2224 botanical, 24 zoological	*Flora Peruviana et Chilensis*, ca. 5000 descriptions
J. C. Mutis	Colombia, 1783–1810	6717 botanical	*Flora Nueva Granada*, ca. 500 descriptions
T. Haenke, L. Née	Pacific, 1789–1794	331 botanical	not yet studied, ca. 800 descriptions
J. Mociño	Guatemala, 1795–1803	119 botanical	*Flora de Guatemala*, 394 descriptions
B. M. Boldo, J. Esteve	Island of Cuba, 1796–1802	66 botanical	*Flora de Cuba*, 743 descriptions
J. Tafalla	Ecuador, 1799–1808	216 botanical	*Flora Huayaquilensis*, 625 descriptions

Today we still do not know why Ruiz published nothing from 1788—the year of his return—until the first years of the nineteenth century. This question still belongs within the realm of the enigmas of the history of Spanish botany. In this period, with the help of the all-powerful Casimiro Gómez Ortega, Ruiz set up an "office of the Flora of Peru," to which José Pavón was also assigned. Although Ruiz and Pavón published with the Sancha printing house, not with the Typographia Regia as did Cavanilles, they do not appear to have lacked the means to finish their task. Perhaps one of the reasons was an unfinished basic education, as a consequence of the early interruption of Ruiz's formative years by his taking on, at only 23 years of age, the management of the enterprise that would take him to America.

What is certain is that later Ruiz found himself distanced from the Real Jardín Botánico due to his confrontation with Cavanilles, and he experienced times of serious economic difficulty and isolation. In spite of that, he worked, revised manuscripts, and took some important works to the publishing house, although the majority would remain unpublished to the present day. Worse yet, after Ruiz's early death not only did his collaborator José Pavón not finish what Ruiz had begun, but, perhaps urged on by economic problems, he also sold off their resources—herbaria, manuscripts, etc.—and did not even manage to publish the works already written that remained in the "office."

This English version of the "diarios" can thus serve as a well-deserved homage to the enlightened Spaniards of that age, who believed they could see in science a road to progress, and to the young botanist from Burgos, the self-sacrificing cultivator of our *scientia amabilis*.

Preface to the English Translation

by
Richard Evans Schultes

Unbelievable has been the odyssey of this document—the complete manuscript of Ruiz's *Relación*—and the story of its translation into English. The steps from Ruiz's original handwritten notes to this published English version of the entire account constitute an extraordinary series of improbable events.

The original and complete manuscript was long thought to be lost. Only a partial copy was known: it was published in Spain in 1931 by Padre Agustín Jesús Barreiro, and later translated into English by Dr. Boris Eric Dahlgren and published in Chicago in 1940 as the *Travels of Ruiz, Pavón, and Dombey in Peru and Chile (1777–1788)*, Botanical Series, Field Museum of Natural History, Volume 21.

During the Second World War, Dr. Jaime Jaramillo-Arango, a Colombian surgeon of the highest intellectual attainment and at that time Colombian ambassador to the Court of St. James's, rediscovered the two later manuscripts in the bombed British Museum (Natural History) in Kensington. Having worked with early Spanish documents during his researches on quinine and the history of malaria, Dr. Jaramillo fortunately was fully aware of the great historic value of this find. He and his wife, María José, set about editing the entire manuscript for publication. In 1952 the Royal Academy of Sciences in Madrid published it in two elegant volumes, the first comprising a faithful rendition of the original journals of Ruiz, and the second a collection of Peruvian and Chilean maps, charts, and illustrations of the period of the Real Expedición Botánica.

Shortly after the appearance of this Spanish publication, Dr. Jaramillo, knowing of my deep interest in South American botany, gave me an inscribed copy. Later, while I was a guest at their country estate in Fusugasugá, Colombia, Dr. Jaramillo and María José suggested that such an important document should be put into English, and they asked me if I would be willing to undertake the translation. That invitation came in 1952, when I was about to begin a 15-month botanical exploration of the jungles of the Apaporis River in the Colombian Amazonia. I agreed to try the assignment and to do it in my "free time" in the field.

During the following months, armed with tear sheets of the galley proof of the Spanish edition and a pocket dictionary, I worked slowly on the translation. It was done in the great round houses of Colombian Indians on days of tropical rains, when botanical collecting was impossible. My desk was a metal box of botanical equipment, my chair a low, hand-hewn stool made by the natives. I frequently worked on into the evening by the light of a candle or a pitch torch prepared by the Indians. Little by little, the translation progressed until, when I finally returned to Bogotá, much of the work was done, but only in a preliminary way. It was contained in six school notebooks and written in lead pencil.

Yet there were many hiatuses. Ruiz had used numerous old Spanish terms, familiar in the late eighteenth century but not today, as well as local Peruvian and Chilean phrases. More often than not, these terms did not appear in the abbreviated dictionary I had in the field, and thus I was not able to translate them properly.

Once back in Bogotá, I gave the six notebooks to Doña María José. With the greatest of care and dedication, she typed the manuscript and filled in some of the omissions. Doña María José has graciously assisted me over the following years as well, in many puzzling aspects of the translation of Don Hipólito's Spanish.

In 1953, after 14 years of residence in the Amazon, I returned to Cambridge, Massachusetts, to take up my duties at Harvard University. Because of many pressing commitments, further work on the translation languished, and little was done for a number of years.

Dr. Jaramillo died in 1962.

It was not until 1974 that I could again devote any sustained attention to Ruiz's *Relación*. In April of that year, I had the opportunity of spending 3 weeks in Bogotá, devoted wholly to the work of polishing my translation. On this occasion I was able to work on the manuscript, aided by Mrs. Jaramillo, in an appropriate setting: the private study of a 400-year-old colonial house that had been the building where the famous Colombian Academy of Letters was founded. Dr. and Mrs. Jaramillo had saved the house from bulldozers and restored it to its historic and pristine glory; Calle 13, Number 5-33, is now a national monument. Though I made measurable progress on the translation, much remained unfinished.

Once again, other occupations delayed the final work, but in July of 1980 I was able to spend a month as a guest at the Rockefeller Foundation's Study and Conference Center at Lake Como, Italy. There, in the peace of an ancient, restored castle with the finest of facilities, I at long last had an uninterrupted opportunity to organize the polishing of the English manuscript. The rest of the work, on several important parts of the manuscript, was finally accomplished during my vacations in 1981 and 1982 on Sutton Island, off the coast of northern Maine, as well as during the summer of 1982 when I was teaching in Mexico, at the Instituto Nacional de Investigaciones sobre Recursos Bióticos Renovables.

Returning to Harvard, I was able to obtain grants to cover the cost of the final typing of the manuscript.

Few are the manuscripts, I am sure, about which can be recounted such an odyssey: handwritten two centuries ago in Lima, Peru; lost for 150 years; found in wartime in a bombed museum in London, by a Colombian ambassador who recognized its scientific and historic merit; published in the original Spanish in Madrid; translated by an American botanist in the depths of the Amazon jungle of Colombia; typed and improved by the discoverer's wife in Bogotá, in the original home of the Colombian Academy of Letters; refined in a sixteenth-century castle in northern Italy, on a rocky island on the New England coast, and in the mountains of Jalapa, Mexico; financially supported in its final phases by American and international institutions and companies; and, finally, published by a botanical press in Portland, Oregon.

Would that Don Hipólito Ruiz could know of the peregrinations of the manuscript into which he put his heart and soul, a record of 11 years of dedication, frustration, privation, and ill health. He would see that his journals, having gone far beyond its value as an account of the accomplishments of Ruiz and his Spanish companions, are of immeasurable significance in modern times.

To gain a perspective today on the travels and writings of Hipólito Ruiz, we must first understand that the Spanish government under King Carlos III demonstrated serious interest in the botanical study of the rich floras of the colonies of the New World. Several government-sponsored explorations were sent out for the purpose of collecting, studying, and illustrating the plants of the Spanish possessions.

The royal expedition to Peru and Chile, under the direction of the botanist Don Hipólito Ruiz, was the first of these explorations. Ruiz and his colleague Don José Pavón spent the 11 years from 1777 to 1788 in the two colonies, primarily in the Andean and coastal areas.

The second expedition, sent to New Granada (Colombia), continued for 33 years. It was officially established in 1783 under the direction of Rev. José Celestino Mutis and included the Colombian naturalist Francisco José de Caldas and a number of artists, mostly Colombians. Following the death of José Celestino Mutis in 1808, the work of the expedition was directed by his nephew, Sinforoso Mutis, until its termination in 1816.

The third botanical expedition went to New Spain (Mexico). It was directed by the Spanish physician and botanist Martín Sessé, who began in 1787 with four assistants including the Mexican physician José Mariano Mociño. After the death of Sessé in 1809, Mociño carried on studies in Europe of the collections of their expedition.

The work of these three expeditions, much of it carried out under incredibly difficult physical conditions, not only had a powerful effect on the early cultural development of these countries, but has also continued to exert strong influence on modern taxonomic and floristic research.

As the surviving record of the first of these Spanish expeditions to the New World, the *Relación* of Ruiz is an extraordinary document. Many of the plant explorers of the eighteenth and nineteenth centuries were men of broad interests and education in natural history, and Don Hipólito Ruiz was no exception. The journals that he kept in Peru and Chile are fantastically detailed, and characteristic of his breadth of interest in science and in local culture. Though much of his journals was necessarily taken up by the descriptions, vernacular names, and local uses of plants, Ruiz also devoted attention to many other topics. These included ecological factors, climate, mineralogical findings, zoological observations, racial characteristics, social and economic conditions in the towns and villages, anthropological observations of Indian life, secular and church architecture, and sundry aspects of the natural history of Peru and Chile. Because they are firsthand accounts written two centuries ago, all of Ruiz's observations are of unique significance.

The journals, consequently, will be of interest to readers involved in any of the numerous fields of biology and to those concerned with other natural sciences, such as geology and mineralogy. They contain fascinating information for students of sociology, government, architecture and town planning, and colonial history. There is also material that conservationists will find helpful in today's quest to protect the environment. In short, while presenting a special historical picture of Peru and Chile, Ruiz's journals are relevant to the problems and interests of modern times.

This English edition of Ruiz's 200-year-old travel narrative does leave scholars with two challenges. First, in this book the Latin names of plants stand alone, without authorities for the names. Confronted by an abundance of new plants, Ruiz and Pavón came up with binomials that served them well in field notes, but these names are often difficult to verify today. Some can be traced to Linnaeus, and a number of others have now been appended by "Ruiz & Pavón"; the rest await taxonomic detective work.

Second, the original published work of Jaime Jaramillo-Arango, from which these journals in English were translated, contains an additional wealth of information in his appendices and indexes. Many an interesting story remains to be discovered within those two Spanish volumes.

Acknowledgments

The kindness and patience of native Indians in the unknown area along the Río Apaporis in the Colombian Amazonia are gratefully remembered. During the initial translation of the Ruiz journals, in their malocas (enormous circular houses) they provided hospitality and peace and quiet on days of torrential rains. Unschooled in our ways, they did not understand what the outside man was putting on paper, but their interest and friendliness is never to be forgotten.

We, Richard Evans Schultes and María José Nemry von Thenen de Jaramillo-Arango, also remember with gratitude the many friends of our own society, especially those in the Republic of Colombia, who helped and encouraged us in many ways during the long spell of translating Ruiz's journals into English.

We are likewise deeply indebted to Dr. Santiago Castroviejo of the Real Jardín Botánico de Madrid, for his advice and assistance in putting us in contact with Spanish experts on obsolete Spanish words of Peru and Chile in the eighteenth century and on the many local usages of the language of that period, and for providing an illuminating foreword. William Moore kindly translated Dr. Castroviejo's foreword from the Spanish.

No small measure of gratitude goes to Miss Kathleen Horton for her meticulous typing of the final draft of the manuscript.

It is a distinct pleasure to acknowledge financial assistance during preparation of the manuscript from the Milton Fund of Harvard University, the World Wildlife Fund, the Marstrand Foundation, the Philip Morris Company, and the Smith, Kline

& French Company. We are most deeply indebted to the Overbrook Foundation for its generosity in providing a grant through Conservation International, and to Dr. Peter Raven, Director of the Missouri Botanical Garden, for obtaining additional funds to help defray the expenses of publication. Their assistance has made it possible to put the price of these extensive journals within the reach of those who would be most interested in the natural history and exploration of South America during the eighteenth century.

Prologue to the Spanish Edition

by
Jaime Jaramillo-Arango

The Royal Academy of Exact, Physical, and Natural Sciences of Madrid published in 1931, in a volume of 500 pages, a narrative of the first of three expeditions sent to the New World by Carlos III—the expedition to Peru and Chile. The work was issued under the title *Relación del Viaje hecho a los Reynos del Perú y Chile por los Botánicos y Dibuxantes enviados para aquella Expedición, extractado de los Diarios por el orden que llevó en ellos su autor Don Hipólito Ruiz.* This work formed part of the praiseworthy efforts of the Academy to publicize the work carried out by the great Spanish scientists who contributed to our knowledge of the American flora and, in particular, by those who took part in the three expeditions under Carlos III's patronage.

In an explanatory note, the commission[1] to which the Academy entrusted this publication stated that it is based upon a manuscript of Don Hipólito Ruiz "which had remained unpublished in the hands of a member of his family," a document which Father Agustín J. Barreiro, O.S.A., an official of the same commission, had discovered and revised. Thus, Father Barreiro was able not only to direct the publication of the document, but also to annotate its text.

In 1940, this work of Barreiro's was translated into English by Dr. B. E. Dahlgren,[2] Chief Curator of the Department of Botany of the Field Museum of Natural History in Chicago.

Apart from the fact that, just as Father Barreiro annotated at the bottom of pages 13 [of his Spanish edition and of the translation by Dahlgren] and 96 [of his Spanish edition; page 67 of the translation by Dahlgren], the chapters referring to the city of Lima and the city of Huánuco de los Caballeros are completely lacking (since they were not found in the original manuscript), a careful examination of this very work reveals passages in which the thread of thought seems to be interrupted and disjointed. In other places, the descriptions of geographic features and natural products of one region appear to be confounded with those of another.

During the course of studies that we carried out recently on the history of quinine (around which so many legends and unfounded tales have grown up),[3] two manuscripts dealing with the travels of Don Hipólito Ruiz, both in his own hand, came to our attention. One of them, comprising 88 pages of untrimmed paper of folio size and written in a fine hand on all four sides, is complete; the other, consisting of 75 sheets of the same paper and size and likewise written on all four sides, is, unfortunately, unfinished.

Here and there in the former manuscript one finds interlinear corrections, marginal notes, grammatical and orthographic changes, etc.; on the contrary, the text of the latter appears to be unaltered in any way. As is quite apparent, the title that the first manuscript originally bore (proving quite clearly that this was the title which Don Hipólito at first thought to give his narrative) is *Compendio del Viage que hizo á los Reynos del Perú y Chile el Botánico Español dn. Hipólito Ruiz en el año de 1777 hasta el de 1788* (Figure 1).

In the second manuscript, the title has been changed for another: *Relación histórica del Viage, que hizo á los Reynos del Perú y Chile el Botánico dn. Hipólito Ruiz en al año de 1777 hasta el de 1788, en cuya época regresó a Madrid* (Figure 2). The term Relación was thus substituted for that of *Compendio*. The 75 sheets of the unannotated work contain only that material found in the first 57 sheets of the complete manuscript. This shows that the second manuscript is not simply a transcription of the first, but that, while engaged in making a new and clean copy of his narrative, Don Hipólito revised and enlarged the material in his work as he went along.

In addition to the many interesting data and descriptions of plants which are lacking in Father Barreiro's publication, both manuscript versions in question contain not only the two chapters about the city of Lima and the city of Huánuco de los Caballeros but also other chapters that likewise are not included nor even mentioned in the Barreiro work. We may cite as examples the "Curious Information Learned from People Who Have Traveled in Peru" (Chapter 13), the "Description of the Villa de Tarma" (Chapter 14), etc. The complete manuscript contains, in addition to the foregoing, two other chapters: "Voyage from the Port of Callao to the Bay of Cádiz" (Chapter 58) and "Trip from Cádiz to Madrid" (Chapter 60). These two chapters are also lacking in the work of the distinguished Augustinian clergyman.

What explanation can there be of our discovery and the gaps that, as we have just pointed out, mar the publication of the Spanish Royal Academy?

Father Barreiro himself gives us the explanation. He not only suspected that a complete copy of Don Hipólito's work must have been in existence; what is more, he made a deliberate search for it. Unfortunately, difficulties that he met forced him to abandon his search. Father Barreiro wrote,[4]

> The manuscript upon which this work is based comprises 67 untrimmed sheets, written on both sides in the hand of Don Hipólito Ruiz. Most of the pages are perfectly legible. Marginal notes and interlinear notes are abundant. Extreme carelessness marks the spelling and punctuation, but we have corrected this part of the manuscript. The description of Lima and of Huánuco are lacking, but undoubtedly these are to be foun in the final copy, which was to be printed. Actually, we tried to locate this copy. We approached the person who, according to reports, had it in his possession, but our efforts failed miser-

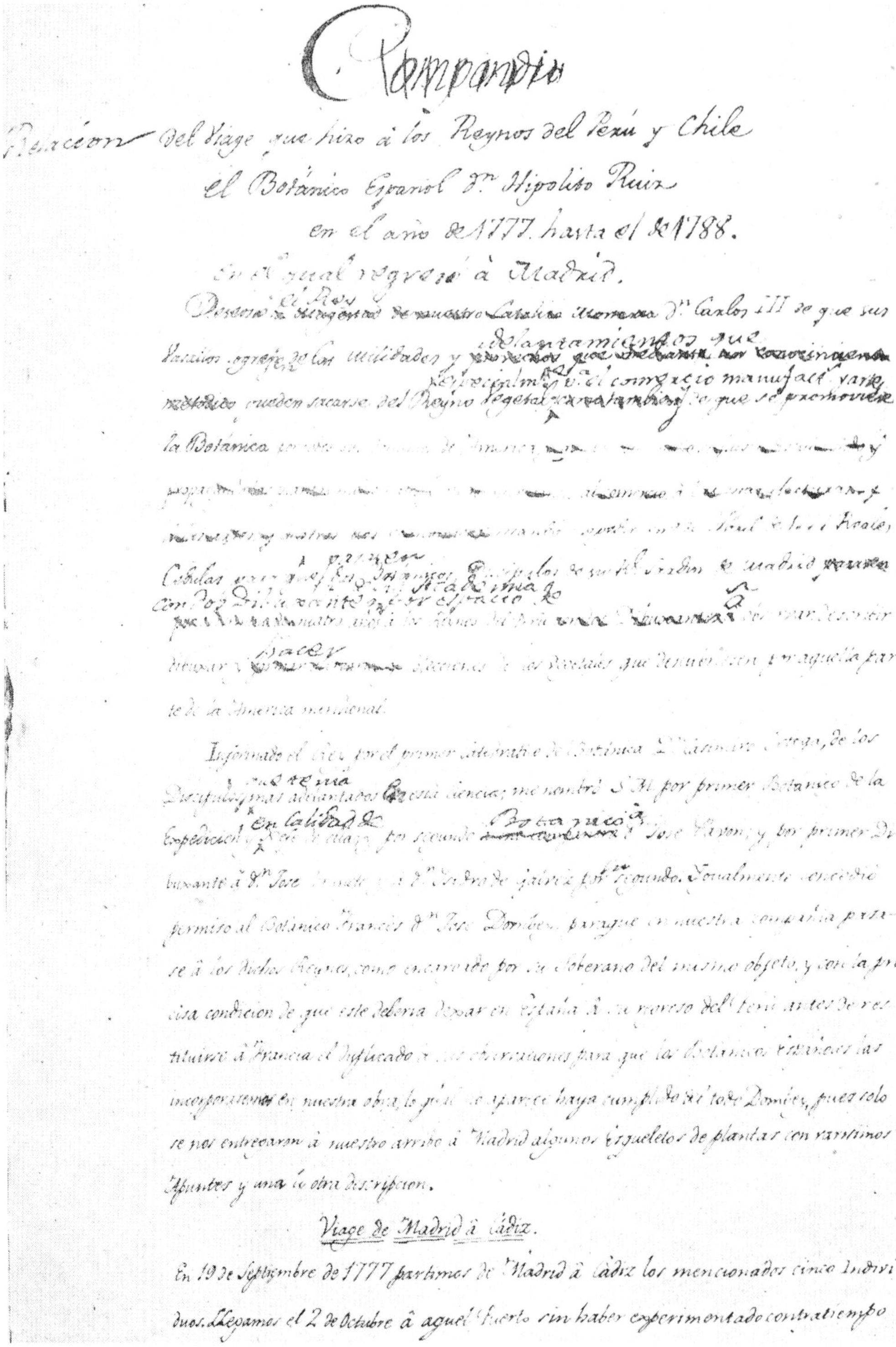

Figure 1. Ruiz's own draft version of page 1 of the *Compendio*. (Courtesy of the British Museum's Department of Botany and Natural History.)

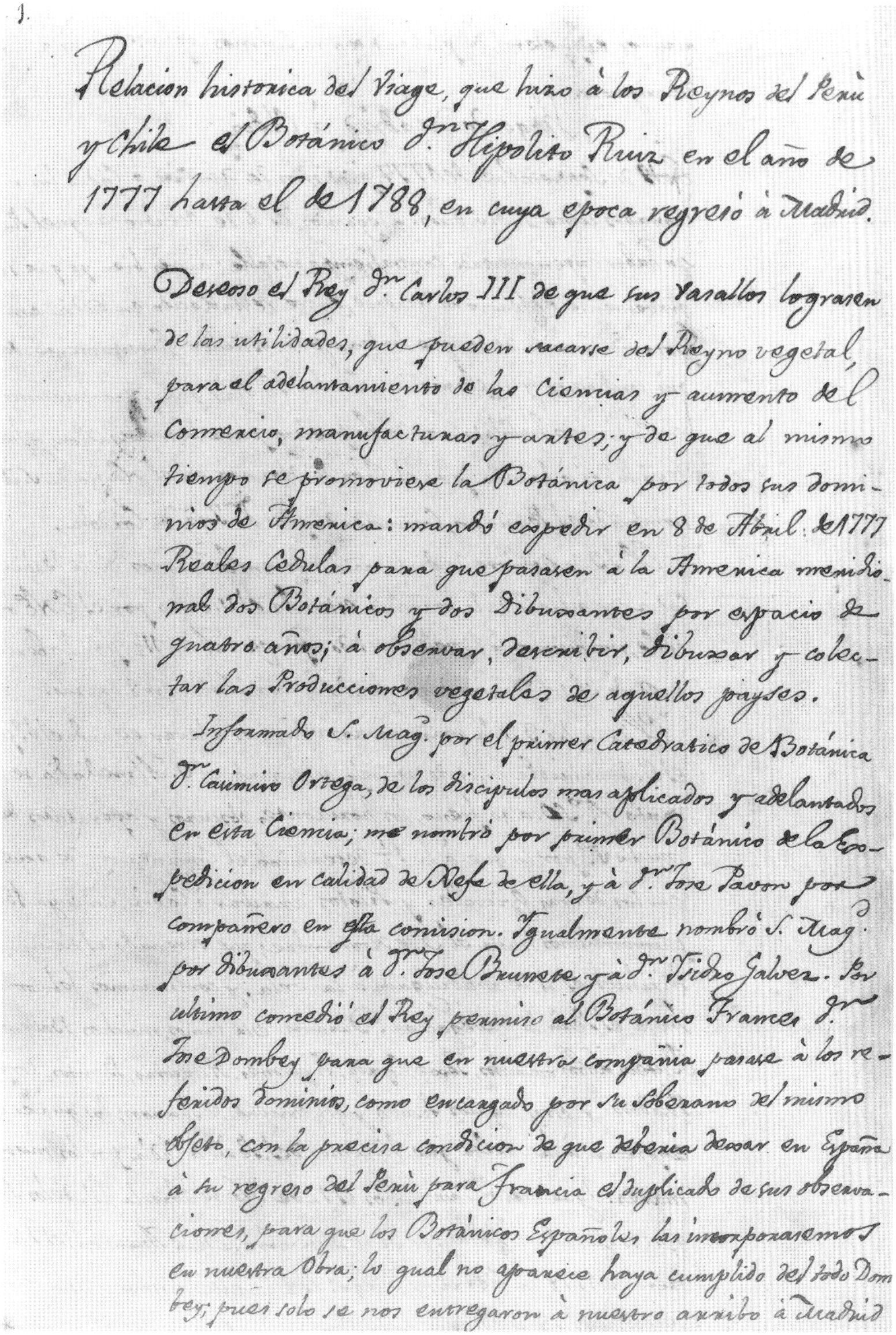

1.

Relacion historica del Viage, que hizo à los Reynos del Perù y Chile el Botánico Dn. Hipolito Ruiz en el año de 1777 hasta el de 1788, en cuya epoca regresó à Madrid.

Deseoso el Rey Dn. Carlos III de que sus vasallos lograsen de las utilidades, que pueden sacarse del Reyno vegetal, para el adelantamiento de las Ciencias y aumento del Comercio, manufacturas y artes; y de que al mismo tiempo se promoviese la Botánica por todos sus dominios de America: mandó expedir en 8 de Abril de 1777 Reales Cedulas para que pasasen à la America meridional dos Botánicos y dos Dibuxantes por espacio de quatro años; à observar, describir, dibuxar y colectar las Producciones vegetales de aquellos payses.

Informado S. Mag. por el primer Catedratico de Botánica Dn. Casimiro Ortega, de los discipulos mas aplicados y adelantados en esta Ciencia; me nombró por primer Botánico de la Expedicion en calidad de Gefe de ella, y à Dn. Jose Pavon por compañero en esta comision. Igualmente nombró S. Mag. por Dibuxantes à Dn. Jose Brunete y à Dn. Isidro Galvez. Por ultimo concedió el Rey permiso al Botánico Frances Dn. Jose Dombey para que en nuestra compañia pasase à los referidos dominios, como encargado por su Soberano del mismo objeto, con la precisa condicion de que deberia dexar en España à su regreso del Perù para Francia el duplicado de sus observaciones, para que los Botánicos Españoles las incorporasemos en nuestra Obra; lo qual no aparece haya cumplido del todo Dombey; pues solo se nos entregaron à nuestro arribo à Madrid

Figure 2. Ruiz's own fair copy of page 1 of the *Relación histórica*. (Courtesy of the British Museum's Department of Botany and Natural History.)

ably when, through a third party, we received a rude and disconcerting answer which we are happy to forgive.

A detailed comparison of Father Barreiro's text with that of the two manuscripts at hand reveals, indeed, that his publication is based upon a first draft of the work of Don Hipólito. A close examination also reveals that our two manuscript copies are second and third drafts, successively amended and enlarged. The chronological relationship of these three copies can be established as follows: Don Hipólito produced the first draft (that of Father Barreiro) directly from his field notes while still in Peru and on his return trip. Back in Spain in 1793, working over the copy that we may, for convenience, call Father Barreiro's, Don Hipólito composed the complete manuscript of 88 (90?; see below) sheets, the first of our two manuscripts to which he gave the title *Compendio del Viage*, etc. Still later, he revised this second copy by making annotations in situ, resulting in a completely corrected and modified text; this text, sometime after 1801, he began to write out in a clean transcription, continuing to correct and amplify the context the while. This is why the 75 sheets of the last copy contain, as we have pointed out above, the material of only the first 57 of the 88 sheets of the complete copy.

These deductions are not mere conjecture. In the various copies, referring to dates when he was still in Peru or when he was making his return trip, Don Hipólito speaks of his work in preparing a fresh transcription of this or that passage: his first draft. Later, in his *Suplemento á la Quinología*, he referred to the *Compendio*, or complete copy of his travels, as being ready for publication. He alludes, in fact, to Don Francisco Antonio Zea's description of the falls of the Tequendama, inserted in volume 8 of the *Anales de Ciencias Naturales de Madrid*, where he states,[5] "The authors of the flora of Peru could publish many poetic and picturesque descriptions [like that of the falls of Tequendama] . . . but we offer to publish these descriptions in the *Compendio* of our travels, which now after 7 years is extracted in 90 pages of fine handwriting, in a simple style . . ."

Finally, armed with the knowledge of the foregoing reference and year (1801), we must conclude that the third copy was prepared later than that date. The title for this last copy was then altered from *Compendio*, etc., to *Relación histórica del Viage*, etc.

Had the difficulties that Father Barreiro encountered in his search for the final transcription of Don Hipólito's work been of a different nature, would this outstanding member of the Spanish Academy have attained his goal? We cannot say.

The two copies with which we are concerned remained undisturbed in the library of the Department of Botany (Natural History) of the British Museum for 107 years. When we say "undisturbed," we ought to qualify this statement by saying "undisturbed by an inquisitive eye," for apparently, in all these years, no glance went beyond their covers and titles. In spite of this peaceful oblivion, however, they suffered extensive physical disturbance in very recent years.

During the last war, these, as well as other valuable manuscripts, were wisely removed from the library of the Museum in London to the Zoological Museum in the little town of Tring, Buckinghamshire, which functions as a dependency of the British Museum. This measure was fortunate. In December 1940, enemy air raids deluged the capital of Britain in the never-to-be-forgotten orgy of fire which destroyed a great part of the center of the city, a hell which only those of us who lived through those hours can fully appreciate. In the course of these bombardments, the imposing home of the Museum of Natural History on Cromwell Road fell victim to the impact of a bomb. The fire which followed this explosion consumed a large number of books. Fire resulting from another bomb that struck the home of the British Museum in Bloomsbury, as the whole world knows, destroyed a quarter of a million priceless volumes, some of them practically irreplaceable.

With such destruction rampant, how fortunate that the Ruiz manuscripts did not perish! And how fortunate that, with the Museum's destruction, the only complete account of the botanical expedition to Peru and Chile, headed by one of the most devoted, disinterested, and capable European naturalists to have visited America, was not forever buried and lost to mankind!

How and why did these two manuscripts (the *Compendio* and the *Relación*) come into the possession of the British Museum? The answer to this question is simple.

When the renowned botanist and naturalist Aylmer Bourke Lambert died in 1842, his library and herbarium were sold at public auction. In the sales effected on the first day of the auction, the 27th of June 1842, the British Museum bought part of the library and herbarium. Among the works and documents thus acquired were the two manuscripts in question. According to the catalogue of the auctioneer, S. Leigh Sotheby, Esq., which is preserved in the library of the Department of Botany of the Museum, the price paid for them was £275.

How and when, then, did Lambert come into possession of these documents?

Our attempts to clarify this second point have so far been almost completely unsuccessful. Lambert, as is well known, translated into English some of the works of Ruiz—his *Descripción del Arbol conocido en el Reyno del Perú con el nombre de Quino-quino* [*Myroxylon peruiferum*] *y su Corteza con el de Quina-quina, muy distinta de la Quina ó Cascarilla*; his *Disertaciones sobre la raiz de la Ratanhia* [*Krameria triandra*], *de la Calaguala* [*Polypodium calahuala*] *y de la China* [*Smilax* or *China peruviana*], *y acerca de la yerba llamada Canchalagua* [*Gentiana canchalagua*]; his *Memoria sobre las virtudes y usos de la raiz de la planta llamada Yallhoy* [*Monnina polystachia*] *en el Peru*, and the *Memoria sobre las virtudes y usos de la Planta llamada en el Perú Bejuco de la Estrella* [*Aristolochia fragrans*]. This, nevertheless, does not necessarily imply that there was any direct relationship between Don Hipólito and Lambert. These works of Ruiz were all published at the end of the eighteenth century (1796–1805), and Lambert obtained a copy of the publications through Don José Pavón (letter from Pavón to Lambert, dated in Madrid the 30th of March 1816; in the Royal Botanic Gardens, Kew). The fact is, in Lambert's correspondence with various botanists and men of science, we have been wholly unable to discover the slightest sign or suggestion that letters were exchanged between these two famous naturalists, Lambert and Ruiz.

Don Hipólito Ruiz died in 1816.

As we have just referred to indirectly, there was correspondence between Lambert and Don José Pavón, Ruiz's companion on the expedition; this correspondence spanned a number of years. The library of the Royal Botanic Gardens at Kew owns a rather extensive collection of letters that date from the earlier to the later years of this correspondence. The earliest of these letters is dated the 12th of August 1814; the last, the 18th of July 1825. We can see, then, that this correspondence spanned at least 11 years. Through purchase, Lambert obtained from Pavón the greater part of the material on the American flora (Peruvian and Mexican) that he (Lambert) had in his herbarium.[6]

We have, however, read this mass of correspondence very carefully, and there is one point that stands out clearly to us: up to the date of the last letter (18th of July 1825), Lambert appears not to have had the slightest knowledge of the existence of Don Hipólito's manuscript of the *Relación* of his travels. Nor does it seem probable that after this date there was further correspondence between Pavón and Lambert. As we can see from the last few letters—particularly from the last one—the relationship between these two botanists, which had been friendly up to that time, was embittered by business misunderstandings. In truth, the relationship became unfriendly in the extreme. Upon whom may we lay the blame? Since this unfriendliness does not have any connection with our study, and since even today we do not have all the evidence necessary to hand down a fair judgment, we refrain from expressing our opinion.

Don José Pavón died in 1840.

Let us suppose for a moment—the evidence to the contrary notwithstanding—that Pavón and Lambert may have resumed their correspondence after 1825. Or, perhaps, that Lambert began to write to the heirs of Don Hipólito Ruiz. Up to now, we have been unable in London to shed any light upon this matter which might clarify it; we have not found the slightest clue in this respect. Also, sad to say, Father Barreiro is now dead. Because he tells us in his "Epílogo" that he tried to communicate with a person who ought to have known something about the last copy of the manuscript, which was ready for the press, we would have liked to get in touch with him in search of further clues. According to our correspondent in Madrid, this outstanding Augustinian clergyman, Father Barreiro, died in that city in 1937, during the Spanish Civil War as a refugee in the Norwegian embassy.

To three expeditions did Carlos III entrust the study of the natural history of the New World: the first was sent to Peru and Chile, the second to New Granada (Colombia), and the third to New Spain (Mexico). It is true that Francisco Hernández, medical advisor to Philip II, was sent to Mexico in 1570 to investigate the flora of that country. It is also true that the chroniclers Gonzalo Fernández de Oviedo, Padre José de Acosta, Fray Antonio Vásquez de Espinosa, Fray Antonio de la Calancha, Fray Bernardino de Sahagún, and Padre Bernabé Cobo, in their accounts of the New World, dedicated various parts of their works to the study of American plants.[7] However, prior to these three Spanish expeditions—in the period which can properly be called the scientific period of botany—only Peter Loefling, Linnaeus's favorite disciple, as a member of the Iturriaga and Alvarado expedition (1754–

1756) officially explored the Guayana, part of which now comprises the states of Sucre and Bolívar in Venezuela. Loefling fell deathly ill with intermittent fever in the Capuchin Mission of San Antonio de Murucurí, whence he was taken to the town of Caroni, near the mouth of the Caroni River along the Orinoco, where he died on the 22nd of February 1756, at the age of 26. His remains were buried under an orange tree behind the church. Loefling's diary and his flora, sometimes called *Flora Cumanensis*, were published in 1758, after his death, together with a biographical note and a critique of his work by Linnaeus.[8]

After the first three expeditions came the 5-year voyage of Malaspina, Pineda, Née, and Haenke around the world. Haenke collected plants from the western coast of Patagonia and Chile to the northern part of America (California and Alaska). Although Malaspina's expedition was planned under Carlos III, it was not until the reign of Carlos IV that it set sail, in July 1789.

The first of the above-mentioned official Spanish expeditions to be organized was the one to Peru and Chile. This was created by a royal decree of the 8th of April 1777. In accord with the suggestion of Don Casimiro Gómez-Ortega, Professor of Botany and Director of the Royal Botanic Garden in Madrid, his two most enthusiastic and outstanding students, Don Hipólito Ruiz and Don José Pavón, were appointed botanists to the expedition. The principal artists were José Brunete and Isidro Gálvez. At the request of the Court of France, His Majesty gave permission to the French botanist, M. Joseph Dombey, to accompany the expedition, on the condition that a copy of his observations be left in Madrid to be incorporated in the final report of the Spanish botanists. Later, on the 14th of November 1784, the personnel of the expedition was increased in Peru: Don Juan Tafalla and Don Francisco Pulgar were included as apprentice botanist and apprentice artist, respectively.

After one unsuccessful attempt to set sail, Ruiz's expedition finally left Cádiz on the 4th of November 1777. It returned on the 12th of September 1788. Dombey already had returned at an earlier date; he boarded the *Peruano*, bound for Europe, in Lima on the 14th of April 1784, and arrived in Cádiz in early May 1785, after a crossing that lasted 1 year and during which they were more than once on the point of being shipwrecked. The studies of the expedition covered not only much of the territory now included in Peru and Chile, but at sundry points also touched areas that presently lie in Ecuador and Bolivia, but at that time formed part of the Viceroyalty of Peru.

The expedition to New Granada was, in point of time, the second royal botanic expedition established by Carlos III for his American dominions. Officially, it was set up in 1783. It had been the dream and obsession of Mutis for nearly 20 years. As early as 1764, 3 years after his arrival in Bogotá, capital of New Granada (today the capital of Colombia), Mutis had sent a petition to the king suggesting the creation of an organization similar to the one sent to Peru and Chile. He proposed an undertaking that would bring honor to the nation, improve public economy, increase commerce, enhance science, create new sources of income for the royal treasury, and thus glorify His Majesty with everlasting fame; be a means of investigating the quinine tree, to determine the best technique for its exploitation and conservation and to sell the best quality bark to the public at the lowest prices; and, finally, pay a debt to humanity in return for the munificence of Providence in having given Spain such boundless and rich possessions.

What Mutis could not win from the Crown in 20 years of repeated requests was won in his name through the influence of the newly appointed Archbishop-Viceroy of New Granada, Señor Don Antonio Caballero y Góngora. The royal decrees that realized Mutis's dreams were promulgated by the end of the year 1783. Mutis was appointed director, first botanist, and astronomer. Participation of the illustrious prelate-viceroy in setting up the expedition was even more direct: he had already created a provisional expedition the 1st of April of that same year. His action was stimulated by news from the central government that the Crown had granted permission for "four travelers who, financed by the Emperor of Germany, planned to become acquainted with both Americas, with the view of discovering and collecting curiosities of natural history." The viceroy was worried lest the honor of initiating the study of the country's natural resources should fall to foreigners. Accordingly, he created the provisional expedition on his own initiative, and he named Mutis its director.

The expedition established its headquarters in Mariquita, a charming town in the warmer zone situated at the foot of the central cordillera of the Andes, not far from the capital. Mutis and his organization worked there for 8 years, collecting plants and establishing a botanical garden. For various reasons, this location was abandoned in favor of Bogotá in 1790. Under the name of Instituto Botánico del Nuevo Reyno de Granada, the expedition became the center of academic life in the colony.

During his visit to Bogotá in 1802, Humboldt spoke of the work of Mutis and of Caldas with warm praise. Mutis was by then well along in years; he died 6 years later, at the age of 75. As a tribute to this outstanding botanist, Humboldt and Bonpland published in their *Aequinoctial Plants* an engraved portrait of Mutis, framing it with the plant that Gronovius had named in honor of Linnaeus, *Linnaea borealis*, on the right-hand side, together with the plant that Linnaeus's son had named in honor of Mutis, *Mutisia*, on the left.

The original members of the Expedición del Nuevo Reyno de Granada were as follows: First, the provisional expedition, created by the Archbishop-Viceroy Caballero y Góngora on the 1st of April 1783, was made up of the director, José Celestino Mutis; the assistant, Padre Eloy Valenzuela; and the artist, Antonio García. Second, the members of the permanent expedition, as constituted by royal decree on the 1st of November 1783, were the first botanist and astronomer, José Celestino Mutis; the second or assistant director, Eloy Valenzuela; the artists, Antonio García and Pedro Caballero; and the assistants, Fray Diego García, Pedro Fermín de Vargas, Bruno Landete and José Camblor (geographer).

Most of the members of this group were Colombians. Two artists were later sent out from Spain: José Calzada, a native of Malaga, and Sebastian Méndez, a native of Lima. Unfortunately, they did not prove to be satisfactory. Mutis was obliged to seek new artists. Since the art school in Quito, Ecuador, enjoyed a well-deserved reputation in those days, Mutis turned to it in his search for collaborators.

A group of five artists was contracted to come to work in Mariquita under the direction of Salvador Rizo, a notable painter and native of Mompox, Colombia. Rizo had been, from the start, in charge of the administration of the expedition and, like Caldas and other companions, was later a martyr of the Independence. This group of artists comprised Antonio Cortés, Nicolás Cortés (brother of Antonio), Antonio Silva, Vicente Sánchez, and Antonio Barrionuevo.

In addition to the aforementioned members, a number of students of Mutis directly or indirectly associated with the Instituto Botánico (which, as we have noted, had become the center of cultural life in Colombia by shifting intellectual activities from literary and philosophical fields to experimentation and investigation) took part in this program. Among these, a number of whom later became famous, the most noteworthy were the following: Francisco José de Caldas, a native of Popayán, a scientist, and a martyr; Caldas himself collected between five and six thousand plants in Ecuador for the Instituto. Francisco Antonio Zea, born in Medellín; he later became assistant director of the Botanical Garden of Madrid and the first Minister Plenipotentiary of Colombia to Great Britain. Jorge Tadeo Lozano, of Bogotá. José Manuel Restrepo, of Medellín.

Quite naturally, during the many years of the expedition (which lasted more than a quarter of a century), various other artists and painters, from one source or another, took part in the work. To name them all would be a long task. Fifteen permanent artists were at work in the expedition when Humboldt visited Bogotá. One name above all is worthy of special mention, that of the famous Colombian painter, Francisco Javier Matiz, whom Humboldt described as "the best painter of flowers in the world."

Despite the great loss suffered when Mutis died, the Instituto Botánico kept up its active program. Sinforoso Mutis followed his uncle as director of the expedition. Later, Caldas himself took over the direction. But from the moment in 1810 when the first sounds of independence rang out across the country and when, to free themselves, the people rose up in bloody battle for 9 years, the expedition began to undergo gradual paralysis and languor.

From more than one point of view the outstanding and many-sided personality of José Celestino Mutis offers extreme contrasts. Considering the times and the environment in which he lived, and the spirit of unrest in which he worked, Mutis's cultural attainments were solid and sound in many fields: he was at once philosopher, mathematician, naturalist, physician, clergyman, professor. His contemporaries justly gave Mutis the title of *sabio* (sage). Notwithstanding these attributes, however, his disposition was distant and misanthropic and, perhaps, a bit selfish. Caldas himself, the student whom Mutis held closest and appreciated most, was obliged to complain of his teacher's personality.

Mutis's *Flora de Bogotá*, which undoubtedly would have constituted the most valuable work of the three expeditions had it been published, has, for all practical purposes, been lost and has left no tangible results to posterity. Of his observations or discoveries made over a period of 25 years as director of the expedition (to say nothing of his 20 years of residence in Colombia prior to the organization of the expedition), Mutis published nothing of permanent interest except his *Arcano de la Quina*, printed in a Bogotá weekly, *El Papel Periódico*, in 1793. This work appeared later in Madrid in a second edition published by Hernández de Gregorio in 1828. Of the rest of his work—excepting his *Iconografia*, which is, after all is said and done, primarily the work of the many artists who collaborated with him over the years—there remains naught but an occasional report or address. His manuscripts, which at the time of his death numbered, according to Sinforoso Mutis,[9] "570 very precise descriptions of plants," have been lost in their entirety. Nevertheless, as we have pointed out, Mutis must be recognized as a great educator and teacher who served as a bellows for the scientific and cultural fire that burns today in Colombia.

Mutis had two angry controversies concerning priority and originality relating to discoveries in the study of the quinine tree: the first was directed against Dr. Sebastián José Lopez-Ruiz, and the second, through Don Francisco Antonio Zea, against Don Hipólito Ruiz. In both cases—especially the second—we must in fairness acknowledge that Mutis was not wholly in the right. It is a fact that Don Hipólito's work,[10] a work of great scientific value and the first treatise specifically on the quinine tree, but never published, antedates the *Arcano de la Quina* by about 2 years.

The third and last of the Spanish expeditions sent out to the New World by Carlos III was that to New Spain. In an interesting recent work, Dr. Harold William Rickett[11] has presented a documented historical reconstruction of this expedition and an interesting biographic summary of the group of investigators who made it up. He has saved from oblivion more than one of the significant facts about the lives and personalities of the expedition's members, one or two of whom were rather odd characters; but all, like the members of the other two expeditions, were outstanding men in their own fields.

Vicente Cervantes was the affable and hard-working teacher who for 30 years occupied the chair of botany in the recently founded botanical garden in Mexico, which had become, as in other countries, the intellectual center of the times.

Martín de Sessé y Lacasta was a competent organizer and director, not only of the expedition but also of the garden; he, like Mutis, strove for a long time to convince "His Majesty to see fit to establish in this city [Mexico] a royal garden with a chair of botany and to study the very fertile provinces of this dominion." Through his perseverance, determination, and skill, Sessé overcame all the hardships and obstacles with which "bureaucracy was constantly blocking the progress of the work of the expedition."

José Mariano Moziño[12] was a brilliant Mexican and native of Oaxaca whose love for botany led him to abandon his own medical career for plant sciences, and who years later was the victim of perplexing circumstances. After having obtained the rare honor of presiding over the Royal Academy of Medicine of Madrid for four consecutive periods, he was forced to flee Spain when the French retired from that country and to seek political refuge in Montpellier, only to have to later beg his colleagues in Madrid to intercede on his behalf for permission to return to Spain.

Don Joseph Longino Martínez, the naturalist, was that member of the expedition who managed to satisfy his wish to remain apart from his colleagues for 11 years; his work, nevertheless, was of great scientific merit, and he succeeded in amassing an important and valuable collection of minerals, animals, and plants.

Jayme Senseve, the apothecary whose correspondence constantly complained of his salary, left us one of the best and most illuminating itineraries of the travels of members of the expedition.

The Expedición Botanica de Nueva España (botanical expedition to New Spain) was created by royal decree on the 27th of October 1786. This document specified that the aims were to "draw, collect natural products, and illustrate and complete the work of Doctor Don Francisco Hernández." A second order, dated the 13th of March 1787, clothed these generalities with particulars, naming the scientific members of the expedition and prescribing their emoluments, privileges, and duties. A third, dated the 23rd of November 1787, gave directions for the operation of the garden, including a plan of instruction in botany.[13]

The general lines along which this expedition was organized were very similar to those which guided the organization of the other two expeditions. All three were scientific expeditions, and the three had as their principal goal the study of the natural history of the New World in its three divisions: mineral, vegetable, and animal. In this way it was to be insured that "his [Carlos III's] subjects take advantage of the benefits that may arise from this study for the advancement of science and the increase of commerce, industry, and art."

Aside from Cervantes, Sessé, Longino Martínez, and Senseve, whom we have already mentioned, the other original members of the expedition to New Spain were Don Juan Diego Castillo, who died in 1793, and the artists Juan de Dios Vicente de la Cerda and Athanasio Echeverría. Moziño joined the expedition as a field assistant on the 21st of March 1790. According to official records, however, he became a member only upon the death of Castillo—and even then as a provisional member—when he was named by the viceroy to succeed Castillo on the 24th of October 1793. He was promoted 1 year later to the rank of permanent member, when the viceroy's appointment was confirmed by royal decree on the 16th of September 1794.

The expedition of Sessé and Moziño took in most of Mexico from the north to the south; that is to say, from the states of California, Sonora, Chihuahua, Coahuila, and Nuevo León to Oaxaca and Chiapas. Collections were made also in Guatemala, Nicaragua, Salvador, Cuba, and Puerto Rico.

Accompanied by Moziño, Sessé went back to Spain in 1803, boarding ship in Vera Cruz in April of that year. The other members of the expedition stayed on in Mexico. Castillo had died in 1793; Longino Martínez died in June 1803, the very month and year that the expedition was expected back in Cádiz. Cervantes preferred to continue the duties appertaining to his chair of botany. Nothing further is known of de la Cerda or of Echeverría.

The text of the flora of New Spain studied by Sessé and Moziño—*Plantae Novae Hispaniae* and *Flora Mexicana*—first went to press in installments, when it was published by the Sociedad Mexicana de Historia Natural in 1886 and 1887. A second edition, complete in one volume, was published in 1893 and 1894 by the Secretaría de Fomento and the Instituto Médico Nacional of the same country. In both cases, the publication unfortunately had to be made without illustrations. The iconography of the expedition, comprising 2500 plates, unfortunately was lost in Barcelona after Moziño's death. This fact we know from the memoirs of de Candolle, for most of these plates were copied by that great Swiss botanist under dramatic circumstances.

When he was in Montpellier, Moziño loaned the illustrations to de Candolle, who conceived the idea of utilizing them in a *Prodromus* of the flora of Mexico, describing in particular the new species. When Moziño decided to return to Spain, he unexpectedly asked de Candolle to return the plates. De Candolle called together almost the entire intellectual community of Geneva, at least all who had any notion of drawing or painting, and in 10 days made copies of the illustrations. Although the projected *Prodromus* was never published, de Candolle—it is now generally recognized—leaned heavily on these plates in preparing descriptions of American plants.

Nor did the herbarium of Sessé and Moziño come to a much luckier end, although fortunately it was not wholly lost. Most of the collection is preserved in Madrid. According to what we read in the letters that passed between Pavón and Lambert[14] (which correspondence we have already discussed) and between Pavón and the equally celebrated botanist Philip Barker Webb,[15] Pavón sold two large collections of Mexican specimens: one to Lambert in 1823–1824, another to Webb at a later period. At the present time, parts of the first sale are preserved in the Delessert Herbarium in Geneva, in the Royal Botanic Gardens at Kew, and in the British Museum. The material in the British Museum is marked "Herb. Pavón."[16] The plants from the second sale are included in the Webb Herbarium in the Botanical Institute of the University of Florence. Pavón was never in Mexico himself; he makes no mention in his letters indicating the collector of these plants. It is known that when the Academy of Medicine, where Moziño kept his property, was destroyed by fire, he (Moziño) moved everything to the botanical office of the renowned authors of the flora of Peru and Chile. In view of all of this information, we strongly suspect that Pavón of motu propio sold part of the Sessé and Moziño herbarium.

Sessé died in 1809, Moziño in 1819.

Today the definitive version of the *Relacion histórica del Viage*, etc., of Don Hipólito Ruiz has finally been brought to light. This is due to the interest and zeal of the Real Academia de Ciencias Exactas, Físicas y Naturales de Madrid in keeping alive the memory of the members and labors of the various expeditions which, subsequent to the Spanish discovery of America, were sent out by the Crown of Spain to investigate the natural history of the New World, and the studies of which, even though available only in fragments, contributed so decisively to knowledge of the American flora in the science of Europe. Don Hipólito's *Relación* comprises the itinerary and complete account of the travels and work accomplished by the earliest of the three great scientific expeditions, mentioned above, that were sent to America by Carlos III. Two-thirds of this work have been transcribed from Don Hipólito's incomplete and final copy; the rest, the last portion, is from the complete, or second, copy of the same work, the *Compendio del Viage*, etc.

We need not praise the scientific value and style of Don Hipólito's work. As a writer, Don Hipólito can compete with any of the famous chroniclers who, in accounts which will live forever, have handed down to us narratives of great events in connection with the Spanish discovery and conquest of America. Some of his descriptions (e.g., that relating to the character and nature of the Indians) can take their place in the classical Spanish literature of all time. Don Hipólito was a man of science; however, in addition to the identification and classification of more than 2000 plants of different genera and species (including 500 new species that are not mentioned in Padre Barreiro's edition) and the execution in colors of drawings of most of these, we must note how deeply interested Don Hipólito and his expedition were in the fields of sociology, politics, administration, and religion—not to mention their contributions to mineralogy and zoology. That today, thanks to the progress made in taxonomy, some of his classifications have been corrected is but natural.

A comprehensive appreciation of the studies of Don Hipólito would, indeed, be too extensive to include in a prologue. We hope, nevertheless, that the time will come when we can realize one of our fondest desires and dedicate a special study to this aspect of his work. Among those contributions of special historical and scientific interest which Ruiz's investigations offer to the student of today, we cannot forgo mention of Don Hipólito's interesting observations or references on the introduction of the potato to Madrid, in 1662, under the name of *patatas manchegas* (under "Plants" in Chapter 3); on the "Source of the Marañón (Amazon River)" (in Chapter 12; under "Marañón River, or the Amazon" in Chapter 20; and in Chapter 27); on quinine bark (under "Quina, or Cascarilla" in Chapter 21); on the description of the properties, use, cultivation, and preparation of coca (under "The Coca Plant" in Chapter 24); on the "Rebellion of Tupac-Amaro" (in Chapters 14 and 32) and of the Indian Curiñancu (under "Religion and Superstitions; Uprising of the Indian Curiñancu" in Chapter 34); etc. Along with technical information such as that referring to the quinine tree, for example, Don Hipólito presents important observations such as those touching upon the social conditions of the Indians of the period (which the author gives us when he touches upon the life and activity of the bark gatherers)—conditions which, sad to say, still hold in some American countries. His notes tell us also how he was the first, even before Bernardino Antonio Gómes (1810) in Portugal, to attempt extraction of the active principle from quinine bark, by means of the separation of its salts. Finally, he tells us that the Peruvian natives, unlike the Indians of Loxa in Ecuador, were, up to that time, completely ignorant of the medical value of quinine bark. In respect to this last point, we may quote Don Hipólito's own words (under "Diseases" in Chapter 21):

> In spite of the abundance of cascarilla or quina recently discovered in Huánuco's forests, nobody employed this specific remedy to treat tertian fevers (malaria) until, during our second trip there, we introduced the use of the extract, prescribing a dose of 2 drams. After taking a few such doses, the patients were completely cured of their fevers.

The foregoing, however, is not all. Here and there, in his botanical descriptions, Don Hipólito's observations on the use by natives of sundry plants as medical agents represent, without a doubt, the most valuable contribution yet made to the study of American ethnomedicine.

In this connection, we recall that only a few years ago our forefathers had recourse to herbal remedies to treat their ills, and that this knowledge has, unfortunately, gradually died out with the voracious and often unscrupulous onslaught of so-called patent medicines. How many of the really great modern remedies—digitalis, ipecacuana, quinine, curare, opium, etc., to mention only a few—are of plant origin, and how many more would be discovered were systematic phytochemical investigation of native plant remedies to be carried out? How many of them would be found to be more effective than some of the highly refined and advertised "injections which stop eruptions and dry up the flux," "extracts and pills which nourish," "elixirs or syrups which stimulate like tonic wines," etc.? At the end of the *Historical Narrative of the Expedition*, as an aid to the reader, we have prepared an "Appendix: Medicinal Plants Mentioned by Ruiz" and an "Index to Latin Names of Plants."

Concerning sickness and its etiology and prevention, it is equally interesting to note here that at that time, as Don Hipólito noted, the Indians believed that certain ailments were transmitted by animals of minute size—sometimes almost imperceptible—and that, even though wholly isolated from contact with other civilizations, they recognized the infectious character of contagious diseases. From this belief arose their logical, though drastic, sanitary custom of burning alive the contagiously ill and those who had been in close contact with them.

Nor is the curious or humorous touch lacking. In discussing plants or animals, Don Hipólito oftentimes records amazing observations, such as the one about the Peruvian bird, the chivillo, which is like its congener the cuckoo, in England (under "Birds" in Chapter 21):

> When the chivillo wants to lay its eggs, it seeks out a huanchaco [called aloica in Chile] nest and deposits an egg there, and similarly finds a nest for every single egg it lays. It contrives to propagate its young by the work of others, for the huanchacos incubate and feed the young chivillos as though they were their own offspring.

Or the following (under "A Depilatory Plant?" in Chapter 31):

> *Mimosa latisiliqua*, yerba de la lancha. Natives say that when horses and mules eat this plant, they lose the hair of their manes and tails, and that the hair is not renewed for a long time. They also say that if a man should wash his head for a number of days in water in which many leaves of the plant have been crushed, he will become completely bald.

Here Don Hipólito adds, "We must not believe that many have undergone this experiment, for nobody wants to be bald. If it had the same effect upon the beard, it would be worth its weight in gold, especially in that country [Peru]." Similar amusing observations abound throughout the manuscript.

Whosoever reads Ruiz's account does not have long to wait before appreciating the sufferings that members of the expedition had to undergo and the difficulties and dangers that they had to overcome. The descriptions of Brunete's death, of Don Hipólito's illness on his trip from Lima to the mountains of Huánuco and Cuchero, of the adventures that befell the travelers in the mountains of Pozuzo and Chacahuassi, etc., merely reflect the many indescribable experiences that those devoted and long-suffering scientists had to face. All this does not even touch upon the almost superhuman willpower which Don Hipólito showed when, on four different occasions, he saw the results of months—yes, even years—of work and sacrifice lost in a matter of seconds in one kind of accident or another. One of these accidents was the fire in Macora that destroyed, among other irreplaceable materials, his manuscript of the journey to Chile, the product of 2 years of labor. Others were the sinking of the *Buen Consejo* and the shipwrecks of the *San Pedro de Alcántara*, first along the Chilean coast, then later off Portugal.

What drives a man to face such dangers and sacrifices? What material return did the members of the expedition receive? Don Hipólito himself answers these questions. Concerning the first, he wrote in the description of his trip from Chacahuassi to Huánuco, "Only the defense of honor or business interests could force one to travel over such an abominable path . . ." (Chapter 56), undergoing "the continual fatigue, falls, blows, heat, thirst, hunger, bad weather, and suffering that fell to the lot of the botanists because of the rough and rugged character of those tangled jungles" (under "Mayco Sickness" in Chapter 49). About the second question, he tells us that, when the time came to set sail from Lima, "We spent every penny that we had earned in Peru and left as poor as church mice, for we had not engaged in any business other than the fulfillment of our mission" (Chapter 57).

Insofar as Don Hipólito's character is concerned, we find that his is perhaps one of the few such works in which the writer hardly mentions himself. When he does so, it is merely incidental to the subject under consideration. That he was a conscientious, patient, studious, observing man—albeit, and perhaps because of these various traits, often demanding and exigent with his companions—is attested to by every page of his manuscript. Even his impulses and his qualms of conscience peer out between the lines. We may cite one example. When, after the fire at Macora, he accused the artists of indifference in the face of such a tragedy and of having failed to come to his aid to try to save something from the disaster—and this notwithstanding the fact that the manager of a neighboring hacienda, from which the fire could be watched, had admonished them to go and help in the rescue work—Don Hipólito decided to omit this accusation from his final manuscript. Thus, in the *Compendio*, upon which the *Relación historica* is based, the paragraph relating to this point is crossed out. It seems, therefore, that Don Hipólito did not want any reference to this mishap to be made in the published work.[17]

Don Hipólito reveals nothing about the character of Don José Pavón, of the artists Brunete and Gálvez, or of those who later joined the expedition, the assistant Tafalla and the artist Pulgar. Does this mean a discreet silence on his part or just a bit of egotism? Perhaps a little of both. The fact is, Don Hipólito's account leaves us in the dark as to just what was Pavón's part in the final work of the expedition. However, this we can deduce without fear of error: Don Hipólito and Pavón had opposite temperaments, and Don Hipólito preferred to do (and actually did) the greater part of the botanical classification. Of the artists, Ruiz preferred Gálvez, whom he chose as a personal companion. The same observation applies to Dombey. Don Hipólito hardly if ever mentions Dombey, except in the preface of his work, where he notes that Dombey "has not met this condition to the letter [that on his return to France from Peru he leave in Spain a duplicate copy of his observations so that the Spanish botanists might incorporate them in their work], for upon our arrival in Madrid he delivered to us merely a few fragments of plants with very few notes and only an occasional description." Such a stipulation was set up when he received permission to accompany the expedition to America. There is no question, nevertheless, that the Spanish botanists were to have benefited greatly from their association with Dombey, for Dombey was an outstanding naturalist.

A few closing words: We do not want to end without acknowledging our indebtedness to the trustees of the British Museum for their kindness in allowing us to publish this manuscript of Don Hipólito's, a document which must be counted as one of the treasures of the Museum.

In like manner, we want to express our gratitude to Dr. John Ramsbottom and to Mr. A. H. G. Alston, former Director and Principal Scientific Officer of the Department of Botany of the British Museum (Natural History), respectively, for the facilities they made available to us during our study and transcription of the manuscript.

The beautiful and interesting maps that illustrate this work were photographed and colored for us with artistic skill and with admirable fidelity by Mr. Harold J. Gowers, from the unpublished works *Descripción Histórico-Geográfica, Política, Eclesiástica y Militar de la América Meridional* [*Historical, Geographical, Political, Ecclesiastical and Military Survey of South America*] (compiled by Padre Fr. Manuel Sobreviela, Missionary of Ocopa, Lima, 1796, manuscript no. 15,740 Plut.) and *Maps of Peru* (manuscript no. 17,671 Plut.), also deposited in the British Museum.

Mlle. Marie-José Nemry (now Mrs. Jaime Jaramillo-Arango) assisted us enthusiastically and with great care in the difficult task of transcribing and revising the manuscript, of comparing the two versions—the *Compendio* and the *Relación*—and of making the various indexes.

Dr. Javier Pulgar-Vidal, a native of Panao, Department of Huánuco (Peru), is the great-great-grandson of the artist Don Francisco Pulgar of the Ruiz and Pavón expedition, and is, like his distinguished ancestor, a devoted naturalist. He has kindly assisted us in checking the indexes of geographic, proper, vernacular, and native names that we have thought it well to add to the ordinary indexes [in the Spanish edition], in order to enhance the value of the manuscript.

In homage to Don Hipólito, we have kept his original orthography [in the Spanish edition]. In this respect, it is of particular interest to note that in the original manuscript—since the author must have gathered the names from the Indians themselves—place names which today are written with a *g* in Spanish usually appear with an *h*: Huallaha = Hualla*g*a; Huayaquil = *G*uayaquil; Huamanha = Huaman*g*a; Yanha = Yan*g*a or Yan*g*as; etc. The aspirate sound of the *h* seems to have been replaced by the guttural sound of the *g*. In other names, this sound has been replaced by that of the double *c*: Pomaysanha = Pomaisan*cc*a; Huallanha = Huallan*cc*a. The letter *g*, furthermore, does not exist in the Runa-shimi (Quechua) language, spoken by the natives of Peru. This is why, in our history of quinine,[18] in the chapter on the etymology of the word quina or quina-quina, we wrote that although Chifflet,[19] Colmenero,[20] Heinrich von Bergen,[21] and other authors state that the natives called the quinine tree gennanaperide, gennaperide, or guananepide, they could not have meant *aborígines* when they used the word *nativos* because the letter *g* does not exist in Quechua. This is the reason that it cannot be found in any of the several dictionaries of the Quechua language.

[In the Spanish edition] the only changes we have made in transcribing the manuscript concern the correction of the punctuation. This we have done for the sake of clarity. We have rearranged Father Barreiro's appendices, placing them in chronologic order and giving each one of them an explanatory title in accord with the contents.[22]

Notes to Prologue to the Spanish Edition

1. Comisión de Estudios Retrospectivos de Historia Natural.
2. *Travels of Ruiz, Pavón, and Dombey in Peru and Chile (1777–1788)* by Hipólito Ruiz, etc. Translation by B. E. Dahlgren, Chief Curator, Department of Botany, Field Museum of Natural History, vol. 21 (Chicago), 1940.
3. Jaime Jaramillo-Arango, "A Critical Review of the Basic Facts in the History of Cinchona," in Journ. Linn. Soc. (London), vol. 53 (March 1949), pages 272–309, plates 10–21, and (in the Spanish text) "Estudio Crítico Acerca de los Hechos Básicos en la Historia de la Quina," in Rev. Real Acad. Cienc. (Madrid), vol. 43 (1949), book 1.
4. For the English-language translation of all the chapters of the "Epilogue by P. Augustín Jesús Barreiro" by B. E. Dahlgren, see *Travels of Ruiz, Pavón, and Dombey in Peru and Chile*, op. cit., pages 243–276. Referred to here is Chapter X, "The journals and the *Viaje* of Ruiz—Date at which it was terminated," etc., pages 273–274.
5. Hipólito Ruiz & Josef Pavón, *Suplemento á la Quinología* (Madrid) (1801), page 115, note.
6. Collection of reference letters, herbarium, Royal Botanic Gardens, Kew, and lists and accounts of shipments in the library, Botany Department, British Museum (Natural History).
7. Gonzalo Fernández de Oviedo y Valdez, *Historia General y Natural de las Indias, Islas y Tierra Firme del Mar Océano* (Madrid) (1851–1855). José de Acosta, *Historia Natural y Moral de las Indias* (Seville) (1590). Francisco Hernández, *Rerum Medicarum Novae Hispaniae Thesaurus seu Plantae, Animalium, Mineralium . . .* (Rome) (1651). Antonio Vásquez de Espinosa, *Compendio y Descripción de las Indias Ocidentales*. Manuscript in the Vatican Library, Barberini Collection, no. 3584. Antonio de la Calancha, *Coronica Moralizada del Orden de San Augustín en el Peru* (terminated in Lima in 1633 and published the first time in Barcelona in 1638). Bernabé Como, *Historia del Nuevo Mundo* (Seville) (1890–1893). Bernardino de Sahagún, *Historia de las Cosas de la Nueva España* (Mexico) (1829–1830).
8. Carl Linnaeus, *Petri Loefling Iter Hispanicum, eller Resa til Spanska Länderna uti Europa och America, Förratad ifrån Ar 1751 til Ar 1756* (Stockholm) (1758).

9. Sinforoso Mutis, Introduccíon a la *Historia de la Quina*. Unpublished manuscript in the library, Jardín Botánico, Madrid.
10. Hipólito Ruiz, *Quinología, o Tratado del Ábol de la Quina ó Cascarilla* (Madrid) (1792); (see "Epilogue by P. Augustín Jesús Barreiro," translated by B. E. Dahlgren, op. cit., Chapter I, pages 243–250).
11. Harold William Rickett, "The Royal Botanical Expedition to New Spain," in Chron. Bot., vol. 2, no. 1 (1947), pages 1–86.
12. Moziño always wrote his name with a *z*, not with a *c*. It seems, therefore, that this original orthography should be kept.
13. Rickett, loc. cit.
14. Letter collection, herbarium, Royal Botanic Gardens, Kew.
15. Letter collection, Instituto Botánico della Universitá de Firenze. We are indebted to Prof. Rodolfo E. Pichi Sermolli for having very kindly made available a copy of this correspondence.
16. Thomas A. Sprague, "Sessé and Mociño's Plantae Novae Hispaniae and Flora Mexicana," in Kew Bull. (1926).
17. The fact that this episode has already appeared in Father Barreiro's publication makes it unnecessary for us to transcribe it in this version and allows us merely to mention it in passing, to the honor of Don Hipólito.
18. Jaramillo-Arango, op. cit.
19. Jean-Jacques Chifflet, *Pulvis Febrifugus Orbis Americani Ventilatus* (Brussels) (1653).
20. Joseph Colmenero, *Reprobación del Pernisioso Abuso de los Polvos de la Corteza de Quarango, o China China*, etc. (Salamanca) (1697).
21. Heinrich von Bergen, *Versuch einer Monographie der China* (Hamburg) (1826), in Edinburgh Med. Surg. Journ., vol. 27 (1827), page 120.
22. For the English-language translation of all of Father Barreiro's appendices by B. E. Dahlgren, see *Travels of Ruiz, Pavón, and Dombey in Peru and Chile*, op. cit., pages 279–332 (publisher's note).

The Journals of Hipólito Ruiz

Historical Narrative of the Expedition Carried Out by the Botanist Don Hipólito Ruiz to Peru and Chile from 1777 to 1788, and the Return Voyage to Madrid

King Carlos III of Spain, desirous that his subjects use their economically valuable plants for the advancement of science and for the increase of commerce, industry, and art, and at the same time to encourage botanical investigation in all his American dominions, promulgated on the 8th of April 1777 royal decrees allowing two botanists and two artists to travel to America to observe, describe, draw, and collect the flora of Peru and Chile for 4 years.

His Majesty, informed by the head professor of botany, Don Casimiro Ortega, of the most studious and best-prepared scholars in this branch of learning, appointed me principal botanist and leader of the expedition, and he named Don José Pavón as my colleague in the commission. Likewise, His Majesty named Don José Brunete and Don Isidro Gálvez as artists. Finally, the king gave his leave that the French botanist Don José (Joseph) Dombey visit these dominions in our company, charged by his sovereign with the same purpose that we had; the only condition was that on his return to France from Peru he leave in Spain a duplicate copy of his observations so that the Spanish botanists might incorporate them in their work. It seems that Dombey has not met this condition to the letter, for upon our arrival in Madrid he delivered to us merely a few fragments of plants with very few notes and only an occasional description.

CHAPTER 1

Trip from Madrid to Cádiz

On the 19th of September 1777 we—the five persons named—left Madrid for Cádiz. We arrived on the 2nd of October in that port with no trouble worthy of note; on the contrary, I, who had left Madrid seriously ill, arrived recovered in Cádiz with little admiration for those who had made mournful predictions concerning my swellings and melancholy. During the 18 days that we remained in Cádiz, we arranged all that was necessary for the trip. We were informed that it would be by Cape Horn in the ship of San Magdalena called *Peruano*, under the command of Don José de Córdoba.

On the 19th of October of that year, we embarked on the Bay of Cádiz; and at nine in the morning, with shifting light winds by the east and north, we raised full sail. At half past eleven, since the wind was calm, we dropped anchor at 4 yards.

On the 20th, at three in the morning, we again set sail, steering westward since the wind was moderate by the east. At midday a fresh, southwesterly wind arose, but the horizons were dark and affected with considerable wind. Consequently, at quarter past one, the captain agreed with other officials and pilots and decided to enter the port of Cádiz, where we stayed until the 3rd of November. With the weather improved, we set sail at four in the morning and continued the trip to Peru very happily.

On the trip we saw many young whales, dolphins, seals, swordfish, sharks, albacores, bonitos (striped tunnies), dorados (giltheads), flying fish, and various other fish, and a diversity of birds that we describe on our return along the same route from Peru to Cádiz. On the 12th of November we also caught sight of the island of Los Salvages and on the 13th that of La Palma, and on the 31st of December the island of La Ascensión. The 7th of February 1778 brought us to Tierra del Fuego, the 8th to the island of Los Estados. On the 15th we saw that we were at 60°19', for on the 2 previous days we could not take readings and could only estimate that we had gone a few minutes beyond 61°. These few days were the most uncomfortable of the whole trip because of the cold, snows, hail, rolling of the ship, and battering of the waves that occasionally entered the ship.

During the entire voyage we saw but one ship, until we arrived at the region of Pisco where, 25 leagues from the port of Callao, we found on the 5th of April two small packet boats carrying slaves of both sexes to Pisco.

On the 2nd of April, at eight in the morning, we saw the Peruvian mainland at a distance of 10 leagues. On the 6th, we caught sight of the island of San Lorenzo, and we believed that we had run aground in the shallow areas before the town of Lurín. On the 8th of April, we anchored in the port of Callao. We disembarked on the 9th and went on to Lima (Figure 3, Plate 1) to present ourselves, together with the officials of the ship, to the viceroy of Peru, His Excellency Don Manuel de Guirior. He received us most courteously and offered us his protection as far as the powers of his office permitted. We were visited by the most distinguished and illustrious people in Lima, and we responded respectfully to all these attentions.

When we had received the viceroy's permits and passport, we began our botanical excursions on the 4th of May in the parks of Lima and the farms and towns of the province of Cercado. We traveled on foot with our presses underarm, collecting whatever we found in these areas. Such work, never before seen by the native inhabitants, was very surprising to them, especially since we always traveled on foot—they were not accustomed to doing this themselves when leaving town to go into the countryside. In all the streets and fields, they stopped to watch attentively and with wonder, pointing their fingers at us and calling us herb-gathering warlocks.

Nonetheless, we three botanists continued collecting on foot until the 22nd of July, during which period we gathered, described, and drew various new plants, as well as others known to us but which had been studied and described superficially and by methods less exact than those of Linnaeus. We adopted the Linnaean system to identify and describe new and already known plants because it is the most favorably received system throughout Europe. For those plants that we identified, we always recorded the generic, specific, and common names, as well as any local names, uses, and medicinal properties of the plants.

CHAPTER 2

Description of the Province of Cercado

The province of Cercado measures 13 leagues long north to south, by 8 leagues wide. It is bounded on the north by the province of Chancay, on the northeast by that of Canta, on the east by that of Huarocherí, on the south by that of Cañete, and on the west by the southern ocean. Its climate, although usually mild—especially when there is no garúa (mist)—tends to foster tertian fevers (malaria), grippe, colds, tetanus, chest ailments, rheumatism, smallpox, vicho or mal del valle (valley

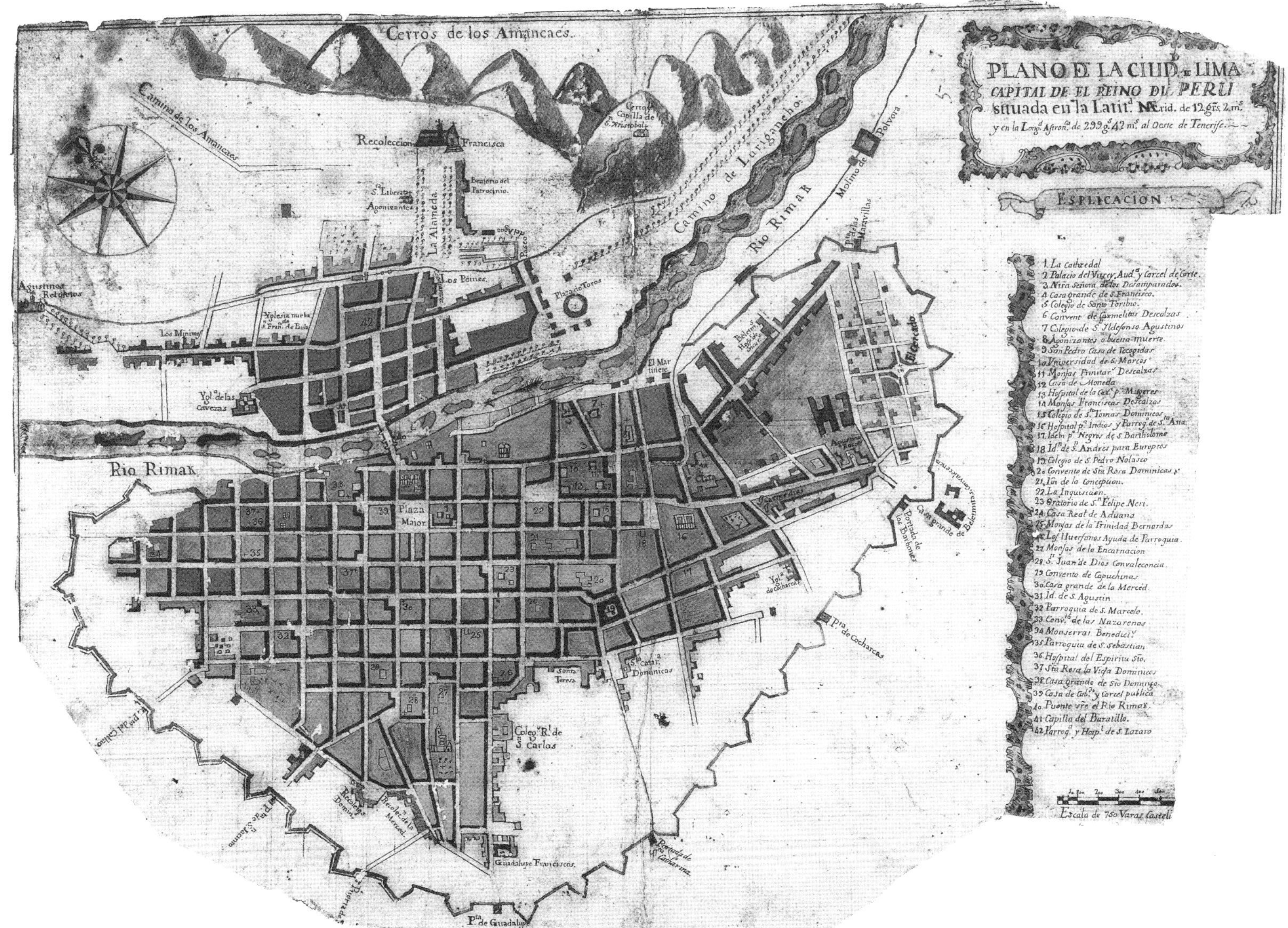

Figure 3. Map of the city of Lima, capital of Peru. From the *Historical, Geographical, Political, Ecclesiastical and Military Survey of South America*, edited by Manuel Sobreviela, missionary of Ocopa, Lima, 1796, folio 35. (Courtesy of the British Museum.)

sickness), a kind of dysentery, and much venereal disease. The cold of the winter season, not felt by those accustomed to colder countries, is rather penetrating for the natives; at that time of year the atmosphere is foggy throughout the morning until noon, and sometimes all day and night. No rain falls except the very fine mist called garúa. There are no storms, but during the spring—October and November—there are great earthquakes. Diseases are cured in the villages with medicines brought in from Lima, but those who cannot afford these drugs use herbs administered in accordance with their means.

Since it does not rain in this region or along the whole coastal area, houses and farm buildings are roofed with wood, canes, branches, and a mortar made of sticky clay. All the fields abound in maize, beans, a little barley, various kinds of squash, green vegetables, root vegetables, fruits, and beautiful and fragrant flowers in the gardens and orchards.

The most important products of these farms are alfalfa and maizillo (a milletlike grass). Taken to Lima to be sold, they provide fodder for all sorts of animals; without these two crops it would be difficult to keep so many animals in the city. Even so, many people take their cattle to pasture on the farms during the winter. There are also a number of sugar cane plantations where some sugar is produced, but most of the harvest goes into guarapo (liquor made from fermented cane juice), miel (molasses, syrup), alfeñique (a paste prepared of sugar and almonds), and chancaca (brown sugar).

The rivers that water these fields are the Rimac, the Carabaillo, and the Lurín, all coming down from the mountain ranges of Canta and Huarocherí. During periods of rain in the mountains, these rivers are filled by the melting of great amounts of snow, and they give enough water to irrigate the whole of this large valley of farms. But in the dry season, water becomes very scarce.

There are seven parishes in addition to those in Lima, the capital of Peru and the head of this province. The first four are Carabaillo with its dependency Lancón; Late with its dependency Rinconada; Lurigancho with its dependency Huachipa; and Bellavista, founded after the great earthquake of the 28th of October 1746 in which the town and garrison of Callao, or San Fernando, were flooded. The bay here, protected by the island of San Lorenzo on the southwest, is deep enough to accommodate all ships of the southern ports of America as well as those arriving from Spain. The fifth parish is the town of Magdalena with its dependency Miraflores. The sixth is Surco with its dependency Chorrillos, the inhabitants of which keep themselves busy fishing and carry their fish to market in Lima every day. The seventh parish is Lurín with its dependency Pachacamac.

CHAPTER 3

Description of the City of Lima

Lima, the capital of Peru, is located 2 leagues from the sea at 12°2'51" south latitude, and at a longitude of 298°59' from the meridian of Tenerife.

The climate is agreeable for those arriving from cold regions, but people living there for 2 or 3 years find it very enervating in winter and very hot in summer. It never rains, however, except for the thick mist called garúa. In summer there is a constant southern breeze, which prevails all the year round and cools the atmosphere. Since this ocean breeze is constant, and as the winds of the nearby mountains are at a higher altitude and therefore cannot counteract the sea breezes, it is impossible for the mist, or garúa, to condense into rain. The temperature in summer usually is about 81 to 84°F (27 to 29°C); in winter it drops to 59°F (15°C).

Notwithstanding the lack of rain, the sun is hardly ever visible except in winter, as it is ordinarily hidden by clouds, which are normal during the summer. These clouds come from the mountains, where they are spent in the form of hail, snow, rain, and lightning—phenomena unknown along the coast because of its low altitude. On the contrary, the coast is plagued with terrible earthquakes, which likewise are felt in the mountains and valleys of the cordillera.

For this reason, the western or coastal slopes of the mountains are devoid of forests except for limited and scattered patches of herbs and shrubs. Where they do exist, such plants spring up during the period of heaviest garúa, or may not appear even then. There is no water but that supplied by the small rivers coming down from the mountains or that which gushes from an occasional spring. The Rimac, which crosses the city of Lima after bathing the mines of the province of Huarocherí, is this kind of river; so also is the great puqueo, or spring, that is brought into Lima through an underground aqueduct for public water supply. There is no lake, unless we count as lakes a few pools formed by discharge from rural irrigation canals: such a pool is the one called Villa where, a short while ago, the magnesium sulfate that now supplies the apothecaries of Lima was discovered.

Potassium nitrate, or saltpeter, abounds along the coastal areas, especially in meadows and low places where cattle urinate frequently. This nitrate is rich in sea salts. Because they do not know how to separate these salts, the inhabitants do not use the saltpeter of the fields and strands of Lima; they resort to the mines in Cumini and Huarocherí, where the nitrate from these sources is purer and almost crystalline. So easy would be the separation of sodium chloride, or common salt, that many hundredweight of pure saltpeter could be procured at an insignificant cost from the fields of Lima—and the common salt might likewise be put to use.

In the valley of Lima and in the neighboring mountains, useful minerals have not been found. Many of these mountains have been explored, and some have mines where silver and gold have been encountered, but the yields have been so poor that the mines have had to be abandoned. In the Cerro de Camacho, 1½ leagues from Lima, layers or accumulations of garnets have formed on the surface, hard by the house on the estate near Lurigancho. At Mangomarca, the boundary of the estate of Zárate, and upstream in the creek as far as the wall on the right bank, outcroppings of quartz and black slate are to be found. Deposits of lime and gypsum are also found there. These deposits are not exploited, because their products can be obtained at low cost and brought in from Chilca. The *amianthus immaturus* of Linnaeus (fine, silky asbestos) is also found. Among the various layers, or strata, in the valley of Lima, there is one of clay. In this clay, one can see numerous caves that have been dug out to extract material for use in ceramics.

This earth is thin in some places, sandy in others. Everywhere it lies over a vast quantity of gravel, proof that the sea once covered the area for 6 or 7 leagues inland. Some speculate and say that when the floodwaters receded they tore these deposits of earth from the mountains and that, since the waters originated far inland, they flowed out and left the various layers of soil that we have mentioned, according to the region from which they came. If this be so, we may infer that this hemisphere was inhabited before the Flood; for, upon excavating a building site in 1757 at a place where the soil was deepest, there was dug up from between the soil and gravel a human skeleton so completely agglutinated to the soil that it was possible to separate only a few bones. The slightest handling caused the bones to fall apart, and nothing could be obtained but a few fragments of the cranium, from which its identification as a human body was established beyond a doubt.

Large timber trees grow in the valleys in spite of the thin soil. Among these, we may mention molle (mastic trees), huaranccos (acacias), jaboncillos, totumos or tutumos (calabash trees, gourd trees), higuerones (species of wild figs), sauces (willows), and cedros (cedars), only recently transplanted to this region. The excellence of climate and soil favors the growth of many other trees that yield fruits and precious woods: nogal del país (native walnut), palto (avocado), lúcumo, pacae (pacay, inga), chirimoyo (cherimoya), anono (anona, custard apple), guanabano (guanabana, soursop), palillo, cerezo (cherry), ciruelo de la tierra (native plum), ciruelo agrio (sour plum), and mamei (mammee). The fruits of most of them have a rind that is rough or else of an unpleasing hue, and they are not allowed to ripen on the tree but are prepared for eating by being plucked green and set aside for some days, wrapped in various materials.

Limo (lime), limón real agrio (true sour lemon), limón dulce (sweet lemon), limón sutil (thin-skinned lemon), naranjo (orange), toronjo (grapefruit), and cidro (citron)—all brought from other countries—bear abundantly the year round. Mulberry, olive, fig, pear, peach, and apricot, taken from Europe to Chile and then to Peru, fruit well. The plums, morello cherries (sour cherries), and cherries of Spain do not fruit in Lima, or else do so very infrequently. Papayas, plátanos (bananas), granadillas and tumbos (kinds of passion fruit), grapes, pepinos de la tierra (native pepinos, fruits of the melon shrub), mitos (small papayas), zapayos or mates or calabazas (gourds, pumpkins, squash), and melons are abundant; and large and delicious watermelons are trafficked for sale from the town of Mala to Lima.

The region produces excellent root vegetables such as camotes or batatas (sweet potatoes), yuca (manioc, cassava), yacones, arracachas (apios, Peruvian parsnips), and papas or patatas (potatoes), all of which enter into the everyday diet, especially among poor people. Excellent green vegetables there are, too: lettuce, endive, celery, cabbages, kidney beans, asparagus, onions, garlic, shallots, tomatoes, hot or sweet peppers, parsley, mint, and others.

The soil is appropriate for all kinds of leguminous crops such as horse beans, peas, chick peas, and many varieties of the common bean or kidney beans or string beans, of which even the most fastidious people are very keen, especially of the variety called pallares (lima beans). On holidays, in the evenings, there is a great consumption of peanuts and chochos or altramuces (lupines), either roasted or boiled together.

The principal crop in these fields is sugar cane; large quantities of alfeñique (almond-paste candy), chancaca (brown sugar), miel (molasses), and guarapo (cane liquor), the drink of the general populace, are prepared from it, but very little sugar. Maize, alfalfa, and maizillo (a milletlike grass) are the chief crops produced by the landholders, because of the great amounts needed as feed for animals. One seldom finds a person who does not have at least one animal. Barley and wheat are cultivated only on a very small scale, because these grains are brought to Lima from Chile.

In the gardens, sundry fragrant and showy plants and flowers are cultivated. In addition to giving delight as ornamentals, they are employed in preparing various compounds called mixturas, to which are added other fragrances such as incense, amber, scented water, liquor of amber, and sometimes musk. Finally, these fields have many wild plants, some of known medicinal value, as I shall outline at the end of this description.

On the beaches, the only marine plant one finds is the cachiyuyo, an enormous species of *Fucus* (wrack) that is occasionally cast up by the sea.

Animals

A great population of donkeys is kept in pastures and cultivated fields. These animals are used to transport alfalfa and maizillo to Lima. There are also many horses. Crossing of the horses and donkeys produces excellent mules, which are called aguilillas (little eagles) on account of their nimble and smooth pace. Furthermore, there are good herds of cows and flocks of sheep; large numbers of these animals are driven down from the mountains to supply the needs of Lima. In addition, there are some goats, small deer, and guinea pigs, and usually a few small foxes as well.

The añaz, or zorrillo (skunk), is a small animal the size of a rabbit. It is partly a vulgarism to say that its urine stinks and that the animal defends itself with it when attacked, for it can be observed that, in addition to the bladder, the skunk possesses two fluid-filled glands located in a natural cavity at the base of the tail. It seems that the animal can eject the fluid from these glands not by compression but only as the result of some external irritation or vibration that is put into action by fear of whatever is pursuing the beast. When one goes to capture the skunk, it shoots off a spray of milky fluid of such a disgusting and obnoxious stench that all within reach of the odor must flee from it. Sometimes sailors notice it more than 4 leagues out to sea; this happened, I was told, to the crew of the *Begona* in the Rio de la Plata in 1753.

There are two great enemies of hens and fruits: rats, and mucamucas (opossums), *Didelphis marsupialis*. This little animal is smaller than a cat and hangs by its tail like a monkey; it bears on the outside of the abdomen a pouch that, when open, exposes the breast and forms two cavities where it carries its offspring when changing its haunts or when frightened by enemies. Pericotes (large rats) or mice are very common; on the other hand, squirrels are rare.

Insects

Aside from an occasional viper or scorpion in the mountains, there are no poisonous animals. There are a number of bothersome mosquitoes in the fields and orchards. In the nearby mountains, during the season when the rains turn the hillsides green, a kind of spider breeds. It measures 4 inches in length and 2 inches in width, is very hairy and brown, has black, shiny, very sharp biting parts as large as a cat's claw, and is extraordinarily agile, but it does not seem to do any particular damage. Concerning the house spider, which is black and large and abundant in dirty places, it has happened that people awake in the morning with their faces covered with blotches—the effects of the bite of this animal.

There are two species of nihuas (jigger fleas or chiggers), also called piques, that burrow into the feet to hide, causing much itching. Although they are tiny they form, upon the negroes and slovenly folk, nests almost the size of a pea or bean; when these nests are dug out of the flesh, they are seen to be made up of great numbers of tiny eggs. When not combated, this pest becomes so common that it sometimes kills these unfortunate people.

In the summertime caterpillars abundantly infest almost all plants except the pacay (*Mimosa inga*). People would be happy to have more of this tree in Lima and be able to admire what happens in the forests of Monzón and Panatahuas with larvae on the pacay. These caterpillars are 2 inches long; when they have fed, they form a mass on the thickest part of the trunk and begin weaving a cloth like thin, corrugated rag paper that usually stretches for more than a yard in length and about a foot in width. When this cloth is finished, they weave a simpler one over it. They continue working thus for six layers; each layer is thinner and whiter than the one before, the final layer having the delicate texture and whiteness of rice paper. When the work is finished, the six layers are freed at their ends. The larvae, now almost in the nymph stage, come together in the middle and, joining all the loose ends in one point, form a sack that resembles a melon. This sack is hung on the nearest twig or whorl until, when it is time for the butterflies to emerge, the whole thing disintegrates. This phenomenon has hitherto gone unobserved, probably because these sweet and tasty caterpillars are hunted by Indians for food, and they are now found only in inaccessible forests. The fabric of the caterpillars can be mistaken for a thin skin because of certain thick fibers and the luster that coats one side. It can also stand soaping and washing, even after a long immersion, without losing either its sheen or its usefulness as a writing material.

Birds

There is neither the abundance nor the variety of birds, especially game birds, that one finds in other countries. There are only two small doves; one is called cuculi or madrugadora (early bird) and is about the size of a wood pigeon, and the other is a little larger than a sparrow. Both are very delicious to eat. One finds an occasional partridge or species of large codorniz (quail) that comes down from the mountains in springtime, and a few ducks and widgeons that cross the irrigation canals.

There are condors, like vultures in size and habit, and three species of buzzard—the black-headed, the red-headed, and a third with a black and white head. Those with red heads usually live in the country. The other two frequent towns, ridding them of all dead flesh with such voracity that in less than half an hour 30 or 40 of them leave nothing more of a mule than the skeleton. And if any animal feeding in the fields has a large sore, these buzzards search it out with their keen sense of smell, even at a distance of 3 or more leagues; though the beast be far from death, one of the birds will descend upon it, picking out its eyes. None of the other birds will draw near until the animal lies prostrate on the ground, when they all assemble promptly and, starting at the hind parts, consume the beast in short order. When they find a carcass, one of the birds first plucks out the eyes, then the others fall upon it like wolves. If an animal has enough strength to defend itself and flee, these birds will follow it without rest until they can accomplish their plunder.

Of the many species of hummingbirds in America, there is only one in the valley of Lima, and this is not one of the most delicate. It is called picaflor (flowerpecker) because, like the other species of this group as well as bees, it lives exclusively on the honey (or nectar) of flowers. To one who did not know this bird and saw it fluttering around flowers, its small size and the noise of its wings might suggest that it was some large bee or fly. Its hue is an iridescent green and can be clearly seen only when the bird comes to rest at close range.

There is another, somewhat larger bird called a negrillo (little black bird). The peculiarity of this bird lies in its jumping round and round on a branch, a habit that it continues persistently for 2 hours or longer. This exercise goes on with no interruption of the bird's constant singing, for each outburst of song calls for a jump into the air of about 2 feet. These birds are of various colors. The birds called fruteros (fruit birds) are of a color between green and yellow, similar to the ones known as gilgueros and the small and medium-sized cotornitas (parrots). The boconcitos (little big-mouths), or sparrows, are brownish along the back with an ashy gray breast; about the size of a gilguero (goldfinch), they have a tender and tasty flesh.

There are, likewise, two species of brown and bright-red birds: the smaller of these is called putilla (little whore) and has a beautiful lake-red (carmine) breast and head, with a gorgeous crest; the larger ones are known as huanchacos or piches. The color of these birds usually changes, the breast remaining red and the rest of the body turning white. His Excellency Señor Jauregui kept one of these varieties; see the description of the characteristics of this bird in our description of Huánuco.

In addition to the birds listed, there are herons, flamingoes, and various other birds of the lagoons and sea, as well as gulls, zambullidores (divers), pájaros ninos (albatrosses), and others.

Fish

The great abundance of birds that dwell along the coast and that cover various islands with their excrement, or guano, which will be mentioned in our description of Chancay, is an indication of the abundance of fish in this sea. In it, one can catch the pexe rey (a kind of sardine), the bagre (catfish), and the camaron (shrimp) that is especially abundant. But these are nothing compared to the anchovetas (small anchovies), bonitos (striped tunnies), cabrillas (sea bass), rodaballos (flounders), and numerous other smaller species that in summertime attract quantities of robalos (similar to bream), corbinas (whiting), chitas, lenguados (sole), meros (grouper), cazones (dogfish), pexes sapos (anglers), sardinas (sardines), and others.

There are also young whales, dolphins, and—according to some reports—swordfish. These reports seemed to be confirmed during the repair of a boat by the discovery of the point of a straight, bonelike lance buried in a plank of the boat. This lance head, which measured about a foot in length, was taken to the inspector general, Don José Antonio de Areche, who kept it in his office.

Shellfish are not found in such abundance as along the coast of Chile, but there is no lack of cangrejos (crabs), ollitas, and almegillas (clams or barnacles) that cover the cliffs and the hulks of ships. We may mention the many-tentacled pulpo (octopus) that measures about a yard in length, the tiny picos (sea urchins), and two species of estrella de mar (starfish).

Towns and Villages

In addition to the many large chacras (farms) or country estates in the beautiful valley of Lima, there are numerous hamlets and the villages of Magdalena, Miraflores, Chorrillos, Surco, Late, and Lurigancho. Another village, San José de Bellavista, grew out of the port of Callao; of the port there remains only the castle of San Fernando, which serves nowadays as a jail and which, with two other forts, constitutes the entire defense of the bay.

Lima

As we have already stated, Lima, the famous City of Kings and emporium of the vast realm of Peru, lies 2 leagues inland from the coast. It was founded by Don Francisco Pizarro, who on the 6th of January 1535 read the proclamation of possession, in the middle of a spacious and pleasant valley that forms a level plain almost triangular in outline.

The streets are laid out in straight lines and are wide, ample, and very beautiful. Its wall comprises 34 bastions within which are 150 squares or islands of about 150 yards each. These cannot be completely enclosed because of the river that crosses the city and divides it from the outskirts, which are called San Lázaro. San Lázaro lies to the north of the city and makes up apparently a third of the area and a fourth of the population of Lima, to which it is connected by a carefully built bridge of five spans. As the city continues to grow, however, it will be necessary to build another bridge to handle the traffic, as the viceroy Don Manuel Amat has already planned.

Lima has about 53,000 inhabitants. The clergy, monks, nuns, and lay sisters number 1936. Spaniards and creoles (Peruvian-born Spanish) number 17,300, Indians about 4000, and negroes about 9000. The remainder are mulattos (white-negro), zambos (Indian-negro), and other social groups based upon sundry types of racial mixtures: chinos (offspring of nonwhite parents); tercerones, quarterones, and quinterones (racial mixtures of three, four, and five generations); salta atrás (throwbacks); tente en al ayre (child of a quadroon and a mulatto); and other indefinable castes. There are one-third more women than men.

The city, including the suburb of San Lázaro, comprises 209 blocks; these are divided, according to the latest map, into 35 districts, 355 streets, and 3641 houses with 8222 doors opening to the street. There are 74 churches, divided among only six parishes: Sagrario, having as its dependency the parish of Corazon de Jesús; Santa Ana, which has that of Salvador; San Marcelo; San Sebastion; and those of Cercado and San Lázaro.

There are 21 monasteries for religious orders: four of Santo Domingo, three of San Francisco, three of San Agustín, three of La Merced, one of Mínimos or Paulinos, two of Agonizantes, one of San Juan de Dios, two of Betlemitas, one of San Felipe Neri, and the Hospicio de Nostra Señora de Monserrate. The Jesuits have four, three active and one vacant. There are 13 convents for nuns: Santa Clara, Encarnación de Canónigas Agustinas, Santa Catalina de Dominicas, Trinidad de Cistercienses, Agustinas del Prado, Mercedarias Descalzas, Santa Rosa, Capuchinas Trinitarias, Nazarenas Carmelitas, and two each of La Concepción and Carmelitas. There are four beaterios (houses of retreat for pious women): Dominicas del Patrocinio, Viterbas de San Francisco, and Copacabana de Indias and Copacabana de Recogidas, both of La Concepción.

There are two schools for girls, La Caridad and Santa Cruz, but they are small and insufficient and very poor, like all else. There is one house for spiritual retreat for women, and two more are being built in the monasteries of San Francisco. La Inclusa has a very small income and is poorly furnished.

There are 12 hospitals: San Andrés, for Spaniards, with its madhouse; Santa María de la Caridad, for Spanish women; Santa Ana, for Indians, both men and women; San Bartholomé, for negroes of both sexes; San Pedro, for the clergy; San Lázaro, for lepers; and two for incurable diseases. To those we add the rest homes of San Juan de Dios, for Spaniards; two of Betlemitas, for Indians of both sexes; and that of San Pedro de Alcántara, almost wholly in ruins, for Spanish women.

A beaterio de camilas (house for pious women) is being built and is used as a hospital for the hopelessly sick, in particular for those affected with the terrible disease of cancer.

This city is the official seat of the viceroy; of the captain general; and of the courts of justice, which are the Real Audiencia (royal high court) and the Chancillería, formed by 10 oidores (judges of the supreme court), a regente (president of the court), a fiscal (legal officer) for civil affairs, five alcades de corte (justices of the peace), and a fiscal for criminal affairs. There is a superior court of accounts and another for successions, and courts of the Holy Office of the Inquisition, of the crusade, and of the consulate; and the city council formed by two ordinary alcaldes (mayors) and seven regidores (aldermen).

The ecclesiastic council, which the archbishop heads, is formed by five bishops, nine canons, six prebends, and six subprebends: the ecclesiastic tribunal, in which the archbishop and the vicar-general take part.

There is a court of royal physicians, with its examiners and legal officer. The city has a university and three colleges: the new San Carlos, which incorporates the two old ones of San Felipe and San Martín; the theological seminary of San Toribio; and that of Principe, for Indian chiefs. There is also a hospice for the poor, which is unoccupied; a foundling home; a house of correction for women; the mint; and a comic theater, a ring for bullfights, and another for cockfights.

Architecture

With respect to architecture, there is little to praise in these buildings. From the remains of repeated earthquakes that nearly leveled the city—especially the one in 1764, the damages of which are still scarcely repaired—we know that in former times there was sturdy construction. The monastery of Santo Domingo with its tower, the theological school of Santo Thomás, the monastery of San Francisco, and several other monasteries are solid and beautiful structures dating from earlier periods, and their strength is due, without doubt, to their excellent foundations. In all the rest, both modern and ancient, one cannot find a shred of anything architecturally outstanding.

The cathedral, which with the archbishop's palace forms one side of the great plaza, is not of any great note, in spite of the excessive cost of its recent renovations; at least its towers could have been constructed differently from those of the other churches. It is a pity to see such great waste of wealth in overdecorating the churches with cedar and other woods. They are crammed full of what are called altarpieces but are, in reality, nothing but monstrosities of art and offense to good taste.

The viceroy's palace occupies the other side of the plaza, taking up a whole block. Neither is this building worth the large sums that must be spent on its renovation every time a new viceroy takes up residence. Having had much experience with the building, Señor Amat invested 30,000 pesos to embellish it for his successor, Señor Don Manuel de Guirior. And when Don Manuel left, barely 4 years later, another large sum was spent when Señor Don Agustín de Jáuregui moved in.

These expenses, as well as those connected with the reception of the viceroys, are met by the municipal council and the city government from their general budget. This is why the general budget suffers greatly and cannot provide for more important public works.

To this palace are connected the courts, the exchequers, the royal treasuries, the hall of arms, the headquarters of the infantry guard, and the court prison. Adjacent to the palace are also a number of stalls where perfumes and other articles are sold, as well as the ironmongers' shops. Behind the palace is the bridge that we have mentioned, and at its entrance stands an ancient arch that Señor Amat decorated and provided with a beautiful clock for the governments of the palace and of the suburb of San Lázaro. This gentleman, who was much interested in military and civil architecture, built a church for the Nazarene nuns, the jewel of all churches in Lima. He renovated the magnificent tower of Santo Domingo. He constructed a magnificent canal, but it remained unfinished due to his absence. In Callao, he improved the castle of San Fernando, and Lima owes other useful and meticulous public works to his enterprise.

Originally, other buildings might have been tall enough to be both useful and beautiful, but they have all been lowered and stunted as a result of the repeated earthquakes. Now the houses are very low, with the exception of a few whose owners, regardless of the threat of earthquakes, have built them up again. Constructed of reed, mud, and wood, they are far from being safe. Because, as we have stated, rains in Lima are infrequent, they also have no tile roofs. Aside from an occasional terrace of baked clay tiles, all the roofs are covered with ashes, which absorb the dense mist of garúa during the winter period.

The whole city is provided with a drainage system and a water supply. Although there are no elaborate fountains except for the beautiful bronze one in the great plaza, nearly every ordinary community is obliged to provide a water pipe in the street for public use. As a result, there is no dearth of water.

Lima spends an unbelievably large part of its income on both aqueducts and buildings. One might say that this is the reason why, notwithstanding its opulence, Lima cannot be compared with the richest cities. On account of repeated earthquakes, a new city must be built every so often; families of moderate means are thus impoverished, and even the wealthy suffer from such an appreciable drain on their fortunes.

Character and Composition of the Inhabitants

It would seem that the makeup of the inhabitants is self-evident. They are as unlike in social and economic rank and complexion as they are alike in their behavior. Hardly a middle-class home can found without faces of all colors; in them we can recognize the races that make up the population. There is the Indian; the cholo (Indian-Spanish); the chino, resulting from the cohabitation of a cholo and a negro woman; the mulatilla, the result of intercourse between a Spaniard and a negro woman; and the zambo, the result of intercourse between a negro and an Indian.

There is likewise the offspring that each of these has begotten with each of the different women of this mixture, which are called tercerones, quarterones, quinterones, salta atrás, etc.

Some of these mixtures are slaves and others are free, according to the position of the mother, even though all might be born in the same household. Few are legitimate offspring and, like as not, all are brought up together. Those children of Spanish blood among them are fed from the breasts of any of the mothers, for the white or Spanish woman does not look upon the nursing of her own children as at all important.

The Indian is sensual and, like his native land, warm of temperament; he easily falls prey to deception, is prone to cowardice, and is drawn more to superstition than to religion. The negro is inclined to be a thief almost from birth and to be arrogant, mercenary, and inclined to all the vices that servitude and recent conversion open up to him. The mulatto is intrepid and bold, vainglorious, pompous, and fond of keeping up false appearances—even with what does not belong to him—and boastful of even his licentious behavior. The germs of all these defects and qualities are as mixed, in as many different ways, as are the results. The sum total of much of this, making up a physical monstrosity, naturally produces a moral monstrosity: this multiplied perversity of tendencies and passions is picked up by the unfortunate Spaniard who is born, reared, and nurtured by them, unless—as rarely happens—some good fortune separates him from it.

Wickedness early lays claim to all the children, so much so that a tendency to thievery is evident even before they attain the age of four. Lewdness usually associated only with adult years and, very frequently, envy and vanity not manifest in any other country are also common in these children, even at the age of 12 or 15. They are possessed by a vivacity, restlessness, and impishness characteristic of persons incapable of exercising common sense and behaving calmly. They are, naturally, troublesome to their families in a proportionate degree. Their intelligence and motivation are usually astonishing. Everything points to the presence of acrid humors and great heat in the blood and in the imagination, which in time engenders very vehement passions, all the stronger when one adds to them the causes of association and the example of so many of similar nature.

All this means merely that the Spaniard born in this country is to be pitied, for he tends to be superficial, haughty, cowardly, false and untrustworthy, light-fingered, and very skillful in the exercise of these traits. We can see, then, that all this is part of the recklessness, lack of honor, fault-finding, pride, and haughtiness that lead them to consider themselves better than their European-born parents, to believe themselves worthy of all honors and employment even though their unfitness is evident, and to give themselves over to such vain and extravagant ideas that any well-balanced man might think them mentally deficient.

This, generally, is really the character of the Spaniard born in Peru—those known as creoles. The same is true of many other Europeans who grow up or settle in Peru. They try to mimic the others in a kind of self-defense calculated to soften the implacable ill will that the natives usually show towards them.

This generality, nevertheless, does not include many honorable and illustrious families. Experience, religious obligations, and social station have led these families to be extremely cautious, and a praiseworthy and overcareful training enables them to correct or alter the natural course of affairs. One finds among them true models of the strictest civility, honor, and virtue, which are passed down to their noble descendants.

Character of the Womenfolk

Womenfolk especially enjoy these prerogatives. Their nature is more flexible, more pious, and more inclined to be honorable than that of men. If they have had any chance at all to have a good upbringing, they find it easy to be virtuous and charitable, generous rather than selfish, and devoted to uprightness. For these reasons, they prefer to marry Spaniards. Nor do they find it hard to do so, for they are good-looking, smart, and skillful. However, before they marry in the present era, when excesses of luxury have corrupted traditional customs by displacing much of the virtue that has always flourished in Lima and by allowing vices to get a foothold, women will take a second look at a European.

Luxury and Dress

To realize to what extent life in Lima is governed by luxury and poverty, it is necessary to stroll through the streets and to visit the homes. In churches, in theaters, and in public places, one meets only ostentation and splendor. If not betrayed by their color, many women would be judged ladies of importance and wealth because of the cleanliness and quality of their clothing. They usually go out wearing a cloak and heavy skirt, with a bodice at night.

At the beginning of this century, dress was like that used in Spain, if we are to judge from paintings, and like that still worn in North America, in New Granada (Colombia), along the coast of Guatemala, in Panama, and as far as Guayaquil. After our return to Spain, dress used by women on the Iberian Peninsula was introduced into Peru. But one style of dress introduced during the present century is unlike that of any other country. It was first taken up by the ladies of the aristocracy, and then by the women of the better families. Between the two, one cannot nowadays see any great difference.

To begin with the footwear: women wear shoes that, far from resting the foot, torture it because of the tightness and narrowness of the fit. For this reason, one must nearly destroy the shoes in order to wear them at all, for the toes must be allowed to arch out of the uppers and show the stocking. Then one is obliged to tread upon the cordovan, because the sole is but 1 inch wide in some places, 2 at the widest part, and 5 inches long. It is common to wear the flaps loose and lopped off, though buckles of gold, gemstones, or diamonds are coming into use more and more as the latest fashion; and that part of the cordovan that used to be embroidered is now painted. Of such shoes, usually made of sheepskin, a middle-class woman needs one pair a day, and the least they cost is from 6 silver reales to 1 peso fuerte. As the shoes break at every step, the women go out carrying needle and thread, and they are not embarrassed to take off their shoes in a doorway or even in church, to repair a shoe in order to return home.

The shoes are worn with stockings made of silk, not of any other material, even among the ordinary people. This part of the costume is preferred by all. They seek stockings of the most delicate and the brightest, sharpest, and most colorful hues, although they may cost 25, 30, or 40 pesos. During the hardships of the war with England, they were sold at 50 pesos fuertes, but the commonest of them cost 6 duros. If the stocking has to be stepped upon when the shoe disintegrates, just how long will that stocking last? Especially when the foot is a part of the body that must be most fastidiously dressed! The women never wash these stockings, for once washed they are not fit even for the servants.

The overskirt, usually a silken brial (skirt), begins almost where the stockings end. It could more correctly be called a kind of kilt, were it closed in front and not worn open. Notwithstanding its being so short—it does not drop over the lower part of the abdomen—16 yards of goods go into it, as well as a like amount for the lining with its stiffening, which folds and swells out like a bell. Some pull their waists in with flannel sashes or with belts of other, lighter material, and this swells them out the more. This habit is referred to as contrabando (smuggling), and it makes them so hideous that only they themselves, and lustful eyes that like nothing better than lewdness in women, can bear the sight. This feminine delirium knows no bounds in luxury and in extravagant methods to improve their appearance.

There has been a recent innovation in favor of decency. Since the overskirts are open at the front, some ladies have made aprons lined with two or more pieces of ribbon, 2 inches wide and as delicate as those of Chinese origin. But we fear that this fashion will not last, since it is not conducive to lewdness, which is what the libertines crave. At the present time, they are wearing skirts made of ribbons, similar to the aprons.

Over the kilt they wear a saya or tunic. It consists of 30 yards of material made of thick, corded silk, and 20 yards of lining. Some have 40 yards of cloth with an equal amount of lining and triple pleats or fringes. They increase the size of the wearer hideously, and it is a monstrous state of affairs to find that a coarse mulatto woman cannot be distinguished from a lady, for both wear the same dress and have the same appearance (Figure 4).

All the rest of the body excepting the arms, which are bare nearly to the shoulders, is covered with rich ribbons, laces, and embroidered veils with many odds and ends of gold, pearls, and oftentimes diamonds, all most costly. As a crowning touch, they wrap around themselves a flannel strip about two-thirds of a yard wide that, in trying to hide everything completely, covers only the upper part of the arms, the neck, and sometimes the chin.

It is customary to wear many flowers on the head, without taking into consideration their price, as long as they are fresh or of the latest fashion. They have succeeded in producing a large white poppy, the seed of which came from Spain; of ladies who flocked to buy them, one paid 4 pesos for one of the flowers, put it in a kerchief, and found it crushed upon arrival home. Since she had coddled herself

Dame Créole du Pérou Vêtue selon l'usage de Lima.
S.ra CRIOLLA DE LIMA.
Dedicado al S.or D.n Joseph Perfecto DE SALAS del Consejo de S.M.
Fiscal de la Real Audiencia de Chile, Assessor General del Virrey del Perú
Por Su mas humilde y Seg.o Servidor
Pedro M. ***
Nunca a Su Nombre el tiempo Será ingrato.

Figure 4. A lady of Lima, Peru. From the *Historical Account of the Voyage to South America*, undertaken under Royal aegis by Jorge Juan and D. Antonio de Ulloa, Madrid, 1748. This and other illustrations were added to the above work in 1774.

with the idea of going abroad wearing her enormous blossom, she instantly sent for another, which cost another 4 pesos. This she put in her hair and, as was to be expected, it fell asunder at the third or fourth jolt of the carriage.

The ariruma, a species of *Amaryllis*, is a yellow flower of six segments joined at the base. At the time of the New Year, when each woman wants to sport one of them, nothing else is of any importance if she cannot wear an ariruma. Herein lies the value of the flower. The flower merchants can sell all they bring in at any price—oftentimes as dearly as 20 or 25 pesos a bud, for they are worthless when they have unfolded. Not only are the flowers an ornament, but the scent adds to their charm. And since, due to the hot climate, the flowers oftentimes lack fragrance, their aroma is reinforced by coating them with resin, by perfuming them, and by bedewing them with scented waters. Later, they are packed in with the clothes and spread about on the furnishings of the house, in order to counteract the native fetidity that the women, especially those who have some racial mixture, often transpire. They consider the puchero, as this preparation of fragrant flowers is called, more important than the cooking pot. Some women are so depraved that, unwilling to buy even 2 reales' worth of bread for their children, they will spend up to 25 pesos every day on flowers.

A gardener's wife who grows jasmines exclusively earns 500 pesos a year from her harvests, and another with one aromo tree (cassie, sweet acacia, false myrrh tree) earns 200. A great many more pesos come in from resin trees, civets, benzoin, and the other kinds of aromatics that women, even negro and zambo women, commonly use as part of their dress.

They are extremely fond of jewelry. According to a conservative estimate, five to six million pesos are represented in the gem trade in Lima. Some wear enough diamonds in the hair to dazzle the eye. So long as earrings are very large and in style, the women do not mind what price they pay for them. They are much addicted to riding in carriages and chaises, even those who cannot afford such luxury, for which reason one finds a disproportionate number of these vehicles in Lima. The same is true of male and female servants, who cannot so much as earn their keep.

Foods

Likewise, at table and on excursions, one finds an immoderate abundance of foods. This is an attempt to imitate the larders and desserts of the important people who come from Europe. Formerly, the most sumptuous tables were made up of six to eight dishes, plentifully served but limited to turkey, chicken, lamb, and veal. Nowadays, every person of note must seek a French cook, and the table is loaded three or four times with everything that the native soil yields—not to mention fruits for sherbets and a great abundance of liquors, all very costly. On holidays in the country, the same expenses and even greater ones are incurred day after day, because various friends and visitors are always present, and their numbers swell. All this food must be brought from town.

This extravagance in entertaining has become so general that we have seen an entire family, living on alms, go to the country to convalesce and for many days set a table such as would grace the home of a wealthy first-born son.

Games and Gambling

The table, with its foods, is not the worst of the expenditures. Gambling occasions even greater outlays of money. The passion for gambling has become almost universal, has ruined many a home, and is destroying even more, including some of the wealthiest. The habit of keeping tally with ounces of gold has crept in, and even the negroes on the street corner want to follow this fatal custom. Men no longer seem to have any other destiny in life or any better occupation. There are countless gambling houses. Shops close their doors so that their owners may go to gambling houses, where there are "sharpers" who loan money at immoderate interest and who will, at their own prices, buy gems, clothing, and any other personal effects a player may have with him. The gentleman, the merchant, the shopkeeper, and whosoever can raise money for a bid—no matter his social class—can all enter these houses. When they get tired of sitting, they roam away to other parts of the establishment where there are ball games, and to the cock-fighting gallery; here they lose just as much money through betting as they did at the card games and dice. The gambling den is filled thrice weekly: there the sons of families, husbands, peasants, and all social ranks are to be found, their absence from business greatly affecting their work and obligations, and everywhere the gamblers must resort to dishonesty to support their gaming passion. Hence, these customs lead to universal chaos. The lower classes wrangle in public places, and on the streets and plazas one sees knots and groups of people fascinated by the gamblers. The government has taken some steps against this vice, but the whole thing has gone so far that no one is considered a man who does not gamble, and gamble for high stakes.

Bullfighting

All this is called entertainment. All the people are prone to succumb to it, wherever it exists, because of their nature: idleness, languor, and exhibitionist tendencies. Similarly, the theaters are attended by great crowds. So many people will attend a bullfight that it is repeated eight or ten times a year, even when there are no toreros (bullfighters), and though the plaza be nothing but a slaughterhouse. The homes and streets have the appearance of uninhabited wastes, yet in the amphitheater all is splendor and lavishness. Rare indeed is the spectator, especially among the ladies, who does not have new clothes made to go to the bull ring. To the cost of these garments and the price of the seat one must add what is spent buying quantities of food and sweets that are sold during the spectacle. These people never weary of entertainment, nor are they frightened off by misfortune—which often befalls them—or by unfavorable weather at certain seasons when it is excessively hot and harmful to the health.

Plays

Plays are presented on Sundays, Thursdays, and holidays, and never fail to pack the theaters, especially in those seasons when the novelty of Italian dance forces the owners of the theaters to enlarge them. I heard it said by an Italian actor, who traveled from Mexico to Lima with his wife and other dancers whom he had trained in this capital, that of all the countries he had visited, none was so profitable as Lima. Though the wealth of Lima was more limited than that of other cities, the curiosity, indolence, and spendthrift temperament of its inhabitants was a treasure house for him. Perhaps he felt this way because he found no obstacle to having the theater enlarged and 5000 pesos a year assigned to him as a salary.

Poverty

We have described Lima as it appears on the surface. But when one peers underneath, one sees nothing but unbelievable poverty. There is the exception of a few houses that have an income from trade or from their extensive estates, but all the rest is mere sham. One sees many ladies riding in carriages, the mules of which have more to eat than the family. Many wear diamonds but have no daily bread, except when they visit the pawnbrokers. Great numbers of women are loaded down with fine trappings, yet their children go bare. Countless people are dazzlingly dressed, although they are in debt for every stitch on their bodies.

This is not paradoxical: in Lima the custom has grown up of making an agreement with clothiers who advance credit for two or three hundred pesos, to be paid in weekly installments of 2 or 3 pesos. The purchasers accept this arrangement, for they know that by tightening their own and their families' belts they can be ready with the payments when they come due. Debts are paid off by dieting. They who yesterday were seen in tatters are today unrecognizable in their extravagant dress, but their meals are reduced to squashes, potatoes, and warm water. The many servants of such false ladies behave likewise. With the pennies they are given for their daily bread—which is the only ready money that they ever see—they, too, dress on the installment plan, eating what luck brings their way. As they say, they can feel no greater woe than being clad in rags.

If it were not for the soup that the monasteries dispense to the poor, many would find themselves in dire straits. Where to all outward appearances one might think there is some affluence, there is usually only a stewpot of food that has come from a religious society, and the masses said by a priest; and these shamefaced people look for more from the religious orders, to which they become indebted and which they frequently deceive with trickery. All this is tolerated because of widespread need, and the burden falls most heavily on the whites, who frequently say, "I wish I were born a slave, for he never lacks food, clothes, or shelter." This is what most frequently vexes them and causes them the deepest worries. They are seen continually being thrown out of one house after the other because they cannot pay rent, and they pledge as security to their landlords their poor furnishings and, not uncommonly, even their most needed articles of clothing.

This poverty has many roots beyond those conditions that we have enumerated. The first was the bringing of negroes into the city. The many and distinct castes of society of which we have spoken, and which make up the greater and humbler portion of the population, spring from intercourse between these negroes and the Indians. The trades and crafts, as well as ordinary manual labor, are left to them; and they carry out their work with the crudity, flaws, and fraud that are endemic to their race and their ineptitude. And this constitutes no small scourge upon the inhabitants in general. Meanwhile, the white inhabitants are excluded, for they do not want to lower themselves to work as servants or learn a trade—nor could they, should they wish to do so, because of the many obstacles in the way. Some of the more decent employments that might be open to them are coveted and snatched away by the mixed or colored portion of the citizenry, in order to hold its own against the white population. Thus the white man is, in the end, the most forsaken, the most indolent, and the one most often resorting to trickery, gambling, and pretense: he lives in constant wretchedness. The mixed-blood part of the population is not far behind in the use of trickery and fraud. If the work be at governmental expense, either half or all the cost must be paid in advance, even at the risk of its loss—a very common occurrence. And if the money is not lost, nothing is done without cunning and cheating, for all the work and service will be of the poorest quality.

The second evil is this plague of women who find no way to use their time. In days gone by, women were wont to keep busy sewing or making a kind of lace that is used in Peru, work in which they are most skillful. But since the arrival from Spain of the lace known as trencilla and of all sorts of embroidery and of many ready-made articles of wear, there has been nothing left for them to do, except fuss with their hair and bedeck themselves with trimmings to improve their looks and to avoid pining away. This is one point that truly merits the government's attention, even if only to put an end to so many offenses against the Creator. There certainly are kinds of small industries that could be set up, but it must be high governmental circles that provide the incentive.

The third reason for poverty, in addition to the others that we have listed, is the dearth of foods and materials of basic need. The authorities ought to revoke the excise taxes and foster abundant production, at the same time curbing speculative buyers who resell imported foodstuffs at twice the price they have paid. Countryfolk who bring in their products should sell them directly to the market, as happens in other places where the municipal authorities do not permit speculation. Bakers are allowed to waste as much flour as they have at hand to produce substandard bread. Fish, the basis of a very valuable trade, is sold a league from the coast at excessive prices. It could be sold cheaper. This was attempted by a number of fishermen who came from Spain in 1777, but a petition by Indian fishermen led to the revocation of the fishing rights that had been granted to Spaniards. The same is true with lard and fats and other articles of food of basic need: they are stored up or hoarded by grocers and other speculators, much to the detriment of the public.

In the final analysis, the causes of Lima's poverty are infinite in number, and perhaps only a viceroy of extraordinary zeal could set things to rights.

CHAPTER 3

Trade

Trade in Lima—both import and export—is rather backward. Imports have shrunk since the division of the viceroyalty of Buenos Aires. Nevertheless, two or three Spanish merchant ships anchor in the port of Callao every year. The new scheme for free trade may increase this number. An increase did come about when the wars with England ended, and 20 ships arrived at Lima in 1 year. Numerous merchants were thrown into bankruptcy by this event, because most articles are on credit, either within the city or without. Nowadays, there exists a wicked custom among the wholesale merchants: one or two tradesmen are loaded with several articles of prime necessity and are permitted to sell at whatever price they choose. This happens, for example, with paper, iron, wax, thread, silk, and so forth.

Peruvian ships carry on a trade in larch planks, ponchos, and exquisite hams from Chiloe; to it they could carry quantities of sardines, cod, and other fish if the source of fish were protected and not destroyed. Luma, cypress, and other woods are brought from Valdivia. From Concepción and Valparaíso they bring in yearly 320,000 bushels of wheat, 13,000,000 pounds of tallow, and large shipments of delicious wines, dried beef, butter, lentils, anise, sesame, walnuts, almonds, native hazelnuts, neat's tongue, and preserved fruits. From Talcahuano comes wood of pellin (roble, a kind of oak), hazel, and pine. Other ports of call supply copper, tin, pitch, and dried and unsalted conger eel. This eel could, with encouragement, become the basis of a good trade like the cod-fishing in the islands of Juan Fernández, but because of indolence the eel trade does not prosper. Toyo, another kind of fresh fish and a food of the poor, is brought from Paita, as are tanned goatskin, soap, rice, cascarilla (quinine bark), cotton, sheetings, and other products.

Guayaquil supplies the cacao, silk cotton, and ginger that are abundant but in very little demand in Lima, as well as wood for all kinds of uses, tobacco, coffee, aceyte (aceite) de María (oil of Mary, a resin), anime (a myrrhlike resin), and jipijapa (Panama) hats, made from one kind of delicate white rush. [Actually not made from a rush but from the bushy, cyclanthaceous *Carludovica palmata*.—Translator] This type of hat is in great demand, notwithstanding the price—from 3 to 7 pesos —while Lima manufactures many hats of a coarser, yellow reed, which satisfy the needs of the ordinary folk, especially the country people. Some hats, customarily arriving from the other coast and made of painted straw, are lighter; but the women, accustomed to going out at night with a hat, prefer them to others and make them more uncomfortable by lining them with golden gauze and other trimmings, thus affording themselves no little elegance and no less torture. From Panama, Guatemala, and Sonsonate are traded pearls, indigo, good cedars, acacia, and other precious woods, as well as sundry articles of furniture inlaid with shells and mother-of-pearl.

Lima's export trade is very limited, unless we take into account those articles or raw materials brought in from the provinces or from the mountains. Of these, cacao, quinine bark, indigo, cotton, silk cotton, oils, and medicinal balsams are exported to Spain. The silver and gold is employed for seals and as bullion for coinage. Made in the textile factories, a type of cheap and light cloth called panete, flannels, and sheetings are sent to the southern ports, as are flour and various liquors. Quantities of liquors are produced in the provinces of Pisco, Ica, and Moquehua, as is oil in Camaná—that is, when the harvest does not fail, as it did in 1782 and 1783, when the price in Lima soared to 16 pesos for 25 pounds. The most substantial export is sugar: annually 5,700,000 pounds down to 320,000 pounds have been sent to Chile. The trade in this commodity, which we may say is Lima's only article of export, is dropping off because the advice (dispatch) boats and those from Janeyro (Rio de Janeiro) supply the provinces of Buenos Aires and Tucumán, which formerly got their sugar from Lima by way of Chile.

Plants

On various occasions during our residence in Lima, from the environs of the city I gathered and described sundry new plants as well as others already known to botanists. Some of these grow also in the mountain valleys east of Lima and in other parts of the coastal region. They are the following:

Canna indica, with the common name of achira; the tuberous roots of this plant have cooling properties and are used as food everywhere in Peru. *Boerhavia viscosa*, pegapega; *B. scandens*, yerba de la purgación (laxative plant), of which an infusion or decoction is used in treating gonorrhea. *Gratiola peruviana*. *Dianthera repens*. *Veronica peregrina*. *Calceolaria biflora* and *C. pinnata*, yerba de la bolsilla (pocket plant); an infusion in warm water helps alleviate venereal infections. *Peperomia aequalifolia*, congona, cultivated in gardens for its fragrance; *P. crystalina*, with an aroma strongly resembling anise, but milder and more delicious; and *P. tuberosa*. *Salvia procumbens*, yerba del gallinazo (herb of the buzzard); an infusion is used for jaundice. *Olea europaea*. *Nictanthes sambac*, diamela, grown in gardens for the fragrance of its flowers. *Jasminum grandiflorum*, jazmín real (royal jasmine); the womenfolk adorn their hair with the flowers, and the half-opened buds are employed in the mixture of flowers called puchero, in which they cast off their delicious aroma more intensely as they unfold. *Verbena nodifolia* and *V. officinalis*. *Valeriana officinalis*, *V. pinnatifida*, and *V. laciniata*. *Commelina fasciculata* and *C. gracilis*. *Tamarindus indica*, found in some gardens. *Cyperus niger* and *C. virgatus*, vara de San José (Saint Joseph's staff), or quernillo; when the root is kept in the mouth it dispels or corrects halitosis, and when infused into liquor and applied to the forehead in a moistened handkerchief it is a powerful palliative for headaches.

Paspalum rubrum, maizillo (small maize), a valuable grass that is cultivated in alfalfa fields and is excellent fodder; *P. dactilon*, grama oficinal (officinal grass). *Saccharum officinarum*, caña de azúcar (sugar cane). *Arundo phragmitis*. *Scoparia dulcis*, escobilla (little brush). *Buddleja connata*; *B. occidentalis*, quisoar. *Galium ovale*. *Spermacoce tenuior*. *Cuscuta corymbiflora*, cabellos de angeles (angels' hair). *Tillaea connata*. *Potamogeton compressum*. *Mirabilis jalapa*, trompetillas (little trumpets), or flor de Panamá (Panama flower); an infusion and decoction of the root of this species may be used as a purgative. *Heliotropium curassavicum* and *H. peruvianum*;

when they make excursions out into the country, members of the fair sex adorn their hair with blossoms of these two plants because of the vanillalike fragrance of the flowers. *Heliotropium pilosum* and *H. synzystachium*. *Cynoglossum pilosum*. *Myosotis granulosa*. *Nolana acutangula*.

Convolvulus sepium and *C. batatas*, camote (sweet potato); the roots are one of the commonest foodstuffs of Peru. *Ipomoea glandulifera*, auroras (morning glories); cultivated in gardens as an ornamental plant, this plant is named for the dawn because the blossoms open in the morning and wither away by noontime. *Datura stramonium*, chamico; *D. arborea*, floripondio, or campanillas (little bells). Because at night the flowers of the floripondio breathe out an odor of musk, the plant also has the common name of almizclillo (little musk). Its leaves, crushed and mixed with lard, are excellent to use as a suppurative and to relieve tumors. *Nicotiana paniculata* and *N. glutinosa*, tabacos cimarrónes (wild tobaccos); and *N. tabacum*, tabaco legítimo (genuine tobacco). *Plumeria rubra*, *P. tricolor*, *P. carinata*, and *P. bicolor*, suches; women use the flowers of all of these species of plumeria to adorn the hair, scenting them and folding in the corolla lobes. *Cordia rotundifolia*, membrillejo, tina; an infusion and decoction of this bush is used in the treatment of jaundice.

Cerbera thevetia, found in some gardens, has been brought in from the jungle provinces of the country. In these regions, both pagan and recently converted Indians make long strings of beads from the kernels of the fruits and hang them around the neck and knees to make a rattling sound in their dances. To make a bead, the bony core of the fruit is burned at one end and, when the pits are taken out, a hole is drilled through the other end; this makes it look like a small and imperfect bell. When strung together on a cord and shaken, the beads rattle like castanets.

Cestrum auriculatum, called both yerba santa (holy plant) and yerba hedionda (stinking plant), referring to the excellent properties of this plant and to its foul odor. Used extensively in Peru to cool and purify the blood, it is the most widely used remedy for chavalongos (typhoidlike fevers) and tabardillos (spotted fever).

Solanum cymosum montanum, papas de lomas (potatoes of the hills); *S. tuberosum*, papas (potatoes). The potato was introduced into Madrid in 1662 under the name of patatas manchegas. The sap from these tubers is sometimes used to dissolve cataracts, and the cooked tubers are applied as a poultice to lessen pain from gout and to alleviate headache of a cold. *Solanum variegatum*, pepino. [Pepino is the common name of the cucumber, *Cucumis sativus*, but in Peru it is still applied to this solanaceous fruit.—Translator] The fruits of this pepino are a favorite food in Peru because of their melonlike flavor, but when eaten in quantities they cause tertian fevers and tenesmic diarrhea. *Solanum angulosum*; this plant is called naranjitas de Quito (little oranges of Quito) because it has fruits the size and color of a small orange and was introduced from Ecuador. The womenfolk like these fruits for their delicate fragrance and the special taste that they impart to the maté beverage, into which they customarily put several drops of juice. They also use them to enhance their mixtures of flowers, which are made more pleasing by the faint aroma of the fruit.

Calydermus erosus, capuli cimarrón (wild cherry); *C. carapamacman*, which is called orzita, torrito, or porroncito de cuero (little crock, little jar, or little leather jug) in reference to the shape of the calyces. *Physalis pubescens*, capuli; ladies appreciate the fruits of this species as much as those of the naranjitas de Quito for their flower mixtures because they have a particular fragrance that can be intensified by daubing them with resin. They are also used with flowers to decorate the hair. Some people eat them for their bittersweet taste; the flavor is not unpleasant. *Physalis angulatum*. *Cedrela odorata*; this tree has been transplanted from the Peruvian jungle to the orchards of Lima. *Xuarezia biflora*, té del Perú (Peruvian tea); this name is derived from the use of the plant, in days gone by, as a substitute for Chinese tea. *Asclepias filiformis*, amarra judíos (Jewish cord); this vernacular name refers, without a doubt, to the long, stringlike branches of the plant that are useful for tying up bundles of faggots and other articles. *Asclepias incarnata*, árbol de la seda (silk tree), chuchumeca (contemptible little chap), or flor de la reina (queen's flower); this species is unusually plentiful in all cultivated plots of Lima, Lurín, Chancay, Huánuco and elsewhere. *Daucus visnaga*, visnaga. *Hydrocotyle vulgaris*, oreja de abad (abbot's ear), or petacones (plump ones). *Tillandsia granulata*, cardo de lomas (thistle of the hills). *Pitcairnia ferruginea*. *Achras lucuma*, lúcumo; this tall, stout tree has an excellent wood for building and for sundry uses in carpentry. It has round fruits that ripen when plucked from the tree and packed for several days in dry leaves, seeds, bran, or other material. The pulp of the fruit, deep yellow like the yolk of an egg, is sweet, pleasant-tasting, and rather cloying; it therefore quickly satisfies the appetite.

Narcissus odorus, called amancas, or camantiray in other parts of Peru, grows in abundance in the Amancas and Camantiray mountains, where many people go in the rainy season to gather the large, yellow flowers to adorn the hair. Combining this narcissus with onions, figs, and the whites of eggs, women concoct a liniment to remove freckles and blemishes from the face. *Narcissus tazetta*, narcisos, was introduced from Spain and is grown in gardens in Peru, as are other exotic species of the lily family such as *Pancratium maritimum* or coronas de rey (king's crowns), *P. allium* or feligranas, etc. *Alstroemeria peregrina*, peregrina (pilgrim), is cultivated in gardens for its splendid flowers and grows wild in the gravelly ravines of the mountains. From its roots some natives prepare a starch, which in Chile is called harina de liutu and which is an appetizing and easily digested food, especially for the sick, infants, and those of delicate health. For an explanation of the method of preparing this starch, see the description of *Alstroemeria ligtu*.

Polyanthes tuberosa, margaritas (daisies). *Ornithogalum corymbosum*, flor de cuenta (bead flower), referring to the black seeds shaped like rosary beads. *Lilium candidum*, azucena (white lily). *Juncus acutus*. *Rumex patientia*, romaza (dock), or lengua de vaca (cow's tongue). *Tropaeolum majus*, mastuerzo (cress), abounds in Lima; *T. peregrinum*, pajarillos amarillos (little yellow birds), is cultivated in gardens as an ornamental and occurs plentifully in mountain ravines. *Oenothera prostrata*, yerba del clavo cimarróna (wild clove plant).

Sapindus saponaria, jaboncillo (little soap) is a leafy tree, 6 to 8 yards tall. Its fruits, known as bolillos or cholocos, have a soapy rind that is used by the poor instead of soap to wash their clothes. *Laurus persea*, palto (avocado tree), is a tall tree with a heavy crown and good wood. Its edible fruits are called paltas or aguacates (avocados, alligator pears); after being plucked they must be made to ripen by wrapping them for four or more days in bran. These fruits are usually eaten with salt, for they are tastier that way; they may also be eaten with honey or sugar, or in salad. The pit will stain white clothing, leaving an indelible mark.

Caesalpinia tara, tara; its pods are a source of ink for writing, and they have various other uses that are described elsewhere. *Cassia tora*, cañafistola cimarrona (wild cassia); an infusion of its fruits and leaves is used as a purgative. *Limonia triphyta*, limoncillo de China (little Chinese lemon); the Chinese make a highly esteemed and pleasant confection from the fruits of this little Asiatic tree, which has been introduced from Panama and is now found in some gardens of Lima. *Jussiaea peruviana* and *J. fruticosa*, flores del clavo (clove flowers), named for the shape of the capsules. *Malpighia nitida*, ciruela de fraile (friar's plum), and *M. punicifolia*, cerezo (cherry); the pleasantly sweet fruits of both these species are eaten, as are the fruits of *Spondias mombin*, known as ciruelo agrio (sour plum). An *Oxalis* species called chullco-chullco or ocas silvestres (wild ocas); Indians apply the crushed roots in a poultice to relieve conditions of goiter and double chin. It is a cooling plant, and its root is very styptic and astringent.

Talinum paniculatum and *T. album*. *Euphorbia maculata*. *Cactus cochenillifer*?, gigantones (giants). *Psidium pyriferum*, huayabo (guayabo, guava), which has edible fruits. *Tetragonia cristallina*. *Sesuvium portulacastrum*, litho. *Rubus jamaicensis*. *Campomanesia palillos*, palillos (little sticks). *Mammea americana*, mamei (mammee, mamey); there are two extremely tall mammee trees in the College of San Carlos of Lima. *Corchorus siliquosus*. *Argemone mexicana*, cardo santo (sacred thistle). *Bixa orellana*, achiote (annatto). *Annona squamosa*, anono (anona, custard apple, sugar apple, sweetsop); *A. tripetala*, chirimoyo (cherimoya); and *A. muricata*, guanabano (guanabana, soursop). *Crescentia cujete*, totumo or tutumo (calabash tree, gourd tree). *Bartsia vivularis*. *Mimulus luteus*. *Dombeya lappacea*. *Dodartia fragilis*. *Lantana camara*. *Waltheria incana*, negrillo. *Melochia pyramidata*. *Sida filiformis*, pilapila; *S. capillaria*, matayerno; and *S. frutescens*, pichana. *Malva himensis* and *M. peruviana*. *Monnina macrostachya* and *M. pterocarpa*. *Erythrina macrocarpa*, frijol del inga (inga bean) and frijol de árbol (tree bean); this species, found only in Huánuco and in one orchard in Lima, was brought in from the mountain regions. Viceroy Amat was very fond of eating its fruit.

Lupinus perennis, chochitos. *Arachis hypogaea*, mani (peanut). *Crotalaria laburnifolia*, cascabelillos (little bells). *Dolichos lablab*, frijol de antibo (antibo bean). *Phaseolus vulgaris*, frijoles (beans); there are many varieties of beans. *Medicago sativa*, alfalfa. *Psoralea americana*, found in some gardens. *Citrus medica*; *C. aurantium*; and *C. peruvianus*, limón sutil (thin-skinned lemon), the fruits of which are in great demand in Peru. *Theobroma cacao*, cacao; there are some small trees in the gardens of Lima that have been brought in from the jungle. *Spilanthes dentatus*, *S. urens*, and *S. multiflorus*, called salivatoria (saliva producer) and used to relieve toothache. *Ageratum conyzoides*?, huarmihuarmi, employed as an excellent aperitif, in a decoction or infusion. *Eupatorium scandens*, yedra (ivy). *Bidens bipinnata*, amores secos (dry loves).

Molina parviflora, *M. scandens*, and *M. ivoefolia*, chilcas. The Indians make extensive use of all species of chilca, which are applied with hot cloths or in a poultice or flour cataplasm, with or without wine or liquor, to relieve colic, flatulence, or edematous inflammation of the legs, or to treat gangrene. Chilcas are also considered to be excellent as pectorals, calmatives and sticking plasters. *Tessaria dentata*, pájaro bobo (stupid bird). *Sobreyra sessilis*. *Cosmos pinnatus*. *Tagetes chinchi*. *Senecio scandens*. *Encelia canescens*. *Achillea urens*, botoncillo (little button). *Helianthus giganteus*. *Vermifuga corymbosa*, contrayerba, or matagusanos (worm killer). *Erigeron canariense*. *Centaurea napifolia*. *Lobelia decurrens*, contoya. *Impatiens balsamina*, nicaraguas, flores de nieve (snow flowers), or flores de San Francisco (flowers of Saint Francis). *Eclipta alba*.

Passiflora punctata, ñorbo (passion flower), grown abundantly in gardens for the violetlike fragrance of its flowers; children eat the pulp of its fruits. *Passiflora minima*, ñorbito (little passion flower); *P. foetida*, with fruits that are much attacked by ants. *Passiflora tiliaefolia*, granadilla (passion fruit). The fruits of this species are the size of a hen's egg and have a bittersweet pulp full of seeds; the pulp whets the appetite and has cooling properties. Many people add sugar and wine, which improves the flavor; still others make a sweet from it with refined sugar. *Passiflora quadrangularis*, tumbo; the fruits of the tumbo are as large as small melons, but because of their excessive acidity are not so highly prized as the granadilla.

Pistia stratiotes, lechuga cimarrona (wild lettuce). *Elaterium pedatum*, caihua; its fruits are stuffed with chopped meat, much as tender pumpkins are in Spain. *Typha angustifolia*, totora; fishing rafts that stay afloat for days are manufactured from this cattail, and an uncooked salad can be prepared from the roots. *Morus nigra*, moral (mulberry). *Xanthium spinosum*, yerba de Juan Alonso; we shall discuss the properties of this plant later in our account. *Amaranthus oleraceus*. *Sagittaria sagittifolia*. *Juglans nigra*, nogal (walnut).

Artocarpus otahetianus, árbol de las mantas (blanket tree). I saw two small trees of this species in bloom in the orchard of Señor Ascona, president of the consulate of Lima. They had been introduced from the islands of Tahiti, where the natives make beautiful blankets from the bark that measure from 11 to 14 feet in length and 7 in width. Such a blanket is prepared with a technique no other than pounding the bark between two flat stones to separate the scabby, juicy, fleshy part from the fibrous layer, which looks like a specially woven cloth. Only close examination convinces one that it is not made by the hand of man. The natives paint it with round spots and figures of various colors and then it is ready for use. I have had two of these blankets that measured 10 feet in length and more than 5½ in width. In the same orchard I saw an árbol del pan (breadfruit tree), or rima; the day before, a mule had eaten its leaves and the bark all around its trunk, thus killing the tree—a source of considerable grief to the owner and all interested people.

Croton balsamiferum? *Acalypha indica*. *Ricinus communis*, higuerilla (castor-oil plant). *Jatropha* (*Manihot*) species, called yuca (manioc, cassava). *Cucurbita lage-*

naria, *C. ovifera*, *C. pepo*, and various other species that are all called zapayos or mates; *C. citrulus*, sandía (watermelon). *Cucumis sativus* and *C. melo*. *Begonia tuberosa*, florecita de San Juan (little flower of Saint John), which is extremely abundant in the Amancas mountains, where many people travel in the wet season; ladies decorate their hair with its flowers and with those of the narcissus called amancas. Eaten fresh, dried and taken as a powder, or drunk in an infusion, the root of this begonia acts as a laxative and cleanses the abdomen of humors. *Salix helix*; *S. hermaphrodita*, sauces (willows). *Populus nigra*, chopo. *Schinus molle*, molle, or falsa pimienta (false pepper). *Cenchrus procumbens*.

Musa sapientium. There are five kinds of bananas in Lima. Four of them are the platano largo (long banana), or platano de la tierra (local banana); the dominico (Dominican banana), or guineo (Guinea banana); the platano anaranjado (orange-colored banana); and the platano amarillo (yellow banana), or Otaheti (Tahitian banana). Ripening after bunches are cut from the plant and hung for several days, when the fruits begin to turn yellow and become tender through a kind of fermentation, all these kinds of bananas have a rather delicate flavor whether eaten fresh, boiled, or fried. The dominico cannot be boiled or fried because it is more fleshy and more likely to ferment; for the same reasons it is dangerous to eat the dominico after drinking wine, aguardiente (brandy), or other fermented liquors.

Mimosa inga, pacae (pacay, inga); *M. sensitiva*, tapateputilla (close up, little whore); *M. fernambucana*, huaranquillo; and *M. prostrata*, huarancco tendido (prostrate huarancco). *Mimosa farnesiana*, aromo (cassie, sweet acacia, false myrrh tree); its flowers are much esteemed in Lima for bouquets and for dressing the hair of womenfolk with a delicate, very mild fragrance. When the seeds of this mimosa are chewed and spit out in the house they cause an unbearable stink like that of human excrement, which can be dispelled by burning scented paper. The *Mimosa* species called huarancco is a leafy, stout tree with wood excellent for fuel, and it provides a beautiful, health-giving shade that cattle appreciate when resting.

Cavalleria oblonga, manglillo (little mangrove); its wood, though light and weak, is burned every day in the kitchens of Lima. *Ficus carica*, higuera (fig); *F. radicans*, higuerón (wild fig). A number of higuerón trees are found growing on the streets that form the alameda, or carriage drive, in Lima; they were brought in from the jungle. *Polypodium vulgare*, raquiraqui. *Acrosticum trifoliatum*. *Phoenix dactylifera*, palma de dátiles (date palm).

In addition to these plants, one finds in the fields, gardens, and cultivated plots many other species that are grown either for their fruits, seeds, roots, and greens, or for the beauty of their blossoms; but since they are very common, it has not seemed necessary to mention them with the others. They include such species as *Vitis vinifera*, *Zea mays*, *Triticum aestivum* or *T. sativum*, *Hordeum vulgare*, *Pastinaca sativa*, *Cichorium intybus*, *Scabiosa leucantha*, *Ocimum basilicum*, *Mentha sativa*, *Amaryllis lutea*, *Narcissus jonquilla*, and many others.

I shall not stop here to describe the uses and properties of all the plants enumerated above, but shall treat of them in the descriptions of those places where I have studied them more carefully than in Lima.

CHAPTER 4

Trip to the Province of Chancay

On the 22nd of July 1778 the five members of the expedition set out together from Lima for the province of Chancay (Plate 2), having been often told about the fertile hills of this area. We spent the first night on the estate of Carabaillo, 3 leagues from the capital. To that point we were accompanied by the Marques de la Real Confianza, owner of another estate, and by the lawyer Don Manuel Eraso and other gentlemen.

On the 23rd we came to the roadside inn of Copacabana, where late in the afternoon we were set upon by a band of thieves led by an outlaw with the evil name of Uracán (Hurricane). This bandit appeared at the inn in disguise, asking for alfalfa for all his animals. Accompanied by two negro women who remained on horseback, Uracán started a dispute with the innkeepers to surprise us and take over our arms and the room in which we were lodged. But once the strategy of that quarrel was discovered, we cut short his scheme by thrusting two pistols into his chest. Instantly surrounding him, we forced him to give up the dagger he had used to frighten unfortunate muleteers and travelers who crossed his path and then rob them of whatever money or gold they were carrying. This we were told by the Conde (Count) de Villar's mayordomo (manager, overseer), who came to the inn with two negro men and shouted that we should truss up the criminal—he was the leader of four other robbers who had gone ahead a little to await the results.

When the two negro women saw Uracán in bonds, they fled to tell his companions, but the mayordomo and his negroes followed them. Since they would not stop when he shouted orders for them to halt, he shot at them. One shot brought down the mare that one of the negro women was riding, whereupon her companion drew her own horse to a halt and waited until the mayordomo and his negroes came up and took them both to the inn. There they were registered and handcuffed and then taken with Uracán to the estate of the Conde de Villar. Once placed in separate rooms, they confessed their plan to rob us while we were sleeping.

With this piece of news, arrangements were made for alternating guards near the gate of the inn, each a half hour at a time, beneath a branching huarancco (mimosa tree). At nine at night, from the huarancco the guard heard the clatter of horses; the four companions of Uracán had arrived. Three times the guard asked in a loud voice, "Who goes there?" and, since there was no answer and the sound of horses' hooves came all the while, he shot in the direction of the gang. The shot perforated the ear of one horse and the thigh of the rider, who happened to be second in command to Uracán; as he fell badly wounded to the ground, his companions fled.

We knew nothing of this entire adventurous episode until the following day, when a traveler brought the news to us at the inn of Alancón. The wounded bandit had recounted the story to the mayordomo, who had found him lying wounded on the ground where he had fallen. The mayordomo took the two thieves and two negro women to Lima. The wounded bandit died on the third day, Uracán was sent in exile to Valdivia, and the two slaves were delivered to their owners because nothing could be proven against them except that they had been kidnapped by the robbers. The two imprisoned thieves were proclaimed by the town crier as fugitives from several jails.

On the 24th we entered Torreblanca, the estate of Don Toribio Bravo de Castilla half a league from the town of Chancay. This gentleman of Lima very generously gave us the hospitality of his home, ordering his mayordomo and servants to help us with whatever we needed during our stay to the end of August. From there we passed on to the town of Huaura, where we were put up in the beautiful hospital that had recently been founded by His Excellency Señor Castañeda.

We remained in Huaura until the 22nd of October, when we returned to Lima with a portion of the collections, descriptions, and drawings of plants gathered from the shores, hills, valleys, and creeks of the province of Chancay. These collections were made with considerable trouble and inconvenience resulting from long hikes made over mountains, deserts, and hills where horses could not easily cross, and from the excessive heat experienced at certain hours of the day.

CHAPTER 5

Description of the Province of Chancay

Twelve leagues north of Lima and half a league from the sea lies the town of Arnedo, capital of the province of Chancay and the first town that one encounters straight out from Lima. Commonly also called Chancay, it has been the place of residence for many magistrates, but nowadays these officials dwell in Huaura.

The jurisdiction of the province of Chancay begins 6 leagues from Lima. It is divided into two territories: the region to the east, called Checras, is cold and mountainous; the warmer region to the west is famous for its coast and valleys. There are 30 leagues of road along the coast from north to south, and 27 leagues from east to west. The province of Chancay is bounded on the Lima side by the province of Cercado, on the north by that of Santa, on the north and northeast by that of Caxatambo, and on the east by that of Canta.

There are various ports along the coast. Going south, the first is Alancón, the largest and quietest; a number of fisherfolk dwell on the beaches of this port and transport their fish to Lima. Going north, one comes to the port of Arnedo, or Chancay, where all the guano, or manure, used for fertilizer in the province, as well as wood brought in from Guayaquil, is unloaded. Farther on is the port of Chancayllo, but since it is small only a few guano boats put in there. Next is the port of Huacho, which is not wide but is deep enough to accommodate some of the larger boats as they pass from Guayaquil to Lima or vice versa. In addition to these ports there are various bays and inlets, but they are rather unsafe for shipping.

Two rivers water this province: in the south the Pasamayo descends from mountains in the province of Chanta and enriches the valley of Arnedo and Pasamayo, and in the north the Huaura falls from the ranges of Caxatambo and irrigates the beautiful valley of Canaverales de Huaura. The Huaura is the larger of the two throughout the year. The direct route to the town of Huarura crosses the river over a single-arch bridge built between two cliffs that confine the river for more than 150 yards. On the town side is a small fort built in days gone by to prevent the passage of enemies, and at the gateway of the bridge are two columns, beneath which are laid two stones. The Spanish royal arms are engraved on one of these stones, and on the other is the following inscription: "In the reign of Philip III the building of this bridge was started and finished in 1611, when Don José de Rivera y Abalos was Commissary." There are inscriptions on two other stones set into the columns; on one is written, "His Excellency Don Juan de Mendoza y Luna, Marqués of Montesclaros, built me when he was viceroy in 1611." On the other is the name of Juan del Corral, the artisan who directed construction of the bridge.

In the mountains of this province and along its cold rills, ocas (edible tubers of *Oxalis* species), massuas (edible tubers of *Tropaeolum tuberosum*), potatoes, arracachas (apios, Peruvian parsnips), and yacones are harvested. In the valleys and deep ravines where the temperature is warm or hot, beans, maize, and wheat are grown. On the punas—high, cold moors where only very small plants can grow—ichu and other grasses abound; these plants support many herds of sheep and cows that are consumed by the landholders of the valleys and their negro help. Some wool is collected from the ganado de Castilla (livestock of Castille), or merino sheep, and is used in the workshops to make coarse cloth; delicious cheese and butter are made from the cows' milk. Vicuñas, llamas, huanacos, and vizcachas (chinchillalike rodents) are kept on the high moors. In the valleys and mountainous watercourses there are deer, bears, foxes, wildcats, and guinea pigs.

On the coast and in the valleys the climate is milder than in Lima. Because the air is clearer, clouds are not so easily formed; thus the sun is not hidden from view all day long as in Lima during most of the winter season. The mild climate notwithstanding, in some places intermittent fevers and other ills are prevalent; they are caused by excessive accumulation of moisture and overbearing heat in all seasons of the year. These conditions also cause an abundance of fleas, chiggers, and mosquitoes—all most troublesome and unbearable insects.

These valleys are extremely fertile for wheat, barley, maize, beans, and sugar cane. Yuca, sweet potatoes, various types of squash and gourds, and all sorts of green vegetables—cabbage, cauliflower, broccoli, lettuce, endive, onions, caihuas, and yuyus (yuyos, amaranth)—grow abundantly. Watermelons, native pepinos (very different from the European), cherimoyas, anonas, guanabanas, guavas, palillos, avocados, ingas, lucumas (eggfruit), granadillas and tumbos (passion fruits), sour plums, friar plums, pears, apples, and quince are very common. Oranges, limes, true lemons, thin-skinned lemons, citron, and grapefruit are extremely abundant. Melons and peaches grow well only in the foothills.

In the gardens and orchards, there is no lack of variety in flowers, for we find arirumas, narcissus, pilillas (*Pancratium littorale*), amancas, coronillas de rey, bead flower, feligranas, peregrinas, jonquils, tulips, lilies, white and multicolored margaritas, iris, gillyflowers, marigolds—commonly called flor de muerte (flowers of death), taconcillos (*Dolichos uncinatus*), pajaritos, ambarinas (scabious, mourning bride), buttercups, anemones, piochas (*Cynanchum* species), passion flowers, carnations, roses, jasmine, larkspur, lupines, albaca (basil?), oregano (wild marjoram), marjoram, mazizez (macises, mace?), chamomile, aromo (cassie, sweet acacia, false myrrh tree), plumerias, orange blossoms, cherimoya blossoms, etc.

In winter, the time of fogs, or garúas, the mountains and hills of this coastal area are clad with a thick and fragrant flowering mantle of many kinds of plants, bringing pleasure to travelers and to those who come for recreation or days in the countryside. The hills of Lachay, situated between Arnedo and Huaura, are famous in Lima for the variety of plants and flowers, and are considered by the common people to be an earthly paradise covered with a multitude of different plants. In reality, about 40 species make up the beautiful and varied floral carpet at Lachay, and there are but a dozen or so species that are more showy and abundant than on the other hills of Lima, Lurín, etc., where the same vegetation prevails but without that exceptional vista so characteristic of Lachay.

With these plants and their roots, a large population of swine, cows, and horses is maintained in winter, which in that area is called the hill season. Because these hills are located on the road from the coast, their cover of grasses supports the livestock of muleteers, for these animals arrive weary from the hot sun and dust of the desert and are anxious to refresh themselves with these succulent grasses.

Maize is the most abundant of harvests in the valley of Arnedo. Besides being the basic food of the negroes and the workers on the estates, this grain is used to fatten up 30,000 head of swine, most of which are brought down from the valley of Huaura and fattened up in Arnedo, and from there transported to Lima for slaughter. Each landholder slaughters on Saturdays, extracting the fat, or lard, and melting it together with bacon fat. This mixture is sold at 2, 2¼, or 2½ reales, so every year the value of the pork fat produced in the province of Chancay can be reckoned at more than 340,000 pesos.

In days gone by, the chief harvests of these valleys were wheat and wine, but nowadays the production of wine has disappeared completely.

The valley of Huaura, more than 10 leagues long and 2 leagues wide in the vicinity of the town but narrowing up to Sayán, is filled with sugar cane plantations. There are landowners in this valley who send to Lima 50,000 pesos' worth of sugar of the best quality, like that of Holland, selling at 3½ to 4 pesos for each arroba (25 pounds).

In this province, guano from the islands off the coast is so essential as fertilizer for maize that without it the harvests are decidedly meager. For each plant two handfuls of guano are thrown into the hill at the time of planting; later, when cultivating or weeding is done, an additional two handfuls are added. In the province as a whole, the yearly consumption of guano amounts to 60,000 fanegadas (fanegada, about 1½ bushels?), each weighing 8 arrobas; the boats carry 600 to 1000 fanegadas. That practice continues, and apparently for ample reason: this guano is nothing but the excrement of birds, those known as guanals and others, which sleep at night on tiny islands 5 miles out to sea off Pisco and near Cañete and Arica, towards the northern part of the coast.

We were told that so many of these birds visit and dwell upon these islands that each year they produce, beyond doubt, as many fanegadas of guano as are used in the provinces of Chancay, Pisco, etc. Furthermore, it is said that some of these tiny islands have in certain years been devoid of this guano, or soil, as some think of it; this is borne out by the discovery of eggs, hardened as though petrified, which had been buried either in this excrement or in the quicklime that generally abounds on these islands in the southern sea. After a period of time, diggers have gone back and again collected unlimited fanegadas of guano from the same islands.

Though the use of this guano was discovered but a few years back, the visits of these birds to the islands dates from time immemorial. Therefore it is not hard to accept the theory that this guano is exclusively a product of the excrement of birds, chemically and physically changed to the consistency of yellow or brownish yellow earth by marine acids, air, sun, and water. It has a heavy odor that is a bit unpleasant to those of us not accustomed to it; even when one takes pains to avoid places where guano is stored, the odor can cause a headache that lasts several hours.

On the hill at Jeguán, near the town of Arnedo, there is a silver mine. Not very long ago it was being worked and yielded from 50 to 80 marks (400 to 640 ounces) of silver per box. Between Jeguán and Torreblanca there are very many guacas, or tombs, of pagan Indians, and from these we took out various tools and clay pots and another thousand artifacts that had been buried with the bodies long before the Spanish conquest.

One league from Huaura, to the north, is a series of strong walls, 3 yards wide at the base and gradually narrower towards the top and about 3 leagues long. According to local lore, the walls separated the territories of certain native chieftains. Beyond the port of Chancayllo are to be found two stones engraved with figures remotely resembling seals; the Indians call them the sea-cow and the sea-bull and are completely convinced that these were animals that left the sea and turned themselves to stone. In truth, they are remarkable stones, and are the only ones that can be seen on all those hills and sandy beaches where seals are abundant, and where there are also great numbers of buzzards that come to devour marine animals left stranded on the beach.

Four leagues from Huaura, to the south, one finds very rich deposits of salt from which the mineral is mined in rectangular pieces weighing 75 to 100 pounds. This salt, as we have explained in our description of Lima, is natural calcium chloride; in the prevailing high humidity a great part of it dissolves very quickly, so in the mountains, forests, and other damp climates it is always kept close to the fire. These mines supply salt to the provinces of Cercado, Caxatambo, Canta, Huarocherí, Tarma, Xauxa, Huánuco, Huamalíes, Conchucos and Huaylas, for use in cooking as well as in the refining of silver. Much of it is also employed in protecting sheep from an insect known as alicuya in Peru and pirhuin in Chile, which attacks the liver and causes rapid loss of weight and death.

This province is divided into nine parishes, which together contain 14,000 souls of all classes of society. The first parish is the town of Arnedo, or Chancay, capital of the province and founded in 1563 when the Conde de Nieva was viceroy. He intended to establish a university there, but his plan was never consummated. Arnedo is the largest town of the province and has the greatest number of inhabitants of all classes, but there are few families of more than moderate means. It has the best buildings and an ample, square plaza in the center of town. A highway, which goes to the coast in one direction and to the valleys and mountains in the other, skirts one side of the parochial residences; in town it is called the main street, where its entire length is perfectly straight. The other streets are laid out without any order. There is a royal hospital and a Franciscan monastery in addition to the parochial residence.

The town is located a quarter league in from the sea, at the entrance to the valley, and is surrounded by farms and orchards that beautify it with diverse cultivated fields and various greenery and fruit trees. The buildings are of one story only, although some have a garret where grain can be stored; they are, like most along the coast, constructed of the same materials and in the same style as those of Lima. This parish has no dependencies, other than San Juan de Huaral and all the numerous estates of the valley that we might consider to be additional dependencies. Most of these estates belong to gentlemen who live in Lima, where they have their principal homes and families, but many of the owners pass the greater part of the year on their plantations and cultivate them with negro slaves.

The second parish is Huacho, the first town past the beaches and hills of Lachay. It is situated 1 mile from the sea at the entrance to the valley of Huaura. Although there are but a few small buildings in the center of town, with a church and a spacious plaza, Huacho is a square league in area and covered with small farms and orchards, each with a hut or small house in which the owner lives with his family. This arrangement makes it the most peaceful and pleasant town on the outskirts of Lima and the only one in Peru that has its chief crops and all kinds of vegetables and fruits within its confines, not only to maintain its own townsfolk but also to provision travelers and to sell in Huaura, Arnedo, and Lima. In this town one finds the best anonas that one can taste in Peru, as well as numerous trees of canafistola (purging cassia) and tamarinds. There is no unoccupied terrain in the town, and cattle are obliged to feed beside the houses all the year round. Huacho, we may truly say, is a tiny garden spot where nothing of the plant kingdom is lacking for the enjoyment, recreation, and support of its citizens, who are hard-working Indians of good character plus a few mestizos (Indian-Spanish). The natives of Huacho supply the town of Huaura with all sorts of foods that the womenfolk take to sell every morning, especially vegetables, fruits, fish, chickens and other fowl, eggs, etc. The women also prepare the best chichas (liquors made from maize) in Peru, known for both their strength and their good flavor.

The third parish is that of the town of Huaura, founded in 1608, with its two dependencies Mazo and Vegueta, small Indian villages located on the seacoast. The parish has a monastery of Franciscan monks that was rebuilt this year, 1781, and a royal hospital completed in 1764 by His Excellency Don Juan de Castañeda Velázquez de Salazar, Bishop of Panamá and later of Cuzco. He died the same year the hospital was finished, and thus he could not endow it as was his pious and charitable plan. The initial foundation of this hospital was financed by the king, and for its support he assigned the head taxes of the villages of Vegueta, Supe, and Barranca, which reduced the sum that each Indian had to pay to 5 reales yearly. Since there were many Indians in those days, the amount assigned for the upkeep and for the care of the sick was sufficient. Today this tax amounts to a mere 34 pesos and with a few lands and annual pensions makes up a yearly income of 250 pesos. This hospital is cross-shaped; the arms and head of the cross contain the sickbeds, and the remainder serves as a chapel. Because the altar is placed in the center of the cross, the patients may hear mass in bed.

The town of Huaura has a single street, straight and nearly a quarter league in length. Its buildings are one story high, like those of Lima. The population is made up of creoles (Peruvian-born Spanish), mestizos, Indians and other races. The highway from the valley or from the coast runs right through the middle of town.

The fourth parish is that of Barranca, 7 leagues from Huaura on the highway straight to the coast, with its dependency Supe, 5 leagues from Barranca.

The fifth parish is Aucallama, founded in 1551. A miraculous image of Our Lady of Rosario is worshipped there; Emperor Carlos V sent it together with its ornaments.

The sixth parish is Sayán, with its dependencies Tapay and Quintay. Quintay belongs to the province of Caxatambo.

The seventh parish is that of Chancas Maray, or Checras, with its dependencies Yuracyaco, Picoy, Parquín, Yucul, Camin, Moyobamba, Pañun, Turpay, Tonhos, and Cheuchín, where there are hot springs visited by many who suffer from rheumatic and venereal ills and who cure themselves by bathing in and drinking these waters for a few days. Our companion M. Dombey went there with the wife of a judge from Lima, who was ill but returned to the capital in the same condition as when she left; he undertook to analyze these waters, but did not finish his analysis nor state what they contained. In the vicinity of the springs Dombey collected a number of new species of plants, some of which we collected simultaneously in Cheuchín in the province of Tarma; there we described them and handed them over to the artists to be drawn.

The eighth parish is the village of Paccho with its dependencies Ayaranca, Huacar, Musca, Llancsanka, Apache, Santa Cruz, Huanasaqui, and Auquimarca.

The ninth parish is the village of Iguari with its dependencies Llancao, Obequet, Huchiuha, Yunhuy, Acotama, and Huaycho.

The plants that we gathered on this first trip through the province of Chancay are as follows: *Salvia biflora*, *S. acutifolia*, *S. cuspidata*, *S. excissa*, and *S. integrifolia*. *Dianthera acuminata* and *D. multiflora*. *Calceolaria biflora*, *C. nutans*, and *C. trifida*. *Jovellana scapiflora*. *Valeriana laciniata*, *V. pinnatifida*, and *V. serrata*. *Commelina fasciculata*. *Cyperus niger*. *Galium ciliatum*. *Isnardia subhastata*. *Heliotropium microstachyum*. *Lithospermum hispidum*. *Anagallis ovalis*. *Convolvulus crenatus* and *C. heterophyllus*. *Ipomoea cuspidata*. *Solanum decurrens* and *S. pinnatifidum*. *Basella lucida* and *B. rubra*. *Physalis prostrata*. *Chenopodium ambrosioides*. *Calyxhymenia prostrata*. *Byttneria cordata*, called yerba de la araña (spider plant) because of properties attributed to it by the natives as a treatment for spider bites; the well-crushed leaves are plastered over the bite. I suspect that this name originated from the form of the flowers rather than from virtues of the plant.

Gilia multifida. *Xuarezia biflora*. *Gentiana quadrangularis*, known as canchalagua cimarrona. *Phelandrium ciliatum*. *Ornithogalum corymbosum*, called flor de cuenta (bead flower) because the seed resembles a rosary bead in form and color. *Epilobium dentatum*. *Jussiaea repens*. *Talinum album*, *T. lingulatum*, and *T. paniculatum*, all called castañuelas (castanets) for the shape of their fleshy leaves, which are used by the natives to soften calluses of the feet and by the fair sex to cleanse blemishes of the face. *Triumfetta lappula*.

Loasa urens, called ortiga de lomas (nettle of the hills) or, in other areas, itapallo; frequently used when cooked or in an infusion as a cleansing agent, laxative, aperitif, or diuretic. Members of the delicate sex usually take an infusion of this plant during a 9-day fast after giving birth, to relieve the afterpains called entuertos and to cleanse themselves of menstruation. An infusion with salt is reputed to be an effective remedy for rheumatic swellings, and the infusion is also given to alleviate asthma. *Loasa punicea*, commonly known as pomaysancca, is more often employed for these ailments and is more highly esteemed.

Mentzelia aspera. *Tetragonia cristallina*; in winter the mountains and hills along the coast are blanketed with this plant so abundantly that it provides excellent food for cows during the entire season. *Stachys pratensis*. *Gardoquia elliptica* and *G. obovata*. *Mimulus luteus*. *Mecardonia ovata*. *Waltheria tomentosa*, known as palo negro (black bush) or ancoacha cimarrona; it grows to 6 feet tall and excellent charcoal is made from its base. *Geranium moschatum* and *G. tuberosum*. *Malva scoparia*, escoba cimarrona (wild broom), which is used by the natives to make common brooms. *Sida multifida* and S. *palmata*. *Gossypium arboreum* and *G. hirsutum*; both species grow spontaneously near the villages and are called algodón (cotton). *Monnina dentata*. *Hedysarum procumbens* and *H. prostratum*. *Orobus biflorus*? *Phaseolus alatus*? *Astragalus rhombeus*. *Lupinus stipulatus*, chochitos. *Indigofera tinctoria*, añil cimarrón (wild indigo).

Bellis pubescens. Erigeron ramosum. Aster divaricatus and *A. verticillatus. Gnaphalium americanum, G. crispum,* and *G. odoratissimum. Senecio stipulatus. Eupatorium valerianum. Tagetes chinchi*; chinchi is the common name for this plant, and the Indians grow it in their gardens as a condiment for the stewed dish called chupe. *Ferraria violacea. Amaranthus gangeticus. Cucumis maderaspatanus. Sycios angulata. Bignonia grandiflora. Betula acutifolia,* aliso, which grows along the banks of rills towards the mountains; its wood is used for fuel. *Equisetum repens* and *E. gangeticus*; silversmiths clean and polish silver with both of these species. *Cenchrus muticus, C. echinatus,* and *C. lappaceus. Ophioglossum vaginans. Polypodium unitum,* called negrillo because of its black stalk and petiole; in Peru this plant is used in an infusion to relieve pain in the side, and the crushed leaves, always with pork fat, are applied as a poultice to the aching area at the same time.

In addition to the plants listed above, almost all those mentioned for Lima also grow in the province of Chancay, as do numerous other species that we shall enumerate in the account of our second trip to this province.

CHAPTER 6

Trip from Huaura to Lima and from Lima to the Village of Lurín

On the 22nd of October 1778 we returned to Lima from Huaura. When we finished drying the plants that we had gathered, described, and drawn in the province of Chancay, we packed them in boxes with other natural products that we had collected in that region.

Having heard of the fertility of the hills and coasts of Lurín, the five members of the expedition set out together for that town on the 5th of December 1778. We passed through the towns of Surco and Miraflores, both located on flat terrain and fanned by gentle breezes. Both towns are also surrounded by extensive and beautiful farms or country estates, orchards, and gardens, which abound in all sorts of shade and fruit trees, vegetables, and flowers. Because of the pleasant environment many families of Lima are continually visiting these towns to spend vacations of a fortnight or longer.

A quarter league beyond Surco we entered the vast plantation of San Juan where sugar, alfeñique (sugar paste with oil of almonds), chancaca (brown sugar), miel (molasses), and guarapo (cane liquor) are produced. A bit farther on, in a place known as Olivar, there is a large grove of olive trees. After this, one finds a stretch of sand that extends to the Lurín River, an arid and sterile desert even in the winter season.

On the left-hand side of the highway are the hills of Lurín. In the wet season these are clad with small plants that make an exquisite carpet when in bloom. This invites many people from Lima to walk and play in these beautiful hills or mountains during the time of flowering.

On the right-hand side, hard by the river, one can see the famous castle of Pachacamac (Plate 3). Here the ancient pagan emperors of Peru had barracks for 5000 soldiers. At the foot of the castle are also ruins of a town that obviously was very large in the time of the Incas. A short distance from these ruins, the aforementioned Lurín River flows through a conduit. When rain falls in the mountains, the river swells so much that fords are obliterated; for this reason chimbadores or vadeadores (men who know the fords) are sent out from Lurín to guide travelers and take them across the river. Notwithstanding this help, a number of people and cattle drown every year. In the dry season this river dries up almost completely, but its banks are always green and clothed with the various trees and plants that make it a beauty spot.

Not far from the river there is the estate of the priests of San Pedro of Lima; it is a sugar plantation like that of San Juan, and 10,000 pesos' worth of sugar, alfeñique, chancaca, etc., are annually produced there. The town of Lurín lies beyond this plantation.

CHAPTER 7

Description of the Village of Lurín

San Pedro de Lurín is located a little less than 6 leagues from Lima. It lies in a broad, green valley 1 mile from the sea and has a mild climate, much healthier than that of Lima and other surrounding towns. Because of this healthy climate, Lurín is a vacation center for some of the viceroys and other gentlemen of the capital and their families.

Lurín has a population of 120 people, all Indians, scattered in a number of huts or shelters. Most of these dwellings are built of quimcha, or canabrava (a kind of reed or bamboo), and of straight timbers that commonly come from willows or from green, leafy trees called huayros, a species of *Erythrina*. Many houses are plastered inside and out with the usual mixture of mud and straw and are often whitened, especially inside, with lime made from seashells. They are square and one story high, with a flat roof like the houses of Lima. Each house has its orchard or small garden, with a variety of flowers and as many as five kinds of suches (*Plumeria* species) with enormous flowers of different hues.

The streets are straight, and only the new ones have fixed names, such as Malambo, La Palma, Mentidero, and La Costilla. In the center of town there is a large, square plaza. On one side of the plaza is the church, and the town hall is opposite. At the beginning of every year three mayors, each with his constable, are named: two for the town and one for the countryside. In addition, there is an Indian governor and a defender for the Indians, posts that are permanent and hereditary.

Lurín is truly a town for recreation, for it is a delight and a pleasure to walk past the masses of flowers that one can see through the reed fences that surround all the gardens, and under the thick foliage of the trees and bushes on the outskirts of the village. There is a beautiful walk that is called the Uña del Diablo (Devil's Fingernail) because one can see upon a stone the impression of the palm of a hand with long fingers.

For the celebration of the festival of San Pedro, patron saint of the town, there is a solemn ceremony in the church, a bullfight with young bulls, dances, and fireworks—without which no holiday is complete in all Peru. For the festival of San Miguel the same celebrations are repeated, and in some years there is a genuine bullfight for which many people come out from Lima to spend a vacation of a fortnight or so. They also celebrate Our Lady of Guadalupe. On the festival of San Nicasio, the favorite holy day of these Indians, the main attraction is a cock-and-duck race. These birds are hung head-down on a pole with a rope, and he who yanks the animal free while riding past on horseback wins the duck or cock. During the procession there are fireworks, and at the end of the festivities, by nightfall, everyone comes to drink chicha (maize liquor), which the mayordomos (managers, overseers) of the estates pass around freely.

Although the soil at Lurín is fertile and yields abundant harvests, the natives are content with sowing only what they need for their own immediate support. Their most important trade is in fish, which is carried to Lima for sale. To sell with their fish, some take along various fruits as well as yuca, sweet potatoes, squash, and beans, the unique foods that sustain these people.

Instead of bread the natives use boiled maize, which they call mote. This is one reason for their large harvests of maize, which is also used to make chicha. A fresh supply of this beverage is prepared daily by first soaking the necessary amount of maize grains in water overnight. The soaked maize is then placed on banana leaves, covered with more leaves, and allowed to germinate; the grains are then dried in the sun and ground into meal between two stones. This meal is boiled with a proportional amount of water, and the strained liquor is set out to ferment in an unglazed earthenware jug. It takes 3 or more days before a winelike odor is generated and the liquor becomes well charged with carbonic acid gas. They describe the drink in this stage as being very sharp or, in other words, fully effervescent like a strong beer.

The inhabitants are organized into two military companies of 50 men each. Their duty is to proceed twice a year to the port of Callao to do work connected with the ships and to help care for patients in the Bellavista Hospital. The militiamen receive a salary of two reales a day while on duty.

The fish most frequently caught in the sea off Lurín are robalos (similar to bream); lenguados (sole); corbinas (whiting); pexes sapos (anglers); pintadillas, a kind of trout; chitas; cabrillas (sea bass); cazones (dogfish); pexes reyes, a kind of sardine that is very delicate, especially when fried; anchovetas (small anchovies); lornas; jureles (spiny fish related to mackerel); bonitos (striped tunnies); chalacos (gobies); and pexe gallo.

The method of fishing in Lurín is the following: two Indians go out to sea, each astride a large bundle of totora reeds or bulrushes tied together well to retain buoyancy in the water. The two fishermen start out together, but when they are a certain distance from shore they cast their nets and move off in opposite directions, as far from each other as the cords of the net will allow. They then return to the shore thus separated so that the net remains taut. Just before touching shore, they approach each other again to close the net; then, both jumping on land at once, by the sheer strength of their arms they pull the net, with the fish, out of the water.

Although Lurín enjoys a mild climate most of the year, there are some tertian fevers (malaria) in the wintertime, or period of garúas. The fevers are cured with an infusion of yerba hedionda (stinking plant), apple, lemon juice, and cream of tartar; the dose of this preparation, which must be taken in fasting, amounts to half a pint for 3 consecutive days. In some years smallpox is rather prevalent. Caracha (itch or scabies) and gonorrhea are always present, both ills being caused by excesses and unhygienic conditions. Some of the women also suffer from tetanus and cancer. The remedies employed as cures are common herbs, taken in prescriptions dictated by the pecuniary condition and family traditions of the individual. Some, however, go to Lima to be treated by professional doctors, with pharmaceutical preparations.

In a small brook that flows from the hills, between two cliffs, there is a spring from which issues very soft, crystalline water that is always cool. Between the town and the sea there are numerous small lagoons in which one can catch the various fish listed above, as well as sundry aquatic birds such as zambullidores (divers), ducks, herons, flamingos, sarapicos, and others.

Beside one of these lagoons, which is called San Pedro de Quilcay, was situated a town of the same name. But its inhabitants had to abandon it because of frequent tidal waves from the sea during earthquakes. Those who did not perish in the last tidal wave resulting from the great earthquake of 1746 moved to the location where the town of Lurín stands today.

About 3 leagues out from the beach at Lurín there are a number of stacks, or small rock islands, strung out along a northwest to southeast line, the first being about 2 leagues from the last. The first is called La Viuda (The Widow) because it stands alone and is located farther out than the others. Next to La Viuda is the famous Pachacamac, largest of the stacks; in it are numerous caves where great flocks of marine birds dwell and reproduce, among which are extraordinary numbers of *Diomedea*, or pájaros niños (albatrosses). Anyone coming near to these caves will flee at once, for the shrieks of the birds are so loud that they deafen the ears and strike terror into the hearts of the bravest and most spirited of men. The shrieking is quite like the neighing of a great herd of asses. On this island much guano is collected to fertilize the maize fields. Farther on is the stack called El Arenisco (The Sandy One); it is small and pyramidal. The next one is known as San Francisco; it is slightly smaller than Pachacamac and has the form of a high cone. The last is El Jorobado (The Hunchback), so called because of its shape; it is the only smaller stack with a name of its own.

Besides the many fruit trees, seeds, vegetables, and flowers enumerated for the province of Chancay, the fields of Lurín support almost the same plants that have been listed for the flora of the environs of Lima. Other species are common here. I collected and described the following:

Dianthera repens. *Heteranthera reniformis*. *Lithospermum dichotomum*, tiquil-tiquil. *Nolana acutangula*, chaves; this plant is an appetizing food for chickens. *Convolvulus secundus*, campanillas de lomas (little bells of the hills), used as a garden ornamental because of the size, beauty, and clear blue color of its flowers; its roots are employed by the Indians as a purgative. *Convolvulus sepium*; an infusion of this milky plant is likewise taken as a laxative. *Evolvulus stipulatus*. *Cordia rotundifolia*, called tina or membrillo (quince) because its leaves resemble those of the quince; an infusion of these leaves finds great use as a remedy for jaundice. *Lycium salsum*, called cachicassa (salty spine) owing to the flavor of its leaves. *Potamogeton compressifolium*. *Atropa umbellata*.

Solanum variegatum, called pepino de la tierra or pepino del país (native pepino). [This fruit and the true cucumber are both called pepino in Peru.—Translator] The fruits of this plant, borne in great abundance, are as large as eggplants, yellowish or whitish, and spotted with purple, violet, or red. Their flavor is similar to that of melons, though not so sweet or agreeable; when eaten to excess they cause tertian fevers and bloody diarrhea, and are harmful for those who suffer from mal de vicho, or dysentery. Because seeds do not form until the second year after the plant is transplanted from germination beds, this pepino is reproduced by means of its stem.

Hydrocotyle vulgaris and *H. umbellata*, called orejas de abad (abbot's ear) or petacones (plump ones) because of the orbicular shape of the leaves. The juice of both species is used as a cure for ulcers of the mouth, and is applied to an infected pimple to bring it to a head and heal it.

Plumeria rubra, suche morado-rosado (violet-pink suche); *P. tricolor*, suche blanco-rosado (white-pink suche); and *P. carinata*, suche turumbaco. These species are milky trees, 6 to 8 yards tall, affording good shade without doing the harm that other lactiferous trees often do. In January, February, and March they make a wonderful garden decoration, as the tips of the branches are covered with thousands of beautiful flowers arranged in corymbs. The leaves are only at the ends of branches, and the flowers are borne in the center of clustered leaves. These species differ from one another merely in the color and size of the flowers. When cut, the trees remain fresh for 2 or 3 years, after which they can take root and grow vigorously just as easily as they would a few days after being cut. This is why they are called suche, which means "pimp."

Alstroemeria peregrina, peregrinas (pilgrims); this plant is abundant in the ravines of the hills of Lima, Lurín, Chancay, and other places. It is grown in gardens for the beauty of its flowers that, though without scent, are large and tinged with various colors. *Amaryllis aurea*, amancae antiguo (ancient amancae); its flowers, with their bright golden hue, are striking in gardens. The tubers are surrounded by a great many bulblets or small onionlike tubers the size of chick-peas; by means of these, multiplication the following year is assured. *Polyanthes tuberosa*, called margaritas blancas (white daisies) or vara de Jese (Jesse's staff). Because the fragrant flowers of this plant are used in the preparation that Peruvians call mixtura, it is cultivated on a large scale; emollient plasters are also prepared from its roots. *Pancratium flavum*; the attractive flower has a splendid orange color that makes it well worth cultivating as a garden ornamental. *Cassia mimosioides*, huaranhillo, and *C. tora*, cañafistola cimarrona (wild cassia); infusions of the leaves of these two species of senna are used as purgatives by natives of Peru. *Bauhinia aculeata*, called uñas de gato (cat's claws) because of the spines on the stem.

Sapindus saponaria, jabonera (soapwort), a leafy tree about 8 to 12 yards tall; its wood has various applications. Its fruits, called cholocos or bolillos, contain four seeds in a rather thick rind or husk that is useful for washing woolen or cotton clothing, for it lathers as much as soap; this characteristic gives the tree its common name. Children use the seeds, the size of a rifle shell, to make toys.

Sesuvium portulacastrum, litho; in Ica and other parts of Peru, from this plant natives obtain barrilla (saltwort or glasswort), which they use in manufacturing glass and soap. *Malva peruviana*, malva común (common mallow); this species is used in Peru as are *M. rotundifolia* and *M. silvestris* in Spain. *Crescentia cujete*, totumo or tutumo (calabash tree, gourd tree), a tree growing to a height of 6 to 8 yards; its branches are clustered, erect, and rodlike, and it is a beautiful dark green. See the uses listed for the fruits of this tree in the description of the province of Chancay. *Lantana salvifolia*, mastrante; in some localities the flowers of this shrub are called cariaquito. In Peru the natives use an infusion or a boiled potage of mastrante to cure jaundice, drinking one or the other in large amounts.

Dolichos uncinatus, frijolitos (little beans) or taconcitos (little heels). *Dolichos lablab*, called frijol de antibo (antibo bean) or, elsewhere, senccapuscu; not withstanding the bitterness of the seeds of this legume, negroes and other peasant folk on the large estates eat them in quantity, lessening their bitter taste somewhat by letting them stand overnight in warm water. *Phaseolus vexillatus*, frijol cimarrón (wild bean). *Crotalaria incana*, called cascabelillos (little bells) because of the noise of the seeds when dry pods shake in the wind. *Hedysarum asperum*, called pega-pega (stick-stick) in reference to the pods and leaves that adhere, by means of their stickiness and roughness, to the clothes of those who walk where the plant grows.

Erythrina corallodendrum, known as huayro or huayruru; this is a tree attaining a height of 8 to 10 yards. Thickly beset with spines, it also bears such an abundance of flowers that from a certain distance it presents the splendid sight of a tree laden with scarlet corals. Its pods, though bitter, are eaten green by natives, who first rinse them. The Indians propagate these trees from cuttings, which in a short time become stout trunks; for this reason they are used for corner posts of huts or houses, and the reeds that make up the quimchas, or walls, are bound to these trunks.

Hypericum quadrangulare. Senecio scandens. Eupatorium scandens, yedra (ivy). *Bidens cuneifolia. Lobelia decurrens*, contoya; natives use an infusion of this plant as a strong laxative, and to halt its drastic action they drink 1 or 2 cups of cold water. *Pistia stratiotes*, called lechuga cimarrona (wild lettuce) because of the placement and color of the leaves. *Passiflora minima*, ñorbo cimarrón (wild passion fruit), and *P. foetida*, ñorbo hediondo (stinking passion fruit).

Mimosa fernambucana, cierrate puta (close up, whore), so named because of the characteristic closing of its leaves when touched; it grows abundantly in all cultivated fields along the coast. *Mimosa punctata*?, tapateputilla (close up, little whore), which is the most sensitive species of plant that I have seen; when it is touched by a hand or anything else, the leaflets instantly contract and fold in such a manner that the plant becomes only a mass of naked twigs. In an entire afternoon I could not collect and press in my papers even one leaf of this mimosa, which grows in sandy and dry places among the trees called huaranccales and is always prostrate. Its sensitivity, rapid as lightning, is truly admirable. A powder made of the leaves is esteemed in Lurín as the best remedy for healing sores.

Mimosa inga, pacae (pacay, inga) or huabo; this is a leafy tree, 15 to 20 yards tall, the stout trunk of which is a source of wood and planks for numerous uses. The pulp of its abundant pods or fruits looks like very white cotton and is juicy, sweet, and tasty. It is thus a favorite of children and especially of the fair sex, who on holidays enjoy a half real's worth of pacays, or huabas, as the fruits of the pacay are called. The seeds nearly all sprout within the very pod or fruit, and they lack the shell or hard membrane that covers the bean of those species of *Mimosa* that are devoid of juicy cotton or spongy pulp. Because they are naked, or protected only by this pulp, the seeds of the pacay shrivel up in a few days when exposed to air; they lose their power of germination if not planted as soon as they are taken out of the pod, or at least before drying sets in. These same conditions apply to those other species of *Mimosa* that are known in Peru by the names of pacaes silvestres and pacaes cimarrones (wild pacays). In my opinion, Linnaeus was in error in putting them all in the one genus *Mimosa*, for they ought to constitute a distinct genus and were so treated by certain botanists both before and during the time of Linnaeus.

Laurus persea, palto (avocado); this is a stout and leafy tree attaining a height of 12 to 28 yards or sometimes more, with wood valued for construction and various other uses. The pulp of its fruits, which are called paltas (avocados), has a color between green and yellowish and is tender and soft as butter, with a taste much like that of fresh nuts, especially if eaten with bread. The usual way of eating paltas is to add a bit of salt, for with salt they are tastier and more appetizing; nevertheless, some people like their delicate flavor with syrup, and others prefer them in salads. These fruits cannot be eaten immediately after picking but must be kept a few days covered with straw, bran, or other wrapping; the more they are covered, the sooner they ripen.

The pulp of avocado alleviates the burning pain of hemorrhoids when applied directly to the afflicted part, without the need of adding oil, saffron, and egg yolk as some people do. The seed, or stone, as it is commonly called, is used as a styptic in cases of dysentery; also, because it contains a permanent red dye, many women are in the habit of using it to mark linens. The largest and most delicious avocados grown in Peru are those of Santa Olalla in the province of Canta, and of the town of Chavín in the province of Huamalíes.

Sagittaria sagittifolia. Gentiana canchalagua, canchalagua; in the hills of Lurín, this plant hardly reaches 6 inches in height. See its uses and properties in our description of the realm of Chile; large amounts grow also in Guayaquil and in Buenos Aires.

CHAPTER 8

Trip from Lurín to Surco, and Return to Lima

On the 3rd of February 1779 we passed from the town of Lurín to that of Surco without any particular adventure along the way. We stayed in Surco until the 6th of March, roaming the fields and orchards. We observed and collected the following plants, which were described and drawn.

Utricularia aphylla. Scoparia dulcis, escobilla (little brush). *Heliotropium pilosum. Cynoglossum pilosum. Ipomoea acuminata* and *I. subrotundifolia*.

Cedrela odorata, cedro (cedar); there are various species of these valuable trees in Surco, Lima, and other towns. They have been transplanted from the hills to these localities in the valleys in recent years, yet some are luxuriant and beautiful trees with straight trunks that measure 20 yards or more in height. These are found on some estates and principally on that of Don Pedro Echervers, an oidor (judge) of the Audiencia of Lima; we were all lodged there during our stay in Surco. Should these trees continue growing as well as they have to the present time, the day will come when the coastal parts of Lima can have profitable plantations of cedars for building boats and many other works of carpentry. The government should encourage this crop by obliging all landowners to plant these trees around their cultivated fields.

Samolus valerandi. *Illecebrum achyranta*; because of its dryness, this plant is preferred to others for wrapping up cherimoyas, anonas, guanabanas, avocados, lúcumas, bananas, ciruelas de fraile (friar's plums), and other fruits for the purpose of ripening and softening them for eating. Without this help they are naturally hard, shriveled, tough, and flavorless, even when picked ripe; but with this slight fermentation they soften and become juicy, delicate, sweet, and tasty. *Cynanchum leucanthum*, piochas (jewels); this spreading and twining plant is very appropriate for covering summer houses and adorning fences and walks in gardens. Its latex is said to have strong laxative properties, and womenfolk dress their hair with the clusters of flowers that are never lacking on the plant. *Anethum parvum*, eneldo cimarrón (wild dill); natives use this plant medicinally in place of dill.

Achras lucuma, lúcumo, a stout tree 15 to 30 yards tall; it has a heavy, beautiful, dark green crown, and bears an abundance of fruits called lúcumas (eggfruit). The fruit is round with a tiny apical teat, weighs from 4 to 10 ounces, is green outside, and has a rather dark yellow pulp, like boiled egg yolk. This pulp cannot be eaten until several days after the fruit has been picked and then kept under cloth, bran, or other material to promote a winelike fermentation. The excellent wood is valuable for many uses because of its grain, color, strength, durability, and the ease with which it can be worked.

Pancratium maritimum, coronas de rey (king's crowns), and *P. littorale*, pilillas; both species are ornamental plants, and the flowers are used by ladies to adorn their hair. *Tropaeolum majus*, mastuerzo (cress) or capuchinas (nasturtium); the natives in Peru frequently use this plant to treat the mouth sores of scurvy, and innkeepers and other interested people pickle the buds, just as is done in Spain with capers. The flowers of mastuerzo are likewise added to uncooked salads, to which they lend a peppery and appetizing flavor.

Larrea glauca. *Poinciana tara*, tara; this beautiful bush, which grows to a height of 4 to 6 yards, is covered with bunches of showy yellow and red flowers. The fruits, of the same colors, are used as a substitute for galls in making the ink that is commonly used in Peru. Furthermore, these pods and the wood are employed in curing, tanning, and dyeing cordovan leathers, and in preparing other types of dye for tinting woolen and cotton fabrics.

Triglochin palustre. *Euphorbia chamaesyce* and *E. hypericifolia*, yerbas de la golondrina (herbs of the swallow); the latex of both species is used to clear up and cure cataracts of the eyes. These plants are also valued by the Indians as purgatives, but their effects are drastic and they must be taken with great care. *Spondias mombin*, ciruelo agrio (sour plum); this treelet grows to a height of 6 yards and has great racemes of flowers and fruits that, each in their season, present a splendid sight. Its fruits are as large as olives and reddish outside, and the pulp when fully ripe is yellow, juicy, bittersweet, and very appetizing.

Cleome triphylla. *Cassia tenuissima*, huaranhillo. *Malva coromandeliana*?, escoba cimarrona (wild broom). *Corchorus siliquosus. Melochia corchorifolia. Dolichos suberectus. Geoffroea spinosa*, called azofaifo (jujube tree) for the color and form of the fruits, which children like to eat. *Ageratum conyzoides*, called huarmihuarmi (woman-woman) because of the properties that an infusion of this plant, taken abundantly, is believed to possess for regulating menstruation. *Bidens tripartita. Sisyrinchium palmifolium. Acalypha indica. Ambrosia maritima*, called artemisia (mugwort) and used in place of medicinal artemisia. *Zizania octandra.*

Juglans nigra, nogal del país (native walnut); this tall and leafy tree is a source of very good wood for various purposes. The young and tender fruits, treated a number of times in hot and cold water before adding sugar, are made into a very tasty sweet like that made from limoncillos. The nuts, when fully dry and ripe, are mixed with honey, peanuts, and other seeds to make another kind of delicious candy.

Psoralea capitata, variously called yerba de San Agustín (Saint Augustine's herb), yerba de la Trinidad (herb of the Trinity), yerba del carnero (sheep's herb), and huallicaya. Natives often utilize the leaves of this plant to cleanse dirty wounds and to aid in the regeneration of flesh; afterwards, leaves of the same plant in powder form are applied to hasten healing. *Erigeron phyladelphycum.*

Castiglionia lobata, piñoncillos (little pine nuts), a bush attaining a height of 5 yards; it is covered with leaves for 4 months of the year, and then it becomes completely denuded except for the fruits, which persist for nearly the entire leafless period. The fruit has three seeds a little larger than pine nuts, each with a shell and a little white nut that is sweet and tasty but strongly laxative. Some people have the habit of taking three or four of these nuts to cleanse the digestive tract, and even children are aware of the properties of these piñoncillo nuts and use them to play tricks on playmates who do not know the plant and its characteristic action. Some mix the latex of the seeds with cow's milk in order to fool their friends, or they may even make them into sweets, thus hiding the joke more completely from unsuspecting victims. To stop the laxative activity brought about by these nuts they administer a glass of cold water, and within a short time the purgative effect stops. These piñoncillos are very abundant in Havana, where the nuts are used in the same way as in Peru.

On the 6th of March 1779 we returned to Lima to coordinate, bundle, and box up the specimens collected to date. These were sent to the king on the ship *Buen Consejo*, which left Callao for Cádiz in the following month of April.

This first shipment included 11 crates of plant specimens and various animal and mineral samples, various packets of seeds, 17 pots of living plants, and 242 drawings of plants in their natural colors.

On the 11th of March Mr. Dombey left Lima for Cheuchín, accompanying a judge's wife who was going to take the baths in the hot springs there. Because of this trip, Dombey entrusted to my care the shipment of seven crates of plant specimens, huaqueros (pottery artifacts), and clay and other curiosities of the mineral kingdom.

Once the 18 crates and 17 pots of living plants were shipped, we requested from the viceroy of Peru the permits and passports necessary to visit the forests of

Tarma and Xauxa. We had heard much about the fertility of these regions and of the abundance of new and valuable plants never before seen and studied by naturalists, just as had been the case with many of those gathered and observed along the coasts of the southern sea by Padre Feuville and José de Jussieu.

Armed with the viceroy's permits and equipped with the necessities for our trip, we Spanish botanists and artists left Lima on the 12th of May by way of the port of Las Maravillas, heading for the gorge of San Matheo.

CHAPTER 9

Trip from Lima to the Province of Tarma

On the 12th of May 1779 we left Lima at noon. We put 6 leagues behind us that day, traveling through farms and sugar plantations, fields of alfalfa, fruit orchards, and vegetable gardens. We spent the night on the Chacalacayo estate in an abandoned hut without undressing, for fear of being surprised by negro outlaws or raiders who had fled from their owners' estates and were roaming the countryside to steal and plunder. The night, therefore, was uncomfortable in the extreme; besides our having to keep a sharp watch for the negroes, fleas and mosquitoes in the hut feasted on our blood to their satisfaction, as they had done on the entire trip. On this day we found *Malesherbia thyrsiflora* on the hills and knolls of Lima.

On the following day, the 13th, we arrived at the town of Surco in the province of Huarocherí. This town consists of about a hundred inhabitants, all Indians except for a few mestizos (Indian-Spanish). The heat of the sun and a plague of mosquitoes made us very uncomfortable on that dangerous trip from the town of San Pedro de Máma to Surco.

On the 14th we passed San Juan de Matucána, a town of some 160 Indians and a few mestizos, and arrived at the town of San Matheo. Here we stayed the night, having traveled for great stretches on foot because of a succession of gullies and dangerous slopes with steps made of small stones laid one atop the other without a trace of any cementing substance. The path thus becomes, along its entire length, a narrow wall of stones at the edge of a steep, rocky mountain slope, covered merely with trodden earth. Should some of the lowermost stones of these steps come loose, as sometimes happens, the rest of the stones would fall with the first, and the same fate would befall anyone who might at that moment be traveling along the path.

On the 15th we had to stay in San Matheo, for the mayors were not in the village. We remained until the next day, when they gave us equipment for our trip, and we left at eleven o'clock for the settlement of San Juan de Chiclla.

On the morning of the 17th we found that we were without the mule drivers loaned to us by the mayors of San Matheo; they had returned to San Matheo with three pack mules. We were left with one muleteer, who alone could not load and control so much baggage along such roads. Though we were in a village of 60 inhabitants, it was only with great difficulty that we replaced the three pack mules. After searching in all the farmhouses we found but one Indian worker from the mining estate of Yauliaco, whom we besought with money ready in our hands, willing to help our driver pack and transport the baggage. Nor did we succeed in this until we used force and helped with the loading ourselves, and when this work had been haphazardly completed the Indian ran away. The loads kept falling, bit by bit, to the ground, whereupon all of us had to become muleteers; so we passed through the estate of Pomacamcha.

The Indian miner had gone ahead to Yauliaco, where he filled the mayordomo (manager, overseer) with all the lies that he could think up in order to create ill feeling between him and us. And he succeeded in his scheme. Taking to the road with several peasants, the mayordomo returned to the mining estate with the first load that he found, and deposited it in his quarters. My three companions, unable to escape the fury of this Biscayan, continued on their way with some of the other pieces of luggage that they had in their care. I arrived with the last of the baggage and the mule driver from Yauliaco, greeted the mayordomo courteously, and asked why those two trunks were still here. He answered me arrogantly, speaking as though he were the most important man in the world.

When I told the mayordomo all that had happened, he calmed down and his manner lost all its fire; he almost pleaded that we spend the night there, and promised that on the following day he would give us the same worker and as many more as we should need to continue on our way. A good Biscayan, Don Juan Unzaguey was ashamed of his initial bullying attitude, and he served us a magnificent supper that evening and an equally splendid dinner the following day. He also supplied us with the three mules that we needed and with the same worker to help our muleteer. Such was the mayordomo's shame that, as his employer Don Pablo Carreras told us several days later, he did not have the courage to take supper or dinner with us in spite of our insistence that he do so, but made excuses that he had already eaten.

We left Yauliaco on the 18th. We had an uneventful trip across the snow-covered peaks of the Andes, with difficulties much more bearable than those of the previous day. But we had just got down onto the puna, or high moor, when dusk fell upon us. It was then that our troubles began because the men in charge of the loaded mules were not with them, and we were traveling through unfamiliar, narrow stretches. At eight o'clock that night we crossed the outlet of the lake called Huascacocha, where we bogged down in a quagmire. One mule was sucked in and drowned. This animal carried two leather trunks containing my clothing, books, papers, and other equipment, all of which suffered such damage that most of it became unusable—especially the clothing, which was dyed in blotches from colored papers that the artists had packed in the trunks.

Notwithstanding the lateness of the hour and the cold of that region, my servant plunged in and cut the cords that were binding the trunks, whereupon we pulled them through the water onto dry land with a long rope. There we left them upside down and continued alone, following the whims of the horses until, at ten that night, we got to the mining estate of Pucará, frozen to the bone and famished. At eleven o'clock the miners of Pucará sent men to fetch the trunks; these arrived on two horses at half past midnight. On the following day we lingered in Pucará to dry the contents of the two trunks in the sun.

In this mining concession, as in the other silver-mining areas between San Juan de Chiclla and Pucará and on the slopes of those mountains and moors, the miners use the native sheep known in Peru by the name of llama, *Camellus llama*, to transport ores from the mines to the smelters.

Instead of firewood, the miners all use champas, a kind of turf growing in the boggy spots that are never lacking in these high moors. The clumps of sod are cut and pulled from the bogs in rectangular blocks, which contain an abundance of tiny herbs with strong, branching rootlets all intertwined. These plants, together with the soil that they hold, provide a good fuel, but when the well-dried turfs are burned they give off, before forming coals or embers, a dense smoke with a very unpleasant odor. Especially unhealthy for persons who are not used to the smoke, it causes headaches, irritation and swelling of the eyes, and even nosebleed. Should one suddenly go outside in the cold to escape the smoke, the throat and even the lips become inflamed, and one nearly suffocates. And those folk who are dedicated to digging the hidden treasure of silver from the heart of the snow-capped mountains and moors of the Andes live in the midst of all this discomfort.

The commonest plants in those moors and humid places where champas are cut are gentians, geraniums, valerians, and certain grasses and diadelphias (diadelphous plants). All of these are small and scrubby or prostrate plants growing on spongy ground, into which horses and mules can sink with extreme ease. When this danger exists, one can see water covering the turf.

On the 20th the four of us with our servants and mule drivers left Pucará, all suffering more or less from headaches, watering eyes, blistered faces, and chapped lips, and smudged with the thick and noxious smoke that is ever-present in the rooms of those gloomy, reeking huts.

Half a league beyond Pucará we passed over a short natural bridge, formed by the waters of a rill that flows under it. Farther on, perhaps half a league from the estate of Pachachaca, we crossed a wide plain called Chaplancca. Measuring 600 paces in length and as many in width, the plain is so level that a brook of crystalline, petrifying water spreads out and flows over the whole surface; this situation has doubtless caused the formation of a gentle and beautiful waterfall that seems to have been purposely chiseled into that spot. A short way from Chaplancca there is another natural bridge under which the waters of this cascade flow swiftly, together with the brook that passes through the first bridge that we mentioned. The waters of various other streamlets springing from the mountains, moors, and ponds on several sides also come together at this spot. A little farther on, this stream joins the famous and sizable Parí River, over which is the first bridge in this region to be made of tarabilla, or ropes. By means of pulleys, people cross from one bank to the other in a leather sack or a box.

At eight at night we arrived at the bridge of La Oroya, built of thick leather cords and chacllas, or slender vines. Since loaded animals could not cross on the bridge, we had to carry the baggage over on our own shoulders and have the horses swim across. We started the task at that inappropriate hour by the light of several bundles of ichu grass, the thatching material of the caretakers' huts at each end of the bridge. Before taking baggage to the other side, Gálvez attempted to get his saddle mule across the bridge. Since only two planks had been placed over the hole where the cords were tied, the mule fell in and an hour was lost rescuing the animal with ropes. This accident taught us to have all the animals cross by swimming. The river at this point is so full and so swift that we lost one mule; the following day the animal was found a short distance below, drowned. We spent more than 3 hours in all this work, and arrived at the town of Oroya at midnight, thoroughly worn out and dead tired. This bridge, about 40 yards across and barely 2 in width, swings from one side to the other as one passes over it, so the mere thought of crossing it at night is shocking and frightening. We succeeded, however, without suffering any accidents beyond those mentioned.

With the help of the workers that the mayors of San Matheo had sent to replace those who had escaped from San Juan de Chiclla, we managed to cross the bridge and leave the town of Oroya by daybreak, entering the capital of Tarma on the 21st. We left all our baggage in the care of the mule drivers, who arrived at Tarma with it at eight o'clock that night. To crown this trip with mishap, a mule disappeared from the corral. It was never again seen, nor did we ever hear any news of its whereabouts, notwithstanding all our investigations to locate the animal.

In spite of our misfortune and travail on this trip, along the way we collected many specimens of precious plants that all the year round adorn the gorge of San Matheo and the little brooks and rills that descend from the mountains to join the Rimac River.

From Lima to San Pedro de Máma, a plain stretches on both sides of the river, filled with continuous fields of sugar cane, alfalfa, sweet potatoes, yuca, yacones, squashes and gourds, beans of several types, and maize, as well as many trees of figs, bananas, pacays, and other native fruit. All this together presents a restful and delightful view of a pleasant, leafy countryside in that wide and fertile plain.

From Chacalacayo to Cocachacra, on the mountain slopes on both sides of the river one sees the remains of sundry villages of pagan Indians; it is obvious that they were sites that had supported large populations. Almost all the mountains between Lima and Cocachacra, on both sides of the river, are arid and without vegetation all the year round; even in the season of garúas there is hardly a green plant on any of them.

Between Cocachacra and Surco the road is crossed by a brook of cool, crystalline water issuing from a small ravine. The natives assured us that this water produces a disease known as verrugas (Carrion's disease, bartonellosis), with infected eruptions that often cause death to those who suffer from the sickness, especially those who arrive in a sweat and drink the water to excess.

In the whole long gorge that spreads out from San Pedro de Máma to the mountain, sunrise and sunset are 1 hour later and 1 hour earlier, respectively, than on the heights and in the open plains. The difference is due to the narrowness of the gorge and the height of the mountains, for the sun cannot penetrate the depths until nine or ten o'clock in the morning, and the towering peaks shut out the rays of light at two or three in the afternoon. When the sun does shine down into the depths of the valley, it produces heat that would be unbearable if it were of longer duration. One could not walk along the stream were it not for the cool breeze that, during those very hours, comes down from the surrounding mountains to alleviate the sun's heat, oftentimes cooling the air too much.

As a result of all these changes of heat and cold, the gorge is clothed with sundry shrubs and herbs throughout the year. Some individuals of each species are almost always in bloom. The climate of the ravine is mild and healthy; only an occasional tertian fever is experienced when the waters begin to swell, and again when they begin to fall—or in what we consider autumn and spring. Ordinarily, the Indians cure their illnesses with herbs, for neither physicians nor surgeons are available; only the mestizos are wont to seek the assistance of a few mediocre barbers.

From the town of Surco to the settlement of San Juan de Chiclla, the canyon through which the river flows is so narrow that, in some places along the slopes, one finds only a few small plots of level land that one might refer to as resting places along the way. Here the natives plant potatoes, ocas (edible tubers of *Oxalis* species), ullucos (edible tubers of *Ullucus tuberosus*), massuas (edible tubers of *Tropaeolum tuberosum*), abas (horse beans), and alfalfa.

From Chiclla onwards the climate is cold, and only a little barley is grown for the fodder with which miners feed their pack animals. Until one arrives at the river, one finds very few plants in addition to those common throughout the region of mountains and moors. But there is no lack of grass for the ganado de Castilla (cattle of Castille, or merino sheep), llamas, huanacos, and vicuñas. Even for cows, horses, and mules there are pockets of ichu and many other grasses that, though small, are succulent and nourishing for all kinds of domestic animals.

The road from San Matheo is extremely narrow and very dangerous along its entire length, following the bank of the river that flows from the mountains to San Pedro de Máma. The river falls within such a narrow course and with such force that the waters form one continuous cascade. In some places these falls are frightening because of the incessant roar of water swirling and pounding against the grotesque rocks that have fallen from the cliffs into the middle of the river. This noise makes it impossible to understand, or to hear, what one traveler says to another, even when shouting. At many points along the way, travelers are completely soaked with the fine spray like garúa, or mist, that is flung far into the air from the rocks against which the water dashes. And then, in other places, the cascades are so beautiful that the white, foaming water looks like snowballs of various sizes, now in constant motion, now at complete rest. The waters form such extraordinary and playful designs that travelers who pass this way for the first time are distracted by their imagination and lost in pleasant contemplation.

Among the many ravines along which this road passes is the slope known as Punta de Diamante (Diamond Point), located between San Juan de Matucána and the inn of Ibiso. Because of its narrowness and steepness, one shudders at the thought of passing this point. A beast of burden must climb to the top in a run, stopping for breath on the little shelves of landings that are found here and there; in no other way can this steep slope be ascended or descended. Should man or beast have the misfortune to fall to the river from this height, it would be useless to undertake a search, for the blows received from the fall and the pounding of the waters against the rocks would dash the victim to pieces in a few short moments.

Many stretches of this road are formed, as we have said, of small, smooth boulders or stones piled one atop the other from the bank of the river to the highest part of the road. Should some of these uncemented stones loosen and become dislodged from their places, that whole stretch of road would be ruined. Nonetheless, the durability of these narrow roads is worthy of admiration. Though simply constructed and a yard wide at most, they have lasted from the days of the Incas to the present time without any maintenance other than occasional mending when needed.

Throughout this ravine in abundance is a species of bird known as cotornita, or small parrot, as well as sundry other little birds of diverse color and song. Their variety serves to entertain the interested traveler along that long, deep, and murky gorge, and to take his mind from its dangers.

CHAPTER 10

Description of the Province of Huarocherí

This province (Plate 4) is bordered on the west by the jurisdiction of Cercado de Lima, which begins 5 leagues from the capital of Peru. To the north it is bordered by the provinces of Canta and Tarma, and on the east by the province of Xauxa. It is 30 leagues long and 26 leagues wide. It enjoys two climates: one more or less warm in the lowlands, valleys, and canyons, and the other more or less cold in the hills, punas or high moors, and mountains.

In the deep gorges and the warm or hot canyons, as well as on the slopes of the lower mountains, the following crops are grown and harvested: potatoes, sweet potatoes, arracachas (apios, Peruvian parsnips), yucas, yacones, ocas, ullucos, massuas, horse beans, porotos or indias (beans), maize, bananas, pacays, palillos, lucumas, cherimoyas, guanabanas, guavas, berries, apples, and quince. These fields are never without alfalfa.

In the mountains, since the ground is covered with snow for most of the year, one finds only the occasional plant in crannies and hollows of rocks and in a few protected places warmed by the sun. On the punas, or moorlands, ichu and other smaller grasses, sedges, diadelphias (diadelphous plants), and sundry other tiny plants grow in plenty. With these the inhabitants maintain large flocks of sheep and herds of cows, horses, and mules, as well as the innumerable llamas that, as we have said, are used by the miners of this province to transport metales, or ores, from the mines to the smelters. These smelters are always located in gorges or canyons at the foot of the mountains, near a supply of grasses for feeding the saddle horses and mules.

Large numbers of huanacos, vicuñas, and vizcachas (chinchillalike rodents) live wild on these punas. Here there are many lakes in which the natives fish for bagres (catfish) and cachuelos, which are delicious fried or boiled. Various kinds of birds inhabit the moors, too: huachas (washers, wagtails), the crop of which is applied to goiter by natives who believe the swelling will be thereby reduced; ducks; swans; treguilles; sarapicos; dominicanos, a kind of eagle; condors or vultures; neverillas; and the birds called llorones (weepers) or burladores (mockers) because they moan as would a human crying, and then laugh heartily when a person, dog, or other animal comes near them. Near and within villages there are aloicas, or calandrias (calandra larks); pichuisas, a kind of sparrow; zorzales (thrushes); papamoscas (flycatchers), or ruiseñores (nightingales); and cascabelillos (little bells), or palomitas.

The source of the Lima River springs from several ponds near the mining estate of Tuctu in the mountains. Others of these ponds or small lakes shed their waters towards the provinces of Yauyos and Cañete and increase the size of the Mala River; the Mala, like the Rimac, flows into the Pacific Ocean. The stream known as Santa Olalla joins the Rimac near San Pedro de Máma. All the other ponds of the punas, large and small, send their waters north to considerably augment the Parí River, which arises in Lake Chinchaycocha, located on the pampas (prairies) of Bombón, between the village of Reyes and the town of Pasco.

Along streams and in higher areas of the mountains grow various medicinal plants in common use. Some Indians take them down to Lima to sell, especially the true calaguala, *Polypodium calahuala*; ratanhia (rhatany), or dental root, *Krameria triandra*; quinchamali, *Quinchamalium*, a new genus described by Molina; pomaysancca, *Loasa punicea*; escorzonera (viper grass); Peruvian sage; and sundry others.

Among the silver mines worked in this province that meet sterling standards, those of Pucará and of the peak of Nuevo Potosí in Yauli, where there are hot springs, are the richest and most productive. From Pucará to the Parí River one finds, as related in the account of our trip from that estate to the town of Oroya, two small natural bridges of one span each in the solid rock, and the plain called Chaplancca, all natural formations. The disease known as verrugas (Carrion's disease, bartonellosis), which is caused, as I have said, by the waters of the little stream that flows between Cocachacra and Surco, is cured by Indians who live in that region with an infusion or decoction of a species of *Mespilus*, as well as with the water of chuño (dried potato, potato starch) drunk in copious amounts.

The Indians of this province are employed in working the mines and transporting ore. The women, whose clothing consists merely of the manta (a kind of shawl), anaco (a native dress), and sucuyes instead of shoes, cultivate the fields, although their mates assist them in sowing and reaping. On holy days the womenfolk take charge of dressing the altars and images, adorning them with bunches of flowers from their gardens and from the fields. In each town, and on each mining estate, there is but one church or chapel, with three or five altars dedicated to various saints.

The province of Huarocherí is divided into 11 parishes. The first parish is that of Huarocherí, head of the province, with its dependencies Calahuaya and Allocá. The second is that of San Lorenzo de Quínti with dependencies Huancayre, Quínti, Tantaranchi, and Ccarhuapampa. The third is that of Olleros with dependencies Matará and Chataccamcha. The fourth is that of Chorillo with dependencies Chontay, Cochahuayco, Huamansica, Sisicaya, Lancca, and Lahuaytambo. The fifth is that of San Cosme and San Damian with dependencies Suniccamcha, Tupicocha, and Santiago de Tuna. The sixth is that of Santa Olalla with dependencies San Gerónimo de Tunán, Chaclla, Xicamarca, and Collata. The gardens of Santa Olalla produce large and delicious avocados, excellent cherimoyas, and other native fruits to be taken to Lima for sale, where they are more highly esteemed than those produced in other localities. The seventh parish is that of Carampoma with dependencies Larao and Huanza. The eighth is that of San Pedro de Casta with dependencies San Juan de Iris, Huachupampa, Chauca, and Otao. The ninth is that of San Juan de Matucána with dependencies Surco, Cocachacra or Cucachacra, San Pedro de Máma, San Bartolomeo, and Santa Inéz. The tenth parish of San Matheo de Huanccor, where the corregidor (chief magistrate) usually resides, is divided by the river into two barrios (districts) called San Antonio and San Matheo; its dependencies are San Miguel de Viso, San Antonio de Yauliaco, and Pomacamcha. The settlement of San Juan de Chiclla is located between Pomacamcha and San Matheo. The eleventh and last parish is that of San Antonio de Yauliaco with its dependencies Pomacocha, the settlement of Carahuacra, Pucará, Pachachaca, Santa Rosa de Yaco or Saco, La Concepción de Paccha, San Cristóbal de Hucumarca, San Francisco Solano del Trapiche, San Gerónimo de Callapampa, Santiago de Huayhuay, San Antonio de Huarí, and San Lucas de Chacapalca. Beyond Pomacamcha lie the mining estates known as Bellavista, Ciracamcha, Yauliaco, Yanacolpa, Tincco or Tincu, and Cassapalca; on the right-hand side, one passes Piedra Parada and, past the mountain and in front of Pucará, one sees Tuctu.

We gathered many curious plants along the road from Chacalacayo to Oroya. We described these later in Tarma, using the notes that I had made in the locality of the collection, the dried specimens, and various living plants of the same species also found growing in the valleys and mountains of the province of Tarma. Those we encountered most abundantly were: *Calceolaria cuneiformis* and *C. viscosa*. *Atropa biflora*. *Malesherbia thyrsiflora*. *Tropaeolum tuberosum*; its tuberous roots, known as massuas, are cultivated for food in various parts of Peru. *Fuchsia verticillata*, molloccantu. *Buddleja incana*, quisoar. *Saxifraga tridactyles*. *Euphorbia tuberosa*, huachanccana; the Indians take the root of this plant to Lima to sell as a purgative, but it must be used with much caution because of its drastic laxative properties. *Mespilus uniflora*; an infusion of this plant is used by natives as a cure for the disease called verrugas. *Loasa punicea*, pomaysancca; in Peru this is taken in an infusion or decoction to induce menstruation. *Duranta plumieri*. *Alonsoa linearis* and *A. lanceolata*. *Thalictrum polygamum*. *Molina tomentosa* and *M. prostrata*, pachataya. *Sapium nitidum*. *Polypodium calahuala*, calaguala. *Agave mexicana*. *Plumbago europaea*. One species of *Dianthera*, one of *Cestrum*, three of *Convolvulus*, two of *Lycium*, one of *Aloe*, one of *Yucca*, two of *Silene*, two of *Lantana*, four of *Sida*, and two of *Lobelia*. Many species of *Tagetes*, of *Cactus*, and of diadelphias (diadelphous plants), syngenesias (syngenesious plants), and cryptogams. I shall discuss these and publish my notes elsewhere.

CHAPTER 11

Arrival of the Spanish Botanists and Artists in Tarma

On the 21st, as soon as we had entered Tarma, capital of the province, the four of us went to the home of the army commander for the town and its borders, Don Francisco Gómez de Toledo, to request lodging; at the moment the governor of the province, Don Juan José de Avellafuentes, was not in town. The military commander immediately gave orders that we be provided with lodgings, and that evening and on the following day entertained us at his own table.

On the 23rd of May 1779 we communicated with the governor, telling him of our arrival and the purposes of our commission in the province under his rule. By return post he wrote to us from the town of Pasco, where he was at that time, offering us all the help that was within his power to give. He also provided assistance in securing equipment, provisions, and other necessities for the excursions and trips that we were to undertake throughout the whole region over which he had jurisdiction.

On the 26th we began the botanical work, continuing until the 21st of April

1780 in the lowlands, ravines, hills, mountains, and canyons of Tarma, as well as in the forests of Huasahuassi and Palca and in the woodlands of Churupallana and Huayabal. We made similar journeys to areas of the province of Xauxa, as far as the sanctuary of Ocopa and the town of Concepción. Nearly all the plants of these regions were new to us, and of great value in the enrichment of botany and materia medica for the benefit of humanity.

CHAPTER 12

Description of the Province of Tarma

The province of Tarma (Plate 5), lying 40 leagues from the city of Lima, is bounded on the southwest by the province of Huarocherí, on the south by that of Xauxa, on the north by the provinces of Huamalíes and Huánuco, on the east by the forests where barbarous Indians live, on the west by the province of Canta and the part of the province of Chancay called Chacras, and on the northwest by the province of Caxatambo.

This province enjoys three different climates: hot, warm-temperate, and cold. The first prevails along the edge of the forest and in deep canyons. The second climate occurs in the valleys and gorges and on the hillsides, where many kinds of seeds and vegetables are sown: barley, maize, alfalfa, horse beans, peas, beans, lupines, pears, peaches, apples, lettuce, endive, cabbage, garlic, onions, potatoes, sweet potatoes, yacones, arracachas, ullucos, and massuas. Growing in the forested areas are yuca, mallicas (yams), ssaqui (*Calla* species), pineapples, papayas, and bananas. In the town of Acotamba there are sloe plums, or blackthorn, and in Tarma a type of Spanish currant. Garden flowers are abundant, especially pinks, narcissus, white and multicolored margaritas, ambarinas or viuditas (scabious, mourning bride), jasmines, and numerous others with which the Indian women dress the altars and images daily, but on festival days above all. There is land suitable for flax, for several plots of this plant have been sown and are growing well. Canaries, European hares, turkeys and other animals from mild climates thrive here. Furthermore, even outside of forested areas there are trees useful for building, such as willows, alders, quisoares (*Buddleja* species), and quinhuares (*Polylepis* species). There is also no dearth of other woods for fuel, though in the town of Tarma most are inferior.

The area of the third climate lies in the cold heights of the mountains and punas (moorlands), where both bitter and sweet quinoas (*Chenopodium* species) grow as

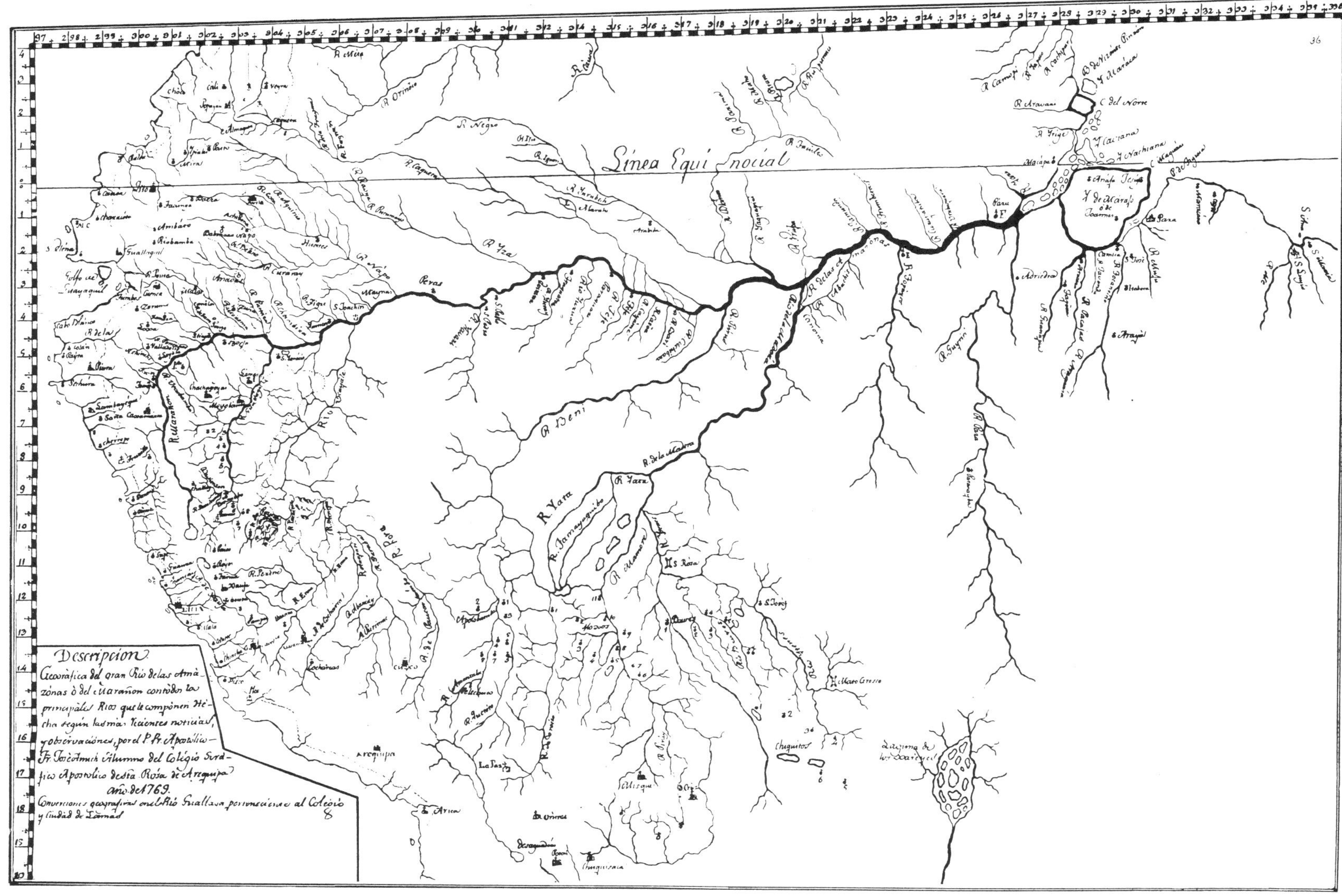

Figure 5. Description of the Amazon, or Marañón River, and all its major tributaries, drawn by José Amich, 1769. From the *Historical, Geographical, Political, Ecclesiastical and Military Survey of South America*, folio 36. (Courtesy of the British Museum.)

well as ocas, maccas, and massuas (three kinds of root vegetables). In localities somewhat less frigid, excellent potatoes are harvested; these are put into sacks to rot in tanks or in running water for a fortnight or longer, and are later crushed with stones and set out to dry in the sun for making what is known as chuño. A very white meal prepared from this chuño is used to make a kind of mash or porridge called mazamorra de chuño, which is a smooth, soft food and very appropriate for those who are sick or of delicate health.

On the punas of Bombón and on other high moors of the province, an infinite number of vicuñas, huanacos, vizcachas, guinea pigs, and uroncillos flourish, and great flocks of sheep are kept. Many of these sheep are taken to Lima for sale, for the meat is the most delicious in the country because of the grasses on which the animals feed. From their wool many pieces of jerga (a coarse cloth for cloaks) are manufactured in the factories of this province. An appreciable portion of the wool produced is also sold to factories in other provinces, only to be bought back as cloth because the looms of the province of Tarma cannot keep abreast of the demands of the mining communities. From the wool of the vicuña and huanaco, alone or mixed with silk and cotton, the womenfolk weave handkerchiefs, scarves, stockings, underwear, gloves, sock-suspenders or garters, sashes, belts or girdles, caps, etc. They adorn these with drawings and inscriptions from models given to them, though they can neither read nor write. They spin the wool themselves, and the work is perfect. From sheep's wool mixed with cotton they make capes of sundry styles and colors, spinning and weaving the wool themselves and dyeing it with infusions of plants.

In gorges near the forests there are deer, foxes, wildcats, small snakes, and a few poisonous serpents and scorpions.

Mines of Yauricocha

In this province are located the famous mines of Cerro de Yauricocha, which are in the most inhospitable part of the punas of Bombón and yield enough ore to keep a hundred mining engineers, spread throughout the territory, working constantly. It is the rare smelter that does not have two, three, or four mills of various types for grinding ores.

Salt Springs

In the town called Yanacachi, which means black salt, there are some saltwater springs. This water, when purified and evaporated, yields salt that is excellent as a condiment for foods.

Source of the Marañón (Amazon River)

Of the numberless lakes that are located in the moorlands and mountains of this province there are three principal ones: Lauricocha, Yauricocha, and Chinchaycocha. Lauricocha, situated at 10°28' south latitude between Chinche and the town of Jesús and bounding upon the province of Huamalíes, gives rise to a little stream.

Crossing through Huamalíes and other provinces, this stream enters the forest and, ever-swelling with the myriad brooks that descend from the hills, mountains, and moors, forms the Marañón, the greatest river known in the world (Figure 5).

The second major lake, Yauricocha, is located at 10°50' south latitude and forms the river that passes by Huánuco, there called the Pillco and in the territory of the Lama Indians known by the name Huallaha. This river is navigable from Cuchero, a town 26 leagues from Huánuco, downstream to its junction with the Marañón at 4°55' south latitude.

And from the third lake, Chinchaycocha, which lies in the middle of the pampas (high prairies) of Reyes, or of Bombón, and stretches from 11° to 11°30' south latitude, flows the Parí River. Crossing the province of Xauxa, this river enters the forest and joins up with the Apurimac; these two, together with the Paro, or Beni, River, make up the great Ucayali River. The Ucayali traverses the pampa of Sacramento and flows into the Marañón in the territory of the Omagua Indians.

The lake of Chinchaycocha is 10 leagues long, stretching from the town of Reyes almost to the town of Vico, and averages from 3 to 6 leagues wide, corresponding with the appearance of its waters, for some parts are very much wider than others. But its whole length is muddy and boggy. It produces bagres (catfish), cachuelos, and beautiful frogs with large hind parts that are very tasty when fried in butter. This lake, surrounded by stretches of reeds and bulrushes, is almost completely impenetrable. In the shallow, muddy parts of the lake there are some little islands where pigs, dogs, and guinea pigs thrive, along with ducks, widgeons, pelicans, parionas, and other different kinds of aquatic birds. The wildness of the guinea pigs, pigs, and dogs shows these animals to be either native to the lake or naturalized in the region for many years. Because it is so hard to find a point of entry to the lake, these animals are seldom bothered by men. Were this lake of a calmer temperament, it would afford the greatest diversion in shooting and fishing while crossing it, and communication from one town to another would be accomplished more rapidly. Not many years ago, a priest from the town of Ccarhuamayo navigated this lake in a small boat and crossed over it to the town of Ondores.

Water Dogs

According to the natives, the dogs of this lake are of a special type: the body and head look like those of a mongrel, the snout is pointed, the nose red, the ears like those of a fox, the tail very hairy, and the eyes glowing and sharp. In their native haunt these dogs are much more agile than they are on land, for in the wild they have very fine hair like that of swine, but after being domesticated for a year or more they grow a long wool like that of other races of dogs of the Peruvian mountains. Their color varies; some are black, others black and white, and still others ashy gray or reddish. On the soles of the paws and feet they have membranes that are useful in swimming, like those of ducks. When the dogs are raised away from water, these membranes fall off after a certain time and the dogs walk awkwardly until domesticated, when they run like other dogs.

Paved Highway of Chinchaycocha

Stretching in a straight line from the town of Reyes to Ccarhuamayo are the ruins of the famous roadway of Chinchaycocha, or of Reyes. There is evidence of its having been one of the best constructed works of the pagan Indians, but at the present time travel over it is almost impossible. In the rainy season the inhabitants of Reyes repair certain bad places in order to make use of it.

Before arriving at Ccarhuamayo, one meets great stands of a kind of rhubarb in certain swampy flats. The roots of this plant are used as a substitute for medicinal rhubarb. In the cold climate of Ondores and Ccarhuamayo, nothing is planted but the root known as maccas, which the natives use as a food. These little potatoes, or potatolike roots, are the size of a hazelnut and very tasty, but hot and aphrodisiac; for this reason many believe that they increase the reproductive capacity of both men and women.

This province has under its jurisdiction other rivers in addition to the three mentioned above, as well as an untold number of brooks and creeks that come down from the mountains and lakes of the punas, forming high and beautiful waterfalls upon entering the gorges and canyons below and winding northward through the dense jungles of the Andes. One of these rivers passes through the town of Tarma—or, rather, the new Villa de Tarma—and, as it leaves the town, joins another stream that descends in a different gorge; this junction is called Tincu or Tincco. Two leagues farther on, the small Acobamba River enters this same river; 4 leagues below that, the Huasahuassi and Siusa, already united, flow into it.

In addition, various other brooks become tributaries, and all together they make up the Chanchamayo River. Farther downstream, the Chanchamayo is known as the Enero, or Perene, River, and it flows on to join the Apurimac, which in its turn empties into the Paro River.

Still another river flows from the town of Rancas, joins up with one that has its source in nearby ponds, and within a short distance enters the Chinchaycocha, or Parí, to which many streams from the pampas and punas of the provinces of Canta, Huarocherí, and Xauxa pay tribute. It then forms a large river that tunnels through a mountain for a distance of 104 yards, where the waters rush through with tremendous force in the rainy season. This river finally crosses the provinces of Xauxa, Anccaraez, and Huanta and, entering the jungles, flows swiftly and in great volume to join up, as we have said, with the Apurimac.

Royal Highway of the Incas

Along the southern gorge, 1 league from the Villa de Tarma on the direct road to Xauxa, the ruins of a fort of the pagan Indians dominate the gorge and, halfway along, cross over the Xauxa road. There is enough evidence to deduce that it was one of the strong forts of the Incas. Following this route one finds, 3 leagues beyond the Villa de Tarma, the great highway of the Incas that was laid out in a straight line from Cuzco to Quito. Although in places it is lost, there remains to this very day a great part of this magnificent work of the emperors of Peru. The highway is made in the style of an avenue, all of cobblestones with here and there a step, almost imperceptible, of the same stones. At certain distances there are resting places that were used by the Incas and their processions, say the natives, for pauses or rests when they traveled the highway. These steps can be seen not only in the ascent and descent of mountainsides, but also in the plains, and at uniform distances from each other along the entire length.

Burial Monument and Silver Coins

Two and a half leagues from the Villa de Tarma along the western gorge, in the middle of a hill lying behind the houses and huts of the Huichay estate, are several narrow rooms in the hollow of a cliff. In that place is a cave that, according to the natives, goes on into the mountain for some leagues. I entered this cave, and all that I saw were several divisions or cells, like sepulchers, placed one atop the other to a height of five stories. Although I studied all of them, I could find no way of entering the abyss or deeper part of the large cave. The little sepulchral vaults or divisions, or narrow cells, are made of stone and loose soil, covered or roofed over with wide slates on which earth mixed with straw has been laid with no attempt to use cement or mortar. Each division has the shape allowed by the cavity where it is located, each has a little window through which a stocky man could just barely squeeze, and there is no other entrance or ventilation. Each one of these cells just barely accommodates one person seated, lying on the side, kneeling, or reclining; in any other position the feet or head would have to be pulled up.

The whole space occupied by the hollow of the cliff is enclosed by strong walls and has several trenches, with only one entrance; it measures 9 quartas (cuartas, handspans) in height and 5 in width. Because more than half the divisions are covered by a part of the cliff hanging like a curtain or shade from the highest part of the hollow, and the lower divisions are hidden or covered by the walls, those who pass this point along the roadway see neither walls nor cells. Everything points to the probability that the hollow in the cliff served the Indians in pagan times either as a severe and confining prison or as a cemetery, rather than as a dwelling place for living and free people. Among the quantities of human bones found there, which would seem to prove that this served as a place of burial for the pagans, pieces of silver the size of a 2-real coin have been found; these are extremely thin and polished on both sides, without indication of having had any seal or inscription.

One mile east of Tarma in the valley called Curis, which means gold, are the ruins of a pagan town. Not far from these ruins there is a gold mine, but since the yield of gold is too low to meet the cost of working the mine, and it is devoid of copper, it is not worked at the present time.

At the edge of the forest there are various forts, manned by the necessary troops and militia to prevent the chunchos (savages), or non-Christian Indians, from advancing beyond the forests. These Indians roam throughout the jungles without a trace of a home, living on the game and fish that they find, and subject to no rule or government.

Because the Indians of the parish of Huancabamba rose in revolt in 1742, and because the converted Indians of Chanchamayo, Quimirí, and Cerro de la Sal likewise rebelled, the exportation of coca, fruit, seeds, balsams, and other products across the boundaries of Tarma was interrupted. To return those Indians to Christianity, a fortified village at Chanchamayo, 18 leagues from the Villa de Tarma, was founded in 1779. This village was founded by order of His Excellency the Viceroy of Peru, Don Manuel de Guirior, at the request of the Reverend Friar Francisco de San José, Roman Catholic missionary of Santa Rosa de Ocopa. The governor of Tarma, Don Juan José de Avellafuentes, gave the necessary assistance for the work; and the commander, Don Francisco Gómez de Toledo, joined in the undertaking with his troops and the cavalry. Also in 1779, on the 10th of June, the road to this village was begun, and on the 13th the governor left with his personnel and troops to complete it.

In spite of the hope at that time of converting a multitude of unbelievers and of taking back into the folds of the church those who had revolted, the lieutenant of Tarma, Don Juan María de Gálvez, ordered the destruction of the fort and town of Chanchamayo in 1785. But later, on orders from his superiors, he had to establish the settlement again, 14 leagues from Tarma in the valley of Vitoc.

In this province, just as in Canta, Huarocherí, Xauxa, Huamancha, Huancavelica, Caxatambo, Huamalíes, Cuzco, and others located between 5° south latitude and 35° south latitude, including the province of Chucuytu, the Indians, both men and women, hunt the wild vicuñas and huanacos that live there. Up to the present time, they have not been able to tame or domesticate these animals in herds or flocks.

To carry out this kind of hunting, the natives fence in one or several hills and then climb up shouting, beating drums, blowing whistles, and snapping whips until they reach the summit or some other place previously agreed upon, usually in a corner where the animals cannot escape. In an open space or where there are not enough people, the natives make a low fence of cords a yard high and hang colored pieces of cloth or wool upon it every few feet; this presents an impassable barrier to the animals. They also hunt on horseback or on foot with the libis, a rope ½ to ¾ yard long and divided into four or more branches of the same length, with a round stone at each tip. When they are near the animal, they swing this apparatus in the air, making several circles so that it will gain considerable momentum. Flung towards the animal with force, it ensnares all 4 feet and the animal falls immobile to the ground. This same instrument is used in the pampas of Buenos Aires to hunt ostriches.

Vicuñas

Vicuñas are very curious animals, and they are greatly distracted by bright colors, especially scarlet or crimson. These animals have a peculiar habit: they always roam in groups of odd numbers, six females with one male or sometimes only four females with one male. As soon as the male sees a person nearby, it leaves the females and, a little way off, stops to watch what has attracted its attention. When the animal is certain that the flock is not in danger of being hunted or chased, it returns to the females without further ado. But when chased, it sets off in swift flight with the females following, running uphill or down with equal ease.

Vicuña wool is softer and darker than that of huanacos; each pelt yields half a pound, the very limit being 12 ounces. The main portion, from the shoulder area, is best because of its greater length and its dark tobacco color.

Huanacos, Llamas, and Alpacas

The huanaco is larger than the vicuña and smaller than the llama, or native sheep. These three animals, and the alpacas of Cuzco, belong to the genus *Camelus* of Linnaeus. The penis of the llama is in a reversed position; because of this, the Indians have made use of some ingenious methods to insure greater certainty in the act of reproduction in llamas. Since these animals are domesticated and are useful in the transport of ores, their procreation is essential.

When a person or a dog chases a llama, it spits out a sort of stinking saliva that causes the persecutor to flee. If more than 125 pounds of ore is loaded on its back, a llama will lie down and refuse to get up, till death; for this reason, the miners have bags that do not hold more than this weight. There are stones of different sizes and colors in the stomachs of all these animals.

Gigantones and Cochinilla

Growing in great abundance on hillsides near the Villa de Tarma is a species of cactus that the natives call gigantones, which is very closely related to *Cactus cochenillifer*. In March and April it is infested with certain small insects belonging to the genus of the cochinilla (cochineal insect), here called pilcay or pircay. Some of the inhabitants, rasping the plants with knives, gather the insects to make a type of red cake, also called pilcay, which is used to dye woolen and cotton goods a scarlet color. Were these plants cultivated, as they are in Mexico, I am sure that in Tarma the people could obtain harvests of cochinilla as large and of as good quality as in Mexico.

In Huamanha, Cuzco, and Tucumán the inhabitants also collect masses or round cakes of pilcay, just as in Tarma but in greater abundance. In Cuzco they call these cakes maccnum, and in Chile they are known by the name of macano. I suspect that the gigantones are but a variety of *Cactus cochenillifer*, or perhaps the other way round, since in Mexico the species is cultivated with care. In Tarma and other provinces of Peru the plant is given no care.

The diseases most frequent in the province of Tarma are tabardillos (spotted fever), pain in the side, colds, and certain tertian fevers (malaria) contracted by those who carry on commerce with the coastal areas. Smallpox is very common and kills many children. Those people who are intemperate and dirty suffer from a rather high incidence of venereal disease, but without the disastrous effects common in Europe.

The natives usually cure their ills with herbs, each plant remedy being used according to the knowledge of the person administering it. In the larger settlements there is usually a mediocre surgeon who attends the whites and mestizos, but the Indians neither call for him nor visit his house for the pharmaceuticals that these doctors customarily buy in the apothecaries of Lima and keep on hand in their homes for treatments.

The men are, in general, lazy and carefree. They are content to work just enough to earn their keep. Most become mule drivers, and for this work they maintain many mules. They are quick to tell the truth, for by nature they are timid; if there is ever any arrogance, it is almost always brought about by drunkenness. The cholos and mestizos (Indian-Spanish), increasing in number, are arrogant, untrustworthy, and extremely indolent. The womenfolk—Indian, cholo, mestizo, and white—are usually humble, hard-working, religious, and seldom seen in a drunken state. When they are not sowing or gathering crops, they are continually spinning cotton or wool, or weaving cloth for their own use or for sale.

The Spanish, or white, women and the mestizo women dress after the fashions of Lima, but most of the Indian women wear the following: lliclias, mantas, anacos, fresadillas, huatanas, and sucuyes.

The lliclia is a piece, a yard square, of flannel or loose woolen cloth or other textile decorated with stripes of various hues, and sometimes with gold and silver stripes and pieces of tisu (metallic cloth). It is thrown over the shoulders and is pinned over the chest with a timpis, a pin or clasp that joins the lliclia like a great needle. The manta is the same as the lliclia, but without ornamentation.

The anaco is a kind of coat or dress that is closed up to the waist and, from the waist up, is open along the sides and secured over each shoulder with a timpis.

The fresadilla is a kind of coarse woolen blanket that can be used as a bed coverlet.

Huatanas are like sock supporters or garters, but are little used among Indian women since most of them go barefoot or wear sucuyes. Sucuyes are pieces of cowhide that cover mainly the soles of the feet like sandals and are worn by Indian men and women instead of shoes.

The Indian women are so attached to weaving that they spin in their homes and out-of-doors, going along the streets and roads spinning. Instead of a distaff they use a forked stick about a quarta (cuarta, handspan) in length; any stick the same length as a distaff can be used, but it must taper towards the top, and a little wheel of maté (gourd) or other material is fastened at the basal end.

Indian women can also be very generous towards a person who has done them a favor; in this characteristic they contrast strongly with the menfolk. They take special care in dressing the altars and images with various kinds of flowers. In the Villa de Tarma, for Holy Wednesday, Maundy Thursday, and Good Friday, the Indians make very special carpets of various colors and shades at the corners of the plaza and in front of the church, using both wild and cultivated plants and flowers for this work. The carpets are rectangular, about 8 to 10 yards long, and made after the sermon in an hour or two. The Indian women bring blossoms and plants, as well as ideas for designing and making the carpets, while their husbands do the work.

The province of Tarma is divided into 13 parishes and has 34,641 inhabitants, including Spaniards, creoles, Indians, mestizos, and others.

The first parish is that of the Villa de Tarma, with a dependency called La Oroya; this parish is entrusted to the Dominicans of Lima. There are 3979 souls in Tarma and 456 in Oroya.

The second parish is that of the town of Acobamba, with 1413 inhabitants. It has four dependencies: Palca, a frontier fort with 450 people; Palcamayo, with 808; Tapuc, with 680; and Picoy, with 424. Since they are located in the gorges, all these towns have a mild climate.

The third parish is that of Reyes, a town 10 leagues west of Tarma with a population of 912. It has three dependencies in the area towards Tarma: Racas, with 146 people; Cacas, with 328; and Huasahuassi, with 308. Huasahuassi lies 5 leagues from Tarma and has a warm climate, whereas the others are cold, being situated on the pampas of Bombón. The name Bombón comes from the explosions that are frequent there during the storms and strikes of lightning produced when the clouds break. To explain the force of the thunderclaps, the Indians said that in those places the clouds make bumbum, or pumpum, words later corrupted by the conquistadors, or Spanish conquerors, in calling that area Bombón. Its real name is puna, or punna, equivalent to páramo, which signifies a heath or moor completely unprotected from the elements of a mountain climate.

The fourth parish is that of Ondores, 6 leagues from Reyes, with Anticona as its dependency; it has 600 inhabitants.

The fifth parish is that of Ccarhuamayo, with 428 people; it has one dependency, Ullcumayo, a frontier fort where 497 people live.

The sixth parish is that of Ninacacca, with a population of 545 and one dependency called Huachón, with 169 souls. Ninacacca means fire hill, and is so named for the hill of flint upon which that village is built. All of these villages are in a cold area.

The seventh parish is that of Paucartambo, with 442 inhabitants, and its dependency Quiparacra, with 216. Both villages are in a warm climate, and they have their own fort and barracks.

The eighth parish is that of the town of Pasco, with a population of 1600. One of its dependencies is Vico, with 367 people. Another is Raco, with 306; near this village are a number of strange quarries, extraordinarily beautiful in distant view of the various shapes and sizes of their tall, creviced cliffs. Naturally arranged like a large, dense woodland, these quarries produce stones to grind ores; some of the stones measure from 9 to 10 handspans in height. A third dependency is the town —or, rather, the mine—of Cerro de Yauricocha, with 2810 souls. Two leagues from there, behind Cerro de Colquijirca, is a fourth dependency, Rancas, with 189 inhabitants; the natives of this town and of Vico work in transporting ores from the mines to the smelters. Six leagues from Pasco lies a fifth dependency, Caxamarquilla, with

170 people. A sixth and last dependency is Yanacachi, with 244 people; the men here also earn their living by carrying ores to the smelters. Both Cerro de Yauricocha and Cerro de Colquijirca are silver mines.

The town of Pasco is located at the end of the pampas of Bombón, 20 leagues from Tarma, 8 from the mountains, 8 from the forests, and 45 from Lima, between two low hills. The people of the town of Pasco and of the mines depend upon other towns and provinces for food, clothing, and other necessities, for they do not produce much except silver, the best meat that can be tasted in all of Peru, considerable cold, and much smoke in the kitchens. Instead of firewood, the fuel is taquia, or sheep dung, and champas, or turf.

The ninth parish is that of Huariaca, with 1500 souls. Its dependencies are Yacán, with 216 people; Ticllacayan, with 108; Chinchan, with 109; Chacos, with 62; Matehuaca, with 208; and Macar, with 102. All these towns have a rather temperate climate.

The tenth parish is that of Parianchacra. Its dependencies are Ccarria, with 1024 souls; Cochacalla with 297; Rondos, with 166; Angasmarca, with 164; Mosca, with 199; and Tusi, with 1229. These towns have a cool climate and are rather too cold at night.

The eleventh parish is that of Tapuc, with 809 people. Its dependencies are Mitos, with 139 souls; Chaupimarca, with 222; Pillau, with 358; Yacán, with 419; and Huayllarsica, with 179. The climate of all these villages is warm.

The twelfth parish is that of Chacayán, with 484 people. Its dependencies are Chancco, with 515 people; Vilcabamba, with 677; Antapirca, with 226; Yanahuanca, with 1102; Villo, with 92; Roco, with 188; and Yamacocha, with 326.

The thirteenth parish is that of Cayna, with 1807 people. Its dependencies are Tanccor, with 355 people; Cauri, with 658; Coquin, with 365; Yamos, with 216; and Paucar, with 211.

The town of Marhos is part of the parish of Jesús, which belongs to the province of Huamalíes, but in civil affairs it is under the jurisdiction of Tarma. Its population is 450. And the town of Yacos, in the same parish, has 191 souls.

Besides the towns that we have mentioned, there are numerous residential estates and groups of hamlets throughout the province of Tarma; these have a small number of inhabitants who are not included in the foregoing enumeration.

CHAPTER 13

Curious Information Learned from People Who Have Traveled in Peru

When Señor Manso was viceroy of Peru and Don Carlos Angulo y Cabrera was chief magistrate of the province of Huamachuco, there lived in the province a family that numbered more than 500, and the original father of all these people was still living. The viceroy commissioned the magistrate to investigate the truth of this story, which was verified and sent to the Ministry of Spain as something very unusual.

In various provinces of Peru, one can find ores of iron oxide, iron, copper, lead, arsenic, sulfur, pyrites, alum, vitriol, ocher, and native verdigris (Paris green), as well as blue, green, yellow, and red earths, and many kinds of clay.

Of the many silver mines that are known in Peru, the most famous are those of Cerro de Yauricocha, near Pasco; those of Chota, near Yauli in the province of Huarocherí; and those of Huayanca, or Huallanca, in the province of Huamalíes. The mines of Huantasaya are extremely rich, and most certainly would be the treasure trove of America in a more favorable location, but they are in a region where there is no water. From this mine one can extract nearly pure papas, or silver nuggets, that weigh 50 pounds or more. The miners who work there gather and use only the papas or chunks of silver; they do not bother to transport other ores for processing.

Of no lesser fame are the mines of Caylloma and Potosí, where there lived a miner by the name of Don Antonio López de Quiroga, a native of Vigo in Galicia. One of the greatest changes of luck ever known befell this man: when he began mining he lived in complete misery, but within a short time he was the wealthiest miner in all America. In quintos (20% taxation) alone, he paid 33 million pesos into the royal coffers. The value of this wealth was enhanced by the generous gifts that he made to help the needy.

The opulence of Quiroga's home, and the variety and novelty of its adornments, were crowned with a rug embroidered entirely in gold and covering the floor of the whole drawing room. The curtains on the walls were done in the same style. Were this not proof enough of his wealth, we have further pieces of evidence. Once, when he became godfather to a baby boy born to the wife of one of the viceroys, he sent the infant 200,000 pesos for swaddling clothes. Moreover, in the church of the patron saint of Spain, Santiago de Galicia, there are treasures and jewels of great value that were donated by this good countryman. Finally, having given 15,000 pesos for the founding of a chaplaincy dedicated to the Blessed Souls of Potosí, and later learning that the draft was over-written by the sum of 500,000 pesos, he paid the whole amount as an endowment. Eventually all that splendor reverted to its previous state, as today one sees the various branches of this once-powerful family reduced to poverty.

There was also in Potosí a certain Salcedo who offered to send the King one bar of assayed silver as a quinto (tax) every day. But his affluence was more short-lived than Quiroga's.

In Cerro de Yauricocha there is a mine called Tajo, now flooded, which previously yielded more than a thousand marks of silver for each casting.

In addition to the quicksilver mines at Huancavelica, two have been discovered near Huánuco, but operation of these has not continued because the poor people who tried to work them could not make them pay. In the province of Huamalíes, near the hamlet of Jesus, there are two other quicksilver mines that give good promise of having rich deposits.

In La Paz there is a mountain called Illimani. The streams that are formed on its slopes from the melting snow bring down sands charged with pure gold; nuggets weighing nearly half an ounce have been collected from them. Judging from the contents of these streams, we might well presume that immense wealth lies hidden within the core of this mountain.

There are hot springs or thermal baths in Cheuchín, in the province of Chancay; in Yauli, in the province of Huarocherí; in the province of Caxamarca; and in Baños, in the province of Huamalíes.

In Chilca there runs a stream with waters capable of petrifying bodies that are thrown into them.

Throughout Peru there is an infinite number of rope and vine bridges built for crossing the rivers.

There are various paved causeways in Peru for transit across the swampy flats and drainage basins of the lagoons, rivers, and lakes. One example of this is the Calzada de los Reyes (imperial causeway of the Incas). Another, a league long, is on the road from Pino in the parish of Coroy, which belongs to the bishopric of La Paz; this causeway protects the main road from the overflow of a lake 80 leagues long and varying in width according to the lands that enclose it. The outlet of this lake lies near Pino; the depth and contours of the bottom have not yet been determined. Within the lake are various islands, one of which is 5 leagues long and inhabited by the Urus Indians. There are various birds and fish in the lake. The river that arises in the lake is 150 yards wide, and to cross it there is a bridge built on eight totora (reed) rafts and fastened with two heavy iron chains. It is on the main road to Cuzco, Lima, and other regions.

The most famous buildings, forts, and towns of the pagan Indians are those of Cuzco; Caxamarca; the fort and palace of La Barranca, 7 leagues from Huaura; and the palace of Thiahuanaco, which means sitting runner. In this palace of Thiahuanaco there is an arch 12 yards long, formed by three rectangular stones a yard wide; two of the stones are standing and the third is laid across them. On the ground there is another stone that is 8 or 9 yards long, 5 or 6 wide, and a yard thick; it is said to have been used by the Incas as a table. These ruins likewise include a group of benches with various seats, evidently serving as a chamber for conferences in the days of the Incas. The higher bench at the head has a water spout to the right of it so the person sitting on that bench may drink.

On the hills along the coast, as well as on the slopes, in the gorges, and on the summits of the Andean range, there are various ruins of the towns of pagan Indians. Near these settlements one finds many huacas, or Indian graves, from which numerous bodies, along with pieces of silver and other curiosities, are often dug. A most amazing thing is that one can find, in many of the sandy places, vessels of chicha (maize liquor) as fresh as though it had just been made, and seeds that sprout at once when planted.

CHAPTER 14

Description of the Villa de Tarma

Up to the year 1784, when the viceroyalty of Peru was divided into seven intendencias, or districts, the capital of the province of Tarma was not honored by having the title of villa. This title was acquired when the intendente (manager, mayor) of these seven divisions, or provinces, went to live there: Tarma, Xauxa, Caxatambo, Huánuco, Huamalíes, Conchucos, and Huaylas. In each one of these provinces there is a subdelegate, instead of a corregidor (chief magistrate) as there was before the revolt of Gabriel Tupac-Amaro in 1780 in Tonccasuca, a town in the province of Tinta. This revolt was set off by the hanging of the corregidor, Don Arriaga, his godfather, and by the imprisonment of numerous Spaniards by that mestizo. He claimed the throne of the Incas in place of a relative who made the same claim, so he could take possession of certain estates of his forebears that were under litigation in the high court in Lima.

The Villa de Tarma is situated in an esplanade, or hollow, between three gorges and a valley. The whole area enjoys a warm climate, is verdant and pleasant, and is surrounded by hills clad with plants most of the year. In the rainy season, the whole narrow valley blooms with a beautiful variety of hues in the vegetation. The gorges to the south and west are each nearly 3 leagues long, and almost a mile wide in places but extremely narrow at the ends. The gorge to the north becomes wider towards the jungles; the valley is probably half a league long. In the depths of these gorges the vegetation is rich throughout the year. Many areas on the hills are covered with six species of giantones, or cactuses. In the low places there are four species of *Cassia*, or senna, three of which have purgative properties as strong as oriental senna; when we arrived in Tarma, the natives began to use these as laxatives, drinking either a cold or hot infusion of any one of these species.

Before the intendencia was established, the secular council of Tarma consisted of the governor of the province and, in his absence, the chief justice, as well as six Indian mayors, each with his alderman, his constable, and his Indian chieftain. But when the township was created, the administrative body that was formed included aldermen, a royal military officer, a constable, a receiver-general, a provincial mayor, and a subdelegate of the district.

In Tarma there are two companies of trained troops, one of infantry and one of cavalry, with their captains and lesser officers. The duty of these troops is to guard the forts in the jungle area of the province, preventing the barbarous tribes that dwell in those forests from coming out to attack.

On the central plaza, which is square and quite ample, are located the barracks and the armory, next to the public jail. Facing the barracks is the town's parish church; the tower of the church is partly in ruins or, we should say, was never finished: there are four bells in it. In the church there are 22 altars dedicated to different saints, but the Chapel of Miracles, Chapel of Sorrows, and Chapel of Our Lady of the Rosary surpass all the rest in ornamentation and spirit of piety. There are three small organs. The patron saint of the town is the glorious Santa Ana (Saint Anne), who is celebrated on her day; and in September there is also a celebration of Our Lady of the Miracle and the Infant, with solemn performances in the church, dances, fires, bullfights, and plays. There is a hermitage of San Sebastián, where one mass is said each year. In the jail is a tiny chapel with a beautiful painting of Our Lady of Sorrows on the wall.

There are three primary schools, the largest of which has 40 children, mostly whites and mestizos.

The buildings are of one story, but some have garrets where roots, fruit, and grain are kept. They are constructed of simple adobe, and the pitched roofs are made of poorly worked wood interwoven with chacllas, or thin reeds, over which are placed tiles set out in more or less narrow channels. The roofs of some houses are not tile, but made of mud mixed with straw or ichu grass, and flat like the roofs of Lima and the entire coastal area of Peru. Since the establishment of the intendencia in Tarma, houses have gradually been made larger and the paving of the streets has been improved. The streets used to have no names, except for the Calle Ancha (Broad Street).

Tarma has two puqueos, or springs, of abundant water. One of them is located on the south side of town, at the foot of a hill near the entrance to the gorge; it has thick water that is harmful if drunk sooner than 24 hours after being drawn, but becomes thinner and safe to drink after that period of time. The other spring lies within the town; its water is not so good as that of the first spring, but with the same effect if it is drunk immediately after being drawn instead of being kept for some hours. Both springs were kept under close watch in the days of Governor

Amat, but now only the one in town is guarded. The shed covering the other spring was completely ruined by the flooding of a river that passes close by it.

There is another spring of very good water at the foot of the valley of Curis. When a visitor from elsewhere has been in Tarma for some time and has come to like the town, or plans to establish himself there, folks say, "So-and-so has drunk the water of Curis." There are also various other puqueos of drinking water on the outskirts of Tarma, smaller but still of rather fair size.

During the 11 months that we remained in the province of Tarma, exploring the area and carrying out botanical excursions in all directions, we discovered in those gorges and at the edge of the forest a considerable number of trees, shrubs, and herbs that had familiar uses, medicinal properties, or economic potential. The following are those that I collected, dried, and described; illustrations were done for nearly all of them.

Jarava icho, called ichu, icho, or ossa. In Huancavelica, the natives use this grass instead of wood to melt cinnabar and extract quicksilver from it. Since one can always find an abundance of this plant, both dry and green, and it burns easily, mule drivers and travelers take advantage of it to warm themselves and to cook in the high moors. When ichu is young, ruminant livestock eat it with relish; it is excellent food for cattle, llamas, huanacos, vicuñas, and alpacas. Deer, mules, and horses also eat it when they cannot find better pasturage. The natives of the mountains and moors thatch their houses or shelters with ichu, and they also use the grass in making rugs and mats, and as bedding in place of ordinary straw mattresses. *Salvia grandiflora*; with red, showy flowers more than 4 inches long, this plant could serve as a garden ornamental. *Salvia plumosa* and *S. fragrantissima*, chenchelcoma or salvia menor (lesser salvia). *Salvia sagittata*, huarmico or salvia real (true salvia); some Indians eat the leaves as a vermifuge. They attribute to the plant excellent medicinal properties for asthma and other respiratory ailments, and they believe that it can make sterile women fecund. It is frequently used to stimulate the appetite, to cleanse and heal wounds, and as a diuretic or tonic.

Justicia incana. *Margyricarpus subfruticosus*, called yerba de la perlilla (herb of the little pearl) for the resemblance of its sweet and tasty fruits to the shape and color of pearls; this plant abounds also along the coasts and in the fields of Chile. *Calceolaria scabra*, *C. uniflora*, and *C. tomentosa*. *Columellia ovalis*, ollus or ulux; this is a shrub 2 yards tall, bitter in the extreme, and admirably effective as a febrifuge when taken in either a cold or warm infusion. *Pinguicula stellata*. *Peperomia pubescens*. *Piper scabrum* and *P. churumayu*, churumayu. *Valeriana connata*, *V. globiflora*, *V. interrupta*, *V. pilosa*, *V. oblongifolia*, *V. rigida*, *V. thyrsiflora*, and *V. lanceolata*, all called huarituru; the natives employ the roots to set bones by crushing the roots and applying them as a poultice.

Cyperus striatus. *Briza media*. *Panicum purpureum*. *Plantago hirsuta* and *P. tomentosa*. *Galium mucronatum*, *G. croceum*, *G. ciliatum*, and *G. corymbosum*. *Aegiphila biflora*. *Paltoria ovalis*. *Alchemilla pinnata*. *Nertera repens*. *Krameria triandra*, pumacuchu or mapato; see the notes on the uses and virtues of this plant in our discussion of the collections made in Huánuco, where it is called ratanhia. *Hedyotis conferta*, *H. juniperifolia*, *H. setosa*, and *H. thymifolia*. *Acaena ovalifolia* and *A. lappacea*. *Embothrium emarginatum*, called catas or machinparrani for the shape of the flowers and follicles, which strongly resemble the genital organs of monkeys; its crushed leaves are applied to contusions by the Indians. From its flowers Indian womenfolk make beautiful bouquets to adorn arches set up in the streets for processions, to dress altars, and to cover the floors of churches.

Buddleja incana, called quisoar, quishuara, or colle; Indians use an infusion of the terminal branchlets to expel viscous and cold humors. The same part of the plant, crushed, mixed with urine, and heated over the fire, forms a poultice to relieve aching molars; it is applied both internally and externally. Some people employ the buds to color food. The trunks of this tree are used in construction and for making plows because of the strength and durability of the wood, which is never attacked by insects.

Cissus obliqua. *Lithospermum aggregatum* and *L. incanum*. *Anchusa leucantha*. *Tournefortia polystachya* and *T. virgata*. *Varronia obliqua* and *V. rugosa*.

Solanum calygnaphalum, nuñunya. *Solanum lycioides*, ama de casa (mistress of the house). *Solanum asperolanatum*, *S. foetidum*, *S. sericeum*, and *S. quercifolium*, menhas. *Solanum habanense* and *S. tomentosum*, hormis. *Lycium obovatum*, espino (thorn). *Datura sanguinea*, called puca-campanilla or floripondio encarnado (red floripondio); when this tree is in bloom, it is extremely beautiful because of the abundance of large, red flowers always hanging like bells, and its round, leafy crown. The leaves are used on the skin to soothe or relieve pain, either in poultices or applied alone and whole. The seeds are narcotic, dulling the senses and mind, and they are sometimes administered with evil intent, as a powder in food. Some natives say that there are people who have gone mad merely by lying down to sleep in the shade of these trees, which are found exclusively in the vicinity of towns at high altitudes.

Cynoglossum revolutum. *Sessea dependens*. *Cervantesia tomentosa*; I ate the fruits, similar to a hazelnut in size and taste, on numerous occasions without their ever causing me harm, but in Peru the plant has no known use. *Atropa biflora*. *Saracha biflora*. *Nicotiana tabacum*, tabaco verdadero (true tobacco). *Rhamnus acuminatus*. *Celastrus triflorus*, known as rurama or, in Muña, picna; this is an evergreen, branchy shrub, and its wood is excellent for making ax handles and other implements requiring strength.

Stereoxylon resinosum, called tiri encarnado or puca tiri or, in other areas, chachacoma; womenfolk use the tips of its branchlets to prepare purple and red dye. *Periphragmos uniflorus*, ccantu; this shrub is found in fences around orchards and farms on the outskirts of towns, and in the ruins of settlements of pagan Indians who esteemed it as a magical plant for their superstitious practices, but at the present time Indian women dress altars and images with its flowering branches. *Ribes luteum* and *R. dependens*. *Desfontainia spinosa*, a shrub that is showy because of its leaves and beautiful red flowers.

Ipomoea subtrilobata. *Ipomoea papyru*, papyru; the tuberous root is highly valued as a purgative. It is administered as the infusion of a small piece of root, from

¼ to 2 drams if fresh, or exactly 2 drams if dry. *Gardenia spinosa*, millucassa. *Psychotria caerulea. Swartia corniculata. Gentiana biflora, G. umbellata, G. subulata, G. maculata*, and *G. quinquepartita. Dichondra repens. Gomphrena purpurea. Chenopodium tuberosum*, ulluco; the roots, boiled and stewed, yield a common food, and an infusion of the entire plant is given as an expectorant or as an aid in childbirth.

Illecebrum lanatum. Achyranthes mucronata. Asclepias cordata. Cynanchum minimum and *C. glandulosum. Fragosa crenata, F. multifida*, and *F. reniformis*, called frutilla del monte (mountain strawberry) for the form of its leaves, which are comparable to those of the strawberry. *Caucalis grandiflora. Oenanthe? pedunculata. Sium biternatum. Sambucus glandulosa*; this shrub grows in settlements in the high mountains and is used in place of sahuco común (common elderberry), or *S. nigra. Viburnum verticillatum. Hydrocotyle asiatica.*

Tillandsia recurvata, T. revoluta, and *T. coarctata. Tillandsia huechle*, commonly called huechle. *Tillandsia usneoides*, variously known as salvagina, saccropa, millmahina, or cotataura; it is used in warm baths to soothe the nerves, rebuild physical strength, and help induce sleep. Indians make various kinds of mattresses of it because it is reputed to repel flies and other insects. It is also used to an appreciable extent as a remedy by those who have backaches and kidney trouble. Crushed and mixed with fat, it is applied as a treatment for hemorrhoids, and the natives assert that it gives admirable results in such ailments. It is very useful as a wrapping for fruit that needs to be ripened off the tree before being eaten, and is no less valuable for packing and boxing up vases and other articles that are easily broken or damaged. This species is extraordinarily abundant in all the gorges and along the margins of hot jungles; it grows on cliffs, trees, and shrubs, often with such vigor that it dries up the host and kills it. In Huánuco there is not a single lúcumo tree that is not covered with this *Tillandsia*.

Pancratium coccineum, margaritas encarnadas (scarlet daisies). *Pancratium viride*; because its flowers, half the size of those of the azucena (white lily, Madonna lily), are totally green, they would be much esteemed by gardeners and by the fair sex as an ornament. *Crinum sagittatum*, margarita amarilla (yellow daisy). *Ornithogalum pyrenaicum.*

Alstroemeria linearis, A. coccinea, A. capitata, and *A. spiralis. Alstroemeria trifida*, piñipiñi. *Alstroemeria crocea*, chocllocopa. All these species are worthy of being introduced to the gardening world because of the color and beauty of their blossoms.

Loranthus luteus and *L. pentandrus. Berberis mucronata* and *B. tortuosa*; the wood of these plants yields an excellent yellow dye. *Triglochin ciliatum.*

Tropaeolum tuberosum, massuas; this plant is cultivated in Peru and its tuberous roots are used as food, boiled or stewed. The roots have the shape of an inverse cone, are reddish or sometimes yellow, and can weigh as much as 4 ounces.

Dodonaea viscosa, chamisa or chamana; its leaves, crushed and applied as a poultice on contusions, have very good and swift healing properties, and in Tarma and other towns the pressed leaves are used as a substitute for firewood.

Coccoloba nitida and *C. carinata*, muyaca; the Indians use an infusion, an excellent diuretic, for ailments of the urinary tract. *Gaultheria alba*; *G. cordifolia*; and *G. hirsuta*, rimincussau. *Fuchsia apetala* and *F. verticillata*, molloccantu or molloccanto; children eat the ripe fruits of this shrub, and womenfolk make a tasty preserve of these fruits and sugar. *Rhexia repens*, olaola; mixed with other plants, it provides a yellow dye. *Rhexia hispida*. *Weinmannia oppositifolia*. *Polygonum subulatum*.

Cassia hirsuta, *C. procumbens*, *C. setacea*, and *C. undecimjuga*; the two last species are known by the common names of pachapacte and hatumpacte. The natives have been using an infusion of the leaves as a purgative since we came to Tarma, and at present they prefer these leaves to those of Oriental senna because of their greater benefit and milder effects.

Melastoma tomentosa, tiri blanco (white tiri); the womenfolk make a yellow dye from this shrub, varying the shade by adding other plants. *Arbutus multiflora*. *Thibaudia*? species, called machamacha, which means intoxicates-intoxicates; its fruits bring on drunkenness if too many are eaten. It acts as an especially strong inebriant for children. *Thibaudia trinervis*, *T. punctata*, *T. nitida*, and *T. lanuginosa*. *Thibaudia alata*, pucasato; the Indian women take its fruits, which are very pleasant-tasting and sweet, to the market of Huánuco for sale. *Ceratostema grandiflora*, called uchu-uchu, meaning pepper-pepper, for the shape and red color of its beautiful, pendent blossoms. The flowers are edible and serve as a condiment and dressing for green salads, as they have a pleasantly acid flavor and the bright red color of the guindilla (cayenne pepper).

Sedum ccallu, known as ccallu (tongue) because the leaves resemble the human tongue; the juice is used to dissolve cloudiness and incipient cataracts of the eyes. *Saxifraga tridactyles*, called puchuppus or siempreviva (everlasting). *Talinum ciliatum*. *Portulaca pilosa*. *Cuphea cordifolia*. *Acunna oblonga*, called rosa-rosa for its abundance of pink blossoms; this plant is an excellent ornamental for the garden.

Cactus melocactus, *C. tuna*, and *C. ficus-indica*. *Cactus cochenillifer* var.? *foliosus*, commonly known as huallanca or gigantones (giants); the name gigantones is also used for the other species listed here, which are abundant in the gorges of this province, and for additional species that we shall discuss elsewhere.

Psidium pyriferum is well-known by its common name, huayabo (guayabo, guava); I shall speak of it in my description of Huánuco. *Psidium nitidum* is called aka or acka; its leaves are aromatic like those of the arrayán (myrtle), and are employed in warm baths for the relief of rheumatic and nervous pains. This shrub bears such a profusion of flowers, the color of sealing wax, that it is a splendid sight.

Rubus roseus, called chilifruta because its fruits resemble those of the freson de Chile (Chilean strawberry) in shape and delicate flavor. *Rubus biserratus*, *R. salvifolius*, and *R. fruticosus*, called siracas or zarzamora (blackberry). *Loasa spiralis*. *Geum urbanum*. *Potentilla prostrata*. *Mespilus uniflora*; its properties were discussed in our list of plants of Huarocherí. *Mespilus ferruginea*, *M. prostrata*, and *M. subspinosa*, called millucassa; children eat its small, rather tasty fruits.

Polylepis emarginata, quinhuar; because the wood of these trees is extremely hard and does not suffer attack from insects, the miners use the trunks for beams in the smelters. The bark peels off the trunk in many layers, very thin like sheets of paper. *Anemone digitata*, arracacha cimarrona (wild idiot). *Anemone pubescens*, called polizones for the orbicular shape of its flowers, which resemble the pendant earrings also called polizones. *Vallea cordata*, curhur; this is a attractive shrub when in flower, as it bears an abundance of pink blossoms. *Thalictrum polygamum*. *Ranunculus cordatus*. *Bartsia hirsuta*, *B. purpurea*, and *B. prostrata*.

Gardoquia conferta and *G. canescens*, called socconche, suyumpay, or chinchi. In Tarma, and likewise in Lima and other places, an infusion of this very fragrant plant is frequently used to relieve melancholy, pain in the side, or nervous breakdown; it is sometimes mixed with wine, and at other times with water and spirits.

Duranta plumieri, tantar blanco (white tantar); *D. tomentosa*, yanacassa or tantar prieto (dark tantar). *Ruellia prostrata*. *Lantana involucrata*. *Rhinanthus rugosa*, *R. glutinosa*, and *R. sagittata*. *Tecoma stans*, ccarhuaccero. *Limosella subulata*. *Alonsoa lanceolata*, huakyansacha. *Virgularia revoluta*, mancapaqui. *Cleome glandulosa*, tacma. *Geranium filiforme*.

Sisymbrium sophiae, ucuspatallan; this plant is very abundant in the province of Tarma, as well as in that of Huamalíes, where it is used as a diuretic. There are people who believe it to be a stronger diuretic than it really is, for they prepare the infusion with the dried plant, in which state it lacks ammonia and is therefore nearly inert.

Monnina salicifolia, called hacchiquiss or pahuata-huinac, meaning growing-by-night, for these people believe that it grows during the night hours and not in the daytime. Members of the fair sex often wash their hair very carefully with water in which the plant has been rubbed, and they are convinced that their hair grows exuberantly with frequent use of this wash. It is at least certain that the saponaceous, or soapy, contents of the plant free dandruff from the scalp and oils from the hair very thoroughly, and that the hair does grow noticeably as a result of this daily cleanliness. The root is extremely bitter and much higher in saponin content than other parts of the plant; these two properties indicate that excellent medicinal virtues, especially for treating dysenteries, reside in these roots. Its effectiveness is not inferior to that of simarouba, or *Quassia divica*, or even to that of *Quassia amara*. The bark of *Monnina polystachia* has also been proven to be effective in dysentery, and in asthmatic ailments as well, when used frequently. Three grains of its powder are taken morning and evening at the beginning of the treatment, and the dose is increased over several months.

Cytisus purpureus. *Hedysarum pubescens*. *Astragalus canescens*, garbancillo (little chick pea); this plant grows in the mountains and moorlands of Peru and is especially abundant in the pampas of Bombón. It brings about severe pains and constant trembling in animals when eaten in excessive amounts, and usually leads to their death, so some people call this plant tembladerilla. *Lupinus argenteus*, quitatauri.

Dalea punctata; in the rainy season, the hillsides of the Villa de Tarma are covered with this plant, which forms a splendid carpet with its green leaflets and myriad bluish spikes. When the rays of the morning sun strike them in that season they breathe forth a certain sweet and very strange fragrance, which suggests that they possess some very useful properties.

Hypericum subulatum, chinchancco; the natives use this plant, very abundant in many parts of Peru, to dye woolen and cotton fabrics a beautiful yellow. *Eupatorium angulatum* and *E. trinerve*. *Hieracium triflorum*. *Tagetes odoratissima*, chinchi. *Cosmos nasturcifolius* and *C. laciniata*.

Gnaphalium trinerve. *Gnaphalium viravira*, called viravira (fat-fat) because the entire plant is covered with a very white and woolly layer that appears greasy or filled with tallow. When crushed and applied as a poultice to contusions and ruptures, viravira is very effective in strengthening and healing sore parts of the body.

Aster pinnatus, *A. tomentosus*, *A. auriculatus*, and *A. foliaceus*, called viravira del monte (wild viravira).

Molina scabra, taya; women use this plant extensively to freshen the air in their rooms, and they apply it crushed as one of the best remedies to strengthen sprains and contusions. *Molina uniflora*, *M. ferruginea*, and *M. cespitosa*. *Molina obovata*, taya hembra (female taya). *Molina emarginata*, taya macho (male taya). Natives use the last four species listed for the same purposes as *Molina scabra*.

Artemisia hirsuta. *Helianthus glutinosus* and *H. lanceolatus*. *Barnadesia? gemina*. *Bacasia spinosa*.

Polymnia resinifera, called puhe or taraca; this plant abounds in Xauxa and Chaclla, where many natives gather the resin that exudes in white crystalline tears. These tears are made into a uniform mass or cake, which after some days loses the color and transparency that the resin had before being gathered, but it does not lose its pleasing aroma, which is much like that of lemon gum. The natives use the resin extensively for broken bones and for neuralgias, applying it in plasters.

Atragene villosa. *Perdicium lanatum*. *Bidens? pinnato-multifida*. *Plazia conferta*. *Mutisia acuminata*, called chichinculma, chiucumpa, or huincus; this is a very beautiful plant for gardens because of the large size of its red flowers. *Sigesbeckia occidentalis*. *Munnozia trinervis*.

Eupatorium subsessile and *E. huaramakia*, huaramakia. *Eupatorium aromaticum*, chilca; the natives employ this plant as a dye, both green and yellow. The crushed leaves are used to cleanse and heal ulcers and, most important, they are applied to relieve the pain of sprains and contusions.

Lobelia purpurea, *L. bicolor*, *L. tomentosa*, and *L. purpureo-viridis*. *Viola obliqua*, *V. parviflora*, and *V. subulata*. *Senecio abrotanifolius*, *S. frutescens*, *S. nitidus*, *S. quercifolius*, and *S. revolutus*. *Cacalia serrata*. *Anguloa uniflora*. *Gongora quinquenervis*. *Epidendrum maculatum*, *E. biflorum*, *E. acuminatum*, *E. croceum*, *E. emarginatum*, *E. lineare*, *E. volubile*, and *E. triflorum*. *Humboldtia aspera* and *H. spiralis*. *Masdevallia uniflora*, rima-rima. *Sobralia dichotoma*. *Cypripedium grandiflorum*. *Satyrium album*, *S. dicolorum*, and *S. luteum*.

Maxillaria alata, *M. cuneiformis*, *M. grandiflora*, and *M. tricolor*. *Maxillaria bi-*

color, called caccacacca, which means joined pavement; where the plant grows, the soil is so densely covered with its pseudobulbs that the ground appears to be intentionally paved with them. These bulbs are so tender and juicy that they are easily chewed, and at the same time there oozes forth an abundant juice that is insipid, fluid, and clear as water. Six bulbs are enough to assuage thirst. In order to avoid descending to the bottom of a gorge to get drinking water, the natives frequently take advantage of this property when traveling through areas where caccacacca abounds.

Orchids

The orchid family is so abundantly represented in the gorges of Huasahuassi and Palca that it would be hard to find another locality where so many species and so many individual plants grow. The ground, the cliffs, and the trees are covered with them. It would seem that, from the time of creation, the natural destiny of these regions was for orchids in preference to the myriad other plants, large and small, that also occur in these most pleasant places and are reached by the sun every day of the year even in the rainy season. Notwithstanding the abundance of orchids in these gorges, the same and other species are not lacking along the lower parts of the mountain slopes or along the edge of the jungle in the provinces of Panatahuas, Huamalíes, Xauxa, etc. Even into the depths of the forests themselves, untold numbers of orchids hang on trees and cliffs.

This large representation of orchids moved me to prepare a monograph of that family. When my manuscripts were burned in Macora, more than 500 descriptions of orchids were consumed; in the shipwreck of the *San Pedro de Alcántara*, we lost more than 200 drawings that, together with 600 drawings of other families of plants, we were sending to the Ministry of Spain. In spite of the difficulty of replacing all those descriptions and drawings, we have succeeded in repairing most of these lamentable losses. We make this note that other botanists, in the years ahead, may visit these localities and complete the monograph.

Sisyrinchium luteum. *Sisyrinchium purgans*, ossapurga or pajapurgante; natives use the roots of this plant as a purgative, controlling its laxative effects with drafts of cold water. It is a strong purgative and must not be taken in excess.

Tacsonia biflora and *T. mamosa*, both called purupuru; and *T. ciliata*, hualhapurupuru. These three species have large, showy, tubular blossoms, quite different from those of other passion flowers, for which reason Antoine Laurent de Jussieu created, quite correctly, a new genus distinct from *Passiflora* of Linnaeus. He gave it the epithet *Tacsonia*, from the vernacular name tacso, which he asserts is commonly applied to these plants by the natives of Peru. It is possible that this common name is used in some provinces, but in those that I have visited I have never heard a name even resembling tacso, which means to be of small stature. It really is not appropriate for any of the species, for they ascend or climb into the highest trees, entwining the very tree tops and even spreading to neighboring trees. That is why the Indians of those forests where I have traveled call the plant purupuru (wanderer- wanderer), from the verb purini, which means to walk or wander. [Tacsa is still the vernacular name in Ecuador.—Translator]

Urtica orbicularifolia. *Urtica spiralis*; a crystalline gum, like gum arabic, weeps from wounds inflicted on its branches. The yield of this gum, which is completely soluble in water, is small. *Urtica fumans*; when this species blooms, as soon as the sun's rays strike it in the morning, a multitude of flowers begin to open and their anthers shower pollen, or a dustlike powder, in such profusion that the air surrounding the plant is filled with a very dense dust. It looks like smoke, and for more than 2 hours, or until no more buds open that day, one can imagine the plant to be burning. No other species of nettle that I have studied opens its flowers with such elastic force as *Urtica fumans*, the smoking nettle.

Croton pulverulentum and *C. striatum*. *Sapium nitidum*, chichis. *Salix pyramidalis*, called sauce prieto (dark willow) or sauce negro (black willow). *Viscum luteum* and *V. sessile*. *Coriaria pinnata*; Indian women dye cottons and woolens a rather bright purplish color with racemes of its fruit.

Clusia? thurifera, árbol del incienso (incense tree); instead of olive incense, in their churches the Peruvians burn the beautiful resin that flows abundantly from these trees. The resin, in amorphous masses often weighing a pound and a half, is between reddish and golden in color and nearly transparent; it is very shiny and hard even when freshly gathered from the tree. Since not all of its components are resinous, some being gums, this material does not melt in oil when placed on the fire, nor does it dissolve completely in alcohol. It fails to burn completely when thrown on the embers, and only the resinous component generates smoke. Though similar, its fragrance is not so pleasing as that of genuine incense. One can buy the resin in Lima at 4 reales of local money per pound, but in Huánuco, Tarma, and other towns a pound costs 1½ to 2 reales of the same money.

Myrica stornutatoria, known as ssayre, tuppassayre, or laurel; the entire shrub is useful for dyeing leather black. Its powdered bark causes repeated sneezing; a small pinch of this snuff will not harm the nostrils as other irritants often do, and when the nose is blown, the irritation and sneezing stops. For these reasons it is used extensively to clear the head and relieve headache. *Betula alnus*, aliso (alder). *Ephedra distachya*. *Atriplex monoica*. *Aralia? digitata*.

Polypodium lineare and *P. serratum*. *Polypodium calahuala*, called calaguala fina (good calaguala) or calaguala verdadera (true calaguala); this is the one that should be used in the apothecaries and in medicine. Its slender roots are very bitter and saponaceous; these properties are not possessed by other roots sold under the name of calaguala. In this respect, see what I have written on calagualas in the dissertation that I published in the first volume of the *Memorias de la Real Academia Médica de Madrid* and in the pamphlet that I published separately, adding various later observations and important notes. *Polypodium crassifolium*, puntu-puntu or lengua de ciervo (deer's tongue); the roots of this species are sold under the name of calaguala gruesa (stout calaguala). Natives use an infusion of the roots to relieve pain in the side. *Polypodium incapcocam*, called cucacuca, incapcocam, or coca del

Inca (coca of the Incas) because, according to the Indians, the Incas used it in place of coca, and also used it, as a powder, instead of tobacco to clear the head. *Polypodium coronarium*, *P. erecto-lineare*, *P. exaltatum*, *P. rhombeum*, *P. scolopendroides*, and *P. virginianum*.

Acrosticum calomelanos, *A. lineare*, *A. marante*, *A. nitidum*, *A. ovatum*, *A. palmatum*, *A. revolutum*, *A. sulphureum*, *A. squamatotomentosum*, and *A. squamatum*. *Acrosticum cuacsaro*; see what I have published about the roots of this plant, which is sold under the name of calaguala de cordoncillo (stringlike calaguala), in the aforementioned dissertation on calaguala.

Pteris liniata. *Pteris ternata*, culantrillo (maidenhair fern). *Pteris tomentosa*, *P. trifoliata*, and *P. triangulata*. *Asplenium acutifolium*, *A. caudatum*, *A. cultrifolium*, *A. falcatolineare*, *A. fissum*, *A. lineatum*, *A. multifidum*, *A. obovatum*, and *A. praemorsum*. *Adiantum capillus-veneris*. *Hemionitis rigida*. *Trichomanes crispum*, *T. lineare*, and *T. obovatum*. *Lycopodium corymbosum*, *L. dichotomum*, *L. lanceolatum*, and *L. subulatum*. *Polytrichum subulatum*. *Bryum nitidum*. *Lichen cinereoviridis*, *L. multifidus*, *L. oculatus*, *L. pallidoviridis*, *L. pyxidatus*, *L. ruber*, and *L. subulatus*.

Many other plants that grow in the forests and other territories of the province of Tarma will be mentioned elsewhere. Because we did not have time to collect and study them in this area, and because they are common in other regions as well, some plants such as the species of quina, or *Cinchona* of Linnaeus, are not included here.

CHAPTER 15

Trip to the Province of Xauxa

To ascertain whether or not the land of the province of Xauxa was rich enough in natural products to merit several months of observation, I left for that province on the 27th of July 1779, accompanied by the artist Don Isidro Gálvez.

Two leagues from Tarma we found the ruins of the famous castle of Tarmatambo, on a site that dominates the entire region. From this point one can see the remains of an Indian town that is located atop a mountain much higher than the castle. Through these ruins runs the Inca highway that connects Cuzco and Quito in a straight line.

Two leagues beyond the castle we left the highway and took our way through a wide plain, more than a league and a half long and covered with grass that is short but of excellent quality for all kinds of cattle. After passing a small mountain, we entered upon another pampa, or plain, somewhat longer than the previous one. At the end of this plain we came upon a puqueo, or spring, with an abundance of cool, crystalline water, free from minerals. It undoubtedly seeps out through an underground system from a lake on the right-hand side of the road about a quarter of a league back. The local people use this water to irrigate two small hedged fields in which they plant wheat and barley, and which yield good harvests, thanks to the water supply. A beautiful plain lies ahead of the site of this spring, abounding in good pasture grasses for cows, sheep, swine, and horses. Beyond this pampa lies another, not as long but just as fertile in grasses as the previous one.

One then comes to a small slope and a stream that arises from the spring mentioned above, and enters onto a vast plain upon which there is a lake about a league long and a mile wide. To the left of this lake are two small hamlets, and one can see numerous little farms dotted all over the plain. Because of the cold climate, however, neither grains nor fruits are sown as in other, more temperate localities. Totora, or bulrushes, and numerous species of aquatic birds are plentiful in the lake. We passed another lake, smaller in its volume of water but much more swampy, before entering the town of Xauxa, where we spent the night.

From about 2 leagues out of Tarma to Xauxa we found only an occasional plant, except grasses, that differed from those species gathered in the high, cold regions of Tarma. Therefore we did not need to stop to collect or observe plants on the whole journey.

On the 28th we left the town of Xauxa for the monastery of Santa Rosa de Ocopa, about 6 leagues from the town. We passed through the villages of Mojón, San Lorenzo, and Apata; towards the west there is a small lake. At one in the afternoon we arrived at Ocopa. We wandered about the nearby fields and hills, and found hardly a plant that we had not already seen elsewhere. In spite of its pampas and cool mountains, the province of Xauxa has a paucity of larger plants, and its flora varies only a little; but on the edge of the tropical forests, the natives say, Xauxa is just as rich in plants as Tarma.

Polymnia resinifera or taraca, *Calceolaria linearis*, and *Polypodium calahuala*—that is, the true and genuine medicinal calaguala and the favorite one in Peru—are the only three larger plants that we found along the road from Xauxa to Ocopa.

CHAPTER 16

Description of the Monastery of Ocopa

The monastery of Santa Rosa de Ocopa (see Figure 6) is located at the foot of the very high mountains that form the boundary of the forests of the pagan Indians, on a beautiful, crescent-shaped plain protected by those same mountains on the west, south, and north. This monastery is enclosed by tall, leafy alisos (alders), or *Betula alnus*. In front of the main wall there is a spacious yard, adorned with similar trees. This yard has various lodgings, called hospedería, to accommodate the faithful who frequently gather for religious retreat there, coming from the entire province and other places. At the back there is a beautiful garden abounding in exquisite vegetables and surrounded by the same alders, which beautify the place very much. There are trees that divide at the roots into three to nine trunks, each stout and nearly equal and supporting an extremely luxuriant crown. The brooklet that supplies the garden and grove of trees has enough water, in spite of its small size, to irrigate even more land.

The interior of the monastery has two cloisters, each with gardens of different kinds of native and European flowers and aromatic herbs. One of these cloisters has the life of Saint Francis of Assisi excellently painted in sections that fill the recesses of the four walls. The other is ornamented with paintings of converted peoples and of expeditions made into various parts of infidel territories. In these last-mentioned paintings, there are representations of the sufferings of apostolic missionaries and their countrymen who accompanied them in the work of conversion.

On the top floor there is another cloister in which there is a register for the Way of the Cross, with a large cross at each angle, a crown of thorns on each cross, and a clock in its case at each corner. The peace, silence, symmetry, and taste with which these mystic ornaments of Ocopa are arranged and installed are conducive to the greatest devotion and a contemplative and penitent life.

Architecturally, this monastery is one of the best in Peru. The facade of the church, the main part of the building that consists of one nave, and all the other interior rooms are superbly built in the modern fashion and painted white in the most artistic manner. The church is spacious, full of light, and tastefully ornamented, as are its altars dedicated to various saints.

The vestry is square and as elaborately ornamented as the church itself. It has a beautiful set of cabinets for the holy ornaments and vessels, which occupy all four

Figure 6. Map of the Mission of Santa Rosa de Ocopa, Peru, drawn by Pedro González Agüeros. From *Maps of Peru*, folio 8. (Courtesy of the British Museum.)

sides; for each cleric there is a chalice with his own mark. The walls are covered with fine Roman paintings, and above them is a row of small squares of white marble depicting the life of Santa Rosa de Lima. Many of the windows of the vestry and of the cloisters are made of small pieces of very transparent stone.

During Lent, on the days of the Porciuncula of Saint Francis, and on many other festival days, great numbers of people from Tarma, Xauxa, and nearby provinces come together here to confess and to receive communion, and many for religious retreat.

From Ocopa, monks are sent out to the villages on the infidel frontier to give spiritual sustenance and instruction in Christian morals and good habits to newly converted Indians. The monastery of Ocopa provides them with the necessities to maintain and successfully carry out their ministries, asking nothing from the natives except that they cultivate a small patch of maize, roots, and vegetables for the support of the fathers. His Catholic Majesty likewise contributes a certain amount of money toward maintaining these doctrines and conversions.

The monastery of Ocopa has a large library of authors in various fields of learning. It is arranged in alphabetic order in a large room and on good shelving made of beautiful wood.

Having wandered around about Ocopa and having seen the monastery, we went on to put up for the night in the town of Concepción, 1 league from the sanctuary. We crossed a small stream that is dangerous to ford in the rainy season. Along its banks *Calceolaria linearis*, which we collected, described, and drew in Concepción, is abundant. In this town there is a company of veteran troops to defend against the thrusts of infidel Indians. There are many residents in this town, which has an extensive market square always supplied with food. In the public square there is a jail that is much more secure than any other in the province and to which, for that very reason, important prisoners are brought.

On the 24th we returned to the town of Xauxa. It is situated at the foot of some low mountains on a very wide and gently sloping plain. Its streets are straight; only the sidewalks of the principal ones are paved, and when it rains many of the streets become great mudholes that impede travel. Though of but one story, with the exception of a few houses that have an upper story, the buildings are very good. They are constructed of earth, lime, and small stones, and are roofed with tiles. The main plaza is square and very large, and the market is well supplied with food at all times. The main church faces onto the plaza on one side and has two priests, and on another side of the plaza there is also a large, beautiful chapel in which masses are said every day.

The climate of Xauxa is cool all year round, and throughout the year the cold is felt here more than in the rest of the valley. The drinking water in Xauxa comes from a spring above the town, on clay soil. Since animals also go to this spring to drink, the water is always grayish blue and often too muddy. This could be prevented if the inhabitants would build a fountain and a drinking trough in the plaza and bring the water in through underground pipes.

CHAPTER 17

Description of the Province of Xauxa

The province of Xauxa (Plate 7) lies 45 leagues from Lima in a flat, spacious valley, or pampa, as it is called there; it has 18 leagues of road from east to west and 12 from north to south. To the north and northeast is the province of Tarma; to the east, the forests of infidel Indians; to the southeast, the province of Huanta; to the south, that of Angaraes, or Anccaraez; to the southwest, that of Yauyos; and to the west, that of Huarocherí.

The climate of this beautiful valley is, in general, rather warm. But in high parts here and there it is quite cold, especially at night, because of the winds that sweep down from the nearby mountain ranges. In winter there are continual freezes and hoarfrosts, and for this reason vegetables often become scarce during that time of year. Alfalfa, though produced near some of the villages around the town of Xauxa, is a failure in these higher areas. Six leagues away, the climate is milder: as one climbs up, the soil is good for sugar cane, and they do indeed grow it there and produce some sugar. Harvests of wheat and barley are heavy. Maize, potatoes, ocas, yacones, arracachas (apios, Peruvian parsnips), green vegetables, flowers, and some fruits are plentiful in gardens and orchards. On the hilltops and along the edge of the forests, yuca, mallicas (yams), papayas, bananas, pineapples and other fruits are gathered.

In the dry season, plants in the greater part of the valley are no more than half a foot tall, except in low spots that are protected from the mountain winds. In springtime, however, the open country is most delightful.

Many swine are raised; delicious hams and savory sausages, famous as far away as Europe, are produced here. In the colder high regions, huge flocks of sheep are kept. Their wool is used in the domestic factories for making much coarse cloth, and the womenfolk weave blankets, cloth of various colors, many ponchos, and other fabrics for their clothing and household use, both cotton and wool. On the highest and coldest moorlands there is an abundance of vicuñas and huanacos. The wool of each of these two animals is collected and mixed either with cotton or silk, or one with the other, for fine weaving into scarves, handkerchiefs, sashes, girdles, garters, socks, caps, slippers, and other objects of wear. In some of the lower ravines on these moors, cattle are also kept.

The Oroya, or Parí, River crosses through the middle of the province of Xauxa. It arises in the lake of Chinchaycocha, which is located on the pampas of Bombón.

It is too shallow to be of much use in irrigating the valley of Xauxa, but in emergencies irrigation ditches can be dug from it to make parts of these arable plains fertile and pleasant. When the Marqués de Cañete was viceroy, a stone bridge of a single arch was built over this river 5 leagues from Xauxa, but the indolence of the natives allowed the waters to destroy it. Another bridge was constructed over the Huancayo River at about the same time; because the inhabitants repair it each year, it still exists and is extremely useful for traffic and communication between those villages. The Huancayo and other smaller rivers of the province of Xauxa flow into the Parí, after having watered extensive stretches of the province.

At a time in the past, the proposition of founding the capital of Peru in the valley of Xauxa was considered, but there were numerous disadvantages that argued against it. One was that the climate was too cold in the rainy season.

There are a number of ancient ruins of settlements in this province, and some old fortifications of the pagan Indians, but these are just barely known nowadays.

In 1742 the Indians of many towns, already converted to Christianity, rose in rebellion and threatened war in this province, as did happen in the forest areas of Tarma and Huánuco, resulting in the loss of the new villages and many inhabitants of Huancabamba, Cerro de la Sal, Metraro, Enero, Quimirí, Tulumayo, Urubamba, and others.

Although various silver mines are found in this province, today the only one being worked is a mine that was discovered in 1779. The others are not rich enough now to exploit commercially. The population of this province is 53,000. Most of this number is made up of Indians and mestizos, for there are hardly 2000 Spaniards or white creoles, and some 60 negro and mulatto slaves. All of these inhabitants are distributed throughout 14 parishes. The chief parish of the province is that of Xauxa, with its dependencies Ricrán and Mojón. The second parish is that of Apata, with dependencies Uchubamba and Huamalí. The third is that of Concepción, where there is a monastery of the fathers of Observantes de San Francisco. The fourth is that of Comas, with its dependency Andamarca, located on the jungle frontier. The fifth is that of San Gerónimo, with dependencies Hualhuas and Quinchuay. The sixth is that of Huancayo, with two priests, and its dependencies Pucará, Huayucachi, Caxas, La Punta, Zapallanca, Miraflores, Hualayo, and Mejorada. The seventh parish is that of Cochanccara, with dependencies Pariahuanca and Acobamba. The eighth is that of Chonhos, with dependencies Cayahuacallancca and Colca. The ninth is that of Chupa, the tenth is that of Sicaya, the eleventh is that of Orcotuna, and the twelfth is that of Mito. The thirteenth is that of Matahuassi and Cincos, with the dependency San Antonio de Huancani. The fourteenth is that of Huaripampa, with its dependency Muquiyauyo.

The very same plants grow in this province as in the cold, high parts of Tarma and in some of its gorges. For this reason we found nothing new except, as pointed out before, *Calceolaria linearis*, an abundance of *Polymnia resinifera*, or taraca, and the genuine calaguala, *Polypodium calahuala*.

CHAPTER 18

Trip from Xauxa to Tarma

On the 30th of July I returned from Xauxa to the Villa de Tarma, certain in my mind that at no season of the year would the valley and mountains of Xauxa offer enough material for some days' work by the members of the botanical expedition unless we were to go into the jungle areas. This we refrained from doing, upon the expert advice of missionaries of Ocopa who informed us that the tropical forests of Tarma were just as abundant in vegetation as those of Xauxa, and had the advantage of being easier and safer to travel through for botanical collecting.

From Tarma we continued to observe, collect, describe, and draw the plants of the gorges of Huichay, Tarmatambo, Curis, Acobamba, and Huillauicham, as well as of the mountains, moors, and slopes around these localities, until the end of September. At this time Mr. Dombey arrived in Tarma, having finished his trip to Cheuchín. My companion Pavón and the artist Brunete went to the fort of Palca, 4 leagues from Tarma, and set off collecting along the new road to Chanchamayo that the missionaries and the governor of Tarma were opening; they traveled as far as a place called Huayabal, 10 leagues from Palca. There they stayed for some days and then betook themselves to Huasahuassi, 5 leagues from Tarma, where on the 2nd of October 1779 I had come with Dombey and the artist Gálvez, skirting the town of Acobamba to the right and the town of Picoy to the left.

On top of the mountain called Portachuelo, on the way to Huasahuassi, we suffered for more than 2 hours from a cold, severe wind. It was accompanied by a dense mist that made it impossible to see anything even 12 paces away. Shortly thereafter, the mist turned into a furious rain that drenched us as we traveled for more than a league, until we started down the gorge. This phenomenon is common at these altitudes. Wet through and through, we entered Huasahuassi at half past three in the afternoon. This is the last town in the part of the province that borders on the realm of the pagan Indians, who are known locally as chunchos. To hold these Indians in check, in this town there is a fort, manned by veteran troops.

Though Huasahuassi is situated at the bottom of the gorge, it has command over the exit route of the Indians. It is built upon the banks of a small but noisy river; the pleasant, crystalline water falls rapidly in some places and beats against the cliffs, with the whitest of froth forming large and small globes and other shapes, making the most beautiful and lovely cascade imaginable.

The inhabitants of this town number hardly more than 40, all Indians and mestizos who very painstakingly cultivate the small plots needed for their food. They keep swine and chickens for household needs, and also some cattle to sell and to provide their families with milk, butter, and cheese. These natives are forced to stand guard at night in the fort along with the veteran soldiers of the active troops. The fort comprises four bastions, each with a cannon. The buildings are low, and thatched like those of other villages of the province, as is the tiny church of a single nave with its vestry.

The heavy jungles, from which the barbarous Indians are wont to make their warlike thrusts, begin 2 leagues from this fort.

On the 3rd of October we made our first excursion. Accompanied by a second lieutenant of the militia and by three peasants, we went down along the river to the hut of the advance sentinel. There we left our horses and continued on foot, collecting in the beautiful, pleasant fields. They were covered with a profusion of plant life, with a perpetual fragrance and aroma so stimulating and vivifying the senses that the place seemed to invite one to leave it nevermore. Of all the plants there, the most plentiful belong to the orchid family. Growing on the surface, their bulbs cover the driest and craggiest parts of the ground like cobblestones, and their strange and beautiful flowers tint that curious natural pavement with varied colors.

We returned to the fort, where the military authorities had put us up, with more than 40 new plants, all different from those we had seen in other places.

On the 12th I went with Gálvez to the town treasurer of Xauxa for the third part of our salaries, and we returned on the 15th to Huasahuassi, where Mr. Dombey had stayed. Pavón, having returned to Tarma from Palca with Brunete, went down to Lima on the 25th with two boxes of dried plant specimens. Brunete remained in Tarma until Pavón's return, and on the 26th of November they both proceeded to Huasahuassi to join up with us.

On the 31st of October 1779, I went with Dombey and Gálvez to the forests of Churupallana, 5 leagues from Huasahuassi. A second lieutenant of the militia, five peasants, and our servants accompanied us on this excursion. We had hardly climbed up that high mountain a league and a half when it began to rain without any interruption until the following day. Because of the water we climbed up the remaining league and a half to Churupallana under the greatest of handicaps, slipping and falling many times in the ascent.

Thoroughly wet through, we took shelter for the night in a very tiny, nearly dismantled shack that the lieutenant had thrown together there for shelter when caring for his cows, which were continuously pastured at this spot. Crowded together in the shack as we were, we could not escape the water even there, for we were rained upon from all sides just as in an open field. The cold, coupled with the soaking, was unbearable. We lighted a large fire of green wood, but before we could get it to burn we were thoroughly smoked and wet to the bone. No one got a wink of sleep that night.

One hour before daybreak we heard, coming from the forest, repeated mournful shrieks like those of someone in pain and calling for help. We all took up positions around the shack in expectancy, bending an ear towards the screams that were repeated every now and again without any change in place of origin. Finally the lieutenant, who had been surprised like the rest of us, heard the shrieks more clearly and recognized them as the cry of birds that in the jungle regions are called almas perdidas (lost souls), which always dwell in the most tangled parts of those dense forests.

As morning began to break through, the blazing colors of dawn increased and the downpour ended, yielding to a dense mist. It was not too thick, however, to prevent us from drying our clothes slightly, although we met with very little success in this task.

We tried to penetrate the forest, but we had hardly taken a step in that direction when Dombey slipped. Since he could not walk by himself, we took him back to the shelter and he remained there, nursing his pains. I left anew with the peasants to gather some of the infinite number of plants that clothe that whole terrain. It was no time before we had collected a good load with which to set off from that spot in order to escape another rainstorm, which was moving in with great fury. We all felt sad to leave that locality without finishing our study of it. According to information that we had obtained, there are quinas, or species of *Cinchona*, in that region, and we thought we had spied a species of this tree on the mountain near our shelter.

When we had gone down hardly a league from Churupallana, we found ourselves free from the dense and foggy mist for the remainder of that day and those following. From that point onwards until we arrived at the fort, we had splendid sun, so hot and radiant that for more than 2 hours we had to hide in the shade along the banks of the Siusa River. Here we likewise gathered plants that we did not already have, taking a variety of specimens of them to describe and draw. At eventide we entered Huasahuassi, wet to the bone and weary from this difficult hike.

On the 3rd of November, we sent to our companions a request for the drawings that they had made on the trip from Palca to Tarma, so that we might avoid duplicating them in Huasahuassi; in this locality one can find many of the same species that grow in the gorge of Palca.

On the 24th Dombey and I went to Lanco, a league and a half from Huasahuassi, to study the orchids that literally blanket that delightful and pleasing place. While there we drank of the watery juice of these orchid bulbs to quench our thirst, and felt no ill effects, on that or the following days.

On the 5th of December 1779, I returned to Tarma with Dombey and Gálvez, and on the 12th Pavón and Brunete came back. They had stayed behind to finish and perfect some of the drawings that they were making in Palca of the living plants also found in Huasahuassi.

We continued our botanical work in Tarma, all five of us, until the 13th of January 1780, when Dombey, Pavón, and Brunete left for Lima; on the 19th I left for the capital with Gálvez.

All the plants that we saw and collected on this long expedition through the province of Tarma and its extremely rich jungles have been enumerated at the end of our description of the Villa de Tarma.

CHAPTER 19

Trip from Tarma to Lima

We have reported how Dombey, Pavón, and Brunete left together for Lima on the 13th of January 1780; they arrived well, notwithstanding a few misfortunes.

On the 19th of the same month, at two o'clock in the afternoon, I left Tarma with the artist Gálvez. We were happily traveling towards the highlands of Oroya when we were overtaken by a strong hailstorm, followed at once by a heavy downpour of rain. It wet us from head to foot and made us lose our way several times, for we did not know which way to turn among the myriad little ponds that sprang up in a short time. Entirely at the mercy of our beasts of burden, we traveled through the murky, wet night wherever they wanted to take us. We got to the town of Oroya after nine o'clock that evening, bristling with the cold and wet to the bone. In this predicament, we were lucky enough to come upon the home of a mestizo who generously offered us his very bed, making it up with sheets that, though woolen, were very clean and suitable for covering us so we two travelers could find a bit of warmth that night. Moreover, this mestizo and his wife, making a brisk fire in the room next to where we slept, patiently worked at drying all our clothes and then strung them on lines to dry during the rest of the night. This done, they lay themselves down to sleep at the foot of our bed, making themselves comfortable on some sheepskins.

Although they were familiar with the road, our own servants got lost, having gone ahead of the mule drivers in the rain and hail. They came to the village of Reyes and slept there, having made a circuit of 5 leagues longer than the road and 8 leagues longer than our route. The mule drivers had the luck to come upon a cave, where they spent the night, and arrived at Oroya the next morning at half past ten. At eleven our servants, with the Indian whom we had sent out to look for them, returned. When we were all together again, we set out from Oroya at one in the afternoon. We counted one mule drowned in crossing the Parí River.

A mile from the bridge the pelting of hail began, and then it rained until we got to Pachachaca, where we put in to await better weather. At five o'clock we resumed our trip, arriving in Pucará at night.

On the 21st of January we left Pucará. We were accompanied up to the cordillera (mountain range) by a miner who had his mine in the mountains. Because of the strong heat of the sun pouring down upon us, we crossed that stretch of snow without feeling the slightest cold.

While descending the hillside at Cassapalca, I had the bad luck of suddenly falling into a narrow gorge formed by erosion. However, I managed at the same time to remain astride the prostrate mule, to the cinch of which my horse had been tied on the right side. Frightened of a chasm that the mule had just crossed, my horse had drawn back from the edge so fast that it cast the mule into the ravine and caused me to fall in on top of the animal. Then, in spite of all its efforts to remain safely above, the horse tumbled down on those of us who were already below. Fortunately, I was able to get the upper part of my body out of the way by leaning sharply to one side when Gálvez shouted from above that the horse was about to fall into the abyss.

Only the mule and the saddle, along with a broken stirrup and spur, were harmed in this strange and unexpected adventure. The mule had both of its rumps bruised and its face skinned against the walls of the gorge. The horse, in struggling to get up and find a way out of the pit, kicked violently. I was able to escape this incessant kicking by crouching on the ground behind the mule, under which my left leg was caught, until I could cut the horse's halter. Once freed, the horse got up with a couple of kicks that skinned my right cheek. This accident drew some blood, but the bleeding served to distract my attention from worrying about what might have resulted from the fall. The horse, when it was loosed from its shackles, set off down the gorge, snorting and puffing with anger and scraping its belly along the walls.

Then I began the work of extricating my leg from under the mule and was soon successful. I also succeeded in making the mule get up, but the animal was so short and fat, and the place so narrow, that it could not get out unless the crevasse were widened. The first thing I did was to take the ruined saddle off the mule and send it up on a rope that Gálvez had dropped down to me from above. This was not enough, so I enlarged the narrow exit with a stone and a knife, whereupon the mule set off after the horse. Both animals were caught at the end of this gorge by a mestizo who had witnessed the fall from afar and had come running up to render his help.

We saddled the mule as best we could and continued our journey to San Matheo, where the saddle was partially repaired and we treated the mule's wounds. We could not, however, fix the stirrup or solder the spur, nor could we repair the handle of the whip, which was dented and split all up one side.

A few days later we learned that, a short while after our falling into that gorge, the same fate overtook another traveler, but he was badly hurt and his horse suffered a broken foot.

On the 22nd we left San Matheo and arrived in San Pedro de Máma in time to spend the night. The next day, we entered Lima without any further trouble except for the heat that we had to bear through all the gorges on this journey. On the 24th of January the servants and mule drivers arrived in Lima, where we all remained until the 23rd of April 1780.

During our stay in Lima, we finished the drying of plants gathered along the road as well as others collected in Lima. We transferred all the specimens that had remained in Lima into new papers in order to free them from a tiny insect that Linnaeus, in his *Systema Naturae*, has named *Termes fatidicum*. The first specimen he saw was in the plant material sent from America by Mr. Loefling. I found another species of insect, even tinier than the first, on some of the plants, but it belongs to a different genus and does not harm specimens. Nevertheless, I dusted the boxes with sulfur before packing the plants.

We arranged all the collections by classes, writing the generic and common names on the specimen sheets, and the material was left boxed up in good condition for travel. I made clean copies of the descriptions that we had drawn up in Tarma, and described various plants that we had recently collected in the vicinity of Lima.

When these tasks had been done, and when permission had been granted to leave boxes of natural products stored in the royal armory, awaiting the opportunity of shipping them off to Spain, we asked for a permit to spend a year in the jungles of Huánuco. These regions are famous for their richness and for the abundance of valuable plants that grow there. Once this permit was secured, we equipped ourselves with necessities for the expedition, and on the 23rd of April the artist Gálvez and I sent off our baggage, including the presses, paper, and other equipment for our work.

CHAPTER 20

First Trip to Huánuco

Accompanied by the artist Gálvez, I left Lima by the gateway of Las Maravillas on the 24th of April 1780. We arrived safely in Cocachacra, early enough to spend the night there. We suffered from oppressive heat during our journey.

On the 25th we got to the smelter of Pomacancha in time to sleep there, having climbed down by night from the crest of the high mountain of Cacray. The descent had been extremely difficult because of darkness brought on by a dense mist that suddenly came up. Near San Juan de Chiclla, we met a miner from the smelter, Don Juan José Martínez, who took us to his own house and offered us generous hospitality that night.

On this same date, the botanist Pavón and the artist Brunete left Lima by the same road. Dombey went by the Canta road, since his mule drivers were in that province, whereas the others were in the provinces of Tarma and Huarocherí.

On the 26th, accompanied by the miner Don Juan José Martínez, we set out from the Pomacancha smelter in a bitter cold wind. We arrived at the cordillera where, a blanket of snow notwithstanding, the sun very thoroughly warmed us.

When we had crossed the mountains and gone past the lake of Huascacocha, which is more than a league in length, we continued without anything in particular happening until we arrived at the Pucará smelter. We had hardly dismounted when a terrible hailstorm let loose and was followed by a long downpour of rain.

On the 27th of April we left Pucará early in the morning and, with no untoward experiences, entered the Villa de Tarma at nightfall. Our mule drivers arrived on the 30th. On the 2nd of May our companions came into Tarma, where we all remained until the 11th, finishing and perfecting some of the descriptions that had been left incomplete on the previous trip. At the same time, I procured reliable information about the following colors that these people use to dye wool and cotton for their weaving.

Scarlet or blood red: Take 8 ounces of pilcay, or pircay, 2 pounds of red tiri, and 1 ounce of alum. Boil all together in 2 gallons of water with the wool or cotton until these fabrics take on the desired hue. Then wash the wool or cotton and set it out to dry.

Pilcay is a dough made of liver with mashed, sun-dried cochineal, formed into cakes of various sizes. The cochineal is gathered in Tarma, but in small amounts because of the indolence and lack of interest among the natives. They could cultivate it in the ravines near the town itself, as well as in those of Acobamba, where it grows wild but is inferior to that produced elsewhere. Tiri is a species of *Melastoma*.

Purplish red: This color is produced in two ways. The first method consists of mixing 2 pints of the lye of quinhuar, *Polylepis emarginata*, with 2 ounces of rosin and the scarlet dye described above. A beautiful purplish red hue is the result.

In the second method, sticks of tara, *Caesalpinia tara*, are split up very fine, then urine is poured over the pieces of wood and they are put out in the sun. The urine is poured over them repeatedly until they are well soaked with it. After the sticks are aired, they are boiled in ordinary water with red tiri and the wool or cotton until the fabric is well dyed.

Yellow: Take equal parts of yellow tiri and of chinchanho, a species of *Hypericum*, with a bit of alum and some wine; boil all this together in ordinary water with the wool or cotton until the fabric is dyed.

Color of aromo: Take 4 ounces of pahuan, which is a species of *Cosmos* or of *Coreopsis*, and cook it in 16 pints of the yellow dye mentioned above, together with the wool. The fabric will come out dyed a beautiful aromo color—that is, the color (deep yellow) of the flower of *Mimosa farnesiana* (aromatic myrrh tree, cassie, sweet acacia).

Orange: In 6 pints of water cook 4 ounces of pahuan until the dye is well extracted. Then put in the wool, previously soaked in an alum solution, and boil it all together until the fabric becomes orange.

Green: Take twigs of chilca macho (male chilca), a species of *Eupatorium*, and boil them together with indigo and urine in ordinary water until the wool or cotton takes on the desired green hue.

Color of cloves: Take the dried fruits of tara and a bit of soot and boil them up together with wool that has been soaked in iron sulfate or copperas (vitriol). The fabric will come out dyed the beautiful color of cloves.

Color of cinnamon: Take equal parts of pahuan and of tara that has been soaked in urine as we have outlined in the recipe for the purplish red dye. Add soot, lemon juice, and alum, then boil all together in ordinary water with the wool or cotton. The result will be a cinnamon color.

Color of raisins: Take bark of the native walnut, *Juglans nigra*, with soot and rosin; boil them together with wool that has been previously soaked in an alum solution.

On the 9th of May 1780, the mule drivers left Tarma with their cargoes. Pavón and Brunete left on the following day. Due to torrential rains, they were soaked in crossing the pampa of Reyes and suffered not a few mishaps. On the 11th, after the weather had improved, I left Tarma with Gálvez and arrived at the village of Reyes, 10 leagues from Tarma; here we spent the night. We had to pass the estate known as Las Casas, noted for its abundant harvests of potatoes and of barley that is short-spiked but gives considerable grain. We likewise crossed a wide pampa, or plain, sparsely covered with short grass.

The village of Reyes is located in the center of the pampa of the same name; because the climate is cold the year round, they grow no major crops here. Only barley is cultivated in the village itself for feeding the horses and for other domestic use, and to sell to travelers in April and May. During the rest of the year, not even this scant relief can be found here, and cattle must be taken off to protected spots where there is pasturage.

Nothing is sown or harvested on the pampa of Reyes except the small roots called maccas, and even these grow well only in the villages of Ondores, Ccarhuamayo, and Ninacacca, and the dependencies of those three parishes. The men of Reyes earn their livelihood as mule drivers, while the womenfolk spin and weave.

On the 12th we left Reyes at seven o'clock in the morning. It was bitterly cold, a result of the frost of the night before and of the dense mist that gathers, almost every day, between four and five o'clock in the morning and lasts until eight or nine, when sun and wind drive it away.

Marañón River, or the Amazon

Half a league from Reyes, the lake of Chinchaycocha begins. It widens out until it nears the village of Vico, and we crossed it by going over the Inca causeway, which is nearly destroyed. Today that great work of the pagan Indians is one continuous mire. We passed through the villages of Ccarhuamayo and Ninacacca, leaving that of Vico to one side, and entered the town of Pasco as night was falling. The day had passed without mishap.

We have already explained in our description of Tarma that three famous rivers, the Marañón, the Ucayali, and the Huallaga (Plate 6), have their respective sources in three lakes in these extensive pampas of pumpúm, or Bombón, as they are called at the present time. These three lakes are not far from one another: the lake of Lauricocha, whence flows the Marañón, is but 4 leagues from that of Chinchaycocha, where the Ucayali has its origin, and 12 leagues from there lies the lake of Yauricocha, where the Huallaga is born. These rivers go in separate directions, flowing many, many leagues from one another, and after having described great curves and bends over that vast realm that is Peru, and having run through almost the whole jungle-covered area, come back and join up in a single river called the Marañón, the greatest river known in the world. Some call this river the Amazon. It is 80 leagues wide where it empties into the sea.

On the 13th of May we left Pasco. The miners of that region go to the royal treasury in Pasco to pay their quintos (20% taxes) and to melt down the silver ore taken from their mines. Pasco is situated at the foot of a lake, which is dammed up so that only enough water to work the grindstones of the smelters can run out. There is, therefore, no shortage of water in the dry season as was common in former times. The streets are not laid out in any order and are unpaved; with the exception of a few short stretches of sidewalk, they are perennial bogs, so it is difficult to travel on them.

The buildings are not so poor as are those in the villages and hamlets on the pampas and punas of Bombón, for numerous miners, businessmen, and silver brokers live there. Constructed of earth and stones and roofed with wood or ichu grass, they are rectangular, conical, or square, and one story high. Very rarely is a building whitewashed without, but most are within, though they are dirty and begrimed with smoke. Usually they are dark inside; they have few windows or, at best, very small ones, for it is constantly cold there throughout the year. For the same reason, the inhabitants have to keep braziers or portable stoves burning with champas and taquia, or turf and sheep dung, all the time. This is why the houses always are full of smoke and stink unbearably. This smell permeates not only the clothing but also the bodies of the people, lasting for many months even though they go to other, warmer climates and remain there for long periods of time.

Only some strong interest could attract people to these places and force them to live there, shut in most of the time and either smoked or frozen. It is impossible to go for a long walk there without resting from time to time to get back one's strength and breathe more easily, as well as to keep from being suffocated by quantities of azotic (nitrogenous) and carbonic-acid gases given off during the calcination of the minerals and from the burning champas. The air is filled with the foul gases known there as beta, which kill even the beasts of burden.

Crossing numerous mining estates and lakes, we climbed down to the ravine called Quinua, a name given to it because of its abundance of the trees known as quinuares or quinhuares. These trees are of great value to miners of the Cerro de Yauricocha as building material for houses and as fuel in the smelters, since their trunks are very strong and their wood burns very slowly in furnaces. We established the genus *Polylepsis* (*Polylepis*) on this tree, taking the generic name from the great number of thin layers, like honey-colored parchment, that progressively peel off from the bark as the tree ages.

We continued on so that we could sleep in Caxamarquilla, a village of very few inhabitants located on the summit of a high mountain and thus in a cold climate. A few families have their homes deep in the ravine, on the riverbank, and consequently enjoy a mild climate the year round. All the people living on the mountain, both high and low, cultivate plots in the lowermost reaches of the gorges, with excellent crops of maize, alfalfa, potatoes, lettuce, massuas, ocas, cabbages, and other vegetables, as well as pinks and other garden flowers. We had hardly come into Caxamarquilla when furious thunder and lightning let loose. It was accompanied by a bombardment of hail that lasted more than an hour without interruption.

On the 14th we left Caxamarquilla. As a result of the hailstorm of the previous day, the potholes and ruts were filled with water and the ground was extremely slippery and impassable. We therefore made our way with greatest difficulty to the village of Huariaca, suffering considerable stumbling and falling. Located upon the side of a mountain, Huariaca is on a slightly sloping plain that is always covered with various herbs and shrubs, most of them in flower the greater part of the year.

From Huariaca onwards, for a league and a half, there are no ruts, or a few shallow ones. Notwithstanding its better condition, this road is much more dangerous because it is wholly along hillsides and cliffs that slope or drop vertically down to the river. After this stretch the road becomes flat and presents no danger for another half league or more, to a point beyond San Rafaél. San Rafaél is a village with few inhabitants, located on a riverbank in a small valley. It enjoys a wonderful climate, even better than that of Huariaca.

Beyond this valley, one climbs a steep mountain along a poor road for more than a league to get to Rondos, a small Indian village. Rondos is built upon a plateau halfway up the mountain. It has a cool climate by day, but the nights are cold. Notwithstanding the variety of bushes, shrubs, a few trees, and especially the good grasses and herbs that clothe the mountain and its glens, the natives cultivate hardly anything except horse beans, quinoa, potatoes, maize, and a few vegetables for their own use. The forests hereabouts are plentifully supplied with deer that roam in herds even along the road. We spent that night in Rondos.

From the smelter and settlement of Quinua to the village of San Rafaél, meat, vegetables, alfalfa, and other food supplies are available all the year, but one cannot find bread of any kind all the way from Pasco to the city of Huánuco.

The gorge is perennially verdant with small plants and large, one or another always in flower. From Pasco to Caxamarquilla, in the lakes we saw but two species of ducks and a bird called huehue. The huehue is as large as a heron, with a dark gray body, a few white feathers on its belly and two long, linear, white feathers on its head, long legs, and a long, thin, sharp beak.

We left Rondos on the 15th, climbing upwards for more than a league on a road full of potholes until we got to the top of the mountain. The road follows along the ridge until it descends to the settlement of Ambo, 5 leagues away from Rondos. At this sparsely populated settlement there is a river that comes down the ravine of Huariaca from the lake of Yauricocha, along with the river that descends through the ravine of Huacar. Here it is called the Pillco, or Pillccuu, River, the name by which it is known in the province of Huánuco.

From Ambo to Huánuco there are 5 leagues of flat road, pleasant and interesting because of the many hamlets, gardens, and orchards that one finds all along the way. The entire stretch is fragrant with the delicious aromas given off by cherimoya, guava, and other native fruit trees, as well as by the lime, limoncillo, lemon, grapefruit, citron, orange, and other citrus trees that are plentiful in the fields there.

We entered the city of Huánuco at three o'clock in the afternoon. We were completely burned up by the strong sun, notwithstanding the fact that the heat was lessened by the north wind that blows through the whole valley from eleven to five o'clock every day. Our companions also entered Huánuco on the same day, and all of us dedicated the next week to preparations for beginning our work.

CHAPTER 21

Description of the Province and City of Huánuco de los Caballeros

The province of Huánuco is bounded on the south by the province of Tarma, on the west by that of Huamalíes, and on the north and east by the jungles of the Panatahuas. It enjoys two climates: the high regions are cold, and the low regions and the ravines are hot.

The valley of Pillco, where Huánuco is situated, is hot and dry from May to November. In spite of rather cool nights, the heat of the day is strong. This heat is tempered a bit by the northerly and east-by-northeasterly winds that, crossing the punas and forests, start to blow down into the valley about eleven o'clock in the morning and continue until sunset or, on some days, until eight in the evening.

Rainfall is exceedingly heavy from November through April, but the rainstorms do not prevent the sun from shining every day nor do they interrupt travel along the streets and out in the country. If it rains in the morning, the water soaks into the ground by afternoon; should a storm come in the afternoon, by the next morning the day is clear and the ground is almost completely dry.

On clear nights, it is so bright that even without a moon one needs no artificial light for traveling. What is really astonishing is that the sun is so hot and penetrating in this valley, surrounded as it is by mountain ranges and high moorlands where it snows and freezes from May to November. The temperature of the valley of Pillco is about the same throughout the year, the highest being from 84 to 86°F (29 to 30°C). From May to November, the overnight reading falls 9 to 11°F at most;

during the rest of the year, the temperature does not vary more than 4°F from morning to afternoon. Thus it is that the vegetation of the valley carries right through the year. Nevertheless, it is easy to distinguish four seasons, especially the winter with its torrential rains and the summer with its droughts. Springtime is characterized by the luxuriance of the flora, and autumn by the withering away of various vegetables and grains that are harvested at that time of year.

Wheat grows very well on mountains and slopes where the temperature is moderately cool. This grain was formerly sowed in the lower regions and on the plains, and then two harvests of very good wheat were garnered. In the high, cool ravines, where sharp frosts are frequent at night, potatoes, ocas, ullucos, massuas, arracachas, yacones, light and dark maize, horse beans, sweet and bitter quinoa, peaches, and sloe plums are grown. The slopes of the lower mountains are excellent for peas, beans, and lentils.

In the valleys and plains, sweet potatoes, yuca, gourds, pumpkins, squash, small melons, watermelons, cardo (artichokes, cardoon?), celery, cabbages, cauliflower, chard, lettuce, endive, garlic, onions, caihuas, and quisiu are cultivated. In the valleys one finds huge cherimoyas, commonly weighing 6 pounds and sometimes as much as 10 or 12 pounds, as well as many varieties of guavas that differ in the size and color of the fruit. There are also avocados, palillos, pacays, bananas, small and savory pears, papayas, apples, quinces, sour plums, friar's plums, cherries or *Prunus virginiana*, lucumas (eggfruit) with or without pits, native nuts, granadillas and tumbos (kinds of passion fruit), tunas (prickly pears), grapes, strawberries, grapefruit, citrons, oranges, limes, sweet lemons, true lemons, and thin-skinned lemons.

Maize is cultivated and gives a plentiful yield in the valleys and low regions. There are beautiful plantings of sugar cane throughout the valley; the juice of the cane is made into guarapo (fermented cane liquor), chancaca (brown sugar), miel (molasses, cane syrup), and alfeñique (almond-paste candy). Barley yields well in the cooler and temperate high regions, but little is sown because larger domestic animals can be maintained on the alfalfa that is available all the year round. Black figs can be found ripe throughout the year. Flax is planted and thrives prodigiously. Considering the terrain and climate of Huánuco, one can see that most of the fruits of Spain could be produced here. The forested regions produce delicious pineapples, some of them weighing as much as 9 pounds; anonos (anonas, custard apples), papayas, and caimitos (fruit of *Achras tetrandra*) are likewise brought out of this part of the province.

Flowers

The gardens offer a variety of ornamental and fragrant plants and flowers, such as large and small pinks, jasmines, amancas (*Narcissus odorus*) of varying colors, aromo (*Mimosa farnesiana*, cassie, sweet acacia, false myrrh tree), gillyflowers, albaca (basil?), amaranth, scabious or mourning bride, flores de San Francisco (*Impatiens balsamina*), white lilies (*Lilium candidum*), carnations, congonitas, larkspur, feligranas (*Pancratium allium*), flor de la Trinidad (Trinity flower), sunflowers, jonquils, iris, mazizes (macises, mace?), marjoram, camomile, white and multicolored margaritas, narcissus, pajaritos, peregrinas (*Alstroemeria peregrina*), piochas (*Cynanchum* species), musk roses, ñorbos (passion flowers), taconcitos (*Dolichos uncinatus*), tulips, fragrant broom, rosemary, and Alexandrian roses grown in the cold dales. There are also white, yellow, and red suches (*Plumeria* species), and other plants and flowers that please the senses of sight and smell and beautify the gardens all year round.

Throughout this province there are many wild plants that have medicinal uses or are otherwise of economic value; these will be discussed along with their respective locations. Among them are the abundant cabullas (cabuyas) and magueys (*Agave* and *Yucca* species), which are useful as hedges around farms and which also yield fiber for making ropes, twine, or thread for sewing. Natives use the stems of these plants to roof their huts and houses and to make stoppers for earthenware jugs, and from the pith they prepare tinder. Wild tuna cactus (prickly pear), infinite in number, is likewise employed as fencing on farms. From the tuna cactus the natives also distill a white gum similar to tragacanth; it is only slightly sticky, but could be used in various ways in medicine and even in the arts.

From gigantones (giant cactuses), equally plentiful in that valley, is gathered a wool that is useful, when mixed with white clay, for whitewashing buildings. It serves the purpose of binding the clay and preventing it from being washed off, which happens when the clay is not mixed with the wool. Though the pilcay, or cochinilla (cochineal insect), occurs in the valley, this insect is not another product of the gigantones there because it is not cultivated as it is in Mexico.

Fish

There are various brooks that gush down from the dales and ravines. Their waters are of sufficient volume to irrigate the orchards and farms of the entire valley of Pillco, so the natives need not use the large river that runs the length of the whole valley. The waters of the river support choques, or cachuelos; short and long bagres (catfish); and fish called huascachallhua, alguillas, ccaspa, and ccachaccachallhua. The first three are very tasty either fried or boiled. Only the ccaspa is eaten dried and powdered with the proper spices to give it some flavor; it is a favorite among the inhabitants of the region. In the same river, but in forested areas, there are corbinas (whiting) and boconcitos, which are delicious either fresh or salted; the Indians sell them either way.

Birds

Various birds occur in the province. The yanamanau is a species of diving duck, black, with tough and very dark meat. The tauriccaray, or sayalejo, is slightly larger than a sparrow and variegated brown in color; it always sleeps in its nest. The male and female stay together in the trees, chirping repeatedly for minutes on end the word "tauriccaray," which means to give chochitos or lupines to eat. With this endless gabbling, which bothers anyone who hears it, it seems as though the male and female dwell in a constant state of warfare with one another. Condors are very common in the mountains. Buzzards are seen occasionally but not at all times. Herons are very rare and are as white as ermine.

The chusecc, or owl, is as large as a hen but has little meat. Its croaks sound like the word "chusecc," repeated and repeated, and when it is harassed it frantically rattles its beak. Sometimes it continues to wag its head, bending it down towards the ground and switching it from side to side. The chusecc is variegated in color, and on its face is a circle of a color different from that of the rest of the body. It roosts in churches. The pacapaca is another species of owl, rather small, which wanders through the villages by night croaking its repeated "pacapaca."

The guardacaballos is the size and color of a large thrush; it lives in large groups in corrals, on farms, and along roads. Its beak is sharp on top and is covered with hairs along the edge and around the nostrils. The rihua, or oropendola (golden oriole), is the size of a small thrush. Its body and head are as yellow as egg yolk, with wing feathers grayish brown above and white underneath. It mimics the calls of other birds that live in the same region. The yuquis, or native thrush, is as large as a European thrush, of grayish brown hue with yellow bill and feet. It walks in little hops, as does the guardacaballos, and has a melodious song that imitates other birds. The quillicsa is a species of kestrel.

The huanchaco, or piche, slightly larger than a sparrow, is brownish with a lake red breast, or sometimes white with red breast. The females, however, have but a small spot of red on the throat. The flights of the huanchaco are short, and it dives precipitately to earth like a bird of prey. The males easily learn songs taught to them, and they have other interesting characteristics such as coming when called, leaving when ordered away, etc. A man from Lima, full of curiosity about the piche, taught one of these birds a little song on a reed flute with so much accuracy that the animal even made the same mistakes, imitating the false notes of the player. They take up three or four different musical notes and please the listener with the flood and sweetness of their song. But all this must be taught to them when they are young, for their natural song is quite tiresome. They can also be taught to fight with a cock, and it is interesting to see them attack the cock until they tire it out and win. It is only indolence on the part of the inhabitants that there are so few well-trained piches, for this bird is so abundant that it is the bane of the farmer in Peru.

The chivillo (cuckoo), black and the size of a thrush, is born in the nest of the huanchaco. When the chivillo wants to lay its eggs, it seeks out a huanchaco nest and deposits an egg there, and similarly finds a nest for every single egg it lays. It contrives to propagate its young by the work of others, for the huanchacos incubate and feed the young chivillos as though they were their own offspring. In Chile the huanchaco is called aloica.

The pito is a magpie, as large as a wild pigeon. It lives in uninhabited spots, among cliffs and crags, where it makes its nest by picking at the rock with its beak. The carpintero is another magpie or woodpecker, the same size as the pito, black above and whitish on the breast, with a red tail. When it walks along the ground, it carries its head high and its tail scraping the ground. Its flights are not high, but short and fast. With its beak it picks at tree trunks and at cliffs, making a loud noise with its rapid-fire hammering.

The pichuisa is smaller than a sparrow, grayish brown and spotted with white and light gray. Dwelling in villages, the male and female are always together but at a regular distance of 20 to 30 yards apart. They call to each other at this distance with the song "pi-chui-sa," each syllable a bit higher in tone and more plaintive than the one before. The texa-pissho, or texuelillo, is the same size and color as a canary or a linnet, and sings like a goldfinch.

The papamosca (flycatcher), or ruisenor (nightingale), smaller than a linnet and tobacco-colored, lives in villages, gardens, and orchards, feeding upon flies and mosquitoes. Its song is extraordinarily pleasing to the ear, especially in the morning and evening.

The santa-rosa, a species of swallow that is white on the breast and belly, and black elsewhere, lives in settlements and along the river banks.

Huinchos is a general name for all kinds of hummingbirds in Huánuco, where they are of various sizes and colors. In Chile these birds enter into crevices on tree trunks, where they attach themselves so securely with their beaks and tiny claws that one would believe that they were nailed there, dead. Thus they remain all during the winter, until the warmth of springtime calls them and they come out to search for the nectar of flowers, which is their food. If one takes them in the wintertime and warms them next to one's breast, they soon begin to move and awaken. Children often do this in play.

The tunqui-pissho is a beautiful bird with a yellow-white breast and belly, black head, and blue body. It chirps the word "tunqui."

There is a wild pigeon, smaller than the domestic one, called urpay; its song sounds like the word "urpay." The cuculi is another pigeon but smaller still and grayish brown in color; its call, sung out in a slow, halting way, is "cu-cu-li." The pacha-urpay, also known as tortolilla, is another small dove; it is slightly larger than *Columba minuta* of Linnaeus. A fly, like a horsefly, always lives on the rump of this bird, never leaving until the bird dies. The song of the pacha-urpay is also "urpay." The ccullcuy, ccullcullu, or cascabelillos (little rattlesnake) is another dove of variegated color, grayish brown and white. When moving from one spot to another, it makes a noise like that of a rattlesnake; when resting, it repeats the calls "ccullcuy" and "ccullcullu." The meat of any of these pigeons, marinated in vinegar, is tender and delicious in proportion to the amount of cooking it is given.

In the province of Huánuco, geese, ducks, turkeys, hens, and domestic pigeons are abundant. As a consequence, chickens, squabs, and fresh eggs for eating are never scarce.

Animals

Among the domestic animals are horses, mules, cows, sheep, swine, and guinea pigs, called ccoyes or cuyes. Animals found in the countryside include deer, a few vicuñas and huanacos in the cold highlands, foxes, gray wildcats, a small species of otter, guinea pigs, huayhuas (weasels), and pericotes, or rats. Abundant in the wet places and irrigation ditches of Huánuco is a very small species of frog; its constant song, similar to that of crickets, annoys everyone both day and night. There are but two snakes known. One of these may be as long as a yard and a half, more or less, and the other is hardly a yard long; neither has a poisonous bite.

Insects

At night a species of very small glowworm, or firefly, is active. Cicadas are very common in the fields, as are various kinds of tiny spiders that are only slightly poisonous. The paltacurus, also very common, resembles a cockroach; its sting, like that of spiders, is often bothersome. There is a wasp whose sting is likewise uncomfortable, but it is a slow insect that spends the daytime hours on the walls of houses, making the little mud tubes in which it sleeps. There are crickets, and small butterflies and moths. When the apple blossoms are out, they are visited by swarms of blowflies called mascull, seen only at that time of year. Dogs devour these flies so ravenously that they may eat nothing else and, as a consequence, wither away and die. Mosquitoes are very rare, but there is a little gnat that is bothersome all year round, especially in orchards and in damp places. Fleas and bedbugs are common, and lice and piques, or chiggers, are plentiful among the poor and dirty. Chiggers infest the feet of swine, as well as the feet of Indians, negroes, and mestizos in great numbers, all of whom generally go barefoot. White inhabitants are likewise often attacked when they do not bathe their feet with care. Wherever guinea pigs are bred, there is always a tremendous plague of minute fleas, unbearable because of their bites.

Mines

There are a number of silver and gold mines, but those that have been discovered up to the present time yield very little ore and consequently are not worked. Across the river from the city of Huánuco there is a gold mine, and some miners vainly tried to make it pay; for a lack of proper tools, they dug down only about 3 yards and then abandoned it. They saw from the very start that the small amount of ore taken out of the hard rock ledge would not pay for the work.

On the plantations of Cochachinchi, 6 leagues away, is a very rich mine of potassium nitrate, or saltpeter; the carriers of Huancavelica go there to get loads of this salt as it comes from the mine. A goodly production of beautiful crystals, well mixed with considerable earth, is reported every year. On the estate of Corpus, in the valley, and in many places along the road between Huánuco and this village, there is an abundance of saltpeter, but no one bothers with it because it is not crystallized like that from the mine.

Stones

Rock crystal occurs on Pinculluyocc, a mountain near the city of Huánuco. Slate is very common on the mountain of Puelles and in its entire vicinity. There are clays of many colors, some of them excellent for pottery. There is also white marl, or calcium carbonate, which the Indians call iscu (lime); they use it to extract and activate the substance and taste of coca.

Natural Products

From the forests of the Panatahuas, commonly called the Huánuco forests, an appreciable amount of incense is exported for use in the churches of Peru. These forests also provide a number of balsams, resins, barks, roots, seeds, fruits, and other plant products, as well as parrots, macaws, parakeets, and four species of monkeys.

Quina, or Cascarilla

Leaving Lamas by way of the Cuchero River in 1776, Don Francisco Renquifo saw cascarilla trees, source of the best Peruvian quina bark, along the road and in the forests surrounding the town. He had previously seen and known this kind of tree in the forests of Loxa. He gathered some samples of bark, took them to Huánuco, and showed them to a number of people. He told them that the inhabitants of Loxa carried on a considerable business in this bark, and he insinuated that they, too, might make large sums of money from the stands of cascarilla trees he had found.

When told of the localities where these trees grew, Don Manuel Alcaraz went to the forests, collected various samples of bark, and took them to Lima to Señor Lavalle, Marqués de Premio Real, who was a dealer in quinine bark. Señor Lavalle was convinced of the quality of the product, and he outfitted Alcaraz and numerous inhabitants of Huánuco to gather as much of this bark as they could. Furthermore, trained peasants from Loxa were sent to teach the people of Huánuco how they had collected in their own region. In 1778, as soon as the natives of Huánuco were skillful in the harvesting and drying of cascarilla, or quina bark, work began in earnest at the sites of Cuchero, Casape, Casapillo, and Cayumba. But this exploitation was carried out in disorder, resulting in serious destruction of the quina groves. In 1779, 50 to 75 thousand pounds of bark were exported yearly to Señor Lavalle.

This merchant, Señor Lavalle, increased his activities considerably in those first years, thanks to the advantageous contract he had made with the exploiters to pay them in Lima from 2½ to 5 pesos per 25 pounds, the highest price then paid for the bark. Then he made another contract that was more favorable to the producers, some of whom could recoup their earlier losses. From 1782 on, all sorts of people trafficked in quinine bark in Huánuco.

In 1788, when the botanists of our expedition left the region after two visits, seven species of quina were known, including three of interest to medicine: Peruviana fina, or true cascarilla cana fina; delgadilla fina of Pillao and Acomayo; and anteada fina, or amarilla boba fina, of Muña. One kind of quina bark is absolutely worthless, and another three kinds are of very little value: morada, azahar, and pata de gallareta.

Don Juan Tafalla, our successor who continued on after our return to Spain, discovered quinine trees in other localities in those extensive forests. He found four more species, two of which have medicinal properties: cascarilla fina of Chicoplaya, or quina de flor pequeña, and quina glandulosa. The other two, cascarilla de hoja aguda and ahorquillada, have no commercial value.

Finally, in 1800 another quina was received in Spain. Called quina de Huánuco, it is valued by dealers and apothecaries for its color, both inside and out, but is inferior to the five medicinally valuable types mentioned above because of its taste, which is not very bitter and is too astringent. For this reason, apothecaries use it and sell it by mixing it with quina calisaya [*Cinchona calisaya*], requesting the chemists with whom they do business to do the same. Thus some have come to believe that it is effective, but the effect is really due to the calisaya alone, for the same miraculous result is obtained from calisaya without mixing it with the woody, astringent quina de Huánuco. Furthermore, this quina de Huánuco never arrives pure, for bundles of it always have from two to seven different species mixed with it.

We botanists who traveled about in these forests witnessed the considerable waste that the bark gatherers left by not stripping all the bark from the stems and trunks because these parts did not have commercial value. Since this bark was not commercially acceptable only because it lacked a good inner surface and fluting, we suggested that an extract of its active substances be produced. An extract would necessarily be more profitable, especially since the surface of such bark was not so densely clad with lichens and other foreign bodies.

As soon as some of the producers in Huánuco had been taught the process of extracting from fresh bark, others followed their example and began to extract. Since that time, the extract of thousands of pounds of bark from these forests has been sold and used in Europe. When fresh bark is well worked and subjected to no more than two infusions and a brief boiling, the extract is highly prized.

At first the price of extract from fresh bark was from 1 to 5 pesos a pound, depending upon its relative purity and consistency. Since then, ignorance and greed have led to the production of much soft, impure, or burned extract, with its effective activity much reduced and its medicinal properties changed. This abuse should receive the government's most serious attention so that it can be corrected; otherwise this business, so interesting for Spain and so very important for mankind, will be lost.

Bread

Bread is not made in any village of the province, except in the city of Huánuco itself. Here they bake both wheat bread and French bread, very white and of excellent taste. Bread is often produced in the form of biscuits so that it may be taken to sell in the forested areas or other parts of the province.

Work of the Natives

The womenfolk make chichas, or very special winelike beverages, from the meal of germinated maize and from quinoa, pineapples, and the fruits of the molle (pepper tree). They also make up boxes of sweets from various kinds of fruit, to take to other provinces and sell. They help the menfolk with sowing and reaping in the fields. With plants and other substances they dye wool and cotton, which they later spin and weave, either alone or mixed with silk, into mantas and lliclias (kinds of shawls), ponchos, garters, handkerchiefs, towels, scarves, tablecloths, napkins, and other articles for their own use or for sale.

The men, in general, either carry out the work of tilling the fields or engage in the muleteer's trade, trafficking in coca, cascarilla or quina, fruits, seeds, and other local products. Some manufacture a local baize fabric or jerga (a coarse cloth for cloaks).

Diseases

In spite of the very mild climate of the valley, which we have already described, the people of Huánuco suffer from chavalongos (typhoidlike fevers) or tabardillos (spotted fever), some pains in the side, digestive disorders and diarrhea, smallpox throughout the year, and sometimes measles or other rashes.

Malaria bothers only those people who travel to Lima or other coastal regions and come back with the disease. In spite of the abundance of cascarilla or quina recently discovered in Huánuco's forests, nobody employed this specific remedy to treat tertian fevers (malaria) until, during our second trip there, we introduced the use of the extract, prescribing a dose of 2 drams. After taking a few such doses, the patients were completely cured of their fevers.

Mal del valle (valley sickness) or vicho, a type of dysentery, attacks women more often than men. They attribute this troublesome and dangerous ailment to the use of capsicum pepper, as well as to chronic or poorly treated venereal disease, such as the kind (syphilis) that is very widespread among the dirty and licentious portion of the population and causes purulent eruptions on the arms and legs. If this disease does not turn into a leprous condition, as sometimes happens, it leaves brownish blotches where the eruptions have been, and these last for years.

One frequently sees empiemas (purulent blisters), or the beginnings of scurvy, around the mouth. Indigestion and diarrhea are common among those who come from other provinces, but they are rapidly cured. People who spend long periods in the forest come out into the valley almost invariably pale and swollen, or bloated, with a condition locally called abombados (bulging) or auriflamados. This sickness does not cause death, but it is uncomfortable and of long duration. It is caused by salty and poorly preserved foods, and by the dampness absorbed by the body in such constantly wet regions where one suffers from excessive sweating.

Finally, goiter is very common in Huánuco. This tumor, or swelling, forms on the neck and grows so large that it becomes unsightly. Whole families suffer from it, and it is hereditary. It is not fatal, for many live with it from childhood to old age, but it is very uncomfortable because it interferes with movement of the head and with breathing.

Even dogs, hens, and swine have goiter. Its cause and its cure are unknown. It does not attack inhabitants of other provinces who come to live in Huánuco, nor do the offspring of such parents have it. If the father or mother suffers from it, the children, or most of them, will inherit it, as we observed in descendants of Europeans and creoles. There are people who have a goiter as large as their head; to carry this enormous weight, they use a kerchief or cap specially made for this purpose, tying it behind the neck.

The Indians and the poor treat their illnesses with herbs, administering them as they learned from their forefathers and in accordance with new observations they themselves make. The affluent are treated in Huánuco by the priests of San Juan de Dios and by the occasional doctor who, without even graduating from the hospitals in Lima, establishes himself there as though he were a great doctor of medicine.

There are four parishes in this province, two of which are in the city of Huánuco: one for Indians, another for Spaniards and others. A third parish is that of the village of Valle and its 10 dependencies.

The first of the dependencies of Valle is Chinchao, with 73 estates in a gorge 18 leagues long. Counting the faithful of Chinchao and of the two parishes of the city of Huánuco, as well as the workers who flock in from other regions to cultivate and harvest coca, which is the chief product of these estates, this gorge has a population of more than 1700 souls. The inhabitants of Chinchao receive spiritual sustenance on only 3 days of the year, when the priest and his assistant, or two curates, come to celebrate all the festivities of the year and to collect the assigned contributions.

A second dependency of Valle, 3 leagues away, is Acomayo; mass is said there on some religious holidays. A third dependency is Pillao, 8 leagues from Valle, where few masses are celebrated during the year. The inhabitants there generally die without spiritual consolation and are buried by their neighbors, with the Indian who usually serves as sacristan, or sexton, taking charge of the burial. A fourth dependency of Valle, 8 leagues away, is Panao, with a population of more than 200 Indians, hard-working and of average means. Until a few years ago they were served by the missionaries of Ocopa, and consequently are well educated in Christian morality, but now they are attached to the parish of Valle and deprived of the spiritual nourishment that they previously had every day.

Two curates, or substitute priests, are designated for the village of Valle itself and five more of its dependencies, each 2 or 3 leagues from Valle: Llacón; Pachacoto, or Quera; Churubamba; Pachabamba; and Pumacuchu. A tenth dependency of Valle is Cani, 7 leagues away; on religious holidays the inhabitants attend mass in Huacar.

The fourth parish in the province of Huánuco is Huacar, with four dependencies: Cayrán, Chaulán, Conchamarca, and Ñausa. Because a priest and two curates administer to the spiritual needs of these villages, the parishioners there are well served.

According to the last census, done in 1787, the number of inhabitants in the province of Huánuco, including all social classes, is 15,000.

CHAPTER 21

Description of the City of León de Huánuco de los Caballeros

Because the city of Huánuco (Figure 7), capital of the province of Huánuco, was founded and populated by caballeros (gentlemen) of nobility and by conquistadors, it is referred to as Huánuco de los Caballeros. The city is also called León de Huánuco because a crowned lion was used on its coat of arms in memory of the fact that Cristóbal Vaca de Castro, the governor who transferred the city to the valley where it is situated at the present time, was a native of León in Castile. After the Spanish inhabitants of Huánuco defeated the tyrant Francisco Hernández Girón, the king added to their coat of arms the body of Girón, standing, and the lion with one paw grasping the tyrant's chest and the other holding a chain around his neck. In addition to these emblems, he honored the city by calling it the "very noble and very loyal city of León de los Caballeros"; this took place when Marqués de Cañete was viceroy.

In 1539, when the tyrant Illatopa was wandering about and invading these parts, Marqués Don Francisco Pizarro sent out Captain Gómez de Alvarado against him. Having driven Illatopa off, the captain then founded a city in a place now called old Huánuco, where today one can see the ruins of that city and of fortifications that the pagans had built for their own defense. These fortifications, it is said, were the best ever constructed in Peru. The ruins are situated on an extensive pampa, or plain, more than 15 leagues long, in the province of Huamalíes. On this plain there are many veins of quartz crystals. Because of the cold climate it is a sterile area, sparsely covered with grass.

In the year 1541, when the delightful valley of Pillco was discovered, Captain Pedro Barroso moved the city of Huánuco to its new location in the valley. After the battle of Chupas, the lawyer Vaca de Castro, governor of Peru, sent Captain Pedro de Puelles to finish the task of settling inhabitants there. At first, because of the wealth that its earliest citizens possessed, Huánuco was one of Peru's most populous cities. During that period, 30 encomiendas (estates of land and inhabitants) were distributed among a similar number of noble and distinguished gentlemen. Of these, some died and others moved to Lima, and after a few years the city began its decline to the poverty seen today. At present the population of Huánuco barely exceeds 6000 souls, counting whites, mestizos, Indians, and cholos, and the number of negro and mulatto slaves is no more than 30.

The beautiful valley of Pillco lies along the highway from Lima, 65 leagues away, at 10° south latitude. The city of Huánuco is built in the middle of this beautiful plain, on the most advantageous point imaginable, where nothing interferes with its dominance. Far from being an obstacle, the mountains to the east and those that surround it on the west afford the city a very delightful diversion all through the year with their greenery and variety of flowers and fruits, and they are a veritable garden in the rainy season. Eight leagues long, the valley is a league across at its widest part, from one mountain range to the other.

The Pillco River waters the valley. It arises, as we have already stated, in Lake

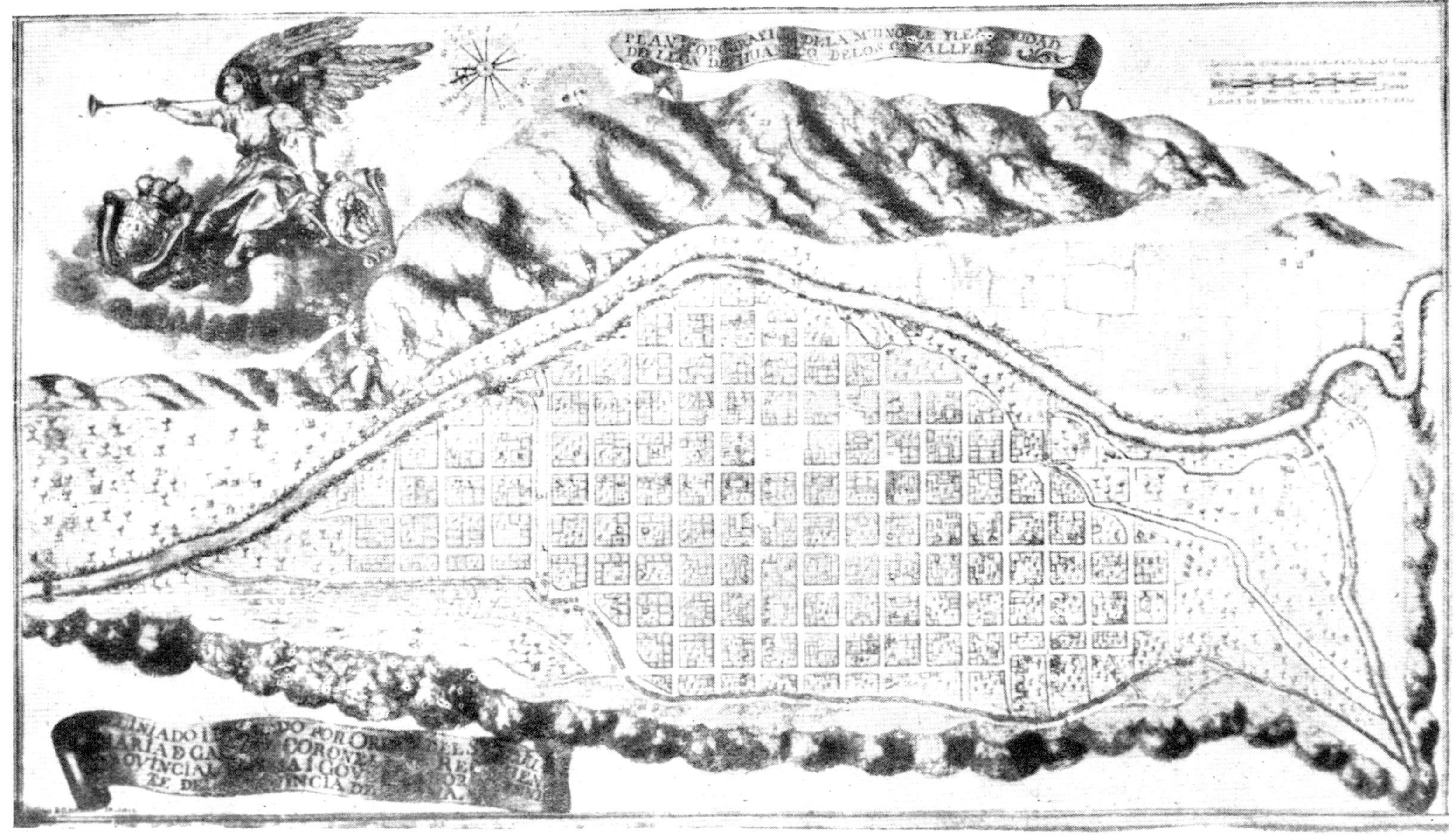

Figure 7. Map of the most noble and loyal city of Léon de Huánuco de los Caballeros, Peru, drawn by Isidro de Galvez; commissioned by Don Juan Maria de Galvez, Colonel of the regiment of Lima province, and Governor of Tarma province. From an original in the War Archives, Lima. (Courtesy of R. P. Rubén Vargas-Ugarte.)

Yauricocha, 21 leagues from Huánuco on the pampas of Bombón in the province of Tarma, and its volume is increased by the numerous rills and brooks that come down from the glens and ravines along the whole length of the valley. The river enters the forests of the Panatahuas near Pillao; it is navigable for 22 leagues from Huánuco, and a wharf is located 2 leagues from Cuchero. The Pillco forms the headwaters of the Huallaha River, which is a tributary of the Marañón, the largest river known in the world.

The city of Huánuco spreads out over 110 blocks; these, with 50 blocks more that are occupied by the suburbs and farm houses at the entrance and exit on the south and north sides, make up the 160 blocks of the street plan of Huánuco. It is rare indeed to find a house without its spacious orchard of fruit trees, plantings of vegetables, maize, or alfalfa, and little flower garden. The streets are straight, running from north to south and from east to west. They are cobbled in part, but generally receive little care and are filled with weeds, grass, and mud. This results from the indolence of the chief of waterworks, who has failed to repair the ditches that cross the city from east to west at every block. Because Huánuco is located on land that is higher than that on either side, the water overflows from breaks in the ditches and forms permanent puddles and mudholes along with tunnels and impenetrable tangles of plant growth.

Though the city's budget is more than 800 pesos a year, public works such as the municipal building, jail, and others are almost in ruins, and there is no evidence of the investment of such an annual sum. The city is divided into four districts: Iscuchaca, Huallayco, San Juan, and La Trinidad. The number of streets, not taking into account those of the suburbs and outlying farms, is 10 running north to south and an equal number running east to west. All are straight from end to end; some are named after the churches, monasteries, and hermitages that are located on them, and the rest are unnamed, except the street named Mercaderes.

Most houses are of one story, but some have two. Foundations are made of lime and pebbles, and the walls of crude adobe; sometimes a front wall is of mortared stone or brick. The interior is whitewashed with lime or plaster, or with white clay kneaded with the wool from a species of gigantones, or cactus, called chunapcapran. Roofs are constructed of the stems of magueys and cabuyas with reed or cane matting, forming a ridge that is covered with tiles manufactured in the city itself, as are bricks and the square tiles needed for floors.

The principal plaza is square, with the main church on one side and the municipal building and jail opposite; the other two sides are occupied by private dwellings. There are four smaller plazas, those of Santo Domingo, San Francisco, San Juan de Dios, and La Merced.

During our stay in Huánuco, as we shall explain below, a public walk lined with trees was built in the district of Huallayco, on the Carrera (Avenue) del Campo. This walk was six blocks in length, stretching from the chapel of Santiago to the river.

A stream running down the slopes of the mountain of Puelles supplies water to all the ditches that irrigate the gardens and orchards of the city.

Formerly, the chief magistrates of Huánuco held jurisdiction in the areas that later contained the provinces of Huamalíes, Huaylas, Conchucos, Chinchaycocha, Caxatambo, and Tarma. After the creation of the provinces, however, they retained only the authority of judges of appeal in the courts of first petition, along with the royal privilege of going to induct the chief magistrates of those provinces in their municipal buildings. By the time the intendencias (management districts of Peru) were established, all these privileges had ended, and today the subdelegate of Huánuco is inducted into office in the Villa de Tarma, it being the capital of that intendencia, or at the royal treasury in Pasco.

The secular city council is composed of 12 perpetual aldermen, one subdelegate, and two mayors, a first and a second named each year by the council; the first mayor is the one who was the second the previous year. The chief of waterworks and the attorney are named each year by the secular city council, as are the mayors and aldermen for the Indians.

There are two parishes in Huánuco: one for Spaniards, mestizos, and other social classes, and another for Indians only. The first, the principal church and most attended, is fitted out with 12 altars, an organ, and four bells. The other church has eight altars, an organ, and three bells.

There are five monasteries, those of Agustinos, Mercedarios, Franciscanos, Dominicanos, and San Juan de Dios; one beaterio (house of retreat for pious women); two hermitages, Santiago and Santa Rufina; and three parish chapels, San Juan, San Pedro, and San Sebastian.

The monastery of San Agustín is the best building of the city, but is much deteriorated at the present time. It has 11 altars, an organ, and three bells. At times it has as many as 16 monks, counting novices, choristers, and clergymen; most of these, however, are acting as assistants to priests of various orders.

The monastery of La Merced has as many monks as that of San Agustín and they are likewise distributed throughout the parishes as assistants to priests. There are no novices. The church has seven altars, an organ, and three bells.

The monastery of San Francisco has four monks who eat in the refectory, but occasionally one of them leaves to serve as a substitute priest. The church has 12 altars, an organ, four bells, and a little shrine at the doorway. Within the monastery there is a hostelry of the apostolic mission priests of Ocopa; here the director resides and sends out supplies and necessities to missionaries located in the last villages that border on the territory of barbarous Indians.

Two or three monks usually live in the monastery of Santo Domingo, which is in ruins, but sometimes there is only the prior and a lay brother. The church has nine altars, an organ, and three bells.

The monastery of San Juan de Dios has five lay brothers and a chaplain priest who provides spiritual nourishment for the sick whom they treat. In the chapel are five altars and two small bells.

In a hermitage or parish chapel there are three altars and one or two small bells.

In the beaterio (house of retreat) there are 12 lay sisters who may leave the congregation whenever they wish, but then they may never return to its fold. Though cloistered, the matron or mother superior may leave in the company of another sister on business of the beaterio. Men and women enter the cloister with the permission of the mother superior, accompanied by her and the servants until they leave by the main door. The sisters educate numerous girls in sewing and in primary lessons. For the spiritual support of these sisters, there is a chaplain; his salary is 1200 pesos, paid from funds left by the founder for the poorest priests of the city. The church has five altars, an organ, and three bells.

Notwithstanding the pleasant climate of the valley of Pillco, the city of Huánuco at the present time is in a poor, very deteriorated state compared with the opulence that characterized it in the past, even long after the suspension of the 30 encomiendas, or estates granted by the king, enjoyed by the early settlers. The causes of this decadence are numerous, varying with the period of time.

One recommendation that I would make for the rehabilitation of the city and the whole province of Huánuco, as well as of its neighbors, is to establish a residency in Huánuco for an intendente (manager, mayor) from Tarma. Another would be to relocate the royal treasury in Huánuco; it was moved to the inappropriate location of Pasco when silver mines were discovered in the Cerro de Yauricocha. My third recommendation would be to name a bishop to supervise and encourage proper spiritual nourishment, which today no inhabitant of that place has, and thus avoid the unfortunate happenings that occur there at the present time.

These frontier forest areas would be populated if there were an intendente and a bishop. The inhabitants would be assured of fair justice, would happily work in the forests, would till and cultivate the soil—all without the opposition of those in power who now make such work impossible. Moreover, if the royal treasury was in Huánuco, the miners of the Cerro de Yauricocha and the mine owners of Huallanca would go there to melt their silver into bars. Having enjoyed for a time the pleasant climate, so much healthier than that of Pasco, they would return to their mines loaded with fruit, seeds, coca, and numerous other products indispensable to their workers. Thus in Huánuco they would leave considerable money, a scarce commodity nowadays in that fertile province.

Perhaps some of the mines, abandoned for lack of laborers, would benefit by way of repopulating the city and the valley. And other mines, richer and of greater interest to commerce and to the king, might be put into operation. Finally, the jungles of those regions would be populated through the incentives of collecting cascarilla, or quina bark, and preparing its extract: more bark could be gathered, and with greater ease.

The cultivation of cacao, coffee, and indigo could be undertaken on a large scale, and trade could be initiated for many plants of medicinal value as well as those useful for dyeing and other arts. These would include the roots of chinaroot, sarsaparilla, rhatany, contrayerba or bejuco de la estrella (star liana), yallhoy (*Monnina polystachia*), and calaguala; the balsams, gums, and resins of copaiba (*Copaifera* species), white balsam, anime, carana, aceyte (aceite) de María, and Peruvian incense; and the fruits of vanilla, ispino, and pinoli. There are also many other animal, vegetable, and mineral products that abound in the vastness of those virgin, fertile jungles.

Character and Nature of the Indians

[According to Ruiz himself, the following paragraph was not to be included in the final copy; it appears only in the rough copy.—Translator]

The present nature and capabilities of the Indians, not only of the province of Huánuco but of the other parts of Peru, have been molded probably in great part by the harsh treatment that these people have received at the hands of the wealthy land owners whose purpose has been to enrich themselves by the sweat of the natives. The Indian hates the European and the white creole; he suspects and distrusts them and even comes to lack confidence in himself. He is lazy or slow in his work. Though oftentimes vigilant in his business transactions, he does not try to enrich himself, but works only enough to eke out a miserable existence. He does not seek honor or dignity or any employment; it would be all the same to him to be a mayor or a constable or a servant. He yearns for novelty, admiring everything. He ponders every problem long and deeply. He tries to cheat and imagines himself cheated. Though surrounded by abundance, he has nothing. He is interested in trinkets, and covets them. He gives little in order to ask for much. He makes haste to collect what is due him but not to pay what he owes. He is an enemy of the truth and is tricky in every way, though he looks innocent. He thinks that he can do more than he really can. He treats his wife like a slave and his mistresses like great ladies. He takes work not because he ought to, but merely for what it gives him at the moment. He gives no thanks for any gift, for he believes that it was given with some ulterior motive, and in this he may not be wrong. He respects nothing but harshness. He sleeps in lust. When entreated he draws away, and when given an order he feigns fatigue. He hates whosoever befriends him, likes no one, and treats even his own kind badly. He generally sleeps dressed. To gain his own ends, he shows cowardice and more misery than he really has. He speaks ill of everything. He affects being devout, yet persists in his idolatry, confusing ceremony with religious worship. He is superstitious. He fears the devil because, according to his belief, the devil wreaks him harm, but generally does not complain about this evil spirit under any circumstances. He makes his devotions a third party to his drunken orgies. He uses drunkenness as an excuse for disputes and deaths, for when intoxicated he is quarrelsome and reckless. He looks for the mysterious in everything he sees. If the word of God be preached, he hardly pays any attention to it. When he seems to be praying, he is often just murmuring. He sometimes lies during confession, will generally perjure himself, and denies what he sees. He occasionally will sell his oath or receive a bribe, and when he dies he leaves them to his relatives for collection. He lives by drink alone, and his diet is poor in the extreme. He sleeps without care. He falls ill as would an animal and recovers in the same way. He breaks faith with his testament and, holding little value on life, he has no fear of death.

Those who live in Huánuco assert that on many nights, in various parts of the city, they see a clear light proceeding along the streets as though from a burning candle. They also say that when it is pursued by someone on foot or on horseback it floats up into space and disappears, usually near a church. I have not seen this light, though I have wandered about at all hours of the night in search of it. I wanted to convince some of these superstitious souls that such a light is natural and nothing but a will-o'-the-wisp, originating from animal matter, which arises from graveyards or other places where there is phosphorescent material.

On the 21st of May 1780, we started our botanical trips in the environs of Huánuco. We continued until the 2nd of July, when we left for the forests of Cuchero. After we returned to the city, we collected plants from September to the 22nd of March 1781 in the glens, mountains, slopes, and ravines of the whole province. During those two periods of time we discovered, gathered, studied, and described the following species, most of which were also illustrated in their natural colors.

Salvia alba, *S. racemosa*, and *S. nodosa*, commonly called socconche. An infusion of any of these three species is employed as a carminative (relieving colic or flatulence), an antiepileptic, or a digestive.

Calceolaria bicolor, *C. dentata*, *C. verticillata*, *C. viscosa*, and *C. pinnata*, called mancapaqui. *Verbena hispida*. *Piper angustifolium*, moho-moho; *P. lineatum*. *Allionia incarnata*. *Callisia repens*. *Acaena amentifolia*. *Buddleja diffusa*. *Calyxhymenia viscosa*. *Spermacoce pilosa* and *S. tenuior*, uspica. *Heliotropium incanum*, *H. lanceolatum*, and *H. parvicalycum*. *Varronia crenata*.

Rauvolfia flexuosa, turucassa; in the morning hours the flowers of this plant breathe out a very pleasant fragrance that permeates the air for a considerable radius. Some people use the branches of this shrub to make small crosses, the arms being formed by its spines.

Psychotria hirsuta. *Solanum angustifolium*, *S. dichotomum*, *S. diffusum*, and *S. spicatum*. *Sessea stipulata*.

Datura stramonium, tonco-tonco or chamico. The name chamico is well known all over Peru because of the criminal use that Indians make of its seeds to intoxicate one another when they feel that they have been wronged, or when they are overtaken by jealousy in a love affair. This practice has given rise to the common Peruvian adage applied whenever a person is pensive, taciturn, or absent-minded, or else too tipsy from drink or other causes: Está chamicado ó chamicada fulano ó fulana (so-and-so is under the influence of chamico).

While we were in Huánuco, it happened that a 10-year-old boy gave powdered seeds of chamico in a piece of bread to a schoolmate, another boy the same age. Within a few hours it began to exercise its narcotic effect, as though the boy had taken wine. Dombey was called in by the boy's parents to administer some remedy, but the boy remained in a permanent stupor in spite of the emetics and other medicines that Dombey prescribed. Before the poisoning he had been intelligent, keen, mischievous, and full of fun in boyhood games, but his former personality was lost forever.

This plant grows in the streets of Huánuco in such abundance that, after this happened, the chief magistrate ordered it all pulled up by the roots and burned. The order was carried out at that time, but upon our second return to Huánuco we found the streets and outskirts of the city just as full of chamico as before.

The natives apply the crushed leaves and seeds of chamico in a poultice to treat piles, with excellent effect. Some people drink the infusion of a few leaves to relieve pain in urinating, or irritation of the skin caused by bitter or strong purgatives. The crushed leaves, mixed with vinegar, are frequently applied as a poultice to the spine or kidneys to reduce fever, relieve rheumatic pain, or bring down the swelling of a hernia.

Achyranthes obovata, yerba del moro hembra (female Moorish herb); *A. rigida*, yerba del moro macho (male Moorish herb). Both species are used in a decoction to stop bleeding; crushed with salt, they are applied to heal sores or scars, with a change of poultice every 24 hours. Finally, these herbs are also used to treat splinter wounds caused by the calyces of the same plants entering the feet of natives who go barefoot; these two species are so common in Huánuco that the plazas and streets are literally paved with them.

Celosia conferta, called yerba de la sangre (blood plant) because of the hemostatic properties of its juice or of a decoction of its tuberous roots. *Eryngium caeruleum*. *Sanicula canadensis*. *Periphragmos uniflorus* and *P. flexuosus*. *Cestrum undulatum*, miu; this plant has the same uses and properties as yerba hedionda (stinking plant). *Gentiana serrata*, *G. minutissima*, and *G. luteo-purpurea*. *Lycium spathulatum*.

Chenopodium dulce, quinoa dulce (sweet quinoa); *C. amarum*, quinoa amarga (bitter quinoa). The young, tender plants, eaten as cooked greens, are called yuyus or yuyus de quinoa. The seeds are extensively utilized in Peru as a food much like rice, and for making chicha de quinoa (a fermented drink).

Narcissus odorus, amancas. This beautiful ornamental plant is more plentiful in Lima and Chancay than in Huánuco. *Loranthus puniceus*, liga.

Agave americana, called pita (thread, fiber), ancaschampaccra, or maguey mexicano (Mexican maguey, century plant). This pita, abundant in ravines and valleys throughout the province, is used to build impregnable fences around farms and orchards, and stockades for all kinds of domestic animals. Indians use an infusion or decoction of the roots to cure rheumatic and venereal pains, drinking it in large doses. The stems, usually 8 or 10 yards long, have a basal circumference of 3 quartas (cuartas, handspans) and taper towards the tip. They are used as beams for roofing houses; though spongy or pithy within, they withstand the weight put upon them. The stems are not attacked by insects, and the pith makes good tinder. Fiber is taken from the fleshy leaves, for several uses. These leaves also yield a honey, or extract, which is excellent for cleansing and healing sores. The honey, as it is called locally, is made by half-roasting the leaves, squeezing the juice out while they are still hot, and then boiling the extract down to the thickness of soft honey. This is applied, without any other agent, to cure not only sores on people, but also ulcers on beasts of burden and wounds on their head or feet. Padre Acosta calls this maguey a marvelous tree because of the many useful products that are made from it: wine, brandy, vinegar, honey, syrup, oil, needles, thread, and twine.

Yucca laevia and *Y. scabra*, called cabullas (cabuyas, cord plants) or magueyes del país (native magueys). Fiber for various uses is obtained from these two plants, just as from the Mexican maguey (century plant). Their stems are used throughout the province for roofing houses. When the outer woody layer of a stem is removed, the heart can be used as tinder; the ends must be burned a bit beforehand so the spark from the flint will kindle it more readily. The pith is also an excellent substitute for cork in making stoppers for bottles, jugs, and other vessels.

Coccoloba carinata, called mullaca or muyaca, is used to treat urinary ailments, as mentioned in our discussion of Tarma. *Cardiospermum biternatum*. *Bauhinia rosea* and *B. aculeata*. *Banisteria fulgens*. *Clethra ferruginea*. *Tribulus maximus*. *Triumfetta subtriloba* and *T. lappula*.

Cuphea ciliata, yerba de la culebra (snake plant). Natives employ a decoction or infusion of this plant to relieve fatigue. *Pineda incana*, lloqui; its strong stems are good for making canes and walking sticks. *Prunus virginiana*, cerezo (cherry); having been introduced from other provinces, this cherry is cultivated in numerous orchards in Huánuco. *Lantana purpurea*. *Bignonia caerulea*.

Jacaranda caerulea, yarabisco; this is a showy tree when in flower. Natives often use the bark to prepare antivenereal and antirheumatic decoctions. The wood is used to make cups in which the natives keep water that they are wont to drink, when desired, in great quantities; they are persuaded that this water has the same virtues as a decoction or infusion of the bark. The powdered leaves are excellent for healing sores after cleansing.

Ruellia ciliata. *Tecoma pentagona*; this tree, very beautiful when in flower, is always abundantly leafy in the province of Huánuco. *Gardoquia striata*, called socconche or pichuisa. *Alonsoa linearis*. *Mimulus subumbellatus*. *Horminum*? *triangulare*.

Lepidium foetidum, known as chichiccara, huanaccara, or mastuerzo silvestre. This herb is frequently employed to treat mal del valle (valley sickness); it is rubbed vigorously in water that is then administered as an enema. Crushed and warmed slightly, the herb is applied as a poultice to cleanse and treat cancerous ulcers. Crushed and mixed with lard, it is applied to the abdomen to relieve swelling brought on by delayed menstruation.

Malva aspera and *M. incana*. *Urena triloba* and *U. biserrata*. *Sida incana*. *Melochia plicata*. *Indigofera argentea*. *Lathyrus incanus*. *Scorzonera ciliata*; *S. peruviana*, the species of escorzonera (viper grass) that is used in Peru as an officinal drug.

Eupatorium scabrum and *E. sagittatum*. *Cineraria perforata*. *Tessaria integrifolia*, pájaro bobo (stupid bird). *Cosmos trifida*. *Vermifuga corymbosa*, called chinapaya, contrayerba, or matagusanos (worm killer). This plant is used extensively in Peru as a poultice applied to the maggot-infested sores and wounds of beasts. *Silphium dichotomum*. *Aster lanuginosus* and *A. lyratus*. *Tagetes integrifolia*, chinchi.

Pectis trifida, known as asccapichana, escoba amarga (bitter broom), or canchalagua cimarrona (wild canchalagua). A low plant, it is extremely bitter and acts as a febrifuge and a tonic for the stomach. Natives use an infusion of it to reduce malarial fevers.

Molina ferruginea, palmito. *Zinnia pauciflora*. *Lobelia hirsuta*, *L. biserrata*, *L. purpurea*, and *L. subpetiolata*. *Viola bicolor* and *V. purpurea*. *Tacsonia subtripartita*. *Ayenia pimpinellaefolia*. *Sycios cirrosa*, calabaza cimarrona (wild calabash). *Bryonia cordifolia*. *Urtica rugosa*. *Phyllanthus niruri*. *Croton nudum*.

Ricinus communis, higuerilla del país (native castor-oil plant); *R. ruber*, higuerilla mexicana (Mexican castor-oil plant). In Huánuco the seeds of both species yield abundant oil, which is used for lighting in houses and for the lamps in churches. The oil is also applied to external tumors to draw out infection.

Dioscorea acuminata. *Mimosa expansa*. *Cavalleria ferruginea*. *Acrosticum acutum*. *Polypodium acanthifolium*, *P. acutifolium*, *P. dichotomum*, *P. furcatum*, *P. racemosum*, *P. trilobum*, and *P. volubile*. *Pteris bipartita*, *P. auriculata*, *P. crenata*, and *P. curvata*. *Asplenium salicifolium*. *Adiantum brachiatum* and *A. trapeziforme*. *Hemionitis falcata*. *Trichomanes fimbriatum* and *T. interruptum*. *Lycopodium nutans*, *L. peregrinum*, and *L. prostratum*. *Marchantia polymorpha*.

CHAPTER 22

Trip to the Forests of Cuchero

Hardly 4 days after I got up from bed after an attack of spotted fever that had struck me down early in June, I made all the arrangements to leave for the forests on the 2nd of July with the two artists. We were following my two botanical colleagues, who had set out the day before. We traveled 3 leagues that first day, with considerable discomfort because of my weakness.

On the 3rd of July we left early in the morning and crossed a high, narrow slope, dangerous because the pathway up was of sharp rock and very rugged. We then came onto a road clothed on both sides with bushes and plants, which made the way very pleasant. This road continued to the village of Acomayo, situated at the entrance to the ravine where the summit of the mountain begins. At a short distance past this Indian village we spent the night under a boulder, where the three of us could hardly fit. We sat all through the night without a wink of sleep because of the ceaseless roar of the rushing brook and the incessant croaking of the infinite number of little frogs that breed in its waters.

At break of day the mule drivers left to bring in the animals, and they found one mule dead. It had languished because its feet had been tied together for grazing. We therefore had to send to Acomayo to fetch another animal.

We traveled about a league and a half through a trail full of brambles, creepers, and other weeds growing across the path from one side to the other. We had to pick our way carefully to avoid falling and getting hurt or being cut to pieces by the spines and prickles of the plants. We found very many deer grazing there without fear of being bothered or hunted.

Half a league onwards, we entered thick woods, on a trail full of ruts and holes; in such a place it is absolutely necessary to let the animals go along at their pleasure. The rider has nothing to do except be careful not to get entangled in the branches of trees obstructing the path. This is why those who go into the jungle areas almost always go on foot, even though they take their beasts of burden, and they go barefoot because of the mud that is permanent in these places.

On the same day we climbed up the high and difficult peak of Carpis, but only with great effort because of the narrowness and depth of the road and because of the high steppingstones, endless bogs, and deep holes that are always found in these passes. Ancient trees fall across the road nearly every day and interrupt transit along these paths, so travelers must carry axes and machetes when leading animals.

At two o'clock in the afternoon we arrived at a tambo, which is a flat, cleared area with a small shelter made of branches and ferns. There travelers can spend the night or take refuge when it rains too heavily.

First Discovery of Quina

In this locality I discovered and described *Cinchona purpurea*, called cascarilla or quina morada (purple quinine tree), the first that I had examined up to that time. At four in the afternoon we entered the village of Chinchao; there, fatigued from that bad road and our sleepless nights, we managed to rest a bit.

On the 5th of July we left Chinchao at eight in the morning. As a result of the rainstorm the night before, the road had become impassable. The mules could not walk without slipping continuously, though some were so skillful that they put their two front feet together and purposely allowed themselves to slide down on sloping ground. Adding to the difficulties of the road itself were the tangles of branches hindering progress, the narrowness of the hillside paths, and the constant climbing uphill and down. We traversed numerous coca farms, for coca is the only plant cultivated commercially in the gorge of Chinchao. The other crops sown are destined exclusively for home consumption, supplementing the food supply brought in from Huánuco. We slept on the Rosapata estate.

On the 6th, at two in the afternoon, we arrived at Cuchero after a trip filled with physical exertion and falls, for the road is now in much worse condition than formerly. The five of us, along with our servants, slept that night in the tiny shelter that my colleague Pavón and Mr. Dombey had occupied the day before. Both Pavón and Dombey told us of the many hardships and mishaps that they, like ourselves, had experienced along the road.

CHAPTER 23

Description of Cuchero

Twenty-six leagues from the city of Huánuco, towards the north, the village of Cuchero is located on a small, level shelf on a mountain. It is dominated by other heights, much more rugged and all covered with large trees, bushes, lianas or vines, and endless other plants of various sizes. This vegetation occupies the ground completely, leaving not the slightest clearing for pastures or farms.

The village of Cuchero occupies a space barely 300 yards long and 50 wide. In this area there are only 11 huts or shelters, with a tiny church and its dwelling for the missionary. This missionary formerly had under his spiritual care twice the current number of Indians. Half of them, however, were recent converts who could not live in Cuchero on foods other than the maize and yuca that they grew in a few small patches on the east side of the village. The missionary, Fray Juan Sugráñez, transferred them 2 years ago to a more appropriate location, where he founded the new village of San Antonio de Chicoplaya.

The quina-bark gatherers, who stayed in the village of Cuchero, then divided the huts among themselves after the other Indians had left for the new settlement. Thus the huts deserted in the old village now serve the bark gatherers as storehouses and shelters.

At Cuchero there is but one entrance and one exit, on a straight road running from north to south to the port. The Pillco River is 2 short leagues down the slope. Here it is a sizable river, for its volume is swollen by waters contributed by the Conchumayo, Cascay, Acomayo, Yanamayo, Panao, Santo Domingo, and Chacahuassi rivers, and many streamlets that come down from all the forested heights around. Half a league from the port of Cuchero, the Pillco River is joined by the Chinchao; another league down, by the Cayumba; and 5 leagues further on, by the Monzón. Continuing through the Pampahermosa region and the village of Lamas, the Pillco grows steadily in size until, near the village of Laguna, it joins the famous Marañón River. In this, its lower course, it is known as the Huallaha (Huallaga).

The Indians of the Pampahermosa go up this river by canoe to the port of Cuchero, a hundred leagues distant, in about 8 days, or 12 at the most; they take only 4 days to return. The Lamista Indians need 2 or 3 months to go up to Cuchero, and they return to Lamas in 20 days, more or less. The Indians trade in some coarse cotton fabrics, tobacco, cacao, parrots, monkeys, magpies, resins, barks, woods, roots, balsams, and medicinal seeds. They also sell the poison (curare) used for shooting game with the zarbatana, or blowgun, for these Indians are extraordinarily skillful in its use.

Poison for Hunting

The Indians make this poison from various lactiferous vines or lianas, preparing and boiling them into a solid extract that is kept in cane or reed tubes. To use this extract, they soften it in the milk of the skin of yuca root, or *Jatropha manihot*, which is plentiful in cultivated plots in these forested areas and valleys of Peru.

Yuca is grown for its tuberous root, which is eaten either boiled or baked. The roots are also used to make an excellent starch or, in some places, a bread called cazabe (cassava cake). An infusion of yuca leaves is used among these people as a bath to treat edematous inflammation.

How Blowguns Are Made and Used

These Indians make their blowguns from the wood of the chonta palm, which is black and extremely hard. They first prepare two half tubes, using fine sand to polish the inner surface as smooth as the bore of a gun. Then they join the two halves neatly, winding them with pita (thread, agave fiber) to make a perfect tube about 7 feet long. The outside is tarred over with various resins, and two tusks of a wild boar or of some other animal are placed near the mouthpiece and precisely adjusted so that no air escapes when the tube is blown to shoot the dart.

The dart is a sliver of cana brava (reed grass) the size of a darning needle, pointed at the tip and fitted out at the other end, or base, with cotton rolled into a little ball just about the diameter of the bore of the blowgun. This cotton causes the dart to fly out violently when the gun is blown, and the dart can take its direction with the same force and without any deviation, straight to its target.

Activity of the Poison and Its Method of Taking Effect

The strength of the poison used is such that it begins immediately to stop the circulation of blood in any bird or animal. To shoot monkeys, the Indians try to break and then again straighten the tip of the dart, for these animals pull the darts out of their bodies so quickly that the poison has no time to take effect. Unless some vital organ is wounded, the animal will not die if the tip of the dart does not remain embedded in the flesh, regardless of how deeply the dart penetrates its body. But if the tip has been bent or broken, the monkey breaks the dart apart when he pulls it out; since the tip remains in the flesh, the poison works efficiently, and the animal falls to the ground beneath the tree. These people eat birds and other animals shot with this poison without the slightest indication of harmful effect to themselves.

On the 9th of this month three tobacco-revenue agents, accompanied by the missionary of Cuchero, set off on this river. They journeyed to Lamas with the purpose of establishing the shipping of tobacco to Cuchero by river, and its transport from there to Huánuco and Lima by mule. A few days after these agents had set out, an official arrived in Cuchero with the countermand that they should all return to Lima without carrying out their previous commission. Thus it would seem that the project of bringing tobacco out from Lamas by river will not be put into effect. In reality, setting up this fluvial transport would have provided a prime motive for the establishment of settlements along the whole stretch of river to Lamas, as well as fostered a sizable trade in quinas, cacao, balsams, gums, resins, barks, woods, seeds, and various fruits abundant in these extensive and fertile jungles.

The climate of Cuchero is always mild. During the day the temperature is 75 to 79°F (24 to 26°C), at night falling 13 to 18°F at the most. Nevertheless, this region has the reputation of being unhealthy, as do all jungle localities where heat, humidity, and stuffiness prevail. There is constant exhalation, especially at night, of nitrogenous and carbonic gases from plants, from decaying vegetable matter, and from bogs and other wet places. As all this contributes to increased transpiration, excessive amounts of water are drunk, breathing is difficult, and the unfortunate inhabitants of such places become bloated and wan. No less harmful to the health of these people is the contaminated water they drink, as well as the foods they eat; their diet is reduced to salted meat, maize, yuca, peas, and beans. They also suffer because they wear no shoes and use little clothing. In this wet climate they wear a sort of undershirt and knee trousers of tocuyo, a kind of thin baize cloth, and they sleep in the same clothes after having worked and sweated in them all day long.

Near Cuchero there are two small springs of fresh water. The water from one of these is piped in to Cuchero by a conduit made of trunks of the tree called tacuna, a species of *Cecropia*. The trunks are split lengthwise to form half tubes, and then it is merely necessary to remove the internal woody partitions that close off the hollow trunk at its articulations. A large amount of clear, fresh water is oftentimes found inside tacuna trunks, and travelers sometimes take it to quench their thirst when no other water is at hand. I have never seen evidence that it is harmful.

There is no grass in Cuchero or anywhere in the vicinity. Because the ground everywhere is covered with forests of very tall trees, shrubs, and smaller plants, the Indians keep no animals except chickens and swine for their own use.

The forests abound in parrots, magpies, wild turkeys and chickens, birds called pájaros arrieros, large doves called pájaros vacas, and various nocturnal birds with a sad song or cackle, such as those known as almas perdidas (lost souls), as well as owls and bats. The bats are very harmful to beasts of burden that spend the night in these places, for they bite repeatedly, principally on the neck, sucking the blood of the animals and also leaving them weakened by the loss of blood that flows from the wounds. There are also numerous small birds with musical and pleasant songs: golden orioles, nightingales, thrushes, hummingbirds of different sizes, and birds of seven colors. Above all, there is the bird called organista (organist), which is fascinating with its warbles and trills; if its song were long instead of short, probably no other bird could compare with it in melody. The organista, the size of a canary, lives on the berries of various species of *Melastoma* that are abundant in the region.

In the forests of Cuchero one encounters some wild boars, bears, monkeys, a species of hare called mischus, armadillos, wild dogs called casonas, wildcats, and opossums. There is also the huayhua, a species of weasel little larger than a house mouse, though longer and more rapid in all its movements. It is brownish along the back and saffron yellow on the abdomen, with a large and bushy tail. The huayhua is easily tamed and is a terrible enemy of mice. I kept one for more than 4 months; if put under my shirt, it would crawl all over my body beneath my clothing without doing any harm. It jumped from the floor to my table to eat. It died when someone accidentally trod upon it.

Ants, horseflies, mosquitoes, and various other small insects abound, and there are numerous small butterflies. Of the three species of bees there, two make very good honey and wax, especially the larger one. Slightly larger than the bee of Spain, from which it differs in having no sting, it deposits its honeycombs in the ground, or sometimes in the rotten trunk of an old tree. The other of these two bees is very small, the size of an ordinary ant. The third bee, black and resembling an ant, does sting and causes a swelling that smarts unbearably for several hours.

Natives say there are snakes as long as 6 yards in the glens near the river. I saw but four little ones and the skins of two large ones that the missionary Fray Juan Sugráñez showed me as soon as I arrived in Cuchero.

On the Rosapata estate I collected a viper, locally called flamón. Though slow in its movements, it is greatly feared by the natives because of the strength of its poison, for the bite of one of these snakes brings on acute pain and swelling in all parts of the body. To escape death, which these people say occurs within 40 hours, they use human excrement diluted with urine or water, drunk and applied externally immediately after the bite. This is, without a doubt, a loathsome remedy, but it is analogous to the volatile alkali employed in similar cases in Europe. The skin of this viper measured 2 yards in length after it was stuffed; I have seen another that was 3½ yards long. Its thickness was slightly less than that of the average wrist, and it was dark gray along the back and darker on the belly, with bright white transverse lines. The head was wide and flattened, and the mouth like that of a toad, with each jaw bearing a single set of curved teeth, all equal except for the larger and more curved fangs. The eyes were lifeless, and the tail measured 6 or 8 fingers in length and was round like the rest of the body. When the Indians saw me take up this snake and cut off its head in order to skin it, they fled a long way from me, crying out that the snake's poison would kill me. But very shortly they were convinced that they were wrong, and were astonished at the work I was doing.

Among the myriad trees and other beautiful plants that clothe those forests, there is an infinite number of cascarillas, or quinas. These produce the cascarilla, or Peruvian quina, most valued in medicine. The quina trees are especially abundant in the Casape, Casapillo, Cayumba, San Cristóbal, and other mountains; in these areas they grow to be huge. There are trees as tall as 30 or 40 yards, with girth and crown in proportion to the height.

To live in Cuchero, one must bring in supplies from Huánuco or elsewhere, for there is naught to be had in Cuchero or on the estates in that long Quebrada de

Cocales (gorge of coca plantations). During the month that we remained in Cuchero, we had much work to do. Since we were not familiar with the country, we took the advice of the natives and imported the most ordinary of foodstuffs that form their diet all year long, and we did not supply ourselves with those articles that could have supplemented our subsistence. We had to eat salted meats, half rotten; maize, boiled in the grain; and roast yuca instead of bread.

False Alarm of an Attack by Barbarous Indians

We had barely finished the month of our residence in Cuchero when, on the 1st of August 1780, after prayers, one of the peasant workers of the quina-bark gatherers, Salinas by name, raised his voice to shout that we were surrounded by more than 3000 chunchos, or barbarous Indians, who wear the black and white cusma, or tunic. In his declaration Salinas assured us that he had seen them, half an hour before sunset, in the cultivated fields of the mayor, Minaya, and that many of the Indians were up in the treetops studying the lay of the land.

This sudden happening, at such an hour, surprised all of us who were gathered there, and Mr. Dombey and Pavón felt obliged to leave the village by the road to Huánuco, the darkness of the night notwithstanding. The night was indeed dark, with a dense fog that had risen during the prayer hour and had flowed in and around all the mountains and through the gorges. The road, clogged with weeds and full of mud, was one series of puddles and precipices. To no avail, we voiced an opinion in conference together: that we should spend the night in the village instead of setting out at such an inappropriate hour, and that we should leave it in the morning hours all together, each with his arms and manuscripts, in the direction of Casapillo. Dombey and Pavón, guided by a boy, left ahead of Gálvez and Brunete who, not knowing the road, shouted to them in order to follow. But when Dombey and Pavón did not answer the calls, Gálvez and Brunete shouted to me that they had stopped and were resting above the water canal, having decided to spend the night there so that they could follow the road in the morning until they caught up with their companions. Since this would be difficult and dangerous because of the others' head start, Gálvez and Brunete then decided to remain in the village with me. They were convinced that not one of the peasants was to be trusted, even those with the best conduct, as we saw later.

Thirty people remained in Cuchero. We resolved that one of those who knew the country best should set out for Casape to bring the people who lived there, with all their arms, to defend the village from the barbarians, should they attack. Little more than an hour later, he came back with 15 men, all armed with knives; there were no more than two sabers among them. Among the 45 of us there were three firearms. One had a bad flint, broken after the first several shots, and no ramrod because it had become entangled with the plug of powder, so the gun had to be fired into the air to empty the barrel. Another was a rusty barrel without a lock, and to fire it the mayor had to use a firebrand (burning piece of wood) and place the charge in the touchhole. The third firearm was in excellent condition and ready.

Nevertheless, we shot several times with each gun, knowing that the barbarians fear firearms very much.

The bark gatherers, the peasant workers, our servants, and we ourselves made ready the other weapons, which were just six sabers, four swords, numerous machetes, and each of us armed with a knife and our courage. We spent the night on watch, some gambling, others resting, and the three of us doing sentinel duty at the exit gate so that no one could escape. Only two men tried to flee, at four in the morning, and we detained them until we knew that the news had been completely false and invented by the said Salinas in order to rob us.

Towards dawn we went to draw water from the river and were astonished by the swift descent of the fog and the great slowness with which it rose, and then its repeated descent and rise. It is an amusing phenomenon, and one worthy of observation because of the speed with which the mist flows down all the ravines, like the falling of a curtain in the theater. All of us became more worried as morning came on, for we were aware that the barbarians usually attack at that time. Once assured of the falseness of the news, however, we stood staring at one other like Don Quixote and Sancho in the adventure of the fulling mills.

In spite of having regained our peace of mind, we made arrangements to leave Cuchero the next day with a mule driver who was taking a number of boxes of food to the bark gatherers.

Mr. Dombey and Pavón took more than 4 hours to get to Casapillo, though that ranch is but a little more than half a league from Cuchero. They suffered great hardships on that bad road, for the darkness of night and the precipices and ruts along the way forced them to proceed mostly on all fours. Sunk up to their knees, they could hardly get out of some of the deep mudholes. The boy who was guiding them did not know his right hand from his left, and he was often completely mistaken on the path, so they were frequently in danger of falling over cliffs or down steep slopes. The three fugitives entered Casapillo at midnight, covered with mud from head to foot, and worn out and weary with sweat and thirst.

The managers and ranch hands at Casapillo were no less surprised than we had been at the reports that my companions gave them. They became alarmed and set up sentinel duty all the rest of the night, shooting from time to time towards the Cuchero road. They thus might have killed one of the peasants who fled from Casape; as he himself later recounted, one of the shots passed right in front of his face.

The following day, as soon as dawn had come, Dombey and Pavón sent two men with one of the managers of Casapillo to inquire after us. All during the night, the subject of their conversation had been our unhappy fate and how, if only we had left Cuchero, we could have escaped from the barbarians.

Since the manager of Casapillo, Juan de Mata, had informed me that Dombey and Pavón were not going to come back to Cuchero but planned to leave for Huánuco, I arranged to use the 12 horses that had just arrived with food for the bark gatherers. When we had loaded them with our baggage and the expedition gear, we left Cuchero at three o'clock in the afternoon on the 2nd of August. We made the trip entirely on foot and with great difficulty; the road was in poor condition and uphill all the way to the estate of Maychaynio, or Rosapata, where we all five spent the night of the 3rd. We had joined Dombey and Pavón on the morning of the 3rd, in the shelter that we made on the 2nd a little beyond Casapillo.

On the 4th, when Dombey and Pavón had been fitted out with horses, they left for Huánuco, leaving their baggage in Cuchero in the care of their servants until they should send for it from Huánuco. I stayed for another month with the artists in the village of Chinchao, continuing my discoveries of new plants and other work.

When my companions arrived in Huánuco, the inhabitants there became alarmed, and a report spread all the way to Lima that the three of us who had remained in Chinchao had been killed by barbarians invading our territory. This report made it necessary for Don Simon Govea, commander of these outlying forest areas, to dispatch Lieutenant Francisco Señas to the region to find out what had happened and to take whatever steps were needed to hold the pagans in check. After Señas arrived in Chinchao, we told him the truth about the fraudulent story and plot of Salinas, and he then returned to Huánuco to inform the commander of all that had happened. With his return, all were reassured in Huánuco, and later in Lima.

During our stay in Cuchero we discovered many new plants. Of these I collected and described the following, and had all of them drawn by the artists.

Discovery of Quina Cana and Quina Roxa de Santa Fe

Cinchona nitida, cascarilla, or quina tree, from which is extracted the true Peruvian quina, or quina cana, as it is called in the trade. This species is numbered among the best quinas, with the most effective properties. It has the best aroma, most pleasing and noticeably bitter, of all that are handled commercially.

Cinchona magnifolia, called flor de azahar, or quina roxa (roja) de Santa Fe according to the terminology of Dr. Mutis, after its presentation to the viceroy by Dr. Sebastian José López in Santa Fe de Bogotá. This species of quina is valued neither in Peru nor in Europe. Its properties are very weak in comparison with many others that are esteemed in medicine and in the trade. This tree is, without a doubt, the tallest and most leafy of all the species of cascarilla, or quina.

Maranta capitata. *Amomum racemosum* and *A. thyrsoideum*. *Justicia punctata* and *J. tenuiflora*. *Calceolaria perfoliata*. *Peperomia concava*, *P. obliqua*, *P. scandens*, and *P. striata*. *Piper acuminatum*, *P. acutifolium*, *P. curvatum*, *P. filiforme*, *P. mite*, *P. obliquum*, *P. ovatum*, *P. polystachium*, and *P. scabrum*. *Sanchezia oblonga*. *Verbena adpressa*. *Commelina nervosa*. *Coccocypselum sessile*. *Ohigginsia aggregata*. *Riqueuria avenia*. *Manettia racemosa*. *Macrocnemum pubescens*.

Sauvagesia ciliata, yerba de San Martín (Saint Martin's herb). The Indians use this plant medicinally in various ways, especially to treat fatigue and chest ailments.

Psychotria lutea, *P. repanda*, and *P. rubra*. *Hippotis triflora*. *Lisianthus quadrangularis*. *Solanum anceps* and *S. ternatum*. *Solanum laciniatum*, called rocotito de monte; Indians eat its raw fruits.

Schwenkfelda umbellata. *Convolvulus quinquefolius*. *Laugeria hirsuta*. *Coffea oc-*

cidentalis. Echites acuminata and *E. subsagittata. Cestrum pulverulentum. Arthrostemma ciliatum. Paullinia striata. Laurus aurantiodora. Melastoma flexuosa, M. grossularioides, M. hispida,* and *M. latifolia.*

Godoya obovata and *G. spathulata*; both species are called laupe. They are beautiful trees and valued for their wood, which is hard and strong for whatever use one wants to make of it.

Clethra obovata, a tall, leafy tree with very good wood for various uses. *Miconia lanuginosa, M. pulverulenta,* and *M. triplinervis. Prunus nitida.*

Bixa orellana, called achote, achiote, or huantura. The seeds are reported to be an excellent diuretic, and are used to color spicy foods. They also serve as a dyestuff, for which reason the tree is cultivated in Peru and Mexico and the seeds exported to Europe.

Gaultheria glauca. Vandellia diffusa. Browallia demissa. Lantana aculeata. Ruellia alata and *R. paniculata. Besleria biflora* and *B. radicans. Monnina polystachia. Negretia planticarpia. Cytisus purpureus*, chucchoclle. *Vismia tomentosa. Palauvia hirsuta.*

Erythrina incarnata, huayruro. This tall tree, abundant in Cuchero and Pozuzo, drops its leaves completely. Before sending out new leaves, the trees burst into such a show of flowers that from far away they look like trees of red coral. When blossoming time is over, the leaves immediately burst forth and the fruits develop along with them.

Theobroma cacao, cacao. This tree is cultivated in various parts of the forested region. When we were there, a resident of Huánuco set out a cacahual, or cacao plantation, just beyond Cuchero.

Hoppea tinctoria. The leaves of this plant dye woolen, cotton, and linen goods a beautiful canary yellow.

Ageratum secundum. Eupatorium hirtum. Senecio pyramidalis. Molina quinquenervis. Lobelia scabra. Pothos volubilis. Cypripedium grandiflorum. Sobralia dichotoma.

Vanilla officinalis, vainilla (vanilla). The Indians gather some of the fruits, or pods, which they take to Huánuco to sell, but the harvest in those forests is small because they have little value there.

Begonia lobata and *B. obliqua. Acalypha pubescens* and *A. purpurea. Cissampelos cordata* and *C. peltata. Citrosma pyriformis. Coussapoa latifolia* and *C. obovata. Ficus striata. Polypodium simile? Lonchitis cultrifolium.*

Palo de Balsas and Tacuna

Heliocarpus glandulosa, palo de balsas (raft tree). This tree is always dioecious throughout these forests; I have never found one that is monoecious or hermaphroditic. Its trunk is greatly valued for making rafts, for the wood is exceedingly porous and lightweight, and it floats better than any other. The trunks are cut and split with the greatest of ease, which is why these people use them to build shelters and huts that must be put up in a few hours. One of these trees can be felled with four or six blows of the ax, no matter how stout it be, for the ax or machete sinks into it as though it were a cabbage stalk.

Cecropia aquifera, tacuna. This is a very tall and leafy tree. Its trunk is hollow with rather closely spaced septa, or divisions, and is usually filled with clear, fresh water. This water can be drunk without any danger, as is often done by the bark gatherers and others who wander through those forests. Split lengthwise, with the septa cut out, these trunks are used instead of aqueducts to conduct water from one place to another. Their large, spreading leaves, which can be used as umbrellas, follow the sun, turning from east to west during the course of the day in much the same way as the sunflower.

Tafalla glauca, aitacupi. These bushes give off tears of resin, very similar in shape, color, and smell to mastic, and for this reason some people call it almáciga (mastic). The resin is used to alleviate headache by applying it to the temples in a plaster.

Clusia rosea, matapalo (tree killer). This name derives from the growth habit of the plant; like ivy, it gets a hold on a tree and enclasps the trunk, eventually damaging and killing its host. It yields a resin, also called matapalo, which is highly esteemed in Peru for treating hernias and ruptures.

Vegetable Ivory

Palma pullipuntu, called pullipuntu. This beautiful plant has no trunk. The fronds, or leaves, and the inflorescence arise from the root, through the developing leaf bases. Its fruits, young but having completed their growth, make up a huge head, all clustered together and united with one another. When this fruiting head is cut across, it provides enough water to quench the thirst of two or three men. When the fruits are a little older, this water becomes a milky juice, somewhat sweet and pleasant tasting, which the natives also use to satisfy their thirst. Then it later turns bitter and cannot be drunk because of its taste. Finally, this sap turns into a very solid, white substance, as hard as ivory. For this reason, the seeds of pullipuntu have been named marfil vegetal (vegetable ivory). From them, craftsmen turn out many small figurines and curiosities for the handles of walking sticks and other implements, as is done with animal ivory. This valuable palm is abundant in the forests of the region.

CHAPTER 24

Description of the Village of Chinchao

Sixteen leagues from the city of Huánuco, towards the north, is the village of Chinchao. It lies on the eastern bank of the river, on a small plateau between the river and the summit of the mountain that forms, on that side, the gorge known as the Quebrada de Chinchao. This village is made up of nine huts or cottages, with twice as many inhabitants. Eleven more souls live scattered on small farms that are spread around the outskirts of the village. There is a small church where mass is offered only when the priest from the parish of Valle, to which Chinchao belongs, comes with two other clergymen to celebrate the holy days of the entire year, all within 3 or 4 days. At this time the priest also collects the pay for burials and other tithes and contributions due the church, in accordance with Indian tariffs and laws.

The construction of the church and houses is of wood and mud, or adobe, with roofs of straw thatching. There is nothing about them that merits attention. The sky is clear and bright in the summertime, but it rains often in other seasons, especially during the winter months, though the sun does shine some part of every day. Winds blow constantly from the north and from the south, thus making the climate eternally mild. On the hottest days the temperature climbs to 84 or 86°F (29 or 30°C); between sunset and dawn it drops 13 to 18°F.

A brook of good water, fresh and crystal clear, flows down the little glen at the entrance to Chinchao. No cattle at all are kept here, for there is no pasturage for them. The scant grass one sees in a few small, artificially made clearings is tough and stiff, but the horses and mules that bring in food and other supplies, and take out coca or quina bark, are obliged to eat it because there is nothing else. In order to have this stubby and worthless grass available, the natives burn those areas during July and August to prevent their being taken over by trees and bushes, to make certain that the grass sends out soft sprouts, and to maintain other herbaceous plants that the mules also eat.

On many market days, there are some foodstuffs in the village of Chinchao because it is on the main road from Huánuco to Cuchero, the road that goes past the 74 coca plantations in the gorge. But these foods include merely four or five common and ordinary things, such as bread in the form of biscuits, potatoes, salted meat, and lard.

In addition to coca, a few roots and fruits are cultivated throughout the gorge of Chinchao for food, such as yuca, achiras (*Canna* species), arracachas (apios, Peruvian parsnips), potatoes, mallicas (yams), ssaqui (*Calla* species), native cabbages, sugar cane, maize, beans, pineapples, bananas, avocados, papayas, and anonas (custard apples). Chicha, or maize wine, is seldom lacking in Chinchao and on those plantations where the houses face onto the main road.

Coca is the only cultivated plant of commercial importance at the present time. Many other crops of equal commercial interest and productivity could be grown, such as cacao, indigo, coffee, and quina bark.

The Coca Plant

Coca is a small bush, 2 to 4 yards tall at the most, with many slender twigs spreading horizontally. It is grown in Peru in the sheltered gorges of Chinchao, Chacahuassi, Pozuzo, and the other provinces contiguous with the forests of the Andean range. It is cultivated for its leaves, which are gathered and sold.

Properties and Use of Coca

The Indians of Peru say the leaves of coca possess the property of restoring to the body the strength spent on long treks and in mining work and other physical exercise. They also assert that the gluten and juice of the leaves, set free during the slow mastication practiced by coca chewers, serve as food and nourishment. Finally, they argue that they are rested and amused by the coca while engaged in what they term chacchan or acullican, which is a process of placing the leaves in the mouth and preparing them for use.

To carry out this operation, the Indian seats himself comfortably, takes the chuspa, or coca pouch—which he always carries hanging from his shoulder and under one arm, as a shepherd or school boy carries his bag—and places it between his thighs. He then slowly opens the pouch and from it, leaf by leaf, takes out the coca; he stretches each leaf, plucks from it the stalk, the nerve, and any foreign matter that it might have, and then places it in his mouth. Here the leaves gradually become moist while the Indian, in the same slow and absent-minded manner, cleans the second batch of leaves and puts it in his mouth. He thus continues with each successive batch.

To more efficiently set free the gluten and other active substances contained in the leaves, he partially chews them and adds to them, from time to time, a little powdered lime from an iscopurus, or small calabash (gourd) carried for this purpose. The lime is extracted from the calabash with a small stick moistened at the tip with saliva; it is then mixed with the soft, moistened mass of leaves in the mouth. Some use sugar; still others used a fixed alkali, especially the ashes of quinoa or sugar cane or other plants, kneaded and made into little balls known as llipta.

When the Indian has put enough leaves in his mouth to make a ball the size of a small nut, he rolls the ball repeatedly from one cheek to the other to soften the leaves and to free them of the green coloring matter that comes out in the first saliva. He usually spits this out and does not swallow any of the juices until that particular aromatic and pleasing flavor that he is waiting for appears. With the ball in his mouth, prepared as we have explained, he returns happy and freshened to carry on his work, swallowing from then on all the juices and substances that the saliva extracts from the coca. This goes on until the coca is left tasteless and weak, which usually takes 2 or 3 hours.

Coca is such a necessity for the Indians who work in the mines that without it they lack the slightest disposition or strength to continue their labors. Because of this, the owners of the mines are very careful that their peasants never feel the want of this stimulant.

For a long time I was convinced that coca is, like tobacco, a habit-forming plant used to keep the Indian happy, but experience has made me change that groundless belief. I have seen positive proof of the wonderful effects of these leaves that appear to be tasteless, odorless, and inert. Moreover, coca is a remedy with proven medicinal properties. As a decoction or infusion it cures dysentery, checks diarrhea, and stimulates delayed menstruation after childbirth; as a powder, mixed with sugar, it corrects acidity and strengthens the teeth.

Cultivation of Coca

To plant coca, those dedicated to the harvest of this leaf make a number of holes about a cubic foot in size. In each hole, they throw about a hundred seeds and half fill it again with earth, leaving the seeds without any care for a year. After that time, the young plants will have grown about a foot and a half. They are transplanted when in bud, after being checked three or four times a year. The small plants are put into holes a foot and a half deep, placing in each hole two stalks crossed a little above the root. They are then half-covered with soil, rather firmly packed in. The transplanting is done in lines 3 quartas (cuartas, handspans) apart, with the holes a little more than a foot from one another.

For the next transplanting, done in November and December, one must wait until it rains. If many young plants have been pulled up, with no chance to set them out because of a dry spell and no watering system available, the plants are tied up into various bundles and placed with their roots in running water. Cared for in this way they will last for 10 or 12 days, and will usually establish themselves more easily after the treatment than when recently pulled from the ground. If the plants are large, as they may be when 2 or 3 years old, the roots and stalk are cut back before transplanting. No more care is given the transplanted coca except weeding to remove plant intruders that arise spontaneously in the plots; for this work a type of spade or hoe is used to scratch the surface of the soil on the paths and to cut or pull out the weeds.

Although the coca bush usually has flowers and fruit most of the year, its main flowering period comes in October and November. Because it is then so covered with flowers and fruit that it has hardly any leaves, the coca harvest at this period of the year is sparse in comparison with the yield of leaves during the other three seasons. When the bushes are old, they are cut 1 yard above the ground so they will sprout new, more vigorous shoots. The coca bush cannot be stripped of its leaves for a year and a half to 2 years after being transplanted, depending upon the soil and the strength of the plant. If the leaves are gathered before that time, the bushes will die from the loss of strength and resistance.

Preparation of Coca Leaves

After the coca leaves are removed from the bushes by the handfuls, they require little processing except to be put in the sun and stirred constantly with bundles of dry twigs so they will air quickly and dry evenly. This seldom is accomplished in 1 day, in spite of the strong heat of the sun in these regions, for clouds and short rainstorms often interrupt the process.

When the leaves are crisp and almost completely dried, they are gathered up and wrapped in large sheets or blankets to ferment, as the natives say, during the night. In this way the leaves become leathery and supple, so they do not shatter no matter how much they are crushed. This process also gives them a better aroma, a more pleasant taste, and a brighter color. The coca gatherers all try to avoid bulging, or rotting, of the leaves, which happens when drying has not been carried out on time or when the leaves are allowed to become too wet, bringing on a strong and fetid fermentation.

Once well prepared, coca is kept in bags of coarse cloth, having been squeezed in as tightly as possible with hands and feet. In Huánuco, 25 pounds of coca leaves fetch from 3 to 7 duros (15 to 35 pesetas).

In Chinchao and throughout the gorge, the same species of animals, birds, and insects that we listed for Cuchero are found. There is likewise little difference in the flora. During the month that we stayed in Chinchao, I made a beautiful collection of dried specimens and drawings, and studied and described the following plants.

Acosta aculeata, montelucuma; its fruit, the size of a hen's egg, is very delicious when ripe. If it were cultivated it would hold an important place among the edible fruits.

Peperomia filiformis, *P. foliiflora*, *P. purpurea*, *P. quadrangularis*, *P. trinervis*, and *P. uniflora*. *Costus ruber*. *Gonzalagunia dependens*. *Coccocypselum lanceolatum* and *C. obovatum*. *Lisianthus corymbosus* and *L. ovalis*. *Heliconia angustifolia* and *H. latifolia*. *Echites spiralis*. *Macrocnemum venosum*; *M. corymbosum*, ccaratu. *Achyranthes geniculata*. *Psychotria truncata*. *Solanum acuminatum*, *S. bifformifolium*, *S. incarceratum*, *S. pubescens*, and *S. obliquum*.

Vegetable Sealing Wax

Amaryllis miniata, called lacre de montaña (wild sealing wax) because the gluten from its bulbs is used in place of sealing wax to seal letters after they are addressed. When this vegetable sealing wax is used, the letter cannot be opened without slitting the paper. If the bulb of this plant is cut transversely, the exposed surface turns red like the color of true sealing wax. The flower is rather large, and for this reason is esteemed for gardens.

Actinophyllum pentandrum. *Fuchsia mitifolia*. *Cornidea umbellata*; this is a tall, leafy tree that is showy when in blossom, with great corymbs of flowers and their enclosing bracts.

Erythroxylon coca, known as coca, or cuca. This same name is applied to the leaves of the plant; some call the bush cocal, but this name is more properly given to the plot or farm where the shrubs are grown. Thus one speaks of so-and-so's cocal, or of the cocales of such and such a locality.

Trilix macrobotryx; this shrub is very beautiful when in flower, and is suitable as a garden plant because of its abundant branches that can be made to grow into any shape one desires.

Clinopodium? bisseratum and *C. procumbens. Dracocephalum? odoratum. Besleria auriculata* and *B. diversicolor. Gesneria frutescens. Mecardonia ovata. Urena cornuta.*

Escobedia scabra, called especia (spice) or azafrán de montaña (wild saffron) because natives use its roots in place of saffron to color condiments. The roots are also employed as a dyestuff for baize fabrics and cotton goods. Some people journey from Huancavelica to these forests and gather many loads of the roots, which they sell in their own territory for 4 reales or more a pound.

Ochroma triloba, huampo; the wood of this leafy tree is excellent for constructing rafts, as it is very light and more buoyant than other woods. Equally valuable for the walls of huts or shelters, it is cut and split with great ease, and its softness makes it easy to fashion any object desired. The flowers are large and beautiful; the capsules, or fruits, are long, plump, and deeply furrowed, and are full of many tiny seeds embedded in a sparse brownish cotton. Because of its softness and lightness, this cotton is appropriate for stuffing pillows, mattresses, cushions, and other articles. When the filling becomes compacted, these pieces of furniture can be exposed to the sun, and in the heat the cotton again becomes as fluffy as when newly stuffed.

Crotalaria retusa? Palauvia biserrata. Ageratum secundum and *A. trinerve. Aster erosus. Molina venosa. Senecio odoratus. Cacalia pubescens. Monnina incarnata*; the bitter, saponaceous root is used instead of soap for washing clothing.

Eupatorium carinatum, E. coriaceum, and *E. obovatum. Eupatorium odoratum*; its flowers are arranged in large corymbs or bunches and have a delightful aroma like that of Peruvian or black balsam. The whole gorge is filled with this fragrance from the time, near midday, when the sun begins to warm the air.

Lobelia hirsuta. Satyrium pubescens. Sobralia amplexicaulis and *S. dichotoma. Serapias ciliata. Sisyrinchium bermudiana? Tacsonia maliformia*, granadilla de mono (monkey's passion fruit); the pulp of its fruits is eaten.

Calla acuminata. Calla polystachia, caqui or ssaqui; the tuberous roots are eaten by the Indians who cultivate the plant for this purpose, but the roots of wild plants are extremely sour and poisonous.

Arum lanceolatum. Arum rosaceum, a vine that climbs on trees and kills them; it has a very acrid, caustic taste. *Pothos hastata, P. sagittato-cordata*, and *P. volubilis. Ficus retusa?*

Urtica geniculata, U. nuda, U. sparsa, and *U. striata. Urtica fumans* is more abundant in Chinchao than in other localities.

Dioscorea triloba, called mallica (yam) or papa de montaña (wild potato). The

Indians cultivate this plant in the coca plots for its tuberous roots, which are rather large and divided into numerous sections much thicker than those of the peony. Purple-red inside, they are soft and good-tasting, either roasted or boiled.

Schinus mayco, mayco. This bush is leafy and showy, but if anyone stands in its shade, it causes an outbreak of unbearable, burning pimples and rashes, especially on the hands and other unclothed parts of the body. Some people are more susceptible to the poison of mayco than others. To cure this uncomfortable and unbearable evil, the natives use *Valeriana pinnatifida*, known there as albergilla, which is half-roasted and applied as hot as can be tolerated.

CHAPTER 25

Trip from Chinchao to Huánuco

On the 1st of September 1780 the artist Gálvez left Chinchao for Huánuco, and on the 3rd Brunete and I left also. We slept in the roadside hut of Pati, very uncomfortably because of the cold wind that entered every chink in the shelter. As we have said, the quina de hoja morada (purple-leaved quina), or quina boba, grows here, as does the cascarilla, or Peruvian quina, *Cinchona nitida*. The difference is that the latter grows on the highest parts of the mountain, and the former on the lower part where the hut is located. Many loads of Peruvian quina were gathered in the high areas of Pati during the years when we were traveling through those regions bounding on the jungle.

On the 4th we left Pati and arrived in time to spend the night in Acomayo. It was a hard trip with much trouble climbing up and down the high peak of Carpis, for the ledges, holes, and poor road completely wore out the travelers and the animals.

We entered the city of Huánuco on the 5th, without any further discomfort along the way except the great heat of that ravine. The mule drivers arrived at six o'clock in the evening.

When I had finished some descriptions begun in Cuchero and Chinchao, and had prepared the dried plant specimens collected in the forests, I put them in order and got them completely ready to be boxed up for safe transport.

I continued plant collecting in the ravines and on the mountains around Huánuco until the 25th of October. During this interval I dried and described various plants to which I have already referred in my description of the province of Huánuco.

I had been told that it would be possible to find some rare plants in the province of Huamalíes. I decided, therefore, to go there with the artist Gálvez to reconnoiter and to ascertain whether there were localities where all of us could work together with useful results.

CHAPTER 26

Trip to the Province of Huamalíes

On the 25th of October 1780, with the artist Gálvez, I left Huánuco for the province of Huamalíes. The morning was very hazy, and when we had gone through the gorge of Higueras a downpour of rain overtook us. This ravine is pleasant and interesting for the fertility of its fields and plots of maize and vegetables, which are cultivated along the riverbank by the Indians of settlements along the way.

Six leagues from Huánuco we left our guide, telling him to return to Huánuco little by little with one of our mules that was worn out with fatigue. We continued our trip with our servant, but half a league farther on he, too, had to go back to Huánuco, taking Gálvez's mule; it had fallen and rolled a long way and was wounded and useless for work. Gálvez had saved his own life by grabbing a small bush when the two of them fell, and he thus escaped unharmed. The mule, however, rolled over six or eight times until it came to the bottom of the cliff, where the animal lay motionless for a long time. Although maimed, it finally got up and was able to walk very slowly with the servant leading it by the halter.

Punishment of Rebellious Indians by Flogging, Haircutting, and Forced Labor

From that point we two continued our journey alone to the village of Chavinillo, 14 leagues from Huánuco. We arrived at five o'clock in the afternoon. There was nothing of note except that the chief magistrate of the province, Don Ignacio de Ulloa, had left the village after dispensing justice in a case of several rebellious Indians. He ordered that their hair be cut and that they be taken off to Quivilla to work. For this reason, we found nobody in Chavinilla except four men and the women of those who had been able to flee from justice and of those who had been sent off to work.

We spent that night in the town council house, stretched out on stone benches upon which there was a little bit of wet ichu straw. This was our mattress, and it succeeded in making us wetter than we were from the rain along the way.

On the 26th we set out for the villages of Cahuac and Ovas, where the chief magistrate had gone with 200 armed mestizos to assist him in meting out punishment to those who had risen in revolt in Ovas. These rebel natives were considered accomplices in the rioting and in the attempted murder of the tax collector, for after insulting and beating him on the road, they carried him off trussed up, with the intent of casting him over a high cliff.

That same afternoon we went to Chupán, together with the chief magistrate's entire party. As soon as he arrived in the village, he ordered the flogging of various other accomplices who had joined up with those of the other two villages to kill the royal tax collector and to cause rebellion in the province.

Chupán, Ovas, Cahuac, and Chavinillo are located on rather high mountains and are cold. There is only pasturage for sheep and cows, and there are good flocks or herds of both these animals. In all these places large plants do not grow; all I saw was the sahuco (sauco, elder), *Sambucus nigra*, in the villages themselves. In lower places in the deep gorges the inhabitants plant potatoes, the only crop of that region.

We left for Quivilla on the 27th, following the chief magistrate's party and the prisoners he was carrying off to forced labor, to pay for their crimes by working in cloth factories.

It rained on the following days and did not let up until the 2nd of November, when we decided to go back to Huánuco. We were satisfied that these places were not suitable for the purposes of our commission. Furthermore, the chief magistrate informed me that we should find nothing of what we sought until we hit the jungle area, because the whole of the province of Huamalíes lay in cold altitudes and its native flora offered very little variety.

CHAPTER 27

Description of the Province of Huamalíes

The province of Huamalíes (Plate 8) is bounded on the north by the province of Patáz, on the southeast by that of Huánuco, on the south by that of Tarma, on the southwest by that of Caxatambo, and on the west and northwest by that of Conchucos. In the north it also abuts on the province of Panatahuas and on the jungles of pagan Indians. Huamalíes is 82 leagues long from north to south and 30 leagues wide from east to west, though in some places it measures but 12 leagues wide. It is divided into heights and gorges, or deep ravines. The climate of the former is cold and bleak, especially in the southern part, and that of the latter is mild.

The principal gorge or narrow valley of this province forms the course of the river that Padre Fritz on his map calls the Marañón. This agrees with the opinion of Mr. de la Condamine, and Brother Manuel Sobreviela supports them in his map drawn up in 1791. This river, as we have explained in our description of Tarma, arises in the lake of Lauricocha. The Patayrondos and Taso rivers flow to join the Monzón, which in turn joins the Pillco, or Huánuco, River 7 leagues below the port of Cuchero.

In the parish of Huacaybamba, some of the farms are so hot throughout the year that this is said to cause its inhabitants to be darker than the rest of the population of the province. The people here are called zambos.

Fruit, vegetables, and seeds are harvested in the lowland areas and warm valleys: cherimoyas, guavas, bananas, figs, tunas (prickly pears), two kinds of peaches, and good pineapples and papayas in the forested areas. In Chavín there are very large, good-tasting avocados. From sugar cane the natives make chancaca (brown sugar), molasses, alfeñique (sugar paste with almonds), and guarapo (fermented cane liquor). There is some wheat and barley, and there are quantities of maize, potatoes, and ocas, and alfalfa for horses and mules. In gardens and orchards, all the year round, Indian women cultivate a variety of flowers for decorating the altars and statues.

The forests of Huamalíes, like all Andean forests, are extraordinarily luxuriant with a variety of trees, bushes, and plants of all sizes. Many plants have known properties and uses; there are fine woods, as well as some resins, gums, and balsams that the Indians gather and take to the villages to sell along with various medicinal seeds and roots. There are also the almendrón or *Caryocar*, vanilla, ispinho (espino?), huampo (*Ochroma* species), and two species of the tallow tree, or *Myristica*. Most important of all, there are various cascarillas, or quinas, from which bark is gathered in goodly amounts. Along the edges of the forests there are some coca plantations; leaves harvested on these farms are taken to Huayanca and Pasco and sold to the mine owners.

Nothing is planted or harvested in the cold heights because of the bleak climate, but large flocks of sheep and herds of cows are maintained and find good food in ichu grass and other herbs. For this reason, there are many ranches on those punas, or moors.

Much wool is produced, and is woven in small mills into considerable amounts of jerga (a coarse cloth) and native clothing. Textiles constitute the chief trade of the province; the cloth is taken to Bombón, Lima, and elsewhere for sale. In addition to the wool produced from sheep of the entire province, the mills buy up large amounts from other regions so the looms will not be idled by a dearth of raw material. These purchases are usually paid for with light cloth and other kinds of fabrics made from that same wool.

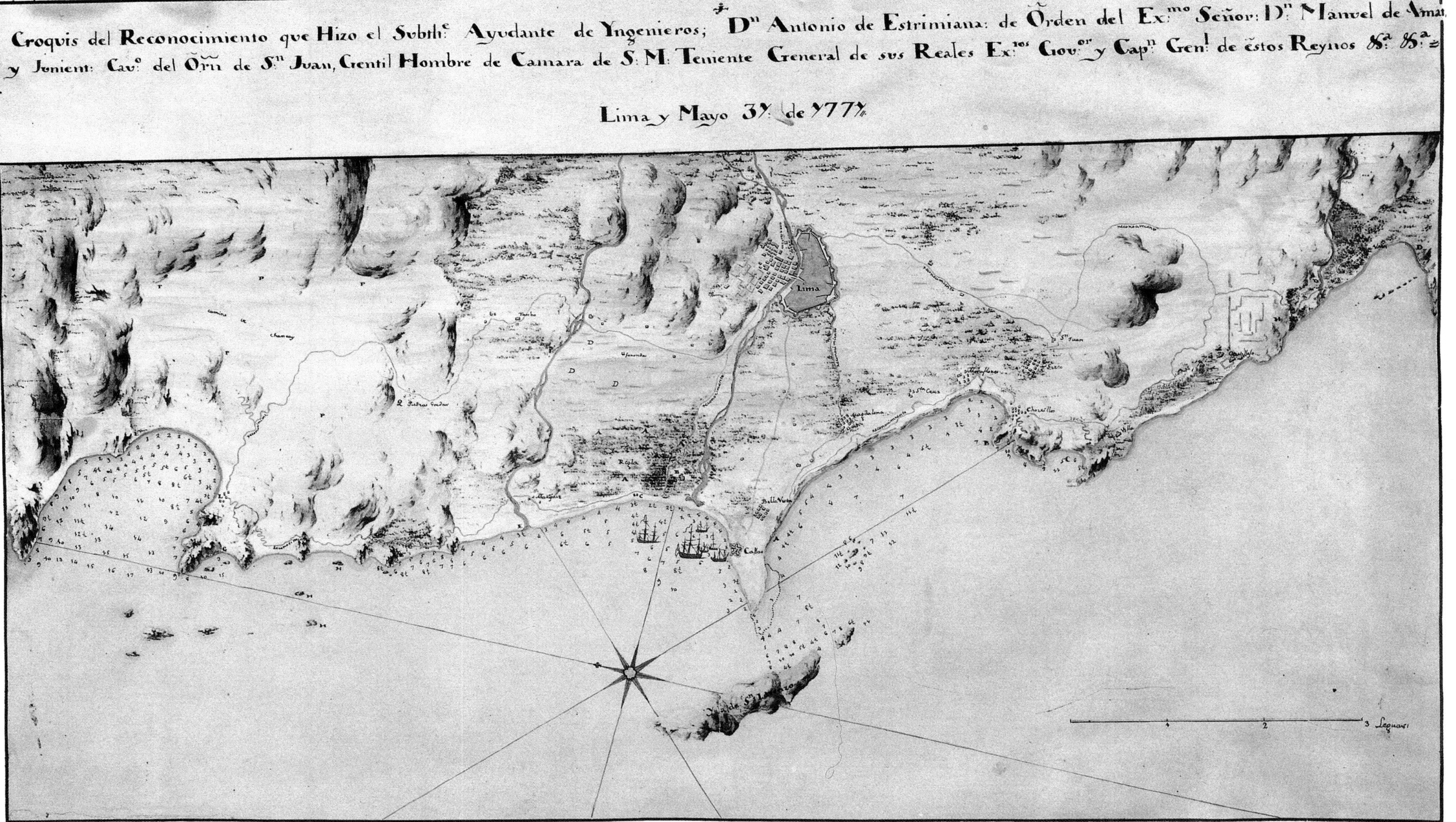

Plate 1. Map of Lima, Peru, and the Coast. Sketch of the survey carried out by Deputy Chief Engineer, Don Antonio de Estrimiana, by order of His Excellency Don Manuel Amat y Junient, Knight of the Order of St. John, Royal Chamberlain, Lieutenant General, Governor and Captain of this realm, Lima, 31 May 1771. From *Maps of Peru*, folio 14. (Courtesy of the British Museum.)

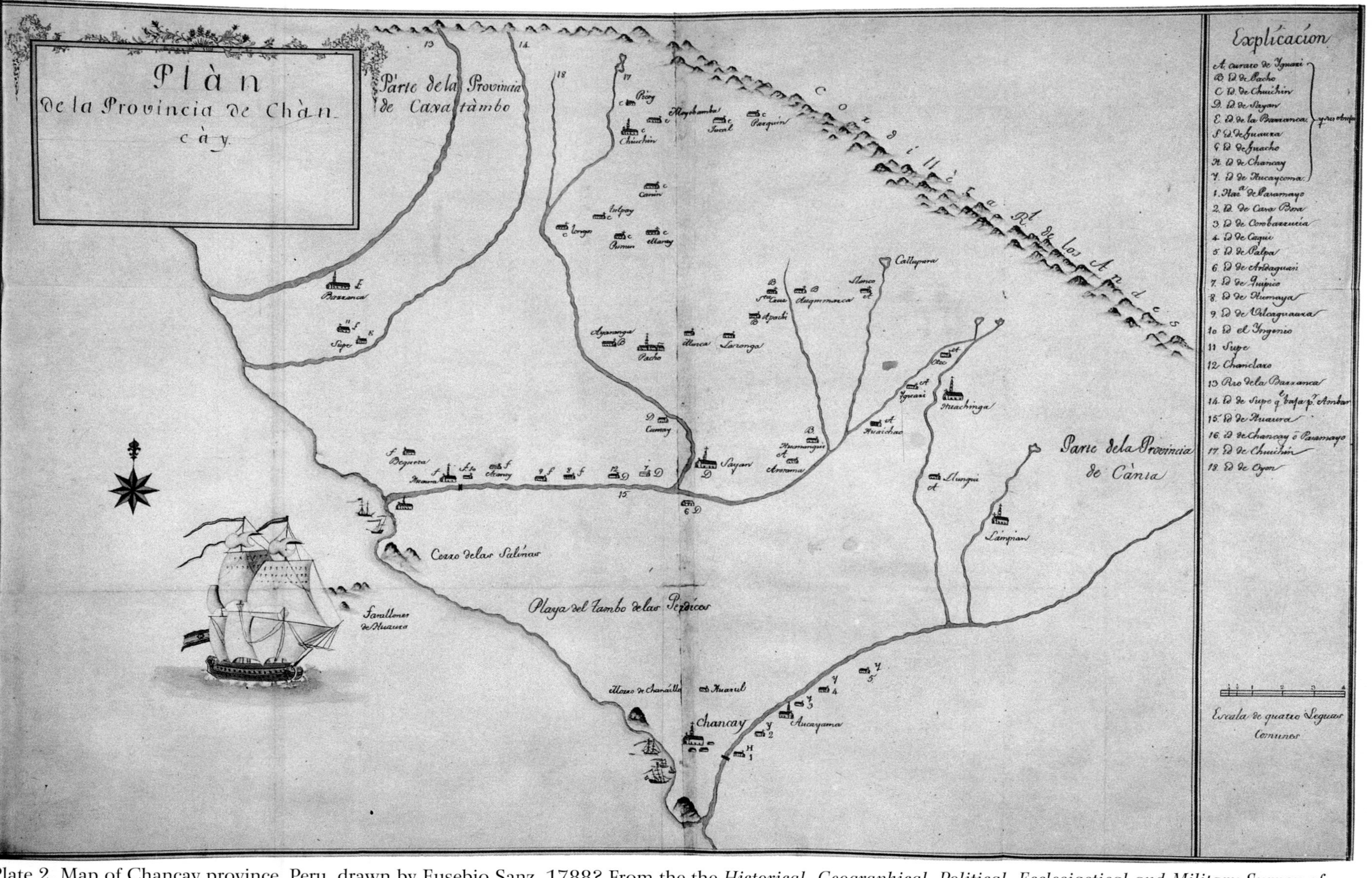

Plate 2. Map of Chancay province, Peru, drawn by Eusebio Sanz, 1788? From the the *Historical, Geographical, Political, Ecclesiastical and Military Survey of South America*, folio 37. (Courtesy of the British Museum.)

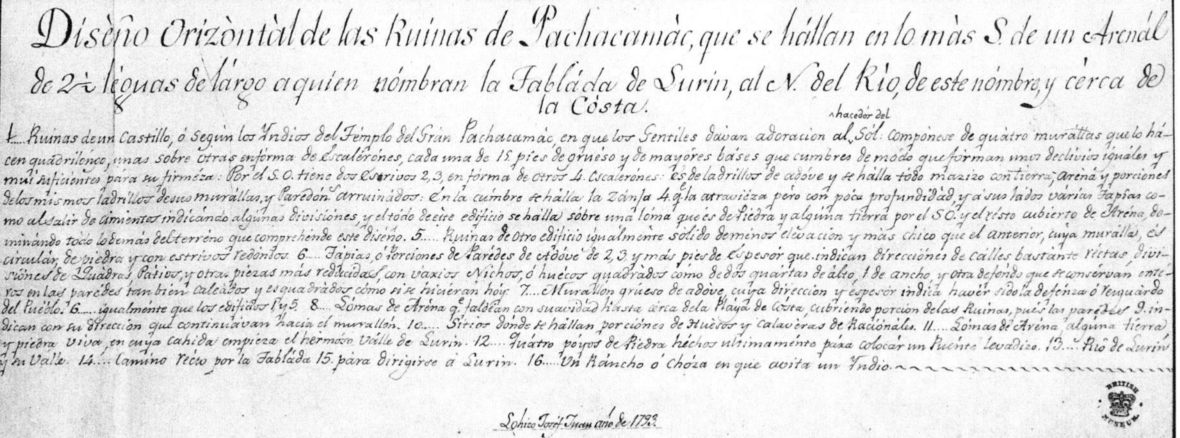

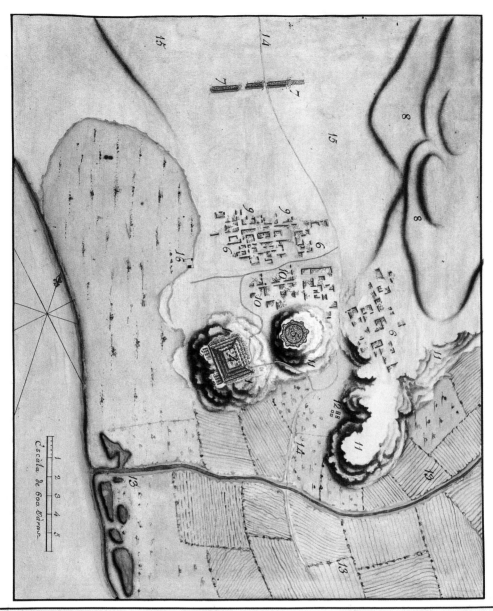

Plate 3. Plan of the ruins of Pachacamac, Peru, which comprise most of the southern part of a sandy coastal area 2½ leagues wide, and include the Lurín Plain to the north of the river of the same name. Drawn by Josef Juan, 1793. (Courtesy of the British Museum.)

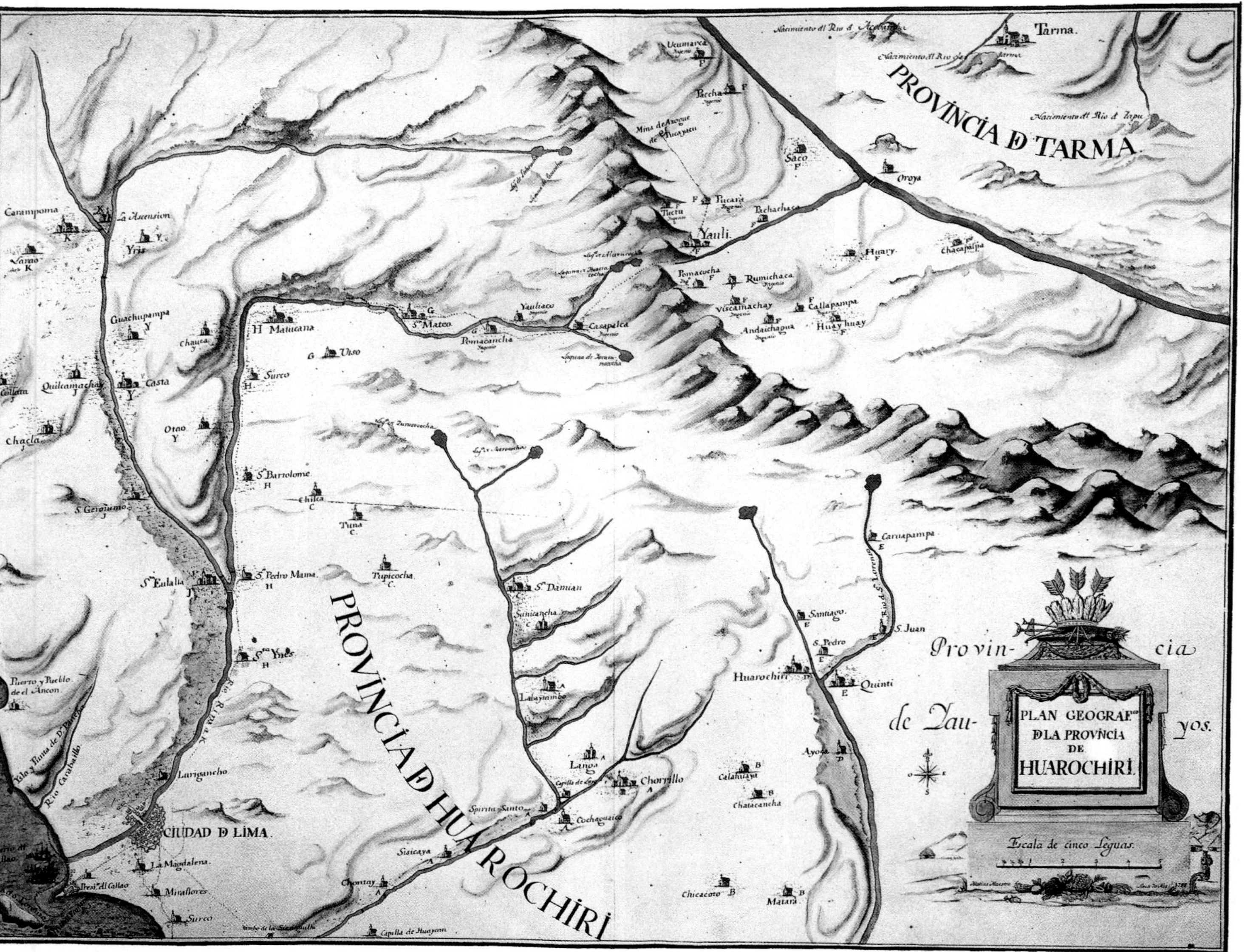

Plate 4. Map of Huarocherí province, Peru, drawn by Matias Maestro, Lima, 20 April 1788. From *Maps of Peru*, folio 13. (Courtesy of the British Museum.)

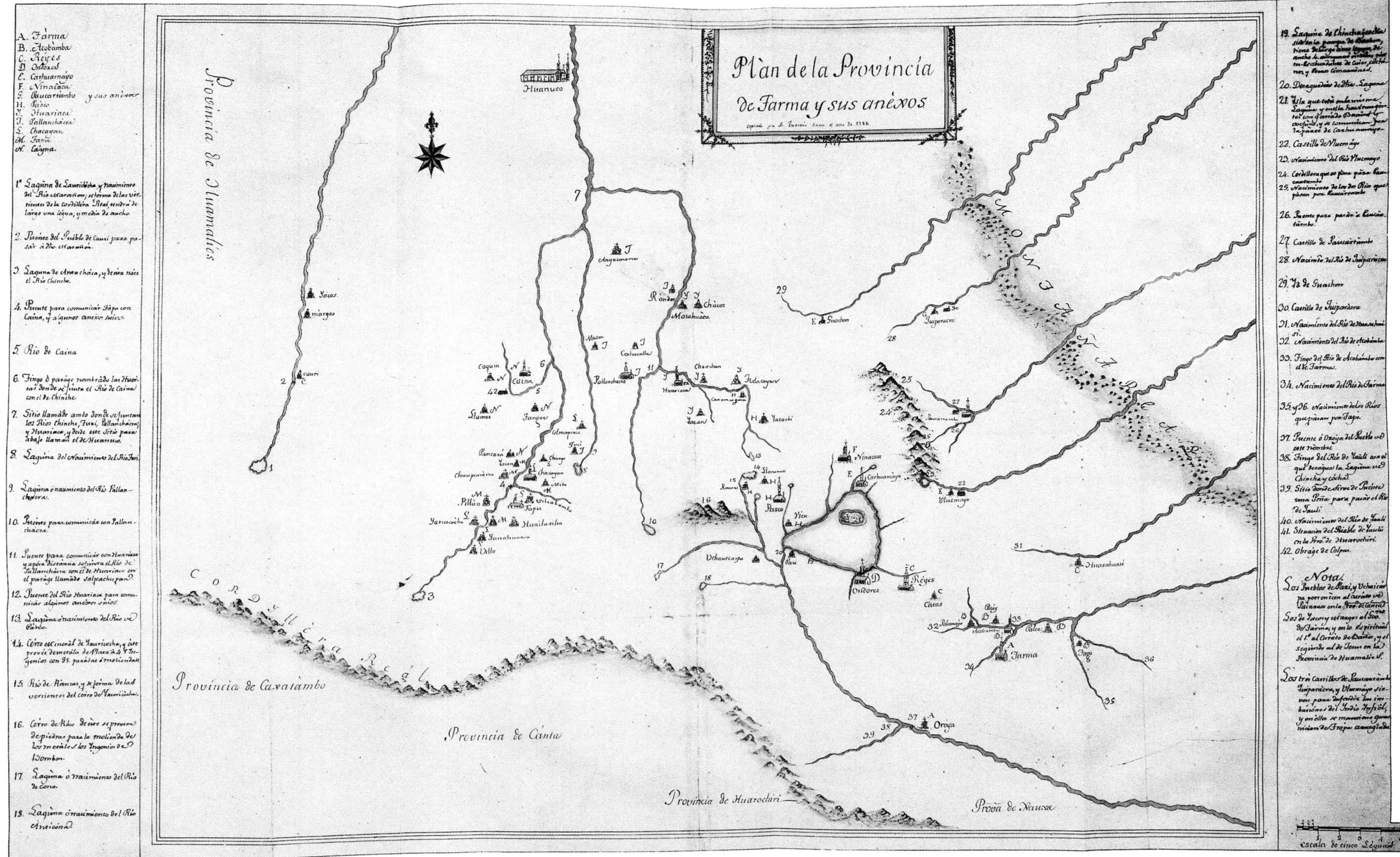

Plate 5. Map of Tarma province, Peru, and surrounding areas, drawn by Eusebio Sanz, 1788. From the *Historical, Geographical, Political, Ecclesiastical and Military Survey of South America*, folio 40. (Courtesy of the British Museum.)

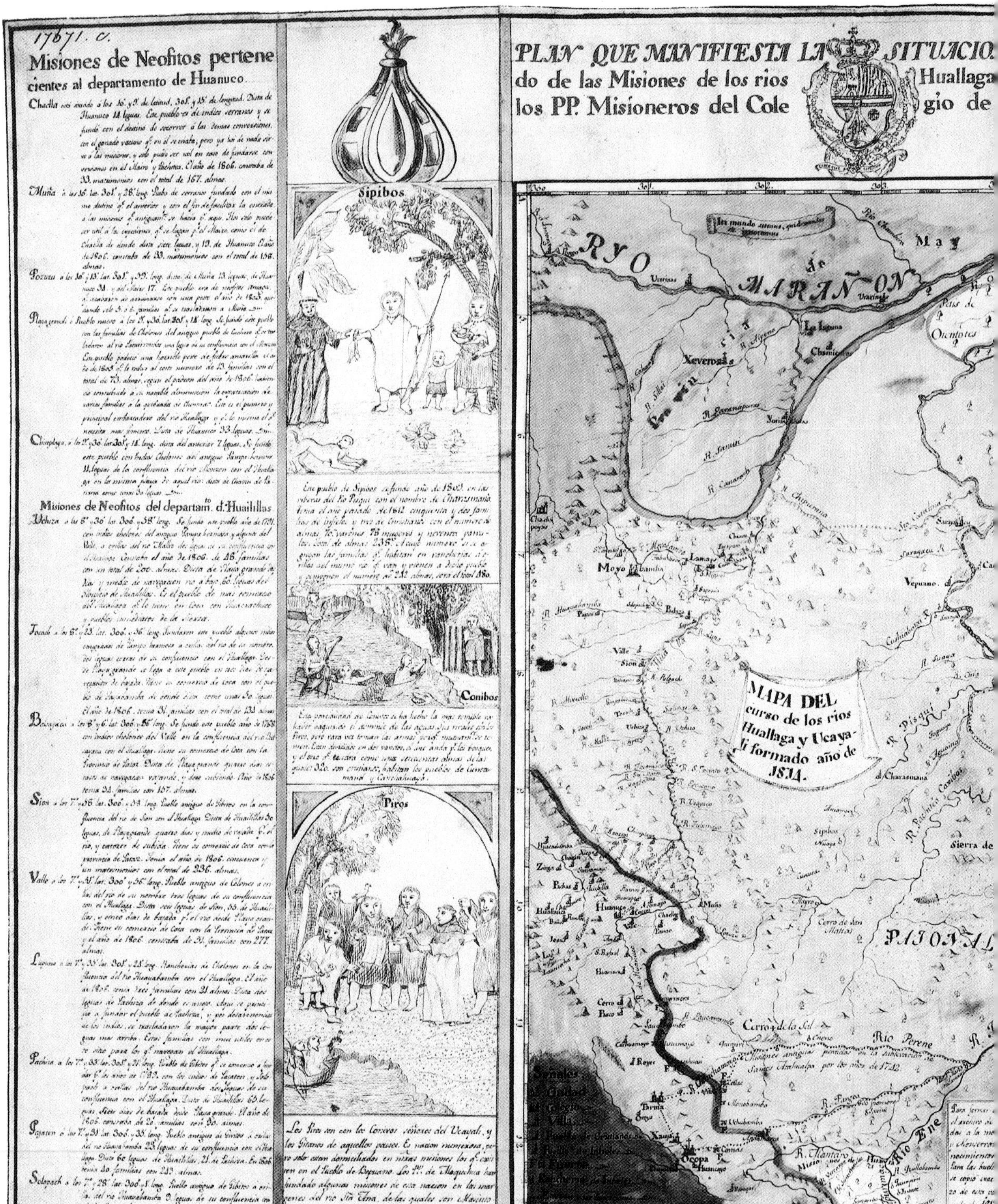

17671. C.

Misiones de Neofitos pertenecientes al departamento de Huanuco.

Chaclla está situado á los 10°. y 3'. de latitud, 301°. y 15'. de longitud. Dista de Huanuco 14 leguas. Este pueblo es de indios serranos y se fundó con el destino de socorrer á las demas conversiones con el ganado vacuno q. en él se criaba, pero ya no de nada sirve á las misiones, y solo puede ser util en caso de fundarse conversiones en el Mairo y Pachitea. El año de 1806. constaba de 33. matrimonios con el total de 167. almas.

Muña á los 10. lat. 301°. y 28'. long. Pueblo de serranos fundado con el mismo destino q. el anterior y con el fin de facilitar la entrada á las misiones q. antiguam.te se hacia p.r aqui. Hoy solo puede ser util á las expediciones q. se hagan p.r el Mairo, como el de Chaclla de donde dista siete leguas, y 13. de Huanuco. El año de 1806. constaba de 33. matrimonios con el total de 158. almas.

Pozuzu á los 10°. y 13'. lat. 301°. y 39'. long. dista de Muña 13 leguas, de Huanuco 34. y del Mairo 17. Este pueblo era de neofitos [illegible], q. acabaron de arruinarse con una peste el año de 1803. quedando solo 5. ó 6. familias q. se trasladaron á Muña.

Playa grande ó Pueblo nuevo á los 8°. y 30'. lat. 301°. y 18'. long. Se fundó este pueblo con las familias de Cholones del antiguo pueblo de Cuchero q. se trasladaron al rio Sataironde una legua de su confluencia con el Monzon. Este pueblo padeció una horrible peste de fiebre amarilla el año de 1803 q. le reduxo al corto numero de 13. familias con el total de 73. almas, segun el padron del año de 1806. habiendo contribuido á su notable disminucion la extravacion de varias familias á la quebrada de [illegible]. Este es el primero y principal embarcadero del rio Huallaga y p.r lo mismo el q. necesita mas fomento. Dista de Huanuco 33 leguas.

Chicoplaya á los 9°. y 30'. lat. 301°. y 18'. long. dista del anterior 7 leguas. Se fundó este pueblo con todos Cholones del antiguo Pampa hermosa 11. leguas de la confluencia del rio Monzon con el Huallaga en la misma playa de aquel rio: dista de Chavin de Pariarca como unas 30 leguas.

Misiones de Neofitos del departam.to d. Huailillas

Uchiza á los 8°. y 30'. lat. 306. y 58'. long. Se fundó este pueblo año de 1781. con indios cholones del antiguo Pampa hermosa y algunos del Valle, á orillas del rio [illegible] dos leguas de su confluencia con el Huallaga. Constaba el año de 1806. de 46. familias con un total de 200. almas. Dista de Playa grande dia y medio de navegacion rio abajo, 60. leguas del Partido de Huailillas. Es el pueblo de mas comercio del Huallaga q. le tiene en coca con Huacrachuco y pueblos inmediatos de la Sierra.

Tocache á los 8°. y 23. lat. 306°. y 36' long. fundaron este pueblo algunos indios emigrados de Pampa hermosa á orillas del rio de su nombre, dos leguas cerca de su confluencia con el Huallaga. Desde Playa grande se llega á este pueblo en tres dias de navegacion de bajada. Tiene su comercio de coca con el pueblo de Tayabamba de donde dista como unas 30 leguas. El año de 1806. tenia 31. familias con el total de 131 almas.

Balsayacu á los 8°. y 6'. lat. 306°. y 56'. long. Se fundó este pueblo año de 1768 con indios cholones del Valle en la confluencia del rio Balsayacu con el Huallaga. Tiene su comercio de coca con la Provincia de Pataz. Dista de Playa grande quatro dias escasos de navegacion bajando, y doce subiendo. Año de 1806 tenia 34. familias con 157. almas.

Sion á los 7°. y 56'. lat. 306°. y 53'. long. Pueblo antiguo de Hibitos en la confluencia del rio de Sion con el Huallaga. Dista de Huailillas 30 leguas, de Playa grande quatro dias y medio de bajada p.r el rio, y catorze de subida. Tiene su comercio de coca con la provincia de Pataz. Tenia el año de 1806. cincuenta y un matrimonios con el total de 236. almas.

Valle á los 7°. y 41'. lat. 306°. y 36'. long. Pueblo antiguo de Cholones á orillas del rio de su nombre tres leguas de su confluencia con el Huallaga. Dista seis leguas de Sion, 35. de Huailillas, y cinco dias de bajada p.r el rio desde Playa grande. Tiene su comercio de coca con la Provincia de Pataz y el año de 1806. constaba de 51. familias con 277. almas.

Lupuna á los 7°. y 35'. lat. 305°. y 25'. long. Rancheria de Cholones en la confluencia del rio Huayabamba con el Huallaga. El año de 1806. tenia tres familias con 21 almas. Dista dos leguas de Pachiza de donde es anexo. Aqui se principió á fundar el pueblo de Pachiza, y por desavenencias de los indios se trasladaron la mayor parte dos leguas mas arriba. Estas familias son muy utiles en este sitio para los q. navegan el Huallaga.

Pachiza á los 7°. y 33'. lat. 305°. y 21'. long. Pueblo de Hibitos q. se comenzó á fundar p.r los años de 1789. con los indios de Pajaten, y Solopach á orillas del rio Huayabamba dos leguas de su confluencia con el Huallaga. Dista de Huailillas 65. leguas siete dias de bajada desde Playa grande. El año de 1806. constaba de 20. familias con 90. almas.

Pajaten á los 7°. y 31'. lat. 306°. y 35'. long. Pueblo antiguo de Hibitos á orillas del rio Huayabamba 23 leguas de su confluencia con el Huallaga. Dista 60 leguas de Huailillas, 21. de Pachiza. En 1806 tenia 40. familias con 243. almas.

Solopach á los 7°. y 28'. lat. 306°. y 1'. long. Pueblo antiguo de Hibitos á orillas del rio Huayabamba 9. leguas de su confluencia con el Huallaga. Dista 14. leguas de Pajaten, y 9. de Pachiza. En 1806. tenia 21. matrimonios con 121. almas.

Nota El año de 1807 se reunieron en Pachiza la mayor parte de las familias de estos tres ultimos pueblos, pero como despues no se insistió en esta reunion, las mas volvieron á sus antiguos pueblos. Todos estos tres pueblos tienen su comercio de cera con la provincia de Pataz, y abundan en balsamo de Copaiba y Cera blanca de q. hacen algun comercio.

Jucusbamba á los 7°. y 55'. lat. 306°. y 12'. long. Se fundó este pueblecito con indios cholones huidos del pueblo del Valle en las cabeceras del rio [illegible]. Es util este pueblo p.a auxiliar á los q. entran desde Huailillas y Provin.a de Pataz á las conversiones del Valle y Sion, pues hasta él se llega á mula, y desde alli comienza el camino á pie. No tengo el padron de aquel pueblo, pero sé q. apenas llegará á 12. familias. Está muy distante de las misiones y por este motivo rara vez es auxiliado de los conversores.

Este pueblo de Sipibos se fundó año de 1809. en las riberas del Rio Pisqui con el nombre de Charasmaná. Tenia el año pasado de 1812 cinquenta y dos familias de infieles y tres de Christianos con el numero de almas 70. varones 78 mugeres y noventa parvulos. Total de almas 238. A cuyo numero si se agregan las familias q. habitan en rancherias á orillas del mismo rio q. van y vienen á dicho pueblo y componen el numero de 242 almas, será el total 480.

Esta parcialidad de Conivos se ha hecho la mas temible por haber adquirido el dominio de las aguas. Sus rivales son los Piros, pero rara vez toman las armas porq. mutuam.te se temen. Estan divididos en dos vandos, el uno anda p.r los bosques, y el otro q. tendrá como unas seiscientas almas de las quales 320. son cristianos, habitan los pueblos de Santamaria y [illegible].

Los Piros son con los Conivos señores del Ucayali, y los Gitanos de aquellos paises. Es nacion numerosa, pero solo estan domiciliados en n.ras misiones los q. existen en el Pueblo de Bepuano. Los P.es de [illegible] han fundado algunas misiones de esta nacion en las margenes del rio Sta Ana, de las quales son [illegible] y Shapa, la primera á los 10°. y 35'. de lat. 304°. y 36' long. En aquellas misiones los llaman Chontaquiros.

Resumen del

	Conversiones	Familias	Almas	Religiosos Conversores
Serranos	Chaclla	33	167	El P. Fr. Juan del Toro
	Muña	33	158	P. Fr. Nicolas Farge
	Pozuzu			
Cholones	Playa Grande	13	73	
	Chicoplaya	32	131	P. Fr. Ramon Basadre
	Uchiza	46	200	P. Fr. Juan Blazquez
	Tocach	31	131	
	Balsayacu	34	157	
	Valle	51	277	
	Jucusbamba			
	Lupuna	3	21	
Total	11	276	1338	4

PLAN QUE MANIFIESTA LA SITUACIO[N]... do de las Misiones de los rios Huallaga... los PP. Misioneros del Colegio de

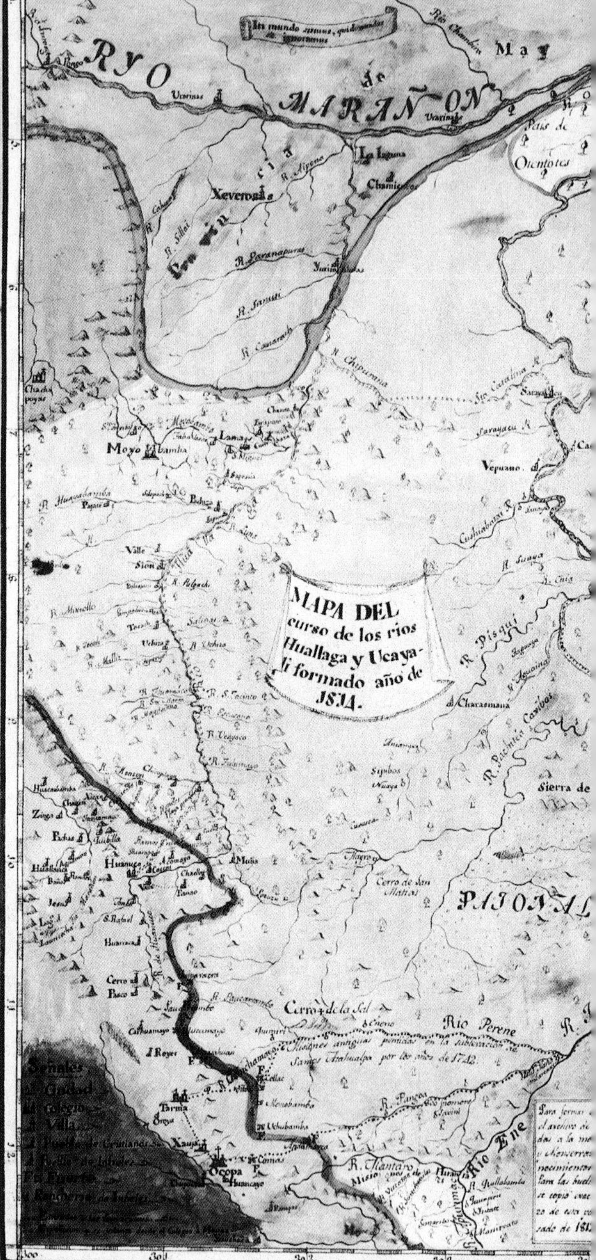

Estado

	Conversiones	Familias	Almas	Religiosos Conversores
Hibitos	Sion	51	236	El P. Fr. Juan Sepeda
	Pachiza	20	90	
	Solopach	21	121	
	Pajaten	40	243	
Hibitos	4	132	690	1
Cholones	11	278	1338	4
Total	15	410	2028	5

Colegio de Ocopa y Abril 24 de 1814.

Fr. Paulo Alonso Carballo

No han llegado los padrones de Chiloe, y se pone aqui el estado de su poblacion como se halla en el mercurio peruano de 13 de Octubre de 1791. en el qual el numero de almas asciende á 15.601 indios, y 11.979 españoles, por todo 27.580. Pero, segun escriben los Misioneros de aq.a Provincia, en el estado presente tiene su poblacion de 37.000. almas. De los Misioneros de Chiloe se hallan dos en el exercito de Chilan q. son los P.P. Fr. Juan Almirall, y Fr. Ysidro Vidal, q. fueron con las tropas á peticion del Governador de aquella Provincia.

No se pone en este plan el estado de las misiones de Manoas, porq. aunq. por real cedula de 15 de Julio de 1802. se mandan entregar á este Colegio, hasta ahora en rigor no se ha verificado por las desavenencias del S.or Gobernador Calvo y del Ill.mo S.r Obispo: ni en la actualidad puede este Colegio hacerse cargo de ellas p.r la falta absoluta de religiosos, pues necesitando 150. p.a estas y demas atenciones indispensables, solo tiene 40. sacerdotes en todos los destinos.

Plate 6. Map showing the courses of the Huallaga and Ucayali Rivers, drawn by Paolo Monso Carballo of the Ocopa Missionaries' College, 1814. From *Maps of Peru*, folio 4. (Courtesy of the British Museum.)

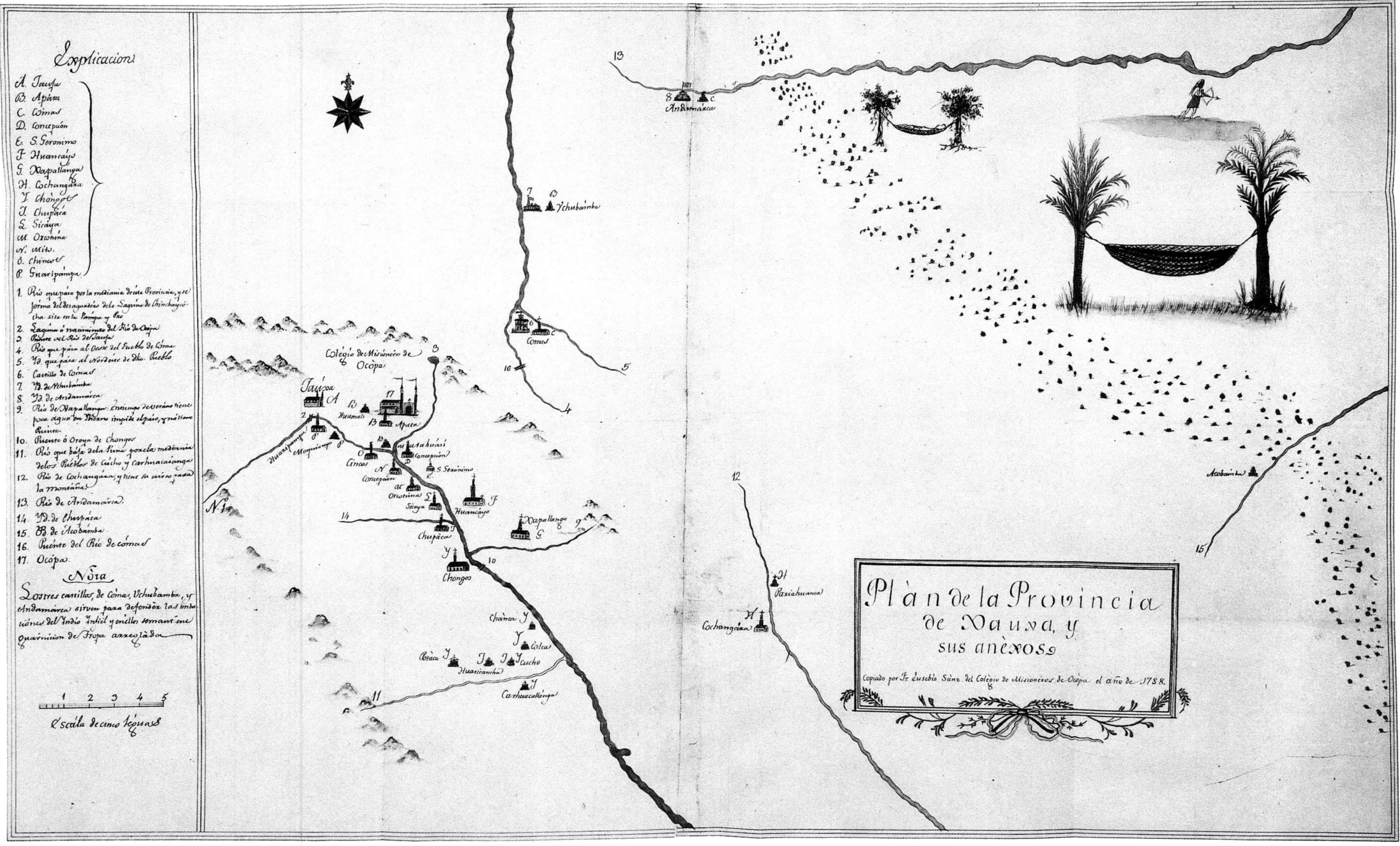

Plate 7. Map of Xauxa province, Peru, and surrounding areas, drawn by Eusebio Sanz of the Ocopa Missionaries' College, 1788. From the *Historical, Geographical, Political, Ecclesiastical and Military Survey of South America*, folio 41. (Courtesy of the British Museum.)

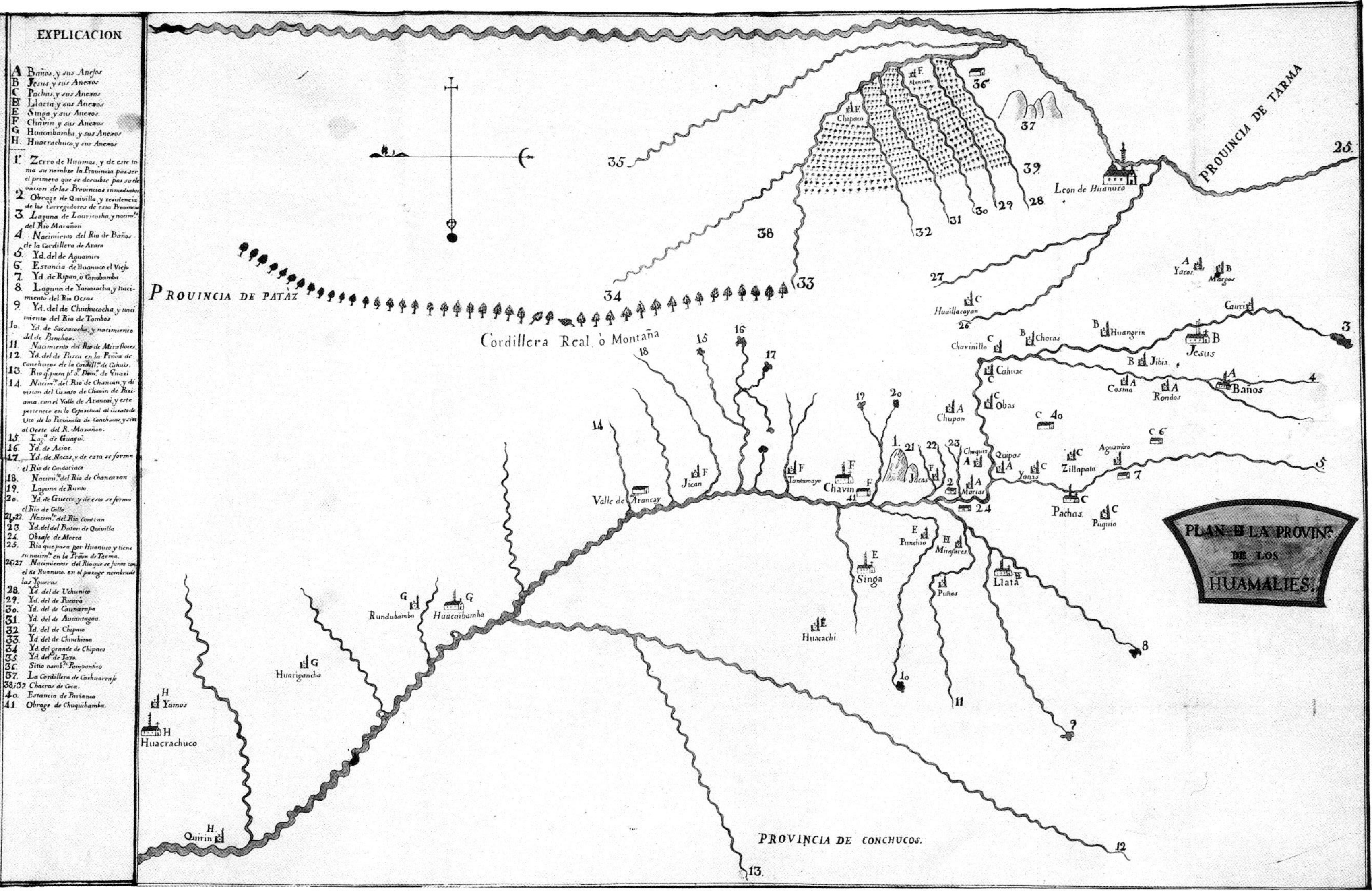

Plate 8. Map of Los Huamalíes province, Peru, by Eusebio Sanz, 1788? From the the *Historical, Geographical, Political, Ecclesiastical and Military Survey of South America*, folio 43. (Courtesy of the British Museum.)

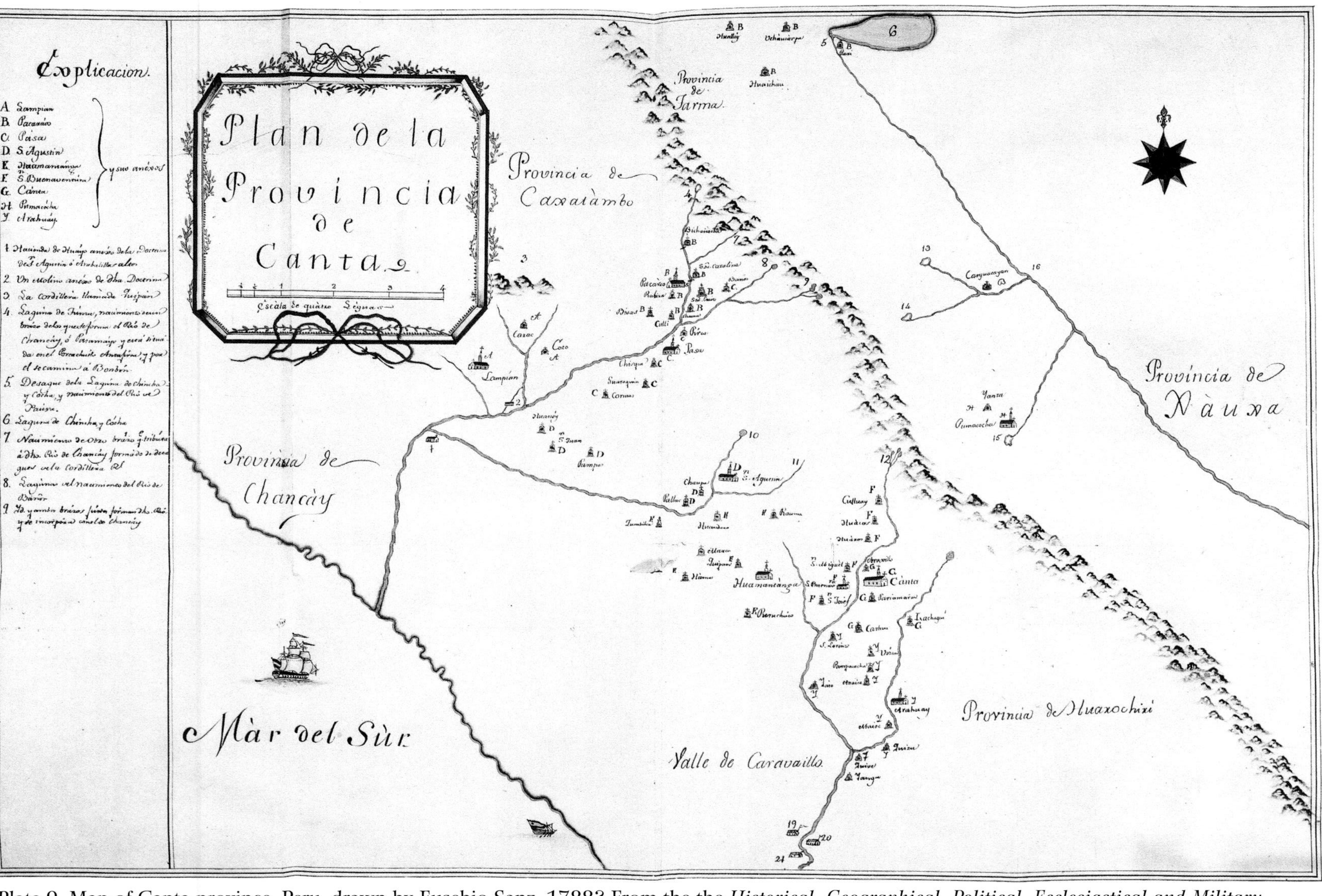

Plate 9. Map of Canta province, Peru, drawn by Eusebio Sanz, 1788? From the the *Historical, Geographical, Political, Ecclesiastical and Military Survey of South America*, folio 38. (Courtesy of the British Museum.)

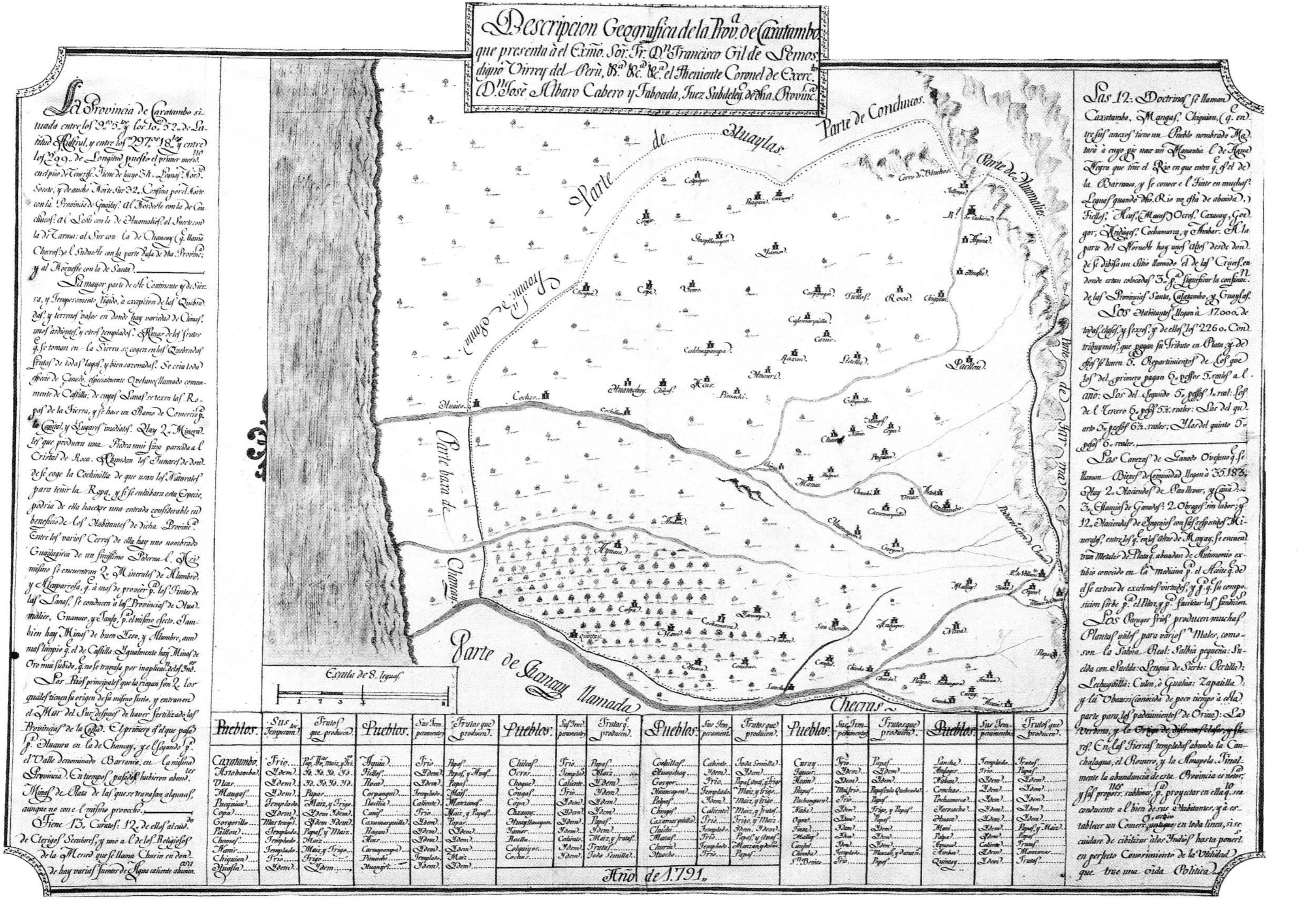

Descripcion Geografica de la Prov.ª de Caxatambo que presenta á el Exmõ. Sõr. Fr. D.n Francisco Gil de Lemos digño Virrey del Perú, &c.ª &c. &c.ª el Theniente Coronel de Exerc.to D.n José Albaro Cabero y Taboada, Juez Subdeleg.o de dha. Provinc.a

Plate 10. Map of Caxatambo Province, Peru, 1791. From the the *Historical, Geographical, Political, Ecclesiastical and Military Survey of South America*, folio 42. (Courtesy of the British Museum.)

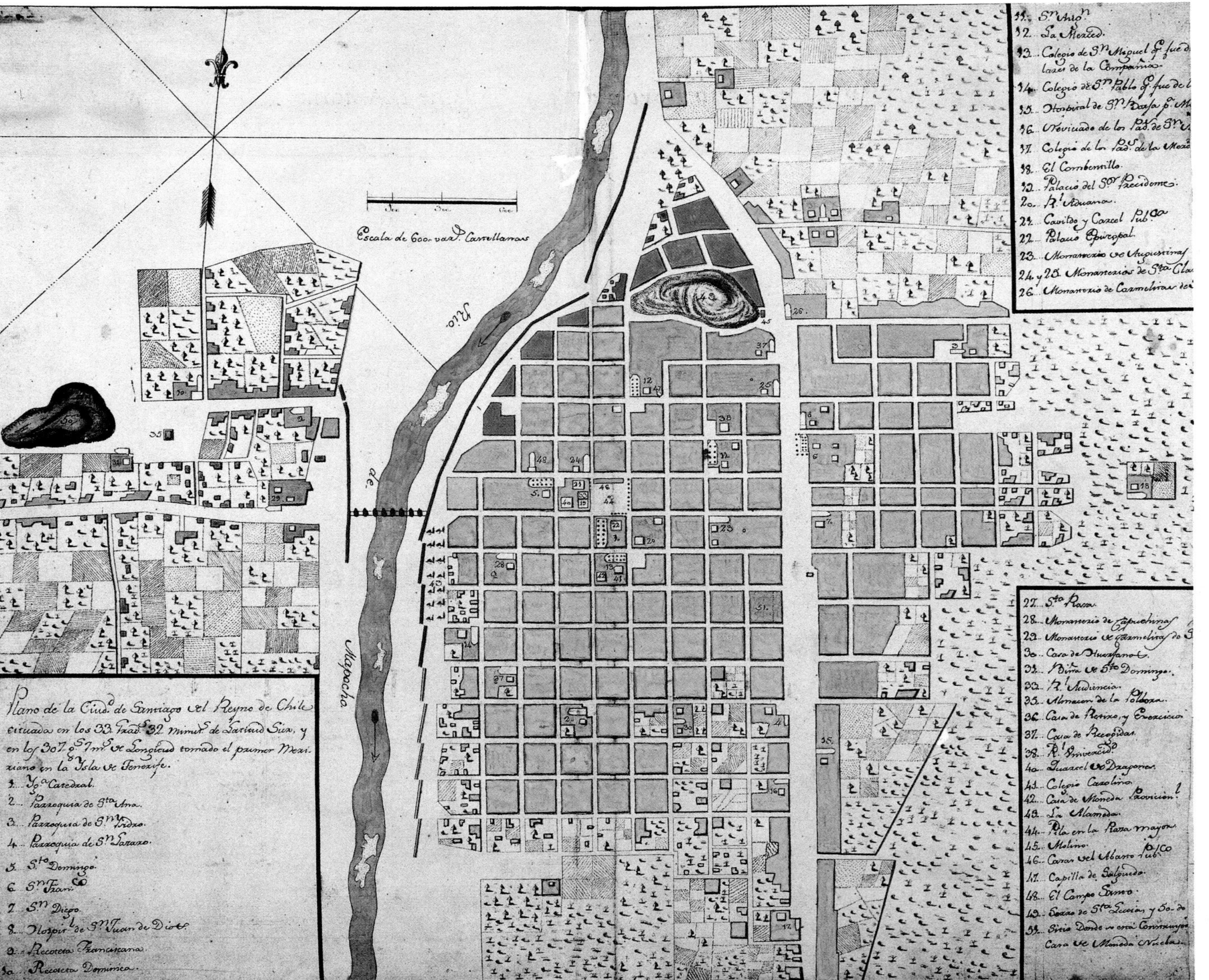

Plate 11. Map of the city of Santiago, Chile. From the the *Historical, Geographical, Political, Ecclesiastical and Military Survey of South America*, folio 51. (Courtesy of the British Museum.)

Silver, Mercury, and Gold

In 1778 and 1779, many mines of high-quality silver were discovered in the mining district of Huayanca. Some of the ores yielded 400 marks (3200 ounces) per box. As a result, a town of more than 500 souls was founded in that locality where in 1776 only vicuñas and huanacos lived.

A quicksilver mine has been discovered on the mountain called Chonta; it has already yielded a small amount of mercury. About 20 years ago, some silver mines were discovered in the region of Ayras. This location is being exploited by only two mine owners, and the place consists of nothing but a few houses, just a short way from Huayanca. There is also some gold ore, but it is not worked because of the high cost of reducing it. In the village of Chavín there are gold panners, and some people have taken out fair amounts of this metal.

Hot Springs; Royal Highway of the Incas; Ruins of Some Inca Palaces, Temples, and Fortifications

Between Aguamiro and Baños there are fountains, or springs, of warm water. The main highway of the Incas, which I mentioned in my description of Tarma, passes near Baños. There, too, the ruins of one of their palaces can be seen; it has a bath (Figure 8), constructed of stones perfectly cut. The remains of a temple and a fortification atop a mountain commanding a view of the river at Quivilla are also found there. Finally, on an extensive pampa, or high, cold heath, known as Huánuco el Viejo (Old Huánuco), 14 leagues from the present location of Huánuco, there are vast numbers of aetites, or eaglestones (nodules of clay ironstone). They are little used by these people.

The province of Huamalíes is divided into eight parishes distributed along both banks of the river. Most villages are in the highland areas.

The first parish is that of the village of Baños, with seven dependencies that are called Rondos, Cosma, Chupán, Quipas, Chuquis, Marías, and Margos, which falls under the jurisdiction of Tarma. The second parish is that of the village of Jesús, with its dependencies Xibia, Huaccrin, Choras, and Yacos, which also belongs to Tarma. The third parish is that of Pachas, with its dependencies Sillapata, Llamas, Aguamiro, Ovas, Cahuac, and Chavinillo or Chavinillos. The fourth is that of Llacta, with its dependencies Puños and Miraflores. The fifth is that of Zinha, with its dependencies Punchao and Huacachi. The sixth is that of Chavín de Pariarca, with its dependencies Tantamayo, Hacas, Xican, Chipaco, and Monzón. The seventh parish is that of Huacaybamba, where sugar cane is the main crop; its dependencies are Rundubamba and Huaricancha. The eighth parish is that of Huacrachuco, where sugar cane is likewise cultivated, with its dependencies Llamas and Quirin.

In the valley of Arancay, located at the eastern part of the Monzón River, there are five farms that ecclesiastically belong to the parish of Uco, which is in the prov-

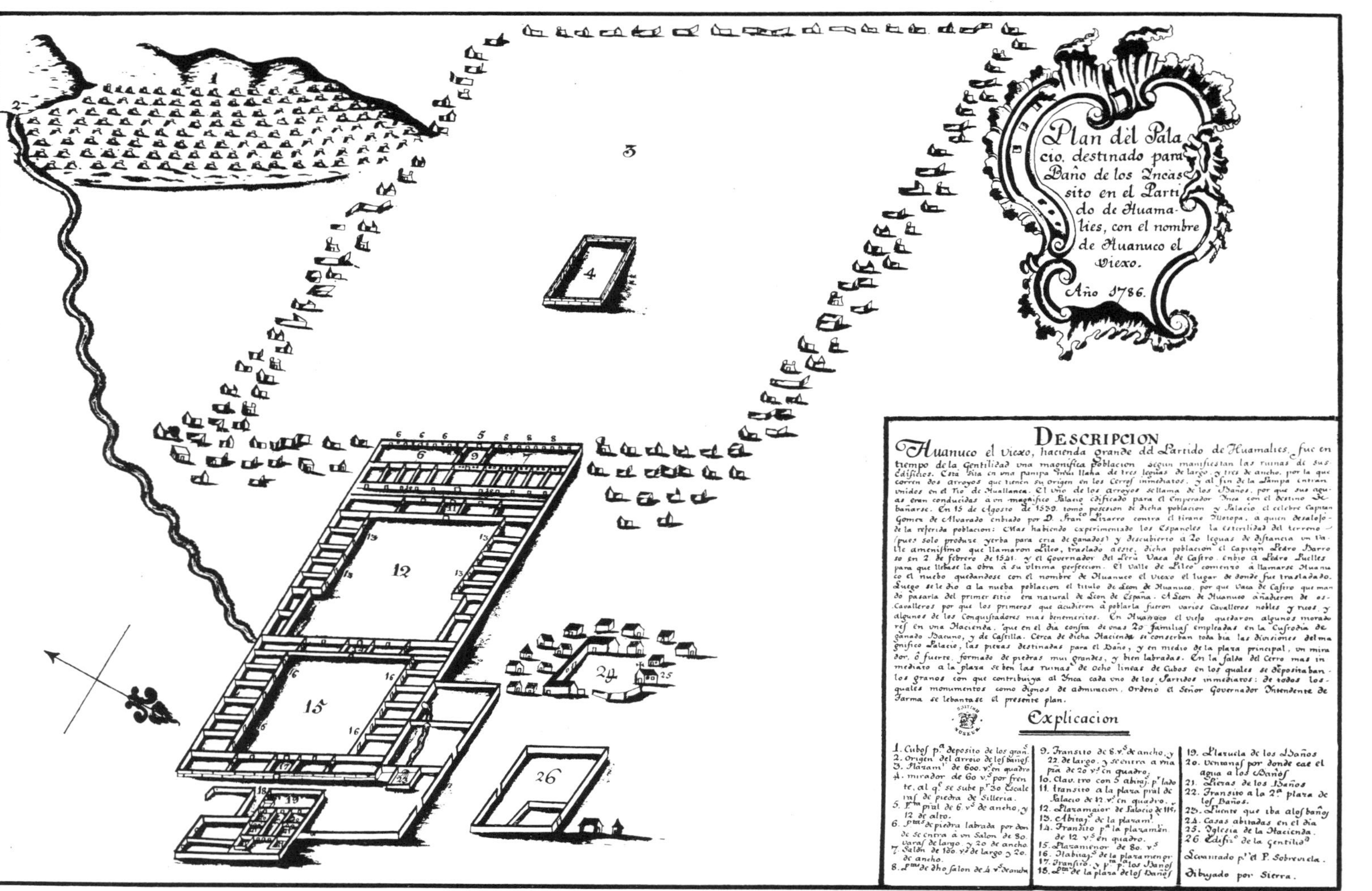

Figure 8. Plan of Inca baths, Peru, situated in the region of Huamalíes and known as Huánuco el Viexo. Drawn by Sobreviela, 1786. From *Maps of Peru*, folio 19. (Courtesy of the British Museum.)

ince of Conchucos. At the great weaving mill of Quivilla, in the center of the province and on the banks of the Marañón River—known as the Quivilla River in that region—the chief magistrates had their residency until 1780. The residency was then established in Huayanca, also known as Huallanca, by the chief magistrate Don Ignacio de Santiago y Ulloa. The discovery and exploitation of the mines was the reason for this change. In Quivilla, which forms a part of the parish of Pachas, there is an excellent cable bridge that the chief magistrate Don Domingo la Cagiga had built out of his own pocket in order to facilitate communication between the villages of one bank and the other. In payment for this beneficence, the Indians treacherously murdered him and set fire to his house in the deepest hours of the night. This bridge is more than 30 yards long and is anchored on enormous cliffs; it is the best bridge I have seen. Though there are only a few leagues between Quivilla and the lake of Lauricocha, the river in that region has a sufficient volume of water all through the year.

Dress and Weaving Among the Indians

Most of the inhabitants of this province are Indians, with some mestizos and very few whites. The Indians dress themselves with black or blue cloth from their own looms. They go barefoot even during the coldest season, or a few of them use the type of sandal known as sucuyes, a piece of rawhide strapped to the sole of the foot with two leather thongs.

The women wear a short skirt, but many use the anaco (native dress), both in the villages and on the farms. They spend their time tending their herds of cattle and spinning wool for the manufacture of jerga, light cloth, blankets, rugs, ponchos, handkerchiefs, and other objects. They also spin cotton for tocuyo (coarse cotton cloth) and for various kinds of cloth that combine cotton or silk and the wool of sheep or of native llamas, vicuñas, or huanacos. Animals, birds, and other figures are represented on these fabrics.

Drunkenness, Quarrels, and Inclination to Fight

The Indians are prone to drunkenness, especially at festive times. In a drunken state they will stir up fights among themselves, sometimes with mestizos, not infrequently with officers of the law, and even with the clergy. In those villages that have an Indian chief, this strife goes on most of the year, for the chiefs are wont to incite the natives of the village and its surroundings. The priests and the officers of the law almost invariably have to use force to keep the chiefs and Indian men under control in such riotous outbreaks.

The women, on the contrary, are peaceful; they are not given to strong drink and they try to keep their husbands out of many of the disputes. They are hardworking in whatever type of labor, and they prove this by their constant attention to their huts or houses and to their families, cattle, and crops, without mixing with the Indian men in their drunken sprees. If, as occasionally happens, the womenfolk do attend these sprees, it is only when they sow or reap their fruit and seeds, for in this work they are accompanied by their husbands and relatives who, at harvest time, are stimulated by the abundance of chicha prepared by the women just to get them to work. For the digging and the task called urias, or weeding the fields, the women work alone.

Festivals and Dances, Piety, Charity, Disposition for Work, Reproduction, and Misery

The Indians love dances. When they hold their dances for Twelfth Night, Corpus Christi, day of the patron saint of the village, etc., the celebrating and drunkenness last for 8 days or longer. If the magistrates and other officials did not make them work to pay tributes to the king, assessments to the magistrates, and debts to the merchants and creditors, the whole year would be a festival for the Indians, for they generally say that 1 day of drunkenness is worth more than a hundred lashes.

Indian men are not very devout, but are superstitious indeed. On the other hand, the women run to the churches and decorate the altars and images every day, and especially on holy days, with various flowers grown in their gardens for this use. They are affable and charitable in the midst of their misery. For this misery they can thank the laziness, and lack of interest in work, of their menfolk. The men waste in drink what their women earn spinning, weaving, and farming.

This indolence on the part of the males and devotion to work on the part of the females is, among the Indians, general throughout Peru. This evil state of affairs is the cause of their slow rate of reproduction and their universal misery. One might speak to the contrary of what Ochno said, "Torquere funiculam Ochno," when he saw that his wife was destroying his wealth.

Light from an Animal Source

On the 2nd of November we said our farewells to the magistrate Don Ignacio de Ulloa, who had extended us such sincere hospitality and was, together with his entire family, most kind and generous to us. We arrived to spend the night in Chavinillos. In the surroundings of the village we found an infinite number of lucernas, or glowworms, which shone so brightly that two of them, inside a cornet of white paper, were enough for a fortnight to allow me to read by night. We cannot doubt that if these animals could be kept and propagated in glass jars we would have a wonderful light for our houses, and could save the expenses of artificial lighting.

We arrived in Huánuco on the 3rd, with no particular trouble along the way. We gathered very few plant specimens.

I stayed on in the city of Huánuco, collecting and describing various new plants gathered in the neighborhood, until the 20th of November. On that date I went to the treasury at Pasco, with power of attorney for my companions, to receive our salaries. I spent the night in San Rafael.

On the 21st, while riding along a slope a league and a half from Huánuco, the man who was our muleteer and guide had to alight from his horse because the animal had become tired out. The mules came to a stop in the narrow pass, and to jog them onward he had to throw a stone. The last mule in the line gave him two kicks in the jowl and he fell unconscious to the ground, his cheekbone broken. Instantly three streams of blood gushed forth from three wounds, and he began to writhe on the ground. If I had not dismounted at once, he would have fallen over the highest cliff of the craggy mountain. I was able to grab him by the feet and tie him onto the slope, until the servant and the other muleteer heard my cries. Then, among all of us, when he had regained consciousness we were able to get out of the narrow pass.

For the time being, we staunched the blood with handkerchiefs soaked in rum. Upon arriving at the first brook, we washed the wounds and applied some balsamic herbs crushed between two stones, and this treatment stopped the flow of blood. He fainted away twice. We led him to the nearest hut, where I again treated his wounds and left him in good care, telling the inhabitants what treatment they should follow until my return.

The rest of us in the party continued on our way, all without the slightest knowledge of the right paths, so we went astray various times on the way. We also suffered considerably with the thunder and lightning, accompanied by some rain and hail, that fell upon us in the heights of Bombón. Not infrequently, we found ourselves surrounded by lakes and knew not where to turn. At long last we got to Pasco at eleven o'clock that night, frozen and bruised.

With the mule driver sick, I left Pasco on the 23rd. I had to wait in Quinua because the servant and mule driver who were bringing my baggage got lost, so we could get only as far as Caxamarquilla.

On the 24th we spent the night in Rondos, having found the wounded muleteer in Huariaca in very good spirits and ready to return to Huánuco along the road through the gorge, which was much shorter. This he did, as soon as he was cured.

On the 25th we entered Huánuco, with no worse luck than a mule being wounded when it rolled down a hillside with the baggage containing the money. The wounded mule recovered in 2 months, after four small pieces of bone were extracted. The lack of these bones left a noticeable depression in that part of its body.

We continued our botanical excursions in the valley and glens near Huánuco until the 22nd of March. During this time we discovered many plants, which we collected, dried, and described; these we have related following our description of Huánuco.

CHAPTER 28

Trip from Huánuco to Lima

On the 22nd of March 1781, we left Huánuco for Lima. The mule drivers and I spent the night in Ambo, and on the 23rd we left for Rondos. I went ahead with my servant to collect various plants on the outskirts of that village. Because they found the road very difficult to travel as a result of the rainstorm that overtook us at midday, the mule drivers slept a league from the village.

The artists Brunete and Gálvez left Huánuco on the 23rd, and Dombey and Pavón left on the 24th. On that same date my mule drivers arrived in Rondos at half past ten in the morning. I had them unpack the paper and the press so I could change the papers and put the plants that I had gathered along the road into the press. At twelve o'clock I left Rondos with the mule drivers, and went along with them until five in the afternoon. Then, in order to escape a furious storm, I went on ahead with my servant and my bedding, leaving the mule drivers in charge of the rest of the load. Since they could not make any progress with the mules on account of the thunder, lightning, and heavy downpour that fell upon them, they decided to remain behind under some overhanging cliffs. This decision was taken lest the mules run the risk of falling down the mountainside or into crevasses along the way.

When the storm overtook me, I was already on the hillside and was therefore obliged to continue on to Huariaca. Night caught up with me a league from the village. I certainly thought I would perish on that gloomy and horrible night. The storm of frightful claps of thunder, the tremendous downpour of rain, and the noise of the river, together with constant flashes of lightning, could bode nothing good along that narrow mountain pass full of precipices and gullies, bad enough even in the full light of a fine day.

Happily, I got out of these straits by following the footsteps of a person whom I had heard walking along ahead of me with a little donkey ever since I had started downhill. My servant no longer answered my calls. I asked the man ahead where he was going, how far from Huariaca we were, and whether or not there were any bad and dangerous spots. He answered every question in Spanish, promising to warn me of the bad places. And he kept his promise. Furthermore, he advised me to let the mule travel at its will, without pulling in the reins even though the mule stumble or slip, as it did three times on loose gravel and in the most exposed places where both man and beast could fall over the cliff to the river below.

When the cliffs and other major dangers were past, I begged my unknown guide to go back to search for my servant, and offered to pay him. He replied that the servant would be arriving shortly. I repeatedly whistled to the servant, but he did not answer. When we had left the roar of the river behind, I renewed my repeated whistling. When he failed to respond, I feared that he must have perished.

The unknown guide informed me that we were now near the village. I stopped for a bit and again called out to my servant and to the guide. Nobody answered me now. Finally, I walked along alone for a long stretch. Then once again I whistled to my servant, and he answered my call very close to me, but he said that that was the first time he had heard me. I asked him about the mule with our bedding and about the other without a load, and he answered that they had lost their way, for he had not heard their footsteps now for a long while.

We arrived at Huariaca at eight o'clock that night, soaked from head to foot. The village priest was astounded that we could have traveled along that stretch on such a night without suffering some accident. As we had lost our mules, he put us up in his house and charged the mayor to send out two Indians at dawn to search for them. The animal with the saddle, without a rider, appeared shortly; it was attracted by the neighing of my horse, to which it was accustomed. The other, with the bedding, was found by the Indians a league and a half from the village, lying down with the load and tired out as a result of carrying it all night long.

I have never been in such immediate danger of losing my life, of falling over a cliff in a place where nobody would have known a thing about it.

The muleteers arrived in Huariaca the next day. All the loads were soaked through, so I was obliged to stay there to take advantage of the beautiful sunny day to dry out the equipment and personal effects that were in the baggage. At two that afternoon the artists arrived; they continued the next day at dawn, leaving their baggage in the care of the mule drivers.

I left later with my muleteers and accompanied them for 2 leagues. Then, fearing another rainstorm, I went on ahead to the Cerro de Yauricocha. I arrived there with no misadventures, suffering only from the cold of those high altitudes, the hindrance of a few bogs, and the inconvenience of rain that caught me at the entrance to the hamlet. The mule drivers arrived the following day, and without any delay we all set out together to sleep, on a sheepskin blanket, at the estate of Diezmo.

On the 29th we left that farm and arrived at night at another, called Palcamayo, at the foot of the Andes. These places called punas have, in spite of their cold climate, an abundance of grasses all through the year. There is plenty of ichu grass and purum-icho (false ichu), both providing good pasturage for cows, horses, huanacos, and vicuñas. Among the herbaceous plants of the punas there are various species of *Gentiana*, and some diadelphias (diadelphous plants), syngenesias (syngenesious plants), and cryptogams.

We left Palcamayo on the 30th. One league from the farm, we were overtaken by a furious storm of thunder and lightning. This was followed by 2 hours of fine hail, which did not let up until we had passed the lofty Cerro de la Viuda, highest peak in those mountain ranges and always snowcapped. At eight at night we entered the village of Culluay, thoroughly wet through and bristling with the cold. As a result of this exposure, the head mule driver suffered a recurrence of the malarial fever that he had contracted on a previous trip to Lima.

We traveled but 4 leagues on the 31st, for some of the mules had become footsore from the wetness and the hard ground of the mountain crags. This often happens; it is not customary for these people to shoe the beasts of burden that travel through the mountains, for an unshod mule can get a better hold on the slopes and in dangerous places where there are loose stones.

On the 1st of April 1781 we slept in a tiny hut near the village of Obragillo. We spent the night of the 2nd of April in another farmer's hut, half a league from Quibo.

From this point on I went ahead of the mule drivers, since no plants occur in that area that are distinct from those found near Lima. I went along the Ríoseco road, a hot and totally sterile place enclosed by two long, unbroken mountain ranges of stone and sand. I passed the estate of Caballero; in its grasslands and pastures of alfalfa and grass, many head of cattle and horses are maintained all year round. At three in the afternoon I got to Lima. My baggage arrived on the 4th.

The artists arrived in Lima on the 8th, with no unhappy experiences on the road through the provinces of Tarma and Huarocherí. Dombey and Pavón turned up in Lima on the 15th, having come on the same road that I had used through the province of Canta. They had been set upon by some bandits who tried to steal their mules at night on the other side of the mountain, from which they had then come with much suffering from the rain and cold.

CHAPTER 29

Description of the Province of Canta

The province of Canta (Plate 9) is bounded on the east and northeast by the province of Tarma, on the west by that of Chancay and a part of Chacras, on the south by the province of Huarocherí, and along the rest of its border by the outskirts of Lima. It extends 24 leagues from north to south and 35 leagues from east to west, forming an oblong.

The climate of the mountainous regions and punas is very cold; at night ice and hoarfrost form, but by day both disappear under the sun's rays. On the slopes and in the ravines of the hills, the climate is mild. The deep gorges are hot throughout the year.

The terrain of Canta is broken and hilly, though in the gorges and on the slopes there are a few small, flat areas where the natives plant and harvest various root crops, fruits, green vegetables, and seeds. These include potatoes, massuas, arracachas, maize, horse beans and other beans, barley, alfalfa and other greens, guavas, granadillas (passion fruit), pacays (ingas), cherimoyas, paltas (avocados), and guanabanas (soursops). In gardens the Indian women grow different kinds of flowers to use in decorating the churches.

In the highlands, where there is plenty of ichu, purum-icho (false ichu), and other short grasses, large flocks of sheep and herds of cows and horses are kept. Llamas, huanacos, vicuñas, and vizcachas (chinchillalike rodents) are abundant on the punas. In these places where wood does not exist, the people burn taquia, or cow dung, and champas, or turf prepared as described in our discussion of the mining area of Pucará.

Descending the mountain towards Culluay, one finds a few mines that yielded much silver when they were worked in former years, sometimes fetching as much as 200 marks (1600 ounces) per box. But today none is being worked in this province. Hematite, alum, and copperas (vitriol) are found in various places, and there are two mountains of lodestone.

The numerous streams that flow down the mountain ranges and ravines form only two rivers. One of these rivers is the Carabaillo, which has its source in the lakes of Hacaybamba and Lorococha and empties into the southern sea between Lima and Chancay. The other river is the Huambra, arising in the lake of Punrun, which is 3 leagues long and 2 wide. The Huambra flows into the Parí River near Oroya, along with waters from the lakes of Huaychaó, Pomacocha, Cullue, and Huayllasrum; the last is 5 leagues long and 2 wide.

In the village of Santa Catalina there is a hot spring, the waters of which find their way to the Carabaillo River. All the water that Lima uses during the year comes from snow on the slopes of Hacaybamba.

This province has 54 villages, and some settlements and estates. The total population is 12,150, most of which is Indian; there are just 60 Spaniards or creoles, and 1730 mestizos.

The villages are organized into nine parishes, the first of which is that of Canta, with its dependencies Chaqui, Ccarhua, Obragillo, and Pariamarca. The second parish is that of Pomacocha, with dependencies Ccarhuacayán and Llanta. The third is that of Parí, with dependencies Uchayucarpa, Huayllay, Huaychaó, Pacaraos, Vichaycocha, Santa Cruz, Santa Catalina, Chaucá, Ravira, Chupas, Culli, and Vircas.

The fourth parish is that of upper Atabillos, with its dependencies Pasachisque, Huaroquin, Ccormo, Pirca, Baños, and Alpamarca. The fifth is that of Lampián, with dependencies Cotoc and Carac. The sixth is that of lower Atabillos, with its dependencies Pallac, Champis, San Agustín, Huascoy, San Juan, and Pampas.

The seventh parish is that of Huamantanha, where there is a much-visited church with a crucifix shrine to worship; its dependencies are Quípan, Marco, Sumbilca, Ama, Huandaro, Rauma, and Puruchuco, where the earth is excellent for making pottery. The eighth parish is that of San Buenaventura, with its dependencies San José, San Miguel, Huácos, Huáros, and Culluay. The ninth parish is that of Arahuay, with its dependencies Biscas, San Lorenzo, Pampacocha, Anaica, Yasu, Mayu, Quisu, Yanha, and Quibe; in Quibe there is a poor little chapel where the glorious Santa Rosa de Lima dwelled for a number of years.

Most natives of this province are mule drivers, working chiefly in the mining districts of the Cerro de Yauricocha to transport ores from the mines to the smelters. For this work they keep many mules. Other men work the mines. The womenfolk tend the fields and care for the family while their husbands are away in the mines. They also spin and weave woolen and cotton goods for domestic use. Women generally wear the anaco (native dress), and many use a short skirt.

Mal de Verrugas

The illness called mal de verrugas (Carrion's disease) is common in some gorges. If the eruptions do not appear rapidly, the result is a long, troublesome, and dangerous illness. A decoction of *Mespilus uniflora*, taken in quantities, is employed to treat these verrugas, or purulent eruptions, which eat away the flesh; this medicine is the only remedy.

Mal de Llagas and Its Agent of Infection

In this province there frequently occurs another ailment, mal de llagas, which causes flesh-consuming ulcers, especially on the face. The cure is not only a long process but also very difficult. For these reasons, along with a lack of good physicians and with utter neglect in the early stages of the disease, many sufferers die. When they do go to the hospitals in Lima for treatment, it is already too late; remedies are of no avail and cannot check the progress of this kind of skin cancer. The natives say that this disease is caused by the bite of a very tiny and almost invisible insect called uta.

Likewise, we observed pains in the side, tabardillos (spotted fever), and some tertian fevers (malaria). The Indians themselves treat these ills with herbs, used according to availability. There are no doctors.

Among the numerous medicines of plant origin that grow plentifully in those gorges, moors, and mountains, one can find genuine calaguala, the one used in Lima and elsewhere in Peru as the most efficacious. One also finds pomaysancca; quinchamali, or chinchimali; and huachanccana, huachancana, or purga de pobres (poor man's laxative). The Indians use the tuberous roots of this last plant, a species of *Euphorbia*, taking about 1 dram in an infusion; when they want to stop the purgative effects of this remedy, they drink a glass of very cold water. In Huánuco a preparation of equal parts of the fresh root and sugar is made up, and a dose of 2 drams of this is given for a milder effect than raw huachanccana.

The number of species of *Cactus* growing in the hot ravines and on the slopes of the hills is considerable. Down in the depths of the valleys there are abundant *Calceolaria*, many syngenesias (syngenesious plants), and some Malvaceae. There are many other delightful plants of known medicinal and economic uses and properties. Among these are *Scorzonera peruviana* and *Loasa grandiflora*, as well as species of *Molina*, *Ambrosia*, *Terrazia*, *Kageneckia*, *Traxinus*, *Saracha*, *Periphragmos*, and others. We have discussed all these plants in our descriptions of the provinces of Huarocherí, Tarma, and Huánuco, and for this reason we refrain from any consideration of them here.

From the 16th of April to the 4th of July 1781 we remained in Lima, drying the plants collected along the way and finishing the descriptions of many of them. I arranged and packed, according to their classes, all that we had collected in the jungles and mountainous areas.

We received news that the ship *Buen Consejo* had been seized by the English, but we had no idea whether or not it had succeeded in unloading its cargo in the Azores before being captured. I therefore spent some time in the valleys and on the mountains near Lima, collecting various plants that are found there, to replace what we thought was lost. We also decided to visit the province of Chancay again with this same purpose in mind, crating up the results of our work in the mountains and roads of Tarma and Huánuco before leaving.

When we had obtained the viceroy's permit and had made preparations for the trip, we sent off the equipment with the mule drivers, who left Lima for Chancay on the 4th of July.

CHAPTER 30

Second Trip to the Province of Chancay

On the 5th of July 1781 the Spanish botanists and artists left Lima for the province of Chancay. Mr. Dombey remained in the capital to join a naval officer and a pilot of the port of Callao in making some observations on the tides of the ocean, at the request of Mr. Lalande and by order of the viceroy.

We arrived at half past seven at night at the estate of Torreblanca, with no mishap beyond the discomfort of the sun's heat on those sandy deserts. We stayed on this estate until the 10th of August, spending many days in the company of the owner, Don Toribio Bravo de Castillo. A gentleman of the most distinguished society of Lima, he was one who took the greatest pains to extend us hospitality in that country. He not only brought us into his house and sat us at his table on the two occasions that we were in Torreblanca, but also accompanied us for several days on our plant-collecting trips in the vicinity.

On the 10th of August we went on to the town of Huaura. We stayed there until the 3rd of September, when we set out for the village of Sayán, 10 leagues inland. We crossed the estate called El Ingenio (The Mill), owned by Don Francisco de la Puente, a gentleman from Lima. This estate, once owned by the Jesuits, measures 1 square league and has two millstones that grind every day to produce from 28 to 30 loaves of fine-quality sugar, each weighing 2 arrobas (about 50 pounds). Each arroba of sugar is worth from 30 to 40 reales of local money. The sugar is like Dutch sugar: pure, white, and extremely solid.

Leaving this estate, we entered that of Pativilca, owned by Don Pedro de la Presa, a gentleman of Lima. Though this estate is larger than the other, at the present time nothing is maintained there but many head of cattle. In former years, extensive harvests of delicious sugar were produced, but the owner abandoned this work when he transferred his slaves to another estate.

From Pativilca we continued on to the estate called Humaya; it is much larger than the two preceding ones. The Jesuits formerly owned it, but today it is the property of the sons of Don Juan Antonio Blanco, who are citizens of Lima. Four or six pairs of oxen grind sugar cane day and night, daily producing 30 to 40 loaves of sugar superior in quality to that of neighboring estates. In order for the sugar mills to continue working, this estate needed 150 more negro slaves than it had; the mills are often stopped for a lack of laborers. Because of high humidity and the excessive heat of the sun, the negroes fall sick oftener on this estate than on others, for the locality is more sheltered.

From Humaya we went on to Quipico, an estate owned by Don Antonio Boza, a gentleman of Lima. It produces from 24 to 30 loaves of sugar of good quality. Quipico is more than 2 leagues long, and its homes, offices, and church are distributed in a manner better than that of all the other villages in the valley. The caldrons, refining machinery, drying equipment, and warehouses of Quipico do not compare unfavorably with those on the estates mentioned above, and are even better than those on the estate of Don Puente. The mills and other workshops associated with sugar production are even more extensive on the Humay estate than on the preceding ones.

We passed the night in Quipico, and remained there for a day because the public prosecutor of Lima, Don Joaquín Galdeano, was visiting the estate. Don Joaquín is from my part of Spain; only the day before, he had received news of his being named a judge in Mexico. He wanted to accompany us in the fields of the plantation to watch us collecting plants.

On Quipico I described the *Momordica operculata* of Linnaeus, which is plentiful along the hedges of the estate. The negroes there employ the dried fruits, which they call jaboncillos (little soaps), in place of dishrags to scour the mates, or calabashes (gourds), from which they eat.

After noontime on the 5th we left for Sayán, in the company of Señor Galdeano. We arrived at three that afternoon. We visited the gorge and mountains in the vicinity, finding no new material for our collection.

As the inhabitants told us that we would find no plants other than those of the coast until we got to the mountain range, we went on to spend the night at Andahuasi, an estate of the Augustinian fathers of Lima that produces from 18 to 20 loaves of sugar daily. On this estate they have finished the construction of spacious, rectangular slaves' quarters with many separate huts arranged along uniform, straight streets, where the negro couples stay at night. Married slaves live apart from single ones, but all under the same lock and key, although each has a key that fits the door of his own hut. The monk who started this estate, only recently and on untilled soil, began the work with nothing but 14 pesos. At the time of our arrival he had progressed so well, by dint of hard work and constancy, that it was yielding about 60 pesos of profit a day above the cost of maintaining laborers and supplying their equipment.

Parkinsonia aculeata is abundant on this estate. I had it sketched here, and it grew in Lima from seeds that I took from Sayán to the little garden of Buenamuerte.

The valley that stretches from Huaura to Sayán is indeed pleasant, fertile, and agreeable because of the many plantations of sugar cane encountered, the diversity of fruits and seeds sown and harvested, and the variety of trees, shrubs, and herbaceous plants growing wild there.

What is astonishing is that most estate owners in this valley are nearly always short of money and workers. This is especially true since the shipments of negroes from Lima have stopped. Most of these landowners annually produce 40 to 60 thousand pesos' worth of sugar, molasses, and chancaca (brown sugar), and they harvest on the same estates much fruit for the maintenance of the help.

CHAPTER 31

Description of the Village of Sayán

The village of Sayán is located at the foot of a mountain of red earth, a kind of blood-colored clay, and at the mouth of a gorge at the end of the range. Here the valley of Huaura begins, and descending the gorge is the river that waters the valley. This river has no ford in the rainy season, when it must be crossed by the stone bridge at Huaura or the one at Sayán, which is built of timbers bound together.

Coming from Huaura, before arriving at Sayán, one sees a large arched rock that has fallen away from the cliff; the road passes beneath it. Round about the village there are various small farms and alfalfa fields with some fruit trees. The houses and shelters are rather far apart, except for the buildings on the plaza where the more affluent mestizos dwell. All the buildings are made of quimcha, or reed grass, plastered with mud inside and out. The inhabitants are mestizos and tax-paying Indians, and most of them live continuously on their little farm plots, where each has his hut.

The mountains, which surround the gorges of Sayán for a distance of 5 leagues beyond the village, are dry and devoid of plants all the year round, for it never rains or even mists heavily there. One league from Sayán the jurisdiction of the province of Caxatambo (Plate 10) begins. Down another ravine there flows a small brook with enough water to irrigate the small farmlands located in the ravine, along both banks of the stream.

Both ravines and almost the whole valley of Huaura are very hot throughout the year. The sky is usually clear both day and night, for neither rains nor garúas, or mists, occur more than 2 leagues inland from the seashore, as is true all along the coasts of Lima, Chancay, Cañete, etc.

On the 6th the artists set off for Lima by way of Huaura, passing us from Andahuasi to Torreblanca through the narrow passages of Jequar. There we suffered much from the heat of the sun's rays reflecting from the sandy stretches and bare mountains and lowlands, to within a league of entering the estate of Retes.

From Retes we crossed to the estate of Esquibel and arrived at Torreblanca, where we met up again with Don Toribio Bravo de Castilla, our benefactor and a lover of botany. This he demonstrated by accompanying us on our walks, not only on his estate but also in Lima and in the mountains of Amancas, and by gathering various plants himself and drying them in presses that he, like ourselves, carried for that purpose.

We explored the mountains of Jequar once again on the 7th, and also collected on the estate of Jequar, owned by Don Mauricio Zuazo, a gentleman of Lima. We gathered various plants and among them *Salsola fragilis*, very plentiful in those fields that are covered with sodium sulfate and are called salitrales, or niter beds. Indeed, in this area there is much niter, or saltpeter, or potassium nitrate; I collected some well-formed crystals of this mineral on the fields of coarse grass.

On all the estates near Arnedo or Chancay large numbers of swine are kept for fattening, to provide lard for Lima and other towns in the province.

During our plant collecting on this second trip to the province of Chancay—along the coasts, in the valleys, on the slopes, and in the mountains—we found various new plants and prepared dried specimens of them, as well as of some that we already knew from Huánuco and the regions around Lima. I described the following plants.

Boerhavia viscosa, called pegajosa (sticky) in reference to the stickiness of the plant, which adheres to the clothing of those who brush by it.

Calceolaria pinnata, called yerba de la bolsilla (pocket herb) for the shape of its flowers. In Peru the plant is commonly used in an infusion or a decoction as an excellent diuretic and aperitif; it is employed especially in treating gonorrhea.

Salvia rhombifolia and *S. excissa*. *Dianthera mucronata*. *Calyxhymenia expansa* and *C. ovata*. *Valeriana pinnatifida*. *Spermacoce tenuior*. *Buddleja occidentalis*. *Cissus compressicaulis*, yedra (ivy). *Tillaea connata*. *Potamogeton compressum*. *Heliotropium synzystachium*. *Salsola fragilis*.

Chenopodium album, yerba del gallinazo (buzzard's herb). Natives frequently use an infusion or a decoction of this plant to cure jaundice.

Solanum repens; *S. peruvianum*, tomate cimarrón (wild tomato), used as a condiment by some people when they cannot get ordinary tomatoes.

Xuarezia biflora, té del Perú (Peruvian tea); many people dry and keep the leaves of this plant to use in place of Chinese tea.

Lycium aggregatum, called mancapaqui, or pot breaker, because its wood explodes and shatters when burned, or at least bumps and overturns pots as it cracks. The leaves are useful as an emollient or a suppurative, and they are crushed, mixed with lard, and applied as a poultice for such purposes.

Campanula biflora. *Physalis angulatum*. *Atropa umbellata*. *Cordia rotundifolia*, called tina or membrillo (quince); an infusion or a decoction is very effective in cases of jaundice, which is frequently treated with this plant in Peru.

Bowlesia palmata. *Allium angulatum*, feligranas, cultivated in gardens as an ornamental; *A. triquetrum*. *Oenothera prostrata*. *Jussiaea peruviana*, flor del clavo (clove flower). *Euphorbia elliptica*. *Bartsia trinervis*.

Cassia tora, cañafistola cimarrona (wild purging cassia). The pulp of the fruits, or pods, is used as a laxative by the natives, as is an infusion of the fresh leaves. The dosage is from a half ounce to an ounce of either pulp or leaves.

Caesalpinia paipai, called paipai. The solid wood of the trunk of this small, leafy tree makes it valuable for various applications in woodworking. The pods of its fruits are also used as black dye and as writing ink. This ink, however, like that made from *Caesalpinia tara*, fades out in a short time; the black color changes to a reddish hue in a few years.

Malpighia nitida, called ciruela de fraile (friar's plum) or ciruela de la tierra (native plum). The flesh of the fruit, which is red, tender, and as soft as butter when ripened in bran or other material, is sweet but cloying, albeit appetizing to many people. The pit, or kernel of the seed, is pleasing like an almond, but causes immediate nausea even when only a few are eaten.

Annona squamosa, anono. This tall, stout, and leafy tree grows wild in the Andean forests of Peru, but along the seacoast it is found only in cultivation. Its fruit, called anona (custard apple, sweetsop), is globose to conical in shape and somewhat resembles a pineapple. The skin is rather thick and leathery, and has scalelike protuberances that are more or less pronounced. The pulp of the fruit is white, tender, sweet, and as soft and smooth as butter. Its flavor is more delicate than that of the chirimoyo (cherimoya), or *Annona tripetala* as described in *Flora Peruviana et Chilensis*, and this is especially true of those fruits grown in the village of Huacho, from where they are sent to Lima as special gifts. The wood is valued for use in carpentry. Since we have not found in the epithet *squamosa* the certain differentiation of this species from the others, we have called ours *Annona pteropetala*, in reference to a character that we believe is of sufficient importance to separate it from the other species of the genus.

Annona muricata, guanábano; this tall, stout, and leafy tree is cultivated in Peru. Its fruit, called guanábana (soursop), is heart-shaped, weighs 1 to 6 pounds, and has white, bittersweet pulp. The fruit is in every way inferior to the anona and the cherimoya, and one cannot eat as much of it as of the other two. Good planks, beams, and boards for construction and other uses are made from the trunks of guanábanos.

Crescentia cujete, totumo or tutumo (calabash tree, gourd tree). This little tree, 6 to 9 yards tall at the most, is always leafy and very pretty, especially when it has blossoms with a few fruits persisting from the previous year. The fruits, called totumas or tutumas (calabashes, gourds), have a very hard shell or husk, and the natives use them in place of jicaras (cucurbit gourds) to make cups for drinking maté or chocolate. They only have to saw through the fruits at the head and remove the seeds and pulp; later, they ornament them with little pieces of silver and gold along the edge and at the base.

Empty totumas are also useful for gathering and keeping balsams and resins. When the totuma is to be used for this purpose, the natives make a small hole in the lower end of it—that is, in the part cut across in the preparation of cups—and remove the flesh. This flesh is cooked with sugar over embers until blended perfectly, and then a sufficient quantity of sweet almond oil is added to make a thick and very tasty syrup. This preparation is very efficacious in treating internal abscesses and alleviating the symptoms of asthma, in a dose of a half ounce to 1 ounce twice a day.

Sida americana and *S. repens*, pilapila; water in which either of these plants has been scraped is frequently used by members of the fair sex as a dressing to stimulate the growth of their hair. *Sida jamaicensis* and *S. cristata*. *Sida capillaria*, matayerno (son-in-law killer).

Sida lutea and *S. frutescens*, pichana (broom). On holidays the negroes on the farms sell the roots of pichana in little bundles at the price of half a real, for cleansing the teeth of tartar. Women also use the roots as a diversion when in the home, out riding, or on visits, keeping them in the mouth without taking them out except to spit.

Malva peruviana, malva común (common mallow). This species is used in the same way as is the mallow in Europe. *Malva coromandeliana*?

Malope moschata, called almizclillo (little musk) for the odor that this plant exhales, much like that of almizcle (musk) but weaker.

Crotalaria incana and *C. laburnifolia*, called cascabelillos (little bells), because the seeds rattle when the dry pods are shaken in the wind or by hand. *Hedysarum prostratum*. *Dolichos soja*?, frijolillos (little beans); the seeds are eaten cooked and are very tasty. It is a cultivated plant. I have never seen it growing wild.

Spilanthes urens, called salivatoria (saliva maker) because the plant activates salivation when chewed. In Peru it is employed to lessen the pain from aching molars.

Galinsoga quadriradiata and *G. quinqueradiata*, pacoyuyo; in Peru both species are known by this vernacular name. These plants are used, without regard to species, to treat ulcers of the mouth; the sores are wiped with the juice of the leaves many times a day.

Eclipta alba. *Bidens cuneiformis*. *Encelia obliqua*. *Sobreyra repens*. *Matricaria tripartita*. *Centaurea napifolia*?, which Indians use in an infusion or a decoction to treat intermittent fevers.

Molina ivoefolia and *M. scandens*; both species are known as chilca. The leaves and terminal shoots of the plants are crushed and applied as a poultice to alleviate the pain of bruises or sprains.

Serapias flava. Satyrium viride. Ferraria violacea. Atriplex crystallina.

Passiflora suberosa?, ñorbo cimarrón (wild passion fruit); *P. foetida*, puchepuche. Children eat the pulp of the ripe fruit of both species, and ants devour them before they fully ripen.

Amaranthus retroflexus and *A. spinosus*, called yuyos cimarrones or yuyus cimarrones (wild yuyos). Several times we ate salads made from the tender young leaves of this plant; they are tasty and a gentle aid to digestion.

Elaterium bifidum, caihua de lomas (caihua of the hills). *Elaterium pedatum*, caihua; this plant is cultivated in Peru. Its fruits are used instead of small squash, filled with minced meat or small meatballs; when cooked, they taste rather like the pepino (cucumber) of Spain. When a woman is sluggish, somewhat stupid, and generally awkward in her movements, Peruvians are wont to compare her with the caihua and say, "So-and-so is a caihua." This simile is applied only to women, not to men; in similar circumstances, men are called candidos.

Mimosa sensitiva, called tapate (close up), ciérrate puta (close up, whore), or ciérrate putilla (close up, little whore), in reference to this plant's property of contracting and folding up its leaflets when touched.

A Depilatory Plant?

Mimosa latisiliqua, yerba de la lancha. Natives say that when horses and mules eat this plant, they lose the hair of their manes and tails, and that the hair is not renewed for a long time. They also say that if a man should wash his head for a number of days in water in which many leaves of the plant have been crushed, he will become completely bald. We must not believe that many have undergone this experiment, for nobody wants to be bald. If it had the same effect upon the beard, it would be worth its weight in gold, especially in that country.

CHAPTER 32

Trip from Chancay to Lima

On the 9th of September 1781 the two Spanish botanists left Torreblanca for Lima. We arrived on the same day, with no problem except uncomfortable heat in the sunny, sandy stretches that exist as far as the heights of Lancón or the plains of Copacabana.

We all remained in Lima until the 19th of December, drying and describing the plants collected on the way from Huaura to Lima, and describing those I found on the outskirts of the capital in gardens and orchards. Among these, I described the following.

Atropa aspera. *Ipomoea hirsuta*, called auroras (dawn) for its flowers. *Weinmannia pinnata*, a shrub transplanted from the mountains to the gardens of Lima for its effectiveness as a febrifuge when taken as a decoction of the leaves.

Parkinsonia aculeata; because of their length, consistency, and flexibility, its petioles can be used to make baskets, scouring tools, and other objects when treated in the same way as linen and hemp.

Hibiscus rosa-chinensis and *H. esculentus*, naju; negroes use the capsules or fresh fruits of these plants to season certain foods, which we found nauseous and unpleasant because of the amount of viscous matter these fruits contain.

Dodartia fragilis. *Cosmos pinnatus*, esteemed for its flowers as ornamentals in gardens. *Helianthus pubescens*.

Tessaria dentata, pájaro bobo (stupid bird). Although it does not last long in the fire, its wood is the one most commonly burned in the kitchens in Lima, along with that of manglillo, another fuel of short duration. The branches of *T. dentata* are also used in the suburbs of Lima for roofing huts.

Llagunoa triphylla, called árbol del rosario (rosary tree) because its black, round seeds resemble common rosary beads, and some people do string them to make rosaries.

Rebellion of Tupac-Amaro

When the collections of dried plant specimens and other natural products that had been gathered in the provinces of Chancay and Lima were arranged, we asked the viceroy for permission to leave them in the royal armory as we had done earlier with the material from Tarma, Huánuco, and the forests of Huánuco. Permission was granted and storage was effected.

We then requested authorization to travel to Chile, since we were full of news of the richness of that country. At that time we also found ourselves disturbed in the provinces of Peru by the rebellion of Gabriel Tupac-Amaro and his brother Diego. These men wanted to crown themselves in Peru, and would have succeeded if the promptness and foresight of Inspector Areche, who went to Cuzco in person, had not at the start put out the fire that was burning on all sides.

When we had obtained the authorization of the viceroy and the inspector to travel to Chile and continue our commission there, we made our preparations and arranged for the voyage with the captain of the ship called *Nuestra Señora de Belén*, which was leaving for Chile to take on a cargo of grains and wines in the port of Talcahuano.

CHAPTER 33

Trip from Peru to Chile

On the 19th of December 1781 the five members of the expedition, with our servants and equipment, set out from Lima for the port of Callao. On the 20th the port authorities visited the ship, and on the 21st we set sail at ten o'clock in the morning. The breeze was very light; at six in the evening we could still see the point of the island of San Lorenzo, near the port of Callao, but shortly thereafter it was hidden from view by dense fog. During the day, our speed had been 2 miles an hour; at night, the south wind disappeared completely.

At nine o'clock on the morning of the 22nd of December, the south wind began to stir and we moved about 2 or 3 miles an hour. The sky remained overcast until evening, when all the clouds were dispersed. We saw many bonitos (striped tunnies), dolphins, and seals.

On the 23rd the day dawned perfectly cloudless; with a south wind and slight swells, we made 3 miles an hour. The sun came out, and the seasick passengers, kept from the dining room for the past 3 days by the heavy seas, returned to meals. We continued sailing with the same wind until the 27th, at 2 to 4½ miles an hour, without having changed the sails since leaving Callao. On the 25th we lost a calf overboard at night; the darkness prevented our rescuing the animal, which was sorely missed on the trip.

From the 28th on, the south wind made the weather cooler. We had numerous squalls or rainfalls, and sailed from 3 to 6 miles an hour.

CHAPTER 33

Phosphorescence in the Ocean

By the 15th of January we found ourselves at 32°2', with no important misadventures on the trip. We had seen nothing in the sea that drew our attention except a few dorados (giltheads), and some phosphorescent flashes all during the previous week. The phosphorescence was so much in evidence on the 15th that the prow and the helm of the ship, as well as its wake, seemed to be on fire as if with burning sulfur or spirits. Some attribute this phosphorescent light to bituminous and oily substances secreted by certain fishes; it is said that these substances, mixed with the saltwater and churned up by the waves and the friction of the ship's passing, offer this sightly phenomenon.

To ascertain whether there are insects in the water, as others suspect, or to observe oily substances, we repeatedly took numerous samples of water in buckets or tubs and studied them under good lenses, but found nothing. We stirred up the water with various instruments in dark places, but very rarely observing a weak, transitory sparkle.

From the 17th to the 26th there was a wind that was too cool, and so strong that we had to pull in all the sails and navigate with none but the great sail and the foresail. There were many squalls, with constant and violent rolling, pitching fore and aft, and incessant creaking of the ship's beams and planks. An endless number of pounding waves threw water into the hatchways, and we suffered from frequent and very bothersome spells of seasickness. All of this made us extremely uneasy, and we kept to our cabins and were strapped down to eat with our plates close to our chests. At six in the morning on the 24th, a Biscayan passenger named Balaya fell overboard and, in spite of our efforts to help him, he was never seen again after falling into the water, for the sea was very choppy and we were sailing at a speed of 7 miles an hour with the two aforementioned sails. This unfortunate man was journeying with sugar and articles of commerce to the city of Concepción. Having gone to relieve himself at the chainwales, he fell overboard with the rolling of the ship.

At eleven on the 26th, from the prow we spied the island of Santa María and, shortly thereafter, the Tetas de Biobio (Teats of Biobio, a headland). The wind had grown in strength, so the sails were hauled in. Towards evening, when the wind had calmed down, they were hoisted again, and the pilot decided to enter the port of Talcahuano by moonlight. We made good progress until midnight, when the wind died down.

At seven in the morning, when the breeze renewed its activity, the sails were again hoisted. One of them flung a British seaman, at work on the topsail of the mizzenmast, into the ocean. However, as the breeze was slight and the sea calm, the ship easily turned around and two oars were put out. The seaman caught onto one of them, and it helped him keep afloat while the boat that the unfortunate man had requested was launched. This was done in all haste, and everyone present assisted in the work. Four seamen went out in the boat, rescued the English sailor about a mile from the ship, and came back with their shipmate without any mishap. On the return he plied the oars himself from the moment he got into the boat, in order to warm himself.

On the 27th, at nine o'clock, a boat that had left Talcahuano with an officer of the navy arrived; it was commanded by Señor Bacaro and had a berth in that port. Our mail was given to this officer, who returned with it to Talcahuano.

On the 28th we were becalmed, and our ship was towed out to sea after weighing anchor. We had set anchor the previous afternoon after having missed a turn, freeing ourselves from against the rocks, and almost touching bottom. The work of the boatswain in loosing the hawser of the anchor had saved us on this occasion, for we had suddenly found ourselves in 4 fathoms of water.

On the 29th the ship set anchor in the port, where it had been towed. On the 30th, after inspection of the ship, we disembarked with our equipment.

With the arrival of the navy from Belen and with its being stationed in Talcahuano, the field commander of Concepción, Don Ambrosio O'Higgins, came there. He introduced himself as the chief of those fortified areas and received us with the utmost friendliness. He at once offered us whatever help was within his power to give us, as well as hospitality in his house whenever we were pleased to avail ourselves of it during our stay in Concepción. In the afternoon, we made our way to this capital of the bishopric without any untoward experiences along the pleasant road, which was clad everywhere with wonderful plants new to us.

Until the 12th of February there were not enough rooms available for all of us and we had to put up in two separate houses. Most of the buildings were inadequate, though the city is only 31 years old, and the present buildings were finished but 17 years ago. The citizens moved from the old site of Penco, or Penco el Viejo, to the present location of Mocha on the 24th of November 1764; floods and destruction caused by the tidal wave and earthquake of the 24th of May 1751 left Penco naught but the remains of ruins and a fortress standing on higher ground. The inhabitants fled to the hills and took refuge in their country houses until the city was founded.

On the 13th of February we began our botanical excursions in those extremely fertile fields. We continued our labors until the 24th, collecting many specimens of plants; most of them represented unknown species. These we studied painstakingly and drew with the greatest of care.

CHAPTER 34

Trip to the Fort of Arauco

On the 24th of February 1782 we left the city of Concepción at half past two in the afternoon. The group included the lieutenant colonel and field commander of the fort, Don Ambrosio O'Higgins y Vallenar, the two artists Brunete and Gálvez, and the two botanists Dombey and Ruiz. Pavón stayed on in the city, fearing to cross the Biobio River. We took our way to the fort of Arauco, where O'Higgins was going to talk with the Indians of that vutalmapu (Indian principality or district).

When we were all on the bank of the Biobio River and the rafts were ready for us to embark, a heavy rainstorm overtook us. Although there was some difference of opinion as to whether we should return to the city or board the rafts, we decided to cross the river. Happily, we succeeded in doing so in little less than half an hour. The river at this season is low, and is but half a league wide, but in the rainy season it swells to about a league in width.

The bed of the river is pure sand, with no stones to hinder the progress of a raft. These rafts are built of five to seven logs, each a handspan in diameter and 3 to 4 yards long, nailed on top of others set out crosswise beneath them. The center logs are longest; the rest are gradually shorter toward the sides. Along the length of the raft is a platform or bench, constructed of small poles bound together with leather thongs, where passengers sit and baggage is piled. At the end of the raft is a short free space for the raftsman, who guides the raft from here with a pole 4 or 5 yards long.

Raftsmen are also wont to tie a raft to the tail of a horse; sometimes on foot and sometimes swimming, the animal pulls the raft from one bank to the other. This method of crossing, however, is more precarious, for the horses oftentimes get stuck in the sand and, thrashing about to free themselves, get their legs sunk deep in the sand or overturn the raft. But on the day we crossed, none of these mishaps occurred. Beasts of burden cross the river swimming, guided by one or two men who, naked and on horseback, lead the animals. The crossing for pack animals is downstream from the raft crossing.

Once we had reached the opposite bank, we saddled and mounted our horses inside the fort of San Pedro. The fortification is built in this place to control the comings and goings of the Indians in case of revolt. An excellent butter is produced at this fort, as well as a high-quality flour of ligtu, or liutu, from the roots of *Alstroemeria ligtu*. As we shall have occasion to describe below, this flour is a starchy meal that is highly valued as a food for babies and for the old and infirm.

We left San Pedro with a military escort and spent the night at Esquadrón, a country house 5 leagues from the fort. The road crossed the plains and was pleasant, clad with leafy trees and plants that are green throughout the year and are a supreme joy to the eye.

Militias of Countryfolk

There are plains a league inland from San Pedro and 2 leagues from the sea. These are called lagunillas (little lakes) because they flood in the rainy season and must be crossed by raft. All along this coastal area, which is royal land, there are numerous pastures for the king's horses. These animals are cared for by many families of guazos (guasos, countryfolk or peasants), who dwell scattered in little hamlets on the wide, pleasant flats. Here they plant and harvest various fruits and seeds for their own use. They are permitted to use these lands on condition that they all serve as militiamen, ready to go out when needed to fight the Indians and pirates who customarily invade these coasts. The militiamen are armed with lances, 3 to 4 yards long. On horseback, they are very skillful with these lances, and run with wondrous speed through the hills and over the plains. The mountainous areas are inhabited by unchristianized Indians. The militia is accustomed to carrying out frequent campaigns against them when they come out to steal cattle and fruit.

Canelo

Our trip was interrupted at Esquadrón by heavy rainfall that lasted from ten o'clock the previous night until ten in the morning on the 25th. We explored the fertile countryside at this locality and collected many plants. Of these collections we studied and drew *Sarmienta repens*, which clothes the trunks and branches of the trees; *Schizanthus pinnatus*; and *Laurus peumo*, a splendid tree that I shall discuss later on.

Our collection also included *Drimys acris*, a tree called canelo (cinnamon) because of the color and flavor of its leaves, wood, and bark. The bark is much more acrid and aromatic than the other parts of the plant, and exudes tears of an aromatic gum. When burned, the wood gives off smoke that irritates the eyes. The bark and leaves keep clothes free from moths, and a decoction of them makes a bath water good for treating convulsions, nervousness, spasms, paralysis, impetigo, scabies, and ringworm of the scalp. Mixed with urine and salt, the decoction is also good for ridding horses of frush (thrush of the feet) and lice, and is widely employed for these purposes. The smoke of canelo purifies the air and is used against contagions and insect pests. An infusion of the tender shoots of canelo intensifies the color of indigo, for which reason it is mixed with the starch of this dyestuff. Some people use an infusion of the shoots as a bath to treat venereal sores; smoke of the leaves and bark may also be applied for this purpose. When the leaves are crushed up and cast into streams or the backwaters of rivers, they kill fish. From the trunk of this beautiful and showy tree the natives cut very good planks and boards for construction.

CHAPTER 34

Canelo in Superstitious Rites of the Indians; Detection and Punishment of Hidden Crimes

The Indians are accustomed to holding their meetings and councils in the shade of the canelo tree, on the pretext of discovering hidden crimes and punishing the guilty individuals. For this superstitious and evil ceremony they call upon the oldest and most renowned machi, or female soothsayer. The Indians all kneel in dead silence around the highest and most leafy canelo tree in the area, with their eyes fixed on the ground respectfully and devotionally. The machi then climbs the tree and from there pours out her incantations, calling upon Pillán, which means God, and casts down a twig or stick for each of the four principal winds, having performed various ceremonies for each wind.

Once this first rite is finished, she harangues all assembled; whereupon, like some divine oracle, by whatever her whim dictates she answers the questions that the chieftains, who called together the council for evil and sinister ends, may ask of her. The machi lays the blame upon those whom they have ordered her to find guilty, and sentence is carried out as though it were laid down by Pillán himself. Finally, she exhorts those assembled with a short sermon, telling them to thank God for the discovery of the true or supposed delinquents.

The machi climbs down from the tree, and the congregation, all standing, give her a little drum to beat. In time with the sound of this drum, they continue the ceremony, jumping and skipping around the canelo tree, until the machi stops beating the drum. Then they all gather round to drink of the abundant supply of chicha (maize liquor) prepared in advance to crown such functions. Almost all of them become drunk after imbibing the chicha, and those who have conflicting opinions about the diabolical sentences given out by the soothsayer are often, under the influence of drink, disposed to kill one other.

The canelo tree is abundant in places that are damp and swampy in the rainy season but dry the rest of the year. Its bark and leaves have a flavor that is stinging and sickening, tart and biting, a little like cinnamon. Because of its spicelike properties, the Indians and some other countryfolk use the bark for flavoring some of their crude stews. Wild doves devour the berries, or fruits, of the canelo; when this tree is in fruit, it is visited by enormous flocks of them. When doves have eaten these fruits, their meat is hard and has an unpleasant taste.

We left Esquadrón on the 26th and, with no mishaps, arrived at the terminus called Coronel, which is 2 leagues from the plains of Esquadrón. Here the company of militiamen was exchanged for another that was armed with lances, always carried erect with the iron spearhead pointing skyward and the staff resting on the stirrup or saddle. In the parade of exchange, the captain of the company sends an official with a saber in his hand to receive the field commander, to salute him, and to tell him that the captain has taken his place at such a locality with his soldiers and is awaiting him. When he has received the answer of the commander, the official leaves with all haste for his company. The captain draws the company into two lines, ready to march off at once when the field commander arrives. Two or three soldiers have already scanned the whole district from nearby heights in order to discover any unusual activity among the Indians.

A league from Coronel we came to Playa Negra (Black Beach), a locality named for the brownish sands there. It is thus distinguished from a place just ahead that has sands lighter in hue and is known as Playa Blanca (White Beach). We climbed the mountain at Corcura, 5 leagues from Coronel; the fort of Corcura is located on that high point. Here the company of militiamen was exchanged in ceremonies similar to those at the previous posts.

When we had descended the mountain, we entered upon a beach or sandbank a quarter of a league long. The Llanista Indians, or those of the plains—that is, those of Santa Juana—find this beach an easy place for their sallies. They make no other sallies between San Pedro and this point along the way, but do make them from San Pedro upstream. And they are wont to use these routes from time to time, as in 1772 when they beheaded a brave official who, in defending himself valiantly from Indian hordes surrounding him in the forest, had cut off the heads of three of the enemy a few days before. He could not free himself, for he was surprised in a hut with two of his soldiers, who were bound and burned alive inside the hut.

Once beyond the beach, we crossed the slope of the Cuesta de Villagra, which has 3 leagues of climbing up and down. This hill was named Villagra after the field commander Villagra, who had a battle there with the Indians. He was killed and buried at this place, and his men were cut to pieces by hordes of Indians, who surrounded and stormed the mountain until all of the soldiers who had taken refuge there were sought out and killed.

At the foot of the Cuesta de Villagra there is another fort, a mile long. Here we ate in the shade of some apple trees and the various other trees that surround it. After we had eaten, we climbed the slopes of Chivilino, where there is always a guard set out by the field commander to preclude the smuggling of arms, foods, wines, liquors, and contraband with which the Spaniards or countryfolk are accustomed to barter with the Indians for ponchos. Commerce in ponchos can be carried on only under license from the field commander; this measure was taken to induce the Indians to cultivate their lands and to prevent their becoming armed and provoking uprisings.

When we had descended Chivilino, we crossed the Araquete River. This name is likewise applied to the beach and flat valley that stretches to the Caranpangue River, 5 leagues from Araquete. In 1 day's riding on this plain, one can find seven roads, wide and straight along their entire length, and formed by various kinds of wild trees indifferently mixed by nature itself, according to Indian belief. It seems impossible that nature could have formed these seven roads all of an equal width, 40 to 50 yards, along the whole 5 leagues of their length, with not one tree, shrub, or bush growing out of line in them.

The trees that form these roads are arrayanes (myrtles), pataguas, boldus or boldos, peumos, maytenes, lithres, and numerous climbers such as voquis, yelmos, and others. [These plants are discussed in detail in Chapters 37 and 40.—Translator] The leafy lacework formed by these climbers and by the branches of the trees, with the diverse greens of the leaves as well as the sizes, colors, and fragrances of the flowers, offers the most beautiful blending of hues and most pleasing country scene imaginable. Strawberry vines with their delicate fruits, and other plants with a variety of flowers, contribute much towards brightening the scene when they cover the pavement. These roads, about the distance of a rifle shot from the sea, lie upon sandy soil, which shows that they are the work of man, not of nature.

Beyond this plain lies the Caranpangue River. This name means lion's face, and is derived perhaps from the great rise and fall of the river, as far as a league inland from the sea. The same difference of level can be observed in the Araquete River. Both rivers have fords when the tide is low, but at high tide they must be crossed by raft. The Caranpangue is about a hundred yards wide at this point. Three leagues upstream from the ford, there is an inlet near a mill. Here there are some little cylindrical stones, rather rectangular, with both ends flat. In the flat end one can make out a cross, similar to a Maltese cross, and this phenomenon can be observed in as many transverse pieces as may be cut. There are stones of various sizes and of diverse colors. Most are whitish with a black cross; others are black with a white cross. There are also bluish and reddish ones, but these are not very common.

Neculgud, or Running Partridge, Governor of the Indians

On the opposite bank of the Caranpangue River, the governor or chief of the Indians there presented himself to the field commander. His name was Neculgud, which means "running partridge," this notwithstanding the fact that he is a very stout man. He appeared at the head of two companies of Indians on horseback, in two lines, armed only with two sabers carried by those who made up the guard for their small banners. Their music was naught but that from some short flutes or small wind instruments called pivilcas, with sad and dismal tones scarcely audible 50 paces away.

When Neculgud had saluted the field commander, he ordered his companies to march at a good gallop, as they are wont to do on such occasions. They were followed by two other companies of our militia, armed with lances. Next came the retinue of the field commander, bringing up the rear of the two lines accompanied by Neculgud, whom they asked whether or not anything unusual had happened in that vutalmapu.

Near the fort of Arauco, there were great numbers of Indian men and women beneath arbors that they had constructed on both sides of the road as temporary dwellings. When the field commander and his retinue passed along the road, these Indians greeted them by repeating again and again, "Mari-mari, Señor; mari-mari, Capitán!"

The two companies of Indians took up their position in two lines at the entrance to the fort, and all our men passed between these lines and entered Arauco. To the music of fife and drum in the fort of Arauco, the field commander and his retinue passed through the barracks of the troops of that frontier garrison.

Welcome to the Field Commander by the Indian Chiefs

Once dismounted, the field commander through interpreters ordered the Indians to join in greeting the chieftains of all the departments, and informed them of the day and hour for a parliamentary meeting. This salutation took up the rest of the afternoon, or approximately an hour and a half.

The ceremony of greeting, which is started by the high chief and by the governor Neculgud and is continued in order of age by the more important chieftains, consists of their presenting themselves one by one, two paces before the field commander. Each removes his hat, bows his head, raises it with naturalness, and approaches the commander with due respect. Then saying, "Mari-mari, Señor," each places his right hand on his left shoulder and, with the left hand—which is holding the hat—gives the commander a light thump on the back. Each then retires directly, with another bow performed in the same place as the first. The field commander answers throughout the ceremony with the same gestures. All of us in the retinue had to bear up under this long and tiresome welcome.

When the ceremony of greeting was ended, the field commander, in the name of the king and of the president of Chile, thanked the chieftains who had put up and helped the troops that had journeyed through their territories to the fort of Valdivia without the slightest harm. Immediately thereafter, he scolded some of the chieftains who had incited others to make trouble against their neighbors. All this he did through interpreters. Many of the principal and more cooperative chieftains offered their allegiance to the field commander in the case of new feuds or suspected summons and uprisings.

At the end of retreat, given after prayers, the chiefs and Indians who remained within the fort left it. The gates of the fort were closed until the next day, which was the day fixed for the parliamentary meeting. It was carried out in the following manner.

Indian Parliament

At nine o'clock in the morning on the 27th, all the Indian chieftains gathered at the great yard of the house of the field commander and, in order of importance and age, took their places upon large planks that had been arranged in several lines, one behind the other. Behind the chieftains stood great numbers of Indian men and women. The field commander presented himself before the chieftains, standing with two interpreters on his left and all of us who were in his retinue on his right. When the greeting was given by the chieftains in the same way as the day before, the field commander began the session with a brief speech, which the interpreter repeated as the commander spoke.

The substance of his speech was limited to telling the chieftains that his Catholic Majesty felt that there was no peace and mutual brotherhood among the Indians themselves, nor good harmony and friendship with the Spaniards. He also said that, if necessary, he had enough troops to stop the disorders, scheming, and bad conduct of the rebels, who would be punished according to their crimes, and that he was confident that the good chieftains would assist him in curbing the arrogance of the wayward.

The field commander thereupon repeated the order that proper sentinels should at no time be absent from the coasts in their territories, that they must be there to observe and immediately report to the fort whenever more than two ships appeared. He also ordered that under no condition should they permit any deserter from Valdivia to pass through their territories, nor should they admit or hide fugitive delinquents, but should take them as prisoners to the fort. He ordered that all thieves, Indian or Spaniard, should be taken to the fort or kept in a secure prison until the commander of the fort was notified and had issued the proper orders for the case. Furthermore, he ordered that whatsoever person, regardless of his social class, who initiated uprisings or promoted discord, quarrels, feuds, or misunderstandings between chieftains be taken prisoner and transported with great security to the fort to stand trial and receive his punishment, in accordance with established laws.

The field commander then requested earnestly that one chieftain come to the assistance of another if the Pehuenches or Huiliches Indians, their bitterest enemies, should stir up trouble or declare war. He advised them to cultivate their lands with seeds and fruits for their own support, and to avoid intoxication and drunken brawls. Lastly, he reiterated to them from his heart how much a good, peaceful, and organized government is to be desired, and he complained about the shortcomings of some chieftains in their districts.

The parliament ended at one o'clock in the afternoon. Every chieftain was offered a small glass of wine, with which they toasted the king and the royal family. Among the chieftains there was one 86 years of age who, in toasting the king, cast the wine into the air above him with the greatest demonstration of joy and happiness, until tears flowed from his eyes. This good elder had walked 85 leagues to be present at the parliament. He showed the greatest satisfaction when he heard that villages were being founded, offering at once to pay for the construction of the church in his area. He begged the field commander to send some missionaries for divine service and the spiritual nourishment of his people, who had been without this help since the last uprising in 1766.

In the afternoon, with the field commander, we visited the living quarters of the chieftains. The womenfolk offered us various kinds of chicha and we reciprocated with a few pieces of money, which they very courteously received. Then we walked the entire length of the hill at Colocolo and the environs of the fort of that name. Here we gathered a number of plants that I described, and I gave the following to the artists to be drawn: *Jovellana punctata*; *Mutisia spinosa*, found in abundance in the ditches of Colocolo; and *Stereoxylon rubrum*. This last plant is known by the common name of ñipa and the natives say a decoction of it lessens neuralgias; they also use the wood to make handles for tools.

During the 3 days of the parliament, the Indian youth spent the time running their horses in the small plaza in front of the fort at Arauco, making them kneel repeatedly, stand on two or three feet, and dance in various ways until the beasts were worn out with fatigue. All of this they carried out with the greatest of skill.

At eight in the morning on the 28th, the chieftains came to take their leave of the commander and his retinue. The same ceremony was observed as on the previous days. The field commander legalized the laws that the council had approved the day before, and reprimanded some who were accused by their companions there of various shortcomings and transgressions. They all gave their thanks to Martin Campo, as they called the governor or field commander, for having given them peace and pardoned their faults. They offered, in one voice, to support him in case one of their number should err in his ways. Repeating their gratitude for the wise and good advice received, they left the parliament to give orders to their troops and to their people to return home. Their return was carried out in 1 day, without one Indian remaining either inside or outside the fort except for Neculgud.

For the convocation of this kind of parliament, there is a royal order that a certain amount of meat and wine be sent, at the expense of the royal exchequer, to the native chieftains for distribution among the Indians. However, as the amount does not usually suffice for these people for the five, six, or more days that the councils customarily last, they bring with them their drinks of chicha and their provisions of ulpo, which is a meal of roasted maize. They are very happy with all of this; most become drunk and pass the days in horse racing, a sport that they are loath to give up when the time of departure draws near.

Appearance, Physique, and Dress of the Indians

In general, these plains or coastal Indians are short and have homely faces in comparison with the Pehuenches or mountain Indians, who are tall, or with the Huiliches or southern Indians, who are progressively taller as one approaches Patagonia or the Strait of Magellan.

The menfolk wear a sort of small jacket, breeches, a waistcoat, and coarse wool socks that are very short and without feet. Some use a shirt of homespun, or those of the chieftains are of linen. They cover themselves with a poncho instead of a cape, wear a turned-down hat, and do not use shoes or any other footwear.

The womenfolk wrap their bodies in a blanket of baize, or thick flannel, tied in at the waist with a sash, girdle, or belt, likewise of baize. The corners of the blanket are fastened with a tupo, or bodkin, so that the whole body is covered with the exception of the arms and the ankles and feet. Upon this blanket are laid two or three smaller ones on the back, each about a yard or a yard and a half square; the two corners of these are placed on the shoulders and are pinned over the chest with more bodkins stuck in horizontally, with the point on the left side and the head or ornamented button on the right. From the two ends of the bodkin they string and hang llancatus, or small colored glass beads and ribbons. Around the neck they wear two, three, or more strings of these glass beads in various colors. They adorn the ears with uples, or pendant earrings, each of which is an extremely thin, small plate of silver, square or crescent-shaped, 2 or 3 inches wide and about half an ounce in weight, with a hook that perforates the ear.

The hair of the women is usually thick, coarse, long, and worn in two braids, each hanging between the ear and the cheek down to the chest; across the forehead they wear a large lock of hair drawn towards each side, which is very becoming. The women walk barefoot, and wear neither a skirt nor petticoats. When engaged in household duties, they pin the two front corners of the small blankets to the back, exposing their bare arms for freer movement in their work. They wait on their husbands even to the saddling of the horses. The youngest married woman obeys the eldest of her husband's wives; though the eldest may be the ugliest, she is the most highly respected of all the women in such a polygamous family. Although they are commonly not beautiful, some of the women have pleasing, good faces and are rather attractive with their kind, black, piercing eyes.

Tendency to Drink; Marriage

Indian men are passionately fond of all kinds of alcoholic beverages and immoderately drink chichas made of maize, apples, huignhan (*Schinus* species), or quinoa until they are drunk. They marry as many women as they can support, with no more ceremony than that of giving presents to the parents of the bride. When one of a man's wives dies, the parents or relatives of the deceased give the husband presents similar to those he gave when he was wedded to the girl.

Religion and Superstitions; Uprising of the Indian Curiñancu

These Indians are very superstitious. They believe whatever the machis, or soothsayers, tell them, for they hold the soothsayers' words to be revealed by Pillán, whom they recognize as the Supreme Being. They do not doubt the immortality of the soul, but they observe no religious ceremonies whatsoever. Read what the abbot Molina relates concerning this subject in Chapter 5, "Sistema de Religion y Funerales," on page 84 of his compendium *Historia Civil del Reyno de Chile*, translated and published in Madrid in 1795 by Don Nicolas de la Cruz.

Among the Llanista Indians (those of the plains) and the Costeno Indians (those of the coast) there live many who were Christians but renounced their religion in the general uprising that took place on the 25th of December 1766. It began at three in the morning in Angol, when the Indian Curiñancu was religious leader of the others. To start the uprising, he stole the horses and mules of the Spaniards, killed one of the Spaniards' servants, and wounded the overseer of the troops, Alberto Fernández, and three of his soldiers. Finding no security in Angol, the field commander, Don Salvador Cabrito, ordered the general roll of the drum on the 31st of December and fell back with his few soldiers to the fort at Nacimiento, which he was happy to enter at the hour of prayer.

The insurrection continued in great force, and the Spaniards lost all the settlements they had held between the Biobio River and the boundaries of Valdivia. These apostates are usually the most crafty and motivated instigators of outbreaks and uprisings, to keep themselves independent and to live in complete liberty without being tied to any village; most dwell in temporary huts.

Bellicose Character, War Dress, and Battle Music of the Indians

The Indians of this country are by nature sullen and warlike. They fight and make frequent forays, always on horseback. They use the lance and the laque (a kind of bola, or lasso with balls), arms that they handle with dexterity. For warfare, they wear a leather doublet made of untanned cowhide or horsehide and a hat of the same material; the hat is formed of two pieces and is ornamented with feathers of various colors arranged in a circle around the crown. Their battle music comes only from little drums and pivilcas, instruments similar to small flutes or clarinets.

Measures Against Contagious Diseases

If an Indian be discovered with a contagious disease or if someone has died of one, the body is burned, dead or alive, with all household furnishings connected with the person. Oftentimes the Indians carry the furnishings to the forest with all those who cared for the sick person and, bound up together, they are cast into a bonfire lest they contaminate the rest.

Political Divisions; Way of Life

The Indians of Chile are divided into four principalities called uthanmapus or vutalmapus (communities or districts). Today they are more or less under the president of Santiago de Chile. The Indians of three vutalmapus—those of the coastal region, the plains, and the slopes of the mountains—cultivate the land to some extent for their support. They plant various kinds of grain, breed all kinds of livestock, and fish in the rivers and along the coast for many kinds of delicious fish and shellfish. The Indians of the fourth vutalmapu—those who are called Pehuenches and live in a part of the mountain range—give themselves over to idleness, slovenliness, and thievery. For this reason they spend a wretched life, feeding upon horse flesh, fat, and pine nuts, or upon whatever they can steal or loot from the farms of Spaniards and Indians in neighboring territories.

Like the Huiliches (Indians of southern Chile), the Pehuenches also attack and plunder travelers in raids on the pampas of Buenos Aires; they usually kill the men and take the women captives to use as their own. From such unions there are among these people many elegant, light-complexioned young men and good-looking women. Some of these prisoners adapt so well to the kind of life characteristic of the natives that they lose all desire to return to their own Christian living, even when an opportunity to do so presents itself. The freedom and way of life have so strong an attraction that both God and kin are forgotten.

The Pehuenches frequently engage in battles with Indians of the coast and the plains, with the Spaniards, and above all with the Huiliches, who also dwell in the mountains, jungles, and border regions of the pampas of Buenos Aires, extending south to where the Patagonians live.

The first vutalmapu is that of the coast, extending from Arauco through Tucapel and Imperial Baxa to Toltén Baxo. The second is that of the plains, beginning in Santa Barbara and continuing through Angol, Ropecura, Imperial Alta, Maguehue, and Toltén Alto. The third lies on the slopes of the mountain mass between Nacimiento, along Chacayco and Renayco, to Quercherchuas. The fourth vutalmapu is located in the mountains and includes only the Pehuenches Indians. These four vutalmapus are distributed among the president, the field commander, the infantry commander, and the sergeant major.

The Huiliches Indians

The Huiliches Indians live in the area immediately to the south of that inhabited by the Pehuenches. They are not subject to any of the four commanders mentioned. They are more barbarous than the Pehuenches and cause more trouble and banditry in the pampas of Buenos Aires. There is evidence that the Huiliches, like the Pehuenches, believe in the immortality of the soul, for they live convinced that after they die they travel across the sea, having provided themselves with food and saddled horses to make the trip more comfortably. Also, helpers at their funerals pray to Pillán, invoking his help and that of the whale to make an easier trip for the deceased.

Longevity of the Indians

There are many among the Indians who are a hundred or more years old; some are 120. Their hair is not gray, and their teeth are still strong and white. This longevity may be due to their way of life or to the gentle climate.

Attitude of the Indians Towards Europeans

All these Indians are openly hostile to Europeans, or we might rather say that they are hostile to the customs and laws of the white man. For this reason it would be very hard to force them to dwell together in villages, if their excesses should continue to be handled in the mild and tolerant way stipulated by the Spanish crown. If the Chileans were permitted to subjugate them by force of arms, the Indians would soon be made to live in villages or towns, putting an end to their raids and frequent plundering of estates, and the murders not uncommon in these operations.

Councils of War

When these Indians engage in general uprisings, and when they light the beacons or bonfires on the mountains for their gatherings, they try to capture a Spaniard for the practice of their cahuin, or council of war. The captive is put into a hole, and in a superstitious ceremony is beaten to death with a war club. The Indians cut out his heart, stick the points of their lances in his blood, and suck it; they then cut off the fingers, hands, and feet, and the pieces are distributed. This act is known as "running the arrow." The chieftains receiving some of these parts of the body of the Spaniard are duty bound—solely because the lot fell to them to receive the pieces—

to rise up in rebellion. For this uprising, they invite with great secrecy the yanaconas, or Indians in the service of Spaniards; though having been purchased, the yanaconas are not treated by the Spaniards as slaves but as free servants.

On their trips, cross-country treks, and uprisings, all these Indians carry along food for a number of days. This food consists of nothing but a little bag or shepherd's pouch of ulpo, or meal of toasted maize, wheat, or barley. They also carry a horn cup, called a huampar, to use in mixing the meal with water. This is the only nourishment they take over periods of many days. When this food gives out, they keep alive by drinking the blood of their horses; if a horse should die because of repeated bleedings, its flesh is also consumed as food.

The Indian men are extremely skillful in the use of the horse and in wielding a lance, laque (bola), club, sword, machete, knife, or dagger when mounted. They fight and attack in platoons. Their ambushes consist of sudden assaults and forays that they call malocas. When any of their men are killed in battle, they take great pains to hide the bodies from the Spaniards. They never have mercy on Spaniards but kill them on the spot.

The Indians are superb swimmers, especially those who live along the coast. When they come together for gathering shellfish, they go out on rafts or in canoes with their womenfolk, who dive into the sea and pry the mollusks loose. The men stay on the rafts to help the women come up from the depths when a signal is given, and to receive and to prepare the catch. When this work is over, the women and children are wont to bathe at once in cold water.

In order to make a lasting peace with these Indians and to establish relations, trade, and intermarriage with them, we Spaniards have tried every means that prudence and diplomacy permit. None, however, has been strong enough to wean the Indian from his wild and barbarous life. The last method tried was gathering them into villages, and some of them accepted this measure. But in 1766 they rose up in revolt, as we have pointed out, and reduced the buildings and churches of Angol and other towns to ashes.

Ambassador Chieftains

The Indians have promised the Spaniards peace and harmony in numerous councils, but any concord has been short-lived. In the last general council, called by the president Don Agustín de Jáuregui on the field of Tapique on the 21st of December 1774, among 18 other points of agreement it was accorded that some of the chieftains would visit the city of Santiago as ambassadors. This agreement is observed up to the present time and, in order to secure a stronger hold upon these ambassadors, 22 young sons of the chiefs or of other important Indians are being educated in the school of San Pablo.

The general councils held with the Indians to discuss peace treaties, or to extend them, are gatherings of all the chieftains and most important Indians. The president of the royal audience, as captain general of the realm, attends these councils, as do the field commander of the fort of Concepción and other military officials. When a council is ended, the president distributes to the Indians hats, knives, scissors, belts, glass beads, and other trinkets of small commercial value but of great worth and esteem to the natives.

CHAPTER 35

Trip from Arauco to Concepción

On the 1st of March 1782, at six o'clock in the morning, we set out from the fort of Arauco with the commanding officer of the fort, the Indian governor Neculgud, and two companies of our militiamen. We went as far as the Caranpangue River, at which point the two leaders and one of the companies returned. The other company stayed with us as far as the Araquete River; from there, those of us remaining in the retinue pressed on by ourselves at full gallop. We entered the fort of Corcura at ten, and left after the field commander gave the orders necessary to make certain repairs.

Fishing on Horseback

We stayed there, however, a short while to witness the fishing on horseback. This is a sport that some of the fishermen play with extreme skill and without danger. When the horses see the waves swelling up towards them, they turn around so that they receive the splash against the rump; the rider, at the same time, bends down so that the water passes over his body. As soon as the wave has spent itself, the horse turns again towards the sea. Thus does the animal gain ground, and soon two horses begin to swim. Then the two mounted fishermen come together to draw taut the net that they have held extended at full length, and the horses pull it in with all the fish.

We ate at the outpost called Capitán, leaving at two o'clock; at four we arrived at the fort of San Pedro. We crossed the Biobio River on horse-drawn rafts and entered the city of Concepción before dark. This rapid trip, at a trot and gallop from Arauco to Concepción, was made with no mishap whatsoever.

We continued our excursions and plant collecting in the fields around Concepción and along the coast until the 24th of April. We went out daily by horse across the fertile fields and through the luxuriant forests, and we studied, collected, dried, and drew a large number of splendid trees and other plants. These we shall discuss below.

CHAPTER 36

Travel and Botanical Forays on Several Estates of the Bishopric of Concepción

On the 24th of April 1782 I went with the artist Gálvez to the estate of Culenco, 12 leagues from the city of Concepción. Eight times we forded the Andalién River at the boundary of Palomares, and we crossed the Nonguen River with no misadventure on the way. Nor did we experience any trouble on the trips we made to the estates of San Salvador, Yeguaraqui, Collico, Chequén, Pelcochin, Loicaca, Santa Rosa, Santa Ana, El Parral, El Rosario, Cangregillo, and Chaymavida.

During our stay in Culenco we explored the fields and forests of all those extensive estates. The fertile lands abound in many kinds of plants, brooks of exquisite waters, and beautiful grasslands on all sides where herds of cattle and horses feed. Few ranch owners sow wheat and barley, for with such abundant pasturage they are content to raise cattle and cultivate one or two vineyards of 40 or 50 thousand vinestocks. They slaughter large numbers of the cattle to make charqui (jerky, dried beef) or corned beef, suet, and tallow, and the rich harvests of the vineyards yield an exquisite wine that, in my opinion, is as good as that of Valdepeñas in Spain.

In the orchards of all these estates, various European fruit trees are grown. These include apples, pears, morello cherries (sour cherries), melocotones (peach grafted onto quince rootstock), walnuts, figs, pines, chestnuts, a few olives, and quinces, which locally are called lucumas and are very fragrant and savory. Cypresses are also grown. Among the various kinds of grapes cultivated, the most exquisite are the muscatels and the Italian grapes. Likewise the pears, called joaquinos, and all the fruits of Europe grow more bountifully in these lands than they do in Spain.

Their new olive groves yield olives that are small as peas, appropriate for pickling. Indeed, when prepared in this way they are tender and tasty; they are eaten by the spoonful, as the pits are easily chewed up and it is not necessary to throw them away. We in Europe could prepare tender or underripe olives in the same way.

Chile, an Earthly Paradise

The forests are full of wild trees that yield precious woods for building and other uses. There are also many plants of medicinal and other commercial value. In short, we might describe Chile as a pleasant and a delightful realm and, from whatever point of view we look at it, we can call it an earthly paradise.

Derivation of the Name Culenco

The name Culenco is derived from the abundance of the plant called culén, or *Psoralea glandulosa*, which is grown in those ravines and valleys. *Mimosa carbonaria*, known as espino, is also very common there, and excellent charcoal is prepared from its wood. Many other species are plentiful as well, but I shall discuss them elsewhere, inasmuch as they are all found throughout the bishopric of Concepción.

CHAPTER 37

Trip from Culenco to Concepción

On the 9th of May 1782 we returned from Culenco to Concepción, with no misfortune whatsoever. We collected some plants and a few seeds along the way.

We continued the excursions and botanical work in the countryside around Concepción until December. From the time of our arrival in Chile until our trip to the fort of Nacimiento, we gathered many plants; I described and had drawn the following.

Calceolaria dentata, *C. rugosa*, *C. scrophulariaefolia*, and *C. sessilis*. All these are commonly called arquenitas or arquenillas. *Jovellana punctata*, also called arquenilla. *Verbena corymbosa*; *V. multifida*, sandialagüen, which Chileans use in a decoction to stimulate menstruation, speed up childbirth, or alleviate a burning sensation during urination.

Gunnera thyrsiflora, called panke or panque; the root of this plant is as thick as a man's thigh and penetrates the ground to a depth of about a yard, usually dividing into two or three branches of equal thickness. The roots are used in tanning and in dyeing leather black. The stalks of the leaves, called nalcas, are edible when fresh, if freed of fibrous material; they have an acid-astringent taste, somewhat like that of sorrel, and are used as a cooling agent, as are the stems, called raguayes. The mucilaginous matter abundant in the tender stems and fresh shoots is applied to the kidneys to lower the temperature of the blood in strong fevers. The root is a good astringent agent in a decoction or powder, and has various therapeutic uses.

Valeriana cornucopiae, *V. crispa*, and *V. hyalinorrhiza*. *Mollugo radiata*. *Nicotiana angustifolia*, tabaco cimarrón (wild tobacco).

Acaena trifida; *A. pinnatifida*, pimpinella cimarrona (wild burnet), used as an excellent diuretic or cooling agent. *Acaena anserinifolia*, broquín; an infusion or decoction is drunk in the morning and afternoon to treat gonorrhea.

Quadria heterophylla, called avellano de Chile (Chilean hazelnut tree) or nebú. Excellent paddles can be made of the wood of this species, for it is flexible but solid; the fruits are taken to Lima for sale under the name of avellanas (hazelnuts).

Plantago hispida. Buddleja globosa, pagnhin, which is a splendid tree in bloom and in fruit; the pendant heads have fruits the size of a small hen's egg. *Cissus striata*, called voqui; this name is also applied by Chileans to a prankish person or a talebearer.

Embothrium lanceolatum, noth'ro; when the Spanish troops were besieged by Indians on the hill at Villagra, they were obliged to make small cakes from the seeds of this bush and eat them toasted or baked to assuage the hunger they experienced before being annihilated by the natives. *Embothrium dentatum*, raral; the bark and leaves are a source of good black dye, while the wood is valuable for building archways. *Embothrium obliquum*.

Cestrum virgatum, called palqui or parqui. Natives employ a decoction or infusion of palqui in the treatment of intermittent fevers, and an infusion of the inner bark is drunk during periods of fasting to cure stomach ills. Lye from the trunks and roots is excellent for cleaning clothing, and the berries yield a dye of a beautiful purplish blue.

Chenopodium dulce, quinoa dulce (sweet quinoa) and *C. amarum*, quinoa amarga (bitter quinoa). Pleasing, strong chicha (liquor) is made from the seeds of these plants in Chile, where the seeds are thus very frequently consumed, just as in Peru. *Chenopodium multifidum*, payco; this is a very fragrant plant. A warm infusion of it is considered by Chileans to be an excellent digestive and is used in place of tea.

Campanula filiformis, hunoperguen. *Periphragmos foetidus*, huevill-huevill; Chileans use an infusion of this plant as a laxative in enemas. *Ribes punctatum. Cynoglossum decurrens* and *C. pauciflorum*.

Villaresia mucronata, huillipatagua; the wood of this tall tree with a stout trunk provides excellent beams and planks for construction and other work. The bark is employed in tanning leathers, and the bark and fresh leaves have strong emetic properties. An infusion of these is commonly used to induce vomiting; in larger doses, the infusion also acts as a purgative.

Rhamnus brachiatus, retamilla, and *R. prostratum*, llaque; Chileans use these two thorny species to fence in farms. With the bark of the roots, which lathers like soap, they wash clothing made of baize (coarse woolen cloth), tocuyo (coarse cotton cloth), and even linen. *Rhamnus verticillatus*, chacay; in Chile an infusion of the bark is a medicinal agent for treating internal abscesses. The wood lasts for many years, and for this reason is used in the construction of farm buildings.

Solanum crispum, nat're; an infusion of this plant can be used with good results in treating a disease called chavalongo, a typhoidlike fever.

Statice armeria. Phlox alternifolia. Lithospermum muricatum. Myosotis corymbosa and *M. gracilis. Aldea pinnata*; writing ink can be made from the leaves of this plant, which grows in abundance in the ravines at Palomares, near the Andalién River.

Celastrus dependens, called maytén or magth'um; this is a showy bush with many hanging branches, evergreen leaves, and an abundance of flowers and fruits. Growing in almost all parts of Chile among small shrubs and herbs, it is known by everyone because it is so conspicuous over its lesser associates. Its young branches are favorite fodder for cows, and its leaves are used in some places as a substitute for senna. The wood is white but rose-colored towards the center, and possesses a good grain that carves and polishes well in making curio pieces.

Maytén is a remedy for the malignant nature of lithre, or lith'i, a species of *Schinus* that ordinarily grows in the same areas as maytén. See our discussion of the properties of lithre in Chapter 40. Divine wisdom surely put lithre and maytén together so that the ravages of the one could be cured by the antidotal action of the other. A poultice of crushed maytén leaves is applied to the purulent sores brought on by the shadow, smoke, or effluvia of lithre, and a purgative infusion of maytén leaves is imbibed at the same time.

Myoschilos oblonga, codocoypo (coypo food); this little bush is one of the very few in Chile that defoliate and bloom before unfolding new leaves. An infusion of its leaves in ordinary water has a light purgative action. The coypo, a species of *Mus*, or mouse, according to Molina, eats the fruits of codocoypo, which are the size of small endrinas (sloe, blackthorn).

Bromelia bicolor and *B. sphacelata*, chupon (sucker). Boys suck and eat the pulp of the fruits with great delight; it is sparse and mixed with seeds, but it separates easily and appeals considerably to boyish tastes because of its sweet flavor.

Pourretia coarctata, called cardón or puya. An excellent extract for setting fractures is obtained from the long stalk of the inflorescence of this plant. The nectar of the flowers is fragrant and tasty, and when applied to an aching ear it lessens the pain and restores this organ. The stem is used in place of cork for the stoppers of jugs and other vessels.

Ornithogalum caeruleum. Ornithogalum plumosum; the white flowers of this plant are covered with a long indumentum that gives them the aspect of felt and makes them all the more splendid and beautiful. *Ornithogalum sympagantherum*, illmu; its bulb, or onion, shaped like a wine bottle, tastes pleasant when boiled or baked. Even in an uncooked state it is palatable and does no harm to the digestion.

Amaryllis formosissima. Alstroemeria salsilla.

Liutu Meal: Its Preparation and Uses

Alstroemeria ligtu, known as liutu; Chileans extract a white starch from its roots. The starch, or meal, is made into a delicate pap or gruel, white and as transparent as jelly, which not only furnishes a soft food for elderly folk and babies but also provides a favorite dish for the sick and those suffering from stomach ailments. The meal is easily digested and lacks any taste or aroma that might make it disagreeable, but with sugar and cinnamon the pap is extremely tasty.

This starch, or arina de liutu (liutu meal) as it is called in Chile, is extracted by grinding the uncooked roots between two stones, and leaching out all the substance with repeated waters until nothing more dissolves out. All the waters are then strained and, after the starch has settled, the remaining liquid is decanted off and discarded. The starch is set out to dry in the sun, and the finished meal is put up in bags or barrels to be sent off for sale. Each peck of meal usually fetches 2 reales in Chilean currency. Great quantities of liutu are produced in the fort of San Pedro and are marketed in Concepción, and from Talcahuano liutu is transported to Lima, where people of taste esteem it very highly.

The other species of *Alstroemeria* likewise yield starch, for all of them have tuberous roots of the same consistency, color, and transparency as those of *A. ligtu.*

Loranthus verticillatus and *L. semicalyculatus*, called ictricgo, michtrin, or quintral; both species yield a black dye. *Herreria stellata*, known as quila or zarzaparilla; the stoloniferous roots of quila are used by Chileans as a substitute for those of *Smilax salsaparilla*. The stems and leaves are excellent cattle fodder, and older stems are used like reed grass or cane for roofing, fuel, and other uses.

Weinmannia corymbosa, tiaca; a small tree, this species has wood that is useful for buildings, for raft poles, and for other carpentry. *Oenothera incurvata*, *O. lineatiflora*, *O. mitis*, and *O. oblonga*. *Fuchsia violacea*, th'ilco; its wood provides a black dye, and an infusion or decoction of the bush gives relief in tabardillos or chavalongos (typhoidlike fevers). *Coccoloba hastata*, quilo. *Francoa lyrata*, llaupanke.

Galvezia punctata, pitau; this is a small, leafy tree with evergreen foliage that is pleasing in sight and smell. Its lustrous leaves are more fragrant when dry; when fresh they easily kindle and burn because of their high resin content. It would seem that this resin might have some useful property.

Laurus peumo, known as peumo; it is a very tall tree and the most luxuriantly leafy in all of Chile. A splendid ornamental, it is a beautiful shade tree, especially when loaded with its red fruits. The fruits, the size of small olives, have little pulp and may not satisfy the tastes of those not accustomed to eating them. Nevertheless, Chileans find them to be very delicious; they cook them in water and, without seasoning, suck the slight pulp around the pits, spitting out the skin and the seeds. Because of a loathsome, bitter taste and odor like that of celery, the pits cause nausea if chewed; for this reason, the natives try to suck the pulp very carefully without crushing the seeds. The wood, bark, and leaves have the same odor and taste as the pits.

The trunks of peumo trees are the source of excellent boards, planks, and beams for buildings and other works. The wood has a good grain and is durable. The bark has astringent properties and yields an orange-colored dye for leather. Chileans say the fruits possess properties valuable in the treatment of dropsy (edema). When the countryfolk, frank and generous people that they are, urge a traveler who happens to arrive at their hut at noon to stop and partake of food, they say in an arrogant and superior tone, "Come, partake of the pot, my friend, the pot that's full of peumo!"

Gomortega nitida, keule; this tree is the tallest and most splendid and leafy tree in Chile except for the pino de Chile (Chile pine). It stands out from other trees at a great distance because of its rich green color and the luster of its leaves. The trunks yield an exquisite dark red wood that polishes up brilliantly. The leaves have an acid-astringent taste and, because of their resin content, they stick to the teeth when chewed. If crushed between the fingers, they give off a fragrance suggestive of rosemary and spirits of turpentine; judging from its aromatic qualities, we might infer that the plant possesses healing properties. The leaves burn freely, even when green.

The beautiful fruits of keule are as large as small hen's eggs, and are lustrous and of a yellow color that invites one to eat them. When eaten to excess, however, they bring on headaches. Although not very juicy, the pulp of the fruit is sweet and pleasant; the nut, or pit, is as hard as stone, with a very thick husk enclosing two or three small seeds in as many chambers. This tree is evergreen and is either in flower or in fruit all year round, sending out its new blossoms when the fruits are ripe or shortly thereafter.

According to the natives, another species of keule grows in the forests from Arauco to Valdivia, but I have seen only the pits of the fruit, which are more pointed at one end and smaller than those of our species.

Sophora oblongifolia, known as mayu or mayo. *Cassia reflexa*, called mayo or mayu; its bark yields a yellow dyestuff. *Silene anglica*. *Gaultheria acuminata*.

Talinum monandrum and *T. nitidum*. *Talinum umbellatum*, called yerba de la mistela (mistela herb) because the flowers impart a crimson color to mistela (a drink made of wine, sugar, and cinnamon). Women of the countryside tint their cheeks with the juice of this herb, and it gives them a bright and attractive blush.

Euphorbia tricuspidata and *E. portulacoides*, pichoa; natives take an infusion or decoction of these as a laxative. They are drastic and terrible purges, but the effect can be held in check by drinking cold water.

Tricuspidaria dependens, patagua, a tree of swampy areas. Good planks are sawn from the trunk of this tree and its bark is valuable for tanning. In some places, a kind of silkworm lives in the patagua tree.

Myrtus revoluta, also called patagua; though its vernacular name is the same as that of *Tricuspidaria dependens*, there are great generic differences between the two trees. *Myrtus revoluta* abounds in many parts of Chile, and those areas where it grows are known as pataguales. It provides beautiful wood for planks and beams; the leaves are not so fragrant as those of the common arrayán (myrtle) and are more astringent. When these leafy trees are in flower, they are very ornamental, and the blossoms breathe out a most delicious aroma that perfumes the whole area where the trees grow. Natives find no difficulty in distinguishing this patagua from the preceding one, albeit the two have the same name. They grow together. In some provinces the two trees sometimes have different names.

Myrtus nuda, arrayán blanco (white myrtle); this name comes from the whitish trunk of the tree, which looks as though it has no bark, or as though all its bark had been stripped away. *Myrtus acuminata*, arrayán colorado (red myrtle); the color of the strong wood gives the tree its common name. The wood is useful for carpentry and for inlay woodworking. Because of the color and polished appearance of its trunk, this tree likewise has the appearance of not having any bark. *Myrtus communis*, known as chequén or arrayán; in Chile this bush grows to a considerable height and really looks like a tree.

Geum urbanum, called quellgon or canelilla (little cinnamon); the second name refers to the odor of the roots, which are used in an infusion or a decoction as an aperitif or to resolve inflammatory lesions. Some people keep pieces of canelilla root in the mouth to counteract the unpleasant smell engendered by decaying teeth, etc.

Loasa laciniata, ortiga brava (fierce nettle); *L. tricolor*, ortiga (nettle). *Anemone digitata*, anemona (anemone).

Azara dentata, *A. integrifolia*, and *A. serrata*, all known as corcolen. The more or less rounded crowns of these little trees make them extremely ornamental, especially when they are in bloom, for they bear countless tiny yellow flowers that give off, like those of the aromo (sweet acacia, false myrrh tree), a most pleasant fragrance that pervades the whole area around a tree. The wood of the slender trunks of corcolen trees is strong and has many uses.

Volkameria verticillata, huanium; the fruits, because their shape, size, and color suggest chaquiras, or glass beads, are called chaquis. When this bush flowers it is completely covered with blossoms, and progressively becomes laden with fruits, charming the eye with its beauty.

Horminum? salvifolium, alhuelagüen. *Mimulus luteus*. *Salpiglossis sinuata*. *Erysimum tuberosum*. *Malva hispida*. *Polygala vulgaris*, clinclin; in Chile a warm infusion of this plant is used as an excellent diuretic. *Hedysarum plumosum*. *Astragalus dependens*. *Lathyrus albus* and *L. lutescens*. *Lotus utriculatus*. *Lupinus rhombeus*.

Aster lanuginosus and *A. repens*. *Santolina tinctoria*, poquil; this plant is valuable as the source of a beautiful and lasting yellow dye. S*olidago secunda*, bullel; this plant also yields a yellow dye. *Mutisia subulata*, called clavel del campo (field carnation) for the color and shape of the large, showy flowers. *Molina concava* and *M. linearis*, romerillo (little rosary); the leaves, crushed and applied to ruptures and bruises, consolidate and strengthen the wounded parts. *Coreopsis bidens?*

Triptilion spinosa, siempre viva (live forever); the flowers of this plant, even when dry, keep their bright and beautiful color for many years. In addition to its being a beautiful ornamental for gardens, this species has excellent properties as a diuretic and is extensively used to treat urinary ailments.

Eupatorium urens. *Santolina scabra*. *Sonchus purpureus*. *Hypochaeris laciniata*. *Boopis laciniata*. *Senecio cavus*. *Viola lutea*; *V. chilensis*, violeta, which is used in Chile in place of the common violet, *V. martia*. *Serapias alba*, *S. lutea*, and *S. plicata*, called gavilu or margaritas. *Croton trinerve*.

Sisyrinchium caducum, *S. cavum*, and *S. alatum*. *Sisyrinchium echinatum*; when pressed and dried between papers, this plant makes a print or outline of the leaves on the sheets, so we may presume that this species might be useful in preparing ink. *Sisyrinchium multiflorum*, known as tekel or huilmo blanco; making an infusion of the roots in water, natives use this plant as a strong laxative. *Sisyrinchium quadriflorum*, huilmo; a decoction or warm infusion of the roots is taken as a purgative or to expel secretions of venereal disease.

Ferraria laques, laques; this plant occurs wild and is abundant in the fields. Its bulbs, or onions, are eaten uncooked, boiled, or baked, and have the savory flavor of hazelnuts. Swine, set out to pasture where laques grow, fatten wonderfully on them, and the meat of these animals is exquisite.

Fagus pellin, called pellin; natives give this name to the tree when it is old. When it is in its prime they call it roble, and when very small or young it is known as gualle. Valuable beams, boards, and planks of lumber are made from the trunks. Roble wood is one of the best known for the keels and keelsons of ships, for gun carriages and wagons, and for many other uses in woodworking. Crushed up and mixed with lime or bran, the bark is used as a tanning material and to dye sole leather a red color.

Roble trees are subject to outgrowths; one kind of growth is called diqueñas and resembles *Lycoperdon*, or a puffball, in shape. It is the size of a chestnut, is white but becomes ruddy at full growth, and is perforated like a honeycomb; in some of the holes there are tiny worms, and we may infer that these growths, or galls, are their nests. Notwithstanding the insipid flavor, suggestive of tender mushrooms, the natives eat these growths uncooked. The other kind of growth is a small gall, reddish and muricate, or covered with small, blunt points. The natives believe that these little points are the fruits of the tree, overlooking the fact that the substance is fungal and full of small worms; these are quite different from the fruits, which are tiny nuts with three seeds.

Sapium fragrans, collihuay. When the roots of collihuay are burned, they give off a fragrance that, though pleasant, causes headaches, especially among those who are near fires of this plant. The milky sap or latex of this species is so caustic that it has cost woodcutters the loss of their sight.

Pavonia sempervirens, laurel de Chile (Chilean laurel); this tree is tall, leafy, ornamental, and green throughout the year. Its wood is white, is easy to work, has a fine, waxy, threadlike grain in the center, and is as fragrant as sassafras. Beautiful beams and planks are sawn from the trunk for use in building and woodworking.

In Chile the leaves of Chilean laurel are substituted for common laurel in preparing pickled fish and other foods. The leaves may have good therapeutic properties, if we are to judge from their fragrance and tonic qualities. Warm baths of the leaves strengthen the nerves, and because of this virtue they are used in treating convulsions, paralysis, and rheumatic spasms. When drunk at each mealtime, an infusion of the leaves relieves rheumatic pain.

Torresia utriculata, ratonero (mouse herb). The swollen rootlets, which are tender, transparent, and the size of seed pearls, are eaten by mice that, seeking food, daily visit the fields where this plant grows.

Lardizabala biternata, called coquillvoqui or taurovoqui. The pulp of the fruit is rather pleasant, and natives eat it with relish. With this creeper they bind the quimchas (reeds or canes), roofs, and rafters of houses; its stems are strong, flexible, and durable.

Dioscorea filiformis and *D. hastata*. *Decostea scandens*, yelmo (helmet); this climbing shrub is evergreen, serving as does ivy to beautify small woods or parks. *Coriaria nervosa*, deu; the entire plant is good material for tanning.

Ruizia fragrans, known as boldu or boldo. This small tree grows to a height of 6 to 12 yards, is evergreen and very leafy, and flowers in August, with a repeat in October. It provides enjoyable shade with its dense foliage, which constantly breathes off a pleasant fragrance that is somewhat similar to that of cinnamon and can be noticed far across the fields. Chileans use the crushed leaves extensively to strengthen the stomach and relieve pain. With the sap of the leaves, extracted with water, they cure earaches; to treat running sores and head colds, they apply leaves that have been half-roasted, bruised, and sprayed with wine. Warm baths prepared with the leaves are taken as unsurpassed cures for rheumatism and dropsy.

Although small, the ripe fruits are sweet and appetizing. In a very tender stage they can be prepared in the same way as olives, and the flavor of well-pickled boldu fruit is even more delicious than that of olives. Some people make rosaries from the pits of the fruit, for they are tough and naturally sculptured as though decorated by the hand of man. Natives also use the leaves as a spice in pickles, in place of common laurel. The wood and branches of boldu have sundry uses in building, and when burned they give off a very pleasant aroma that is never irksome. Lastly, barrels made of the wood of this species improve the quality of wine stored in them for some time.

Because of its luxuriant foliage, beautiful greenness, and delicate aroma, and because an infusion of its leaves can be used daily in place of tea, the boldu is surely a tree worthy of being propagated as a garden ornamental.

Schinus dependens, called huighan or huignan; this tree, 6 to 10 yards tall, has many hanging branches, especially when it is in flower and fruit. Its trunk exudes a resin that, applied to the temples and behind the ears, lessens toothache or pain in the cheek. Musicians prefer its wood above all others for violin bows.

From the ripe fruits of huighan, Chileans make an excellent chicha that has diuretic properties and is believed to be efficacious against dropsy. Recently three people in Concepción were cured of dropsy by frequent use of this chicha. Though the drink is not agreeable to our palate, the Indians invariably take it at every meal. Its taste and smell, like the taste and smell of all parts of the tree itself, suggest black pepper. The chicha is made by scraping the fruits in water to free the sweet or sugar-bearing portions, and this mixture is then set out to ferment for 3 or 4 days until it is wine-colored and heavily charged with carbonic acid gas.

Kageneckia oblonga, guayo colorado (red guayo); because its reddish wood is strong, this showy tree with a rather stout trunk is useful for many things. The red color is intensified by alkali, and for this reason pieces of the wood are put into urine before being turned on a lathe to make walking sticks and other objects. The bark is employed in tanning skins, and natives use the seeds as a purgative.

Mimosa carbonaria, espino. This tree is wondrous for the fragrance of its flowers, which are yellow and arranged in small heads, and for the beautiful shade that its leafy crown provides for cattle. The pods are nutritious fodder for horses and mules. The best charcoal known comes from the trunks of espino, for it burns in the brazier for 40 hours or longer if one is careful to scrape together the live embers and cover them with ashes. The ashes, too, are useful, for they come out white and are good for making lye. Forked poles to support trees, stanchions for farm buildings, props for vines, and other articles requiring strength are also made from the trunks of espino.

CHAPTER 38

Trip to the Province of Rere and the Fort of Nacimiento

In December 1782 the two artists and three botanists set out for the fort of Nacimiento, located at the foot of the mountain range. It was in the forests of this area that the royal order to fell Chile pines, to repair the masts and spars and other internal parts of His Majesty's ships, was being carried out. We passed through Hualqui, capital of the province of Puchacay, which is bordered on the west by Concepción, on the south by the Biobio River, on the east by the province of Rere, and on the north by that of Itata. Puchacay consists of three parishes, those of the Villa de San Juan Bautista de Hualqui, of La Florida, and of Conuto.

We passed the night in Huilquilemu, or Estancia del Rey, capital of the province of Rere. The magistrate, Don Miguel Montero, very generously put us up in his house. He also informed us of the scarcity of plants in the vicinity of Nacimiento; for this reason we divided our party into two groups. My companion Pavón and the artist Brunete went on to Nacimiento, and the artist Gálvez and I stayed in Huilquilemu. Dombey accompanied Pavón, and after 5 days all three returned to Concepción because they had not found enough to keep them busy in the vicinity of Nacimiento.

Pavón left Nacimiento with an official of the navy who was in charge of the felling of the pines. It was Pavón's intention to study these trees in the mountains, and he gathered both flowering and fruiting material for all of us to examine, as I learned later, for he brought to me in Huilquilemu branches with strobili, or little cones, and aments, or staminate inflorescences. When we three botanists together had studied the Chile pine, we decided one and all that it belonged to the genus *Pinus* of Linnaeus, even though the pistillate and staminate flowers are found on separate trees.

Since the magistrate of Rere assured me that numerous plants were to be found in his province that differed from those of Concepción, I remained with Gálvez in Huilquilemu for a month. During that time I explored the vicinity, sometimes in the company of the magistrate, and collected various plants. The species are discussed below.

CHAPTER 39

Description of the Province of Rere

The province of Rere is bounded on the west and northwest by the province of Puchacay, and on the east and south by the frontier forts that are built along the mountain range to hold back approaching Indians. The capital of this province is the town of Huilquilemu, or Buena Esperanza; today it is called San Luis Gonzaga or Estancia del Rey. There is a parish church in this same village, where the faithful of the surrounding farms and ranches, except for those who live in districts that have chapels where services are held on religious holidays, come together for mass and other religious ceremonies.

The climate of the province is like that of Concepción with but slight differences, for which reason the region has excellent harvests of wheat. The harvests of grapes are not large, and the grapes are inferior in quality in comparison with those of Ñipas and other estates in the provinces of Itata and Puchacay. Very large numbers of cattle are slaughtered here for preparing charqui (beef jerky), suet, and tallow. The beautiful pastures of the region likewise support some flocks of sheep and goats.

There are river beds where small grains of gold are washed out. The yields are rather good, considering that the gold-bearing beds are washed to a depth of only 2 to 5 yards. It is common to find nuggets—or papas, as they call them there—weighing half an ounce, and there have been some that weigh half a pound or 2 pounds. Two leagues or a bit farther from San Luis Gonzaga, in the vicinity of the Biobio River, there are mountains where one can find a kind of rounded stone; some of the stones are the shape and size of rifle shot and others are larger than nuts. I gathered two bags full of both types merely by scratching around on the surface of the ground with a knife.

During my stay in Rere I collected and had drawn some new plants, which I shall discuss herewith.

Calceolaria alba, arquenita blanca. *Oldenlandia uniflora*. *Navarretia involucrata*. *Fragosa spinosa*. *Stereoxylon virgatum*; *S. pulverulentum*, madroño. *Stereoxylon revolutum*, called liun or siete camisas (seven shirts) for the bark that peels off in successive membranes or thin sheets.

Eryngium ciliatum, achupalla; *E. trifidum*, anisillo (little anise). *Eryngium tripode*, calcha; the lower portions of the stems of this plant are subterranean and always white, like hilled endive; they are as tender and as tasty as endive in fresh salad.

Fabiana imbricata, pichi; at first sight, this bush somewhat resembles the taray.

It is plentiful on the sandbanks and beaches of rivers and estuaries in the provinces of Rere and Itata, where it is believed to possess wonderful anthelmintic properties for curing sheep and goats of pirhuin (pirguin or alicuya, a parasitic insect), an ailment that wipes out entire flocks. This is why the farmers, who are experts in diagnosing this disease, immediately take the affected animals to pastures where pichi occurs. On this fodder the animals get better and fatten up in a few days, and the insects are not found in the livers of the animals when they are slaughtered. This same ailment occurs in Peru among goats when they feed upon poor pastures, as in forested regions where there is neither grass nor any other fodder plant for ruminant animals or horses.

Alstroemeria revoluta, *A. haemantha*, *A. salsilla*, and *A. versicolor*; all these species have showy flowers for gardening, and the swollen roots are very useful as sources of the starch, or meal, called ligtu or liutu.

Tropaeolum hexaphyllum, pajarillos (little birds); this is a beautiful plant for gardens because of the color and large size of the flowers. *Stachys lanuginosa*. *Gardoquia multiflora*. *Carthamus ciliatus*. *Aster multifidus*. *Chaetanthera ciliata* and *C. serrata*. *Sisyrinchium campanulatum*.

Smegmadermas emarginata, quillay, a tall and heavily crowned tree. Its stout trunk provides excellent beams, planks, and boards for buildings, as well as timbers for mills and mines, because the wood is more durable in wet places than in dry ones. Natives make small balls of the crushed bark for use as soap in washing clothes. A decoction of the bark is used in enemas to treat those afflicted with hysteria. These trees grow in almost all parts of Chile, abounding especially in the provinces of Concepción, Puchacay, Itata, and Maule.

A short way from San Luis Gonzaga there is a small brook plentifully supplied with shrimps, or crabs, of delicious flavor.

CHAPTER 40

Trip from Rere to Concepción

In January 1783 I returned to Concepción with the artist Gálvez, with no problems worthy of note on the way.

We stayed in Concepción until the 29th of March, exploring and collecting in the countryside around Concepción, Cauquenes, and Puchacay. During this interval we dried and drew a goodly number of plants; those that I described are listed below.

Campanula denticulata. *Hydrocotyle althymilaefolia*; this plant produces a delightful aroma, very similar to that of the balm mint. *Apium graveolens*, called panul or apio silvestre (wild celery); natives eat the raw leaves to stop hemorrhages from the mouth and to treat pulmonary troubles.

Linum confertum, merulagüen. An infusion or decoction of this plant is frequently prescribed to treat lung ailments or the cough of a cold. Crushed and mixed with wine, it can be applied as a poultice to dissolve various kinds of tumors.

Oenothera grandiflora, guadalagüen. Chileans maintain that the juice or warm infusions of this plant cure internal abscesses. Although it is a prostrate herb, *O. grandiflora* is very showy because of its large white flowers; like those of all other species of *Oenothera* that I have observed, its flowers usually begin to open after sunset. Two hours after sunrise on the following day, they change color, wrinkle up, and completely wither away.

Sophora alata, called pilo or pelu. A low tree, it has a showy, almost perfectly rounded crown. The trunk has durable, white wood, excellent for the keels of ships; the pods, or fruits, are the source of a black dyestuff.

Oxalis prostrata, yerba de la perdiz (partridge herb). In the springtime this plant is so abundant that the fields along the coast are covered with it. It forms a beautiful carpet with the green of its leaves and the golden hue of its flowers. The leaves, slightly acid, are tasty in salads.

Aristotelia glandulosa, maqui. Womenfolk prepare a pleasant, acid-sweet fermented drink of the fruits of maqui; it is extremely refreshing. The fresh shoots, crushed and applied to the back and the area of the kidneys, lessen excessive heat in these parts of the body during fevers; when chewed, they cleanse and heal sores of the mouth. Binding cord is made of the hammered bark, and the light and flexible wood is excellent for lath in ceilings, for barrel hoops, and for musical instruments. The fruits, sweetened with sugar, are appetizers, and as such are set out on the table before meals; the natives refresh themselves in the afternoon by putting one or two spoonfuls of the crushed fruit in a glass of water with a bit of sugar.

Laurus revoluta, called lingue or linge. This tree is very common in the bishopric of Concepción and in various parts of Santiago. Its trunk is valued for building and as a source of a solid, mottled wood from which levers, troughs, and trays are made. The bark is used to make bags and shoe soles. Doves that eat the fruit of lingue have bitter-tasting meat, and the fruit is very harmful to ruminant livestock.

Loasa multifida, ortiga (nettle). *Stemodia maritima*. *Hissopus*? *punctata*. *Erigeron canadense* and *E. scabrum*. *Arbutus racemosa*.

Molina oblonga, *M. racemosa*, *M. reticulata*, and *M. viscosa*. All these species are balsamic plants with glutinous and comforting properties; they are rich in a resin that has a very pleasant aroma, even when burning.

Fagus oblongifolia, pellin. This leafy tree provides excellent wood for buildings, gun carriages, keels and keelsons, stanchions, and other works of carpentry, for it is strong and long-lasting under water. Chileans use the bark to dye woolens a dark purple. Pellin is one of the few trees in Chile that lose their leaves in winter.

Pinus chilensis, pino de Chile (Chile pine). The description of this tree, which I began in Huilquilemu with the material gathered by Pavón in the mountains of Nacimiento, was completed with the fruiting collections that I made from three trees I found in flower and fruit in a dale near the bridge of Talcahuano. I had a drawing made.

This splendid tree grows as tall as 50 yards or more. Although it is dioecious, the fruits correspond exactly in structure to those of *Pinus pinea* of Linnaeus, according to the examinations made by Mr. Dombey, Don José Pavón, and myself in Huilquilemu and in Concepción. We all agreed to classify it as a new species of *Pinus* and as the most valuable of all species known thus far on account of its wood, resin, and fruits. The wood is white with an excellent grain for working, and is recommended for the masts of ships and for many other works of carpentry.

The enormous cones of the Chile pine often contain up to half an almud or zelemin (peck) of piñones (pine nuts, Chile nuts), and sometimes much more. The piñones are larger than acorns, in the shape of an elongated wedge. They have the consistency and the inner and outer color of chestnuts, and likewise have the flavor of chestnuts when eaten raw, boiled, or roasted. Piñones that have been covered with snow, during the season when snow persists in these mountains, are even tastier than those gathered just after they fall. Though the cones usually are thickly covered with resin, in the ripe stage some scales come loose easily and the rest will then fall off with the piñones.

Piñones form a main part of the diet of the Indian tribes known as the Pehuenches and Huiliches; they make small boiled or baked cakes of them, which they use in place of bread. The Indians also make very tasty orchatas (horchatas, starchy drinks) from piñones.

According to the natives, the forests of this species of pine stretch over 200 leagues; that is, from 36° almost to the Strait of Magellan.

The resin, which flows plentifully, has sundry important economic and medicinal applications. When natives who are engaged in felling these trees gash themselves severely, they apply the resin of the tree to the wound, and there is no doubt that it produces the desired effect. It is also found to be very comforting in cases of rupture or bruises.

In his *Historia de Chile*, Padre Ignacio Molina describes the Chile pine and places it in the genus *Pinus* of Linnaeus. The gentleman Lamarck created a new genus for it, *Dombeya*, in honor of my companion Mr. Dombey. Antoine Laurent de Jussieu based his genus *Araucaria* upon the same tree, no doubt taking the name from his belief that the tree grows in Arauco; this locality, however, is coastal territory, and the tree grows in the mountains many leagues from the sea, at least 40 or 50 leagues inland.

The name *Araucaria* was adopted by my companion Pavón in a description of the Chile pine that he presented to the Royal Academy of Medicine in Madrid; this work was taken in great part from my manuscripts. His only reason for using this name was his wish to please another person. This I have shown to be the case in my *Respuesta, para Desengaño del Publico, á la Impugnacion que ha Divulgado Pre-*

maturamente el Presbitero Don José Antonio Cavanilles contra el Prodromo de la Flora del Perú (Reply, for the Enlightenment of the Public, to the Opposition Prematurely Set Forth by the Clergyman Don Antonio José Cavanilles Against the Prodromus of the Flora of Peru); I published this document in Madrid in 1794.

Schinus frondosus, called lithre or lithi. A stout tree, this species attains a height of 20 yards and is very showy with its evergreen foliage and rounded crown. It is much more luxuriant in springtime than in winter. It gives such splendid shade that it is the most inviting of trees for anyone wanting to nap under it, but its shade is so damaging that many people find purulent sores on themselves after resting under the tree. These sores occur especially on the parts of the body exposed during the siesta, and are accompanied by high fevers. Smoke from the burning wood of this tree, and vapors given off when woodchoppers fell it, are equally noxious. As we explained in our description of mayten (*Celastrus dependens*), that bush is the antidote for lithre poisoning; maize grains chewed up and applied to the sores likewise act as a cure.

In spite of the noxious nature of the lithre, the trunk of this tree is the source of wood that is excellent for the keels of ships, for it becomes more solid when under water. Beautiful beams, planks, and boards for buildings are also cut from the trunks of lithre trees, as are carriage axles and wheels, plowshares, and other implements requiring strength.

During our stay in the bishopric of Concepción we made a collection of many different kinds of wood, worked into small boards. The beauty of their various colors, grains, and hardness constitutes one of the great works of the Creator. However, these were all lost, together with our other extensive collections of natural products of Chile, when the ship *San Pedro de Alcántara* foundered and sank. Each month we also sent from Chile to the Ministry of the Indies multiple packets of the seeds that we found in those pleasant fields and forests and along those most fertile coasts.

CHAPTER 41

Description of the Province of Concepción, and Notes on the Natural Products of the Bishoprics of Santiago and Concepción in Chile

The province of Concepción is confined to the small area running from west to east between the coast and the boundaries of the provinces of Cauquenes and Puchacay, which are located about 2 leagues northeast and east of Concepción; from north to south it extends from the Andalién River to the Biobio River. The settlements located in this province are Mochita, Quebrada de Carcamo, Quebrada de Palomares, Hualpén, and the ports of Penco el Viejo and San Vicente. There are few boats in either of these ports, although we saw the launching of the ship San Miguel in 1783 in San Vicente, which is situated behind the Tetas de Biobio (Teats of Biobio, a headland). The port of Talcahuano is also in this province; it has a large bay, with the small island of Quiriquina, 2 leagues long, at the mouth. Those who arrive from Peru or other areas with smallpox or other epidemic diseases are quarantined here. The bay has two mouths; the larger one is on the north, where boats of all sizes enter, and the smaller is on the south, accommodating only small craft.

In Talcahuano, populated by only 30 souls, the warehouses for fruits and other products of the region destined for Peru are located. Four to six ships a year come from Peru to carry away these products, and they bring sugar and other colonial or European merchandise from Lima. There is a fortress on the hill at Talcahuano to prevent the entrance of any enemy ship into that bay, and its commander is both the military and the political governor of the fort.

This province has three parishes: that of Concepción, which includes the cathedral; that of Hualqui; and that of Talcahuano.

The city of Concepción (Figure 9) was founded by Valdivia in 1550 on the port of Penco el Viejo, and is located at 36°43' south latitude and at a longitude of 303° 18' from the meridian of Tenerife. In 1567 the Real Audiencia (royal high court) was established there, but it was discontinued in 1573 and set up again in 1609 in the city of Santiago.

Concepción was laid waste several times by Indians and by earthquakes. The worst destruction occurred on the 8th of July 1730; after an earthquake, the sea rose up in a tidal wave that flooded the greater part of the city. On the 24th of May

Figure 9. Map of the town of Concepción, Chile, or Penco. From Frézier's *Voyage to the South Sea*, London, 1717. (Courtesy of the British Museum.)

1751, after another earthquake, the sea invaded the city twice. The first wave warned the people of threatening destruction and made them all flee to the mountains, mostly with nothing more than their shirts, for it came about in the middle of the night. With the second of these two tidal waves, the sea flooded and ruined everything in the town, and for this reason the settlement was moved on the 24th of November 1764 to the valley of Mocha, 3 leagues from Penco, near the Biobio River and at the foot of the mountain called Puntilla, where the powderhouse is located.

The streets of Concepción are laid out in lines from northeast to southwest and from northwest to southeast. Because of the small number of inhabitants and the short time of their occupancy, the surface of the streets is sandy and very uneven. The single-story houses are built of wood, lime from seashells, pebbles, and adobe, and are roofed with tiles. Most have rooms or wooden partitions, since wood is the most available and least expensive building material because of its abundance in the fields and forests round about.

There are 10,000 inhabitants, most of whom dwell on their estates, or campanas, as they call them, most of the year. The men are usually of good stature, robust, serious, good-looking, and businesslike in their dealings. They dress after the fashion of Spain, but they wear ponchos instead of capes for riding. The women are of medium stature, good-looking, robust, affable, and gifted, and they dress according to the style in Lima, except that their skirts are a little longer.

Politically, the city is governed by a municipal council composed of a chief magistrate, two ordinary mayors, four aldermen, a royal lieutenant, and other corresponding offices.

The ecclesiastical council consists of the bishop, a dean, an archdeacon, one office of a magisterial canon and another of a canon of mercy. Although the number should be greater, according to regulations, up to the present time small tithes have prevented the establishment of a full complement.

There is a small cathedral located next to the bishop's palace, on one side of the large plaza in the center of the city. In this cathedral Nuestra Señora de las Nieves (Our Lady of the Snows) is worshipped, and the faithful have obtained many miraculous benefits through the intercession of this image.

There are five religious monasteries: the Augustinian, the Mercedarian, the Franciscan, the Dominican, and that of San Juan de Dios. There is a convent of barefoot Trinitarians, as well as a theological college and a house of religious retreat.

Though this city is unwalled, it is the principal military stronghold of the entire frontier. The field commander and the sergeant major of the realm have their residences here. Formerly, the captain general and president of the royal high court of Santiago lived here 6 months of the year and in Santiago the remaining 6 months. At present, he resides permanently in this capital. The royal treasury with its accountant and treasurer, the royal customs office, and various merchants of native and European goods are also established here.

The bishop lives in this city. He has jurisdiction over the six provinces, or districts, of Concepción, Cauquenes, Chillán, Itata, Puchacay, and Rere. None has an income, and the magistrates have no salary other than the sparse judicial taxes. For this reason, these posts are not very desirable and are not sought after in the court. Therefore these municipalities, as well as those of the bishopric of Santiago, are almost always provided for by the captain general of the realm.

In addition to the divisions to which we have referred, there are three other political units belonging to Chile that are cared for by His Majesty. They are Chiloe, Valdivia, and Valparaíso, with jurisdiction over the large island of Juan Fernández, the commander of which is both the military and the political governor.

Throughout the bishopric of Concepción, the temperature in all four seasons is milder than that of Spain, with which country Chile has much in common so far as agricultural production is concerned. In winter the cold is not so severe as in Spain, nor is the heat so extreme in summer. For this reason, the trees are evergreen and more or less leafy and luxuriant all year round, especially along the seashore where the spray from the ocean beats directly upon them. The sky is beautiful, and in good weather the nights are very clear, even when there is no moon.

The commonest, as well as the healthiest, winds come from the south and southwest. The north wind brings with it heavy rains. The east wind, known as puelche, comes from the mountains and is cold and extremely dry, causing palsies, convulsions, and colds that turn into a kind of fever called chavalongos or tabardillos. These fevers may also be brought on by sunstroke, which is very harmful. Natives treat the fevers by bathing the head in cold water and by taking infusions of various herbs with meals. When a puelche blows for many days, it portends earthquakes.

The coldest days this year in Concepción were the 4th and 5th of July, when the mercury dropped to 43°F (6°C). On July 25 of this same year, with the puelche (east wind) prevailing, there was an earthquake at 25 minutes past seven in the morning, and a number of long, violent claps of thunder with flashes of lightning followed it on the same day.

Animals

This bishopric, like the entire country of Chile, is blessed with extremely fertile pasture lands. All kinds of cattle and domestic animals are raised, and poultry and wild animals are plentiful. The domestic animals are cows, sheep, swine, goats, and excellent horses and mules. Among the wild animals is the pagi, or leoncillo (puma); I treated the skin of one, which measured 7 quartas (cuartas, handspans) long, with aromatic plants and sent it to Spain aboard the *San Pedro de Alcántara*. There are also small wolves; four kinds of foxes, which are called the garú, payne-garú, chilla, and culpeu; and two types of wildcats, which are called the colo-colo and guiña. Like a skunk, a little animal called the chinque violently throws off a stinking liquid when chased; its black pelt has a white band surrounding the loin. Other wild animals include deer, chilihueques (llamas), a kind of weasel called the quiqui or uron, moles, field rats, and mice.

In the mountains there are vicuñas and huanacos. In the lakes, rivers, and coastal inlets there are seals such as the lame; the thopel-lame, or small sea lion; urines, or sea wolves; cats, or chinchimenes; bears; nutrias; a type of nutria called the guillin or guillino; and a kind of mouse called the coypu.

Amphibious Horse?

I am told that there lives in the lake of Avendaño a kind of amphibious horse, several of which have been occasionally observed to come out on land. In 1723 a guazo (huazo, peasant) lassoed one of these horses, but it plunged at once into the water and exerted such strength that the peasant would have been dragged down with his own horse to the bottom of the lake, had he not cut the rope quickly. In the lake of Papal, 2 leagues from Avendaño, one of these horses was found floating dead, and it was dragged from the lake in the presence of the local magistrate and of many people who had gathered to see the curiosity. This amphibian was twice the size of an ordinary horse, with a long and slender neck, small ears, and an abundance of thick, long hair on the neck and tail. Its delicate legs and feet had neither knees nor ankles, and were apparently of cartilage instead of bone, terminating in a kind of soft, divided membrane, like fins. The body was entirely sorrel-colored. In their ignorance, these simple folk were satisfied by this imperfect description.

Fowl

The domestic and wild poultry used for food are achaus, or hens; turkeys; ducks; geese; doves; small turtledoves; partridges; wild chickens; thrushes; loycas, or aloycas (aloicas, a kind of robin redbreast); pirenes; sius, or gilgueros (goldfinches); and papagayos, or cotorritas (a type of small parrot or parakeet), the young of which are called tricahues and are very delicious. These papagayos breed on the most inaccessible cliffs along rivers; there the countryfolk catch them with a boldness that is frightening, by going over the edge of an escarpment tied onto a rope secured at the other end to a tree or, if there be no tree, to a horse. These people never stop to think that their lives hang on the strength of the rope and on the horse's loyalty and tameness. If even one of these conditions fails, they will either fall straight to the waters below, alone or with the horse, or be dragged along if the animal becomes frightened.

Origin of the Name of Chile

In addition to the edible birds of farm and forest, in Chile there are to be found thencas, or calendra larks, that mimic the songs of other birds; thrushes; flycatchers with melodious songs; three species of *Trochilus* of diverse sizes and colors, called pigdas or picaflores (hummingbirds); diucas, morning-callers with delightful songs who live in villages; and woodpeckers of the species *Picus pitius*, who drill the trunks of trees with their beaks and make a great noise with their continuous hammering and pecking. The thili, trichli, or chili is a kind of thrush from which it is said the country of Chile took its name.

The pillu, or cigueña (stork), is a kind of white-plumed heron from which wonderful writing quills are obtained. Treguilles are perpetual sentries of the day and night; when they hear the noise of a person or animal, they start up in flight, ceaselessly repeating the sound "treguill" and thus warning their kind that something is amiss nearby. They always dwell in humid places and on lakeshores.

Hualas and urus are pests of gardens and fields alike; though they are small birds, their crops are always full of beans, peas, or even horse beans. In Chile there are also buzzards, some with black heads and others with red; small eagles, known as dominicanos because of the white and black coloration of their feathers; condors; large eagles, such as the gnancu and calquin; sparrow hawks; owls; herons; kingfishers; swallows; bats; piuques; cuckoos; and chinchones, night birds with a sad song that Indians believe brings bad luck if they hear it.

Water Birds

In lakes and along the coast there is an abundance of potojuncos; rabijuncos; pájaros niños, or *Diomedea* (albatrosses); gulls; alcatraces (pelicans) with gorgeous plumage; pardelas; cormorants; ducks; zambullidores, a kind of diving duck; flamingoes; geese; swans; bandurias (red American ibis); piuquenes (a kind of wild turkey); woodcocks; and hualas, or coscorobas, a type of wild goose that cackles "coscoroba," whence the name.

Fish and Shellfish

Fish and shellfish are plentiful along the coast and in the rivers, estuaries, and lakes of Chile. There are trout in the rivers, as well as corbinas (whiting), eels, puyeques, a kind of sardine called the pexe rey, and ahogagatos. Very abundant in the ocean is the robalo, a delicious fish—in fact, one of the most savory known. In the ocean there are also corbinas, cabrillas (sea bass), lenguados (sole), pexe rey, pexe gallo, pexe perro, puyequenes, tunnies, lisas (mullet), pintadillas (a kind of trout), dorados (giltheads), cauques, sardines, small anchovies, tollos (spotted dogfish), conger eels, vieja, pampanitos, chichi, gerguillas, bocones (a kind of anchovy), pintaroxas (dogfish), vagres (bagres, catfish), chalacos (gobies), tembladerillas (electric rays), and rollizos. Young sharks are called cazones (dogfish) and are esteemed as a tasty food; sailors eat the meat of adult sharks, but I did not find it agreeable. There are also octopuses, a kind of manta (devilfish), and, lastly, very large whales that approach the island of Quiriquina in great numbers.

Shellfish are abundant along the Chilean coast, and the most valued are the mollusks known as choros (mussels), cholhuas, and dollimes, in particular the females of all these. They can be distinguished from the males by the color of their flesh, which is yellow like egg yolk, and by their flavor and consistency. The flesh of the males is grayish and whitish, sticky, cloying, and marly or clayey; often they are full of minute pearls, among which are found some as large as peas or even small chickpeas. However, owing to their poor shine and their tiny size, no pains are taken to gather them. In the flesh of the females, which is mostly a mass of eggs, pearls are very rarely found. These mussels occur in rivers and lakes as well as in the sea.

There are four species of apancoras, or sea crabs, called talicunas, reynas, remaderas, and peludas. There are likewise two species of shrimps or crayfish, one of which lives in rivers, lakes, and estuaries and is delicious. The other lives in soil, into which it digs like a mole; for this reason naturalists call it *Cancer talpa* (mole crab). Because of the hardness of its shell and the sparsity of its flesh, this last species is not usually eaten. In estuaries and rivers there is a very small apancora (crab) that also is not eaten, for the same reasons given for *Cancer talpa*.

Exceedingly common along the coast are sea urchins; picos; tracas; navajuelas; chapes; petacones; palancanas or afeytaderas; locos (abalone), the flesh of which must be pounded with a stick to soften it; and pipes, a kind of limpet that sticks to large fish and to other mollusks and shells. In Coquimbo there are oysters; peninpenin or miembro (penis), so called for its shape; potos, also called rosas holonturies or anemonas de mar (sea anemones); piures; starfish; and other various small snails and shellfish. In rivers, estuaries, and lakes one finds frogs weighing up to 2 pounds; the legs of these animals are very tasty.

Noxious Animals

In summertime, when it rains, the fields are full of large toads. The brooks are populated by myriads of tiny toads, continuously chirping and, like crickets, bothering the hearer day and night. There are two kinds of small snakes, but their bite is harmless. Scorpions live under rocks in the ravines.

Of the numerous species of domestic and field spiders, three are more worthy of note than the others. One is large and hairy, while another is hairless and only one-sixth the size of the hairy type. Both of these kinds are harmless and carry their young around on their backs. A third species, much smaller than the second and grayish with red beneath, has a most poisonous and often deadly sting that causes extremely sharp pain, with convulsions and cramping of the arms and legs. These symptoms increase towards nightfall and are maintained at the height of their intensity until the following dawn, when the pains gradually lessen and the cramps begin to leave the limbs. By midday the patient feels normal again, and in good health. The danger of stinging is greatest during the summer season, when this spider is found in pasture grasses.

Insects

Among the various insects in the Chilean fauna, the best known is a species of silkworm found in the ravines of Petorca and of the mountain range. Usually living on Chilean laurel, or *Pavonia sempervirens*, fireflies give off in the dark a beautiful phosphorescent light, which is stimulated by a violent movement that the animal frequently makes by doubling up the forward half of its body without spreading its wings. There are concunas, a kind of caterpillar, of various colors and sizes; one of the largest of these lives in the huighanes (*Schinus dependens*). Butterflies of different hues hatch from these caterpillars. One also finds pinathras, or pinath'as; that is, meat flies of a distinct species.

The ordinary mosquito also abounds. There is also a smaller kind of mosquito that breeds in cow dung, flying in swarms around pens and filling the air with a fragrance like that of amber. Some people gather these tiny mosquitoes to put in their clothing to scent the cloth. Might we, perhaps, attribute the fragrance of these insects to the *Geranium moschatum* that grows abundantly in the fields and that cows eat greedily?

Fleas are very common, and in Santiago there are some nihuas (jigger fleas, chiggers), or *Pulex penetrans*, also known as piques. There are bedbugs in Santiago as well as in some other localities. In Laxa, near Huilquilemu, Spanish flies breed, and they are more efficacious than those of Europe. Flies are infinite in number. At the beginning of winter they completely cover the walls of the stables of Santiago, piling up on one another as if they were swarms of ants.

Fruits and Seeds

In the bishoprics of Concepción and Santiago, the plant kingdom is no less prolific than the animal kingdom. In addition to the wheat, barley, vegetables, wines, fruits, flax, hemp, beans, quinoa, false saffron, oregano (wild marjoram), and other seeds that are harvested abundantly on the various lands of this region, there are all sorts of greens and delicate vegetables that have been brought from Spain and cultivated and propagated here. There is no lack of beautiful flowers in gardens throughout the year; the women cultivate them with their own hands for pleasure.

Among the fruits we may list the famous frutilla or Chilean strawberry, *Fragaria chiloensis*, the fruit of which can grow to an ounce in weight, a huge size compared with that of the European strawberry, *Fragaria vesca*. And they are just as delicious, albeit somewhat sweeter. Their fragrance, taste, and size vary somewhat, according to the soil in which they grow. In the gardens at Palomares and Concepción, where I have eaten many of these strawberries, they are excellent from all points of view.

In addition to the strawberry, Chile has the following fruits: piñones (pine nuts), different from those of Europe; hazelnuts; maqui (*Aristotelia glandulosa*); coquilvoqui (*Lardizabala biternata*); boldu, or boldo (*Ruizia fragrans*); queule; lucumas (eggfruit); coconuts; murtillas (myrtus berries); and other wild fruits. Were these brought into cultivation, they would be esteemed in any part of the world.

Of European fruits, Chile grows the following: piñones (pine nuts); walnuts; almonds; melocotones (peaches grown on quince rootstock); duraznos (several kinds of peaches); peladillos (clingstone peaches); pears; guindas (morello cherries, sour cherries); plums; oranges; lemons; quinces; and the excellent pero Joaquino (Joaquin pear), which is sent up to Lima as a gift. Apples grow in such abundance that fields around Concepción, on the road to Arauco, and in other places are overgrown with these trees in a wild state. It is a pleasure to see them on all sides, loaded with great bunches of fruit and with their branches bent down and sprawling to the very ground. Fascinating to the eye are the reds and yellows of the apples, which load the trees so heavily that one can hardly see branches, trunks, or leaves.

Woods

The countryside is generally full of trees and shrubs that have valuable woods for building and for other domestic uses, or have some medicinal property, as reported in our discussions of the localities where they are native. Chileans employ all of these medicinal plants, guided by traditions passed down to them from their forefathers and by their own experiences acquired in curing their various ills.

The trees and shrubs with the best timber for buildings and for other construction and carpentry work are: the gigantic Chile pines, which provide excellent masts for ships; pellines (roble); raulíes (a kind of southern beech), with pink wood that is easily worked and bark that provides a red dyestuff; lithres, good for making keels; nebú, or hazel tree, appropriate for making oars; queule; laurel; peumo; lusna; coihue; belloto; lingue; aceytunillo (satinwood); quillay (soapbark); red guayo; wild lúcumo; algarrobo (carob tree); espino (hawthorn); molle de Chile; canelo (cinnamon); boldu; myrtles of different species; patahua (whitewood); huillipatahua; pilo; pitao; mañihue; maytén; corcolen; huayacanes (guaiacum); coquito palms; European pines; cypress; walnuts; and olives and other fruit trees of Spain, including chestnuts, all of which are economically very important.

The uses, properties, and applications of all these trees and shrubs will be considered when we describe them. To avoid repetition, we do not discuss them here.

The Mineral Kingdom

The mineral kingdom is no less abundantly represented in Chile than are the plant and animal kingdoms.

In the province of Rere, in the locality known as Quilacoya, there are several gold-washing sites where nuggets and powdered gold of 21 carats, 1 grain are produced. Much gold has been gathered, not only in Quilacoya but also near Huilquilemu. Since this land affords its inhabitants an abundance of food and a comfortable life, there are few who work the gold that nature has so lavishly set before them, almost on the surface of the sands of the river banks. The natives assert that in the bishopric of Concepción there are other veins of gold, silver, copper, and iron, but these are likewise unworked for lack of manpower.

In the bishopric of Santiago a number of gold, silver, and copper mines are worked. In the municipality of Maule, on the mountain called Chivato, there are three gold mines on a single vein. Two of these mines yield from 25 to 30 pesos per box, and the third yields from 50 to 80 pesos per box; the quality of this gold is 20 carats, 2 grains. From the mine of Don Ignacio Zapata, 100,000 pesos' worth of gold was taken, but the mine was completely flooded when a vein of water was struck 185 yards underground. Zapata lost about 200,000 pesos in ores that were beyond reach, since the condition of the ground did not permit tunneling. In this same municipality, in the mountain called Lomablanca, there are other gold mines that yield from 70 to 80 pesos per box; the metal is 16-carat, 15-carat, or 14-carat gold. In these same mines a rich find, known as the mula muerta (dead mule), was made; this yielded more than 16,000 pesos from only two boxes. Each box is composed of 10 loads of earth, or ore; each load weighs 350 pounds.

In the municipality of Colchagua, or San Fernando, there are various mines. The most famous are those in the village of Nancagua, and among these the most outstanding are the ones called Cocinilla and Millaque. These two mines yield 100 pesos per box, in 18-carat and 20-carat gold. In the same mountain there is another mine, known as the Descubrimiento de los Catas, that yields gold of 17 carats. This municipality has numerous other mines, but they are of little economic importance at the present time.

In the municipality of Rancagua, or Santa Cruz de Triana, there is an open mine called Alhue, which means devil, where much gold is mined; its quality varies from 13 carats to 21 carats, 2 grains. Another mine, located in the Altos de Salinas, yields gold of 18 or 19 carats. When this mine was first discovered, it yielded many thousands of pesos' worth of gold, fetching from 200 to 300 pesos per box. At the present time it is worked by Manuel Venegas. Here also are situated the silver mines known as San Pedro Nolasco and San Simón; these mines have been worked by Don Agustín Castillo, Don Manuel Mena, Don Miguel Fernández Quintana, Don José Palma, and Don Agustín Tapia. The silver from these mines fetches from 20 to 40 marks per box; its quality is 11 dineros, 2 grains (266 grains).

In the mountains known as Los Potreros, which belong to the Jesuits, Don Xavier Palacios has worked several mines of copper mixed with silver. Though no one knows how much this ore fetches, or no one has kept records of it, the metal is known to have been sold in the city of Santiago for 150 pesos per quintal (hundredweight).

The gold mines known as Tiltil, El Guindo, Chicauma, Lampa, Caren, Durazno, Membrillego, and El Manzano are in the municipality of Santiago de Chile. The quality of the gold from these mines is from 20 carats to 21 carats, 2 grains, but at the present time the mines yield little more than enough to cover the cost of keeping them open. The gold produced by the Durazno mine is 13-carat, but production is very low; rich veins are found occasionally, but work is greatly hampered by much water. At Tiltil there are copper mines not more than 30 to 37 yards deep; the yield of copper from these mines varies from 16 to 18 quintales (hundredweight) per box. The quality of this metal is superior for hammering but not for smelting.

The beds of gold known as La Dormida, from which more than 100,000 pesos' worth of ore have been taken, are located in the municipality of Quillota. Though they have been nearly mined out, they are still yielding gold. Gold from La Dormida attained a quality of 23 carats, 3 grains. In the same place there are the beds of Culiguay, which yield gold of 21 to 22 carats. The mine called La Ligua is also in this same municipality; it was a very rich mine, yielding 22-carat gold, but at the present time it is running out. The same concession has the old mine of Mazón, which yielded from 4000 to 6000 pesos per box. Nowadays, however, it is in ruins, and what is mined from it barely meets the operating costs.

On the mountain at Petorca there is a mine called La Corrida de Bronce, yielding from 500 to 1000 pesos per box, or 200 pesos when the ore was less fine. From one year to another it yields 100,000 pesos' worth of 17-carat to 19-carat gold. Don Antonio Mura, Don José Sepulveda, and Don Francisco Larrañaga have worked this mine.

On this same outcrop there is a mine called Arcaya, the property of Don Martín Brito. It is an extremely deep mine. In 1780 an Indian miner came upon a rich vein in the very bottom of the pit. He covered the vein over in order to steal it and, conspiring with eight companions, went by night to take out the ore. The discoverer of the vein went down first to bring up the metal to show his companions. When he loaded his quipe (bag) with the metal, he was seized with a great fright, imagining that he saw a horrible person without hair, and left the mine sorely distraught to tell his fellow thieves about the fearful vision he had just seen.

The others would not believe his tale, and six of them went down with the Indian, leaving two behind as sentinels at the entrance to the pit. When the sentinels realized that the other seven were long delayed in coming up, they too went down. They had not gone 20 paces when they found one of their companions lying on the ground as though asleep. They shook him lightly to awaken him and went on their way, coming soon upon a second companion likewise stretched out on the ground. But they saw that he was dead, as was the first, to whom they returned for a more detailed examination.

They betook themselves straightaway to the village and informed the authorities who, as soon as morning dawned, visited the mine, finding all seven dead with no sign whatsoever of any wound. The natives attributed this catastrophe to divine punishment, but more likely it was due to carbonic acid gas or azotic (nitrogenous) gas in the pit. One of the two miners who escaped this tragedy was an apostate of the religion of the Dominican monastery of Santiago de Chile; penitent for what had happened to his companions, he died suddenly in the vicinity of Renca while returning to his monastery.

The owners of the Arcaya mine say that they can get laborers to work only with the greatest of difficulty; the miners dislike the extreme depth of the pit and the frightful noises they hear down below.

Usually only criminals and persons of questionable character seek work in such mines. This is true even for many other mines where conditions are better. Many people also prefer to work in a rich mine for half the normal wage rather than in a poor one at double the salary. They are obsessed with the idea that they can appropriate the ore for themselves. This is due partly to the fact that only the name of the veta (lode or vein), not the name of the guia (select metal), is mentioned in the permit and title that the mine owners obtain from the king. This is the main reason that workers are able to steal the best metal.

In Petorca there is another mining concession, called Yerro Viejo. Although its output is small, its gold is of finer quality than others we have mentioned from this municipality.

In Quillota is another mine, Illapel, where there are many workings very close together, as well as others rather far apart. This mine and that of Petorca are the richest in all Chile, in that they yield the most gold. The metal from Illapel is finer than that from Petorca, for it varies from 20 carats to 22½ carats. There is still another concession between Petorca and Illapel, called Pupio; although this mine is not very productive, its gold is 22-carat. Lastly, Las Bacas is a mine located near Illapel. It has large quantities of water that is pumped out with a screw at the expense of an incredible amount of hard labor. It yields a pound of gold per box, 21-carat and of outstanding color.

Several silver mines with considerable amounts of copper were found in the municipality of Aconcagua; much of this metal was sent to Spain. Because they did not know how to work the silver, miners abandoned the workings when the copper ran out, but present-day owners have put them into production once more. Each box of ore fetches from 25 to 30 marks, while the guia, or select metal, brings in twice that price. It is silver of high quality. Copper mining has waned appreciably in this valley, since most of the miners have gone into silver mining. The local magistrate of this section cannot meet his financial obligations on the basis of income from mining taxes as does the magistrate of Quillota, who yearly collects from 1600 to 2000 pesos in taxes, with each mine paying 6 pesos. The magistrate of Aconcagua is thus forced to meet his governmental expenses with taxes levied upon the harvests of wheat that are subsequently sent to the port of Valparaíso.

In the municipality of Coquimbo, the Talca mine in the past yielded a pound of gold per box, and the guia, or select metal, was worth as much as 600 pesos. Today the mine is so run-down that only pirquiñeros, or free-lance miners, work it, without a salary. This mining village has two streets of houses and huts that have been abandoned by their owners as a result of the poverty that befell the mine called Las Amolanas, which was very rich around 1750 and yielded gold of 21 carats. There is another mine in Chillamahuida, which is being worked and yields gold of 22 carats, 2 grains. It cannot be plated, for it is extremely soft and curls upon itself.

There is a copper mine in the valley of Limari, worked by Don José Guerrero in company with the Indians and the inhabitants of Coquimbo. In 1778 and 1780 several silver mines were discovered in the same valley. Surface studies indicated that the mines had promise of being very rich, but the ore ran out slightly below the surface; as a consequence, work was suspended. Near the valley there is a mountain, Anacollo, with gold mines that are still being worked, notwithstanding the low quality of their metal.

There are also quicksilver mines, but these are not being worked because they have not been developed, and it is impossible to know whether or not they could be put into economic production without a technical study of the subsoil. Once, while I was seriously ill, my companion Don José Dombey went to examine that mine and analyze its metal, at the request of Don Thomás Alvarez de Acebedo, regent of the Real Audiencia of Santiago de Chile. This was on the 21st of May 1783.

However, as he lacked the necessary chemical training, Dombey returned from Coquimbo to Santiago with two mule loads of ore without having made any analysis in the field. I understand that Dombey, and others with less knowledge of chemistry than he had, made some distillations of the ore in Santiago. These experiments failed to come out as the manipulators thought they would, or as predicted by the mine owners. Without my consent they sent the two loads of ore to Lima, where I saw it in the customs house in two leather bags, but I do not know how the whole matter ended. The ignorance of the one and the curiosity of the others led to the failure of these tests to provide the knowledge sought by the government. Although Santiago had very good professors of pharmacy as well as expert miners, the government entrusted the job to those who understood neither chemistry nor mining.

Finally, between Coquimbo and Copiapó there is another gold mine, called the Quebrada Honda, which has had its ups and downs. Today its production is 1 pound of gold per box, of 21½ carats.

In the municipality of Copiapó, the last settlement in Chile at the edge of those vast, uninhabited stretches separating Chile from Peru, there is an open mine that produces gold, silver, and copper. The gold, which is found on the surface, is of 22 carats, 2 grains. In 1772 and the years following, silver deposits were discovered. One of these is worked by Don Francisco Vercasacir and lies almost on the surface. The ores of this mine are so rich that the discovery of pure ingots has been expected at any moment. With the arrival from Peru of various mining interests, more mines of the same metal were discovered. Between the Quebrada Honda and Copiapó there is a valley called Huasco, where there are many copper mines; their entire output usually goes to Spain. The best of these mines are Cortés and Corbalán. These mines continue up into the mountains, where the copper-mining concession called La Jarilla, worked by Don Jacinto Pérez, is situated.

Besides the gold, silver, and copper mines mentioned here, there are many others throughout Chile, so one might truthfully say that, from Huasco to Valdivia, the country is one great gold, silver, and copper mine. There is the difference that some of the mines that have been recently discovered are of low production, in comparison with those that have been actively worked up to the present time. From one year to another, Chile exports from 14 to 16 quintales (hundredweight) of copper, an amount much smaller than that given by Father Molina on page 100 of his compendium entitled *Historia del Reyno de Chile*.

Along with the specimens that I sent on the ship *San Pedro de Alcántara*, I forwarded to His Majesty samples of ore from each of the mines that we have mentioned, gathered during my travels in Chile. Among them was a small chest full of the most valuable pieces of silver and gold ore that I could get from the miners, either as gifts or through purchase.

[The finished copy of the *Relación Histórica del Viage*, etc., of Don Hipólito ends here. The continuation of the work begins at the third paragraph of the first page of sheet number 57 of the *Compendio del Viage*, etc., of the same writer. As we have explained in our Prologue, this *Compendio* really represents the second rough draft of the *Relación Histórica del Viage*, etc.—J. Jaramillo-Arango]

In Coquimbo and other parts of Chile, lead, tin, and iron are found. As I have mentioned in my description of the province of Rere, a kind of round stone of iron is found on the mountain of Tanahuillin, near the Biobio River and 2 leagues from Huilquilemu. These stones, the size of musket shot, represent a veritable mine of iron. The inhabitants of Chile assert that similar balls, in varying conditions of formation, are found in other parts of Chile, and that they are of different sizes up to the size of a hen's egg. I procured several pieces of these stones, and all of them proved to be clayey iron ores, naturally formed more or less consistently into rounded, heavy shapes.

Stones and Earths

Lodestone is found in Copiapó and at a locality 12 leagues from Santiago, towards the coast.

The gold mines of Maule are all rich in bronze (copper), which makes it hard to work the gold from these and other mines. From all of them, however, beautiful pieces are extracted.

Arenilla, or polvos de cartas (a fine sand used to dry writing paper), is found in various places in Chile. There is a good mine on the estate at Culenco, 12 leagues from Concepción, and another on the island of Quiriquina.

Sulfur, yellow and exceedingly pure, occurs in the mines of Copiapó.

Brea de mina (mine tar, mine pitch), or petroleo (petroleum), occurs in the province of Maule and in the mountains, but the inhabitants there do not know how to refine it to the same quality as that of the petroleo brought to Lima from Realejo and Nicaragua.

Brea vegetal (vegetable tar, vegetable pitch) is extracted by boiling the shrub called pájaro bobo (crazy bird), *Tessaria dentata*, in the same way that laudanum is obtained from the jara (rockrose), *Cistus ladanifer*.

There are a few coal mines in Chile. One is located near Talcahuano, on the road to Concepción; another is close to the road leading to Penco el Viejo, and another is near the fort of Nacimiento.

On the flood banks of the stream at Millanantum, 600 paces from Nacimiento, there is asbestos in the form of amianthus. These stones have the color and consistency of chalcedony and are used as flint for striking fire. The natives believe they are the roots and trunks of fossilized willows, for they are shaped like pieces of the branch, root, or trunk of these trees, which abound in the same region. I believe that they are referable to the *amianthus immaturus* of Linnaeus as described in his *Systema Naturae*.

Piedras de cruz (stones of the cross) are found on a flood bank 4 leagues from Arauco, as I point out in my description of our trip to that fort.

Rock crystal occurs in Alhue, a territory of the province of Rancagua, and in the province of Maule.

Amethysts are to be found in the province of Maule; in the province of Petorca, 2 leagues from the town of Petorca on the mountain known as Polcura; and in the province of Quillota between Pupio and Filama, where the finest occur.

Coarse topazes, as well as some of medium quality, are mined in the province of Maule.

There are jaspers of various colors in several parts of Chile. Those found near Santiago are a very beautiful white color.

A hard, red marble is found on the mountain of San Cristóbal de Chile; a soft, white one is quarried on the mountain of Santo Domingo.

There are quarries of excellent masonry stone in Chile. Very beautiful stones are produced near Santiago.

A plentiful supply of pumice stone has been produced by the 14 volcanoes that range from Copiapó to the Tierras Magallánicas (Magellan lands).

Many of the mountains of Chile have numerous limestone quarries.

The lime most commonly used in Chile is extracted from the shells of different mollusks and calcined to a perfect whiteness. This lime is rather slack. In various places there are deposits of these and other kinds of shells that are worked as sources of lime, although appreciable quantities are collected along the coast for the same purpose.

Gypsum, a special kind that is easily calcined, is dug from a hill at the foot of the mountains near Santiago. Once calcined, it is taken to different parts of Chile for sale to be used in wine presses, where it is spread over the crushed grapes to facilitate the extraction of juice and to hasten fermentation. An arroba (25 pounds) of this gypsum is worth from 2 to 3 reales in Santiago, and 8 reales in Concepción.

In Chile there is talc of a very pure whiteness. In some places it is as transparent as glass.

There are three kinds of mica: golden, silver, and black.

Rovo is a black clay, soft to the touch, found in boggy places and used in dyeing cloth black.

Colos is a kind of clay, in a more or less pure state and of different colors: red, red-purple, yellow, buff, purple, blue, and greenish. These earths are employed in painting churches, facades, halls, and the wainscots and baseboards of houses. They are also used to color pots, earthen crocks, pitchers, jugs, clay vessels, and other types of pottery. Colos occurs in abundance near Penco el Viejo and in other parts of the country.

Rap, or gredas (clay), is a kind of marl or potter's clay used to make the pots, dishes, cups, jars, drinking mugs, and pitchers of various shapes that we Europeans call "Indian." This earth is mixed with water, freed of sand and other impurities, and strained through thin cloth several times. The largest particles are allowed to settle out and then the mixture is left to stand, the water being decanted off at intervals, until the softest and finest sediment is left in the bottom of the vessels. This material slowly takes on a consistency that allows it to be worked and shaped into any article desired.

It is necessary to dry these pieces in the shade, for the heat of the sun would cause the material to crack or split. If an article should split, the crack is covered with a bit of the same clay. When dry, the objects are burnished and polished as highly as possible with fine touchstone or some other very soft material, until the potter can see his face in the finished product. Then the pottery pieces are either baked or left unbaked, depending upon the use for which they are destined, and they are decorated with appropriate colors. The black color given to the pitchers and drinking cups is obtained by half-baking them in little piles with the burned straw of any kind of grass, without the use of ovens. In this industry, as in the manufacture of capes, shawls, sashes, and other textiles, the Indian has progressed very little since the Conquest, for pottery very similar to that made today is found in ancient Indian graves. Chilean ponchos (capes) differ from those of Peru by being made of a single piece, whereas the Peruvian ones are made of two or four pieces.

Two kinds of alum, white and red polcura, are employed among the natives to steep fabrics that are about to be dyed. They are found in various places. The waters of the Mapocho River contain sulfate of alum.

Rock salt is mined near Copiapó.

Common lake salt occurs on the other side of the mountains, in the provinces of Maule and Colchagua, or San Fernando.

According to the natives, salt from springs also occurs on the other side of the mountain range, where it is found in the shape of little tubes or cylinders.

Niter, or saltpeter, is also produced in some of the valleys, on pastures where cattle frequently graze.

Common salt is collected along the coast at Vichuquen, Bucalemu, and Bojeruca.

Rather large crystals of sulfate of soda are formed at the edges of some springs.

Arenilla verde, a green sand collected in Coquimbo, is used by some people as powder to dry their writing.

Sulfate of magnesium occurs in the waters of the Maypo River.

Hot Springs

Hot springs of waters with extremely efficacious properties are found in the province of Chillán and in the territory of Colchagua in the province of Cauquenes. There are also warm springs in Colina, 12 leagues from Santiago.

Resins

The Chile pine, huighan, lithre, and a species of *Helianthus* all yield resins. *Helianthus* is plentiful in Coquimbo, and in Chile its resin is called the incense of Coquimbo.

Rivers

There are several rivers that water Chile from Huasco to Arauco and in the region of Mendoza. The largest and most notable rivers are the Colorado, Tachal, San Juan, Mendoza, Tunuyan, Choapa, Huasco, Limari, Ligua, Longotoma, Aconcagua, Mapocho, Maypo, Claro, Tinguirica, Cachapual, Lontue, Teno, Maule or Itata, Andalién or Andarién, Laxa, Biobio, Araquete, and Caranpangue. The last six are tidal; that is, they rise and fall with the tide, and can be navigated with rafts and boats. When Molina states on page 44 that the Maule and Biobio can be navigated with ocean boats, he is in error, unless he is referring only to their estuaries. Besides these rivers, there are many estuaries and streams of both fresh and salt water. From Arauco to Chiloe one finds the following rivers: the Cautén, Toltén, Valdivia, Chaivín, Bueno, Sin Fondo, and Nahuelhuapi.

Lakes

Chile has numerous lakes, including the Nahuelhuapi, Villarica or Lauquén, Tahuatahua, Aculén, Ridahuel, Quinél, Huanacache, Papal, Avendaño, Choapa, Bojeruca, Cahuil, and Bucalemu. Seven leagues from San Fernando, in the province of Colchagua, there is a lake upon which floats a large island formed of the roots of trees and shrubs all twined together. It holds excellent soil, supporting a beautiful turf of grasses that invites cows and horses to frequently enter this floating mass, particularly when breezes blow it against the shore. When the island is blown out to the middle of the lake, the animals live on it for many days until it once again nears the banks.

Ports

The chief ports of Chile are Coquimbo, Valparaíso, and Talcahuano. Collumu is also an excellent port. Penco el Viejo and San Vicente, as well as various other coves along the coast, are not visited by shipping.

Articles of Commerce

The active trade of Chile with Peru and other areas is based upon the following products: copper; gold; huge harvests of wheat, of which 230,000 fanegas (approximately 368,000 bushels) were shipped to Callao in 1780; barley; cecina, or charqui (jerky, dried salted beef); lard, which in Chile is used instead of butter and oil for cooking; suet or tallow, of which some 30,000 quintales (hundredweight) are exported annually to Peru; hides; cordovan leather; sole leather; dressed sheepskin; chamois leather; cheeses, the most valued coming from Chanco; butter, the most delicious of which comes from San Pedro, a fort on the banks of the Biobio River; liquors and excellent wines, the highest quality of which are produced in the provinces of Puchacay and Itata, and that of Ñipas enjoys the greatest reputation; walnuts; guindas (morello cherries); hazelnuts; almonds; coquitos (palm nuts); lentils; oregano (wild marjoram), and false saffron.

Other products, such as olive oil, are trafficked exclusively within the borders of Chile itself. This oil is produced only in small amounts, is greenish and fatty, and does not have very good flavor. The oil from Coquimbo is superior in quality. In time, the cultivation of olive trees will certainly increase and the quality will improve. An appreciable manufacture of soap is carried on in Santiago with tallow and the lye from espino. Espino, a species of *Mimosa*, is the source of an excellent wood for fuel that can be made into a kind of charcoal that burns in a brazier up to 24 hours, or will maintain live coals up to 48 hours if the fire is banked.

Flax and hemp are harvested in the province of Quillota, where the inhabitants produce cordage, rope, twine, and oakum; all these products are purchased by boats visiting Valparaíso. Baize (coarse woolen cloth), cordellates (grogram, coarse fabric of silk and wool), and jerga (coarse native cloth for cloaks) are made in Chillán and elsewhere, as are excellent capes, ponchos, counterpanes, blankets, rugs, and saddle blankets. Quantities of shaggy woolen runners, used over rugs in drawing rooms during the winter season, are manufactured in Petorca.

From sugar cane, which is grown in Quillota, molasses is prepared; a delicious syrup, called miel de cocos (coconut honey), is made from the young shoots of the coquito palm.

There is a special rush that people use in place of cotton for candle wicks. It burns with a beautiful bluish light, gives off little smoke, is easily snuffed out, lasts longer than cotton wicks, and does not cause headaches. If dropped on the ground, the rush wicking breaks into a number of pieces, depending upon the strength of the blow.

It is said that barrilla, or caustic soda, occurs along the coast, but I have not found it.

An excellent flour is made from liutu roots, as we have already explained; it is called harina de liutu and is in demand in Lima and elsewhere. Quantities of this flour are prepared in the port of San Pedro and in that whole general area.

There is a very popular drink in Chile called ullpu, which is prepared with a spoonful of toasted cornmeal, sugar, cinnamon, and a huampar (horn cup) or glass of water. Many people, lacking maize, use wheat flour, barley meal, or horse-bean meal and dissolve it in water without any other special addition. It is a favorite drink of the Indians. The meal from horse beans, dissolved in water, is taken in Chile as an efficacious remedy for shortness of breath.

The principal export trade from Peru to Chile is in sugar and some European clothing and fancy goods.

We can see, then, that Chile, with its fine climate, its products, and the friendly character of its people, is one of the most desirable and enviable countries on the face of the globe.

CHAPTER 42

Trip to the City of Santiago, Capital of Chile

When we had boxed up the dried plant specimens, seeds, ores, stones, woods, and other samples of the natural products of the bishopric of Concepción, and had made preparations for a trip of 150 leagues, we set out from Concepción on the 29th of March 1783. I was accompanied by the two artists and by a soldier whom the aide-de-camp, Don Ambrosio O'Higgins, had assigned to go with us as far as Santiago. My companion Don José Pavón left on the 31st with Mr. Dombey, accompanied by another soldier.

On the 30th we slept in Potreros del Rey, in the province of Cauquenes. Here I gathered a few plants and set them out to dry. On the following day we entered the province of Chillán, spending the night in a farmhouse.

In April of 1783 we continued our trip, accompanied by the mule drivers. We went through the provinces of Chillán and Itata, where we had to cross the river by boat and send the horses across swimming.

In Talco, capital of the province of Maule, we stopped 2 days to rest the animals and to pay a visit to the gold mines. We secured some fine pieces of ore. The magistrate of Talco offered us his hospitality, and we were visited by the most distinguished people of that beautiful town.

From Maule we went on to the province of Colchagua, staying overnight in the village of San Fernando, in the magistrate's home. This official treated us with the greatest of kindness. In a vineyard behind this gentleman's house, we saw more than 4000 fanegas (bushels) of wheat that he had dumped as fertilizer because the grain was spoiled. From Colchagua we continued on to the province of Rancagua, and spent the night in the capital there.

On the 15th of April, Tuesday of Easter week, we arrived at the city of Santiago de Chile without having had any mishap on the trip, not even a slight rainstorm. We had successfully forded the many smaller rivers that lie between Concepción and Santiago, crossing only the Itata by boat and the Maypo by bridge. The road is generally over flat terrain; though there are some mountains, they are so low as to barely deserve the name.

On this whole trip, I saw hardly any plants that were different from those already collected in the provinces of Concepción, Cauquenes, Rere, and Puchacay, and on the coasts of Arauco. The only species occurring in abundance is a small tree, some 6 or 7 yards tall, known as espino; it is a species of *Mimosa*. When in full bloom it spreads a sweet fragrance over the whole countryside. These trees are valuable as material for building corrals on farms, as props for grapevines, and as uprights in buildings. The wood is useful for making cartwheels, doorsills, and hoops, and for turning on a lathe. The pods, or fruits, are good fodder for horses and mules. The seeds, like those of other species of *Mimosa*, give off a disagreeable odor when chewed up and spit out indoors, but the odor can be counteracted with burned paper. The rind of the pod makes a black ink. Charcoal made from the wood of this species burns a long time and supplies strong heat.

In the province of Rancagua we found the carob tree, *Mimosa ceratonia*?, which we had not encountered in other provinces previously visited on this trip.

There are very few villages along this road, though one finds many grain and cattle ranches of all sorts, with good and roomy houses. The owners receive travelers into their homes with kind hospitality, and even offer them meals with extreme liberality, as we found from our experiences in many places.

Arriving in Santiago, we five companions went on horseback, as is the local custom, to present ourselves to Señor Presidente (president, mayor, head magistrate) Don Ambrosio Benavides. He received us very affably, offered us his protection, and invited us to come to his table whenever we wished to dine with him. Bishop Alday gave us a similar invitation, as did the regent of the audiencia (court), Don Tomás Alvarez de Acebedo. We did dine with each of these leading officials, and each offered for our enjoyment the most outstanding foods of the area, the finest liquors of Chile, and even those of various European countries. Following the example of these three authorities, all the nobility of Santiago paid us visits and plied us with daily invitations to their homes throughout our stay in the city.

As a result of this trip and of our zealous plant-collecting activities, I fell ill with a kind of typhoidlike fever, known locally as chavalongo, a few days after my arrival in Santiago. I was feverish for 25 days, and for another 25 after getting out of bed I had a sharp pain on the right side of my chest. This pain made it impossible for me to yawn, sneeze, cough, or laugh, and I was unable to do any work at all.

When I was sickest during this attack, the regent decided to send my companion Mr. Dombey to make a survey of the quicksilver mines at Coquimbo. This he did on the 21st of May. Dombey requested that one of the two artists accompany him on this trip, but the regent did not grant the escort, so Dombey went alone. He returned to Santiago in a few days, bringing samples of ore from various mine openings for analysis. At that time it was claimed that the yield was 1 ounce of mercury for every 3 pounds of ore, according to Mr. Dombey's analysis in Santiago. For this reason the regent sent to the superintendent in Lima two leather bags of ore that Dombey had left deposited in the warehouse at the customs office. I have not heard the results of this shipment. The miners of Coquimbo assert that their mines do not yield enough to make working these holdings worth their while, and many of them have given up the extraction of quicksilver as many times as they have undertaken it.

An earthquake occurred in Santiago on the 25th of May; although rather strong, it was of short duration and did no damage.

Heavy Rains and Floods

At half past ten on the morning of the 15th of June 1783, a heavy downpour of rain started, and it kept on without interruption until two in the afternoon on the 17th. This, together with the melting of snows on the mountaintops, caused most of the rivers in the bishopric of Santiago to swell to such size that those able to judge calculated a loss of two million pesos in damages to the farms of the area. The Mapocho River, which flows through Santiago, rose so much that, besides sweeping away many ranches and numerous houses along its banks, it overflowed into two parts of the city itself.

The river broke a dam up on the peak of Santa Lucía, and flooded many houses and monasteries of the district of La Cañada and on the Santo Domingo road. Downstream from the bridge it also broke the cutwaters and swept away an entire avenue of trees that had been planted in the days of Señor Guil, as well as more than 300 huts and ranches of the poorer classes. The poor inhabitants were left completely destitute, as we could see on the morning of the 17th when we found them seeking shelter behind garden walls. Many were in nightshirts, covered with the mud that the waters had left on the streets and in their ruined homes. The confusion and shouting lasted throughout the day, saddening all of us who witnessed it.

The floods took away a great part of the stone bridge that connected the city with the district of Chimba. The dikes of Chimba were also destroyed, as was the famous convent of Carmen below; the nuns climbed up into the tower, praying and calling for help from the city with white handkerchiefs. Three men, who fortunately were able to cross the furious river on horseback, came to their aid. Gaining entrance to the convent over the mud walls of the orchard, they passed the nuns out through a hole in the wall, placing them on the horses and carrying them to a Dominican convent that was nearly completed in the same district.

Although all the doors of the church of Carmen were closed, the water entered and flooded it to a depth of more than a yard, leaving much silt. The gardens, cells, and other rooms of the nuns were completely flooded and filled with sand and clay to a depth of nearly 5 feet. The furnishings and images that the nuns had in their rooms were swept away with the flood. Such was the destruction of this convent that it would have cost 100,000 pesos to rebuild it.

The beautiful country house of one Don Luis Zañartu, built in this part of the city opposite the convent when the convent, bridge, and cutwater were erected, was likewise flooded out. In 1 day the Mapocho River destroyed all these magnificent structures, built at a cost of many thousands of pesos.

Many orchards, meadows, and cultivated fields were inundated, and the flood struck such fear into the hearts of the people and livestock in villages along the river that many fled, in tremendous confusion, to the highest mountains to save their lives. The inhabitants and animals of Carrizal, where 45 houses were washed away, fled to the hills.

Many extraordinary things happened with this flood. For example, some people, taken by surprise, found themselves isolated and seeking safety on the roofs of their houses, expecting to be drowned at any moment. Others climbed trees and there suffered the fury of the storm until the waters receded. Still others escaped by swimming and took refuge in the hills. The news arrived in Santiago that there was a sick man bedridden in a house already surrounded by water. Four men went to his aid; as they were swimming towards the house, the river swept both house and patient downstream.

A cradle with a tiny sleeping child was floating down the river, and a man on the bank, thinking it was clothing, most fortunately caught hold of the swaddling band and pulled the child out alive. This was done when the cradle had already been borne a quarter of a league by the flood, for the parents had followed the cradle for a long way, finally losing sight of it and returning brokenhearted without their baby. The next day they learned of the rescue through bills posted on walls in Santiago.

The Mapocho River carried off two carriages, the property of Señor Guil y Cuirior, that were in an enclosure near the convent of Carmen.

Santiago was in a state of great confusion on the second and third days of the storm, with prayers, weeping, and wailing audible on all sides.

Once the storm ceased, the river fell in a few hours. Along the banks and on the sandbars were found many pieces of furniture. Among these were a chest with 260 pesos, a pair of silver spurs, rugs, pictures, and an entire image of Saint John standing with an unbroken glass chalice in his hands. A cart was hanging in a tree, more than 4 feet above the ground. In short, there was a whole series of objects too numerous to list.

During our stay in Santiago we collected and drew various plants, and I corrected and completed numerous descriptions begun at other times. I described the following plants.

Cactus horridus, known as quiscas or solsomata; this cactus has spines 9 inches long, so smooth and hard that they can be used in place of steel needles to make stockings. *Renanthes*? *spinosa*, huañil. *Solanum quercifolium*. *Moscharia pinnatifida*, called almizclillo for the fragrance that the flowers give off as they open, before ten o'clock in the morning.

Lithospermum tinctorium, so called because it yields a blue dye when trodden upon by horses. When pressed between drying papers, specimens of this plant leave their shape, albeit imperfectly outlined, traced upon the sheets.

Schinus procera, molle de Chile. This is a tall, leafy tree with solid wood that is employed for pillars, wagon shafts, and the posts of houses. When applied to the temples, its resin is said to alleviate headache.

Sapium collihuai; this seems to be a variety of the collihuai of (the province of) Rere. *Rhamnus canescens*. *Rhamnus dependens*, called trebol (clover) or trebul; the bark of this plant is utilized for cleansing and washing the head, and is used in place of calaguala to reduce and resolve the bruises of blows and falls. *Tropaeolum filiforme*.

Sisymbrium sophiae and *Thlaspi bursapastoris* are abundant in Santiago, as is *Rumex patientia*, hualtata. The purplish leaves of hualtata are used to draw out infection, and the green leaves are used to resolve bruises, for the natives believe they have different properties, but either is applied to the back to cool the blood.

Sanicula marilandica, pata de león (lion's foot). *Hedysarum plumosum*. *Cynoglossum lineare*.

Eccremocarpus scaber. When collecting this plant, 2 leagues from Santiago, we had the most amusing adventure imaginable. I was with my companion Pavón and an expert apothecary, Don Fulgencio Rodenas, botanist for the Jesuits. In his enthusiasm to study botany, Don Rodenas had come out with me for a second time. It happened that my new pupil, who had no experience in plant collecting, dismounted from his horse, as had his two companions and my slave. Without tying the animal, our friend sat down to put some plant specimens in the press; when he was most preoccupied with his work, the distant neighing of a mare excited his horse. The animal, without its master's permission, set off at top speed, neighing across the fields, taking with it the saddlebags containing the lunch and leaving our budding botanist standing. He set off with my negro in search of the horse, but after a long while they returned, both tired of wandering about without locating the animal. The apothecary came back weary and sweating, with the empty saddle bags and the saddle blanket on his shoulders; he lay down, worn out and not knowing what to do about continuing the trip.

When he had rested a bit, Don Rodenas set off for a farmhouse on one of our horses, to ask for an animal so that he might go along with us. They rented him a nag, half dead and as thin as a reed, sluggish beyond description, and capable only of a very stiff and lazy trot.

Heavily laden with a handful of plants and his portfolio, which was nothing but a filthy sheepskin that had once been the binding of some old book, and six or eight sheets of rag paper all crumpled up, our friend was really a botanical martyr, patiently bearing the constant pounding of his skinny trotter. His portfolio fell every few moments, and I advised him to put it under his buttocks. Probably because of this, a few paces farther on he toppled to the ground—his person, his portfolio, and his bunches of plants all together. None of this deterred him, however, for he valiantly mounted the nag again and followed us to the farthest parts of the ravine of Ramón.

There, after examining the flora, we sat down to eat our lunch by the side of a crystalline brook falling there from the mountains. During our lunch we recalled the various mishaps on this second collecting trip, comparing them with some of the adventures of the famous Don Quixote. These pleasantries provided a very amusing sauce for our cold and simple repast.

In spite of the hardships suffered by this learned professor, he was determined to continue his plant collecting with me. He probably would have attained his goal had we not received orders from the superintendent of Peru, requiring us to leave for Lima to return to Spain from that city; the 4 years' duration allotted to our commission was already long overspent.

CHAPTER 43

Description of the City of Santiago in Chile

The city of Santiago (Plate 11) is located at 33°35' south latitude and at a longitude of 307° (from the meridian of Tenerife), at the foot of the peak of Santa Lucía, some 5 leagues from the mountain range, and on the southern bank of the Mapocho River. It is on a beautiful and extensive plain, which is slightly sloping and open to the breezes.

On the northern bank of the river are two districts of the city, Cañadilla and Chimba, and on the southern bank, four blocks from the central plaza, there is a street some 50 yards wide and 1800 yards long, called La Cañada. From east to west the city has 13? blocks, all the same size, and from north to south there are 9? blocks, with a number of other straight streets. The central plaza is a block square, with the side facing south occupied by the palace of the president and the Real Audiencia, and the opposite side by houses and shops with porticos. The cathedral and the bishop's palace are on the side facing east, and across from these buildings are various private houses, the jail, and the meat market.

Though mostly single-storied, the buildings are spacious and beautiful with a garden in a central patio, visible from the street, and a large yard at the entrance. They are constructed of stones, lime, and adobe, and are roofed with tiles; the baseboards, halls, patios, and gardens are painted with different colored earths, lending unusual beauty. Some houses have a main room.

The streets are cobbled, and an open ditch of running water passes through the center of the houses; outside, in the street, the ditch is covered over. Although the air is pure and the sky beautiful most of the year, in the winter season dense fogs, very harmful to the health of the population, arise from the irrigation ditches and the river.

In all of Chile, the only audiencia (high court) is the one in Santiago, which was established in 1609 and is composed of the president, who is the governor and captain general of the country, along with a regent, five judges, two fiscal officers, a chief constable, and a chancellor. There is a chief accountant of royal finance, as well as an accountant and a treasurer of the royal coffers. The civil council is composed of a chief magistrate, two ordinary mayors, 12 aldermen, and other officers. The ecclesiastical council is made up of the bishop and five other dignitaries: a dean, an archdeacon, a precentor, the headmaster of the school, and a treasurer. There are also four canons of mercy and three prebends.

At the present moment, an Italian architect is completing a magnificent and sumptuous cathedral under the direction and care of the most worthy bishop, Señor Doctor Don Manuel de Alday.

There is a mint, where 700,000 to 800,000 pesos in gold doubloons and 200,000 to 300,000 pesos in silver coins are minted yearly. There is a university called San Felipe; it has 10 professorships. There is a seminary for creole Spaniards, and a Jesuit seminary in San Pedro for Indians.

There are five regular orders: that of La Merced, which was the first to enter Chile to evangelize; that of Santo Domingo; that of San Agustín; that of San Francisco; and that of San Juan de Dios. In addition to the principal monasteries, the order of Santo Domingo has a new house of retreat in Chimba and a chapel nearby, called La Viña, that is dedicated to Our Lady of the Rosary. The order of La Merced has a school below La Cañada; that of San Agustín has another in the same part of the city; and that of San Francisco has a school called San Diego, a small monastery called Monte Alverne, outside of the city, and a house of retreat in Chimba.

Of the seven convents, two are of Santa Clara; the old one was founded for the nuns that were gathered together from the cities laid waste in the general uprising of the Indians, and another was recently founded. There is also a convent of Concepción, belonging to the order of San Agustín. Two convents of Carmen, one in the city and the other in Cañadilla, are of the reformed discipline of Santa Teresa. There is a convent of Capuchinas, and one of Nuestra Señora de Pastoriza de Santa Rosa, of the Dominicans.

There is a house of seclusion, a house of meditation, a home for foundlings, a chapel of La Caridad, and another of San Lázaro. Besides the cathedral with two priests, there are the parish churches of Santa Ana, San Isidro, and San Borja. The district under the jurisdiction of this municipality includes the parishes of Tango, of Nuñosa (Ñuñoa) with four subparishes, of Colina with five, and of Renca with four. The holy image of Santo Cristo del Espino is venerated in the church of Renca.

There is one company of dragoons, and the brilliant regiment of mounted militia that I saw in formation on the main plaza during the 3 holy days of Easter week. They went through their drill with the greatest of skill.

The number of inhabitants of this municipality runs over 34,000. Included in this number are many illustrious families and some descendants of the original conquerors of Chile. There are very few Indians or other races, for the great majority of people are Spanish or creole, one and another of good stature, elegant appearance, and good education, correct in their business transactions and gentlemanly in their behavior.

The fair sex, besides having natural beauty enhanced by natural cleanliness, is affable and attentive, unusually generous, and well endowed with other gifts of humanity. The women are so dedicated to music that one can hardly find a young lady who does not know how to play one or more instruments with great skill and precision. They likewise are given to singing, either from pure love of the art or from training in it by nuns. In the evenings they make up excellent orchestras and enjoy the decorous diversion of music.

The Chilean is generally charitable and generous towards strangers and the helpless. They hold social gatherings in a friendly mood and enter happily into popular country diversions, going to these affairs in carts adorned with awnings and cushions, taking all kinds of musical instruments, and playing and singing in high glee without disputes or quarrels of any sort.

The bishopric of Santiago consists of 11 provinces: Copiapó, Coquimbo, Aconcagua, Quillota, Valparaíso, Melipilla, Santiago, Rancagua, Colchagua, Maule, and Cuyo. All of the grains and other natural products to which we have referred in our description of the bishopric of Concepción grow in these provinces.

Note: In the fire at Macora, of which I shall speak below, I lost my diary of 3½ years, including the pages of my notes on Chile. For this reason, I have not been able to insert here the descriptions of all of the provinces of this country, descriptions that I wrote out in great detail during my stay in Chile. It is likewise impossible for me to specify individually the localities and territories of the natural products that I saw and collected, or of those for which I had reliable information to pass along to the magistrates or other educated and interested persons.

CHAPTER 44

Trip from Santiago to Valparaíso and from Valparaíso to the Port of Callao

On the 5th of October 1783 all five of us left Santiago together. With no special adventure, we arrived by nightfall at a point on the banks of the Mapocho River, just 3 leagues from the city. We crossed the provinces of Aconcagua and Quillota and, without mishap, arrived in Valparaíso on the 9th, where we stayed until the 14th, awaiting the sailing of the ship *Nuestra Señora de las Mercedes*. We set sail for Callao at half past two in the afternoon on the 15th, with a favorable wind.

On the way from Santiago to Valparaíso and in the vicinity of that port, I collected a number of plants, describing the following species.

Suriana apetala. *Aristolochia vaginans*; the leaves of this plant give off an unpleasant odor resembling that of the skunk, but the flowers are even more strongly imbued with this odor. *Lobelia purpurea*, tuppa. *Helianthus resinosus*, called maravillas or, in Coquimbo, árbol del incienso; this plant is the source of the resin that is burned in churches in place of incense. *Stachys hastata*, salvio macho (male sage); this species is used in the same way as is *Salvia officinalis* in Europe. *Fuchsia rosea*. *Polygala* aff. *tricolor*. *Eupatorium salvifolium*, barbas de viejo (old man's whiskers).

We entered the port of Callao on the 3rd of November 1783 by night, and dropped anchor in the morning, on the 4th. Our trip had been excellent except for the poor and scanty meals that the captain offered us, but the cunning old codger spiced the frugal fare with little anecdotes and jokes.

Since the 4th and 5th were holidays, we could not unload our baggage until the 6th. We sent it on to Lima, where our boxes were deposited in the royal customs until we could put them on board the *San Pedro de Alcántara*, ready to return with them to Spain.

We stayed in Lima, awaiting the sailing of this ship, until April. During that time I worked on the various plants that I had brought from Chile in leather cases, and packed them securely for transporting. I also packed other samples of natural products—plants, animals, and minerals. I finished some descriptions and copied those that I had made in Peru and Chile into two folio volumes to send them by the inspector, Don Jorge Escobedo, to the Ministry of the Indies. This was the only thing among our select shipment on board the *San Pedro de Alcántara* that was saved. I described *Psoralea americana* and *Theobroma cacao*. I labeled 800 drawings, which were lost in this shipment, with their generic and specific names, and made a list of them. Finally, I again explored the mountains and the countryside of Lima to collect and describe new plants appearing in that season.

Then, with our equipment ready and all preparations for sailing back to Spain finished, we received a royal order to continue our commission in the forests of Tarma, Huánuco, and Cuchero. For this work we had again to supply ourselves with the necessary equipment, all of which we had sold at a very low price a few days before.

The First Great Loss of Botanical Material Suffered When the *San Pedro de Alcántara* Was Overtaken by a Storm off the Coast of Chile

Complying with royal orders, we had sent on the *San Pedro de Alcántara* 55 boxes of dried plants, seeds, and wood; gold, silver, and copper ores; quadrupeds, birds, and dried specimens of fish; shells, stones, earths, and other interesting samples of natural products; and Indian artifacts and clothing. There were 800 drawings, done in their correct colors, and six hothouse cases with 33 flowerpots of valuable Peruvian and Chilean trees. We had placed this material under the care of an intelligent servant for the duration of the trip, and in Lima he had received 50 pesos in advance for this work. But he, as well as the ship's officers who had offered to care for the living specimens with the greatest diligence, was obliged to throw the collections overboard at 45° because of the severe storm that they suffered, which forced them to take cover in Chile and then return to Callao.

Return of Dombey

Our companion Don José Dombey, with his collection, embarked on the ship *Peruano* and thus arrived in Cádiz, from which port he continued on to France.

CHAPTER 45

Trip from Lima to the Forests of Huánuco and Cuchero

As a result of the trip that we had just made to Chile, of the disadvantageous sale of our equipment for overland travel, and of the expenses incurred in making preparations for our sailing to Europe, we were left without the means necessary to undertake new trips. We explained our impossible situation to the general superintendent of Peru, who saw the justice of our plea and offered to send the king a petition to increase our salaries. For the interval of awaiting the arrival of the order, he also arranged for us to be paid 1 year's salary in advance. With this help, we outfitted ourselves with the barest of essentials. I personally spent 1004 pesos of my advance.

Supplied with the most necessary equipment for the trip to Huánuco, I left Lima with my companion Don José Pavón at half past noon on the 12th of May 1784. We spent the night in the country, 2 leagues from the capital. We had no trouble other than experiencing two earthquakes, one at eight that evening and the other at dawn the following day.

On the 13th we went on to Yanha, where I described *Mimosa spicata*, *Clematis vitalba*?, and *Hedysarum mimosioideum*.

On the 14th we journeyed 1 league, staying overnight in a farmhouse. Here I described *Hydrolea urens*, *Cactus squamatus*, *C. lanatus*, and *C. erinaceus*. In the afternoon I had a somewhat unsteady pulse and was quite short of breath.

On the 15th we spent the night out in the country near the village of Yaso, where I described *Cactus echinatus* and *C. cancelatus*, as well as *Oxalis ockas*, known as ocas. The tuberous roots of ocas are called apilla; they are a common and tasty food, but cause flatulence. The stem and leaves are called chullco—that is, sorrel—and are used as a cooling agent in high fevers and tabardillos (typhoidlike fevers) and to treat painful urination, choking, sore throat, and jaundice. My feeling of indisposition became more serious and was accompanied by headache and high fever.

On the 16th we went on to the outpost called Carrizal, where we again slept out in the open. As a result, I felt sicker than during the previous days and could not describe any of the plants that my companion and my servant had collected.

We arrived at San Buena Ventura, capital of the province of Canta, on the 17th. We stopped there over the 18th to rest our animals and to see if my condition might take a turn for the better. But a sharp pain in my right side attacked me, and it prevented my coughing, yawning, sneezing, laughing, or assuming any natural position. Although the chief magistrate insisted that I move into his house and remain there until I was well again, we left on the 19th for the town of Culluay. Here I felt very weak.

On the 20th, in spite of my being worn out with sickness, we climbed to the top of the mountain called Cerro de la Viuda. Night overtook us on this mountain and our beasts were weary, so we were forced to spend the night there, where it is always snowy, with no more shelter than a small canvas. We made ourselves as comfortable as we could under the tarpaulin, surrounded by our baggage. Although we were crowded closely together and were warmly dressed, the cold went through my body until I no longer had any feeling, as if I were made of cotton. My companion thought that I was about to die in that place. There was no fuel, so it was impossible for him to give me warm food or water to drink, or to take any other means of bringing on sleep and lessening the terrible pains in my abdomen, which attacked me with strong tenesmus and intense thirst. At daybreak I quenched my thirst by sending my servant to break the ice to get drinking water.

On the 21st my companions had to put me up on my horse, for I could not mount unaided. We continued our journey, arriving by nightfall at the estate of Palcamayo, where hoarfrost more than 2 inches thick fell upon us. The following day we went into Diezmo, where I had some relief from the pain in my side.

On the 23rd we entered the town of Pasco, where we remained until the 27th for me to undergo medical treatment before continuing our journey. My weakness, my lack of appetite, and the seriousness of my illness had made it utterly impossible for me to go on.

On the 27th, when I had grown a bit stronger, we left for Caxamarquilla. There, thanks to the lettuce and apples that I was able to eat, I began to feel better. We arrived at Huariaca on the 28th, and I repeated the lettuce salad with marked effect.

On the 29th we left Huariaca. Half a league from town, one of my companion's pack mules fell into the river with two cases, so we stopped there all day to dry out our clothes and everything else that had been soaked. Because of this, my sickness returned and the pain in my side came back, even stronger. On the 30th we went on as far as the village of Rondos, where I felt worse as a result of my exposure the day before.

On the 31st we went down to the mining site at Ambo, where I arrived completely played out from the high fevers, and lacking the strength to stand on my feet. On the morning of the 1st of June, my companion found himself without a mule driver; fearing that he would be put in jail because of various debts that he had contracted in Huánuco, the driver had fled with his mules. But we got a mule driver in Ambo and continued on to Huánuco, where I went to bed and got well again in a few days.

The artists Brunete and Gálvez arrived in Huánuco 4 days after us, having traveled with no misadventure whatsoever.

When we had all rested from the trip and I had regained my health, we made the necessary preparations of food for 3 months in the forests of Pozuzo, 45 leagues from Huánuco. Because of information that had come to us concerning the fertility and luxuriance of that area, which bounded upon the region of the Carapacho Indians, we were determined to go and spend time there.

CHAPTER 46

Trip to the Forests of Pozuzo

On the 5th of July we sent 50 sheep ahead as a supply of food. I alone managed to leave Huánuco at noon on the 8th, with 21 mule loads of food, paper, presses, books, and other equipment necessary for my own use and for that of the expedition. I spent the night out in the country, near the village of Valle.

On the 9th I arrived at Tambillo, 8 leagues from Huánuco, to spend the night. There I described *Ambrosia crispa*, known as marco; Indians put it beneath the saddle blankets of mules, convinced that it keeps the animals from tiring out on long trips. I also described *Cestrum confertum*, *C. conglomeratum*, and *Rhexia hispida*; this last-named plant is called cachiquis and is employed as a yellow dyestuff. In this same locality I found in abundance, among many other plants, *Psoralea glandulosa*. The local name of this species is hualhua; it is used in the same way as it is among Chileans, who call it culén.

I went on to the village of Panao on the 10th, and stayed over on the 11th to change mules. On that same day, my companion Don José Pavón left Huánuco. In Panao I gathered a number of plants, corrected some descriptions, and described *Ornithogalum compressifolium*, *Perdicium lanatum*, *Dalea punctata*, *Gardoquia revoluta*, and *Utricularia unifolia*.

On the 12th I left Panao with 15 Indians, to accompany the pack mules along the narrow and dangerous mountain passes. I slept in the village of Chaclla, the first settlement of the missionary priests of Ocopa. It is located on a high and beautiful plain in a cool climate, and is provided with an abundance of pasturage.

On the 13th I came to spend the night at the outpost called Llamapañaui, where I examined the *Smilax china* that I had collected a league before, and I described *Dalechampia rosea*. On that day I gathered many very interesting plants, notwithstanding the difficult road, especially near Cuerno Retorcido and Torre sin Agua. Before arriving at these places, one encounters the entrances to several silver mines that have been left abandoned by their discoverers because they lacked the means of exploiting them.

On the 14th I entered the town of Muña, another village under the jurisdiction of the Ocopa missionaries, having crossed over the ravine and river of Santo Domingo and the high peak of the same name. The hard and dangerous ascent of this peak, along the area of the river, climbs 40 long and excessively steep slopes. Descending the other side of this mountain is another stream; after crossing this stream, one begins to climb up to the village of Muña on a mountain that is more dangerous and difficult than the first. This is particularly true of the Ladera de la Cormilla, so narrow and high that it makes one tremble to cross it even on foot, though there are those who dare to go across it on horseback. Here I collected various new plants.

On the 15th I left Muña and stayed overnight 3 leagues away, near Tambo Nuevo, in a green valley that abounds in ichu grass even though it is cold and covered with water from almost daily rains. For this reason, and in spite of dense and clammy fog, the mule drivers stopped there to give the animals pasturage and let them rest from their hard climb from Muña, and to prepare to continue the next day and climb the rest of that high mountain.

The summit of this mountain is devoid of trees and other large plants, with the exception of *Stereoxylon corymbosum*, known by the common name of suiba. This tree grows to a height of about 10 yards. Its trunk and branches are so densely covered with blackish mosses and lichens that it looks like a tree that has been singed, or dressed in mourning clothes. The wood burns so poorly and with so much smoke that one cannot bear the pain it causes to the eyes, with its fire giving off so little heat in return.

Among the smaller plants there, two species of *Ranunculus* are plentiful; one has a large and beautiful rose-colored flower, the other a completely green blossom. Also abundant are *Swartia corniculata*, two species of *Gentiana*, one of *Hedyotis*, and two syngenesias (syngenesious plants). I could not describe these plants, for I was sick and had severe tenesmus that almost prevented my continuing the trip on the 16th, when I was obliged to walk a league and a half because of the grazing and the continuous rain. The rain was accompanied by an intense cold that swept down from the Portachuelo, which we had crossed that day, bringing with it snow and hail and a stout wind. We took shelter in a glen, somewhat protected from the cold from the mountaintop. In spite of six fires, however, we spent a freezing night made extremely uncomfortable by the dense smoke given off by the suiba, which we burned as fuel.

From Portachuelo one can see a crescent of Andean peaks, covered with snow, and a great expanse of mountain ranges, clad with trees and also in half-moon shapes, extending to the Pampa del Sacramento. All this is a most magnificent and wonderful sight.

We left the glen on the 17th, harassed by the cold, the wind, the fog, and clouds of small, white mosquitoes called huahaches. These flies are so tiny that they are just barely visible to the naked eye, but they bite with an unbearable sting that lasts for an hour or more, without causing a rash or any other visible evidence. We slept at a spot called La Playa, where we were drenched in a rainstorm that lasted throughout the night, nearly until dawn. Here the mule drivers had to go into the forest to forage for reed grass to feed the animals.

On the 18th we went on to Tramo. Here I felt considerable alleviation of my abdominal pains and tenesmus, which had prevented my collecting many plants that I later gathered in those most delightful of forests.

We entered Pozuzo on the 19th to the accompaniment of chiming bells, for the missionary priest, in his pleasure at our arrival in that far off wilderness, ordered the bells rung. He was stationed there to provide spiritual guidance to the 14 souls that made up the village.

Three leagues ahead of Pozuzo there are various springs of briny waters, which are sufficient to make the river water brackish and give it a bitter and disagreeable taste.

On the 20th I made all the necessary preparations for starting work. Pavón arrived in Pozuzo on the 21st, and the artists came on the following day. They had all had a good trip, with no more than the normal discomfort presented by that hilly road full of dangerous and difficult slopes and mountain cliffs.

We began working on the 23rd of July and continued until the 20th of September, when the artists left Pozuzo for Huánuco. Pavón and I could not leave until the 27th of September, when the mule drivers arrived with our animals.

During our stay in Pozuzo we collected many fruits and seeds, numerous kinds of wood, and other natural specimens. Three hundred plants were drawn, and 314 were dried. I corrected some 250 descriptions of plants that I had worked out in Cuchero, Chinchao, and elsewhere, and I described about 400 species, which I discuss below.

A fear of wildcats, bears, wild boars, and other large beasts that lurk in the thick fastness of those forests, along with the difficulty of getting about in the luxuriant jungles, made it impossible for me to examine great numbers of the extremely tall trees, lianas, palms, and valuable plants that completely clothe the high and low mountains, the glens between them, their slopes, and the shores of the river. Although we had to go about on foot, and in some cases even had to clear our way in order to get through, we penetrated as far as the Huancabamba River, which joins up with the Pozuzo River 2 leagues below the village. These two streams form a river of appreciable size.

Many days we walked from 4 to 8 leagues into the forests; we usually returned to the village by nightfall, cut to pieces by the thorns and tangles, out of breath, thirsty, and weary, albeit loaded down with beautiful plants. Not a few times we had narrow escapes from death from the frequent and constant falling of rotten trees, from rocks falling off the cliffs and from the avalanches of earth that followed these rock slips, especially after rains, and from the great gashes in the forests made by the giant trees that our laborers felled for our examination. As a result, when we had finished our work and were about to leave Pozuzo, we were little short of being naked, and our legs and thighs were covered with sores from our daily plant collecting forays. These sores were so irritating that scratching with our nails was not enough, and we would grab some instrument and inevitably cut our flesh in scratching. There was no cure for this condition, save several days of rest and washings with lemon water.

CHAPTER 47

Description of the Village of Pozuzo

Pozuzo is the outlying Spanish settlement in these regions. It is located at 10°18' south latitude, in a deep gorge that is 4 to 8 leagues wide. It is surrounded by high, uninterrupted mountains that are entirely covered with stout and leafy trees, shrubs, lianas and vines, and herbaceous plants. Because there is no pasturage for animals to be found anywhere, the 50 sheep that we took in to feed our expedition wasted away so much that they became transparent as parchment. A number of them also died from pirhuin (pirguin, alicuya); these are insects, shaped like watermelon seeds, that attack the liver.

This gorge is bathed by a river that collects the waters that come down from Portachuelo de Muña, from the slopes of ravines, and from various briny springs along the banks of the river itself. The bed of this river consists of boulders mixed with sand and clay. There are lisas (mullet), cachuelas (a kind of anchovy), and boconcitos, all delicious fish that may weigh up to 3 pounds. In the sand and soil there are particles of gold; we collected some one day when we went panning in the dirt on the river banks.

Three leagues ahead of Pozuzo the gorge starts to widen, and a little more than a league downstream from the village it becomes so narrow again that there is no space except that occupied by the bed of the river itself. The river is too deep to be used to irrigate the small cultivated plots of the natives, so they take advantage of certain springs that tumble down the slopes.

In its path the spring water leaves stalactites, or a white, calcareous crust, of various shapes. Notwithstanding its mineral content, this water is drunk by the inhabitants, causing poor health, pale complexion, and a bloated appearance. Their natural laziness prevents their drinking the waters of a brook called Chinizo, at the most only a quarter of a league from the village. We fetched our daily supply from this brook, for the water is fresh, soft, and crystalline, without the slightest sign of having alumina, gypsum, or any other minerals or salts in solution, unlike the waters of all the other brooks and springs of the region. Our advice to the Indians to stop drinking these mineral-laden, injurious waters was to little avail. Only the missionary priest took our advice; from that time on, he had water fetched from Chinizo for his use.

The village of Pozuzo comprises but 15 huts, a church, the house of the missionary priest—known locally as the monastery—and a hut for the travelers who occasionally visit this unhappy little settlement. At the present time there are only 14 inhabitants, all poor and miserable. They are small in stature and have ugly faces. The men dress in breeches and waistcoat with a homespun cotton shirt, and go barefoot. The womenfolk, who are even poorer specimens of humankind than the men, dress in a short skirt and a bodice and likewise wear no shoes. In all of this misery, they are strongly addicted to chicha (fermented liquor) and to sexual excesses. The missionary is obliged to dwell among these people, most of the time alone and without anyone with whom he may converse, for all these Indians spend their days in their coca plots chewing coca leaves. The use of this drug puts their mouths in a most filthy condition, as loathsome as their very persons.

There is no meadow or clearing in the whole vicinity of Pozuzo, for the Indians have tiny cultivated plots for yuca, sweet potatoes, maize, ssaqui (*Calla* species), and wild beans—the daily nourishment of these people—on the slopes of the mountains and along the river's edge. The missionary priest usually cultivates rice, which grows very well and gives abundant harvests without any irrigation other than that provided by the heavens. Peanuts and sugar cane also grow well and are planted in small amounts as delicacies in the diet. In their plots the Indians also cultivate a kind of diadelphous plant known as verbasco (barbasco), which they employ as a fish poison.

Anonas (custard apples), caimitos, guavas, sweet oranges, sour oranges, true lemons, and thin-skinned lemons appear to be growing wild, but the places where these trees grow seem to indicate a previously larger settlement and former inhabitants who were a more industrious lot than those of today. Finally, there are some truly wild fruits that are appetizing, such as a species of *Spondias* called manzanas de monte (wild apples), two species of *Celtis* called atpuallín, a kind of palm called cacharpurin, and others. Pineapples, bananas, and papayas are grown in the coca fields and have exquisite flavor.

The only business or commerce of this village is coca. Travelers who arrive at Pozuzo buy coca leaves, paying for this product with cloth of various kinds, ribbons, glass beads, and other trinkets that the local people use as adornments, for holidays and their drunken parties when they drink maize chicha. These same traveling merchants also buy maize and maize bread from the Indians of Pozuzo.

The Indians eat the young shoots of the chonta and other palms, and any animal or bird that they can kill with their arrow or shotgun. This makes them lazy. If the missionary did not make them sow and cultivate the few crops that we have mentioned, they would be content to live the life of the savage, naked like the other barbarian Indians of their tribe, the Carapacha (naked ones).

The climate of Pozuzo is rather too humid and hot all through the year, and one sweats excessively. The heat is tempered by winds from the north that blow from about eleven in the morning until sundown. Without this blessing, at noon one could not walk about outdoors in open fields unprotected by trees. Although rainstorms and downpours are frequent, the natives have never seen a bolt of lightning strike. It rains excessively from November through April; for this reason, the locality is unhealthy and will continue to be so until it is cleared of its dense forest.

The natives cannot explain the ills that beset them, but it can be seen that their bodies are wracked by constant pain, that they are covered with infected sores, that they are weak, pale, and wan, and that their span of life is short. They treat their afflictions with herbs.

The forests abound with deer; jaguars; wildcats; bears; anteaters, or *Mirmecofagus americanus*; wild boars; granbestias; sahinos; huamataros; mischus, a species of hare; mucumucus (opossums); and huayhuas (weasels). The most common birds are the pichicapapanes, novengasaqui, yasefue, woodpeckers, hummingbirds, cuiches or pájaros hediondos (stinking birds), quianquianes, birds called jandagueros because of their song, seven-colored birds, organistas (organ birds), oropendolas (golden orioles), flycatchers, nightingales, and the occasional heron or duck. Mosquitoes are very rare and are not bothersome. There are no reptiles, nor noxious insects except for different kinds of small ants. The bite of one of these ants, which lives in the stem of the palo santo, *Triplaris octandra*, is unbearably painful, and the sting lasts for several hours. There is a great diversity of butterflies, of beautiful hues. There is also a species of bee that produces very good honey and wax; this insect builds its honeycombs in tree trunks or in the ground.

There are two bridges, made of lianas, crossing the Pozuzo River; one is near the village and the other is 2 leagues downstream where that stream joins up with the Huancabamba River. This second bridge is the one that is crossed on the way to Mayro or the Pampa del Sacramento, but it is almost always in a rotting condition, for it is used only when missionaries make trips into the Indian country beyond to convert the infidels. At one end of this bridge a large number of palms grow, including the chonta real (royal palm), chonta silvestre (wild palm), camona, cuyol, siasia, and palmitos. It is the pleasantest spot in the whole ravine.

About 3 leagues ahead of Pozuzo, there are several coca fields belonging to miserable wretches who are hunted down by the law and by important townspeople because of debt. They have fled the towns, abandoning their families, to escape incarceration.

Among the many plants of the luxuriant forests of Pozuzo, I collected and described the following.

Justicia spicata. *Sanchezia ovata*. *Peperomia alata*, *P. dependens*, *P. emarginata*, *P. pilosa*, and *P. septemnervia*. *Dianthera ciliata*, *D. appendiculata*, and *D. secundiflora*. *Piper unguiculatum* and *P. hexandrum*. *Verbena virgata*.

Fagara coriandriodora, called culantro in reference to the corianderlike odor of its leaves. It is a small tree, 10 to 12 yards tall, leafy, dioecious, with hermaphroditic staminate and pistillate flowers. The trunk, though barely as thick as a man's thigh at the most, is of a hard wood that almost resists iron.

Rivina secunda. *Spigelia anthelmia*. *Hamelia secunda*. *Gardenia longiflora*, iscumnin; its white corolla is more than a handspan in length. The fruits are 3 inches long, cylindrical, and yellow; Indians eat the sweet pulp.

Cerdana alliodora, called árbol del ajo (garlic tree) in reference to the odor of the leaves and bark, which Indians use in condiments. These trees are tall but not very solid, and are visited by a kind of small ant. The bite of this ant produces a rash that lasts 16 to 20 hours, stinging severely at first but soon abating.

These ants completely destroy the leaves of the garlic tree; they cut them into triangular bits, carry the pieces to their burrows, and place them symmetrically one upon the other without wasting any space. To carry these leaf bits to their hills, the ants grasp them by the shortest angle, putting the sharpest and longest up and the third forward, and walk swiftly. Thus they look like many tiny boats with lateen sails bending to all sides, depending upon the way the wind blows. It matters little that the leaf fragment be six times the size of the ant.

There are so many insects engaged in this activity all day long that they have worn paths about 9 inches wide leading from the trees to the anthills. Opening up and studying several hills, I sometimes found more than 50 pounds of leaves neatly arranged, one overlapping the other; even though some water might leak in, only the upper layers can be wetted, for the rest are placed like tiles and shed the water. The natives call these ants tragineras (carriers) because of their ceaseless labor.

Cinchona grandiflora, azuzeno; this is a tree of low stature, varying from 6 to 8 yards in height. The flowers are about half as large as those of the azuzena (azucena, white lily), and the fruits are an inch and a half long. *Cinchona rosea*, asmonich?; this species is an extraordinarily leafy tree, 20 to 30 yards tall. When in bloom it offers a superb sight, with racemes of flowers at the tip of each branch. The Indians adorn the altars and images of their churches with these blossoms. The barks of both of these species of *Cinchona* are scarcely bitter. The trunk of *C. rosea* is stout and appears to be hollowed out in places, but its wood has a good grain. The same ants that destroy the leaves of *Cerdana alliodora*, or árbol del ajo, likewise attack the leaves of *Cinchona rosea*, so one seldom finds a branch with the leaves entire unless the tree has not yet flowered.

Capsicum frutescens, arnaucho, and *C. pubescens*, rocoto; both species abound in Peru, but the first is extremely variable.

Tabernaemontana corymbosa. This tall, stout, very leafy tree contains so much latex that when it is felled the milk spatters all over the ground. When incisions are made in the bark, a large amount of the white, juicy latex oozes forth; it later coagulates into a dark red resin.

Solanum mite and *S. grandiflorum*. *Convolvulus cymosus*. *Ipomoea angulata* and *I. villosa*. *Cestrum lanuginosum*.

Strychnos brachiata, called comida de venado (deer's food) because deer come down from the hills in search of the fruits for food. *Strychnos auriculata*, abilla; the seeds of this species yield much oil when pressed, and Indians use them in a variety of ways.

Achyranthes paposa. *Cynanchum macrocarpum* and *C. pentagonum*. *Tournefor-*

tia volubilis and *T. longifolia*. *Aralia globosa*, a leafy tree, 10 to 15 yards tall. *Juanulloa parasitica*.

Pourretia lanuginosa. *Aechmea paniculata*. *Crinum? luteum*; its beautiful flowers are yellow, becoming green at the tip. *Alstroemeria fimbriata*.

Achras tetrandra, caimito. This is a tree about 16 yards tall, very leafy and beautifully green. Its fruits, the size of duck eggs and the color of peaches, are delicious when ripe.

Bromelia incarnata; this plant is very showy with its red leaves, bracts, and flowers.

Bromelia ananas, called piñas (pinecones, pineapples) for the shape of their impressive and beautiful fruits. The fruits vary in weight from 4 to 8 pounds, and have superb flavor when cut ripe and bright yellow; in this state they can be eaten without adding sugar. Pineapples also do not have to be stored covered over for several days after picking, as is commonly practiced to give fruits an appearance of goodness when they have been plucked in an underripe condition.

The pineapple plant is a small bunch of flowers growing on one stalk, like the aloe. It sends forth many shoots from the roots and from the axils of the leaves, each shoot eventually producing a pineapple at the tip of its short stem. If the fruits are cut before ripening properly, the quality of their flavor is lower; sometimes one cannot eat such fruit because of the acidity and viscosity, which can set the teeth unbearably on edge and bring on indigestion and abdominal cramps.

A tasty and exquisite chicha, or beer, is prepared from pineapple, and the fruit lends a pleasant flavor to lemonades and other beers. Pineapples are set on the table, cut into wheel-shaped slices, as an appetizer. Everyone knows of the superiority of this fruit, when it is absolutely ripe, over all others of the New World, insofar as its bittersweet flavor, its special fragrance, and its cooling properties are concerned.

The nuns of Huánuco are especially skillful in making a sweet of the pineapple, which they prepare by first peeling the fruit and then parboiling or cooking it in water to remove the acidity and viscosity. The nuns then take out the meat of the heart of the pineapple, comprising about half the pulp; this meat is then crushed together with almonds, raisins, sugar, and cinnamon to form a soft mass. This mixture is then stuffed into the bore of the original pineapple, which has been boiled in sugar water. The whole is then given two or three baths of sugar water, and the result is an extraordinarily savory pineapple weighing 3 to 6 pounds. Because of the tedious work required in their preparation, these pineapples fetch a high price.

Lastly, any skilled cook can prepare crushed sweets and jellies of exquisite taste and delightful fragrance from pineapples that have been boiled to remove the viscosity.

Paullinia pinnata, *P. rubicaulis*, *P. gracilis*, *P. obliqua*, *P. lacticinosa*, *P. hirsuta*, and *P. rubra*; all of these species are climbers.

Guarea abrupta and *G. ferruginea*. *Guarea purpurea*, yecheñor; Indian women employ this plant to dye their cotton and woolen goods a purplish hue. *Neea verticillata*; the fruits of this plant are used by the Indians to stain their feet, hands, and faces purple, and are also the source of a bright dye for cotton cloth.

Laurus pubescens and *L. purpurea*. *Laurus fragrans*, mucamuca; its seeds are aromatic and are a tonic for the stomach. Indians gather them to sell to the traveling merchants who visit the region.

Cassia procera, cañafistola; this tree is 30 to 40 yards tall, is extremely leafy, and has a stout trunk. The pods of cañafistola are 4 to 6 inches long, with a bittersweet pulp that is the laxative of these Indians.

Heisteria coccinea, a leafy tree, 12 to 14 yards tall. *Swietenia macrocarpa*; more than 40 yards tall, this tree has a massive trunk that is the source of a valuable wood.

Quinoquino

Myroxylon peruiferum, quinoquino. This is a very tall and leafy tree, with a stout, straight, smooth trunk that is ashy gray, as are the branches. The inner bark is a straw-colored white. Depending upon the amount of resin with which it is impregnated, the outer bark is more or less spotted, compacted, and tough, as well as sometimes reddish or greenish yellow or dark chestnut in color. It has an aromatic-balsamic taste and aroma that is similar to red Peruvian balsam, which is sold in apothecaries and pharmacies under the name balsamo blanco.

The resin from the quinoquino is called estoraque in Peru, and is used to fumigate rooms. A pomade of the fruits, called pepitas or semillas de quinoquino, is made into a powder together with the bark and mixed with tallow or resins; this is applied as a poultice to reduce headache. The fresh leaves, crushed, will heal new wounds, and the same properties are claimed for the resin and the bark, for both are renowned as admirable balsamic and curative agents. An oil called quinaquina is prepared from the fruits.

Four ounces of the fruit of quinoquino are bruised and infused in a pint of wine for 24 hours; this is cooked over slow heat with a pound and a half of ordinary oil until it is dry. Then a pound of turpentine and, finally, an ounce and a half of incense and an equal amount of myrrh are added. They say this balm is marvelously effective in treating ulcers of the chest, agglutinating and healing the open sores.

Indians saw straight planks from the trunk of the quinoquino, preferring the wood of this tree to all others because of its strength and durability. At the tips of the branches, in the parts farthest from the main trunk, one finds, more often in this tree than in others, the nests of certain birds—poccochycuis, cuiches, or hediondos—where their eggs or young are safe from monkeys and other arboreal animals. See the description of the quinoquino that I have given in the appendix of my *Quinología*, published in Madrid in 1792; there the reader will find all the other interesting annotations concerning this plant.

Banisteria papiliona, *B. auriculata*, and *B. flavelliformis*; all these species are vines. *Joveolaria cordata*. *Erythroxylon stipulatum*. *Oxalis frutescens*. *Euphorbia erosa*. *Heliocarpus serratus*.

Psidium rugosum, huayabo (guayabo) de monte (wild guava), a small tree, 12 to 15 yards tall. Its wood is good, but the fruit contains hardly any pulp.

Myrtus limbosa; this tree, 4 yards tall, has delightfully fragrant flowers. *Cactus parasiticus. Prunus amara*, a tree 10 to 12 yards tall, with bitter fruit. *Calyptrantes paniculata*, a bush 4 yards tall with exceedingly sweet-scented flowers.

Calyplectus acuminatus, called cabeza de monge (cabeza de monje, monk's head) in reference to the shape of the fruit; this tree is very tall, stout, and leafy.

Bixa muricata, known as maxpachín or achote de monte (wild achiote). Natives color their food and dye a variety of objects with the seeds of this tree, as they do with the seeds of achiote, or *Bixa orellana*.

Aceyte de María

Verticillaria balsamifera, aceyte (aceite) de María (oil of Mary). This tree is very attractive because the leaves are disposed in whorls, and the leaves and branches are a brilliant green. It exudes a greenish resin that the local Indians call balsamo or aceyte de María. The resin is gathered in abundance during the rainy season and is kept in pieces of bamboo stem for sale to traveling merchants.

Trillis auriculata. Gualteria lutea. Gesneria hirta, G. verticillata, G. violacea, and *G. viscosa*.

Bignonia alba.On the morning of the 17th of September we saw a host of small trees in flower, clothing the slopes of the peak of Pozuzo, which is on the other side of the river and opposite the village. The trees were so laden with flowers that they looked as though snow had fallen upon them. This phenomenon caused us to cross the river to study the place, and we found that the trees were *Bignonia alba*, wholly leafless but covered with large, white flowers. On the 19th there was hardly a flower to be found; they had already become young fruits. This is one of the few treelets in these forests that shed their leaves.

Bignonia brachiata, B. clavata, B. lanuginosa, B. planisiliqua, and *B. muricata*. All these are climbers that lose their leaves in summer or early autumn.

Besleria radicans. Gomara racemosa. Erinus prostratus. Cleome aculeata and *C. longisiliqua*.

Cavanillesia umbellata, called árbol del tambor (drum tree) because the bark of this tree is used for the hoops of drums. The tree attains a height of 30 to 40 yards and has a disproportionately stout trunk. The wood is soft and spongy, between cork and mushroom in consistency, and an ax cuts into it as easily as into a pumpkin. Though it was of such great girth that two men could not embrace it, the tree we ordered felled was thus cut down in a few blows of the ax, without even tiring the axman. The branches, similarly swollen, are nearly semiglobose in shape. This is one of the few trees of these forests that drop their leaves and flowers before sprouting new leaves at the beginning of autumn—that is, in November. Its flowers are so ephemeral that the young fruits attain full size in 4 days' time. As the fruits have five, or sometimes four, large wings, during their period of ripening in the crown of the tree they appear to be myriad little lanterns, set out intentionally on the twigs. The wood of the árbol del tambor, being so porous, is extremely lightweight and can be used extensively for buoys and rafts.

Sun Cotton

Bombax aculeatum, inich'; the cotton of this stout, tall, leafy tree is called algodón del sol (sun cotton) or zarbatana (blowgun cotton). It is snow-white and valuable as stuffing for pillows, mattresses, cushions, and sofas. It is very soft and, when put out in the sun, has the property of fluffing up again after being compressed.

Bombax microcarpum. This tree grows to a height of more than 40 yards and is stout and leafy. Its scanty cotton is the color of tobacco or of vicuña wool. The tree we ordered the laborers to cut down for study might have killed my companion Pavón and me, had we not taken flight with all haste when we heard one of the men shout. The crown of the felled tree took up a great circle of land where we had been standing, busily cutting a slender bush. As it fell, the giant cut off the top of that bush and even stripped the bark from its branches, as it did to all the other trees that became trapped beneath its mass.

Erythrina glandulosa and *E. articulata*; both are called villcatauri and are tall, massive trees with straight trunks and heavy foliage. The wood is white and has a good grain, but is soft and not durable. Both these species, like the rest of the genus, defoliate and flower in July and August before sprouting new leaves. When in blossom the trees are a splendid sight, with flowers the color of red coral. A few days after the flowers have wilted away, the new leaves burst forth and the tree becomes beautifully and luxuriantly green.

Abrus? volubilis; its seeds, which the Indians call huairurus, are red with one black spot where they are attached to the pod.

Negretia spinosa, called llamapañaui, which means eye of the llama. Indians say the seed is an effective antidote for snake bites and insect stings. It is pulverized and applied to the bite, and about a dram of seed that has been soaked in water is taken internally. The prickles, or bristles, in some places called picapica, penetrate the skin very easily and cause extreme smarting and discomfort. Some people say that half a scruple (1/6 dram) of these prickles, drunk in a cup of chocolate, milk, or sugared water, has an excellent effect as an anthelmintic.

Securidaca punctata and *S. scandens*. *Polygala rhombiflora*. *Galega hirsuta*.

Dolichos umbellatus, frijol de monte (wild bean). Indians eat the beans fresh as well as dried; they are tasty, but bring on considerable flatulence.

Clitoria? pubescens. *Elephantopus spicatus*. *Lobelia coccinea* and *L. laciniata*. *Bletia catenulata* and *B. ensiformis*. *Satyrium dicolorum* and *S. plantagineum*.

Vanilla volubilis, vaynilla (vainilla, vanilla); Indians gather the fruits for sale to traveling merchants.

Gongora quinquenervis. *Sobralia biflora* and *S. dichotoma*. *Epidendrum coronatum*, *E. cristatum*, *E. viride*, and *E. equitans*. *Aristolochia caudata*. *Passiflora vespertilis*, *P. vesicularis*, *P. serrata*, and *P. rubra*. *Pothos apetala*, *P. geniculata*, *P. cordato-sagittata*, *P. laciniata*, and *P. umbellata*. *Arum auritum*, *A. lanceolatum*, *A. lineatum*, *A. parviflorum*, *A. tripartitum*, and *A. volubile*.

Calla bracteata, *C. pinnata*, *C. radicans*, and *C. undulata*. *Calla nuda*; its root is believed to have properties effective in the treatment of snake bites.

Cynomorium punuchrin, puñuchrin. The catkins of this plant look like groups of club-shaped fungi attached to long, much-branched roots; Indians use them to restore energy spent on long walking trips or on hard work. They take an infusion of the catkins in warm water or eat the small heads, or inflorescences. The name puñuchrin undoubtedly comes from the verb puñuchini, which means to put to sleep.

Dragon's Blood

Croton gummiferum, called sangre de drago (dragon's blood) in reference to the sticky, resinous, blood-red sap that oozes out abundantly from wounds. This substance is gathered and sold as sangre de drago. The tree is 10 to 12 yards tall and has a semiglobose, very leafy crown that provides beautiful shade; the trunk is straight and rather grayish. The taste, color, and astringency of the gum-resin are such as would recommend its use in medicine.

Acalypha betuloides and *A. polygama*. *Tragia peltata*. *Betula acuminata*. *Phyllanthus foetida*. *Urtica aculeata* and *U. baccifera*. *Jatropha urens*. *Begonia cucullata*, *B. purpurea*, and *B. repens*.

Cecropia canescens, tacuna; this is a beautiful and very tall tree. Its hollow, articulated trunk often has clear, drinkable water between the septae, which Indians drink to quench their thirst when traveling through forests where there is no water.

Coussapoa radicans, chichillica; this is a tall, stout, and leafy tree. From its larger branches and the upper parts of its trunk arise roots which enclasp the trunks of neighboring trees and thus grow down to the soil. Indians employ the bark to make nets and pillacas, a kind of bag in which they gather coca leaves or fruits and transport them to their homes. The bark is like coarse hemp and is also used by the natives for binding the beams of their houses.

Clarisia racemosa, tulpay, and *C. biflora*, yasmich? Both species are massive trees, more than 50 yards tall, and sources of excellent lumber. When these trees are tapped or slashed, so much milky juice oozes out that the ground is covered with it. The juice coagulates to form a white resin that, upon exposure to the air, turns brownish and retains some elasticity. It is excellent for waterproofing, and Indians cover their blowguns and other tools with it. The bark of the tulpay is blood red, and the color of the roots is brighter still. The roots stretch out horizontally and are exposed in many places on the surface of the soil, giving the impression that blood has been shed all around the tree.

Tallow Tree

Myristica longifolia, called árbol de sebo (tallow tree) because abundant quantities of thick oil, like the fat or oil from cacao, can be expressed from the seeds. Indians light their houses with this fatty oil, which has no appreciable odor or taste other than a soft, oily savor. To extract the oil, the seeds are finely crushed and heated, and the warm mass is pressed between two stones.

Olmedia aspera and *O. laevis*. An extremely white latex flows from any wound made on the trunk of either of these trees. The latex, upon exposure to air, coagulates to form a perfectly elastic resin of a reddish chestnut hue. Probably these and other species of the same genus are the source in other regions of the renowned *resina elastica* (gum elastic) that has so many uses in the manufacture of a large variety of artifacts. [Ruiz was in error in this assumption. He was undoubtedly referring to the rubber produced by various species of the euphorbiaceous genus *Hevea*, which had been described only a few years before by Aublet in his *Histoire des Plantes de la Guyanne Française* (1775).—Translator]

Anguria triloba and *A. trifoliata*.

Smilax china, called purampuí or santo palo; Indians frequently use an infusion of its roots to relieve rheumatic pains or to very effectively induce sweating. For native uses of this plant in Peru, see my *Memoria sobre la Raíz de China*, published in the first volume of the notes of the Real Academia Medica de Madrid in 1797.

Carica septemlobata, papayo; its fruit, called papaya, is as large as a small melon and has a similar flavor. To have it ripen with its best flavor, one must make several lengthwise cuts in the rind the day before it is to be used, in order to drain off the milky latex that gives it a rather bitter taste.

Clusia radicans, pullapullquelpuan. This species is a small tree, 12 to 15 yards tall. It is very leafy, and a beautiful sight when in fruit. The fruit has the appearance of an apple or, more exactly, of a mangosteen; it is a rosy white color and, like the rest of the tree, is full of resin. Indians gather the resin, which is used in place of incense or to fill cracks.

Triplaris octandra, called palo santo, chupillo, or tisackeiro. This tree is erect and grows to a height of 10 to 15 yards; its branching is somewhat pyramidal. The curious shape of its crown and the large size of its leaves lend the tree an exceptional beauty in the flowering season. This is especially true of the pistillate, or female, individuals, which have larger flowers than the staminate trees. The flowers are a splendid red and are borne in large clusters that delight the eye. The upper parts of the trunk, as well as the branches, are hollow and articulated and, in Pozuzo, are inhabited by a kind of ant. We encountered an infinite number of these insects in every tree we felled; their stings bring on an unbearable smarting and raise a rash that lasts, in some instances, more than 8 hours.

Aristolochia fragrans, known as contrayerba or bejuco de la estrella (star vine). I could not find flowers of this creeper in Pozuzo, but when I transplanted it to the garden of the Padres Agonizantes (an order of friars for the care of the dying) in Lima, it did flower luxuriantly under the care of Padre Francisco Laguna. He had the artist Pulgar draw it, and Tafalla wrote up a description of it (see Chapter 48).

The root of this plant is rather long and as thick as a man's wrist, with thick bark that is brittle when dried out and endowed with a special fragrance. When cut crosswise, the woody portions show, as do many other plants, the design of a star, whence the name of bejuco de la estrella. The Cholone Indians employ the root to cure rheumatic and venereal pains, drinking a decoction of it at night. Not only the natives, but likewise the missionaries, state categorically that a few hours after drinking such a potion the patient breaks out in a profuse sweat that continues for 3 days, and that on the fourth day he is completely well and can leave his sickbed, without any bad aftereffect that would hinder his working. I have used this root in Peru to relieve toothache, upon the recommendation of Father Francisco González Laguna. One might expect that in time this root will find an important use in medicine, for its aroma and taste bespeak excellent properties, making it valuable for a number of therapeutic applications and surpassing those of *Serpentaria virginiana*.

Genus aff. *Panax*, species *trinervis*. *Ficus gemina*, *F. hirsuta*, and *F. retusa*? *Gimbernatia oblonga*; this tall, leafy tree has a stout trunk, the source of strong and easily worked wood for a number of purposes.

Mimosa nodosa and *M. quadrijuga*; both species are known as pacae de monte (wild pacay). These are trees of 10 yards' height or more. Their wood is of good quality, and the pulp of their fruits, sparse though it be, is as tasty and sweet as that of the cultivated pacay, or *Mimosa inga*.

Celtis biflora and *C. spinosa*; both are called atpuallín, and Indians eat the fruits of both species. The fruits are as large as yellow cherries, and sweet. *Celtis scabra*, chichillicas; the bark of this plant is used for the same purposes as is the bark of *Coussapoa radicans*.

Gouania? *tomentosa*. *Carludovica acuminata*. *Carludovica palmata*; its stems are shaped like slender, straight, and flexible reeds.

Martinezia ensiformis and *M. linearis*. *Martinezia interrupta*, cuyol. *Martinezia ciliata*, chonta; the trunk of this palm is beset with long, black, penetrating spines. The outer part of the wood is black, solid, and extremely hard, but is easy to work. Indians use it for their bows and arrows, with the arrowheads, quivers, poles, and blowguns beautifully polished. The fresh shoots, known as palmitos, are tender and tasty when raw or cooked, but they are reputed to be a coarse food. I have eaten them in salads and cooked, and have felt no ill effect from them.

Nunnezharia fragrans, chutaslium. The flowers of this diminutive palm give off a delightful fragrance, better than that of the Florentine iris. This fragrance is wafted over long distances through the forest. *Morenia fragrans*, siasia, a very showy palm. *Iriartea delthoidea*, camona, a tall and frondose palm.

Calamus? *hamatus*, cacharpurin. A climber, this palm sends forth many straight stems and grasps with spurs like fishhooks that are on the tips of the leaves. The name cacharpurin, which means walking strap, refers to this climbing habit. The fruits are borne in large clusters and have sweet yellow meat of good flavor when well ripened. From the stems are made beautiful canes or walking sticks, straight, black, and lustrous, that are so flexible they may be bent until one end touches the other without snapping, if they be well seasoned and cured in smoke.

There are, in addition to the plants we have mentioned, so very many trees, shrubs, bushes, and herbs in these forests at Pozuzo that it would be difficult to study them thoroughly in a hundred years, even if one botanist followed another in immediate succession during that period of time. We have examined only the forest areas along footpaths and in certain partly cleared spots, and we lacked the time to investigate more than the most striking plants that were in flower or fruit in that season.

Among the myriad trees in Pozuzo and in the region around this settlement, there are woods worthy of the highest appreciation because of their colors, grains, and other characteristics. Along the slopes of the mountains on the eastern side of the village there are extremely tall cedros (cedars), *Cedrela odorata*, the crowns of which are extraordinarily wide and provide wonderful shade. There are cedars with a circumference of more than 8 yards. Two such giants, which we had cut for making boxes, brought down many other smaller trees when they fell, and tore loose much soil and gravel from the mountainside. They made such a frightful crash that we thought for a moment it might be a great earthquake or landslide; we were having lunch in the village at the time, having sent the laborers to fell the cedars in the morning. Four men took 6 hours to bring down the two trees.

In Pozuzo we received a letter from Don José Dombey from Janeyro (Rio de Janeiro), notifying us of his arrival in that region. Among the plants that he reported having studied there were many of those that we were collecting, drawing, and describing at the same time in Pozuzo.

CHAPTER 48

Trip from Pozuzo to Huánuco

On the 20th of September the artists left Pozuzo for Huánuco. We stayed on until the 27th, when our mule drivers arrived, and left about midday. Nothing was worthy of note other than the lack of good food, for we had to eat boiled maize in place of bread, baked yuca roots, and a little bit of salted meat that had gone bad. We arrived to sleep that night at Tramo, and spent the following night in Cussi. All the afternoon of the 28th, from two o'clock on, we were punished by a heavy rainstorm. Three of my companion Pavón's mules were tired out, but the driver had the good luck of being able to change them along the way. We would otherwise have been obliged to leave our baggage on that desolate road until we arrived at the village of Muña.

On the 29th we stayed overnight at Alto de la Playa, where a dense fog descended upon us until dawn on the 30th; my mule drivers then went on to Muña to rest and feed the animals. Pavón's driver was unable to do this because his fourth mule had tired, and two of the others had died the day before. In spite of the discomforts of this bad path, we collected various plants that we found in fruit between Pozuzo and Muña.

On the 1st of October my mule drivers stopped in Muña, and that afternoon Pavón's men came in, with their mules worn out from hunger and injured by the tangle of underbrush along the path. On the 2nd the mule drivers from Panao made up their minds to carry my baggage and that of the expedition over the Cuesta de Santo Domingo, but the driver from Huánuco could not take Pavón's packs before the 3rd, so we stayed overnight in the village of Chaclla. On the 4th I ordered my men to wait for Pavón's, and we all started out together from Chaclla on the 5th, determined to spend the night in Portachuelo de Panao. Pavón's driver, however, could not drive his animals up to that height, so we had to sleep along the banks of the river. We had a short rainstorm on the 5th. On the 6th I arrived in Huánuco; my companion, not wishing to forsake his baggage, passed the night in Yanamayo and got to Huánuco on the 7th, having had another mule die on the way.

In spite of the misfortunes of this trip and the lack of food that handicapped us until we got to Muña, we collected a very good number of plants from Pozuzo to Portachuelo de Panao. We finished drying these collections in Huánuco.

On the 12th I reported our discoveries in Pozuzo and its forests to the Ministry of the Indies, sending an ample package of seeds to the Royal Botanic Garden. I likewise sent packages of seeds in three different mails in the succeeding months, during which time I put my dried plants in order, put finishing touches on the descriptions, and boxed up the dried specimens, along with seeds and other collections, ready for shipment to Spain.

The Indians of Panao brought to me in Huánuco the loads of raíz de China (China root) for which I had contracted with them. After cleaning and drying these roots, I packed them carefully in five boxes. I also packed up two boxes full of roots of contrayerba and of bejuco de la estrella (star vine).

Tafalla and Pulgar Join the Expedition

On the 14th of November the superintendent of Peru ordered two young men to join our expedition: one to learn botany, the other to learn the art of drawing plants. The purpose was for them to continue working after our return to Spain and to check up on questions and problems that we might communicate from Spain during the preparation of the flora of Peru. On the 20th of November, Don Juan Tafalla began his study of botany under our direction, and Don Francisco Pulgar came under the tutelage of the artists.

I spent the whole month of January 1785 in bed with a kind of tabardillo (typhoidlike fever), similar to the attacks I had suffered in the past. I recovered in early February, although I had a sharp pain in my side, back, and kidneys for more than a fortnight. Once well, I continued until June recopying the descriptions of plants from the trip to Pozuzo and perfecting the descriptions of others from the vicinity of Huánuco. This work also served as lessons for our new assistant, Tafalla.

On the 12th of May 1785 I notified the Ministry of the Indies that we were planning a trip to the forests of the gorge of Chinchao and Cuchero.

CHAPTER 49

Trip to the Forests of Chinchao

Preparations were made for travel to Marimarchahua (Maimarchao), a coca plantation in the gorge of Chinchao, and on the 10th of June 1785 we sent two men on ahead with 55 sheep for our food. On the 12th Pavón, Tafalla, and I started out, and we arrived at Chulqui to spend the night.

We continued on from Chulqui on the 13th. About 3 leagues from Huánuco, Tafalla's mule fled. He chased it and returned to Huánuco that night, worn out not only from the chase but also from the weight of the saddle blanket that he had to carry from the spot where the mule dashed away. He lost a sack with his clothing and 20 duros (coins), but later retrieved it, nearly intact, from the magistrate of the village of Cascay. Because one of the mule drivers was unable to continue on to the village of Acomayo, where our other companions had gone, Don José Pavón and I slept on the pampa of Mayubamba.

On the 14th we joined up with the first of the mule drivers, and late that night we encamped beyond the roadside inn of Pati, where we arrived under considerable hardship from a very bad road full of pools of water. We collected a number of plants, which we put out to dry. On the 15th we stayed overnight beyond Chinchao, on a small, flat area by the side of the road.

We got to the estate of Macora on the 16th. Pavón, in the company of Don Mathías Trabuco, mayordomo (manager, overseer) of the estate, had gone on ahead to this location in the belief that it was more appropriate for our work than Marimarchahua, and with the idea that the mayordomo might provide us with food and give us information about the forests of the region.

We spent the 17th and 18th in getting everything ready that we needed to start our excursions and collecting. We continued our work there until the 6th of August, the day of the unfortunate fire of which I shall write below.

Tafalla arrived at Macora on the 19th after having gone to Marimarchahua, the place we had previously settled upon as our residence. On the 22nd the three artists, Brunete, Gálvez, and Pulgar, arrived in Macora. They began to draw plants on the 24th, and continued this work until the 5th of August, when, contrary to our wishes, the mule drivers arrived to take us back to Huánuco.

During our stay in Macora we made various excursions into the forests, discovered a great many wonderful trees and other plants, and prepared specimens of them all. We gathered a large number of seeds, many samples of bark, roots, and some gums and resins, and various specimens of birds killed with a shotgun or with a blowgun by an Indian from Pampahermosa, who very rarely lost a shot no matter how tiny the bird might be. I described not only the plants that were being drawn but also many others that we had no time to draw. Finally, I corrected numerous descriptions and finished other studies on this first visit to the forests of Cuchero and Chinchao.

Once, when I had gone into the forests a day farther than we usually went, the laborers with me lost the way back, for we had wandered about for 2 hours in the dark of night without knowing where we were and without any hope of finding the path. The guides decided to sleep in the forest, but I ordered them to throw away the plants they were carrying and follow me. Though we had to clamber down several banks and steep slopes, within the half hour we found ourselves in the coca fields of the estate of Mesapata. We were half naked, barefoot, and torn by the tangle of underbrush and the repeated falls that we had suffered. At last we arrived at Macora at ten o'clock that night, exhausted from such a hike and fighting the forest.

My companions Don José Pavón and Don Juan Tafalla had already made plans to set out and search for us the following day with their guns. They hoped that we might hear the shots, had we not perished as all had suspected.

Mayco Sickness

As a result of our daily trips, we botanists found our legs covered with rashes, as had happened in Pozuzo. The rashes turned into very bothersome, stinging sores that forced us to scratch for hours on end during the night, until we had broken the skin on our legs and brought on considerable bleeding. The only way of avoiding this malady was to refrain from walking through the woods or to remain quiet like the artists, who never suffered from this unbearable affliction.

Pavón also contracted another skin disease, called mal de mayco (mayco sickness). It is similar to scabies in its irritating discomfort, but breaks out into rather transparent, purulent sores with a feverish smarting that afflicts the hands, the back of the knee joint, and sometimes the neck. This illness comes, according to the experience of the natives, from the shade of two species of *Schinus*. Some of the natives described them to us as dioecious, and it is true that all the species of *Schinus* that I examined in Chile and Peru were dioecious, and the shade of all of them is more or less harmful. Mal de mayco is cured with albergilla, or our *Valeriana pinnatifida*. The albergilla is half-roasted by the handful in embers, and applied to the sores as hot as can be stood. With this treatment they are cured in 8 or 10 days, as in the case of Pavón on two occasions and of the missionary priest of Muña. While suffering from this disease, the patient finds work next to impossible.

The artists escaped this affliction too, because they did not go out into the field as we did. They also did not share in the continual fatigue, falls, blows, heat, thirst, hunger, bad weather, and suffering that fell to the lot of the botanists because of the rough and rugged character of those tangled jungles.

On the 12th of July 1785 we sent three laborers to the new village of Chicoplaya for the purposes of studying the roads and of bringing us some information about the region, so we might decide upon the advisability of going there. They returned in 10 days, loaded down with many kinds of strange seeds and other curiosities that they had acquired from the Indians or collected themselves in the forests. They returned by way of the Cuchero River in order to avoid the many hardships met on their overland journey to the locality.

An Indian of the Cholon tribe arrived at Macora with the laborers. He was a native of Pampahermosa, and he remained with us for several days. He shot birds for us with his blowpipe, an instrument that, as we have already stated, he used with exceptional skill, killing even the tiniest of hummingbirds without in any way damaging their most delicate parts. He was equally skillful in the use of the bow and arrow, which he employed in hunting all sorts of larger animals. We asked that he continue working with us on our trips in America and also in Spain, and he, apparently in all good faith, agreed to do it. When we thought him most content and obliged, he went to Cuchero under the pretext of some errand; from there he returned to his native forests, leaving us completely tricked.

Before leaving Huánuco, we had resolved to spend at least 3 months in the jungle regions, but the artists, probably tired of living in uninhabited places, decided among themselves to return to Huánuco at the beginning of August. To save appearances in this premature return, they tried to say that they were becoming sick. To convince the mayordomo of the estate and other local people, with whom they talked every day and who could see that they were in good health, they used another means: they convinced them that there were few plants to draw. Not for one moment did we suspect their plans, until we saw their mule drivers arrive. The mayordomo told us what he had heard concerning the small amount of work they had to do.

Until then, we had never guessed why the artists were doing two or three drawings a day without putting on the finishing touches; for this reason, not a few of the drawings done on this trip and others were incomplete. In addition to hurrying their work, the artists never wanted to begin by drawing the separate parts, except in the case of new genera, but added them after the completion of the picture with less perfection than if they had been done before the specimens wilted.

On the 6th of August, when the artists' mule drivers arrived, I asked the reason for their return before completion of the time that we had decided upon for our stay in the forests. Since their answers were anything but satisfactory, I retired to our hut, where my companion was sick with mal de mayco and was out of sorts because of this desertion on the part of the artists.

Fire at Macora

On the 6th, after we had sent a man off to Huánuco with our correspondence, 10 seedlings of a certain tree, and a large package of the coffee that we had only just discovered in these forests, all to be delivered to the ministry, the mules arrived to take the artists' baggage away. In order to avoid fresh annoyance with the desertion of the artists, I set off for the forest with three laborers to cut boards for making boxes and to collect plants to describe.

At five o'clock in the evening, when we were returning to Macora, one of the laborers noticed from a high point on the road that the estate had been reduced to ashes. The shock and grief that this new setback caused us was unspeakable, and it affected me especially, since I had all of my writings and collections in that terrible fire.

Without wasting an instant, we rushed down the hillside, several times rolling down the slope, and arrived at Macora almost bereft of life. We rushed through the burning area, where the flames were just finishing their destruction of the three houses with all their furnishings, as well as all our equipment, plant specimens, books, manuscripts, supplies, and the many samples of local objects that we had gathered together in our huge house and in the mayordomo's house. My first words were questions about my manuscripts, but I learned from my companion Pavón and from Tafalla that all had been devoured in the conflagration. They themselves had escaped by chance; except for a few furnishings that had been within their reach, they had to leave everything behind when the flames surrounded them and forced them to flee for their lives as the fire spread rapidly from one place to the next.

I had hardly heard these words when, neither thinking of the danger to which I was exposing myself nor heeding the cries of those present, I ran into the embers and flames to look for my manuscripts, but in vain after so many hours of burning. Two workers came in after me and pulled me from the danger to which my grief had impelled me. Nevertheless, I did manage to save some scraps of Tournefort's plates. In this mad dash, I filled one of my shoes with the pewter of the inkwell that had melted next to the plates.

At one o'clock in the morning I was still running hither and yon like a man possessed, threatening the mayordomo and damning the artists and anyone else who was on the scene. At that late hour, wearied to the point of death from my ravings, I heeded the words of an elderly man who was there, Don Agustín Ruiz, and sat down. I was worn out, hoarse, woebegone and pensive in the midst of this scene of waste. The others were lying down, fatigued from trying to save the houses and their contents by throwing water from a nearby irrigation ditch upon the flames. Although we were surrounded by fire, we felt cold throughout the night.

At seven the next morning, when my mind was calmer and I was able to listen more attentively to the story of such an unforeseen and saddening mishap, I asked how it had come about. They told me that shortly after I had left for the forest the mayordomo of the estate, wanting to take advantage of the good weather to burn over a felled area to the north of the group of buildings, started a fire at the foot of a hill; the houses were located at the top of the hill. The wind from the north grew stronger than usual at about half past ten in the morning, the very hour when the artists set off. The fire spread with unbelievable speed throughout the dried brush, as if by gunpowder, and the flames, bypassing the chapel, suddenly reached the roof of our house, which was nearest to the felled area. It had only just been vacated by the artists.

The fire was noticed from the mayordomo's house by Don Agustín Ruiz, who sped to it with others and shouted out a warning to Pavón and Tafalla and to the servants and laborers who were at work within the house. Two laborers immediately climbed to the roof to put out the blaze, but just then the chapel caught fire, and the flames from this new conflagration spread with increased violence to the entire roof of our building.

With no further hope of controlling the fire, they began amidst general confusion to take out furnishings with no system or order, each in the other's way, so that some were able to enter only two or three times before the whole roof caved in on top of everything that we had gathered under it. Since much of our material was hanging on the walls or on raised wooden platforms that we had made to keep it dry, the men were thus handicapped in grabbing it quickly. Only Pavón was slightly burned on the calf when he came out through the burning doorway, just as the roof came down. Then a number of men came up to throw water on the house, but were so few that the water served merely to increase the fire.

The fire fighters were so tired out from this effort that they could not save the furniture from the main house, where the mayordomo lived. This house was the last to go up in flames, along with two huts that were used as kitchens.

Numerous people from neighboring estates came to our aid when they saw such a frightful sight, but arrived too late to help.

[The following statement is scratched out in the original text: Only the artists kept on their way, without being moved by compassion, although the owner of a neighboring estate from which they witnessed the conflagration insisted, as he later told us, that they go to the assistance of their companions.—J. Jaramillo-Arango]

The following morning at seven, various farmers of the entire district arrived, each with whatever food he could bring for our immediate needs. We thanked them and, much against their will, made them take pay for it. Dawn had hardly come when all of them together began to put out the fire of our house to retrieve the pieces of money that were scattered about in the rubble and embers.

The mayordomo, Don Mathías Trabuco, had fled from Macora when he knew that I was returning there. He feared that I, as the one who had suffered the greatest loss, would take measures against him. We did not see him again until he was made a prisoner in Huánuco; the unhappy creature spent 5 months in jail after his trial, for something he probably had done with no evil intent but merely with thoughtlessness and oversight. We put these, our feelings on the matter, in a petition that we presented, requesting a notarized statement of the truth of the mishap. The magistrate, Don Juan María de Gálvez, ordered that we be given such a statement, but his councilor judged the accident unjustly; he had interest in the buildings of the estate, the property of his mother-in-law. The councilor dallied with the case until we returned to Spain, when we paid off Trabuco with a few bushels of quinine bark and extract.

In this fire I lost all the clothing and equipment that I had taken from Huánuco for my own use; all the natural history specimens gathered in the forests of the region over a period of nearly 2 months; my diaries covering 3½ years; the botanical descriptions of 4 years, including those of some 600 plants studied in previous years and later corrected and brought to completion through the study of additional living material in Pozuzo and the gorge of Chinchao; my works of Linnaeus, Murray, Plumier, and Jacquin, as well as other books in botany and various other sciences; the presses and paper for drying plants and for writing; six saddles with reins, halters, saddle blankets, and other similar equipment; and two rifles, pistols, and sabers. We also lost the greater part of my companion Pavón's equipment and my assistant Tafalla's clothing, as well as that of the servants and laborers; all of our 2 months' food supply; and the zinc plates and some silver articles, all of which had melted down and were mixed together in the embers. A conservative estimate of the damage we suffered on that day—exclusive of our manuscripts and collections—would run to 4000 or 5000 pesos. I alone had to put out 2404 pesos fuertes to equip myself with the necessary articles again, having become like another Simonides, but I was most disconsolate because of the loss of my botanical manuscripts and diaries, which covered the period from my Chilean trip to the day of the fire.

We gathered together the remains left after the fire and packed them as best we could in two cases that Pavón had saved. Some plant specimens and seeds had been drying on the threshing floor at the time of the fire, and these we packed up in pieces of the canvas of our tents, which had not been completely burned. We then went on to a small, neglected building on the estate at Malqui, each carrying on his back as much as he could. We arrived weary and sore, although the trip was only half a league and all downhill.

We spent the night in utter discomfort in that hut at Malqui, for a furious thunder and lightning storm began. At ten that night it turned into a tremendous downpour that wet most of our battered baggage. Not even with all our digging of drainage ditches and little gutters around the hut, with stones and pieces of iron, could we stop the water from running in over the floor.

The rains kept up until noon the following day. Notwithstanding the tragic mishaps that had befallen us, we tried again to collect and dry specimens of plants growing near the hut. We pressed them between handfuls of half-burned paper that, before the fire, had been left strewn over the threshing floor to dry. I also began to describe these plants, writing with a pencil on rag paper.

When the storm had abated, we set out along the road to procure mules from the traveling merchants who come to these regions unloaded to take out coca. When we had succeeded in getting enough animals to carry the few effects left after the fire, and had made up the loads with pieces of canvas and the bark of chichillica, we left Malqui at eight in the morning on the 9th. We all traveled on foot until we found saddle mules, which were really pack mules that we contracted along the road from the merchants. Some of the farm folk provided us with saddles, but the servants and laborers who could mount the beasts with cargo harnesses went along, taking turns riding in this way. We stayed overnight in the village of Chinchao, where I described a few plants while Pavón and Tafalla changed papers on those that we had collected along the road.

We spent the night of the 10th in the inn at Pati. Along the way we collected various plants, and I described six of them. On the 11th we passed over the high and difficult ridge of Carpis happily and without rain, arriving for the night at the estate of Chulqui.

We got to Huánuco at noon on the 12th. The inhabitants all came to the doors of their houses to see the vestiges of the fire, as evidenced by the pieces of canvas in which our plants and seeds were packed.

We continued the work of drying the plants and seeds collected along the way until the 17th, and we described some of those that had arrived still fresh in bunches. On the 17th two companies of the regiments of Estremadura and Soria arrived in Huánuco. These were led by Don Diego de Herrera and Don Juan Vives, their captains, and were on their way to enter the region of the Mayro River and establish settlements there, and to establish navigation and communication with the Portuguese.

The magistrate of Tarma, Don Juan María de Gálvez, arrived in Huánuco on the 19th, accompanied by numerous personages from Pasco, the civic council, several priests, military authorities, and various others who had left Huánuco to go out and meet him at the settlement of Ambo, 5 leagues from the city. There they received him with a ringing of bells and a display of fireworks, and the militia was lined up in formation from the entrance of the city to the house in the principal plaza that was placed at his disposal. This top authority of the province of Tarma, and leader of the expedition to the Mayro, had hardly dismounted when he gave orders to the magistrate to invite the botanists along with the civic and ecclesiastic councils, the leaders of the religious orders, and the principal citizens of Huánuco to come together in a great meeting to discuss the penetration of the Mayro area.

Notwithstanding the great excitement that this arrival of dignitaries caused throughout the countryside, I described three plants and continued other tasks connected with my work.

On the 20th all of those invited met together in the magistrate's house. The councilor opened the meeting, setting forth the reasons for going into the Mayro area. After all had spoken, each in his turn, it was decided that such an undertaking could not be carried out until the following year, for the rainy season was about to begin and the path from Pozuzo to Mayro was not yet opened up. This path was indispensable for the passage of all food and supplies on the backs of porters, until such time as the path could be widened and made large enough for mule traffic.

When the meeting was over, the magistrate expressed his desire to see the city and the surrounding countryside. Various members of the planning committee went out with him. When he arrived at the place called Carrera del Campo, he explained how useful it would be in beautifying the city to make an avenue of trees of different species to serve as a public park for recreation and to provide shade and a pleasing environment. When he found that all were in agreement with this idea, he commissioned the subdelegate and two aldermen to put the plan into effect in the shortest time possible, in the company of the botanists. It was done in a fortnight: four streets with two small squares at the ends were planted with trees.

For the rest of the month, I described various plants of which my earlier descriptions were burned in Macora. We continued drying many other specimens from the mountains of Huánuco and the vicinity. In September I accomplished much, making collections and drawings of many of the plants destroyed at Macora; I later perfected the descriptions of these plants, little by little, with living material.

On the 11th of September I wrote to the Ministry of the Indies about the events that had taken place in Macora, communicating the news to the director, Don Casimiro Ortega, to the superintendent for Peru, Don Jorge Escobedo, and to the officer in charge of natural history and botany, the Reverend Father Francisco Gonzáles Laguna.

On the 16th Pavón and I presented a memorandum to the magistrate of Tarma, asking him for a certified statement of what had happened at Macora so that, at whatever future date, we might have it as an authenticated document. He ordered his councilor to do this when he had taken down the necessary evidence from all the witnesses who were then available. Perhaps purposely, the councilor neglected to carry out the remaining business until the magistrate was obliged to again order him to do it. However, because the mayordomo, Don Mathías Trabuco, did not present himself in court for fear of punishment, the affair was brought to a standstill for the time being, and the magistrate and his retinue went on to the province of Huamalíes.

On the 7th of October 1785, the Ministry of the Indies ordered me and my companion to again collect specimens of the trees lost on the *San Pedro de Alcántara* at 45° south latitude. From then until the 14th, I continued describing various plants and replied to the superintendent about the fire at Macora, sending him in the same post a package of seeds saved from the flames that he might forward it on to the Ministry of the Indies, to which I had written to tell about the ill fortune that had befallen the expedition.

I fell sick on the 15th and was abed until the 4th of November. I then got up, but not without some difficulty because of pain and weakness that, as previously, attacked my right side. It was not until the 14th of November that I began anew to describe plants and to copy off the descriptions made after the fire. I continued this work until the 17th of December, when I fell ill again with the same sickness. On the first day of 1786 I got up, suffering from the same pain in my side and without any appetite. It was not until the 23rd when, thanks to lemonades and four bleedings, I regained my health and got rid of the fever and dry cough that had kept me in low spirits until the 22nd of February. I then began to eat fruits, greens, and fresh fish, and became completely well on this diet.

The rest of the month of February, and all during March, I repeated a large number of descriptions; I also corrected not a few descriptions of plants collected along the coastal regions that occur in Huánuco as well, especially members of the Malvaceae. It seemed to me that the genera *Palauva* (*Palaua*), *Dombeja* (*Dombeya*), *Pavonia*, and *Ruizia*, which the abbot Don Antonio José Cavanilles had published with others as new, were really not new genera but represented species of *Malope*, *Pentapetes*, *Urena*, and *Malva*.

Weakened by repeated attacks of sickness, and believing that the tasks of the expedition were too hard for me and were daily becoming more demanding, I wrote on the 11th of March 1786 to His Excellency, Minister for the Indies. I requested my return to Spain and informed him that I lacked the strength necessary to continue on as I had done in the past.

On the 13th of March, Tafalla and the artist Gálvez went to the royal treasury at Pasco to claim the salaries for all of us. Tafalla returned with his salary on the 25th, bringing also that of his companion Pulgar, but Gálvez stayed on for several days awaiting the arrival of money at the treasury so he could receive the pay for the rest of us.

On the 9th of April I received a letter from Gálvez informing me that one of his mules, with 4000 duros (coins), had fallen over a cliff along the Huariaca River and that I should come without delay to see if something could be done to salvage the money bags, for the river was extremely swollen. I left early in the morning on the 10th with Pulgar and my servant. That day I arrived at Ollerías, where Pulgar and I spent the night fully clothed because the servant had not been able to arrive with the beds. Untold numbers of guinea pigs, and the lice that these little animals breed, kept us awake all night long.

When we entered Huariaca on the 11th, I was told that Gálvez with all of the Indians of a nearby settlement had succeeded in salvaging the money from the waters, and that he had gone to Rondos the previous afternoon by way of a road other than ours. Without tarrying in Huariaca, we turned our steps back towards Huánuco, where we arrived at half past eleven that night. We were tired and sore, having journeyed 20 leagues that day and from ten in the morning the day before, over rough terrain. In spite of the hard trip, I took six plants to Huánuco and described them on the following day, after having sent off my post with a package of seeds for the Ministry of the Indies.

On the 10th of May we sent 28 bundles of living plants to Lima with Don Juan Tafalla, and on the 27th we sent a similar shipment of different and beautiful seedling trees with Pulgar. With all of this we not only replaced the losses that we had suffered when the *San Pedro de Alcántara* went down, but even greatly increased the lot with 40 specimens of quinine trees, a variety of laupes (species of *Godoya*), weinmannias, laurels, árbol del sebo (tallow tree), incenses, yasmich, tulpay, santo palo, coca, turucasa or *Porlieria*, quinoquinos, *Bombax*, and many other plants peculiar to the forests of Panatahuas and the valley of Huánuco.

On the 12th of May I presented to the general superintendent our urgent need for additional help to continue exploring the jungle areas, and I sent him an accurate accounting of the extraordinary expenses we had incurred for laborers on these trips and for transporting the effects of the expedition.

On the 7th of June I received an order from the Ministry of the Indies for the assistants to stop work as soon as we received notification that we were to return to Spain. By virtue of this information, I made known my wish that the royal order be kept, but at the same time I had to point out to His Majesty the diligence and progress shown by the assistants and the importance of the continuation of their commission after our return to Spain, that they might answer and solve doubts and queries that might arise from Madrid, as well as amplify the work with new discoveries that they might make. I manifested the same feelings to the superintendent for Peru and to the faculty director, Don Casimiro Ortega.

I described and dried various new plants. I corrected and made new copies of numerous descriptions.

On the 9th of July the assistants returned from Lima, having left 56 bundles of living plants in the hands of the Reverend Father Francisco González Laguna, and brought with them the help needed for penetrating the jungles. They had had the good fortune of arriving in Lima with nearly all the plants from Huánuco still alive; only an occasional one had died from the mistreatment of the rough trip and the cold of the highland moors.

Shipwreck of the *San Pedro de Alcántara*

We learned on the 19th of July that the *San Pedro de Alcántara* had foundered off the coast of Portugal and that only some 300 passengers had been saved. On the 30th we heard that the wealth of silver and gold and a few random chests had been taken off the ship; at that time we had hopes that our 53 boxes of dried plants, drawings, metals, and specimens of other natural products might be figured in among the cargo that had been saved.

Subsequent to the fire at Macora, until the end of July 1786, I described the following plants. Most had been described before the fire, in Macora and in Huánuco.

Amomum racemosum, achyra de monte (wild achira). The seeds of this plant, 3 bushels of which were burned in Macora, are even more aromatic than those of cardamom; if they are kept between papers, these seeds give off so much oil that the paper is completely spotted. They are no less oily or useful for medicinal purposes than the seeds of *Amomum thyrsoideum*, which is plentiful in Cuchero and in the forests of Macora and even in the greater part of the gorge of Chinchao.

Costus argentum; *C. scaber*, called purum piña or falsa piña (false pineapple). *Canna paniculata*, achyra de montaña (jungle achira); natives eat the roots cooked, like those of *Canna indica*, the common achira. *Acosta aculeata*, called caimito de monte (wild caimito) for the similarity of the fruits to those of *Achras caimito*.

Boerhavia viscosa, pegajosa (sticky plant). *Boerhavia scandens*, called yerba de la purgación (laxative herb) because of its use and properties against gonorrhea, in an infusion or decoction.

Dianthera hirsuta. *Justicia mucronata*. *Peperomia concava*, *P. filiformis*, *P. foliiflora*, *P. purpurea*, *P. tetragona*, and *P. trinervis*.

Piper carpunya, carpunya. This is a bush 4 or 5 yards tall. The aromatic leaves become more fragrant when very dry, and natives of delicate taste have the habit of drinking 1 or 2 cups of an infusion of the leaves as an aid to digestion. The infusion is made by dropping the leaves into boiling water, and it is drunk as hot as possible. They prefer it to real tea. *Piper dichotomum*; the leaves of this species can be used as a substitute for those of carpunya, for they are almost equally fragrant and tasty.

Hippocratea viridis. Anthodon decussatum. Calyxhymenia viscosa. Dorstenia tubicina; the roots of this plant are as fragrant as those of *D. contrajerva*, and we might suspect that they have similar properties.

Krameria triandra, called ratanhia, pumacuchu, or mapato. This shrub grows abundantly in the provinces of Huánuco, Tarma, Canta, and Huarocherí. Its root has such outstanding styptic properties that it will staunch any flow of blood. The dose is an infusion or decoction of half an ounce of dry root, or a dram of its water extract diluted with 2 or 3 ounces of ordinary water. This root is good for cleansing and strengthening the teeth, and it was already used for this purpose in Peru when I discovered its great efficiency as a styptic. Its efficiency surpasses that of all other herbs currently employed to staunch the flow of blood, and it lacks the evil aftereffects that other astringents bring on. Experiments with more than a thousand persons who have taken the extract under the care of the best physicians bear out this statement. See my "Memoria sobre la Ratanhia," published in the first volume of the *Memorias de la Academia Medica de Madrid* in 1797, wherein all of our present knowledge concerning this medicinal agent is set forth.

Galium lappaceum. Buddleja diffusa, quisoar. *Callicarpa globifera. Ohigginsia aggregata. Cissus lobata. Spermacoce gracilis. Chiococca ovata.*

Ceanothus? aculeatus; this shrub is 5 yards tall and has abundant seeds with a fragrant oil, similar to that of oranges. *Ceanothus granulosus*; this is a very leafy shrub, 5 to 7 yards tall.

Lisianthus acutangulus, L. oblongus, and *L. ovalis. Lisianthus perianthogonus*; this fruit-bearing plant is very beautiful for gardens because of the large size of its pink flowers.

Mirabilis jalapa, called trompetillas (little trumpets) or flor de Panamá (Panama flower). The roots, in a decoction, have mild laxative properties. It is plentiful in all the valleys and gardens throughout Peru.

Ipomoea glandulifera, called auroras (dawn) in reference to the habit of its flowers opening in the morning, remaining open until eleven or twelve o'clock the same morning, and then wilting down and shedding pollen after the sun has beaten down upon the flowers for some 2 or 3 hours. The flowers of all species of *Ipomoea* and *Convolvulus* that I have encountered are ephemerous. The stems ooze a large quantity of latex when cut.

Coffee

Coffea tetrandra. Coffea subsessilis. Coffea occidentalis, café (coffee); this vernacular name was introduced by the Spaniards among the natives who did not know it, and later the local inhabitants began to cultivate it. This plant bears an abundance of one-seeded fruits, though many have two seeds. The mature seed is as large as that of the best oriental coffee.

Hirtella racemosa.

Rhus atrum. This is a small tree, 6 to 8 yards tall. The sap in its bark and stems yields an ink as lustrous and black as printer's ink. It is weak in color when freshly written but becomes blacker as it dries, acquiring a brilliance like that of patent leather.

Tobacco

Nicotiana tabacum, tabaco verdadero (genuine tobacco). Although the tobacco plant is cultivated with rich harvests in various parts of Peru, it grows wild in all the valleys and warm forests. The cultivated leaf is made up into long cigars or bundles and is called tabaco de andullo (twisted tobacco).

Physalis pubescens, capuli. Children and women eat the bittersweet fruits with no harmful effect. The ladies mix them in with their floral bouquets, spraying them with perfume to give them more fragrance than nature meant them to have. They then place them in the hair among the other florets with which these stylish people adorn themselves.

Solanum pubescens. *Solanum incanum*, called yuruhuacta (white sword) for the white color of the underside of the leaves. Natives apply the leaves with the upper side down to bring ulcers or sores to a head, and then apply them with the underside down to heal the sores. *Solanum lycioides*; this species is more abundant in Huánuco than in Tarma.

Convolvulus quinquefolius. *Cestrum longiflorum* and *C. racemosum*.

Alzatea verticillata. The trunk of this tall, leafy tree, which I studied above Mesapata, is divided into six equally stout parts that form a kind of garden arbor at the base and then join together into a single trunk about 10 feet from the ground. Farther up, the trunk splits again into five stout and leafy branches, with the central one erect, the four outer ones open, and all of them subdivided into whorled branchlets, also erect.

Macrocnemum pubescens and *M. venosum*. *Psychotria acuminata*, *P. angustifolia*, *P. coronata*, *P. glandulosa*, *P. tinctoria*, *P. umbellata*, and *P. viridis*. *Staphylea serrata*. *Achyranthes secundum*. *Cynanchum lanceolatum* and *C. lanuginosum*. *Stapelia? volubilis*. *Echites acuminata*. *Pourretia paniculata* and *P. lanuginosa*. *Loranthus retroflexus* and *L. triflorus*. *Heliconia discolor*. *Ornithogalum rubrum*. *Tovaria pendula*.

Plant Hygrometer

Porlieria hygrometra, turucasa. In Chile, this species is called guayacan, and its wood is used in that country to make billiard balls, cups, spoons, hammer handles, and other tools; it is preferred over other woods for its strength and resistance. In Huánuco these bushes are used to make fences, and the wood is also employed as a material for ax handles and other tools.

The leaves of the turucasa open during the day and fold up as in sleep at night, so tightly that one might judge the bush to be leafless. The leaves begin to unfold half an hour and some minutes before sunrise, and they are fully opened a little more than an hour after the sun has come out. They begin to fold up 30 to 40 minutes before sunset, and are completely "asleep" a little more than an hour after the sun has gone down.

If it is going to rain the following day or if the weather is going to be overcast, the leaves of turucasa always foretell it the evening before, for they delay their contraction by half an hour or so; the length of the delay depends upon either the amount of humidity that will be in the air the next day or the time that the rain will start. I believe that atmospheric moisture makes the leaflets more lax, and that for this reason they delay longer in contracting under moist conditions than when the weather is dry and, because they are more rigid, fold up more quickly.

I do not doubt that we might observe this same phenomenon in many plants with compound or pinnate leaves, such as species of *Mimosa*, *Cassia*, *Poinciana*, *Caesalpinia*, *Bauhinia*, and other members of the Leguminosae. But we must still make exact observations to fix the hours of the activity of the leaflets and to correlate it with the weather. This I did with 24 pots of different seedling trees on the trip from the port of Callao to the bay of Cádiz, making daily and exact observations from the 16th of June 1788 to the 12th of September. On that last date I landed happily with the plants, having brought them successfully from Lima to the port of Santa María. Of the 87 living plants that I took out of Peru, 77 arrived in good condition after 5 months and 12 days of ocean voyage around Cape Horn. On the 16th of November I delivered them to the Royal Botanic Garden in Madrid, and 68 were still alive in spite of the severity of the weather that overtook me that year while traveling from Sierra Morena to Madrid.

Oenothera lyrata. *Guarea acuminata*. *Rhexia grandiflora*. *Semarillaria acutangula*, *S. obovata*, and *S. subrotunda*, all called monte lucumas; Indians eat the fleshy, white, sweet arils that half-envelop the seeds.

Laurus alba, *L. caerulea*, *L. crassifolia*, *L. foetida*, *L. obovata*, and *L. pubescens*. All of these species are small trees, more or less leafy; they have only slightly aromatic bark, but their wood is of economic value.

Spondias mombin, ciruelas agrias (sour plums). This is a small tree about 5 or 6 yards tall, leafy and bearing red fruit as large as medium-sized olives and of a bittersweet, rather agreeable taste.

Malpighia nitida, called ciruela del país (native plum) or ciruela de fraile (friar's plum); this tree is cultivated in Peru, as is *Spondias mombin*. When the fruits have reached a suitable stage of ripening, they are gathered and packed in bran or in leaves so that the heat and slight fermentation engendered will complete the ripening process and soften the sweet, cloying, red flesh. The seeds, also sweet and rather like fresh almonds in flavor, have purgative properties and bring on nausea.

Cassia viminea. *Trichilia acuminata* and *T. trifoliata*. *Vaccinium* aff. *bicolor*. *Melastoma acuminata*, *M. caerulea*, *M. carinata*, *M. nitida*, *M. sericea*, and *M. serrulata*. *Banisteria rugosa*. *Chaetocrater pubescens* and *C. serrata*. *Murraya racemosa*.

Bocconia frutescens, called palo amarillo (yellow wood) in reference to the color of the sap, which can be employed to dye cottons, woolens, or coarse hempen cloth.

Miconia pulverulenta. Talinum dichotomum. Triumfetta fructicosa. Valdesia repens and *V. ovalis. Acunna oblonga*, rosa-rosa. *Portulaca pentandra* and *P. cristallina.*

Euphorbia peplus? In Peru, most species of *Euphorbia* are known by the vernacular name of yerba de la golondrina (swallow's herb). The latex is used to cure cataracts of the eyes.

Psidium pyriferum, called sahuintu or huayabo (guayabo, guava); this leafy tree is 8 to 12 yards tall. Its trunk looks as though it has no bark, for it is smooth and a dark, tawny brown. The leaves and fruits have a certain fragrance, somewhat like that of arrayán (myrtle); also like myrtle, they possess styptic properties, so some people chew the leaves to comfort and strengthen the teeth. Many people find the flavor of the fruits pleasant. The fruits are made into a very good sweet, like pear preserve; when made from underripe fruit, the preserve is used as a therapeutic agent to control excessive menstruation and pregnancy. Even when well-ripened fruits are used, the effects are the same, albeit less efficacious.

The shape, color, and size of the fruits of this guava vary so much that one can find more than 10 varieties in Huánuco. These all have special names: verde sahuintu, puca sahuintu, ccarha sahuintu, yurac sahuintu, etc., meaning green guava, red, yellow, white, etc. Guavas are so abundant in the valley of Huánuco that the natives of that region are called huayaberos, a word that also signifies tricksters or fibbers. To say "What a monstrous fib!" in Peru, they say "Que huayaba tan gorda!" (What a fat guava!).

Campomanesia palillos, palillo; this tree, like the previous one, is cultivated in Peru. There the fragrant fruit, known as palillo, is eaten and is also put into floral bouquets because of its sweet scent. The leaves have a pleasant smell, and the wood is good for many uses, as is that of guava trees.

Rubus fruticosus?, siraca; the fruit of this shrub has a pleasant taste, and is somewhat larger than that of the zarzamora (common name for *R. fruticosus*).

Myrtus pseudopimenta. The berries of this little tree have an aroma rather like that of Tabasco or malagueta peppers. *Prunus nigra*, a tree 10 to 15 yards tall.

Marcgravia calyptrata, called purumhigos—that is, higos falsos (false figs)—or higos de monte (wild figs). When the fruits of this climbing shrub are very ripe and opened, they provide a favorite food of the Indians, in spite of the insipid flavor. They are very similar to opened figs with red pulp.

Lettsomia tomentosa and *L. lanata*; these species are low shrubs, 3 to 4 yards tall and extremely showy.

Annona reticulata, chirimoyo (cherimoya). In all the valleys and warmer regions of Peru, the natives cultivate this beautiful, leafy tree, which attains a height of 12 to 14 yards at the most. The branches extend horizontally in a partly pendent position, making a splendid crown that provides pleasant shade because of its density and the exquisite fragrance of its flowers. These flowers are green but whitish toward the base, with a brown spot at the base of each petal.

In Huánuco, some of the chirimoyas (cherimoyas), as the fruits of this tree are called, grow to a weight of 10 or 12 pounds, although the usual size is from 2 to 6 pounds. I have never seen larger cherimoyas elsewhere in Peru, for they normally weigh ½ to 1½ pounds, and generally less. The cherimoya is more or less conical in shape, or sometimes nearly round. The rind is also variable, sometimes smooth and sometimes rough, with small, latticelike squares. These markings are hardly noticeable in many fruits, and those fruits with the squares definitely marked are called chirimoyas reales (genuine cherimoyas). When there are raised points, more or less blunt, in addition to these squares, the fruits are called chirimoyas de cabeza de negrito (cherimoyas of the head of a little negro). If the fruits have been plucked in a good stage of ripening, the pulp of the cherimoya is white, juicy, sweet, and very tender, but even when ripe they cannot be eaten unless a kind of fermentation is allowed to set in. This is brought about more rapidly by packing the fruit in straw or leaves or by covering it with cloth or bran or similar material.

Members of the fair sex like to mix the flowers of the cherimoya in floral bouquets to lend their delightful fragrance. The trunks of these trees are the source of beams and excellent boards for a variety of uses. The fruits hang down when small, and the stalk grows along with the fruit; thus, when woody and strong, the stalk can support a weight of more than 12 pounds. The first cherimoya set before us at a meal in Huánuco weighed 14 pounds, but after that we never saw one over 12. Usually, the larger the fruit the fewer the seeds it bears. As a food, the cherimoya is delicious and, if used in moderation, is very healthy.

Annona lutea, anona amarilla (yellow anona, yellow custard apple). This name refers to the yellow color of the fruit when it ripens on the tree itself. Neither the cherimoyas nor the guanabanas, different species of the same genus, ripen yellow upon the tree, and when ripened by fermentation they keep their green color. The pulp of the anona amarilla seems to me even more delicious than that of the ordinary anona, and it is edible as soon as the ripe fruit is plucked from the tree. This tree grows to a height of more than 20 yards and is beautifully leafy. The trunk is proportionately stout. The fruits that I have seen hardly ever weigh more than a pound, and are covered with large scales; they are round, but narrowed near the apex. These splendid trees grow in forested areas, and an occasional one can be found in the coca plantations.

Annona microcarpa is a leafy little tree, 10 to 12 yards tall. The fruits are small; in the forests where I saw this species growing, they weighed 2 ounces at the most.

Mollinedia lanceolata, *M. repanda*, and *M. serrata*; these species are low shrubs with sparse foliage.

Porcelia dependens, called plátanos de monte (wild bananas) for the shape of the fruit, rather like that of a banana. It is a tall, leafy tree with one straight, stout trunk that supplies good wood for various uses in carpentry. The fruits, borne in bunches of as many as nine for each flower, are as long as the distance between an extended index finger and thumb, are cylindrical, and have protuberances. Between the seeds there is a sweet, yellow pulp that is pleasant to the taste; it is edible after the fruits have been fermented by being packed in cloth or other warm material.

Gualteria dependens and *G. hirsuta*, both small shrubs. *Pineda incana*, lloqui, a bush 4 to 5 yards tall; from its stems are made very strong canes and walking sticks.

Mendozia racemosa and *M. aspera*, both climbing plants. *Gesneria frutescens. Cleome coccinea* and *C. concava*.

A species of *Nepeta* known as muña or ccoa. Natives employ a saltwater decoction of this plant to treat liver complaints, headache, or the swellings of dropsy or gout. A warm infusion is taken for an aperitif and diuretic, to treat severe cholera or melancholy, to cleanse the spleen, or to reduce obstructions. *Nepeta ciliata* and *N. calyciclausa*; both species are called hupaimuña.

Bombax polyandrum, or *Carolinea*?, inich'. This extremely leafy tree rises to a height of more than 40 yards; it has a stout trunk, with pulpy wood. The capsules are as large as small melons and contain, together with the seeds, a soft cotton as white as snow. This cotton is an excellent material for stuffing mattresses, pillows, sofas, chairs, cushions, and similar furnishings. The fiber can be spun into thread when mixed with wool from vicuñas, huanacos, or other animals, but it is hard to spin alone. When compressed, it can be fluffed up again by merely putting it out to sun, and because of this property it is called algodón del sol (sun cotton). When the capsules are ripe and begin to split open, the cotton surrounding the seeds begins to come out, increasing in volume so much that each fruit forms an extraordinarily white, bulky ball as soon as the sun has beat down upon it in full force.

Urena villosa and *U. hamata*, both called lausahacha. Womenfolk are accustomed to wash their hair with the mucilaginous material extracted with cold water from these two plants. It is used to lessen dandruff, to cleanse the hair of excess oil, and to stimulate growth.

Erythrina articulata, huillcatauri. *Negretia mitis*, llamapañaui. *Crotalaria trigona. Trifolium hirsutum. Hedysarum pilosum* and *H. virgatum. Indigofera anil*, añil; añil, or indigo, used for making ink and paint, is extracted from this plant.

Palauvia lanceolata. Achillea urens. Achillea lutea, botoncillo (little button); this plant is poisonous to guinea pigs. *Elephantopus tuberosus* and *E. capitatus*.

Vermifuga corymbosa, called matagusanos (worm killer), contrayerba, or chinapaya. If pounded up with salt, this plant is more efficacious in killing maggots in animals than when applied alone.

Pectis trifida, called asccapichana, escoba cimarrona (wild broom), or canchalagua cimarrona. This herb is an excellent febrifuge and a tonic for the stomach; it is extremely bitter.

Eupatorium canescens and *E. sambucinum. Tagetes chinchi. Tagetes anisiodora*, anís-anís; this is the smallest species of the genus, but has the best fragrance.

Coreopsis trifida. Cacalia punctata. Orchis punctata. Epidendrum cordatum and *E. ferrugineum. Maxillaria ramosa. Rodriguezia lanceolata* and *R. ensiformis. Limodorum croceum* and *L. lineare. Satyrium virescens. Humboldtia acutifolia* and *H. polystachia. Calla caniculata. Pothos perforata*.

Arum aliaceum, named for the extremely penetrating odor of garlic that is effused when the plant is stepped upon or wounded. It is a caustic plant.

Sobralia amplexicaulis; its beautiful, large, purplish red flowers are highly fragrant.

Croton ciliatum, called huanarpo macho (male huanarpo) or higos del duende (figs of the ghosts). The natives assert that an infusion of the root of this milky plant is a strong aphrodisiac. They also say that an infusion of the huanarpo hembra (female huanarpo) is its antidote. There is no difference between these two plants except that the former has red flowers, whereas those of the latter are white.

Phyllanthus gemina, a bush 3 to 5 yards tall.

Cucurbita fragrans, called upe or shupe. Natives eat the fruits, or calabazas (calabashes, gourds), of this climbing plant in a stew called locro. They also adorn their homes and churches with it, for it gives off a sweet fragrance for months on end without any noticeable weakening of the perfume throughout the year. They replace them with fresh calabashes every year. The fruits are cylindrical, more than a foot long, and of a ruddy hue on the outside.

Cucumis purpureus and *C. quinquelobatus. Begonia ciliata. Synziganthera purpurea*, a slender shrub about 5 or 6 yards tall.

Urtica diaphana. Urtica globifolia, piñipiñi; this prostrate herb has entirely glossy leaves, like grains of millet, that are more or less fleshy and thick. It is the only plant I have seen with glossy leaves.

Cynomorium placentoeforme, hatun puñuchrin. This plant has the form of a reddish fungal cake upon which there are many large red catkins, or webs, like cloves the size of a hen's egg. Indians eat them to restore energy spent on long walks and hard physical labor. A cold infusion of the plant is drunk for the same purpose.

Ephedra distachya?, called suelda consuelda in reference to the properties of the plant as a boneset; it is applied as a poultice. *Zannichellia palustris. Elaterium glandulosum.*

Carica monoica, col de montaña (cabbage of the forest). Though the fruits of this species, because of their tastelessness, are not eaten as are those of the other species, Indians do cook the leaves in place of cabbage. The natives of Pampahermosa carry seeds of *Carica monoica* to the gorge of Chinchao, where it is grown in abundance.

Myristica longifolia and *M. oblongifolia*; both species are known as árbol del sebo (tallow tree). The Indians extract from the seeds a thick oil, like cacao fat, for use in lighting. The extraction is simple: the seeds are crushed and pressed between two stones. The seeds of the first species are the size of a nutmeg; those of the second are the size of a hen's egg. They are odorless and tasteless, except for the softness and fatty sensation caused in the mouth by the oily substance. This oil could be used in the manufacture of wonderful candles.

Tafalla triflora, aitacupi. The resin of this plant is called almaciga (mastic) on account of its resemblance to mastic in color, shape, aroma, and consistency. It is collected in some regions and used in comfort plasters. The whole treelet, usually some 6 yards in height, gives off a pleasing fragrance, and the resin oozes out spontaneously in white tears.

Smilax lanceolata; its long, fibrous roots are used for the same purposes as those of zarzaparilla (sarsaparilla).

Coussapoa obovata and *C. triloba*; both species are tall trees with a stout trunk and a wonderfully thick crown of leaves.

Cecropia aspera, *C. coriacea*, and *C. digitata*. These trees, known as tacunas, grow to a height of 30 to 40 yards. The trunks are straight and articulated, with the upper sections or joints hollow. In these hollow parts there is often clear and potable water, which has no disagreeable taste. Some trunks are hollow nearly to the ground, and almost all of the joints contain water. They are splendid trees, and their huge leaves follow the sun on its daily round and at night bend their upper surface down towards the ground until, at dawn, they rise up and direct their faces towards the sun. The leaves are divided into 9, 11, or 13 radial sections and can be used as parasols.

Schinus aculeatus, huillca. This is a tall, leafy tree with a corpulent trunk completely beset with basally swollen spines that look like little nipples, with the point of the spine in the center of the swelling.

Schinus molle, molle. It is said that among the Incas, at the time of Inca rule, this tree was called árbol de la vida (tree of life) because of its properties and uses. One treatment for dropsy or gout consists of a bath of a salty infusion of the leaves and bark of the molle. Indians prepare from the fruit a fermented drink that is sweet and pleasant to their taste. The fruit is also used in treating dropsy. The ripe fruits are merely rubbed in water to free the sugary part, and the resulting liquor is allowed to ferment.

In Peru, even the most educated people are convinced that the fruit of the molle is the source of the true pepper of the East, and that it does not have the commercial value of oriental pepper merely because they do not know how to process it. There are some people who, because of its taste and its similarity in size and aroma to the real pepper, mix molle seeds with the eastern spice. This irresponsibility, carrying considerable hazard to health, ought to be punished severely, especially if it is continued after a warning has been given against this harmful adulteration. Terrible hemorrhoids, as well as that illness known as vicho or mal del valle, are brought on by the practice of eating molle seeds.

The white, fragrant resin from molle is an excellent boneset if applied in the form of a plaster, and it can be used to heal and close up ulcers. The ashes of the resin contain a special fixed alkali that is used for refining sugar, making dyes, and washing clothes. The wood is strong and it lasts a long while as a fuel, but the smoke from it causes headaches. Beautiful boards, beams, and wood for a variety of uses are hewn from the trunks. There are trees that reach a height of 20 to 25 yards, with large crowns.

Olmedia aspera; this tree yields a white latex when incisions are made in the trunk. The latex coagulates into a reddish resin that is very elastic.

Tafalla laciniata. *Clavija lanceolata*.

Mimosa planisiliqua, huillca; this tree, 10 to 15 yards tall, has good wood. *Mimosa farnesiana*, called aromo for the particular fragrance of the flowers, which are used by womenfolk to adorn the hair and are one of the elements in puchero, a mixture of fragrant flowers that Peruvians prepare. When chewed and spit out in any room, the seeds give off an unbearable stink like that of human excrement, but no such odor can be noticed when the seeds are not chewed. Every garden in Lima and other towns in the warmer areas has a tree of aromo.

Gimbernatia obovata, chunchu. This tree is tall and leafy; it has a stout trunk of very hard wood, which is extremely valuable for a number of uses.

Aralia or *Panax* aff. *ferruginea*; a treelet 8 to 10 yards tall. *Populus glandulosa*; this leafy tree has a stout trunk that is useful in many ways.

Izquierda aggregata. *Ficus acuminata*, *F. cordata*, and *F. lineata*. *Carludovica latifolia* and *C. angustifolia*. *Martinezia lanceolata*.

Vegetable Ivory

Pullipuntu macrocarpon and *P. microcarpon*, both known as pullipuntu. These two frondose palms have the inflorescence at the base of the trunk. The fruits are borne in clusters and are joined together in large bunches or heads covered with rounded projections in the shape of obovate, five-angled masses. When young, these fruits are filled with a crystalline liquid, like water, that is often used by travelers throughout these forests when drinking water is lacking. After a few days this water turns milky and acid, and later it coagulates into a sweet, tasty beverage that gradually becomes solid and hard. It is finally converted into a kind of ivory and is called marfil vegetal (vegetable ivory). Like ivory of animal origin, it keeps its white color excellently, even after being worked and exposed for many days to the air. Many little figures or trinkets can be shaped from these fruits, more easily than from real ivory, for the vegetable ivory does not split as does that of the teeth, tusks, or bones of marine and land animals.

CHAPTER 50

Trip to the Forests of Muña

On the 2nd of August 1785, we botanists left for the village of Muña. By nightfall we arrived at Taullan, near the village of Valle. On the 3rd we went on to Tambillo, with nothing worthy of note except the great heat of the ravine. We passed the village of Panao on the 4th and spent the night at Huamanmayo.

On the 5th we got beyond the village of Chaclla and stayed overnight in Piñapata, where we suffered from the severe cold of the hoarfrost that is frequent all through the year in that region. We collected a few new plants there.

On the 6th we slept at the top of the peak of Santo Domingo. The ascent of this peak is accomplished over a steep and dangerous path consisting of 39 winding flights of steps, in addition to the climb from the river to the beginning of the steps. We entered Muña in good form on the 7th, having gathered on the way a large number of plants; we set them out to dry.

From the 8th to the 12th, we busied ourselves in building a large hut of wood and branches to accommodate our equipment and our beds, for the hut that the missionary priest and magistrate of Muña had set aside for us was extremely small. In addition, we set up our field tents as a place where we might work more comfortably and with better light, and as a storage place at night for the presses and plant specimens with which we were working. Last, I corrected various descriptions made on the trip to Pozuzo that were burned in the fire at Macora.

On the 13th of August we began our trips through the thick jungle of the region. By walking long distances, and by working hard in the forests, we found a large number of new plants.

On the 15th the artists arrived in Muña and, living in the priest's house, they began their work on the 16th.

Confirmation of the News of the Loss of the *San Pedro de Alcántara* off the Coast of Portugal

The letters that the artists brought in for me from Huánuco informed me from Lima that the report of the loss of the *San Pedro de Alcántara*, which hit the Roca de Papona (Papona Rock) off Portugal, was true. There was some doubt, however, as to whether the 53 chests of specimens and drawings had been saved along with the boxes of silver and gold that had been sent from Callao in the same consignment with our material.

We stayed in Muña until the 24th of September, when we returned to Huánuco because the rains had started and it was impossible to work comfortably or profitably.

CHAPTER 51

Description of the Village of Muña

Muña is located at 10° south latitude, nearly opposite Huánuco, to the east of the city and 24 leagues away. It is situated on a tableland formed by a mountain that is 5 leagues of continual ascent from the river to its summit. One and a half leagues from the river, Muña is situated in a protected spot that is safe from the south, east, and west winds. Only the north wind blows over the village; as a result, the excessive heat of the sun is tempered by winds from the north that commence at eleven in the morning and continue cooling into the night.

Near Muña, at a place called Rinconada, the natives plant seeds and roots for their food. This place is fertile and is suitable for growing all kinds of seeds and fruits, although the local inhabitants are content with maize, beans, potatoes, sweet potatoes, squashes, arracachas, achiras, and a few poorly cultivated green vegetables.

Although good pastures are to be found between Muña and the river, the natives keep no animals beyond a few mules or small horses for traffic to Pozuzo and Huánuco. Most of the Indians spend their time gathering quinine bark, which abounds in the forests. Besides the cascarilla, or quina, they collect the types known as quina amarilla (yellow quinine tree) and quina de la hoja morada (purple-leaved quinine tree). They also harvest small amounts of incense, which they take to Huánuco to sell to the churches.

There are two small brooks of very good water in Muña, which come down from the mountain through two gorges. The wild animals and birds are the same as those found in other forested areas. Red-headed buzzards are common.

Near Muña, on the slopes of a mountain at Rinconada, there is an abundance of a kind of black slate. It occurs in long, rectangular slabs, more or less like perfect bars. I collected one specimen, which I have kept, that is about 3 handspans long. Of its four flat surfaces, two opposite faces are polished and one of the remaining two is more highly polished than the other, but all four surfaces are sufficiently smooth to use with oil as a whetstone for any sharp-edged instrument. The ends are cut diagonally. The surfaces of some of these slates are very dark gray. I saw so many in this locality that, a little way off, they looked like the trunks of burned trees piled up there.

There are no more than 40 inhabitants in Muña, and all are Indians except for the occasional mestizo; they are governed and helped by a missionary priest of Ocopa who lives among them. One never sees disorder or fighting, which is commonplace in other villages where there is no one to control their drinking feasts. The Indians of Muña are very obedient to the orders of the priest, whether given by him or through the mayor. All go to church both morning and night to sing praises and prayers to God and to the Virgin before leaving for work or before lying down to sleep. On work days the priest holds mass very early so that all who wish may hear it, but on festival days not one Indian misses the service, unless he be sick, for the mayor and priest stand watch at the door of the church to see who is absent.

In the church, the women occupy the center and the men the two sides. The elder men sit farthest from the center so that irreverence among the youngsters, sitting nearer the middle, can be noticed and punished; this leads to greater respect and reverence on their part. Before mass the people pray and sing Christian teachings, and after the service they give thanks, singing praises in their own tongue. Every night, they say the rosary before singing praises and thanksgiving to the Holy Trinity and the Most Holy Virgin.

On work days, only the mayor wears a cloak, but on holidays all married men come to church dressed that way; the single men come in ordinary dress. The men dress in a waistcoat, breeches, jacket, and shirt; the women wear a short skirt, bodice, and shirt. The clothes are wholly simple and ordinary. The Indians mostly go barefoot, but on rare occasions will wear sucuyes, a kind of slipper. The womenfolk wear a shawl of red flannel to church.

Although these Indians have no source of wealth, they have all they need for food and clothing. Each inhabitant has his own little house or hut and the land he needs for cultivation, and the people do not place too high a value on temporal goods.

While we stayed in Muña, I corrected many of the descriptions previously written in other localities where we had worked. I also described the following plants, most of which were also drawn.

Justicia racemosa. Salvia incurva and *S. galeata. Calceolaria heterophylla. Peperomia acuminata.*

Valeriana decussata. Valeriana paniculata, macae; the root of this plant can be used medicinally in place of *Valeriana officinalis*, for it has the same taste and almost the same fragrance, or odor. It is very abundant in Muña.

Spermacoce corymbosa. Buddleja spicata. Callicarpa cordifolia. Ohigginsia obovata and *O. verticillata.*

Embothrium emarginatum, known as catas, picahuai, or machinparrani; this is a low tree, 3 to 4 yards tall, with red flowers. Clusters of its flowers are used by Indian women to dress altars and images, and in various parts of Peru they use the branches to make arches for processions. A powder made from the leaves is applied to ulcers to dry them up and start the growth of new flesh. *Embothrium pinnatum*, called pacopaco; this is a taller, more leafy tree, with bark of a very disagreeable odor. *Embothrium monospermum*, pacopaco de la sierra; this is another small tree, 3 to 4 yards tall.

Cascarillo Bobo Amarillo

Cinchona angustifolia, called cascarillo bobo amarillo (weak yellow quinine bark) for the color of the interior of its extremely bitter bark. In my opinion, this bark ought to be as highly valued in medicine as that of the officinal quinine tree, which is also found in the forests of Muña. Other cascarillas likewise occurring in the region are the purple-leaved, the one called azahar, and the one called pata de gallareta (widgeon foot).

Periphragmos flexuosus, a bush 4 to 5 yards tall.

Lygodisodea foetida, called yurahuanium or bejuco blanco (white vine). The very long stem of this vine is used in place of esparto grass rope to bind beams in country houses, for it is flexible and strong. It gives off an unpleasant odor, like that of rotten cabbages.

Solanum acutifolium, S. incurvum, S. lanceolatum, S. lineatum, S. pendulum, S. scabrum, and *S. sessile. Solanum stellatum*, called huircacassa or campucassa; the spines of this shrub produce blisters full of lymph if they penetrate the flesh. This fluid turns to pus, but the blisters break open and are cured by applying the partially roasted leaves of the same plant to the affected areas. *Solanum granulosum*, chuculate.

Nicotiana tomentosa, a plant which grows to a height of 3 yards; the tobacco prepared from its leaves is of low quality.

Heliotropium oppositifolium. Saracha punctata. Psychotria alba.

Lisianthus revolutus. Lisianthus viscosus; both the calyx and the peduncles of this bush are covered with a white crystalline gum that dissolves completely in water and crackles in the fire. It is plentiful around Huánuco.

Portlandia corymbosa; the bark of this bush is rather bitter, and at a short distance the white flowers look like those of jasmine. *Laugeria stipulata*, a tall, leafy tree; its stout trunk provides strong wood that has many uses. *Cestrum rigidum*; this much-branched bush is very heavily loaded with leaves and yellow flowers.

Stereoxylon pendulum, pumachilca. When this small tree is in bloom, it offers a splendid sight with its long, pendent clusters of red flowers. It grows to be about 6 yards tall. The wood has the strength needed for tool handles and various other uses. Because the leaves and especially the young shoots are covered with a resin that has soothing properties, they are crushed and applied to bruises and contusions.

Huertea glandulosa, cedro macho (male cedar); this tall tree is the source of good wood for planks, boards, and beams.

Celastrus lutescens; this tree has very good wood, for various uses. *Celastrus corymbosus*, called picna or, in Huasahuassi, rurama. Three to four yards tall, this bush is profusely branched and its twigs are heavily clad with leaves. The twigs are like little sticks arranged in clusters. It is a shrub that is very appropriate for gardens, for any shape desired can be formed of it. The wood is strong and is excellent for tool handles. When kept in paper, the seeds stain the paper with oil within a few days, which would lead us to believe that a considerable amount of oil might be obtained by pressing the seeds. The flowering and fruiting of this plant are so heavy that the branches can hardly be seen.

Gentiana violacea. Echites glandulosa. Asclepias reticulata. Hydrocotyle tenuis. Fragosa corymbosa. Gumillea viscosa. Staphylea serrata, a bush 4 yards tall. *Sambucus nigra.*

Berberis lutea, called ccarhuacassa or palo amarillo (yellow wood). This bush, up to 6 yards tall, has strong wood that is the source of an excellent canary-yellow dye.

Tillandsia juncia, T. panniculata, T. parviflora, and *T. recurva. Tradescantia deflexa. Alstroemeria punicea, A. secunda*, and *A. tomentosa*; all have very showy flowers.

Loranthus grandiflorus, moma; this species has flowers as long as the distance between an extended index finger and thumb; they are red with a yellow tube and are the prettiest I have seen. *Loranthus dependens*, liga.

Gilibertia umbellata; a bush 6 to 8 yards tall, with the odor of fennel. *Actinophyllum acuminatum, A. angulatum*, and *A. pedicellatum*; these bushes are showy because their leaves, composed of small leaflets, are borne in whorls.

Rhexia alba, R. quinquenervia, and *R. trinervia. Tropaeolum discolor. Fuchsia grandiflora, F. involucrata, F. parviflora, F. pubescens*, and *F. punicea. Melastoma repens*, olaola; this is used, together with various other plants, as a yellow dye.

Andromeda aff. *cordifolia* and *Andromeda* aff. *punctata. Axinaea lanceolata* and *A. purpurea. Brunellia aculeata* and *B. inervis*; both are trees reaching a height of 12 to 15 yards, with good wood.

Eugenia procera, a tall, leafy tree more than 30 yards tall; its wood is strong and, like the leaves, pleasant-smelling. *Marcgravia pentandra*; this is a low bush, 4 to 5 yards tall, with clusters of very fragrant flowers. *Eccremocarpus viridis*; it has large, yellowish green flowers.

Negretia elliptica and *N. inflexa*, called llamapañaui (llama's eye) in reference to the shape of the seeds, which are believed to be an antidote for the stings of small insects. They are taken in the form of a powder in two doses, and the powder is dusted over the bites of the venomous animal.

Palauvia glabra. Bacasia corymbosa. Soliva pedicellata. Mutisia lanata, a beautiful plant for gardens. *Munnozia lanceolata. Molina latifolia.*

Cypripedium grandiflorum, rima-rima. *Anguloa uniflora*, flor del Espíritu Santo (flower of the Holy Spirit). *Sobralia dichotoma*, tahuatahua; its flowers are splendid, for they are large, purple, and fragrant.

Maxillaria ciliata, M. grandiflora, M. longipetala, and *M. undulata. Epidendrum corymbosum*, flor de todo el año (flower of the whole year); *E. nutans, E. paniculatum*, and *E. parviflorum. Fernandezia conferta, F. ensiformis, F. laxa*, and *F. punctata. Humboldtia cordata, H. contorta, H. oblonga, H. parviflora*, and *H. revoluta. Pothos acaulis. Arum tuberosum.*

Llagunoa nitida, árbol de cuentas de rosario (rosary-bead tree); this bush attains a height of 4 or 5 yards. *Acalypha glandulosa* and *A. granulata.*

Begonia coccinea, B. hirsuta, B. incarnata, B. monadelpha, B. parviflora, B. rosea, and *B. utriculata*; all are low plants with beautiful flowers. *Jatropha aphrodisiaca,* simayuca; according to the Indians, the root of this plant has aphrodisiac properties.

Urtica citriodora, so named for the odor given off by its leaves. *Urtica cymosa, U. dauciodora, U. hirsuta, U. longifolia, U. punctata,* and *U. rugosa.*

Morus nigra and *M. spinosa. Citrosma muricata, C. ovalis, C. pyriformis,* and *C. tomentosa*; on all of these trees there is a kind of liquid that looks like saliva. *Tafalla scabra,* aitacupi. *Carica glandulosa,* monte papaya (papaya of the forest).

Schinus oblongifolia and *S. aurantiodora*; both species are called mayco. The shade of both these bushes causes a stinging and painful rash that develops into infected sores, accompanied by fever. Indians maintain that the shade of the latter species is more harmful than that of the former. We have discussed the effects of this poison and its antidotes elsewhere.

Cecropia alba and *C. tubulosa,* called tacunas. Both species are tall, beautiful trees and very leafy. Their large leaves are divided like a wheel into 9, 11, or 13 segments; they follow the sun, keeping the upper surface always towards the sun's rays.

Thurifera macrocarpa and *T. rotundicapsula,* árboles de incienso (incense trees). A beautiful, crystalline resin, used in the churches of Peru, is procured from both of these species. These trees are tall, leafy, and very beautiful, especially the first of the two. They grow to a height of 40 yards or more.

Synziganthera purpurea. Clavija macrocarpa; *C. spathulata,* called monte lucuma (wild lucuma) for the shape of its fruits. Although both species are low shrubs, they have large leaves.

Mimosa punicea, known as huaita-rebozo (shawl huaita) in reference to the red color of the clustered flowers, which have the same bright hue as the shawls commonly worn by Indian women. The species is also called monte pacae (wild pacay), since it resembles *Mimosa inga,* the true pacay.

Cavalleria dentata, C. dependens, C. ferruginea, C. latifolia, and *C. pellucida,* called manglillos or lucumas. These are trees or shrubs, 5 to 12 yards tall.

Celtis aspera, chichillica; Indians weave nets, baskets, and other common homespun objects from the untreated bark of this tree. They also often use the bark as a binder and as rope.

Adiantum reniforme. Carludovica trigona. Morenia fragrans, siasia; this is a low palm.

CHAPTER 52

Trip from Muña to Huánuco

On the 20th of September the three artists returned to Huánuco. On the 24th we three botanists left Muña and, with no trouble along the way, arrived by nightfall at Llamapañaui, where we were overtaken by a brief shower.

On the 25th we left Llamapañaui. A short way out, when we were climbing a winding mountain path, one of our pack mules was pushed by another. The animal rolled down the hillside a few yards, to the turn in the road where Don José Pavón was riding. The pack mule bumped into his animal, and the fall was thus interrupted, but a disastrous accident was prevented only because Pavón had hastily dismounted before the falling mule hit his own animal.

From that point on, we continued happily on our way, climbing the peaks known as Torre sin Agua (Tower without Water) and Cuerno Retorcido (Twisted Horn). We climbed these on foot, along a narrow and sandy path that was devoid of all vegetation because of a brush fire that was burning over the whole mountain that day. We had supper in the village of Chaclla and went a league farther on to stay overnight. In the final hours of the day we were overtaken by a rainstorm that, with short breaks, lasted until nine o'clock the following morning, when we began to pack our mules. It started in again at eleven o'clock and rained for more than an hour.

We entered the village of Panao to buy foodstuffs, and there we found the priest and his assistants celebrating the holy days for the entire year. All of the holy days are thus celebrated in 8 consecutive days. We slept on a mountain opposite Panao, where we collected numerous plants to dry and describe. On the 27th we stayed overnight in Yanamayo, where we had a short rain after putting up our tents. On the 28th we arrived at Huánuco.

Cascarillo de Pata de Gallareta

Along the road we gathered a good number of plants, which we put out to dry. Among these, I described *Embothrium monospermum* and *Cinchona ovata. Cinchona ovata* is called cascarillo de pata de gallareta (widgeon-foot quinine tree) for the outside color of its light, spongy bark.

In the months of October, November, and December 1786, I finished drying the plants collected in Muña and along the way. I put the specimens in order by classes and packed them well, together with many seeds, roots, barks, and other curiosities and specimens of natural history that I had gathered.

Each month, I sent the Ministry of the Indies various packets of fresh seed for the Royal Botanic Garden in Madrid, and at the same time I reported on the progress of our work and our discoveries.

On the 23rd of November the artist Brunete went to Lima, asserting that he had reasons to make the trip.

On the 12th of January 1787, Pavón and his assistant Pulgar left Huánuco to accompany 73 chests of dried plants and other specimens, 586 drawings, and 18 pots of living plants, which included 40 young quinine trees, or *Cinchona officinalis*, and other valuable trees gathered from the forests. All this cargo was sent to Spain on the ships *Brillante* and *Pilar*, addressed to His Majesty through His Excellency the Minister of the Indies.

Abbot Cavanilles and the Malvaceae

When the descriptions of the plants that I had worked on in Muña, along the road to Muña, and in Huánuco were perfected and copied onto clean sheets, I resumed my collecting activities. I dedicated my collecting to the surroundings of Huánuco and to those plants that I thought might have been lost on board the *San Pedro de Alcántara*, even though I had not received any definite report that our chests of specimens had gone down with the ship. I corrected the descriptions of many plants, and I gave very special study to the Malvaceae, which are plentiful near Huánuco. I engaged in this study because the abbot Don Antonio Cavanilles said that he had found nine new genera of this family in the collections of various French botanists; in the four printed pages that he had sent us from Paris, outlining the characters of these genera, I found no solid bases for separating them from genera already published. I was therefore anxious to clarify my suspicions, as I succeeded in doing for some of the plants, and to prove that Cavanilles was in error in the examinations that he had made upon dried material in Paris.

As the artists were not certain of the loss of the 800 drawings sent aboard the *San Pedro*, they began the task of repeating their work until such time as they should know definitely about the loss.

Towards the end of April a kind of croup attacked me, and it went away only after two bleedings and a copious sweating that I had on the 2nd of May. On that day I received a messenger from Pavón, asking me to send a power of attorney to him in Pasco so he might claim our salaries at the treasury on his way back from Lima.

On the 12th of May Pavón and Pulgar arrived in Huánuco with 12 mule loads of paper and other equipment for the trip that we had planned to the forests of Pillao.

Sickness and Death of the Artist Brunete

On the 16th of May, at nine o'clock in the morning, I received a messenger bearing a letter from the paymaster of the treasury at Pasco, notifying me that the artist José Brunete was at his home so ill that he had already received the last sacraments. He transmitted to me the artist's request that I come to Pasco as soon as possible.

I left Huánuco at three that same afternoon with Gálvez, and we stayed overnight at Ambo. On the 17th, when we arrived at Huariaca, I received a second letter from the paymaster and another from the subdelegate of the province, both announcing the death of Brunete and requesting me to come without delay to receive his personal effects, for he had named me his first executor. We slept that night in Huariaca and arrived at Pasco on the 18th. Brunete's servants and the subdelegate and the paymaster gave me the following details of the final illness of our artist.

On his return from Lima to Huánuco with his two servants, Brunete had suffered the misfortune of having the mule that was carrying his bed, clothing, and other personal effects fall headlong down the high and dangerous slope of Pacrón. This accident obliged him to spend the night there, for he had sent the servants to the village of Canta in search of people to help recover the effects strewn about from the traveling cases. The cases had been torn to bits by the rocks on the steep slope and on the opposite bank of the river, against which the mule was dashed and crushed. After the shock of this accident and the bad night spent at this place, Brunete's servants noticed a change in his expression, a sadness, and difficulty in breathing. All these symptoms increased as they neared the mountain range, the highland moors, and the mining fields.

When they arrived in Pasco, Brunete decided to await the mail from Lima in the paymaster's house. The paymaster, like the servants, observed that he was worse every day, and so weary that he had to stop to regain his strength after every 10 or 12 steps. Brunete attributed his fatigue to the gases or vapors that were continually pouring forth from the mining operations in the nearby mountains, for these did tire out and choke many mules arriving wearily at Pasco.

On the evening of the 11th, the paymaster noticed that Brunete fell asleep during conversation. He asked him if he felt any change in his condition and, although Brunete repeatedly answered in the negative, the paymaster made him go to bed. He had hardly fallen asleep when the others heard such extraordinary mumbling and strong snoring that they woke him up and asked him if he felt worse. He replied that he felt a slight oppression in the chest and had some difficulty in breathing. When they had given him several cups of hot water with sugar, he fell into a more peaceful sleep.

On the 12th Brunete went to mass, and on the way back to the house the paymaster, Don Agustín de Morales, and others noticed a change in Brunete's expression and told him to go to bed. They called the surgeon who attended everyone in the village, so that he might prescribe some medical treatment. The ointment, enema, and warm water that he prescribed produced no favorable effect, and Brunete continued to be even more fatigued. By nightfall he was overtaken by heavy drowsiness. On the 13th he had confession and asked for the holy oils. His illness grew steadily worse, and between eight and nine on the evening of the 14th he died in the place that he hated most in life, for every time he had experienced its rigorous climate he had felt strangely ill. On the morning of the 16th he was buried in the churchyard at Pasco in accordance with the paymaster's arrangements, with a brilliant company in attendance at the funeral.

On the 19th of May, an inventory of Brunete's belongings was made in the presence of the judge and the necessary witnesses, and all was passed over to me, together with the receipts of the expenditures of the burial. After having finished all the details with the subdelegate, Don Francisco Cuéllar, and having taken charge of Brunete's belongings, I left Pasco with Gálvez on the 21st and spent the night at Huariaca. We waited there until the 22nd for the mule driver who had the baggage and, having exchanged our beast of burden, we continued on to arrive at Olerías by nightfall. We got to Huánuco on the 23rd and auctioned off Brunete's belongings on the 3 subsequent days.

I used the rest of the month to copy rough drafts of various plant descriptions onto clean sheets.

On the 11th of June I informed the general superintendent of the royal treasury of Peru, the Ministry of the Indies, and the director of botanical expeditions about the death of Brunete, so that they might inform his sister. I repeated my report of his death on the 11th of July.

I continued until August to again collect those plants of the Huánuco area that had been lost on the ship *San Pedro*, and to prepare new descriptions of them.

CHAPTER 53

Trip to Pillao and Its Forests

When the preparation of supplies and other necessities for our botanical work was done, I left Huánuco on the 3rd of August in the company of Pavón and Tafalla, and we arrived to spend the night in Chulquillo, an estate 3 leagues from the city. There are four date palms on this farm, but the fruit does not ripen because there is no staminate tree to pollinate the pistillate flowers. The owner of the estate asked us why he never could harvest dates.

We arrived at the village of Pillao on the 4th, having experienced no inconvenience other than the intense heat of the sun. A variety of plants grow in the ravine and on the slopes of the mountain along the way. The following are abundant: species of *Calceolaria*, species of *Piper*, *Macrocnemum coriaceum* or ccaratu, various kinds of *Tillandsia*, *Poinciana bijuga*, different species of *Cactus* or gigantones, *Ru-*

bus siraca, three arboreal species of *Bignonia*, not a few orchids, and species of *Cavalleria* or manglillos. There are also many other large and small plants and good pasture grasses.

On the 5th we pitched our field tents in front of the hut that the mayor had indicated as ours, and we put everything in order for working the following day. The work began with our first trip into the forests of the local mountains.

On the 10th the artists Gálvez and Pulgar arrived in Pillao, and they began drawing the next day. We continued our work in the forests and mountains of Pillao until the 25th of September. During that period we collected many specimens of new plants, as well as seeds, roots, and barks with known medicinal properties.

CHAPTER 54

Description of the Village of Pillao

The village of Pillao is located 12 leagues north-northeast of Huánuco. It lies near the eminence of a high, extensive mountain and has a mild climate by day, but the nights are cold. Hoarfrosts and freezes are not infrequent, and fogs are common in the rainy season. During the dry season there is no lack of clouds and brief rains. For these reasons, the Indians suffer from colds and rheumatic pains, although the conditions of the region are generally healthy. They treat these ills with herbs that the womenfolk prescribe and with enemas applied by using a cow's bladder with a little reed tube inserted in the mouth of the bladder.

From the village to the Huánuco River, which skirts the base of the mountain, there is a league and a half of steep climb. Nevertheless, the ground is clad with good pasture grass and with low shrubs, bushes, and trees. Similarly, all the area from the village upwards on the mountainside is covered with this kind of vegetation, and there are even lofty forests where slender quinine trees and an infinity of other plants, large and small, grow. The Indians keep a few head of cattle and some mules on these pleasant and excellent pasturelands. The mules are employed in the trafficking of quinine bark and coca, the only commerce of the area. Four leagues into the hinterland, the dense and closed jungle begins, and there no pasturage whatsoever can be found.

The fields of Pillao are good for growing all sorts of grain, but the few inhabitants let them lie uncultivated. They content themselves with the few seeds and roots essential to their diet, such as maize, beans, a few poorly cultivated vegetables, yucas, and potatoes of excellent flavor, a few mule loads of which are often taken to Huánuco for sale.

There are hardly more than 55 souls living in Pillao. All are Indians, poor in the midst of the wealth offered by these wide expanses of unappropriated forests that stretch over to and border upon the territory of the infidel Indians. Pillao is the last Spanish outpost in that direction.

Pillao falls under the civil jurisdiction of the governor of the jungle areas and under the ecclesiastical control of the parish of Valle. Most of the year, the village has no spiritual leadership, but it did have this benefit when it belonged to the jurisdiction of the Ocopa missionaries as the outlying post of their missions in these regions.

The huts and church of Pillao are made of mud, adobe, lime, and small stones, and are roofed with timber and straw thatch. They are not set close together, as a precaution against any fire that might break out. Behind each little house there is a garden with vegetables and various flowers. The Indian women take great pains in decorating the altars and images with flowers.

The fish in the river include some vagres (bagres, catfish) and cachuelos of excellent flavor. In various spots there are indications of silver and gold deposits, and even in the village itself we excavated an outcrop and showed that it was the ramification of a gold deposit, as proven by the colors of the earth dug up in 2 days by six laborers. The water of the brooks and freshets is very good, but in the high plains there are some small streams that are unhealthy because they are running or stagnant on chalky or nitrate-bearing soils.

Sparrows, or greenfinches, and thrushes are plentiful in the village and the surrounding countryside. In the fields there are excellent turkey hens, as well as a wild fowl that is called the haraco for its repetitive "haraco-manan-haraco" song; the meat of this bird is very tender and tasty. The birds called trequilles are also abundant, as are Dominican birds, condors, woodpeckers, and various other smaller birds of the forests and lagoons. Parrots fly past in the morning and evening in enormous flocks and spread throughout all parts of the mountains, searching for fruit and other food. There are deer, and a species of hare called mischus or missus; occasionally wildcats, boars, or bears lurk in the jungle.

CHAPTER 55

Trip to Chacahuassi, or House at the Bridge

In spite of our difficulties in getting mules for the trip to the jungles, we left Pillao for Chacahuassi on the 26th of September. We spent the first night on the mountain at Sillcay.

On the 27th, we had hardly gone a quarter of a league from Sillcay when we entered upon a narrow road, which for more than 2 leagues was rendered next to impassable by bogs, swamps, and the holes made by animals and filled with water by the rains. On those high peaks the rains last the year through; though there are some sunny hours nearly every day, a day without rain or mist is extremely rare. We spent more than 6 hours covering those 2 leagues. There was hardly a mule that did not fall down and stick in the mire at least 10 times, and occasionally all of them at once were bogged down or wallowing in those narrow, muddy stretches.

Our Indian mule drivers were worn out, not only from contending with the animals but also from fighting against terrain where they sank above their knees and where they could not run in any direction to prod the animals. They were so weary and depressed that we ourselves found it necessary to raise their spirits by dismounting and helping them to unload, load, and pull the mules out of the mud. Had we not taken this course, we would not have got through that short stretch of hell until the following day. To complete the circus, when we were almost out of that boggy part of the road, two of our pack mules fell over a bank of turf down into a thicket of trees and bushes. We had to cut down the vegetation in order to extricate the animals, and with ropes we helped them get to their feet and climb back up the turf to the road. The mule drivers, animals, and loads were completely covered with mud.

It cut into our hearts to see these unfortunate men, uncomplaining and long-suffering by nature, almost mad with desperation. At long last we reached firm ground, but for more than a league the road continued to be narrow and beset with high stepping-stones covered with loose, coarse gravel. Along that stretch the mules suffered in the extreme from stones rolling down behind them and from the swaying of their loads. With feet and legs wounded by the gravel and stones, the animals arrived sore and worn out at Iscutunam, a league and a half from Chacahuassi. Although that spot had only sparse pasturage of very poor quality, we were obliged to spend the night there because darkness had fallen more than an hour before our arrival. It was an uncomfortable place indeed, for the clearing was small and the soil steep and wet. The area is surrounded by a variety of trees, among which *Cinchona purpurea*, or cascarilla de hoja morada (purple-leaved quinine tree), is plentiful.

On the 28th, when we had climbed down to the river from Iscutunam, we ascended another mountain with a steep winding path, the descent of which is extremely dangerous, especially for pack mules and riding animals. Even for men who try to walk over the thick, slippery sand of the road with shoes there is considerable peril.

We finally arrived at Chacahuassi. The name Chacahuassi means "house at the bridge," for at this spot there is a liana bridge giving access to the other side of the river, where the natives gather quinine bark, or cascarilla fina (fine quinine bark), and extract its active constituents.

In this narrow space we felt as though we were confined in the deepest of dungeons, for the sun peeped in only at high noon, and only on clear nights, rare at this time of year, could one could tell the stars of heaven. Then would we look about us at the three towering and inaccessible peaks—clad with a blanket of tall trees, shrubs, and bushes from their highest crags to the banks of the deafening rivers that rushed down the slopes—and our spirits would fall so low that nothing but the wish to fulfill our mission could force us to keep the spark of life alive.

Despite the depths to which our spirits had sunk, we sent off the muleteers, as well as the Indians who, under orders from the chief magistrate of Pillao and at our expense, went on ahead to throw up a shelter. We had to fence the shelter in with trunks of balsa wood, for we had hardly arrived when a heavy downpour set in and, because of the small eaves of the shelter, water beat in on all sides. On the 29th this fencing was finished, and the Indians followed the mule drivers back to Pillao. We stayed on alone, except for four quinine-bark gatherers who lived there in other huts. Two of them had built their huts on our side of the Chico River, and the other two lived on the opposite side in huts located on two small plots of coca owned by the Indians of Pillao.

Rain accompanied the nightfall, and it kept up through the next day with no break at all. The Grande River swelled so much that its headlong, roaring current filled us with horrible fright. At seven in the morning, a shaking of the earth caused us great concern, for we were in such a deep, narrow ravine. At noon we felt a sudden and terrible landslide of several cliffs that slid down from the mountain opposite us to the large river below, carrying enormous amounts of soil, rocks, and trees. This landslide lasted, with repeated interruptions, for more than half an hour. It started again in the afternoon and did not let up until the rain stopped. Such loosening and slipping of mountains and trees are frequent in the jungle regions during the rainy season. He who travels at this time of year along the narrow and abominable footpaths does so at considerable risk of losing his life.

Chacahuassi is located at the foot of one of the three extraordinarily high and craggy mountains that enclose this deep, narrow, triangular ravine that is bathed by two walled-in rivers. These rivers descend from the south and from the east, join in this ravine with an unceasing roar, and rush on together with the greatest force imaginable through the northern ravine towards Cuchero.

There exists not the slightest clearing in the vicinity of Chacahuassi; the three or four tiny plots of coca are on the steep mountainside or on the river banks, on craggy terrain and choking in a tangle of bush and isolated by precipices. No one may move about this area at night without putting one's very life in peril.

The river that flows through the southern ravine is the same one that flows through Huánuco, where it is called the Pillco, but in this area it is of much greater volume, and its waters are much saltier as a result of the many mineral-rich springs that feed it from Huánuco on. In this river there are many kinds of fish: bagres (vagres, catfish), boconcitos, cachuelos (a kind of small anchovy), and corbinas (whiting), all up to half a yard long and weighing as much as 6 pounds, but there are no fishermen to take advantage of this ready supply of food.

There are few species of birds in this deep dungeon; the commonest ones are cuiches or poccochycuis, tunquis, quianquianes, and flycatchers. Half a league from the bridge along the road to Pillao, however, one hears the warbling and sweet trilling of numerous birds of many colors and sizes. Among these are the nightingale, the golden oriole, and the organ bird.

There are few showy butterflies, but there is no lack of small moths that flit about the candles and, with burned wings, fall together with a multitude of mosquitoes and other insects of all sizes. All these pests increased our discomfort by combining their annoying presence with that of the crickets, locusts, and frogs that bothered us both day and night in that murky chasm with their tuneless singing and disagreeable and ceaseless buzzing and chirping. This cacophonous orchestra, accompanied by the perpetual roar of the rivers, forced us to carry on our conversations in shouts and to often repeat what we had said. All of this set our heads to spinning, and put us so out of sorts with ourselves that at times we seemed to be insane, or at other times stupid deaf mutes weighed down with a profound melancholy. We were disheartened that we could not escape to a more peaceful spot, and that we could not find a place where conversation might be carried on in a more nearly normal way. Even our reading distracted us instead of providing the usual entertainment and amusement.

The heat is excessive, and the atmosphere is muggy as a result of the frequent rains occasioned by dense mists that continually arise from the rivers. This is particularly true between the months of September and May. Everything about this dark and dismal place makes it unhealthy, and the foodstuffs that we took in with us rotted and molded with the greatest ease. Even the small quantities of coca harvested here are of low quality because of the humidity and lack of sun. The very Indians who cultivate the coca hardly care to chew it.

Just outside of Chacahuassi there are small fields of sugar cane, for chewing and for making a fermented drink called guarapo, which the Indians and negroes like. In these small plots of cane and coca are also produced excellent pineapples or *Bromelia ananas*, bananas, papayas, hot peppers, yuca (manioc, cassava), sweet potatoes, and ssaquis (species of *Canna*).

In the morning and late afternoon, flocks of parrots and parakeets can be seen flying over the peaks. There are so many of them that they look like clouds, casting shadows on the ground below. Every day great packs of monkeys go down to the river's edge, jumping from tree to tree with a loud screeching and uproar. They are of all sorts: black, red, large and ugly, tiny and attractive.

The bridge that spans the Grande River, upon which the harvesters and laborers cross to fetch quinine bark, is 70 yards long and made of three liana ropes spliced together with great skill. The two lateral ropes are the handrails and the central one serves as the walkway. Other slender lianas or vines are twined at intervals from one of the handrails to the other, and these are knotted fast around the central rope. The three heavy ropes are thus securely tied together to form a keel-shaped bridge with very thin handrails.

Crossing on such a bridge is dangerous. The Indians of Pillao build the bridge anew every year, or more often if necessary, but sometimes they merely repair it by replacing the slender transversal vines that have broken or stretched too much. When these vines have broken or slackened, the traveler cannot reach the handrails. This happened to my companion Pavón once in the middle of the bridge; had not one of our men run up to help him, he would have been in grave danger of falling through to his death in the river, for he had missed the handrail. The day after this incident, one of the Indian bark gatherers, crossing the bridge with a load of 75 pounds of bark on his back, lost his load. Only by supreme effort on his own part did he escape falling through and perishing in the river, and he did receive a wound on the neck.

Only an interest in gathering quinine—that precious and universally employed specific medicine—could bring a man to dwell in these gloomy solitudes in the midst of untold discomforts and misery, living and working almost naked, sustaining himself on ccamcha, or toasted maize, and coca when the supply of salted meat, peas, or beans gives out, constantly wet in the dense jungle growth, and plodding along endless cliffs and slopes so dangerous that even the thought of them strikes terror into the heart. Yet these bark gatherers abide here for many days at a time, through long periods of frequent rains and fog so thick that day looks like darkest night.

When the bridge is down, the Indians cross this and other rivers on rafts made of the wood of two species of *Bombax* or of huampo, a species of *Heliocarpus*. All three of these trees are tall and massive, with straight trunks and very light, spongy wood. From the bark of chuima, a species of *Bombax*, they also make ropes for crossing the rivers. They tie the ropes to trees or rocks and cross with a quipe (sack) or bale of 75 pounds of bark, which they have carried on their backs 4, 5, or 6 leagues down from the forests. Many times, the force of the river sweeps away the loads, and sometimes Indians are drowned trying to cross the river in this way.

As the heat is so intense in these deep gorges, and the air excessively muggy, any exertion easily engenders sweating. Those who are unaccustomed to traveling through such jungle growth are afflicted with an untold number of rashes, especially on the legs. The itching of these rashes begins in the afternoon and keeps up almost all night long, and one is obliged to scratch until the flesh is exposed. This has often happened to us after arriving back at our camp from the forest; there have been times when scratching with our fingernails did not assuage the itching, and we had to use the back of a knife.

Economic Condition of the Indian Bark Gatherers and Its Repercussion in the Destruction of the Stands of Quinine Trees

Indians in the villages of Acomayo and Panao, and especially those in Pillao, have harvested many thousands of bushels of quinine bark every year, yet they are penniless and practically always in debt for one or two hundred bushels. The intrinsic value of this amount of bark is much greater than the worth of the Indians' huts, plantings, and cattle. This obvious truth will shock those who do not know that the buyers get back the money that the Indians receive for the bark, usually in advance, by strange and not always honest methods. And this is not the worst, because most of the Indians die without spiritual help. We have witnessed this on several occasions. Then their burial, which by regulation does not cost more than 4½ pesos, is not paid up with 50 or sometimes even 100 pesos and the debt will never be fully canceled, because the priests or their intermediaries keep the accounts according to their own whims and never settle debts even though they may have been paid thrice over.

The functions of the church enable the clergy to monopolize everything, and the Indians celebrate church pageantry only as a pretext for putting on drunken festivals. The clergy change and delay the orders so that the faithful first bring in the bushels that they must have to pay their debts to various merchants who have informed the priest about debts still outstanding. Furthermore, when the merchants are not of the priest's kin, they stand little chance of receiving their payment in full.

Those who engage in this business try to advance merchandise to the Indians in addition to money, such as light cloth, baize, clothing, and other effects. All wares are scandalously priced, so the natives are constantly in debt for them. This method of exploitation has retarded the agricultural pursuits of these frontier villages in the jungle regions; because food is scarce, the local habitants fall easy prey to sickness, and every year the settlements are poorer and poorer.

In 1784, the 55 Indians of Pillao harvested 25,000 pounds of quinine bark in only 8 days; were we to appraise the value of the buildings of the whole village, we would not find it to equal that of 2500 pounds of bark.

The Indians, lazy and poor workers by nature, are sentenced and punished under orders from the judges and priests if they do not pay their debts promptly. In order to free themselves from these debts, they have to gather as much bark as they can in a short time, felling all the trees that they can find in 1 or 2 days. Then when they go out to strip off the bark, they may find the trees too dried out; being unable to peel off the bark easily, they take only a portion of the bark from some of the trunks and leave a large number, completely unworked, to rot away.

Another practice equally damaging to the forests is the indiscriminate felling of both old and young trees. For example, less than 10 years ago the Indians at Pillao had quinine trees within a league or two of the village. Now, in 1787, they have to penetrate the jungle for more than 40 leagues to get bark, and then carry it on their backs for 5 or 6 leagues.

The same wasteful exploitation of the quinine tree is going on in Cuchero, Sapán, Cayumba, Muña, and Panao, and in the provinces of Huamalíes, Tarma, and Xauxa. According to a conservative estimate, the forests of these provinces have yielded more than 3½ million pounds of quinine in 8 years. Moreover, this calculation does not include the many pounds of fresh bark from which the extract was made and the even greater amounts of dried, stale, and destroyed bark.

On the 11th of October, 3000 pounds of bark and 6 pounds of extract were taken to Huánuco from the bridge of Pillao. I was thus able to observe again the harmful method used by the bark buyers to cram the bark into rough burlap bags. The bark was still wet and somewhat moldy on the inner surface, and they put it into sacks by stamping it down with their feet, breaking it up considerably in the process so they could stuff in more of it. Then they sent it on to Huánuco with no special care and with nothing to protect the sacks from the mist and rain except a few sheets of the same burlap, which of course affords no protection whatsoever from the elements.

On October 12th of this same year, Don Jorge Escobedo, general superintendent, sent me notice that my companions and I must, by royal order, return to Lima to prepare to go back to Spain. I communicated this at once to my companions. It was the happiest news that I could possibly give them, for it meant a change and a rest from the constant labor, fatigue, and misery that we had undergone in those wild forest tangles and chasms, traveling through wild jungles poorly fed and wholly worn out in order to carry out the mission entrusted to us by the king.

During the trips we made through the forests of Pillao and Chacahuassi, I collected and prepared dried specimens of a large number of plants, some of which were also drawn. I described the following.

Canna iridiflora, achyra (achira). Indians cultivate this plant in their gardens for the beauty of its variegated flowers, and for the tuberous roots that are edible when cooked and flavored with condiments. These roots are similar to those of *Canna indica*, which is also called achyra.

Costus laevis. *Salvia acuminata*. *Veronica rotundifolia*, *V. peregrina*, and *V. serpillifolia*. *Pinguicula involuta*. *Calceolaria umbellata*.

Columellia corymbosa, a stout tree; its wood is excellent for a variety of uses. The leaves are intensely bitter and are, according to Indian belief, wonderfully efficacious in treating intermittent fevers.

Piper granulosum, *P. ovale*, *P. nitidum*, *P. asperum*, *P. crocatum*, *P. betulinum*, *P. punctatum*, *P. longifolium*, and *P. secundum*. All of these species are rather tall bushes and more or less aromatic.

Peperomia variegata, *P. rhombea*, and *P. secunda*. *Justicia longistamina*. *Xyris lutea*.

Milium chinense, maíz de Guinea (Guinea maize). The Indians of Pampamarca,

Pueblo Nuevo, and other places in the forested areas of the Panatahuas, Carapachos, and Cholones sow this plant for its grain. Toasted or made into ccamcha, it may be used to prepare a very white flour that is used in a gruel called puchas or ullpus. This flour is whiter than that of either maize or European wheat, and it has a better flavor.

Scirpus fragrans; this plant is fed as pasturage to animals, and its roots have the fragrance of spikenard. *Cissus compressicaulis*. *Spermacoce capitata*. *Cuscuta odorata*, cabellos de angeles (angel's tresses). *Acoema globosa*. *Alchemilla rotundiflora* and *A. tripartita*. *Buddleja incana*, quisoar; its wood is solid, durable, and valuable for buildings. *Hedyotis filiformis*. *Basella diffusa*, uspica; this plant is used as a condiment for locro (a kind of meat and vegetable stew), which is a very common dish in Peru. *Myosotis humilis*.

Cascarillo Fino Delgado, Cascarilla Azahar, and Cascarilla Boba de Hoja Morada

Cinchona hirsuta, cascarillo fino delgado. This tree grows to a height of 4 to 8 yards; its thin bark is as highly esteemed in medicine and commerce as that of quina de Loxa (*C. officinalis*). It is abundant in the highlands of Pillao, occurring with other trees and smaller plants. See my "Tratado de las Quinas," in which I report observations made about this species on my trips. Equally abundant elsewhere in the forests of Panatahuas is *Cinchona lutescens*, or azahar. *Cinchona purpurea*, or cascarilla boba de hoja morada, is abundant in Iscutunam and Chacahuassi.

Stapelia hirta. *Psychotria caerulea* and *P. violacea*. *Stereoxylon patens*, tassta; *S. paniculatum*. *Gentiana violacea*.

Solanum nitidum, *S. nutans*, and *S. oblongum*. *Solanum stellatum*, called campucassa or, in Panao, huircacassa; its partially toasted leaves have the property of drawing out splinters that have penetrated the flesh in any part of the body, or of bringing an infected sore to a head. *Solanum granulosum*, chuculate.

Bowlesia lobata. *Heliconia tricolor*; the floral spike of this plant is three-colored and very showy. *Villaresia emarginata*. *Nycterisiton ferruginea*, called chicchimicuna, or bat food; this tall, leafy tree has a straight trunk and strong wood with a good grain. *Cynanchum acuminatum*. *Sauvagesia subtriflora*, yerba de San Martín (Saint Martin's herb); natives use a decoction of this plant in treating chest ailments.

Heliconia angustifolia. *Varronia dichotoma*. *Echites laxa*. *Anthericum* aff. *falcatum*. *Alstroemeria tomentosa*. *Pourretia simpaganthera*.

Loranthus luteus, enlahora, a bush 10 to 12 yards tall; unlike other species of the genus, it is not a parasite. With its profusion of yellow flowers, it is a splendid sight to see in bloom.

Tovaria pendula. *Actinophyllum conicum*; like all other species of the genus, this bush produces small tears of a white, crystalline gum that is entirely soluble in water. *Vaccinium dependens*, sachsauro; like box, this is a beautiful bush for gardens.

Weinmannia ovalis, machi. This beautifully leafy tree attains a height of 20 to

25 yards; from its wood the Indians make excellent boards for buildings, chests, and other carpentry. *Weinmannia pubescens*, *W. ovata*, and *W. alata* are equally leafy, and their wood is also good for a variety of purposes.

Guarea nitida, a tree 12 to 15 yards tall. *Neea oppositifolia*; its fruits are a dark purplish color. *Gualteria rubra* and *G. alata*. *Phytolacca icosandra*; this plant is abundant in the village of Pillao itself, and the Indian women use the ripe fruits to make a dye for cotton.

Cuellaria ferruginea and *C. revoluta*, both good timber trees, 10 to 15 yards tall. *Arbutus parviflora*, called macha because the ripened fruits, though tasty and sweet, are intoxicating when eaten in excessive amounts.

Andromeda aff. *glauca*, congama. *Andromeda* aff. *mellifera*, called sumacmisqui, meaning rich honey, for the very sweet nectar within the flowers, which the Indians like to suck for the sweet taste. *Andromeda* aff. *bracteata*, pucasato; Indian women take its delicious red fruits, bittersweet and juicy, to sell in the market at Huánuco.

Foveolaria ferruginea, *F. ovata*, and *F. oblonga*; all are leafy trees with good wood for a number of uses. *Erythroxylon patens*. *Turraea quinata*. *Miconia emarginata*. *Prunus ovalis*, a tree 10 to 20 yards tall, with wood of some value. *Mespilus ferruginea*, llinlli; this leafy bush grows to a height of 8 to 12 yards.

Abatia rugosa, called tauhac-tauhac, yoriturp, or galgaretama. This beautiful bush is plentiful not only in Pillao itself, where it serves as fencing for gardens, but also in Rondos and other villages in the high, cold regions. It certainly has been introduced there from the forests to beautify enclosures with its racemes of yellow flowers. *Rhincotheca spinosa*, a bush that is likewise used for fencing in Pillao.

Marcgravia monopetala. *Marcgravia pentapetala*, called purumhigos, which means false figs; this name alludes to the shape and substance of the fruits, which resemble those of the true fig. Indians eat them when they are well-ripened.

Celsia aff. *ovata*; *Celsia* aff. *linearis*. *Antirrhinum avenium*. *Ruellia curvata*. *Melochia cordifolia*.

Polygala aff. *discolor*, mascca; Indian women prepare a wash from the bark of its roots to cleanse the hair and stimulate its growth. The bark is intensely bitter and forms a lather like that of soap.

Cytisus canescens, chuccho'clle; its stems and twigs are useful for making bags. Guinea pigs are very fond of the leaves, which the Indian women gather fresh every day to feed these animals. *Glycyrrhiza? undulata*. *Hypericum subulatum* and *H. corymbosum*; both plants, known as chinchanho, provide the Indians with a yellow dye for cottons and woolens. They may be used alone, or together with other plants.

Melaleuca coriacea; a bush 10 yards tall. *Ternstroemia globosa* and *T. quinquepartita*, beautiful bushes for gardens because of the shapes to which they may be trained. *Cineraria linearis* and *C. lanceolata*. *Munnozia corymbosa* and *M. venosissima*. *Senecio foetidus*. *Perdicium lanatum*.

Molina corymbosa, *M. nitida*, *M. incana*, *M. prostrata*, and *M. salicifolia*; all are shrubs that are resin-bearing, balsamic, aromatic, and tonic.

Anthemis striata, called virgenhacha or manzanilla cimarrona (wild camomile). *Anthemis palescens*; the roots of this plant are more peppery and promote salivation more efficiently than the pellitory plant. The stimulation and pungency on the tongue last for more than 6 hours.

Eupatorium stridens; when crushed in the hands, the leaves of this composite crackle considerably. *Elephantopus capitatus*. *Epidendrum scabrum*. *Fernandezia denticulata*, *F. graminifolia*, and *F. haemathodes*. *Humboldtia lanceolata*. *Passiflora rosea*, puru-puru; children eat the fruits of this plant. *Maxillaria longipetala*, *M. ligulata*, *M. hastata*, and *M. paniculata*.

Sisyrinchium anceps. *Sisyrinchium ocsapurga*, known as palma-palma or paja-purgante; the latter name refers to the laxative properties of a decoction of the roots. A slight tasting of these roots leaves a pungent, bitter taste in the mouth for more than 6 hours and can be the cause of considerable discomfort. I judge from this that its purgative properties are too drastic and ought to be used more cautiously than the Indians are wont to do.

Betula nigra, ramram. Indians use the bark of ramram, soaked in urine, to give color to sole leather and to dye cottons and woolens a cinnamon hue. This bark also serves as tannin. The leaves are pounded up with lard and applied as a poultice to cleanse and heal ulcers; they are used without lard to treat inflammations. When applied to fresh wounds, the leaves staunch the flow of blood.

Olyra latifolia, called bombilla in reference to the use of the culmos, or hollow stalks, of this grass to make the bombillas, or straws, for drinking the beverage known as maté or other hot drinks, according to Peruvian custom. This grass is an excellent food for animals; as such, it deserves to be propagated throughout the world, for besides being a useful fodder it is an impressively large grass with a profusion of broad leaves.

Eriocaulon vaginans and *E. parvum*. *Croton acutifolium*. *Synziganthera purpurea*. *Juniperus* aff., a beautiful, frondose tree. *Cissampelos villosa*. *Chondrodendron tomentosum*.

Dillinia aff. *rubra*, árbol de incienso (incense tree); like other species of the genus, this tree yields a resin called incienso (incense) in Peru. It is employed in the churches and is similar to that used in Europe.

Tafalla racemosa, *T. laevis*, and *T. angustifolia*, aitacupi. These small trees are 8 to 10 yards tall, resinous, and fragrant, as are the other species of the genus, which are all known by the same vernacular name. The resin of these species is called almaciga; it oozes out in the form of small, white, transparent tears like those of mastic.

Clusia rosea, matapalo (tree killer); see my notes on the properties and uses of the resin of this species in the chapter on Cuchero. *Clusia trioecia*; it is as abundant as *C. rosea* and yields a resin that has the same uses. *Clusia decussata*.

Fagara coriandriodora, called culantro (coriander) because its odor resembles that of coriander. The wood is extremely hard; though the tree is not tall, it is leafy and has a relatively stout trunk. In Chacahuassi I observed that this tree is polygamo-dioecious.

Acladodea pinnata. This little tree has a single trunk with no branches whatsoever. The leaves are borne at the tip; though emerging from various places, they give the appearance of a parasol, in a manner similar to that of tree ferns and palms. One large and beautiful cluster of flowers is borne at the very tip of the trunk. This is the only tree I have seen that lacks branches and puts forth but one inflorescence, which remains inserted lateral to the new growth that appears on the tree.

Celtis spinosa, called atpuallín in Pozuzo. *Cavalleria venosissima*.

Acrosticum cuacsaro, called cuacsaro, which means masked sword. The roots are sold commercially as true calaguala, but they lack the medicinal virtues of that calaguala, which is a species of *Polypodium*. I have discussed this falsification in my article on the calagualas that was published in the first volume of the Royal Academy of Medicine of Madrid in 1797.

CHAPTER 56

Trip from Chacahuassi to Huánuco

On the 22nd of October 1787 we left Chacahuassi and spent the night in Iscutunam, where we collected a few plants and put them up to dry. We had a little rain on the way.

On the 23rd we left Iscutunam. Half a league out, two of our pack mules tired out; one remained at that very spot, completely fatigued, and the other went on for another quarter of a league, where we left it after shifting the cargo to my servant's saddle mule. Once unloaded, the wearied animal became so furious that if anyone approached it, it would attack in a frenzy. In one of these frenzies it bit Tafalla and tore a piece out of the side of his coat. Then, turning half way around, it bit one of the Indians on the calf of the leg and ran after him like a wild beast for 10 paces, until the Indian took shelter behind a tree within the forest. In both cases, we spectators were at first astonished and later nearly died of laughter, just recalling the actions and noises of a bull and bullfighters, as frightened as if they were in the claws of a lion.

The wild animal was abandoned there on the spot, and we continued on our way. Some 200 yards farther on, Tafalla's saddle mule seemed so tired that it was necessary to take off its saddle, load it on my servant's mule, and leave the weary mule there at that place. From this point on, Tafalla and the servant went on foot.

A little farther ahead, another tired pack mule fell down into a little glen, from which all of us together had to pull it by hand. We took off half its load and had one of the mule drivers carry the other half until we had climbed up the difficult hill at Saria, where this last mule was wholly worn out with fatigue. Its half load was transferred to the saddle mule of Pavón's servant, and the mule driver carried the other half from Achapatunam to Torrehuassi, along half a league of sloping path and bogs.

When the last of us arrived at the camping place, we found that the muleteer who had gone on ahead had put up the tents in a spot covered with short grass but full of puddles of water. There we found our assistant Tafalla, who had gone on ahead after he had dismounted. He was in bed, trembling from the cold and from a high fever that was probably brought on by the fatigue of the trip and by the perpetual chill of that high mountain pass. That night we thought he would die, but with hot water and sugar and several blankets he sweated considerably and improved enough to continue the next day on mule back. During the night we had a heavy rainstorm for 3 hours, which drenched most of our baggage.

The 24th dawned with a dense mist. Only with difficulty were we able to round up the mules, and it was rather late when we had finished loading them. Shortly after leaving, we were overtaken by a heavy downpour. With this, the pack mules bogged down more frequently, and the mule drivers were unable to extricate them alone. So, just as we had done on the way in, we served as their assistants until the storm was over and they could control the mules themselves. Those of us who were mounted had to dismount as often as the animals were caught in the boggy sites. Thus, continually falling down, we made the greater part of the way on foot, through bogs, mudholes, mire, and pools of water. Nor was there any way of avoiding this troublesome handicap for the worst 2 leagues of the path. We finished this stretch soaked to the bone and bathed in mud from head to foot. On one occasion my mule sank into the mire up to its head, and I up to my waist. Both of us had to be pulled out with ropes while my companions enjoyed the sight, which really was a laughable one, for it looked as though we had fallen through some trapdoor.

From Chacahuassi to Achapatunam there are 5 leagues of very arduous and dangerous climbing. The road lies on a continuous and narrow slope, is rocky and gravelly under foot, and is beset with cramped, high stepping stones. In that area there is also what they call a beta, which is a vein of silver ore with antimony that gives off gases that can wear down the most resistant of animals, even killing many of the mules that pass. This is borne out by the skeletons and bones that line the way. The thinness of the air in these high Andean woodlands is also a contributing factor.

Three leagues of the road between Achapatunam and Sillcay are perpetual marsh, especially the 2 leagues nearest Torrehuassi. If any animal arrives weary and worn at this boggy stretch, it usually ends its life there. Because of this problem, the drivers like to pass this piece of road in the morning, before the animals have become tired out with a day of excessively difficult travel. Only the defense of honor or business interests could force one to travel over such an abominable path as that between Pillao and Chacahuassi.

A little before nightfall we arrived at Pillao, where we stayed all day on the 25th to dry out our baggage and clean the mud from the mule loads. We left at noon on the 26th and traveled the 3 leagues to Tincuc, at the junction of the Acomayo and Huánuco rivers. There was a short rainstorm on the way. On the 27th we got to Huánuco with no trouble, save the excessive heat of the sun in the gorge.

From the 28th of October to the end of December of the same year, we continued to dry the specimens that we had collected in the forested regions and along the way in our travels. We likewise took care of the seeds, bark, roots, and other plant parts gathered on that trip. I finished descriptions that I had started in various places, and worked on those of new plants from the vicinity of Huánuco. To the Ministry of the Indies I reported the progress made on this last trip and at the same time sent the seeds gathered in the forests and along the trails of the Huánuco area. After identifying the plants, we put all the dried specimens into bundles. All of our collections were then boxed up for transport to Lima and shipment to Spain. Last, I corrected the descriptions of many species of Malvaceae and copied a number of descriptions from rough draft to permanent form.

Towards the middle of December we asked for mules to make the trip to Lima; we did not get them until the end of January 1788. On the 17th of January we received 32 mules from the province of Huamalíes and the village of Chaucha. These we turned over to the use of our field men, who left on the same day with 25 loads of crates and other effects. On the 24th the remainder of the mules that we needed arrived from the village of Chaulán. We sent the rest of the cargo on with the muleteers so that they might spend the night outside the city, as is the general custom among the Indian mule drivers, and not lose a moment the following day.

It rained almost all day long on the 25th, which prevented our leaving Huánuco. Because of this delay, I was able to describe a species of *Berberis*, known locally as ccarhuascassa, which means yellow spine. Indian women use the wood of this bush to dye their cottons and coarse woolen textiles a beautiful, permanent yellow. Indian men employ the wood in making handles for axes, hoes, and other tools that must have strength and resistance.

CHAPTER 57

Trip from Huánuco to Lima

On the 26th of January 1788, I left Huánuco with my companion Pavón and our servants. We stayed overnight in the village of Chaucha. We were not able to catch up with the mule drivers until the 27th, when we joined them on the road that leads down from the village of Ronda. We arrived by nightfall at Huariaca, where our assistants and the cargo in their care were waiting.

On the 28th we all left Huariaca. We passed through Yacán, a tiny hamlet surrounded by alders; even from afar the traveler can appreciate the evergreen beauty of the trees. We slept in one of the numerous dairy farms that dot this region, which is high and cold. It is also crossed by poor trails that are clogged with mud and puddles of water, and wind along the edges of cliffs. Here I collected and described a species of *Nicotiana*.

We arrived at the town of Pasco on the 29th, crossing the mining area of Cerro de Yauricocha with no discomfort other than repeated hailstorms and rains along the boggy path. On the 30th we waited in Pasco to change mules, and on the 31st we arrived by nightfall at the ranch called Diezmo.

On the 1st of February 1788 we spent the night on the pampa of Palcamayo, having traveled all day in repeated rainstorms. The night of the 2nd, we slept on the pampa of Huacaybamba in hail, snow, and rain. All the ice that is used in Lima throughout the year, in the refreshment stalls and cafés as well as in private homes, is taken from this locality. On the 3rd we entered Obragillo, after a safe trip across the mountains and down the painfully hard, rocky footpaths from the famous Cerro de la Viuda to the village of Culluay.

We stayed in Obragillo until the 7th because of a lack of mules. During this delay, I prepared some dried specimens of plants of that vicinity and wrote up a new description of *Cestrum auriculatum*, commonly known as yerba hedionda (stinkweed); its properties and uses are referred to elsewhere. I also collected the following species.

Lycium umbellatum, quiebra ollas (pot breaker). *Molina scandens*, chilca; this plant has an abundant balsamic and tonic resin. *Physalis subtriflora*. *Verbena cuneata*, cultivated in Mayubamba.

Salvia ovata and *S. linearis*. *Calceolaria angustifolia*, *C. crenata*, *C. cuneiformis*, *C. inflexa*, *C. maculata*, *C. nutans*, *C. pulverulenta*, *C. trifida*, and *C. virgata*. *Valeriana virgata*. *Galium hirsutum*. *Saracha contorta*, *S. procumbens*, and *S. dentata*. *Achyranthes purpureo-violacea*.

Periphragmos uniflorus, ccantu. This species is a beautiful bush used to adorn the fences of orchards and farms. It is said that pagan Indians use it in their divinations and superstitions.

Baitaria acaulis. Rhinanthus luteus. Scutellaria coccinea. Pancratium uncinatum, chihuanhuaita.

Euphorbia tuberosa, huachanccana. The roots of this plant are employed as a purgative in various parts of Peru. The Indians of Canta take them to Lima, along with other herbs of known medicinal properties, to sell on the street corners. The effects of this purgative are strong, but the Indians moderate its action by merely drinking a glass of cold water.

Staehelina sarmentacea, called rincri-rincri, which means ear-ear, in reference to the shape of the leaves. *Kageneckia lanceolata*; the bark and leaves of this plant, which are bitter, are taken as an infusion in the treatment of fever.

Carica canescens, mito. Its ripe fruits are the size of ordinary lemons; they are tasty and have a pleasant aroma. This species of papaya is plentiful in the hot gorges and valleys of Canta, Huarocherí, and the fields around Lima, growing in dry, rocky, sunny locations.

On the 7th the mayor, using his authority, forced the Indians to bring the beasts of burden that they had offered a few days back but had not produced. When they found themselves in jail, they sent their womenfolk to fetch the animals. In this way we were able to leave Obragillo, albeit rather late in the day. We spent the night at the foot of the mountain at Pacrón. It was here that Brunete's mule had fallen over the crag and caused him the night of exposure and other sufferings that had then overtaken him on the days following the accident, in the mountains and highland moors.

On the 8th we climbed and safely crossed over the ridge and peak at Pacrón and slept in Checta. On the 9th we stayed overnight on the estate of Cavallero, and on the 10th we traveled from that point to Lima, with no further inconvenience except the great heat along the way.

When we had deposited the boxes of specimens in the customs house, we went in search of rooms that could accommodate our baggage. It arrived in Lima the following day, together with the rest of our boxes of specimens, which we also left in the customs.

On the 14th we presented ourselves to the viceroy and to the general superintendent. For our benefit, they both repeated the order for us to return to Spain on one of the ships that was making preparations to sail.

For the remainder of this month, I continued drying specimens of plants gathered along the trails. I described *Verbena citriodora*, commonly known as cedrón. I had sent seeds of this plant to Lima from Chile, and it had grown luxuriantly. The species had originally come from Buenos Aires to Santiago de Chile, and from there to Lima.

I likewise studied and wrote a complete description of *Cerbera salicifolia*, one of the numerous curious and exotic plants cultivated by the Reverend Father Francisco González Laguna in his cemetery in Lima, the Jardín de la Buenamuerte. Indians make strings of beads from the shells of the fruits of this plant. Because the beads make a rattling noise, they are used as castanets in native dances; they are hung around the neck and on the arms and legs. These beads are made by burning the stones, or nuts, of the *Cerbera* on one side so that they can be opened and the pits removed; this also hardens them to make them more sonorous.

Finally, in Lima I described *Limonia trifoliata*, commonly called limoncillo de China (little Chinese lemon). From the fruits of this species are prepared the sweets known as limoncillos de China. This is not an indigenous Peruvian species, but was recently imported from Asia to Panama, and then to Lima. At the time I left, there were only two plants in Lima, one in the school of San Pablo and the other in the Buenamuerte cemetery.

I was summoned to the offices of the viceroy to be given a letter from His Excellency the Minister of Justice of the Indies, Don Antonio Porlier, announcing His Majesty's satisfaction with our work and our important collections. His Excellency the Viceroy, Don Theodoro Croix, proposed to me that one of us, the two botanists, remain in Peru to found a botanic garden, which His Majesty had ordered established. His Excellency considered our assistant Tafalla too young and inexperienced to occupy the post. My answer to His Excellency and to his secretary, Don Esteban Varea, was that Tafalla was indeed sufficiently learned in botany to carry out the duties of such a post, that we (botanists) both had been called to the court to publish our flora, and that, insofar as I was concerned, I could take no other course than that of obedience to the crown. His Excellency thought very highly of my way of thinking and did not continue to press his propositions.

When the plants collected on the road to Lima had been dried and packaged up according to classes, I had them boxed up well for transport, along with various seeds, samples of ore, and specimens of many other natural products. I made final copies of various descriptions, and ordered pots made for transporting the living plant material to Madrid. These plants had been deposited in the garden of the Buenamuerte cemetery under the zealous care of the Reverend Father Francisco González Laguna, who had taken the very greatest of pains in their cultivation from the time we had sent them from Huánuco.

In the name of all of us, I requested the viceroy's permission to return to Spain with our scientific material. On the 26th we went to bid farewell to Don Jorge Escobedo, who left for Cádiz on the 27th aboard the ship *Concordia*.

Since the viceroy had declared that our boxes of specimens were to be divided between two ships, the *Dragon* and the *Jason*, I went to discuss with the first mates of both frigates the location in which the boxes should be stored. We agreed that between decks was the best; after I had acquainted the viceroy with my choice, I ordered that the material be so stored.

I presented the probate officer with the executor's report for the estate of the artist Brunete, requesting of Señor Moreno that the effects of my late companion be sent to his sister, Dona Agustina, on the very ships that were getting ready to set sail after ours. He promised me that he would attend to this matter without delay, and assured me that Brunete's property would not be impounded in vaults, as was usually the case.

In March 1788 the three of us made a request to the viceroy for our back pay and for several months' pay in advance, in order that we might cancel our accounts and outfit ourselves with essentials for the sea voyage. He made everything difficult, especially concerning the order of the treasury officials in Lima to suspend payment from the treasury office in Pasco. This was done in spite of our having received nothing without the order of the general superintendency, in which office all bills and receipts of payments made to us in Pasco were found. In the face of this evidence, we were paid everything that was owed us and for several months in advance, and we were thus able to take care of our bills and buy the necessities for the trip. We spent every penny that we had earned in Peru and left as poor as church mice, for we had not engaged in any business other than the fulfillment of our mission.

On the 18th my two companions went to Callao to take care of our boxes of specimens, as had been arranged with the captains of the *Dragon* and the *Jason*.

I made a request to the viceroy for a cabin for the pots of plants. He ordered a cabin hard by the one already assigned to me, so that I might care for the plants and continue writing up my botanical observations, and this I did during the voyage.

I solicited the legal papers concerning the fire at Macora and was requested to give a certificate suspending the sentence passed by the councilor of Tarma, Don Bartolomé Bedoya, which charged up the expenses of the case against Don Mathías Trabuco, administrator of the estate, to those of us who had suffered the losses.

On the 30th our permits to embark were given to us, and we went to say our farewells to the viceroy that very evening. He ordered me to return the next day to fetch the certificate of the fire at Macora.

We left Lima for the port of Callao on the 31st. We put our equipment on the frigate *Dragon*, along with the 24 pots of living plants that had been brought down from Lima in six hothouse cases. On board, however, they were not kept in the glass cases, but on the floor of the cabin. The pots were arranged so that they would not be injured by the rolling of the ship, and could be taken out on deck whenever desirable.

CHAPTER 58

Voyage from the Port of Callao to the Bay of Cádiz

After clearing papers with customs and with the captain of the port at Callao, we set sail at midnight on the 31st of March 1788. On board there were some 70 men of the Soria regiment; these Spaniards were almost the only survivors of the entire regiment. When we were a league from port we dropped anchor to await the first mate, who was ashore laying in last-minute stores.

On the 1st of April, at three in the afternoon, the sails were raised against a south to south-southeasterly breeze. At half past six we saw the northern point of the island of San Lorenzo and from it took a bearing of 5° east, to the south-southeast. When night fell, the sky and horizon were filled with fleecy, bright clouds of many colors, the sea was quiet to the south, and there was a light south-southeasterly wind. At dawn the frigate *Jason* passed to the starboard, likewise bound for Cádiz, and by noon of the next day she was lost to sight.

On the 2nd, dawn showed the horizon to be rather cloudy, so we could not see the shoreline clearly. Observations gave our position as 12°13' south latitude. In the early afternoon, we saw several young whales on both sides of the ship, as well as a few gulls and pardelas, both aquatic birds.

On the 3rd our position was 12°46'. At half past one in the afternoon, the shoals of Ormigas were seen lying off to the north. We saw more young whales and sea birds. Most of the officers of the Soria regiment, as well as my two companions, were seasick. On the 4th we were at 13°35' south latitude.

When dawn broke on the 5th, we observed a ship to the windward of our prow, 2½ leagues away. We later learned that this was the *Jason*, and we gained upon her by half a league an hour, so that at sundown she was lost to sight. We were then at 14°45'.

On the 6th we were not able to make observations, but calculated our position at 16°45'. We saw various kinds of marine birds, and many bonitos (striped tunnies) and flying fish. On this day I began the work of making fresh copies of the botanical descriptions that I had in rough form, and I continued on the following days whenever time permitted.

Because the sky and horizon were overcast on the 7th, no observations could be made. We saw many bonitos, flying fish, and albacores, as well as the birds known locally as rabiahorcados (frigate birds), pamperitos, and gulls.

On the 8th our observations put us at 17°53'. In the morning we saw a few birds, and there was a squall at seven that morning.

Our position on the 9th was 18°47', and 19°47' south latitude on the 10th. On these 2 days we saw no birds or fish.

The 11th found us at 20°45', and we saw several white birds. The weather was fair, so I had all the pots of living plants taken out on deck as had been done on the previous days and added humus to some of them.

The 12th brought us to 20°55'. We observed some gulls, as well as other small birds that were a little larger than pamperos but of the same color. I set the pots out on deck to water them and put them back in the cabin at sundown as on previous days.

Our position on the 13th was observed to be 21°3'. The weather was calm, and this enabled us to see a few dorados (giltheads) near the prow and stern of the ship. An occasional gull also wheeled into sight. I took the pots out on deck and they were watered by a squall.

On the 14th the sun showed us to be at 21°23'. A few dorados and small gulls were sighted.

On the 15th we found ourselves to be at 22°8', and at six o'clock that same evening we were becalmed. I took the pots out into the sun.

Our position on the 16th was 22°34'. I sunned the pots on deck on this day, too.

On the 17th we were at 23°24' south latitude. I took all the pots out on deck; after I had sprinkled them in the morning, they were watered again by a rain.

The 18th found us at 24°8'. I aired the plants on deck. We saw an occasional small bird and some albacores, and caught three of the albacores.

Our position on the 19th was observed to be 24°34'. I put the plants out on deck.

We found ourselves completely becalmed at 24°54' on the 20th. I again put the potted plants out on deck. We saw a few dorados as well as albacores, of which we caught two; some pardelas were also observed.

Our position on the 21st was 24°59'. I sunned the plants on deck. We saw a few pardelas.

The 22nd brought us to 26°13'. I aired the potted plants and finished making clean copies of the botanical descriptions.

Our position on the 23rd was calculated at 28°47'. At midnight we were becalmed. I sunned the potted plants and started work on the index of botanical and vernacular names in the plant descriptions. We observed a few pardelas.

We found ourselves at 29°30' on the 24th. Pavón took the pots out in the sun and sprinkled them. A few pardelas were seen.

On the 25th we were at 31°6'. I took the potted plants out to sun and, in the afternoon, had Pavón replace them in the cabin. We saw a few pardelas.

We were at 33°25' on the 26th. It rained most of the day, and there was considerable swell. We therefore did not take the potted plants out of the cabin, and I could not write from ten o'clock in the morning on because of the rolling of the ship. Some pardelas were seen.

On the 27th we arrived at 34°35', according to the pilot's computations, for he could take no readings. I did not take the plants from the cabin on account of the rolling of the ship. There were squalls and calms during the day.

Our computations on the 28th put us at 36°31'. I set the plants out on deck, and they were watered by a squall. We saw a great number of golfines, or bufeos (dolphins), a very large fish. I saw an occasional pardela.

We judged that our position on the 29th was 38°45'. I did not want the servant to take out the pots because of the rolling, and there were squalls. We saw some birds: pardelas, pamperitos, and tableros (checkerboard birds).

Our observations on the 30th showed us to be at 39°58'. The birds that we saw included pamperitos, tableros, white carneros, and black carneros. Again, I was unable to write anything except the entry in my diary.

On the first day of May 1788, computation placed us at 41°18'. From eleven o'clock until one, I had the potted plants out on deck. We saw many carneros and tableros.

On the 2nd we computed our position as 42°48'. There were snow squalls almost all day; for this reason, I did not take the potted plants out on deck but merely opened the cabin door to change the air. All the rest of this month, we saw large numbers of white, black, and chestnut-colored carneros; tableros; and, on some days, pardelas.

On the 3rd our observations of the sun put us at 43°34'. Because of the cold and the continued rolling of the ship, I did not take the plants out, nor could I continue work on my botanical index.

On the 4th we calculated our position as 44°41'. Again, I was unable to take out the plants, and the cold and rolling prevented my writing.

Our position on the 5th was 45°35'. As on the several preceding days, the weather made it necessary to keep the potted plants in the cabin, but I opened the door to ventilate the room.

We were at 46°51' on the 6th. Because of the cold and the swell, I did not take the plants out of the cabin until the 28th of this month. I also did not water them until the 28th, since I noted that many of them were losing their leaves.

On the 7th our computed position was 47°52'. On the following days, I was unable to continue writing on account of the cold and the swell.

The 8th found us at 49°30' south latitude, and on the 10th we were at 50°11'. It snowed a little on the 10th.

Our observations on the 11th placed us at 51°5'; the sea had a very heavy swell. These swells continued on the 12th, when we arrived at 53°11'. Our position on the 13th was calculated as 55°25'; we had snowstorms.

Calculations on the 14th put us at 56°49'; snow and hail fell. We were at 58° 21', according to computations, on the 15th; again, we had snow and hail.

On the 16th we observed by the sun that our position was 58°32'; there were intermittent snow flurries. On the 17th we were at 58°47'; snow with intermittent rain fell, and we caught sight of two whales to port.

We computed our position on the 18th as 59°3'. This was the greatest latitude to which we sailed; from then on, we began to turn. There were slight snow flurries, and the swell, which had us worn out with the ship's rolling, died down.

Our observations on the 19th put us at 58°45', and on the 20th we found ourselves at 58°2'. It rained at intervals on the 20th.

On the 21st we judged that we were at 57°; we saw some stems of the seaweed known as cachiyuyo (wrack). The 22nd found us at 56°2'. On the 23rd our calculated position was 55°37', and there were squalls and fog.

On the 24th we arrived at 52°14', according to our observations. We saw numerous dolphins and some cachiyuyo plants. There were slight squalls.

The 25th brought us to 51°40'; we saw some birds, smaller than carneros and of a chocolate color. On the 26th our calculations put us at 51°34'; it rained and snowed most of the day. Observations on the 27th showed us to be at 50°58'.

On the 28th we were at 48°50'. I took my potted plants out of the cabin to sprinkle them with water from the ship's store, and put them back directly in the cabin because of the cold; they were on deck no longer than an hour. Even though about 20 days had passed since the plants were last watered, and some could withstand longer periods without water, I ventured to sprinkle some and wash the others. There was a little snow. We saw two species of birds that were unknown to the ship's crew.

We arrived at 46°20' on the 29th; there were snow flurries at intervals. On the 30th we were at 44°58'; on the 31st, at 43°55'.

The 1st of June 1788 found us, according to dead reckoning, at 42°52'. We saw some tableros, chestnut-colored carneros, and other birds the size and shape of carneros but with a white stripe beneath each wing. Up to the 20th of this month we saw fewer and fewer carneros and tableros, and after the 20th we saw none at all.

I kept the potted plants in the cabin until the 6th on account of the cold weather, but every so often I set the door of the cabin ajar to change the air, for by now most of the leaves had fallen off or turned yellow.

On the 2nd our calculations put us at 42°43' south latitude. We were becalmed. At half past two in the afternoon, we saw a rather large whale.

Our observations on the 3rd put us at 42°8'. In addition to carneros and tableros, we continued seeing an occasional pardela until the 26th, but none from that day on.

On the 4th we were at 40°46'; besides other birds, we noticed a few chorlitos (curlews, plovers). Our position on the 5th was 39° south latitude; a few chorlitos were sighted.

On the 6th we arrived at 37°35'. I took the pots out on deck to loosen the soil, to snip off the branches that had dried up or been frozen, and to wash the leaves free of salt, which by tasting I found to be coating them. A few chorlitos came into sight.

The 7th found us at 36°16'. Again, I took the plants out on deck and continued work on my botanical index. We saw great numbers of chorlitos.

On the 8th we were at 34°50'. We saw a few chorlitos. I had the pots taken out on deck and continued with the botanical index.

We were at 30°49' on the 9th. I had Pavón take the pots out on deck. We saw a great many chorlitos.

On the 10th we arrived at 33°28'. Because the day was overcast and cold, I did not have the potted plants brought out; I merely opened the cabin door. We sighted some chorlitos.

On the 11th, by dead reckoning, we found ourselves at 33°10'. I had the plants brought out in the sun. Only a few chorlitos came into sight.

Our calculations on the 12th put us at 32°33'. It rained most of the day; as it was too cold to set the plants out on deck, I opened the cabin door to change the air. We again saw only a few chorlitos.

Our position on the 13th was 32°7'. The plants remained in the cabin because of the rainstorm, the cold, and the tossing of the ship. At half past five in the afternoon a ship was sighted, and by eleven o'clock we knew that it was fleeing from us towards the shores of Guinea. By dawn it had been lost to sight. From this day onward, we saw no more chorlitos.

On the 14th we were at 32°7'. I took the plants out of the cabin.

On the 15th we found ourselves at 31°34' by dead reckoning. I set the plants out on deck and put them back in the cabin at noon, as there was a rainstorm threatening.

Our calculations placed us at 31°9' on the 16th. I did not take the plants from the cabin. From this day on, I kept a detailed diary in which I recorded the hour in the morning that the *Porlieria hygrometra* started to unfurl its leaves, and the hour in the afternoon that it began to curl them up again. I had observed this plant, not only in its native haunts in Huánuco but likewise from the 1st of April to the 15th of June on the high seas, and I saw that the hour varied, both in the morning and in the afternoon. This variation depends upon whether or not there is to be calm or stormy weather on the following day; I gave that explanation in my chapter on Huánuco, "Trip to the Forests of Chinchao," where I discussed this bush.

We calculated our position on the 17th as 30°50'. In the afternoon I put my plants out on deck. I sowed a number of seeds in pots, but none sprouted.

Our position on the 18th was 29°14'. I took the potted plants out of the cabin. At eight o'clock, a whale hove into sight.

Our calculations put us at 28°26' on the 19th. I took the pots out of the cabin and, after a squall had watered them, put them back at two in the afternoon.

On the 20th, according to computation, we were at 27°23'. I took the plants out to sun. From this day on, we began to see the phosphorescent sparkle churned up by the rudder, the prow, and the waves of the sea. This was the last day that we saw tableros, and no carneros were observed from the 18th on.

The 21st saw us at 25°51'. I took the potted plants from the cabin and fenced in each pot with sticks, for protection from the wind and from damage by the servant in handling them.

On the 22nd we were at 24°7'. The pots were once again set out on deck, and I finished the work of fencing them with sticks. Several whales came into sight, and we noticed some small birds that were slightly larger than pamperos and nearly the same color.

Observation placed us at 22°25' on the 23rd. I took the plants out on deck and sprinkled them in the afternoon.

On the 24th we arrived at 20°45'. I again put the plants out to sun.

We were at 18°50' on the 25th. The plants were again set out on deck to sun. We saw flying fish, a few albacores, and two pardelas.

Calculations set us at 16°27' on the 26th. I put the plants out to sun. One pardela was seen, but from this day on no more came into sight. We saw several dolphins; a sailor wounded one with a harpoon, but the others escaped and were seen no more that day.

The position we calculated for the 27th was 14°12'. The sea was choppy and the swell was strong, so I did not take my plants out on deck. We saw some flying fish and a penguin.

On the 28th we were at 12°25'. I took the plants out and sprinkled them. We saw numerous flying fish and a penguin, perhaps the same one that we had seen the day before.

On the 29th our position was 10°32'. Because the sea was choppy, I did not take the plants out of the cabin. We saw numerous flying fish and bonitos.

Our position on the 30th was observed to be 8°33' south latitude. I took the plants out in the sun and watered them. We saw some flying fish and dorados, a gull, and two of the birds called piqueros.

The pájaro tablero (checkerboard bird) is as large as a domestic pigeon, perhaps a bit larger. From its beak to the tip of its tail, it is a third shorter than the distance from the tip of one extended wing to the tip of the other. It is very similar to a gull in the head, beak, and neck. The beak is black and measures 12 lines (an inch) in length. The nostrils are elongated. The back is somewhat flattened. The feet are short, black, and slightly spotted, and the toes are joined by membranes or webs, like those of a duck. The eyes are large and sharp. In flight the wings are held almost horizontally and straight and are obliquely rounded at the anterior end, sharp at the posterior tip, and bent slightly back at the outer articulation. The tail, entire and rounded, is very short in comparison with the body and wings.

The feathers of the throat, breast, and belly are all white, and the inner ones are more delicate than the outer ones. The feathers of the face, head, and neck, down to the beginning of the back, are black, whereas those of the back, tail, and upper part of the wings are black and white. When the bird is in flight, these feathers form spots of various shapes. The four largest spots, those near the wing articulation, are deltoid; the rest, although not constant in size and shape, tend to be rather square, forming something like a checkerboard pattern, and this peculiarity gives rise to the name pájaro tablero (checkerboard bird). The tail and the wings are black at the margins of both sides, and ashy white in the center, although lighter in the area that forms part of the two spots on the articulations of each wing.

The flight of the tablero, very swift and similar to that of a gull, is circular. From time to time these birds may move their wings like a duck to climb higher, but they usually do not flap them, save for alternate tilting of the flight upwards and downwards. They fly in great flocks, which leads us to presume that they are polygamous. They follow ships, flying in the wake of the vessel to gather up whatever offal may be thrown overboard, and whenever some piece of bread, meat, or other food is swallowed up by the waves, they dive into the water to snatch it up.

Tableros have little flesh and what they have is purplish, although it whitens up a little when cooked. After cooking, the meat is hard and has the flavor of an unpleasant shellfish. Like gulls, they have a low, short cackle. Sailors customarily catch them with bent pins and small fishhooks to eat the flesh and to use the skin for tobacco pouches. They fly no higher than 40 feet, always skimming the water.

Another marine bird is commonly known as the pájaro carnero; like the tablero, it ranges from 30° south latitude to beyond 60°, and to 200 leagues at sea off the Patagonian coast. When its wings are not spread, the carnero is as large as vulture; with its wings fully open, its body, which resembles that of a gull, is the size of that of a duck. The body measures a little more than a third of the distance from the tip of one wing to the tip of the other. The head resembles that of a gull, as do the neck and tail. The beak is 2 inches long, linear and straight, flat and somewhat ridged below, and semicylindrical above with a spoonlike convexity towards the sharp tip. The eyes are large and keen. The wings, from the tip of one to the tip of the other, measure more than 3 feet in most specimens. The feet are short, corresponding to the body, and are webbed. The wings are wedge-shaped and turned back, though very slightly, and end in a point. They are spread horizontally and occasionally are bent like a bow, but the commonest movement is an alternating flap, accompanied by a wagging motion of the head from one side to the other. From time to time, the wings are beaten to create a wind for the purpose of climbing. The path of this bird consists of large or small circles, climbing up and down, never getting higher than 20 yards from the water; the bird usually skims right over the surface of the sea. The tail is very short.

Some specimens of carnero have wholly light brown plumage, and in others it is almost black; many are rusty brown, with variations of black and white on the body and under the wings, or totally black on the upper surface of the wing and on the hind extremities. In some cases there is a black ruff on the neck.

Though these birds follow the ship in great numbers, they always fly in pairs, from which we might infer that they are not polygamous. Only below 38°, white carneros are seen, two by two; they are very rare, much rarer than those of other colors. They follow in the wake of the vessel to gather up bits of offal that are cast overboard. Their cackle has a deep and lazy tone but otherwise resembles that of a gull.

There was another kind of bird that seemed to belong to the genus of the carneros. It occurred from 30° to 60°. It is half the size of the carnero and is entirely chocolate-colored, although a few individuals have white on the face. The wings are more sickle-shaped than are those of the carnero. Like the carnero, it flies in pairs, but it is not so common. I could not ascertain any common name for this bird.

On the 1st of July 1788, our position was 6°26'. I put the plants out to sun and watered some of them. We saw two piqueros and many flying fish.

On the 2nd, observations placed us at 4°16'. I set the plants out in the sun and sprinkled them in the afternoon. We saw two piqueros, numerous dolphins, an occasional albacore, an infinite number of flying fish, a squid, and the *Notilis papyraceus striis violaceis* of Linnaeus.

On the 3rd we found ourselves 2°18'. I took the plants out on deck. We saw two piqueros and an abundance of *Nautilus*, which the sailors call barquillas (little boats) in reference to their shape.

Our position on the 4th was 0°38' south latitude. I put the plants out on deck under an awning.

On the 5th I again put the plants out under the awning. We saw a piquero, a great many albacores, and flying fish being chased by them.

On the 6th I set my plants out under the awning. We saw many flying fish and some albacores.

On the 7th I set the plants out on deck, watered them, and washed them carefully. We saw one piquero, two small black birds, a few pamperitos, and several albacores.

At half past ten on the morning of the 8th, we caught sight of a ship going south. As the sea was calm, we put a boat in the water and the two pilots and an officer of the Soria regiment, with the necessary sailors, paid a visit to the ship, which was Portuguese. They brought back information about the longitude and reported that the ship, a packet boat, was transporting 300 slaves of both sexes to Janeyro (Rio de Janeiro).

I set my plants out under the awning. We saw great numbers of dolphins, several albacores, bonitos, and more than 40 sharks off the stern of the vessel. The sailors caught three of the sharks; under the fins of these fish they found a number of the very small sucking fish known as remoras. Some *Nautilus* and pamperitos were observed.

There were squalls on the 9th. I put my plants out under the awning. A number of albacores and many dorados and flying fish were sighted. One of the flying fish fell onto the ship, and I kept it to describe.

Because it rained all day long, I did not take the plants out of the cabin on the tenth. We saw some corbinas (whiting), sharks, dorados, and flying fish, one of which jumped into the prow and I preserved it in spirits.

On the 11th I put the pots out under the awning, but put them back at three o'clock that afternoon to prevent their becoming too wet. We saw several sharks, two of which the sailors caught.

I put the plants out in the sun on the 12th. We got a glimpse of numerous small fish called romerillos (little pilot fish); the sailors caught one for me to describe. There were also many of the tiny polyps that the sailors call aguas malas (bad waters). This little creature looks like a toadstool with the stalk cleft into four equal parts at the base, and with folds or fringes along the margins. There are eight long threads, compressed like bristles, along the margin. This animal has a viscous-crystalline color, with violet stripes.

On the 13th I put the plants out on deck. We saw some bonitos and great numbers of polyps.

On the 14th we spied a Portuguese ship at six in the morning. At a distance of 2 leagues, it ran up the Portuguese flag with a pennant and fired a cannon shot. We ran up the Spanish colors and received the Portuguese captain on board our frigate. After he had given us the news from Europe, he retired to his corvette with a gift of food from our captain, in return for a similar gift that he had brought us and for his offer of whatever foods we needed. He was bound for Pernambuco. I had set the plants out on deck, and their fresh green color surprised the Portuguese captain, who remarked with admiration how vigorous they looked after such a long trip at sea. I poked the soil of the pots to free the plants from some tiny insects and to allow the water to sink in better.

I set out the plants again on the 15th but put them back in the cabin at two o'clock in the afternoon, for a long and heavy rainstorm came up. We saw many polyps, and a black bird the size of a domestic dove with a slender, curved, awl-shaped bill as long as its body.

On the 16th I put the plants out in the sun. We were becalmed for 4½ hours. We saw great numbers of bonitos and albacores, of which the sailors caught several.

Our position on the 17th was 10°58' (north latitude). I put out the plants but soon replaced them in the cabin, as a strong rainstorm was brewing. We caught sight of three huge sharks, one of which was hooked but escaped and carried off the fishhook after breaking the line. The sailors caught a number of bonitos.

On the 18th we arrived at 11°23'. I took the plants out on deck but had to put them back in the cabin after midday on account of a heavy downpour. During the rainfall we noticed multitudes of tiny globules of water that formed on the deck; they looked like quicksilver and lasted a long while before disappearing. We saw an infinite number of bonitos and dolphins.

On the 19th I put the plants out on deck. A few sharks came into sight, and the sailors caught several bonitos.

On the 20th I had Pavón set out the plants, and they were out until after sundown, when we put them back in the cabin. Two large whales with red backs were observed, as well as many flying fish and albacore and one pardela.

Our position on the 21st was 12°47'. I had the potted plants taken out, and they remained out on deck all night, under the care of our servant. I watered them and fenced in some of the pots with sticks to protect the plants.

On the 23rd I cleaned the plants to remove the eggs of a fly that was destroying the buds, especially of *Platanus otahetianus* and two species of *Laurus*. They were left out on deck in the care of the servant and were watered, when a slight squall came up suddenly.

On the 24th the plants remained on deck all day and night. I revised my description of *Amaryllis miniata*, as my plant had come into beautiful flower. We saw flying fish, bonitos, and albacores.

On the 25th I described *Pancratium luteocarneum*, which was in bloom. The flower has the form of a bugle 3 inches long, for which reason they call it flor del clarín (bugle flower) in Lima. We saw an infinite number of flying fish, bonitos, and albacores.

On the 26th I had the pots taken out on deck; Pavón, not noticing that they were moist, began to water them, but he stopped when I called his attention to their moist condition. We saw some bonitos, albacores, and flying fish.

The plants were kept in the cabin on the 27th, on account of a strong wind and the ship's rolling. We saw untold numbers of flying fish and albacores.

On the 28th we likewise kept the plants in the cabin because of strong wind and repeated squalls. Again we saw a great many flying fish, bonitos, and albacores, and a bird resembling a black swallow.

I put the plants out on deck on the 29th, but in the afternoon I replaced them on account of the squalls and high wind. We saw countless flying fish and bonitos.

The plants remained in the cabin on the 30th, for the sea was choppy and the wind strong. Many flying fish and albacores came into sight.

On the 31st I took the plants out but had them put back very early in the afternoon because of the wind. We saw some mats of sargazo (sargasso, gulfweed).

On the 1st of August 1788, our position was found to be 22°58'. Because of the strong winds, I did not take out the plants. We observed a great many flying fish.

On the 2nd we were at 24°37'. I took the plants out of the cabin. At half past six in the morning, we saw several mats of sargasso, or *Fucus natans*. I had a piece fetched aboard to examine the fructification, which Linnaeus had described. Though I spent the whole day studying it, I could see nothing, until at night I managed to ensnare a plant from the tangle and noticed a bright phosphorescent glow that passed swiftly over many parts of the plant as far as its tips, which I then saw were actually tiny spikes. The next day I saw that they were the flowers of the plant, and later I verified this, as is shown by the exact description that I wrote, and upon which I worked until we were nearly at Cádiz in order to make it even more exact. At six in the evening we spied a small vessel coming from the direction of the coast of Guinea and sailing towards South America.

On the 3rd, observation showed us to be at 26°1'. I took out the plants and sprinkled them. At half past eight in the morning, we sighted a ship bound in the direction of the Windward Islands. Shortly before this one was lost to view, another came into sight on the windward side of our prow, passing in front of us at eleven o'clock at a distance of 1 mile. It raised the French flag, and we answered by showing the Spanish colors. As we sailed towards her, she put to and awaited us until, at half past eleven, she passed on our starboard side. When the officers of each ship had exchanged questions, we were informed that she was sailing to Puerto Frances and that the longitude that she brought from Paris was 42°. We saw several bonitos and flying fish and some mats of sargasso.

On the 4th we were at 27°29'. I took the plants out of the cabin and sprinkled those that had not been watered the day before. I worked on the description of *Fucus natans*, and observed the plant in great abundance.

Our position on the 5th was 28°49'. I put the plants out on deck and continued my observations on the sargasso until we were very near Cádiz. We saw some flying fish.

On the 6th, observation placed us at 30°18'. I took the plants out again and watered them. We saw great quantities of sargasso, many flying fish, and a gull that was ashy brown and white.

On the 7th we found ourselves to be at 31°38'. I put the plants out on deck. An abundance of sargasso was seen, and I put up some flowering specimens to dry.

We were at 32°31' on the 8th. I took the plants from the cabin and described a tiny species of *Astacus* (crayfish), which I discovered entwined in a sargasso plant. I found the sargasso more fully in flower than on previous days. We saw a bird called the rabiahorcado (frigate bird).

On the 9th we were at 32°58'. I took the plants out and watered them. I began to make the final, clean copy of the index to my first volume of botanical descriptions, which I finished compiling this very day.

The 10th found us at 33°26'. I took out the plants and watered some that I had not sprinkled the day before. From then on, I continued copying my index to the first volume. We saw two tortoises, a huge polyp, a dorado, and a bird that was medium-sized and black.

On the 11th we arrived at 34°15'. I put out the plants and sprinkled those that needed water. We saw four dorados.

On the 12th our observations gave us a position of 34°21'. We had a calm sea. At dawn we sighted a vessel to port, about 4 leagues away. I took the plants out on deck. We saw some dorados and one rabijunco (frigate bird).

On the 13th our position was 34°21', the same as the day before, for we were completely becalmed. The vessel that we had seen the day before was 2 miles away, on the starboard side. I took out the plants and watered all of them. I finished the index of Latin names and began to copy the index of common names. At half past five in the morning, the other ship hoisted the Portuguese flag, and we answered by raising the Spanish. At eight o'clock, from the top of the masts, the mastmen spied three ships to windward.

On the 14th our observations put us at 34°14'. I put out the plants. During the morning the Portuguese ship was a league away from us; at a distance of 5 or 6 leagues, off the starboard side, we saw two other ships. We continued becalmed.

On the 15th the three ships were sighted to starboard, at distances of 3, 4, and 5 leagues. A northeast wind began to blow. I put out my plants and watered them. We saw several dolphins and dorados.

Our position on the 16th was 34°43'. I put out the plants and, finishing the index to the first volume, began on the second. All day long we saw sargasso, numerous dorados, and a few dolphins. We were caught again in a dead calm. Of the three ships, we could see only the two off our prow, 3 and 4 leagues away.

On the 17th we were at 34°29'. I put out the pots. The two vessels were in sight 2 and 3 leagues off our prow, one to leeward and the other to windward. We saw a huge tortoise beside our ship. At half past five in the afternoon we lost sight of the ships, with breezes from the northwest and haze on the horizon.

The 18th found us at 35°50'. I put the plants out. We saw some albacores, flying fish, and dorados.

Our position on the 19th was 36°58'. I put the plants out and watered them. We caught sight of dorados and albacores.

We arrived at 37°26' on the 20th. I had the plants put out on deck. We saw a kind of small black bird, very many dolphins, albacores, and some tunnies.

On the 21st we were at 37°42'. I put out the plants and watered them. We sighted a manta ray, surrounded by great numbers of romeritos (pilot fish), two pegadores (sucking fish), and one dorado.

Our position on the 22nd was 38°3'. I put out the pots to sun. We spied three ships, one in the morning and two in the afternoon. One of these ran up Anglo-American colors; both were sailing in the same direction.

On the 23rd we were at 39°22'. I took the plants out and watered them. We sighted a vessel 5 leagues off the stern of our ship.

The 24th placed us at 40°3'. The plants were left in the cabin because the sea was choppy. A small black bird was seen.

On the 25th we found our position to be 39°59'. I put the plants out and sprinkled them. We saw various birds. At daybreak we sighted a ship 4 leagues off our prow. She dropped her sails and waited for us. Our captain ran up the flag and pennant. At half past nine we spoke with them and learned that she was the royal ship *San Julián*, captained by Don Juan Moreno, naval commander, who was transporting troops of the Ibernian regiment from Havana to Cádiz. We informed him that we stood in need of fresh food, and he replied that he was in the same condition.

On the 26th we were at 40°. I took the plants out, and finished my index to the second volume. I started work on the third volume, that of the separate notebooks. We saw some small birds and polyps. At ten o'clock the *San Julián* lowered a boat, and an officer of that ship boarded ours with a calf, two turkeys, several hens, and diverse other articles sent to us by Don Juan Moreno. We informed the officer that we needed certain medicines, and these were likewise sent over to us. The northern lights were observed today.

Our position on the 27th was 40°8'. I put the plants out on deck. The officers and men of the *San Julián*, who had seen them on deck the day before, admired the freshness of the foliage after such a long ocean voyage. We saw sea breams, polyps, culebrillas enrroscadas, and three white birds as well as several brownish ones. We followed in the wake of the *San Julián*. From eight o'clock in the evening until midnight, when the horizon was covered with driving clouds, we saw the northern lights, which began with several whitish beams that later became flaming red. The brightness and redness spread from Ursa Major nearly to Ursa Minor, with white beams, like opaque rays of the sun, flashing from time to time.

I took out the plants on the 28th and watered them. I also finished the botanical indexes. We saw some birds and the northern lights.

On the 29th I put the plants out and sprinkled some of them. We sighted various birds and a tortoise. A vessel crossed the path of the *San Julián* in the distance, sailing towards the south.

I put out the plants on the 30th and watered those that needed it. We sailed more than a league to the lee of the *San Julián*, for the wind on our prow had grown in strength during the night.

On the 31st I did not take the plants out, for the sea was choppy and the wind chill. The *San Julián* sent us a message to hoist all sails. Later, with signal flags, the captain of the *San Julián* warned our captain not to leave the wake of his ship. We caught sight of various birds.

On the 1st of September 1788, our position was observed to be 39°. I did not take out the plants, on account of the cold and rainy wind. The captain of the *San Julián* repeated his advice to our captain that we put ourselves to windward of his stern.

On the 2nd we were at 38°12'. I took out the plants and watered them. We saw a few dorados and various birds. The *San Julián* had put us too far to windward of her stern. At half past nine in the morning, off our prow, we spied a packet boat that raised the Portuguese flag; at half past twelve an officer pulled alongside in a yawl to talk with the *San Julián*. We laid by, awaiting the *San Julián*, which was progressing slowly in spite of having all its sails hoisted.

On the 3rd our position was 37°44'. I put the plants out on deck. By six o'clock, the *San Julián* succeeded in putting itself ahead of us. In the morning two ships were sighted, and in the afternoon, two more. We saw a number of birds, some gulls, and the northern lights.

The 4th found us at 37°17'. I did not put out the plants, as the wind was strong and the sea choppy. We left the *San Julián* to our stern.

On the 5th we were at 36°57'. I took the plants out of the cabin and watered them. At dawn the *San Julián* was only a short distance off our prow. We saw two ships sailing southeast. At night, the northern lights played again.

On the 6th we arrived at 36°22'. I put out the plants and watered some of them in the afternoon. We sighted a French frigate. When the *San Julián* fired a cannon shot to call her she changed her course, which had been from the north to the south, but at the second shot she luffed to converse with us. Because a small land bird was observed in the afternoon, the captain of the *San Julián* ordered soundings to be made from midnight on, for he believed us to be near land.

Our position on the 7th was 36°13'. Because of the strong, chill wind, I did not put out the plants. When day broke, the *San Julián* was off our prow and another ship 3 leagues off our stern, following in our wake.

On the 8th, observations placed us at 36°1'. I took the plants out of the cabin.

We caught sight of the coast of Spain. In the afternoon we saw some castle turrets about 9 leagues away.

The 9th brought us to within sight of the coast of Cádiz, and we saw a number of ships. At noon we cast anchor 4 leagues from Cádiz, for the pilot could not take us in with the prevailing levanter, or east wind. The frigate *Sabina*, on her way to Montevideo, left Cádiz, as did the *Placeres*, sailing to Lima, and a brigantine following a northern course. The *San Julián* cast anchor at the mouth of the harbor, and the ship *Catalana* entered the port, setting anchor at six o'clock in the evening.

We spent the 10th at the entrance to the port; because the wind was against us, we were unable to do more than tack. Little fishing boats brought us fruit, bread, and fish. The plants remained in the cabin.

On the 11th we tacked again and dropped anchor in the mouth of the harbor. I did not take the plants from the cabin. The fishing boats continued to supply us with fresh food.

On the 12th we landed at Cádiz with our baggage. The potted plants were taken to the port of Santa María. Don Pedro Gutiérrez Rodríguez, apothecary of that port, had orders from the president of the board of trade to keep the plants there until they were sent to Madrid. As representative of the Royal Botanic Garden, Don Rodríguez was in charge of such affairs in this part of the country.

CHAPTER 59

Descriptions of the Birds, Shellfish, and Fish Collected During the Voyage

The pamperito is a bird found more than 200 leagues out at sea, from 17° (north latitude) to 40° south latitude. It is the size and shape of a large swallow and must surely belong to the genus *Hirundo*. In flight it skims the surface of the sea with great speed and does not climb more than 3 or 4 yards. The feathers of the belly and breast are white, as are those at the base of the tail; the rest of the body is black. I could not get even one specimen of these small birds upon which to base a more complete description.

The piquero is a bird that we encountered from 12° south latitude to the line (equator?). It is the size of a domestic duck; the body is white, and the face and part of the head and neck are black. The tail is short and rounded. The tips of the wings are black. The wings are held straight horizontally, with two small undulations corresponding to the articulations. The bill is round, awl-shaped, straight, and not very long. In flight the wings flap continually, except for short intermissions when they are held still. The piquero zooms down rapidly, like a bird of prey, and dives into the water to catch flying fish.

The birds called rabiahorcados or rabijuncos (frigate birds) are found at sea from 10° south latitude to 24° (north latitude) and near the line. They are the size of a kite and are black, with the wings curving backwards. The tail is long and slender, and from time to time it spreads open to form a fork. This bird flies so high that, like some birds of prey, it is lost to sight.

A fish known as the pexe remora or pegador (remora, sucking fish) is commonly found attached under the fins of sharks. The largest that I have seen were 4 inches long, but seamen tell me that they have seen specimens as long as a foot and a half and as heavy as a pound. The body tapers gradually from the head towards the tip of the tail. The flanks are rather flat, with the top of the back as far as the mouth entirely flat and the belly rounded and slightly broader.

On the head and a short part of the back, the remora has an armature of 18 rows of cartilaginous or semibony scales, parallel and slanting towards the back. The ragged edges of the scales are beset with fine, straight teeth that are disposed in a jumbled manner, with the outer ones gradually increasing in size over the inner ones. Longitudinally, other scales are divided by a line of the same consistency and are encircled by a membranaceous-cartilaginous margin. All of this together forms an elongated figure with which the fish sticks to sharks so firmly that it is impossible to tear it off by pulling backwards.

Between the margin and the last anterior row of scales, there is a U-shaped canal or depression with two apertures. One of these apertures corresponds to the palate, which no doubt serves to suck some substance extracted from the sharks with the teeth and which may also serve to inhale or attach more easily and more firmly.

The skin of the remora is soft, without scales, and totally brownish, though in some specimens there is an occasional white spot.

The fins, including that of the tail, are seven, all very minutely lined with a number of the tiny bones of which they are composed. The tail fin is divided into two parts for more than half its length. The fin that runs from the anal opening to near the base of the tail is semitriangular, like that above the tail fin. The two fins at the side of the head are elongate-obovate; the pectoral fins, joined at their bases by a thin membrane, are triangular.

The eyes of the remora, located at the sides of the mouth, are round, with the iris pearly white and the pupil round and black; around the iris there are some minute black specks similar to the black spots or points seen on the scales. The nose opens between the eyes and the upper jaw and consists of a single round nostril; in the anterior part of the nostril there is a small concavity of the same shape, but it is not open as is the nostril of the nose. There is no beard whatsoever. On each side there are four gills covered with a single scale or scaly covering; their inner surface is denticulate. From the tail to the belly there is a straight line on both flanks;

it curves upwards from the belly to the upper part of the back and continues straight to the base of the head.

The head, compressed from top to bottom, is flat above and scarcely convex beneath. The lower jaw consists of a semicircular bone, shaped like a bow; it protrudes a line (1⁄12 inch) farther than the upper jaw, which is likewise semicircular, but on the sides it slants downward. When open, the lower jaw expands considerably. There are six rows of curved teeth in each jaw. These teeth are so small and so mixed together that it is hard to make out the rows. The teeth are larger towards the outer rows. The palate is rather concave and is beset at the edges with rows of tiny points, similar to the teeth in shape and consistency.

These fish, which seem to be constructed hind end forwards, are good to eat when roasted or fried.

The pexe volador (flying fish) is plentiful in the sea between the Tropic of Capricorn and the Tropic of Cancer. Its body is commonly about 7 inches long, though some reach about 11 inches. The flanks are flat, the back flattened. The body is equally linear from the anal opening to the head, but it gradually becomes slenderer towards the tip of the tail. The back is somewhat wider than the belly. The ventral skin is whitish. The dorsal skin is bluish and covered with small scales that are smooth, shiny, transparent, a little convex, rhomboid, and disposed in six ranks in the shape of a fan; that is, starting from a central point, they diverge or separate towards the head. The lateral line is straight on both flanks from the tip of the tail to behind the lateral fins, and is equidistant from the back and the belly.

The flying fish has seven fins, counting the end of the tail that is bifurcated nearly to its base, like a very open forked stick, with the lower segment one-third longer than the upper. The tail is made up of many slender spines or bones, the inner ones gradually becoming shorter; the spines are joined by a membrane, which is thicker than that of the other fins. The fin that runs from the anus to the tip of the tail measures 6 lines (6⁄12 inch) in width at its insertion and gradually narrows down; it has 14 spines joined by a thin, transparent membrane that resembles the skin of an onion. The upper tail fin is inserted nearer the head than the lower one; though the spines of both are the same in number, those of the upper tail fin differ in being branched instead of entire.

The two pectoral fins are located in the space between the gills and the anus, and are triangular or fan-shaped and as long as they are wide; they have six branched spines, each one divided four times and subdivided into forked ramifications. These two fins are set as far apart as their length, and their membranes are like those of the two aforementioned fins.

The lateral fins arise near the base of the head. As long as the body, they are triangular in shape and as wide as they are long. They have 16 unequal spines, the inner ones being the shortest; all of these spines divide and divide again into two parts. The membrane is like that of the other fins.

The head of the flying fish is obovate-triangular and in proportion to the size of the body. The eyes, located in the middle of the side of the head, are large, protruding, and round, with a pearly white iris and a large black pupil. The nose is placed anterior to the eyes, with one triangular nostril on each side; above each nostril is an elongated hole, half as large as the nostril. This fish has no hairs, beard, or bristles. When open, the small, symmetrical, round mouth juts forward 3 lines ($^{3}/_{12}$ inch), forming a snout. The jawbones, palate, and tongue are devoid of teeth. There are four gills on each side, covered with a sinewy membrane and a scale.

The fins of many small specimens of flying fish are not so large as those described, attaining only half the length of the body; for this reason, it seems to me that there are two different species. Fried or cooked, they are very tasty. Flying fish move in schools; when chased by albacores, dolphins, and other large fish, they use their ability to fly to try to escape the enemy, but the pursuers follow their flight under water and catch them when they fall back into the sea.

The fish called pexe romerito, pampano, or pampanito (harvest fish, pilot fish) occurs from 6° to 12° north latitude, and a number can be seen around the rudder when the wind is low and the sea calm. It is 7 inches long. From the middle of the body to the head it is of equal width, and from the middle of the body back to the tail it becomes gradually more slender. The dorsal and ventral parts of the body are acutely angled, and the flanks are flat-convex with a sharp ridge on each side at the end of the tail. The markings consist of seven black lines that band the whole body, alternating with seven white lines. The belly is white with a bluish cast, whereas the back is deep blue. Smooth and very shiny, the skin is covered with extremely small, thin scales covering all parts. The lateral line runs from the tail to the gills.

The fins are all light black. The tail fin is forked to the middle into two equal segments an inch long, with white tips; the tail segments are made up of many bony spines that are gradually shorter towards the center. The fin that runs from the anal opening nearly to the end of the tail has 16 forked spines; at its insertion it measures 5 lines ($^{5}/_{12}$ inch), gradually narrowing down towards the tip. The fin above the tail is straight from the middle of the body to the slenderest part of the tail; it has 26 forked spines and measures 6 lines ($^{6}/_{12}$ inch) at its widest part. The two pectoral fins are located 4 lines ($^{4}/_{12}$ inch) from the gills, arising so close together that it looks as though they were joined at the base. Made up of five branched spines, the pectoral fins are triangular to deltoid-cuneiform in shape; they are as long as they are wide, but not more than 6 lines ($^{6}/_{12}$ inch). The two lateral fins, located behind the gills, are obovate and have 20 spines; they are as large as the pectoral fins.

The pexe romerito has four gills, protected by two scales; the lower one is three times the size of the upper one. Underneath these scales can be seen a membrane with six scales, forming six curved lines. The round eyes are very close to the end of the upper jaw, with a black pupil and a pearly white iris with a definite bluish cast; the eyes are in proportion to the size of the fish. The nose has two nostrils on each side, transversely elongated and located 1½ lines (between $^{1}/_{12}$ and $^{2}/_{12}$ inch) from the upper jaw. When opened, the mouth is oval and somewhat expanded, and the lower jaw hardly protrudes beyond the upper. Both jawbones have an infinite number of teeth that are barely visible to the naked eye, but they can be seen with a lens and can be felt, as can the scales of the palate. Fried or cooked, these little fish are delicious.

The pexe dorado (gilthead) is an abundant fish in the northern sea between 30° and 38°. It is usually about a yard long and is laterally rather compressed and flat. Its skin is covered with little golden scales and blue spots, and its body is tapered from the head to the tail.

The tail fin, cleft nearly to the base into two equal parts, is a little less than a foot long and looks like a forked stick; each part consists of 17 tiny branched bones or ribs. The dorsal fin, extending from the back of the head to the tail and gradually narrowing, resembles a saw and has 49 bones, of which the largest are divided and the smallest bifurcated. The lateral fins are 4 or 5 inches long and sickle-shaped, with 17 small bony ribs that are divided two, three, or four times. The pectoral fins, joined at the base, are only slightly smaller than the laterals and are similar in shape.

The dorado has four covered gills. Its eyes are round and in proportion to the size of its body. The teeth are small and not in any special order. This fish, fried or stewed, is a delicacy.

Astacus minuta, cangrejillo (crayfish) is a tiny crustacean that lives entangled in the sargasso. It resembles a tick in shape and is red with a few white and sorrel-colored spots. The body is obovate-rhomboidal, flattened beneath and convex above, wider towards the front, and acutely angled at the margins. Towards the tail the body is semicircular and rather truncated.

The eyes of the cangrejillo protrude and are tipped forward, but when the animal draws them in they are horizontal. The tail of the male is more slender than that of the females; it is almost triangular, somewhat elongated, compressed, and made up of six joints. The tail of the female is rounded, somewhat flattened, has cilia and hairs along the edge, and consists of 12 joints. Both the male and female may draw the tail in and fold it up against the belly. On each side there are four small limbs that are hairy at the tip, as well as a claw or thickened limb near the front of the body. There are two straight, short, threadlike antennae between the eyes and two stouter ones that are awl-shaped and twisted. The animal walks sideways.

The polipo (polyp), or aguas malas, is found in northern waters from 6° to 12°; it floats about in great abundance during calm periods. It looks like a mushroom and has a viscous consistency. Out of water, it melts away easily to an almost watery mess that stinks of shellfish. It is the same color as the water and is marked with violet stripes.

The crown or cap of the polipo is orbicular, concave beneath, and convex above; the four-sided body is cleft from the base almost to the middle into four equal, membranaceous parts that are pleated and marked with violet streaks. These four parts of the body serve to propel the animal as they contract and expand from time to time. This motion may be noted also in the central part of the crown, from the edge of which hang eight long, thin filaments that become extremely slender towards their tips and are in constant movement, acting as fins to keep the animal floating on the surface. There is a hole like a small pipe or tube that goes right through the center of the crown to the cleft parts of the animal's body. This pipe contracts and dilates uniformly with the rest of the body to allow it to swim or to attract food. The animal submerges by inclining its crown and comes up again by tipping upwards the convex part.

Sailors call these animals aguas malas (bad waters), a name that fits them well when one considers their strange shape, their viscous substance, and their curious habit of stinging and burning those parts of the human body that come into contact with them.

From the 13th of September 1788 to the 18th of October, we remained in Cádiz. During this stay I spent 10 days in bed, but two bloodlettings improved my health in a few days. My companions Pavón and Gálvez left Cádiz for Madrid on the 18th.

CHAPTER 60

Trip from Cádiz to Madrid

On the 27th of October 1788, boarding in the bay of Cádiz, I sailed to the port of Santa María, where I spent the 28th awaiting the coaches that were to carry the cases of living plants to the Royal Botanic Garden of Madrid. In the vicinity of Santa María I saw, among other plants, *Passerina dioica*, two species of *Asparagus*, *Salicornia diandra*, *Chamaerops humilis*, *Carlina*, *Thymus*, *Sium*, *Verbena*, *Atriplex*, and various species of *Salsola*.

On the 29th we left Santa María with the 23 cases of living plants that were left of the 24 that I had brought from Lima. We spent the night in Xerez (Jerez) de la Frontera, with nothing untoward happening. We left there on the 30th and slept in Cortijo del Cuervo; it rained during most of the trip, until we arrived at the inn. There I had the cases taken out of the coaches to water the plants and add earth to them. On the 31st we arrived at Cortijo de las Torres, having experienced some difficulties with the coaches as a result of the poor condition of the road.

On the 1st of November 1788 we stopped to spend the night in Utrera, where I took the plants out into the sun. On the 2nd we had lunch in Alcalá de los Panaderos and spent the night in Carmona. The night of the 3rd saw us in La Luisiana, and on the 4th we slept in Carlota. We arrived in Córdoba on the 5th, where I again removed the cases from the coaches and took the plants out to sun. On the 7th we ate lunch in Aldea de Río and slept in Anduxar (Andujar), where I gave the plants more sun. The night of the 8th was spent in Guarroman.

On the 9th, after having lunch in La Carolina, we spent the night in Puerto del Rey; from there we had cold weather until we arrived in Madrid. On the 10th we stayed overnight in Valdepeñas, after a downpour on the way. The night of the 11th was spent in Villarta; we had a long rain the last 2 leagues before arriving, and that storm made us feel colder than we had on the previous days. We went on to Tembleque on the 12th, in rain from two o'clock in the afternoon until ten at night. On the 13th we slept in Ocaña; it rained and we were very cold. On the 14th lunch was taken in Aranjuez, and we arrived at Valdemoro at five o'clock in the afternoon; during the night it rained, snowed, and was cold and very windy. On the 15th we stayed in Valdemoro because of the intensity of the wind, rain, and snow.

On the 16th we arrived in Madrid with the cases of living plants, which I took to the Royal Botanic Garden. The next day we transferred the plants to clay pots and sent half of them to Aranjuez in accord with the king's orders.

In Sierra Morena, I described a species of *Schinus* that is known in that locality by the name lentisco.

APPENDIX

Medicinal Plants Mentioned by Ruiz, from the List Compiled by Jaime Jaramillo-Arango

Indian or Spanish Names, with Corresponding Latin Names

Achiote, *Bixa orellana*
Achote, *Bixa orellana*
Acka, aka, *Psydium nitidum*
Aitacupi, *Tafalla glauca*
Alberjilla, *Valeriana pinnatifida*
Amarilla boba fina de Muña, *Cinchona angustifolia*
Ancaschampaccra, *Agave americana*
Anteada fina, *Cinchona angustifolia*
Apio silvestre, *Apium graveolens*
Asccapichana, *Pectis trifida*

Bejuco de la estrella, *Aristolochia fragrans*
Boldo, boldu, *Ruizia fragrans*
Broquin, *Acaena anserinifolia*

Calaguala fina, *Polypodium calahuala*
Calaguala gruesa, *Polypodium crassifolium*
Calaguala verdadera, *Polypodium calahuala*
Camantiray, *Narcissus odorus*
Campanillas, *Datura arborea*
Campanillas de lomas, *Convolvulus secundus*
Campucassa, *Solanum stellatum*
Canchalagua cimarrona, *Pectis trifida*
Canelilla, *Geum urbanum*
Cañafistola, *Cassia procera, C. tora*
Cañafistola cimarrona, *Cassia procera, C. tora*
Capuchinas, *Tropaeolum majus*
Cardón, *Pourretia coarctata*
Carpunya, *Piper carpunya*
Cascarilla cana fina, *Cinchona nitida*
Cascarilla fina de Chicoplaya, *Cinchona calisaya*
Cascarillo, *Cinchona angustifolia, C. calisaya, C. hirsuta, C. magnifolia, C. nitida*
Castañuelas, *Talinum album, T. lingulatum, T. paniculatum*
Catas, *Embothrium emarginatum*
Ccallu, *Sedum ccallu*
Ccoa, *Nepeta* species
Chacay, *Rhamnus verticillatus*
Chamico, *Datura stramonium*
Chichiccara, *Lepidium foetidum*
Chilcas, *Molina ivoefolia, M. parviflora, M. scandens*
Chinapaya, *Vermifuga corymbosa*
Chinchi, *Gardoquia canescens*
Chullco-chullco, *Oxalis ockas*
Clinclin, *Polygala vulgaris*
Coca, *Erythroxylon coca*
Codocoypo, *Myoschilos oblonga*
Colle, *Buddleja incana*
Contoya, *Lobelia decurrens*
Contrayerba, *Aristolochia fragrans, Vermifuga corymbosa*
Cuca-cuca, *Polypodium incapcocam*

Escoba amarga, *Pectis trifida*

Flor de azahar, *Cinchona magnifolia*
Flor de Panamá, *Mirabilis jalapa*
Floripondio, *Datura arborea*
Floripondio encarnado, *Datura sanguinea*

Guadalagüen, *Oenothera grandiflora*
Guayo colorado, *Kageneckia oblonga*

Hacchiquiss, *Monnina salicifolia*
Hatumpacte, *Cassia undecimjuga*
Hatun puñuchrin, *Cynomorium placentoe-forme*

Higos del duende, *Croton ciliatum*
Higuerilla mexicana, *Ricinus ruber*
Huachanccana, *Euphorbia tuberosa*
Huallicaya, *Psoralea capitata*
Hualtata, *Rumex patientia*
Huanarpo macho, *Croton ciliatum*
Huantura, *Bixa orellana*
Huanuccara, *Lepidium foetidum*
Huarituru, *Valeriana lanceolata*
Huarmi-huarmi, *Ageratum conyzoides*
Huarmico, *Salvia sagittata*
Huayabo, *Psydium pyriferum*
Huevill-huevill, *Periphragmos foetidus*
Huighan, huignan, *Schinus dependens*
Huillipatagua, *Villaresia mucronata*
Huilmo, *Sisyrinchium quadriflorum*
Huilmo blanco, *Sisyrinchium multiflorum*
Huircacassa, *Solanum stellatum*

Inca-cuca, *Polypodium incapcocam*
Incapcocam, *Polypodium incapcocam*
Itapallo, *Loasa urens*

Laurel de Chile, *Pavonia sempervirens*
Lausahacha, *Urena hamata, U. villosa*
Lengua de ciervo, *Polypodium crassifolium*
Ligtu, liutu, *Alstroemeria ligtu*
Llamapañaui, *Negretia elliptica, N. inflexa, N. spinosa*

Macae, *Valeriana paniculata*
Machinparrani, *Embothrium emarginatum*
Magth'um, *Celastrus dependens*
Maguey Mexicano, *Agave americana*
Mancapaqui, *Lycium aggregatum*
Mapato, *Krameria triandra*
Maqui, *Aristotelia glandulosa*
Margaritas blancas, *Polyanthes tuberosa*
Mascca, *Polygala* aff. *discolor*
Mastrante, *Lantana salvifolia*
Mastuerzo, *Tropaeolum majus*
Mastuerzo silvestre, *Lepidium foetidum*
Matagusanos, *Vermifuga corymbosa*
Matapalo, *Clusia rosea*
Maytén, *Celastrus dependens*
Membrillejo, *Cordia rotundifolia*
Membrillo, *Cordia rotundifolia*
Merulagüen, *Linum confertum*
Miu, *Cestrum undulatum*
Molle, *Schinus molle*
Muña, *Nepeta* species

Nat're, *Solanum crispum*
Ñipa, *Stereoxylon rubrum*

Occas, okas silvestres, *Oxalis ockas*
Ollus, *Columellia ovalis*
Orejas de abad, *Hydrocotyle umbellata, H. vulgaris*
Ortiga de lomas, *Loasa urens*
Ossapurga, *Sisyrinchium purgans*

Pachapacte, *Cassia setacea*
Pacoyuyo, *Galinsoga quadriradiata, G. quinqueradiata*
Pahuata-huinac, *Monnina salicifolia*
Paja purgante, *Sisyrinchium purgans, S. ocsapurga*
Palma-palma, *Sisyrinchium ocsapurga*
Palqui, Parqui, *Cestrum virgatum*
Palto, *Laurus persea*
Panke, panque, *Gunnera thyrsiflora*
Panul, *Apium graveolens*
Papas comunes, *Solanum cymosum montanum, S. tuberosum*
Papas de lomas, *Solanum cymosum montanum, S. tuberosum*
Papyru, *Ipomoea papyru*
Payco, *Chenopodium multifidum*
Peruviana fina, *Cinchona nitida*
Petacones, *Hydrocotyle umbellata, H. vulgaris*
Peumo, *Laurus peumo*
Picahuai, *Embothrium emarginatum*
Pichana, *Sida frutescens*
Pichi, *Fabiana imbricata*
Pichoa, *Euphorbia portulacoides*
Pila-pila, *Sida americana, S. repens*
Pimpinella cimarrona, *Acaena pinnatifida*
Pino de Chile, *Pinus chilensis*
Piñoncillos, *Castiglionia lobata*
Piochas, *Cynanchum leucanthum*
Pomaysancca, *Loasa punicea*
Puca-campanilla, *Datura sanguinea*
Puhe, *Polymnia resinifera*
Pullapullquelpuan, *Clusia radicans*
Pumachilca, *Stereoxylon pendulum*
Pumacuchu, *Krameria triandra*
Puntu-puntu, *Polypodium crassifolium*

Puñuchrin, *Cynomorium punuchrin*
Purampuí, *Smilax china, S. peruviana*
Purga de pobres, *Euphorbia tuberosa*
Puya, *Pourretia coarctata*

Quebec-quebec, *Lobelia decurrens*
Quellgon, *Geum urbanum*
Quila, *Herreria stellata*
Quillay, *Smegmadermas emarginata*
Quina, quino, *Cinchona angustifolia, C. calisaya, C. hirsuta, C. magnifolia, C. nitida*
Quina calisaya, *Cinchona calisaya*
Quina de flor pequeña, *Cinchona calisaya*
Quina glandulosa, *Cinchona calisaya*
Quina roxa de Santa Fe, *Cinchona magnifolia*
Quino, *see* Quina
Quino-quino, *Myroxylon peruiferum*
Quishuara, quisoar, *Buddleja incana*

Ramram, *Betula nigra*
Ratanhia, *Krameria triandra*
Remedio contra culebras, *Calla nuda*
Romerillo, *Molina concava, M. linearis*

Sahuintu, *Psydium pyriferum*
Salivatoria, *Spilanthes urens*
Salvia real, *Salvia sagittata*
Sandia-lagüen, *Verbena multifida*
Santo palo, *Smilax china, S. peruviana*
Siempreviva, *Triptilion spinosa*
Simayuca, *Jatropha aphrodisiaca*
Socconche, *Gardoquia canescens, Salvia nodosa*
Ssayre, *Myrica stornutatoria*
Suelda consuelda, *Ephedra distachya*?
Suyumpay, *Gardoquia canescens*

Tapateputilla, *Mimosa punctata*?
Taraca, *Polymnia resinifera*
Taya, *Molina scabra*
Taya macho, *Molina emarginata*
Tekel, *Sisyrinchium multiflorum*
Th'ilco, *Fuchsia violacea*
Tina, *Cordia rotundifolia*
Tonco-tonco, *Datura stramonium*
Totumo, *Crescentia cujete*
Trebol, trebul, *Rhamnus dependens*
Trompetillas, *Mirabilis jalapa*
Tuppassayre, *Myrica stornutatoria*

Ucuspatallan, *Sisymbrium sophiae*
Ulluco, *Chenopodium tuberosum*
Ulux, *Columellia ovalis*

Vara de Jese, *Polyanthes tuberosa*
Vira-vira, *Gnaphalium viravira*

Yallhoy, *Monnina polystachia*
Yarabisco, *Jacaranda caerulea*
Yerba de la araña, *Byttneria cordata*
Yerba de la bolsilla, *Calceolaria pinnata*
Yerba de la culebra, *Cuphea ciliata*
Yerba de la golondrina, *Euphorbia chamaesyce, E. hypericifolia*
Yerba de la lancha, *Mimosa latisiliqua*
Yerba de la purgación, *Boerhavia scandens*
Yerba de la sangre, *Celosia conferta*
Yerba del gallinazo, *Chenopodium album*
Yerba del moro hembra, *Achyranthes obovata*
Yerba del moro macho, *Achyranthes rigida*
Yerba de San Agustín, *Psoralea capitata*
Yerba de San Martín, *Sauvagesia ciliata, S. subtriflora*
Yerba hedionda, *Cestrum auriculatum*
Yerba santa, *Cestrum auriculatum*
Yuca, *Jatropha manihot*
Yurahuacta, *Solanum incanum*
Yuyos, yuyus cimarrones, *Amaranthus retroflexus, A. spinosus*

Zarzaparrilla, *Herreria stellata*

No Common Names Given
Columellia corymbosa
Kageneckia lanceolata
Mespilus uniflora
Weinmannia pinnata

Index to Latin Names of Plants